ON THE PRECIPICE

STALIN, THE RED ARMY LEADERSHIP AND THE ROAD TO STALINGRAD 1931-1942

Peter Mezhiritsky

Translated and edited by Stuart Britton

Helion & Company Ltd

Helion & Company Limited
26 Willow Road
Solihull
West Midlands
B91 1UE
England
Tel. 0121 705 3393
Fax 0121 711 4075
Email: info@helion.co.uk
Website: www.helion.co.uk

Published by Helion & Company 2012

Designed and typeset by Farr out Publications, Wokingham, Berkshire
Cover designed by Farr out Publications, Wokingham, Berkshire
Printed by Gutenberg Press Limited, Tarxien, Malta

Originally published as *Chitaia Marshala Zhukova* 4th ed. (New York: Libes, 2008).

Front cover: 'The captain of the country of Soviets is leading us from victory to victory', contemporary Soviet propaganda poster.

ISBN 978-1-907677-72-4

British Library Cataloguing-in-Publication Data
A catalogue record for this book is available from the British Library

For details of other military history titles published by Helion & Company Limited contact the above address, or visit our website: http://www.helion.co.uk.

We always welcome receiving book proposals from prospective authors.

Contents

List of Photographs

List of Maps

All maps from: Earl F. Ziemke & Magna E. Bauer, *Moscow to Stalingrad: Decision in the East* (Washington, D.C.: Center of Military History, 1987).

Translator's Notes

Pull up a chair, pour a glass of your favorite beverage, and help yourself to some of the black bread and pickled vegetables on the table. Sit down with the author, Peter Mezhiritsky, as you discuss Stalin, the Red Army, and the Second World War – you in your mind, Peter through the pages of his *On the Precipice*. It is a very Russian experience, as the author discusses the war, Russian history, Russian culture, Russian literature and film, even Russian family life, all as they relate to Stalin's foreign and domestic policies that, as the author argues, practically invited a German attack in 1941. This book is not about Marshal Zhukov. It is an examination of Stalin's terror, his purge of the Red Army and mistakes in foreign policy and wartime leadership, all through the lens of Zhukov's memoirs. For example, the author offers the following statistics: "In the Great Patriotic War, the Red Army lost 199 generals either killed or taken prisoner. In the purge, 598 of them perished – an amount of losses equivalent to three wars of such never before seen savagery and fury."

Due to its conversational style, the narrative does not flow in a straight line. Rather, it deflects, eddies and churns, while a topic may slip under the surface, only to re-emerge later. Along the way, the reader will gain many new insights and hit upon provocative re-interpretations of history, all of which the author makes quite plausible with his forceful arguments. Mezhiritsky addresses such questions as: Why did Stalin agree to the Non-Aggression Pact with Hitler? Was Stalin planning a preemptive attack in July 1941? How close was Zhukov to falling victim to Stalin's purge of the military? How did he later repay Marshal Budenny, who spoke out on his behalf? What propelled Stalin to keep pushing the 1942 Khar'kov offensive when it was already clear that the *Wehrmacht* had initiated a devastating counterblow? Did Vasilevsky and Zhukov deliberately mislead Stalin when proposing Operation Saturn to encircle the German forces at Stalingrad? Was this operation, which has long held a glittering place in both Soviet/Russian and Western historiography, indeed the Red Army's main operation in November 1942? Or did it achieve this status simply by its results?

However, looking at the horrendous losses in the Great Patriotic War – approximately 14,500,000 in the Red Army alone, though the true number will likely never be known – the author's central questions, the ones he addresses throughout the book, is "How and why did all this happen?" It is timely to ask these questions: after decades of absence, the Moscow government put up small posters of Stalin around the city as it prepared to celebrate Victory Day, the anniversary of Nazi Germany's surrender on 9 May 1945. You may not agree with all of the author's informed speculation and provocative conjectures, but he will force you to stop and think as he challenges numerous existing interpretations and myths of the Second World War and its origins.

A note on the translation: The author primarily rests his case upon the 2nd (1974) edition of Zhukov's memoirs, which is available in English translation through the Soviet publishing house Progress Publishers. For the most part, to avoid confusion, I have used the existing English translation. However, as the author himself notes, the English translation was often incomplete or failed to adhere closely to the original Russian. Since sometimes

Mezhiritsky addresses a specific word or phrase, which may not have been present in the existing English translation, I have at times adjusted the English translation to fit more closely to the original Russian, or to Mezhiritsky's discussion. In addition, the author also occasionally cites from later editions of the Zhukov's memoirs, some of which differ in striking ways from earlier editions, as censorship relaxed. These later editions have not been translated into English yet, so the translation of these quotes is my own. Otherwise, I want to express my sincere thanks to Peter Mezhiritsky, who always stood by to assist me during the translation process. I only regret that I was unable to capture much of the lyricism and clever word play of the original Russian. Any errors in translation are, of course, my own.

Preface to the English Edition

On 9 May 1965, I, a young writer at the time, was in Moscow. The 20th Anniversary of Victory Day was being touchingly marked. The government had instituted the practice of a "Minute of Silence", and the text of the address to the people was read out over the airwaves by Iurii Levitan, whose voice had shaken us in the war with the gloomy, and then celebratory summaries from the Sovinformburo. The next day I met with an acquaintance, an executive editor on the staff of the journal *Oktiabr'* [*October*], and he fervently described how they had marked Victory Day at the Central House of Literature, and how that night several Marshals had arrived there, including Zhukov. The delight had been warmed up by a preceding round of libations. The writers were shouting "Hurrah!" and rocked the Marshals with their overwhelming enthusiasm. Zhukov received an ovation, and many were sobbing. The ecstasy had reached its apogee. Repeating the words of a venerable Party orator, my acquaintance told me that "if Stalin had arrived, we would have greeted him on our knees."

After this war, after those losses, greet Stalin on their knees? Stalin?

Looking back over my life, I find that the war made and still makes the strongest impression in it. Like many Soviet children of those years, I expected a war, but not like the one that broke out. Having taken in the entire bundle of communist brainwashing, children of the USSR dreamed about a triumphant campaign of the proletariat against the bourgeoisie. However, the war turned out to be a World War – all against all. It concluded with a triumph, but one purchased at a cost more characteristic of defeats.

Stalin was our Beloved Father and Teacher, and without hesitation we would have given our children's lives for him. With the years we learned the truth about his fatherhood and teaching. Was it possible for hatred to be more immense than that great love it had come to replace?

What about our childhood songs? Those are the ones that burn into our flesh and bones, and that dissolve into our blood. We are touched by these melodies even today, although its already been a long time since we were part of that war, and nothing now even remains of the regime that ordered and implanted these songs in us.

> The White Army's coming back with its Baron black,
> Trying to force us to take the Tsar back,
> But from the taiga to the British seas cold
> Our Red Army's the strongest of all.
> Let our Red Army men
> With a grip won't relent
> Each horny clasp on their bayonet
> For we must labor
> And never waver
> And fight this last fight to the death!

We intoxicatingly sang these songs in their exalted minor key, our voices rising at the end of the refrain; we sang them at the top of our lungs at our kindergartens and schools, repeating their melodies on holidays, when orchestras resounded in the squares and singing throngs strode along the streets, festooned with red bunting and the portraits of our kind leaders and invincible commanders. The entire country sang: "We want not a single inch of an alien land, but we shall not give away even a yard of ours!" These songs resounded across the land – and just at the very same time, covered by the slogan of a fraternal reunion of peoples, far more than inches were seized from other nations' territories. Perhaps it was just through these songs that my childhood turned out to be welded to the steel carcass of war, and from the evening of 21 June 1941, day after day it unfolded against the backdrop of *Sovinformburo* announcements, some of which I remember word for word even today. My uncles and cousins didn't return from the war. And the defeats of our beloved Red Army? Of our invincible Army! It had defeated the Japanese at Lake Khasan and had drubbed them at Khalkhin-Gol. It had reintegrated the brotherly peoples of western Belorussia and the western Ukraine. It had pulverized the perfidious Finns into snow powder, our Red Army!

Is it possible to imagine our shock, our childhood disillusionment and resentment as we fled under bombings and machine-gun bursts, seeing only German Messerschmitts above our heads and not even hearing the engines of our own *iastrebki* [fighters]? What of the announcements of cities, abandoned in the very heart of our Motherland? The foe seized our recently reintegrated and reunited Ukraine, Belorussia, Moldavia, Lithuania, Latvia and Estonia, leaving us with not an inch; then he was at the Don, in the Caucasus, and had turned up on the Volga, which with just a glance at the map caused your eyes to blink with disbelief. How did this happen? Why??

I had to experience a similar shock once again twenty years later, in a movie theater, while watching the film *Geroi ne umiraiut* [*Heroes don't die*],[1] when the wise and humane faces of the eradicated army commanders gazed down at us from the screen. The film made it clear to me that prior to 1937 the Red Army truly was one of the strongest in the world, headed by educated commanders and contemporary thinkers. That Red Army was capable not only of rapidly implementing a mobilization, but also of providing effective military training to the new recruits. After the severe trials and enormous sacrifices of the Great Patriotic War, this was a shocking discovery.

Watching the film, however, didn't lead to immediate enlightenment. I had to rid myself of a multitude of other illusions – and from the pernicious influence of self-censorship. Yet this turned out to be impossible without leaving the country in which I'd been born, together with which I'd suffered so much, and in which I'd spent the greater part of my life. For this, another decade had to pass. Only then did I begin to put down on paper the pain of all the losses – not only emotionally, but also analytically. This pain even guided my hand when still during the Cold War I was writing my first novel free from censorship, *Toska po Londonu* [*Longing for London*], which contained two parallel stories: one about Stalin in the Kremlin between 1941 and 1945, and the other about a dissident writer, who couldn't

---

1 This was a documentary film by the Central Movie Studio of Documentary Films, which contained the best chroniclers of films about the Red Army prior to the purges. The film was dedicated to the memory of the executed top brass of the Red Army (Tukhachevsky, Bliukher, Egorov, Uborevich, Iakir) and was authorized for public screening in connection with the wave of de-Stalinization, but the circulation was limited and it was restricted to viewings only at documentary film theaters, which could only be found in major cities.

endure emigration and returned not long before perestroika to his native city, which had been left desolated by the war. The conscience of the first character wasn't troubled by the losses. The second was tormented not only with the question "How did this happen?", but also "Why?" Why had such enormous losses been necessary?

When, back in the USSR, I had once stirred myself to take up again the war's events, the catastrophe of 1941 remained without an intelligible explanation from the men who had been formally responsible for it – Zhukov, Vasilevsky and others. Not authorized to enter the military archives, I time and again pored over the pages of the memoirs and recollections of other generals – and still found no clarity. Stalin's miscalculation, yes, was understandable, but such losses? It might have been possible to avoid these encirclements that the *Wehrmacht* had created!

In America, the events of 1941 became accessible in narratives written by the German side. Sparks sprayed from the collision of viewpoints, sparks that illuminated the memoirs of Soviet military commanders which were well-known to me, but full of omissions and half-truths. As a result, back in the 1980s, I had developed a hypothetical basis for an explanation of the catastrophic losses of the 1941 campaign. This hypothesis was later confirmed by the uniquely meticulous studies of the great scholar of our war, David Glantz.

The fruit of my clarification about the events, however, became the fact that the military aspect in a novel I had been writing at that time began to smother the lyrical side of it. The novel was dying. With an improbable effort I managed to convince myself that I would write another book, one focused on the analysis of the past.

I was writing this other book feverishly after finishing my novel, as David Glantz was already conducting his gigantic research of "the Russian war". However, I wasn't aware of his efforts yet. Sixteen years passed from the time of the first edition of this book. Over this time, myths were falling and facts were surfacing. Almost by himself, David Glantz managed to make the West aware of where in reality the fate of the Second World War was decided. For the West it hasn't been easy to digest this, not for the least reason because of Winston Churchill, who had brilliantly set forth his version of history in his book *The Second World War*.[2] Everything is in it, but its guideposts are not Hitler's pivoting to the East to invade the USSR, not the enormous battles of 1941-1942, not Stalingrad, Kursk and the "Belorussian Balcony"[3], but Africa, El-Alamein and the landing in Normandy. Churchill's authority is enormous, and so was his influence on the British and American interpretation of the war -- the Soviet Army's role in the war was largely ignored. Two reasons, beside the Cold War, contributed to this. First was the inevitable (given the laurels of victory that crowned the USSR) tacit agreement with the proposition that a dictatorship is superior to a democracy in extreme circumstances, which the Western democracies didn't wish to advertise. The second reason, and the main one, was the fact that the USSR was itself an aggressive power (and remained so to the very end of its existence). As the British historian Norman Davies expresses this in one paradoxical phrase: "The axis powers are joined on the criminal list by the Soviet Union, which also turns out to have been the principal victor."[4]

Although the book became popular, it would have been unsurprising if it would have had to wait for its translation into English (since until the present day the memoirs of

---

2   Published in Russian in 1991 by the Voenizdat in Moscow.

3   Editor's note: This is the reference to the German salient in Belorussia occupied by Army Group Center, which was smashed by Operation Bagration in the summer of 1944.

4   *The Sunday Times*, 6 November 2006.

many Soviet military commanders have still not been translated, while Soviet publishing agencies produced the English translation of Zhukov's and Vasilevsky's memoirs, even as they knowingly screened the contents). Only through a happy chain of coincidences did fate, in the form of the young historian Yan Mann, put me in touch with the great historian of our war David Glantz and his reliable colleague, my scrupulous and exacting translator Stuart Britton. Through the efforts of these enthusiasts my book has become accessible to the Western reader, and my gratitude to these dedicated Good Samaritans is eternal. I vastly appreciate Mr. Britton for his immeasurable efforts to preserve my rhythm and style; he succeeded in preserving both, as far as I understand this marvelous English language.

Already the first edition of my book was warmly reviewed by my wonderful friend Mark Raeff, a professor at Columbia University. His comments inspired me to continue working on the book.

On this occasion, I would also like to express my indebtedness to the very first reader of the first edition of this book, Oleg Pridachin. I am sincerely grateful to all who read subsequent editions of the book, offered their comments, and expressed their support for my long years of work: the superb ethnologist and exacting reviewer, Dr. Anatoly Liberman of the University of Minnesota; veterans Ion Degen, Boris Gorbachevsky and David Rakhman; Dr. Yury Polsky of West Chester University; poetess Valentina Sinkevich; my friends Vadim Smolensky, Mark Leykin, Feliks Uzilevsky, Valentina and Aleksander Kucher, Vladi Malakhov, Anatolii Yarkho, and Feliks Press. By rights, my greatest gratitude belongs to my son Mikhail, who helped me a lot, and my wife, Janna, who is a most discriminating reader and demanding editor.

There remains to remind the reader that Marshal Zhukov is not the main character in this sad tale. He only performs a role as the most authoritative witness to the accusations against Stalin, who was the real organizer and instigator of all our losses.

One may ask why not simply read Zhukov's memoirs, or why his memoirs needed such extended commentary. Or why didn't Zhukov and Vasilevsky, the *Stavka*'s two pillars, offer explanations in their memoirs of the rationale for the bloody tactics of 1941, which therefore forced it to be dug out intuitively? Alas, the answer is short and clear: the reason is Soviet censorship.

Just one example: Marshal Zhukov, in his memoirs, assessed the situation at Moscow axis after Operation Typhoon as "serious". For decades we did not know how serious it had been, although in 1966 in an interview with writer Konstantin Simonov, given in the reserved Soviet manner, Marshal Zhukov admitted that between October 6 and 13, 1941, Moscow was defenseless.[5] The interview was given on the 25th Anniversary of the victorious Battle of Moscow. Guess what, dear reader? The authorities ordered the transcript to be destroyed. Taking a great risk, the journalist Vladimir Pozner saved one copy and put it in an archive, where nobody would even think to look for it, in The Studio of Animated Cartoons, where it rested until the son of the journalist decided it was safe to reveal the truth. The interview was made public to the Russian people on the 65th Anniversary of Victory Day, 57 years after Stalin death. That was the amount of time necessary to reveal a bit of the truth to the Russians audience. So, how can a reader count upon the truthfulness of the Marshals' memoirs written under Communist Party pressure and heavy Soviet censorship? How can a reader see through the Marshal's restrained words, stating that the situation on some front sector had become "serious" when the situation was actually

---

5   At time of publication, available at http://www.statehistory.ru/732/Intervyu-Zhukova-Simonovu/

catastrophic? However, that was the typical style of all memoirs written in the Soviet era. So, little wonder that the truth had to be obtained by reading between the lines of the memoirs, combined with reading of a lot of memoirs others than those written by Soviets.

I've worked over the five editions of this book (with intervals) for one and a half decades, and even now continue to write it and rewrite it in my thoughts. The aspects of the purges and its consequences are endless, as are the aspects of the war, and an analysis of the events, with which the history of the USSR is strewn, leads me to repeat humbly Flaubert's words: "Work cannot be completed; it can only be stopped".

Peter Mezhiritsky
San Diego 2010

Abbreviations

APN	*Agenstvo pechati "Novosti"*, or The "Novost" Press Agency
CC CPSU	The Central Committee of the Communist Party of the Soviet Union
CHON	Special Designation Unit
CPSU	Communist Party of the Soviet Union
DAP	*Deutsche Arbeiter Partei*, or German Worker's Party
EPRON	Special Designation Expedition for Underwater Work
GHQ	General Headquarters
GKO	*Gosudarstvennyj komitet oborony* or The State Defense Committee
GRU	*Glavnoye Razvedyvatel'noye Upravleniy,* or the General Staff's Chief Intelligence Agency
GTO	*Gotov k trudu I oborone* or, Ready for Labour and Defense
HQ	Headquarters
KKUKS	*Kavaleriiskie kursy dlya usovershenstvovania komandnogo sostava* or Cavalry Courses for Improving the Command Staff
KUVNAS	Courses for Improving the Higher Command Staff
MOPR	*Mezhdunarodnaia organizatsiia pomoshchi rabochim* or, International Organization of Assistance to Workers
NEP	New Economic Policy
NKVD	*Narodnyi kommisariat vnutrennykh del*, or People's Commissariat of Internal Affairs
NSDAP	National-Socialist German Workers Party
OGPU	*Ob'edinennoe Gosudarstvennoe Politicheskoe Upravlenie* or Government Secret Police
OKH	*Oberkommando des Heeres*, or High Command of the Army
OKW	*Oberkommando der Wehrmacht*, or High Command of the Armed Forces
RKKA	Workers' and Peasants' Red Army, more commonly known as The Red Army
SA	*Sturmabteilung,* more popularly known as 'Storm Troopers', the paramilitary wing of the Nazi Party and, in effect, Hitler's own private army
SIS	Secret Intelligence Service
SMERSH	The counter-intelligence agency within the Red Army
SS	*Schustzstaffel,* a major paramilitary organization closely affiliated to the Nazi Party
Stavka	Headquarters of the Soviet Armed Forces
TASS	*Informatsionnoye telegrafnoye agentstvo Rossii,* or Information Telegraph Agency of Russia
TsK KPSS	*Tsentralniy Komitet Kommunistitcheskoi Partii Sovetskogo Soyuza* or The Central Committee of the Communist Party of the Soviet Union
TsK VKP(b)	Central Committee of the All-union Communist Party (Bolshevik)
USSR	Union of the Soviet Socialist Republics

Wehrmacht   The unified armed forces of Nazi Germany in existence between 1935 and 1945

Part One

In memory of all those who fell in the Second World War.

In memory of all the martyrs, not yet deemed worthy of monuments and who didn't survive to take part in the Second World War.

1

Interlude: Children ...

... often died in families. Indeed, in his as well. Yet he, the third born, unfortunately survived in order to destroy tens of millions of people ruthlessly.

Of course, I'm not speaking about Zhukov. I'm talking about his patron, the Supreme High Commander and Generalissimo, Stalin.

Zhukov, though, survived – fortunately. (I anticipate that such an assertion will find many who oppose it. Considered among Russia's national heroes, Zhukov nevertheless provokes the frenzied howling of neo-Stalinists, who strive to overturn the truth by praising Stalin for the Victory, and blaming Zhukov for the losses.) In the Marshal's memoirs *Vospominaniia i razmyshleniia* (*Remembrances and Reflections*) he hardly touched upon the losses. As a professional, he didn't even begin to try to exonerate himself: A commander's duty is to avoid defeats and to conquer, while the cost is a secondary matter. The casualties – not Zhukov's fault, but not without his participation – were countless, even in vain. However, they were not the victims of the repressions. The strong little boy would live a glorious life, and become a great commander and an idol to millions. In the pantheon of Russian military glory his name stands equal to the names of Peter Rumiantsev and Mikhail Kutuzov. His fame has not been besmirched by the disgrace of repression, like the fame of Suvorov, whose title of Field Marshal had been bestowed by Empress Catherine for the brutal suppression of the Warsaw uprising of 1794. At that time, the banks of the Vistula River had been covered by a medley of the remains of young ladies, children, Jews, Polish nobles and an assortment of random victims. "Speed, assessment, hitting power ..."[1]

History is mocking and repeats itself in ways that are difficult to recognize. One hundred and fifty years later, our hero also faced the problem of a Warsaw uprising. The medley of corpses was now the Nazis' doing, while Stalin kept watch from the Kremlin as his foes consumed each other. It was left for Zhukov to justify his inaction – and he did, thank you. Thanks for the humble admission of his guilt. Zhukov could hardly have been accused seriously; he was a weapon in someone else's hands.

Indeed, he remained a weapon. The brilliant tactician never played any independent role in politics – fortunately so, I think.

Fate placed him in an exceptional situation. Stalin's purges, directed at the liquidation of personalities, struck down more than a few strong-willed people even among those, who weren't drawn into Stalin's orbit. Zhukov was a strong-willed man – and would remain one. Happily for Zhukov. Happily for the country. He climbed the hierarchical staircase to the highest step not too soon, and so his head remained on his shoulders. With his character, that was a great fortune. In the eviscerated Red Army, he wound up in the necessary place at the necessary time – Chief of the General Staff of the Red Army on that fateful day 22 June 1941. At that time and in those conditions, the key talent was the ability and character to

---

1   Editor's note: Field Marshal Suvorov was famous for his military aphorisms, such as "Train hard, fight easy" and "Perish yourself, but save your comrade." This is another of Suvorov's sayings, a well-known, succinct distillation of Suvorov's philosophy of war.

defend one's opinions. Zhukov did this. He proposed singularly acceptable solutions, and insisted upon them. In that situation under Stalin, no one could have managed to do more.

A fulfilled life. A visible result. He never had the love of his superiors, but glory didn't pass him by. His name has never disappeared and never will disappear from lips and printed pages.

The memoirs that Zhukov left behind are brief and distinguished.[2] Though sparing in words, these memoirs are valuable. His omissions are, for the most part, compulsory. There are minimal excuses and none whatsoever regarding Zhukov's personal decisions.

This book doesn't aim to topple Zhukov from his rightful place on the pedestal. It has been written with respect for the great commander, for his role in the war, and for the personal courage he demonstrated. At his post as Chief of the General Staff at the start of the war, his courage was topped only by a senselessness and selflessness of the highest order – of the same sort that gripped those heroes who hurled themselves beneath enemy tanks with grenade bundles.

After all, this book is not about Zhukov ...

---

2   We, the war's contemporaries, waited a long time for them – the memoirs of the saviors of the Fatherland. The memoirs of all the main military commanders were ghost-written, and in the special case of a particularly prominent individual, the memoirist was assigned journalists by the Party apparatus. Typically in such cases, friendly relations developed between the man dictating his memoirs and the scribes, and the journalists would affably explain to the veterans how to avoid censorship and how to present the material connected with mistakes, defeats, and heavy losses. Exceptions are not only rare, but singular. Only Marshal A. M. Vasilevsky wrote his own memoirs by himself, with the same censorship limitations, certainly. They were not published by Voenizdat [the Soviet military publisher], but by Politizdat [the Soviet political publisher]. Zhukov's memoirs were also not published by Voenizdat, as would have been natural. They came out from the APN [*Agenstvo pechati "Novosti"* – "Novost" Press Agency]. Through my friend, a laureate of international competitions, the violinist Rafail Sobolevsky, who was a friend of the Marshal's family, I became aware of the pressure on the Marshal from the Party clique while the memoirs were being written. They demanded silence first and foremost from the Marshal, the omission of unpleasant facts and out of favor heroes, and instructed him to replace them with the glorification of trifles.

2

His origin, according to Zhukov

The childless widow Annushka Zhukov adopted an infant boy, the future father of Georgii Konstantinovich, from a children's shelter. It is known only that a woman had left the infant on the doorstep of the orphanage with a note: "My son's name is Konstantin."[1]

His father's own biography has been shaped and crafted so as to make him out to be a Gavroche of the First Russian Revolution.[2] Soviet power, presumed to remain proletarian forever, prompted such a story in order to give an appropriate revolutionary stamp to Zhukov's background. Zhukov dedicated his life and sword to this power. An interpretation of his father's biography beneficial to it ideologically was a small sacrifice.

The later photographs of the Marshal are remarkable. Of course, the years of power have given rise to an imperious expression on his face. With the years, even ordinary faces acquire significance. The features of the commander, however, suggest portraits of grandees. Although his mother was a simple peasant, perhaps Marshal of the Soviet Union Georgii Konstantinovich Zhukov was not.

It is easy to brush the thin coating of ideology from his memoirs – all these ritualistic dances around Marxism and around Lenin personally, which supposedly even country folk knew about back in 1905. We know, though: Lenin attached himself to the villagers, but the villagers – not to Lenin.

---

1   Although I am not an expert in 19th century mode of life, I do know that there were no orphanages in Russian villages. So, if there was no chance to get an abortion, it was normal practice to hire a cabman to take an illegitimate child of unlawful love to an orphanage. Konstantin by no means could be a name for a country boy of peasant origin. Thus we must assume that Konstantin's mother was a city woman, and that naturally his father was as well. From which it is clear that we can only guess at the genes of the future commander.

2   Editor's note: Gavroche is an impoverished character in Victor Hugo's *Les Miserables*, who as a lad joins the Paris uprising of 1834 and is killed while carrying supplies to those manning the street barricades.

3

Interlude: A fixed interest ...

... in such insignificant details can prompt bewilderment. However, more significant incongruities will appear ahead, and they have a direct relationship to our theme.

From Zhukov's childhood, his apprenticeship in Moscow, the First World War and the Russian Civil War, I won't single out any facts or character aspect, other than to say that the young Georgii was just like the mother, and Ustin'ia Artem'evna was a strong woman, easily able to lift full bags of grain. Zhukov was of medium height. He comported himself just like his character, and what a character he turned out to be! His pugnaciousness showed on his face. There was hardly anyone prepared to offend this young boy, lad, soldier, and *unteroffizier*[1]

---

1 Editor's note: An *unteroffizier* is an old German rank, also used by the Tsarist Russian Army, which is very roughly comparable to "junior non-commissioned officer". In World War II, an *unteroffizier* in the German *Wehrmacht* was comparable to the American rank of sergeant.

4

Military Education 1

The year is 1916. The place is an *unteroffizier* training detachment in the city of Izium, Khar'kov Guberniia. The trainees were unlucky with their commanding *unteroffizier*. He turned out to be a brawler, who liked to knock his subordinates off their feet. The *unteroffizier* particularly disliked Zhukov, but for some reason avoided striking him. For some reason ...

> Looking back now on the old [Tsarist] army's training detachment in general I must say that they taught us well, particularly with respect to formation drills. Every graduate fully mastered equestrian skills, weaponry, and methods to train soldiers. It is not a coincident that many *unteroffiziers* of the old army ... became skilled military commanders in the Red Army.

"Many" ... "Skilled" ... Not Budenny; this swashbuckler, a full Cavalier of St. George[1], hadn't even learned how to read a map. This merits a mention here, because he with his squadron baggage was entrusted with the command of *fronts* in the Great Patriotic War.

Where did Georgii Konstantinovich acquire his skill? Not in the *unteroffizier* training detachment. They didn't teach strategy there. Topography and maps – perhaps, I don't know; but reserves, logistics, the ability to maneuver troops and to organize the rear? Whatever, let's proceed.

The year is 1924. Division commander Gai is asking the young regiment commander how he works to better himself. Zhukov replies that he reads a lot and analyzes operations of the First World War. Gai observed that this wasn't much, and sent Zhukov to the Higher Cavalry School in Leningrad.

Division commander Gai didn't overlook the young regiment commander. He didn't allow Zhukov to linger too long in one place, and gave him a boost upward. G. D. Gai was one of the first commanders of proletarian origin to be arrested (if not the very first). I note this, because it directly touches upon the future leader and his actions ...

Zhukov was considered among the best young officers at the school: the exams turned out to be easy, even formal. How else could they have been for such graduates? Had they been any more demanding, guys like Eremenko definitely wouldn't have passed them, and Eremenko was not one of the worst to survive the purges intact. His sense of optimism nicely served the Stalingrad defense. Of course, had there been no purges, which boosted Eremenko to such a high rank, matters might have never reached the need for a defense of Stalingrad.

V. M. Primakov was commanding the Higher Cavalry School, and Zhukov observes that he (Primakov) "was the product of an intellectual family." The orphan Vitalii Primakov

---

1   Editor's note: In the First World War, Budenny earned all four degrees of the St. George Cross, a medal for non-commissioned officers who demonstrated extreme acts of courage in the face of the enemy. Anyone who earned all four degrees of the St. George Cross became known as a full Cavalier of St. George.

G.D.Gai

V.M. Primakov (courtesy of Nina Young)

L.D. Trotsky

was adopted by the great Ukrainian writer Kotsiubinsky and later married his daughter. During his final year of study in high school, Primakov was arrested for revolutionary propaganda. The student later proved to be a gifted military man. A legendary commander of the Chervonnyi Cossacks and a man of letters, who had mastered the spoken and written word, Primakov, of course, made quite an impression on his tongue-tied and inelegantly-writing peers.

The Higher Cavalry School was re-formed into the Cavalry Courses for Improving the Command Staff (*Kavaleriiskie kursy dlya usovershenstvovania komandnogo sostava –* KKUKS). The period of training was reduced from two years to one year. Their haste was due to a shortage of commanders.

Significantly, though the First World War and Civil Wars are over, the country's army continues to grow, at a time when its government is proposing a program of complete disarmament to the entire world. Increasing arms, while agitating for disarmament ... What is that – counting upon gullibility? Then all these talks about disarmament are just a propaganda stunt? The army is growing, and there aren't enough officers ... Incidentally, there are plenty of officers available, with requisite education, though they had received their commissions in the Tsarist era. But Trotsky had been removed, and Stalin doesn't like the officers of the former Tsarist army: they do not have the proper mindset or they have preconceptions ... It is the same sort of problem that Hitler faces with his officers, with their preconceptions, with their consciences... Yet the Red Army is still growing, and more proletarian commanders have to be graduated from the Courses. We, at our

Polytechnic Institute, were stuffed with military education for five years[2], going over some material repeatedly. A total of four hours a week, but then we had already acquired the general concepts. Even those of us who were on the verge of failing academically didn't need to learn the difference between degrees of temperature and degrees of angles, or to study the concept of scale, the foundations of physics, descriptive geometry, or the distinction between acid and alkaline. Teach those who have no spatial awareness how to read a map. It isn't easy for an untrained person to read a map and see the terrain in his mind's eye. Yet what if the commander is located far from the battlefield, and has no other way to see the theater of combat operations? I'm not even speaking of the planning of offensive operations based on the terrain, occupied by the enemy's forces.

That's just a map; and what about the rest of what a commander needs to know? What about chemical warfare, and as part of it the analysis of the difference between decontamination and de-activation? Airplanes, tanks ... They guzzle fuel, so you'd better stockpile it. What about many other things? Lubricants? Transportation? Communications?

Oh, one year is not enough! Even just to train a good regiment commander, not to mention a commander like Zhukov. Moreover, at the Courses the main subject of study remained the cavalry sortie. Zhukov writes: "Training at the KKUKS concluded with a forced march to the Volkhov River. Here we learned how to swim with the horse and how to force a crossing of a water barrier."

The training regimen wasn't dense with the learning the tasks that a Chief of the General Staff or a Deputy Supreme Commander would have to face. Clearly, the main subject matter still lies ahead. Well then, let's proceed.

In 1927 Zhukov is commanding the 39th Regiment of the 7th Cavalry Division. The division commander is Dmitrii Arkad'evich Shmidt, formerly known as David Aronovich Gutman. ("A clever man" – the Marshal has to say about his commander at the time). Unexpectedly, Egorov, Chief of Staff of the RKKA [Workers' and Peasants' Red Army, known familiarly as the Red Army] and a former colonel in the Tsarist army, arrives at the regiment. The meeting became an event. There was a discussion about forming a second echelon of forces. Zhukov complained about the shortage of personnel in his regiment, and asked how they were to form a second echelon with the available men... Egorov replied, "But we have no other way out. One mustn't underestimate the foe. We need to prepare seriously for the war, to prepare to fight with an intelligent, wily, strong enemy."

Let's remember those words. Apart from the formal bows in the direction of Marxism and the CPSU (Communist Party of the Soviet Union), which were plainly not in Zhukov's style, there are no superfluous words in his memoirs. He had a reason for mentioning second echelons. In their absence lies a secret of the horrors of 1941, though not the entire secret ... yet the Chief of Staff of the Red Army is not making polite chit-chat with the inquisitive regiment commander here. Reading Egorov's reply, you begin to sense just who destroyed the flower of the Red Army's thinking as it confronted an intelligent, wily, strong foe ...

In 1929, Zhukov was sent to the Courses for Improving the Higher Command Staff (KUVNAS). There he studied tactics and the operational art. Book discussions became more concrete. The books of Frunze, Tukhachevsky, Egorov, Shaposhnikov, Uborevich and Iakir appeared.

---

2   In the USSR every man while earning a higher education degree had to receive a military education and the junior lieutenant's rank as well. The requirements were tough. Those who could not pass the state military exam were refused the civil degree also.

Zhukov's memoirs contain a distinctly angry passage on the subject of B. M. Shaposhnikov's book about the role of an army's general staff, *Mozg armii* [*The Brain of the Army*]:

It is a past matter, but then, even as now, I believe that the title of the book ... is incorrect as it applies to the Red Army. The 'brain' of the Red Army from its very first days has been the TsK VKP(b) [Central Committee of the All-union Communist Party (Bolshevik)], since not a single major military question was settled without the participation of the Central Committee. This title applies more to the old Tsarist army, where the 'brain' actually was its General Staff.

It is possible that not everyone will agree, but this passage – together with this identification of the "brain" in each case – actually does hit the bulls-eye. It is of course a past matter, as the Marshal stated, but this observation in his memoirs *Vospominaniia i razmyshleniia* then, even as now (using Zhukov's expression) is striking, like no other in the book. It is, if you will, the book's semantic center and a doubtless continuation of an old argument. Someone may see in this passage a high regard for the leading role of the Party, which taught everything to everyone: writers how to write (starting the list with the most painful personally), announcers how to speak, doctors how to treat, teachers how to teach, and military men, of course, how to fight.

Here for the first time Zhukov reveals the source of our failures and losses in the war. This place in the memoirs has been written with the heavy pen of Georgii Konstantinovich himself, in anger and spite. On the surface the statement is irreproachable. What did this TsK VKP(b) alone mean in the epoch of the CPSU? There is also the mention of the Tsarist army, where its General Staff *actually* was the brain (which Zhukov couldn't know first-hand, but knew from the acknowledgements of his senior colleague Shaposhnikov, who was a colonel on the Tsarist army's general staff). Zhukov's writing style may not be the most elegant, but it mustn't be forgotten that he knew all the ins and outs of the leading role of the Party, and he was quite familiar with writing documents for later Party review. However, Zhukov was a man who put meaning above all else, who meant what he said, and in this passage he achieved it. His point is clear, and further on in his memoirs, he pays respect to the list of repressed marshals and army commanders, and stresses his admiration for the personality of Tukhachevsky, and his high regard for Triandafillov.

Vladimir Kiriakovich Triandafillov was a gifted military thinker and a Deputy Chief of Staff of the Red Army, who headed its Operations Department.[3] He wrote two books: *Razmakh operatsii sovremennykh armii* [The Scale of Operations of Modern Armies] (Moscow, 1926) and *Kharakter operatsii sovremennykh armii* [The Nature of Operations of Modern Armies] (Moscow-Leningrad, 1929). In 1931, Triandafillov presented a report to the staff of the Red Army, "Basic questions of tactics and operational art." The report laid out a theory of deep battle and represented an attempt, as Triandafillov himself wrote, "... to grope for a common, general line in the development of tactics and operations" in light of the use of new types of weapons and combat equipment.

The work remained unfinished. On 12 July 1931[4], a plane crash killed a group of Red

---

3   Subsequently, this post was occupied by Vasilevsky, Vatutin and Antonov.
4   Twelve years later, on 12 July 1943, as if marking the anniversary of the death of the Red Army's leading reformers, two tank armadas collided on the field at Prokhorovka. On this day, the Red Army seized the

V.K. Triandafillov

Army General Staff officers together with the aircraft's crew. Among the victims was the Deputy Chief of the Red Army's Branch of Mechanization and Motorization Kalinovsky. Triandafillov was the senior officer on the flight, which was being conducted by a "special designation" air detachment. (Back then there were a lot of "special designations": CHON – special designation unit; EPRON – special designation expedition for underwater work. However, in the context of events, the name of the air detachment sounds sinister ...).

The 19th century German writer Ludwig Berne once observed: "When Pythagoras unveiled his famous theorem, he sacrificed 100 bulls to the gods. Ever since, when a new truth is revealed, all the beasts tremble."

The cavalrymen and partisan Cossacks were disturbed by Triandafillov's thoughts. They in turn alarmed the Great Leader, Stalin. He, incidentally, was growing concerned even before Triandafillov's report and always relied upon his old comrades in the cavalry and partisans. Together with them, he had achieved his "legendary" exploits in the Russian Civil War; these partisans were dearer to him than any relative. This is not an exaggeration. One need only imagine how the leader thirsted for power over the Red Army, and how insignificant was his authority (deservedly so) and pitiful was his role in it: he and his cronies had merely been swashbucklers of the First Cavalry Army, one of Stalin's commands in the Russian Civil War! They even convinced Stalin, that he, the Leader and Luminary, would himself at his own leisure elaborate the theory of deep battle. There was no general line for which to grope. There was only one line – their line. The leader could test the theory

strategic initiative and never let it go until the end of the war. Hardly anyone recalled the name of those, to whom the Red Army owed the mechanization of its forces and the development of a military doctrine befitting them.

in practice. He had no need for any Triandafillov; and so the right to think strategically henceforth became a prerogative for only Comrade Stalin.

Perhaps, everything wasn't this way. Perhaps the cavalrymen were afraid to fly, and they had no need to do it; they possessed a lot of leisure, time had no value to them, and duties were no burden. Triandafillov, on the other hand, in order to save time, flew, and according to the law of chance, subjected himself to a great risk; who knows? ...

In a word, the best offensive theorist in the Red Army had perished. In the Tsarist army, Triandafillov had been a staff captain. The cup had passed him by, as it also passed by Shaposhnikov. Triandafillov was actually lucky; he had an easy death. However, as Zhukov said in his memoirs, "His works, connected with the future war and [occupying] the most important position in Soviet military strategy and operational art, were unfortunately never completed." This recognition, from the lips of a commander who played a decisive role in that war, tragically signifies much in terms of our immense military losses: he would have liked to have gone to war armed with a strategic doctrine and a developed set of operational principles ... By the way, the sense of regret expressed on this topic draws us further into our investigation: after all, Zhukov's mastery had to have been distilled somewhere, but where?

In the spring of 1931, the KUVNAS [Courses for Improving the Higher Command Staff] audience returned to their units. Just six months – this was plainly insufficient. Plainly insufficient for Khalkhin-gol alone.

5

Interlude: February ...

... of the year 1964 proved to be cold and damp. There was no sun; in L'vov, Ukraine, that February it never appeared and neither did it "under Poland", namely, until the blessed arrival of Soviet power – "the sun from the East".[1] The cold was nipping, down to around 0° C. On a day like that, having received some comp time after my duty as a night director at the factory, I was sitting in a movie theater that showed documentary films. This somewhat long, crooked hall had formerly been a factory shop and was totally unsuitable for a movie theater. The view from the back rows was poor, the heating wasn't working, and the damp cold was penetrating to the bones. However, I realized that I was utterly frozen only when the screen went dark. The film from the Central Studio of Documentary Films, *Geroi ne umiraiut*, directed by S. Bubrik, showed photographs that I had not seen many times before, but would later see repeatedly – the young, intelligent faces of the Red Army's upper command, Zhukov's peers and teachers.

Then the camera lens passed over their books, which had savage stamps on their covers: BANNED. Banned – what, military thought?

Precisely. From the learned higher command staff of the Red Army, only Shaposhnikov survived;[2] bestowed the title of Marshal, but broken morally, capable only of proposing and never insisting.

Sitting with benumbed feet in the unheated hall, though, for the first time I saw the cadres of the legendary maneuvers of the Kiev Military District, 12-17 September 1935.[3] They were playing out an operation to encircle Kiev and the city's defense – like what unfolded day to day, six years later, until the city's surrender. The "enemy" launched a concentric attack from two directions. The infantry rose to the attack after a powerful artillery preparation and advanced behind a wall of artillery fire. After breaking through the defense into operational space, mobile formations of tanks and cavalry moved out. At the location of the intended link-up to close the ring, a mass airborne landing, like history had never known, was conducted. It had the participation of 2,953 men equipped with, in addition to their carbines, 29 heavy machine guns, 10 field guns, light tanks, and six vehicles. Later, in 1940 the commander of the Kiev Special Military District General of

---

1 Editor's note: L'vov was part of Poland from that country's independence in 1918 until that area's seizure by Soviet troops in 1939 as part of the secret protocols to the Molotov-von Ribbentrop Non-Aggression Pact.

2 Shaposhnikov, in addition to his unmilitary-like manners and other merits, was plainly gifted with a diplomatic touch as well. The insinuations against Tukhachevsky created material against Shaposhnikov as well, but this material was never pursued. Not a single living soul spoke poorly about Shaposhnikov. This was a Christ in military dress. He exerted colossal influence on the course of the initial stage of the Great Patriotic War – as an adviser. The shock of the purges shortened his life.

3 Editor's note: The 1935 Kiev maneuvers were designed to test Triandafillov's and Tukhachevsky's theories of deep combat, which were quite similar to the *Blitzkrieg* doctrine adopted by the Germans. In the maneuvers the theory collided against Iakir's and Uborevich's theory of active defense and a following counteroffensive, which became later the basis of the Soviet victorious strategy in the Great Patriotic War.

At the September 1935 Kiev maneuvers. From left to right:
A.I. Egorov, I.E. Iakir, K.E. Voroshilov and S.M. Budenny.

the Army Zhukov, in reply to a question from Stalin about air-dropped tanks in Bessarabia, would answer that the frightened Romanians were only imagining this; there were still no such tanks. So in 1940 there weren't any, but back in 1935 there were!

Observing the exercises, the Deputy Chief of Staff of the French Army General Loiseau wrote, "The parachute drop of a large combat unit, which I witnessed at Kiev, I consider to be a fact without precedent in the world." The English General Wavell reported to his government: "If I hadn't been a witness to this myself, I would never believe that such an operation was at all possible." Professor von der Heydte[4] recognized that the parachute accomplishments of the Russians served as a stimulus to the birth of the *Wehrmacht's* airborne forces, the *Fallschirmjäger*, which played a major role in Belgium, Crete and Norway.

As a child of the war, I had listened, holding my breath, to ominous reports and the description of assaults on heights, taken only after repeated bloody frontal attacks. I'd been tormented by the daily spectacle of cripples, just a little older than myself, who'd been left abandoned to the streets by Mother Russia to beg for alms. Later I had learned as well about the absurd lack of cooperation between not only different types of forces, but even within mixed formations. This intelligent warfare I was seeing on the screen made such an impression on me; it was as if a Christmas tree ornament had exploded in my hands and wounded me. This meant that prior to the purges the Red Army had mastered it all! Yet it had all been taken away from the Red Army by the purges! The ability to defeat the foe at little cost!

The maneuvers were directed by the commander of the Kiev Military District, I. E. Iakir, one of the most penetrating military minds of the 20th century, the recognized leader of the Red Army.[5] These maneuvers were notable not because at them, for the

---

4   Baron Friedrich August von der Heydte, a professor of international law, a veteran of the Crete campaign, a cousin of Klaus von Stauffenberg and an early participant in the plot to assassinate Hitler, as a colonel in 1944 was head of the *Wehrmacht* parachute school.

5   That's how Iakir was evaluated by Stalin, who put testimony into the mouths of the victims of the bloody feast, regarding what Iakir had ostensibly planned in the People's Commissariat of the Navy after Voroshilov's removal. However, this is just what the Army would have wanted. In the 1920s and beginning of the 1930s, the leading doctrine of the Red Army was the doctrine of smashing, which had also been worked out by Triandafillov. "...Iakir attributed little importance to the strategy of destruction.

first time in world practice the new theory of deep battle was being worked out, but also because they were not bilateral, but trilateral: another part of the Red Army troops had represented Polish infantry divisions. At the time, Poland's relationship with the Soviet Union remained rocky. Iakir personally directed the "Polish" formations, combining this with his overall command duties.

For show in order to warn a potential aggressor, the maneuvers were staged so as to ensure the defeat of the "Aggressor" and conducted with the use of an unforeseen airborne landing by the adversary. However, the attempt to encircle the city was repulsed. Kiev remained standing. One can't help but think that six years later, the experience of these maneuvers would have helped hold the *Wehrmacht* outside the walls of Kiev for as long as it took to grind the plans of Operation Barbarossa into the dust.

At a time when the defeated Germany, which had been kicked out of the family of European nations after the First World War, was looking for ties, Russia was in the same situation. The two sides reached an agreement. The 1922 Treaty of Rappallo knocked a hole in the wall of isolation surrounding each government. Under the terms of the agreement and the secret protocols attached to it – secret protocols already at that time had entered the practice of agreements between countries – the Red Army and the German *Reichswehr* established contact. The Germans built factories inside the Soviet Union that produced weapons, including chemical weapons, which had been banned to Germany under the terms of the Treaty of Versailles. In return, Germany shared technology with the USSR and trained Soviet engineers. Within the framework of cooperation, Germany also trained Red Army commanders, who went to Germany in order to undergo an intense program on strategy and tactics. Meanwhile, *Reichswehr* officers, including the famous Guderian, looked in on the latest Russian novelties and drove tanks around the grounds of the Kazan Tank School, which was subsequently reorganized into an intelligence school.[6] The *Reichswehr* overcame the Versailles dam with the Rappallo breach.

Iakir, while studying at the German General Staff Academy in 1927-1928 was invited to give a lecture there on operations of the Russian Civil War. The march of Iakir's own group of forces, which had been bled white in preceding fighting, from the area of Birzula-Golta through the enemy rear to Zhitomir and Kiev became a classic model of a withdrawal

---

He worked urgently at strategic defense and induced his commander colleagues to do so. The first systems of echeloned defenses were born in the Ukrainian Military District; partisan bases were first developed there in case of retreat. Tukhachevsky's conversion to strategic defense came about under the unobtrusive but firm influence of Iakir." (Geller and Rapoport, *High Treason*)

6   My co-worker, a Colonel (ret.) I. A. Kirgizov once told me in confidence – this was back in 1967 – that in 1941 he had been a student of an intelligence school in Kazan', where they were training cadres for a lengthy residence in China. There were approximately 80 officers in the school with ranks ranging from lieutenant to brigade commander. The training was solid and included not only the Chinese language, but also the history and etiquette, including knowledge of all the ceremonies. They instructed the students how to behave, for which they invited famous actors, in particular Nikita Lian'-Kun', who had played the role of Kublai Khan in Sergei Eisentein's film *Aleksandr Nevsky*. In October 1941 the school, despite Molotov's protests, was abolished at Stalin's personal order, and all its students were assigned to the General Staff. "We spent the entire war messing around in headquarters no lower than the division-level," Kirgizov acknowledged, and who had the rank of lieutenant in 1941, "and no one made any use of us, other than one man – brigade commander Rybalko."

out of enemy encirclement.

Once when the great von Moltke[7] was compared to Frederick the Great in a burst of effusive praise, he thought for a moment, then rejected the comparison. He had never conducted the most difficult operation in war – a retreat. Iakir retreated with his wounded, artillery, and a wagon train. However, he not only moved for the sole purpose of linking-up again with his own side, he also created havoc in the enemy rear areas in the process. Searching for the least path of resistance as he retreated, he considered the tactical situation as well as the political situation. Playing with the animosities among the opposing forces, he literally slipped through their combat formations.

After the lecture ended, the delighted von Hindenburg gave Iakir a copy of von Schlieffen's book *Cannae* with an inscription, the gist of which was "From the *Reichswehr*'s senior strategist to the Red Army's youngest strategist."

The Red Army's youngest strategist was the first of eight condemned army commanders to be taken away from the courtroom for immediate execution. After him went Primakov, who back during the Polish campaign had disrespectfully addressed the future General Secretary over the telephone, when the latter had withdrawn his 1st Cavalry Army from the Warsaw axis back to L'vov and had simultaneously demanded the Chervonnyi Cossack Corps from Primakov, who was not subordinate to Stalin. From that same time, Stalin had grown to despise Tukhachevsky as well. This Adonis of a *front* commander by his entire appearance alone vexed the yellow-eyed Stalin. It would have been still better had he been quiet ... Having weakened the axis of the main attack (an action which he would later repeat in 1941-1942), Stalin contributed to the collapse of the Warsaw campaign (which had not been promising even without this error), but blamed Tukhachevsky for the failure. The latter defended himself in a mocking and vigorous style.[8] What Zhukov thought of Tukhachevsky is sufficiently clear in the first draft of his memoir, which percolated through the Communist Party apparatus. However, let's all the same turn to

---

7 Helmurth Karl Bernhard Moltke (1800-1891), Count and German General Field Marshal and Chief of the Prussian (then Imperial) General Staff, was factually the Supreme Commander of the Prussian Army in the Franco-Prussian War of 1870-1871. He was a supporter of the idea of deploying the Prussian Army close to the national borders and initiating surprise attacks, launching forces from different areas toward a common objective ("March separately – fight together") in order to take the enemy in the flanks and to destroy him in a grand battle, and then to obtain victory in a rapid war. He can indeed be considered the founder of the idea of "*Blitzkrieg*", which became so attractive to the Prussian school of war.

8 During the Polish campaign, Tukhachevsky, who earned distinction for successfully routing General Denikin in earlier battles, commanded the main offensive of Red Army forces advancing north of Warsaw. Meanwhile, Stalin was the main political commissar assigned to the forces of the Southwestern Front under the command of Egorov, whose units included the now infamous First Cavalry Army, or Konarmiia, led by Semyon Budenny, which was attacking near Lwow. The Southwestern Front failed to quickly execute the orders received from Moscow to move north from Lwow to Warsaw. Stalin, as chief political commissar, refused to cosign with Egorov the Moscow order to move north and join Tukhachevsky's Western Group and was recalled for his insubordination. The army was turned back at Warsaw and dreams of fomenting revolution to the west were crushed. Tukhachevsky, in a fateful move, assigned the blame for the defeat to the failures of Stalin's Southwestern Front and went on to analyze those failures in his lectures at the Military Academy. What made matters worse, perhaps, is that even Vladimir Lenin agreed with Tukhachevsky's assessment, asking, "Who on earth would want to get to Warsaw by going through Lwow?" Some twenty years later, Stalin apparently placed the blame for the failed campaign squarely on Tukhachevsky's shoulders, charging him for his "criminal delay." (Sally W. Stoecker, *Forging Stalin's Army*, Westview Press, 1998.)

his memoirs' 12th edition[9]: "We always sensed that he played the main leading role in the People's Commissariat of Defense."

Later, Zhukov has this to say about a speech that Tukhachevsky gave to an assembly of Party functionaries in 1931:

> At the time I was struck by the fact that he had almost nothing to say about Stalin. Sitting next to me at the assembly was the chief of the Red Army's signals troops, the old underground Bolshevik Longva (Author's note: one of the first to disappear in the purges), who told me that Tukhachevsky was not a toady, and that he wouldn't extol Stalin, who had unjustly accused Tukhachevsky for the failure of our operations around Warsaw.

Of course, everyone was supposed to sing the praises of the Leader in any public address. It was striking if someone didn't; in this case, striking to Zhukov, not just anyone. This means that at the podium, Zhukov, like the others ...

Continuing his thoughts on Tukhachevsky, Zhukov says:

> Recalling Tukhachevsky in the first days of the Great Patriotic War, *we always thought of his mental far-sightedness and the narrow-mindedness of those* who couldn't see beyond the ends of their noses, as a result of which our leadership was not able to develop powerful armored forces in a timely fashion, but were instead creating them during the war itself.

The emphasis is mine; the expression is clumsy, which makes it even more convincing. The Marshal wasn't a virtuoso of the pen, but this is his own genuine expression.

Sitting in the freezing movie theater, I swallowed bitter tears.

Not all the novelties of 1935 were applied even at Stalingrad. In the area of Kalach, where the ring was closed around Paulus's army, likely the Red Army leadership was itching to employ a paratroop landing. They didn't conduct one. The weather shut down flight operations, and this, that and the other...

Of course, the creation of airborne forces was not Iakir's or Tukhachevsky's personal idea, nor was it their sole decision to demonstrate what the Red Army was now capable of doing. The aviation industry was still not at all the trump card of the USSR, but having recommended this pageant, the army commanders knew how quick the *Reichswehr* was with mimicking and adopting. One had to have a lot of confidence in oneself in order to demonstrate such an airborne landing to a potential adversary. The army commanders had this confidence. They knew that they had opened a large gap in front of the best armies in Europe. In 1937, that gap was eliminated.

---

9   The Marshal's *Vospominaniia i razmyshleniia* [Recollections and thoughts] immediately became so popular in Russia that it was published every three to four years in enormous printings. The first, 1969 edition, was heavily pruned by the censors. Later, as new editions came out, the demands of the censors were softened, until at last perestroika made the entire text, dictated or written by the Marshal, accessible to readers. While writing this manuscript, I had in my hands the 2nd Edition, which was published in August 1974; that is, already after the memoirs' author had passed away. Although later editions became available to me as I worked on this manuscript, I decided to stick with the 2nd Edition, in order to be able to show the readers simultaneously how Soviet ideology redacted and distorted history, in particular the history of the Second World War.

There is no better praise for the Kiev maneuvers than the facial expressions of the military attaches in attendance. The gentlemen were stunned by the grand display of the military spectacle. Everything had been foreseen, everything scripted, and the "foe" wasn't allowed a moment of rest; surprise followed surprise, and the blows came one after the other. Content with the troops' level of training, the commander was modestly demonstrating it with the maneuvers. The professionals – Tukhachevsky and Egorov – were satisfied. The eyes of People's Commissar Voroshilov were indifferent; the whiskers of Budenny were puzzled.

By the end of the maneuvers in 1935, Iakir had become an Army General, 1st Rank. Budenny and Voroshilov, though, became Marshals.

At the time, Zhukov was a division commander in Belorussia, and he wasn't present at the maneuvers. However, this was still a time when the creative experience of any military district was studied everywhere. There are no grounds to speak of a Hannibals or a Scipio in the 20th century. Scipio had to concern himself most with ordering allies to deliver a certain amount of fodder, while Hannibal had to direct elephants with their drivers to a necessary place. Not a single great commander of the past could manage with the scale of modern military operations and the diversity of equipment without specialized training.

Capabilities in combination with at least a minimal education would explain Zhukov's success in his first military operation of his life. The point is, though, that by then, Zhukov didn't even have a minimal education. The Course for Improving the Command Staff of the Army is the final training academy in Zhukov's service record, while the 1935-1936 maneuvers were the last significant military event in the country. The years of banned books and lives ensued. Then there was Khalkhin-gol. Zhukov's maturity at Khalkhin-gol is inexplicable. Possibly, other sources will explain it.

6

Military Education 2

I n the first edition of this book, I introduced the testimony of the German General von Mellenthin that Zhukov received a solid military education from *Reichswehr* training courses within the framework of the aforementioned military cooperation between the two armies stemming from the Treaty of Rappallo. Even until recent times, this matter was kept concealed from the Russian reader, and my mention of the German component in Zhukov's education was met with the dagger points of Russian veterans even in America (which should have been expected). Not knowing when it was, and doubting in the date that von Mellenthin gives, I dated his training in Germany from the beginning of the 1930s.[1]

Von Mellenthin, the scion of an ancient Prussian line and on his mother's side a direct descendent of Frederick the Great, began World War II as a major and ended it as a major-general in the position as Chief of Staff of Army Group G on the Western Front. Today, von Mellenthin's book has become mandatory reading for all generals. Writing in it about the grand offensive of Soviet forces on the Middle Don against the Italian 8th Army, the timing of which was so successfully chosen that it instantly put an end to all of von Manstein's hopes to free Paulus's army, von Mellenthin mentions Zhukov. Precisely in relation to the timing of this offensive, there is an amusing digression in von Mellenthin's narration of this episode of the war to which we will later return when discussing the Red Army's Stalingrad offensive operation. Here, however, I'm speaking about something else. Having mentioned Zhukov, von Mellenthin makes a juicy statement:

> It is not generally realized that Zhukov previously received much of his early training in Germany … For a time he was attached to the cavalry regiment in which Colonel Dingler was serving as a subaltern. Dingler has vivid recollections of the uproarious behavior conduct of Zhukov and his companions, and the vast quantities of liquor which they were accustomed to consume after dinner. But in the military sphere it is clear that Zhukov's time was not wasted.[2]

It is an irony of fate. Zhukov, who received a formidable mastery of warfare from the *Reichswehr*, became a weapon in the defeat of the *Wehrmacht*. Just as the enemy gave a hand to the military education of its eventual conqueror, the USSR gave one to the re-arming of the foe. Why conceal this? It didn't embarrass those, whose names Marshal Zhukov

---

1   One respected Soviet veteran (and later author's friend) living in the United States, after a presentation of the book (at which he was not present, though heard about later through conversations), searched out the author in order to tear him to pieces, and upon finding him, shouted at the top of his lungs that the author was lying. Today, the fact that Zhukov received training in Germany is recognized, though sullenly so. In the Russian translation of von Mellenthin's book *Panzer Battles*, this remark has been omitted, as well as other unpleasant passages. It turned out that Zhukov's training in Germany took place almost immediately after Rappallo, that is somewhere around 1923-1924.

2   Major-General F. W. von Mellenthin, *Panzer Battles* (Ballantine Books, NY, 12th printing, 1990), p. 233, n. 2.

mentioned with special respect. The Soviet and German military schools were running neck and neck in their development. Zhukov's cover-up of the fact of his time in Germany is, I would say, of a persistent nature:

> In April 1941 ... Stalin called me:
>> 'Japan's Minister of Foreign Affairs Matsuoka is returning to his homeland after a visit to Germany' he said. 'You must receive him politely.'
>> 'What are your instructions?'
>> 'Mantsuoka simply wants to get acquainted with you.'

> I didn't even start to puzzle over the matter: plainly, Mantsuoka still had the events of Khalkhin-Gol fresh in his memory.
> Several days later the chief of Department of Foreign Relations of the People's Commissariat of Defense informed me that Mantsuoka and an interpreter would appear before me within two hours. Precisely at the appointed time, the door opened, and Yosuke Mantsuoka entered, bowing deeply.
> I politely greeted him, inquired about his health and asked whether he was tired from the trip. The minister replied noncommittally:
>> 'I love long journeys. It was my first time in Europe. Have you ever been in European countries?' he asked in return.
>>> 'Unfortunately, no' I replied, 'but at a suitable time I will of course try to visit. I've read a lot about Germany, Italy and England, but even the best book cannot provide a complete picture of a country. You get a much better understanding of a nation, its customs and its ways through a personal visit and contacts.'"

Zhukov had read von Mellenthin's book and was indirectly contradicting him. However, he passed over in silence von Mellenthin's remark about Zhukov's training in Germany. If von Mellenthin was mistaken, then why didn't the Marshal openly say so?

Not wishing to touch upon this topic in the pages of his memoirs, the Marshal understands that he needs to explain the source of his military knowledge to the readers:

> "As the commander of the 6th Corps, I labored intensively over operational-strategic questions, since I believed I still had much to learn in this area. My personal working-out of operational-tactical assignments at sessions of divisional and corps command games, command staff exercises, force maneuvers, etc."

That is just it – "etc.", since now he is referring to other levels of command – corps, 6th Corps, almost the army!

There is the testimony of Bagramian that Zhukov often remained behind to pore over maps, even as his peers were leaving for some recreation or amusement. Possibly that's just the way it was in Germany as well. Brigade commander Zhukov was not the only Red Army officer to receive training there...

So, he learned from the future enemy. After all, in the military sphere the foe had long been considered the world's leading specialist. It was no shame to study under the enemy's tutelage; this had been a Russian tradition since Peter the Great. Why not acknowledge it?

There is no reliable explanation. Likely it was not permitted by the editor. In the first edition of his memoirs Zhukov wrote nothing about his studies in Germany, and he didn't live until such permission might have been granted... Incidentally, nothing remains of his time in Germany in his papers either. Perhaps he fell short in his studies there. Von Mellenthin believes that with respect to military matters, Zhukov didn't waste any time in vain. However, the self-demanding Marshal knew that in his youth he lost time over libations, and never learned about the German people, their ways and customs at a time when all this could have been gained for free, while he was posted in Germany, and not later, when such knowledge would come at a high price. Perhaps he could have learned even more about the Germans than their ways and customs. Possibly there were more substantive gaps in his knowledge. No one knew this other than him, and no one will ever know. Had I been in the Marshal's place while writing the memoirs, I would not have mentioned the fact of military training in Germany either.

7

A Promotion

It occurred after his foreign assignment and work as a Red Army cavalry inspector. In describing this period Zhukov gives much attention to the General Headquarters of the Workers' and Peasants' Red Army and is filled with admiration for its global designs. However, the cavalry inspectorate was not subordinate to the General Headquarters, but to Budenny personally – an exception that permitted Stalin to create his own body of troops, like the Red Army's Mamelukes. Zhukov was far from the Red Army's General Headquarters, and this served to link the fates of Budenny and Zhukov, facilitated Zhukov's subsequent rise in command, and possibly saved his life during the time of the purges.

A description of events between 1931 and 1933 is lacking in Zhukov's memoirs because of the absence of any noteworthy events. At the time Zhukov, it must be supposed, had adequate possibilities for drinking sessions with the legendary hero of the Russian Civil War and to get closer to him, but this was not in any way a result of sycophancy. They became close through Budenny's initiative, and this was natural, given their similar background and cultural level at that time. Zhukov, like Budenny, was a dashing cavalryman, and an equine expert and lover of horses. He, a horseman and campaigner to the core, was interested in nothing else beyond military matters. To his great luck, his hobby coincided with his career. Incidentally, the horseman was also a disciple of mechanization and increasing force mobility.

His promotion to division commander was deserved. Higher command asked Zhukov to accept the promotion, and he agreed. However, Zhukov didn't assume command of just any division! He took over the 4th Don Voroshilov Cavalry Division, which at one time had been the nucleus of the 1st Cavalry Army. Its chiefs were men, who had been close to the ruling elite. Formerly the division had been based in Gatchina, Peterhof, and Tsarskoe Selo – in places specially equipped and adapted for housing mounted Guards units, with stables, equestrian arenas, parade grounds and training fields. As a result of negligence, bungling or intrigue (all three occurred; among those who fell in the repressions, many were casualties of the settling of personal scores in all the government institutions, and even more so in the army), the division was hastily transferred to Slutsk in Belorussia, a remote, backwoods place unequipped for a cavalry division. Under tsarism, this would have contributed to an improvement in the local gene pool. Under socialism, as Zhukov describes:

' ... the superbly trained division has become a poor construction unit' ... With his characteristic hot-headedness [Belorussian Military District commander] Uborevich reported to the People's Commissar of Defense Voroshilov on the condition of the 4th Cavalry Division and was demanding the immediate removal of the division commander Kletkin. ... Uborevich's report was extremely unpleasant for Voroshilov: he had been tied by blood for many years to this division, and had more than once gone on the attack in its ranks.

Thus, Zhukov was appointed commander of the Voroshilov Cavalry Division, and by the will of fate he was thrown together with those who during the purges happened to suffer significantly less than others.

The further development of relations between Budenny and Zhukov is curious. Amidst the purges, during an inquiry into a personal matter which was described in later editions of Zhukov's memoirs, then corps commander Zhukov was accused of boorishness and arrogance (Let those without sin ...), the baptism of his newborn daughter Ella, and worst of all being close to the enemy of the people Uborevich. Budenny was undoubtedly asked about Zhukov. I assume that the cavalry chief stood up for his swashbuckling drinking buddy. Later Zhukov didn't forget this and bailed his former commander out of trouble in what was now not a paper matter, but the battle for Moscow – and mentioned this more modestly in his memoirs than it really deserved...

Its new commander didn't find the division in such a shabby state as the District commander Uborevich had described to People's Commissar Voroshilov – with the clear intention to nettle him: they were, after all, in opposing circles. Zhukov, who was not inclined to paying compliments, twice in different places in his memoirs calls attention to 3rd Cavalry Corps commander L. Ia. Vainer, to whom the subordinate 4th Cavalry Division and the entire corps owed their combat training. Even before arriving at his new post, when asked about the 4th Cavalry Division, Zhukov replied that he "... was well-acquainted with the commander of the 3rd Cavalry Corps L. Ia. Vainer; I consider him to be a capable military commander." Then again: " ... the 3rd Chongar Kuban-Ter Division, which was excellently trained, stood out, especially in the areas of tactics, fire and mounted maneuver (in other words, in all categories of evaluation – author's note). Its former commander L. Ia Vainer, who exerted much effort and energy for this, must be given his due ..."

Don't even try to find Vainer's name among the list of heroes of the Great Patriotic War.[1] Corps commander Vainer refused to believe in the guilt of the army commanders and disappeared in the purge. Dovator[2], the corps commander's worthy disciple, was at the time of the purges a squadron commander in Vainer's division, then Vainer's corps, so his life was spared. But that is by the way...

Of course, in his new post Zhukov exerted his extraordinary energy to raise the division to a higher level of readiness. He slept little – and didn't allow others to sleep either. Within a year, Uborevich once again made a surprise attempt to vex the pitiful People's Commissar [Voroshilov], but failed to catch Zhukov unawares. The 4th Cavalry Division was unexpectedly alerted and ordered to march to the border, but Zhukov's troopers

---

1   E. M. Temkina, the widow of N. A. Iung, the Commissar of the 3rd Cavalry Corps, remembers Vainer as a charming, affable man. As it turns out, my own relative, Arkadii Radomysel'sky, served in the 3rd Cavalry Corps and with the modest rank of sergeant was Vainer's comrade: they competed in billiards. I felt a tingle, when Radomysel'sky told me how once he had encountered his commander and had straightened up to salute him, when Vainer had grabbed him by the arm – he was a strapping man of peasant stock – and told him, "Arkadii, none of your clever tricks today; we'll play honestly for a small stake." Yes, we know that there are two kinds of upbringing and education, a playful one and a strict one. They are equally effective in terms of results, but produce personalities in the one case and only mechanical executors in the other. Stalin destroyed the first school of thought and imposed the dominion of the second. As a result of wars and purges it is prevalent in modern Russia in genetics, history, and linguistics ... in all of life itself.

2   Editor's note: Lev Mikhailovich Dovator, Major-General and Hero of the Soviet Union, commanded a cavalry group that became famous for a daring raid into the German rear in the Smolensk area in August-September 1941. Later, as commander of the 2nd Guards Cavalry Corps, he was killed in action in December 1941 near the village of Ruza in Moscow Oblast.

The first marshals. Seated left to right: M.N. Tukhachevsky, K.E. Voroshilov, A.I. Egorov. Standing: S.M. Budenny and V.K. Briukher.

showed class and conducted the training march in commendable fashion. Uborevich had badly wanted to embarrass and reprimand the division that bore the name of Voroshilov with this surprise order – but failed. People's Commissar Voroshilov remained contented .... Zhukov notes:

> The year 1935 was marked for us by major events. ... The division was awarded for its training successes with a higher government honor – the Order of Lenin. I was also awarded with the Order of Lenin. That year was memorable for us military men for another measure, undertaken by the Party to raise the authority of the command cadres – the introduction of personal military titles. Bliukher, Budenny, Voroshilov, Egorov and Tukhachevsky became the first Marshals of the Soviet Union.

It was around this time, apparently, that Zhukov's friendship with Uborevich began. The army commander valued Zhukov's professionalism, and no matter how much contempt he held for Voroshilov, he didn't transfer this attitude to the People's Commissar's protégé, the hard-working and straightforward brigade commander in charge of the 4th Cavalry Division. So Uborevich recommended Zhukov for a promotion. Zhukov received the second bar on his collar patch and became a division commander; he remained at this rank until 1937. (We'll note that Rokossovsky at the time was soaring up the ladder of ranks in advance of Zhukov. He had been a division commander and Zhukov's direct superior back in 1931). It is impossible not to notice Zhukov's measured advance up the service ladder – without any particularly noteworthy rises (prior to 1937) but also without any falls. In this way,

Zhukov was a self-made man: an ardent supporter of discipline and almost the caricature of a campaigner. He was also a model combat commander, which in combination with his ordinary, non-academic education – and I will emphasize this, because it is important for understanding how he was drawn into the Stalinist camp – secured his advancement. No one saw him as a rival, and the swashbucklers of the Budenny-type recognized themselves. Not one of those staff eggheads, you understand, a real campaigner, like one of our own!

To be sure, he was indeed one of them, but with a talent that he himself didn't yet know. This was something also that proved fortunate for him.

Zhukov commanded the 4th Don Cavalry Division for four years, and under other circumstances he would have remained in this post. The Workers' and Peasants' Red Army was refilling its command ranks with capable commanders, whom moreover had graduated from the Frunze General Staff Academy – a superb, by the way, military training establishment. Under a normal institution of authority, under an army led by such reformists as Tukhachevsky, Iakir, Uborevich and others, men like Zhukov would have been the norm at the division command level. Such an army was invincible. "Don't touch us – and we won't touch you, but if you lay a finger on us, we'll give you no quarter." Just try to attack an army, where at the head of each division and corps is a Zhukov, a Rokossovsky, a Tolbukhin or a Govorov!

In 1937 this abundance of command cadres came to a rapid and grim end. Zhukov writes, "The foremost military men were arrested, which could not but tell upon the development of our armed forces and upon their combat readiness. In 1937, by order of the People's Commissar of Defense I was appointed commander of the Belorussian Military District's 3rd Cavalry Corps." This was in place of Vainer.

The vacancies multiplied at a frightening pace. Zhukov spent four years at one post, and then they moved him twice in one year .... He writes:

> "In connection with appointment of the commander of the 6th Cossack Corps Goriachev to the post of deputy commander of the Kiev Special Military District ... (Author's note: Ahem, Iakir had been executed, and Uborevich and Kork too; now there were three districts without commanders – reshuffling!) ... I was offered command of this corps. I eagerly accepted the offer. The 6th Corps of the Belorussian Military District was superior to the 3rd Corps in training and its general condition ..."

A rising tide lifts all boats...

Goriachev was an inspirational commander; his soldiers called him "Chapai".[3] Stalin brought him together with Bliukher and placed them on the tribunal, which would conduct the trial of the first doomed men. The Supreme Leader was preparing his devilish dishes for future consumption. All the members of the tribunal (except for Budenny) were suspected of sympathizing with the accused; all were being readied for the next trial – this time as the victims. However, for the first trial, Stalin needed judges of very high reputation and standing; in the rush of what was happening the fiery Goriachev didn't get the drift of what he was hearing, although he had been compelled to sign the verdict. Supposing only that he was being slow to catch on and that everything was clear to the other members of the tribunal, he believed that the next day he would have another conversation with them and,

---

3   Editor's note: Vasilii Ivanovich Chapaev, known familiarly as "Chapai", was a celebrated Red Army commander during the Russian Civil War, later immortalized in a 1934 Soviet film *Chapaev*.

if necessary, write a protest, a special opinion ... Did he really think that the sentence would be execution? That "tomorrow" would never come, and that the sentence would be carried out immediately? From his perspective, he likely believed that there was no need to hurry; these weren't revolutionary times. After all, these weren't just ordinary people on trial!

However, what Goriachev didn't understand was that this was indeed a revolution, a counter-revolution. It was put into motion, once Stalin had gathered sufficient power, in order to crush the army. There were whispers that Bliukher was appointed to command the firing squad at the execution of his friends. Loyal to his oath, the stunned Bliukher ... This, most likely, is slander. The army commanders were not put in front of a firing squad; they were put to death in the Stalinist style, with a bullet to the back of the head, in order to keep them from looking the victim in the eye.

I know about Goriachev from the words of E. Temkina, the widow of N. Iung, the commissar of Zhukov's corps, who fell as a victim of his disbelief a year later. With the fervor characteristic to him, which is so harmful to one's health and at that time also to the lives of still quite young people, Goriachev did not keep his doubts over the accusations and supposed conspiracies sufficiently concealed.

To arrest such "Chapaevs" at their command posts in their corps – oh, this was a thankless job! Any Special Department men who arrived to make the arrest would simply be carved into unappetizing pieces. However, the genius criminal got around this problem. He worked out methods for all of life's occasions and situations. Goriachev was promoted and transferred to the Kiev District, where he became a deputy commander and was simply just another hero of the Civil War. No subordinate combat formations surrounded him, no revolt was threatened; here it was possible to arrest him without any trouble.[4] However, Goriachev already knew the price he would pay for this promotion and made fools of the Chekists[5] – he put a pistol to his head. In his day, he could always hit the most important target ...

Primakov exchanged shots with the Chekists who had come to arrest him, until he got in touch with Voroshilov, who guaranteed him his security. Trusting, naïve people ...

In order to pick up Iung, he was transferred to the Novosibirsk Military District, but arrested en route while in Moscow. The new chief of the Red Army's Main Political Directorate, Mekhlis[6], ordered Iung to come by to see him at his office, personally took away his pistol, and handed him over to the Chekists. A year later he would also hand Mikhail Kol'tsov[7] over to the NKVD [*Narodnyi Komissariat vnutrennykh del*, or People's

4   Vainer, like Goriachev, was not arrested at his corps. In order to seize him in August 1937, he had been forced to go to Mongolia as a military adviser.

5   Editor's note: This is a popular nickname for agents of the Cheka (and even of the later KGB) – an abbreviation for the All-Russian Extraordinary Commission for the Struggle with Counter-revolution and Sabotage. This was the Bolshevik secret police and an early predecessor of the KGB.

6   L. Mekhlis isn't worth remembering, but he did exist. He was a real stooge of Stalin's, a hard-bitten instrument of the purge. Mekhlis became the chief of the Red Army's Main Political Directorate. The purge of the Red Army can be explained neatly by this change in command of the Political Directorate: in place of Gamarnik, Mekhlis. He didn't arrest only Iung; he was fond of such assignments. He ended badly, this Mekhlis. On the day before Stalin's death, his faithful lapdog departed and was buried with unusual pomp. Mekhlis showed particularly great zeal in the shakeup of the Red Army. If Stalin had a presentiment of his own death, then doubtlessly he didn't wish to leave Mekhlis among the witnesses. Did Stalin bump off his faithful dog, or was Mekhlis's death a natural one? Interesting ...

7   Editor's note: Mikhail Kol'tsov was a Soviet journalist famous for his satirical essays and founder of the popular satirical journal *Krokodil*. As a *Pravda* correspondent, he travelled to Spain to cover the Spanish

Commissariat of Internal Affairs].

In a word, Zhukov was offered Goriachev's corps, which previously had been Vainer's. The results of the purge manifested themselves immediately. Zhukov recalls:

> In the autumn of 1937, district-wide maneuvers were conducted in the Belorussian Military District, at which generals and officers of the German General Staff were present as guests. People's Commissar of Defense Voroshilov and Chief of the General Staff Shaposhnikov observed the maneuvers.
>
> New people, who still had an insufficient amount of knowledge and command experience, had arrived in the District's forces. They had to do a great amount of work on themselves in order to become worthy military commanders ...

And – that's all. Not a word of praise for the maneuvers. Any commentary is totally lacking.

If one exchanges the order of the quoted paragraphs, it will become evident that the German guests might have been overwhelmingly tempted by the obvious weakening of the Red Army. The decline in the level of command in comparison with the Kiev Military District's 1935 maneuvers or the Belorussian Military District's maneuvers a year later was ruinous. In O. Suvenirov's richly detailed and factual book *Tragediia RKKA* [*Tragedy of the RKKA*] dramatic data are presented on the rise in the number of accidents and catastrophes, on the decline in discipline and trust toward commanders and commissars, and on alcohol abuse, which has always plagued the army, but which became an epidemic means of escape during the purge. Here indeed is what the German military attaché, Brigadier General Koestring reported back to Berlin: "The [Red] Army does not present a significant factor of defense."

Meanwhile, the purge was far from over. Even before the end of the terrible year of 1937, Zhukov became the deputy commander of the Belorussian Military District's forces, replacing Ye. I. Kovtiukh, the Russian Civil War hero who appeared as the legendary Kozhukh in Aleksandr Serafimovich's novel *Zhelezni Potok* [*The Iron Flood*], and who graduated from the Red Army's Academy in 1922, at a time when genuine luminaries of military science were still being taught there. Eremenko[8] took Zhukov's place in command of the 6th Cossack Corps. They had completed the very same courses of instruction. So why not?

Eremenko in place of Goriachev. Zhukov in place of Kovtiukh. Who then in place of Vainer? However, this is still not the worst of the replacements that occurred; still not the lieutenants that took the place of colonels; not the colonels that replaced top army commanders. The worse still lay ahead ...

Civil War and also became Stalin's personal ideological representative. He was summoned back to Moscow and arrested in 1938 for "anti-Soviet activities". Sentenced to death, he was later executed.

8   Editor's note: Andrey Ivanovich Eremenko, later Marshal of the Soviet Union and commander of several different Red Army *fronts* during World War II, including the Stalingrad Front.

8

About the purge ...

The Marshal speaks with deep bitterness in his memoirs about the purge in the Red Army:

> Of the old military specialists (in the army), there remained only people who had been tested by life and were dedicated to Soviet power. By the year 1937, workers and peasants comprised more than 70% of the Komsomol members in the army, and more than half of the commanders were Communist Party members and Komsomol members. All the more unnatural then were the unjustified mass arrests, in violation of socialist justice, which took place in the army in 1937, and completely failed to correspond to either the composition of the army or to the concrete situation in the country, which had developed by that year.

To a certain degree, these words reflect Zhukov's attitude toward the mass repressions: the brainwashing affected all levels. However, it is beyond doubt that the phrasing here and in similar places in Zhukov's memoirs was suggested to the Marshal – and accepted by him, since he was always indifferent to empty prattle. However, such wording diverts the reader from the essence of the matter, although for the Soviet people at the time of the memoir's first publication it sounded familiar and even sensible. No one, other than foreign historians and Soviet dissidents, realized that the old military specialists were just as honorable as the new ones. Moreover, no one who did clearly understand the reasons for the purge of the generation, which was purged, searched for explanations for the mass destruction of people, which was unprecedented even on the scale of Eastern satraps.

Literally every word of these quoted comments, attributed to Zhukov, are preposterous – partially in view of the level of censorship at the time of the memoir's first publication (the end of the 1960s, dissidents, Czechoslovakia) and partially in view of the fact that the debate over the causes of the purge of the Red Army continues even to the present day for some reason, and the last word will be said only when history schoolbooks write that it was a logical step of Stalin in his suppression of potential opposition. Any man or woman may be regarded as a potential oppositionist, so, mass terror may become a necessary instrument for tyranny. However, it was impossible to begin mass terror, without having first suppressed the army, which remained the last guarantor of freedom, and capable of responding to the destruction of the flower of the nation with a military *coup d'état*. Yet if you begin with the army, then later everything will be permissible. It seems that for future generations it is much more difficult to acknowledge this, than it was for Stalin to set out on this path.

So, Zhukov's following words are colorless and employ expressions conventional for that time:

> ... unnatural then were the unjustified mass arrests, in violation of socialist justice, which took place in the army in 1937, and completely failed to correspond to either

the essence of the regime or to the concrete situation in the country, which had developed by that year.

These unnaturally smooth words of the journalist, who knew the market conditions and who wrote this example of *belles-lettres* on behalf of Zhukov, do not reflect either the Marshal's character or his vocabulary ...

Of course, the mass arrests were not at all unnatural and fully corresponded to both the essence of the regime – the dictatorship of the proletariat (no one protested this expression, which is how the Party clerics called their rule) – and the concrete situation in the country, the regime of Stalin's personal dictatorship. This was a dictatorship atop a dictatorship.

Unjustified? Everything depends upon the point of view you assume. If you accept the slogan "Think about the Motherland before yourself!" which was pounded into our heads, then of course the mass arrests were unjustified, since the Great Leader and Father should have thought about the costs of his accomplishments – the millions of people dying of famine, killed in the purges, and destroyed in the war, which was lost and then won again at the cost of enormous blood. If however you are guided by the logic of a tyrant, then the mass arrests were more than justified: in order to preserve the lives of the working masses, the army commander scum might at a convenient moment encroach upon the tyrant's power and upon his sacrosanct life.

Was this possibility excluded? Who knows ... indeed in a war with such a catastrophic beginning a change of power is natural. In a difficult hour for the country, opponents, who have foreseen another turn of events, appear to replace the existing failed policies. Such a thing has happened in England, in France, and in many other places.

However, in the Soviet Union the opponents were destroyed far ahead of time. They were annihilated indiscriminately.

The academician Suvenirov concluded his book with the pathetic call, "Save the army!" This is accurate, but it is only part of the matter. Regarding the purges, it should have been said "Save the opposition! It is your last chance in extraordinary circumstances!" Had these purged commanders survived and been around, there could not have been the scenes in the Kremlin on 22 June 1941, when the dimensions of the catastrophe were beginning to become clear. The Leader would not have gone off into hysterics, and there would have been no one to comfort him, and he would not have gone into hiding in the first critical days of the war. The army commanders saw the rising German threat in the 1930s and were preparing for it. Is it really difficult to believe that, desperate to replace the irreplaceable Leader, who had become now both Great and Wise, and who had grown from day to day, like a rotten mushroom under a torrent of praise, the best military commanders, precisely those whom he destroyed first, were ready to overthrow him? One should not underestimate the entire leadership of the USSR; there were intelligent, courageous men in it. The intelligent people, by 1937, had been scrubbed out of the Party apparatus and they could only be found now in the institutions of the army and economic administration.

Another matter – did a military *coup d'état* have any chances for success? Under ordinary circumstances – no; the all-pervading NKVD-OGPU apparatus kept them under a lid. Stalin dismissed and replaced anyone who displayed open opposition to him, while the army commanders were all too familiar with those who were breathing down the backs of their necks.

The German generals of Prussian aristocracy faced the very same problem when they were in disagreement with Hitler. If they resigned in protest, cut-throats from among the storm troopers would replace them – men without knowledge and without morals. Things would then be even worse.

Both the German generals and the Red Army commanders were late to realize that things could not be any worse. That history with all its sympathies would find no excuse for them. Both one group and the other should have more energetically intervened in the internal affairs of their respective countries.

The Germans nevertheless began to act. However, the Kreisau Circle[1], homogenous in composition, was also indecisive like the Red Army commanders. Its members, connected by links of friendship between their grandfathers and great grandfathers, or else by bonds of kinship, had full confidence in their partners (which is why their intentions remained a secret right up to the attempt on Hitler's life). Officers, who had been drawn into the discussions, but who rejected the physical elimination of the Führer, abandoned the circle, but their understanding of honor prevented them from disclosing the contents of the discussions. Wavering men were joining the group and then leaving it again; as a result, the Germans needed more than three years of war, the hopelessness of the situation and a firm moral standing before the realization of an attempt on Hitler's life. Major-General Henning von Treskow, the committed leader of the plot, being asked once by von Stauffenberg whether or not the assassination attempt made any sense, now that the Allies were in France and were hardly likely to enter into negotiations with any German government, replied,

> The attempt is necessary, and as soon as possible. The Berlin action (the attempt to seize power) must take place, even if it proves unsuccessful. Sense no longer lies in whether or not the plot achieves a practical goal, but in demonstrating to the world and history that the German resistance was ready to put everything on the line. In comparison with this, everything else is just a trifling matter.

The Red Army leadership never achieved such a high note. The argument is not convincing that the USSR in 1937 had still not been brought to such a point of despair as Germany would be in seven years later. The strangulation of the peasantry had already occurred, and arrests of the best people were gathering pace. The leaders of the Workers' and Peasants' Red Army did not intervene in the political life of the country for a number of reasons.

The first and most important reason: the military commanders began to shy away from politics. Seeing what a turn the revolution had taken, they were regretting their military-political activity. The first Russian historians of the tragedy of the Red Army, Geller and Rapoport, explain it this way: the best Red Army commanders were Bolsheviks (we will excuse the authors for this statement, since they wrote their book in 1977 and intended it for publication in the USSR). The Bolshevism of such men as Gamarnik and Iakir, according to the authors:

> ... was neither affected nor forced as was many officers' ... Iakir piously believed in the Party ideals. For him, the interests of the Party, the task of building socialism stood

---

1   Editor's note: The Kreisau Circle was the name given by the German Gestapo to an opposition group centered around Helmuth James, Graf von Moltke, Peter Yorck von Wartenburg and Adam von Trott zu Solz – all conservative men from the traditional German aristocracy and gentry.

first, before personal and professional considerations. It is in these high principles combined with altruism, absence of career ambitions, and profound decency, one should search for the source of Iakir's strength and greatness."

If the expression "piously believed in the Party ideals" confuses someone, then two notions should be considered: firstly, at the time of writing the book, the authors could not say anything else; secondly, under the concept of "Party ideals", they hardly had in mind the exultation of the pompous ceremonies of the Party Congresses. As far as building socialism, this was already a universal slogan, an ideal of all mankind, toward which all civilized countries were already successfully approaching. However, what actually bound the military commanders was the key Party doctrine of "unity of the Party" – the backbone of Bolshevism. The threat of a schism is indeed the most sinister nightmare of any organization. The American philosopher Barrows Dunham devoted his 1964 book, *Heroes and Heretics: A Political History of Western Thought*, to the argument that heretics are the most intense proponents of change, and that organizations at all times have been destroying them without hesitation, since not only their actions, but also their views can threaten a schism. Yet the Red Army's commanders, who believed in the ideal of unity of the Party, were ready to part with their own lives, if only not to harm the Party. We are left to regret that these idealists were the idols of army. Without their leading call, neither their subordinates nor their service peers could implement anything, or even begin to ponder an act.

The second reason was the crowding and jostling on the service ladder that was taking place at the time. The competition was artificially heated up by the transfer of part of the NKVD's cadres into the army, by the transfer of officers from the army to civilian posts, the unmerited acquisition of ranks, and the fomented competition between the service branches. I will speak in more detail about this later. In the meantime I will limit myself to citing the most prominent scholar of the Red Army, John Erickson. In his book *The Road to Stalingrad*, speaking of those who were in the majority in the army and who headed it after the liquidation of the army commanders, he notes:

> The men who followed Tukhachevsky lacked also that insight into the probable forms of modern mobile war which had so preoccupied the purged commanders; they lacked any intellectual curiosity because they disposed of no intellect, either singly or as a group. They mouthed slogans but understood nothing of principles, they paraded statistics about fire-power without grasping any of the implications of the new weapons their own designers were developing, they were martial in a swaggering sense without the least grasp of the professionalism necessary to the military.

The third reason consisted of the fact that by the time the arrests of military men had been started and the time to react had arrived, Stalin had managed both by the whip and the carrot to pound his name into the intellectually impoverished brains of the obedient population. Now any attempt at his removal might turn into a struggle, and then the idealists would be confronted with a question, which Stalin never asked himself: "Again blood in the streets?" The matter reached the point of acknowledging nonexistent guilt, and then the desire to avoid torture and anxiety over their families' fates began to work on them. Iakir simply traded his life for the life of his wife and son, and apparently found a way to force Stalin – against his practice – to carry out his promise.

A detailed analysis of the extreme bloodiness of the purge is possible only against the backdrop of a meticulous medical-psychological portrait of Stalin with a necessary consideration of the traditions in the environment of his path from childhood to Supreme Leader – the family, the clan, the government and the Party. However, I will finish with an excerpt from Zhukov's memoir. He had been trained by the executed generals. Even if their contribution to the defense of the country is limited to Zhukov's military education alone, then they should deserve a pedestal. Many monuments have been raised in the country to fictional characters, but not even one has yet been constructed to honor these commanders.

Thus, that which Zhukov wrote was published only in the 10th edition of his memoirs already after the empire had collapsed. The many-paged insert indeed contains that episode, in which the scythe flashed over the head of Zhukov himself. If he survived, then it is not because he was innocent. Vainer and Goriachev were also not guilty.

> "In the armed forces, the majority of district and fleet commanders, members of military councils, corps commanders, and commanders of divisions and units was arrested ... A *terrible situation had arisen* in the country. No one trusted anyone else, people began to fear one another, to avoid meetings or any sort of conversations, and if one was necessary, they tried to speak in the presence of third-party eyewitnesses. An unprecedented epidemic of slander developed. All too often, people slandered totally honorable people, and sometimes even their own close friends. All of this grew from the fear to be suspected of being disloyal. This *terrible situation* continued to heat up (emphasis the author's)."

Any commentary is superfluous, and I quoted this fragment from the 10th edition for the following reasons:

Firstly, so as to bring the reader's attention to the Marshal's uncharacteristic use of the epithet "terrible", which he applied twice in a short paragraph and which one does not encounter anywhere else in the memoir, even when Zhukov is speaking about a truly terrible war.

Secondly, in order to illustrate one of the reasons for Zhukov's survival in the purges. He understood before it was too late that he had to keep his mouth shut. (Nevertheless, the main thing consisted in his personal courage and his driving desire to live. Zhukov forcefully and capably defended himself whenever he had to do it.)

Thirdly, in order to show once more how Zhukov's genuine opinion differs from that which was permissible for publication. In a similar fashion, censorship not only distorted what he wrote, but what he thought as well.

9

Marvellous Timeliness: Some Facts

W hen access to the Soviet archives was opened, three things occurred. First, documents began to be falsified, truncating them or else even supplementing them, but preserving the reference file number as a sign of credibility. Second, some authors began to endow the Leader with the genius of forethought and depicted the Red Army in 1941 in the posture of preparing a preemptive attack. Stalin simply ran out of time, they say. Third, the hypothesis about a supposed commanders' plot against the Leader was construed as a fact. Falling for ostensibly "documented" publications in the yellow press, even I myself used the word "plot" in the first edition of this book. Some people wanted to believe in a plot in order to rationalize Stalin's violence against the Red Army. I wanted to believe it in order to attribute a noble impulse to the army commanders and at least in doing so find solace in the idea that in conspiring against the tyrant bestraddling the entire country, they at least didn't die in vain. Alas, the facts don't allow this.

Unfortunately, the fundamental book on the topic of the Red Army's tragedy, V. Rapoport's and Iu. Alekseev's (a pseudonym for Iurii Geller) *Izmena Rodine* [translated into English under the title *High Treason*], which received only a limited printing at a time when books were still being published in large volumes, came into my hands only after the publication of the first edition of this book. However, this also has a positive aspect: it allowed me to work more freely with the material I had. As well, Geller's and Rapoport's lack of knowledge about prior research on the subject[1] made their book more independent and interesting. Its main value is that it was created on native soil and is accurate in its basic assessments of the actors in the historical drama. Here is how they describe the Red Army prior to Stalin's purge:

> The RKKA [Workers' and Peasants' Red Army] in the middle of the 1930s was a magnificent, first-class army, the best in the country's history. At that time, the most advanced army in Europe and, unquestionably, the most cerebral. Granted, it was used politically, often shamelessly so, but all the same the RKKA more than any other institution (of the USSR of those times) carried within it a revolutionary spirit; a liberation from the age-old fetters of servitude, stagnation and ignorance; a striving for limitless improvement; and a boundless optimism. A new generation of military thinkers had grown up in the army, who took on the most difficult tasks and resolved

---

1   In essence, in their book the Russian historians re-created the bicycle without even knowing it. A quarter of a century before them, in 1962, the leading British historian John Erickson, a professor at Edinburgh University, published a book which remains unique even today: *The Soviet High Command*. Up to the present day, this precise piece of research, as accurate as a diagnosis, has still not been translated into the Russian language and leaves Russia ignorant of the motivations behind the unprecedented destruction of a magnificent army, since the translation of this book conclusively answers all the questions connected with Stalin's purge. Incidentally, a translation of such a book into Russian would demand a re-examination of attitudes toward Russia's characteristic authoritarian rule, which seems improbably in this predominantly Eastern country.

many of them in splendid fashion. It is impossible to imagine that this RKKA would yield half the country to Hitler.

Let us grant that this description is rapturous. The RKKA in fact was inferior to the German *Wehrmacht* in the education of its officer class and in the methodical training of its soldiers. It doesn't really matter – before the purge there was no one willing to mess around with the RKKA. This is a fact, confirmed by history.

The international atmosphere was tense in the 1930s. The peace in Europe didn't deceive the army commanders. An associate of Iakir, the brigade commander I. Dubinsky, after 16 years of imprisonment cautiously passed along stories about the perished army commanders. One regards a speech that Iakir made in front of his Kiev Military District's soldiers: he was explaining the aim of the maneuvers as a means to intimidate the aggressor (everyone knew the identity of this aggressor), in order to maintain the peace for another two or three years and win the time needed for reequipping the army. That was why Iakir revealed his trump cards before the stunned audience; he still had a number of secrets, such as: a network of partisan-commando bases, already deployed in case of the occupation of our territory; and underwater crossings, designed not only for infantry, but also for tanks (a fact that historians know, but prefer to keep silent, so as to not stir up oppressive memories about the blood-drenched river bridgeheads of the Great Patriotic War). So Iakir, in disclosing the innovations, wasn't bluffing when he lamented with a well-acted innocence to the guest military attaches that he couldn't reveal everything due to the lack of time. The intention was to intimidate, to win time and to reach such a state of readiness that there would no longer be any need to intimidate; potential aggressors would themselves be cowed.

Time was short, but there was still enough. Yet the future ... there was no future.

There is a saying that "a job well begun is half done". However, my task here is daunting, the topic is painful, and there is no sense that the beginning was well enough begun for having something half done. There are a lot of facts, and all are jostling to be first in line.

There was for example once a man called Iakov Okhotnikov ... Nevertheless, we won't start with him.

On 5 July 1936, the division commander Dmitrii Shmidt was arrested; a legendary figure, the commander of the 2nd Division of the Chervonnyi Cossacks Corps, then subsequently the commander of the 7th Division (in which role he was Zhukov's commander) and the commander of the so-called 2nd *Dikaia* (Wild or Savage) Division of volunteers drawn from the Caucasus Mountain nationalities. At the time of his arrest, though, he was commanding the Red Army's sole heavy tank brigade. (Dubinsky, who had been repressed and by some miracle managed to survive, was appointed to replace Shmidt.) Gutman-Shmidt was a man of such bravery that it even astonished the veteran swashbucklers of the Russian Civil War. Eduard Bagritsky dedicated his famous poem "*Duma pro Opanasa*" to him. Trotsky's expulsion from the Party in 1927 had enraged Shmidt. At the time he was commanding the *Dikaia* Division and arrived at the Party Congress dressed in the uniform of his division, in a Circassian *cherkeska* [overcoat] with cartridge pouches. Zhukov mentions his commander was a man who always expressed his thoughts succinctly. Here is an example of his brevity, which even the Spartans would envy.

During a break between sessions of the Congress, Shmidt searched out Stalin and told him harshly, making a gesture, as if snatching out an imaginary saber (all Congress delegates were obliged to enter the building unarmed), "Watch out, Koba [Stalin's early nickname], I'll cut off your ears!" Stalin went pale – and remained silent.

Naïve people; they thought they could bring Stalin to reason. However, everything began long before this episode ...

History is a search for ties between events, which on a surface seem to be not connected. But what I am facing now is a need to expound miracles. Not just individual miracles – a continuous string of them, or if miracles aren't an accepted explanation, then the work will have to be turned over to an entire generation of historians, or even not just one generation.

The death of an unwanted is a source of joy for any tyrant. In the 1920s, fate began to bestow just such gifts upon a man with decaying teeth who was then picking his way toward power.

The first miracle occurred in Tiflis on a July day in 1922. Simon Ter-Petrosian[2], who was known by the nickname Kamo, fell under an automobile while on his bicycle, it seems, the only automobile in the city at that time, and did it so successfully that he was killed instantly. He knew much about the new General Secretary, much, like no one else. In the old days, together they had robbed a Tiflis bank, the Leader's first bit of dirty business. He knew about Koba's contacts with the *Okhranka* [the Russian Empire's secret police] – and with all this knowledge, he slipped up. It is mind-boggling, since he was a superman, a terrorist, a trained commando, a superb shot, always ready for ambushes, ready to defend himself. Such a gift, indeed such a gift ... There are rumors that the General Secretary was in Tiflis at the time of the accident. Incidentally, was this necessary? Except perhaps to summon Ter-Petrosian for a meeting and to know when and where he would be walking or riding ...

The second gift became Efraim Skliansky, a deputy chairman of the Revolutionary Military Council and Chief of Staff of the Red Army. He was a military doctor by profession, a military genius by attribute. The entire executive office of the Revolutionary Military Council fit inside his head. He alone coordinated the operations of all the *fronts* of the Civil War. In 1924, Trotsky was removed from the Revolutionary Military Council and Skliansky along with him. He was transferred to civilian work. He lived for 33 years and drowned in the summer of 1925 in Pennsylvania while on a business trip. A serious contender for the post of People's Commissar for Military and Navy Affairs had passed away. Should something happen to Frunze, God forbid, this would make it possible, nevertheless, for Stalin to advance his good friend, the malleable Klim Voroshilov to the

---

2   Here it is time to recall G. D. Gai – Gaik Bzhishkian, the man who didn't overlook the young regiment commander Zhukov and gave his career an upward nudge. It is time to recall corps commander Gai, the chief of the Department of Military Art of the Military Airborne Academy. Gaik Bzhishkian was born in 1887, arrested in July 1935, and that, it would seem, was the first arrest among the army commanders of a proletarian origin, we'll note. Gai's connections in the Armenian community made the circumstances of Ter-Petrosian's puzzling death known to him. However, his contacts with Okhotnikov, who had a direct connection to the country's Air Force, also cannot be excluded as the reason for his arrest. At the time, Okhotnikov was serving a three-year exile in Magadan. Geller's and Rapoport's description of the arrested Gai's hair-raising adventures is of a notably venomous and dramatic nature.

Members of the Revolutionary Military Council: the commander of the Belorussian Military District I.P. Uborevich, chief of the Red Army's Main Political Administration Ia.B. Gamarnik, commander of the Red Army's Cavalry S.M. Budenny, People's Commissar of Defense and chairman of the Revolutionary Military Council K.E. Voroshilov, commander-in-chief of the Air Force P.I. Baranov, commander-in-chief of Soviet Naval Forces R.A. Muklevich, and deputy People's Commissar of Defense S.S. Kamenev. A 1930 photo.

army leadership, thought it might be a bit awkward.

If only we could find out who sent Skliansky to the USA. Why? Did he know how to swim? Who went with him on the trip? Who hauled him to the lake? Who drowned him? All these questions might still be answered.

Skliansky parted from life on 27 August 1925. Within two months, Frunze, the People's Commissar for Military and Naval Affairs, followed him in death, while lying prostrate on an operating table. How badly he didn't want to undergo this operation ...[3] The path for Stalin's henchman was swept clear crudely and conspicuously.

On 6 November 1925, at a session of the highest country military organ, the Revolutionary-Military Council, after many hours of heated bargaining and over the vocal opposition of Council member Muklevich[4], Voroshilov became the Commissar for Military and Naval Affairs. The ability to bargain, an Eastern trait, was Stalin's strong attribute. The

---

3   Zhukov's comment on this subject in his memoirs is reserved and characteristic for him: "After the death of Mikhail Vasil'evich Frunze (*at 40 years of age*) ... [Emphasis the author's].

4   Muklevich, Romual'd Adamovich, (Nov. 25, 1890 – Feb. 9, 1938); member of the Communist Party from 1906. Muklevich enlisted in the navy in 1912. He fought in the February and October Revolutions of 1917 and in the storming of the Winter Palace, before joining the Red Army in 1918. He served as commissar of the Military Academy of the RKKA from 1922 to 1925, became assistant chief of the air forces of the RKKA in 1925, and from August 1926 he was chief of the naval forces of the USSR and a member of the Revolutionary Military Council of the USSR. He became inspector of the naval forces of the RKKA in 1931, head of the Central Board of the Shipbuilding Industry in 1934 and deputy people's commissar of the defense industry in late 1936. Muklevich was a member of the Central Executive Committee and the All-Russian Central Executive Committee at several convocations.

M.V. Frunze, the first People's Commissar of Military and Naval Affairs.

candidate, the insignificance of whom was satisfying to both sides, went through. (The General Secretary was still not omnipotent. Later he would kick those who had bartered with him out of the army. Then he arrested them. Then he killed them ...)

A gift? Well, let us say, a fact. But what a fact!

How could the Army witness this and silently tolerate it?

(Here I will work in something extraneous, but timely: on 6 August 1925, the commander of the 2nd Cavalry Corps Grigorii Kotovsky was murdered – a legendary man, the Robin Hood of southern Russia, Iakir's comrade-in-arms during the heroic campaign of the Red Army's Southern group of forces. The hand of this brave man was quick to reach his saber, but the series of strange deaths in the RKKA begins precisely with his murder. It was just a misfortune, but an extremely timely misfortune. Kotovsky was an uncontrollable sort, with a passion for justice that didn't exclude personal terror, and who moreover literally had the ability to penetrate walls ... The rumor was that he was murdered by his adjutant in a fit of jealousy. Nonsense. A stranger killed him, a man named Zaider, who got off with light punishment. Soon, though, he himself was murdered ...)

The next stroke of good fortune was Dzerzhinsky. Not the man, but his death. Monastically pure, he was particularly dangerous. He was a possible candidate to replace Stalin. So he died, all of a sudden! On 20 July 1926. There was no way to undermine this pillar of the Party, except to kill him. Of course, Stalin would have done this, but Dzerzhinsky up and died himself. What luck!

The circumstances surrounding his death have been described in Geller's and Rapoport's book:

G.I. Kotovsky.

According to published diagnosis, he died of a heart attack during a meeting of the Central Committee, at which he twice engaged Kamenev and Piatakov in angry debate. The text of those speeches surprises one by the insignificance of the subject matter discussed. It seems unlikely that a man so sick would find it necessary to speak out twice on such an ordinary matter. It is said that Stalin deliberately poured oil on the fire to drag out the meeting. Finally, Dzerzhinsky collapsed before the eyes of his comrades, with some of whom he had managed to quarrel so irreparably. Knowing Stalin's ways, one can surmise that aid was not given in time or not entirely properly.

Fortuitous happenstance after fortuitous happenstance!

We will not find out the underlying reasons for the list of coincidences that delighted the General Secretary even before the start of the mass terror. The list was lengthened with the death in an air crash of one more friend of justice, corps commander Fabritsius (a four-time recipient of the Order of the Red Banner for the Russian Civil War, but more modest than Kotovsky). Was this plane crash in the summer of 1929 a repetition of the crash of the plane carrying the officers of the General Staff of the RKKA? Was the murder of the potential terrorist Kotovsky a repetition of Kirov's murder? How many eliminations of potential avengers below the level of Kotovsky preceded Frunze's elimination, which was key in saddling the army? Incidentally, Kotovsky was murdered at a time when he was thinking over on offer from Frunze to become Frunze's deputy. Such a tandem would have been deadly dangerous to the Leader. Into which post was the opposition designing to advance Fabritsius in 1929? I don't know.

Some may think that this author is inflating these events for the sake of sensationalism.

Dzerzhinsky and Stalin. Smiling at "Iron Felix", Stalin conveniently dumped all the new responsibilities on him, the burden of which was back-breaking even for a healthy man...

This isn't so. A dislike of Stalin isn't blinding the author's eyes; he understands that some of these events might be coincidental. However, such an abundance of coincidences isn't accidental.

Stalin's "luckiness" even prompts doubt in whether Sverdlov's death was natural.[5] This tough cookie knew Stalin back from their days of Siberian exile together. Exiled people in their inactivity become talkative, and Stalin divulged so much about himself and his character that Sverdlov never mentioned his name again until the end of his life.

How did the Army endure Voroshilov? How did it stomach the elimination of the popular Frunze? After the revolutionary blood-letting, their hands didn't reach for their weapons. They wanted to resolve everything by parliamentary means.

However, on the day of the 10th Anniversary of the October Revolution, there was a disturbance, right on the podium of Lenin's Mausoleum. On this day, a parallel demonstration by Trotskyists was anticipated, and the life of the Leader, aside from

---

5   Editor's note: Iakov Sverdlov (1885-1919) was a revolutionary activist who later became a close ally of Lenin and helped plan the October Revolution, and a key Party and government leader in the early days of the Russian Soviet Federated Socialist Republic as Chairman of the All-Russian Central Executive Committee. He was an architect of the Red Terror, the Bolshevik terror campaign against opponents of the revolution, and has been implicated in the execution of Tsar Nicholas II and his family. He had a phenomenal memory and possessed a genius for organization. Officially, Sverdlov died of influenza in 1918, though some say he died of tuberculosis. The circumstances of his death became an official state secret in the Soviet Union.

Ia.F. Fabritsius.

the Chekists, was to be protected by military academy students. That's how Geller and Rapoport explain it.

Who made this decision? Stalin? The Cheka? The academy commandants? The parallel execution of any duties can be fraught with confusion and complications. I will introduce the description of what happened from the book by Geller and Rapoport, who treat what happened as a misunderstanding.

On the morning of 7 November 1927, the chief of the Frunze Military Academy, R. P. Eideman (who was later among the first victims of the trial of the army commanders) issued a special pass to three Academy attendees. Let's remember the names of the heroes: Iakov Okhotnikov (there's that name!), Vladimir Petenko and Arkadii Geller. They passed across the grounds of the Kremlin, but Georgian bodyguards were standing at the gates of the tunnel leading to the podium, where the Academy pass no longer had any authority. The fellows shoved aside the bodyguards and leaped up onto the podium. Security guards rushed toward them.

An excellent beginning for a righteous deed! However ...

Guards jumped the newcomers, but Okhotnikov got loose and leaped toward Stalin, whom he somehow considered responsible for the annoying confusion (Correct! But of what exactly?) and with his fist (Well, he found something to use) gave Stalin a rap on the back of the head. At the last moment (before what?), a bodyguard produced a knife – it was forbidden to shoot – and wounded Okhotnikov in the hand. Officers present intervened and ended the scuffle. (The parenthetical comments are the author's).

Pity.

In my essay *"Apologiia Iakira"* ["Iakir's Apology"], published in 1999 in the New York Russian-language *Interesnaia Gazeta* [*Newspaper Digest*], I interpreted this act by the young officers as an assassination attempt. I no longer believe so. One only has to picture the situation preceding this punch to nape of the Chief's neck: the zealous security surrounding Stalin, comprised of Georgian bodyguards and Cheka officials; and the three academy attendees, who must have raised quite a commotion on their way to the podium, having burst through a gate and pushed their way through to the stands of the then wooden Mausoleum before climbing it. It must have allowed time for others to intervene, but they were so fervent in their desire to reach the beloved Chief, who had slaughtered their excessively independent People's Commissar and then named the distant city of Pishpek after him. It is an amusing bit of irony, this practice. It became one of the Chief's main pastimes – to name cities in honor of those who had been eliminated, so their names would ring victoriously in the news reports from the provinces: Leningrad, Kotovsk (there were two of those, one in the center of the country), Dneprodzershinks, Kuibyshev, Ordzhonokidze, and the many cities and towns named after the humble yet unfittingly popular Kirov (Kirovograd, Kirovsk, Kirovobad, Kirovokan ...).

Geller's and Rapoport's description is comical in that it starts with a conception of zealous lackeys. If so, then it was a Chaplin-esque diligence, and their target Stalin, upon whom a dust speck wasn't given the chance to fall, receives a cuff to the nape. However, the first *samizdat* (self-published manuscript), Pilniak's *"Povest' nepogashennoi Luny"* [*"Tale of the Unextinguished Moon"*] was circulating from hand to hand at that time. The tale reveals no names; everything is transparent without them. Pilniak is strongly implying that the real purpose of the fiendish surgical procedure that killed Frunze is clear: it was murder. Perhaps the young officers did have a motive? However, if they were really intent upon assassination, they needed something other than fists! Sabers couldn't be deployed on the podium. They needed pistols, without which there could be no assassination.

As I see it now, it was an act of amateurs. Their chief, corps commander Eideman, was also acting like an amateur. They didn't discuss it? Avoided using words? Like-minded people understand each other without words? That's how they understood each other.

None of these so-called tyrant-killers was close to Stalin. Okhotnikov was entirely Iakir's man – he'd been an assistant to Iakir during the Southern Group's heroic campaign. They were even related. So, did Iakir have a part in it too? Where's the evidence?

However, Stalin didn't need evidence. Suspicions were enough for him. Proof, when it was necessary, he obtained *through the voluntary confession of the suspect.*[6]

One gets the impression that a decision had been made to frighten the Leader, to throw a scare into the criminal. Who made this decision? Not Iakir; he was a realist. Had he been drawn into the discussion, he would have proposed to see it through to the end, and would have found the means. However, in 1927 Iakir still hadn't ripened to the point of opposing Stalin, but after the crushing of the peasants in the early 1930s, it was already too late. Of course, one could resign from the army and save his good name; or, acknowledging the irreversibility of the Leader's criminal actions, albeit in the name of the revolution, one could go with the current and attempt to soften the situation in each new case that came along. Iakir, like many others, and like the German generals did later with their own

---

6   The typical formula in Stalin's trials where there was not any proof of any misdeeds by the convicted except their own confessions, obtained by torture or intimidation of victims.

On the podium in front of the Lenin Mausoleum, overlooking the 1934 May Day parade. Sixth from left (with his face toward the viewer) is the deputy People's Commissar for Military and Naval Affairs R.A. Muklevich, seventh from the left is the People's Commissar K.E. Voroshilov, twelfth from the left is first deputy People's Commissar M.N. Tukhachevsky, and to his left (the tallest figure in the photo) is the commander of the Red Army Air Force Ia.I. Alksnis.

dictator, chose the latter option.

Before Frunze's murder, the military's attitude toward Stalin didn't go further than a condescending contempt in that circle, where the talents of the Leader were being quoted at their genuine worth. Indeed, although two years passed after the elimination of Frunze, the action of the young officers, followers of Trotsky as an alternative to Stalin (one should recall Lenin's testament[7]) was more like a secret undertaking, and carried out in the certainty that for this act of hooliganism, if indeed they would even be judged, then the punishment would not be harsh. Stalin wasn't omnipotent, and they had the army behind them, and it was time to remind the little Soso [a childhood nickname for Stalin] of this! (They didn't even think what might happen to them, if there was no army behind them. In the middle of the 1920s, this thought truly couldn't enter their minds).

In a word, the true face of the Leader still wasn't so distinct, and Iakir wasn't a Trotsky supporter, like Shmidt and Okhotnikov were. He, so to say, was a Gamarnik follower, a supporter of ideas, not personalities. [Ian Gamarnik was a strong supporter of the drive to convert the Soviet Union into a militarily invincible but still peaceful country]. None of the leaders were comparable to Lenin; all of them had shortcomings. A new round of a power struggle seemed inexpedient. Experience was persuasive that the achievement of political aims, especially not fully defined ones, could not be settled without blood. Besides, Iakir still believed in collegiality.

The Leader, however, so clearly sensed the breath of death during the incident on the podium that on that same day of 7 November, he experienced a nervous collapse. A second nervous breakdown would occur on 22 June 1941.

To treat Stalin's first breakdown in 1927, two of the country's top doctors were

---

7   Editor's note: In his testament on his colleagues, written on 23 December 1922 but not opened until after his death, Lenin had issued a warning about Stalin's "boundless power" and suggested that he would not be able to use this power "with sufficient caution". In an addendum written ten days later, Lenin bluntly asserted the Stalin was "too rude", which was a fault "intolerable in the office of the general secretary". He urged that Stalin be removed from the post.

summoned, both luminaries of Russian science – Yudin and Bekhterev. Bekhterev's diagnosis – paranoia – would cost him his life.[8]

The entire country would treat the Leader's second breakdown with all its blood in 1941 ... .

8   After the autopsy, which confirmed that Bekhterev and his wife had been poisoned by a cake sent at
     Stalin's behest to the hotel where the couple was being housed as guests of the government, colleagues at
     Bekhterev's institute immediately cremated the professor's body. For the next several months, Chekists
     searched for the body, and interrogated employees of the morgue and the staff at the institute. Plainly, the
     Leader doubted the professor's death and feared the disclosure of information about his pathology. Years
     later it was revealed that Bekhterev's ashes, after a period of wandering among his colleagues' apartments,
     were concealed by them in a full bust of Stalin, which had been erected in a vestibule at the entrance of the
     institute in Leningrad.

10

The Great Leader and Teacher

L et's imagine Stalin's line of thinking. He was getting his grip on power, and it begins with the police and army.

Things were not difficult with the police. For the police bloodhounds, the head of the Party automatically became their master. The police didn't have either the popularity of the Red Army heroes of the Civil War, nor the sense of self-worth inherent in the veterans. It was also much easier to dispose of them in case of need. However, within the army, the appointment of Voroshilov didn't enhance respect for Stalin. The Civil War was incredibly pitiless and, not without reason, created famous names. The Red Army soldiers carried the glorious reputation of their commanders to every corner of the country and multiplied the legends surrounding them, and around their own selves at the same time. A line from a very popular cavalry song in the 1920s and 1930s went: "We are Red cavalrymen, and talkative *bylinniki* [legendary ancient Slavic epic poets] will tell stories about us." In order to snatch a bit of military glory for himself, the Leader had to tie his name to them and their exploits. He didn't have any of his own; their fabrication still lay ahead.

To saddle such an army was not a simple matter. Well, intransigent opponents would die in accidents; others would retire due to age or would be transferred to civilian jobs and eliminated inconspicuously; some could be sent abroad on missions, a little further from Moscow, a little closer to the line of fire. If they survived, their connection with associates would nonetheless be weaker. Someone might be bought off with money and someone else with a woman. A person could be pitted against someone else; in this, undeserved promotions would help. Keep shuffling and shuffling them, and don't allow them to become friends. Oh, and promote the young commanders, who didn't have any particular fame stemming from the Civil War.

Military men were speculating about Stalin's complicity in the deaths, but he, on the other hand, didn't have to guess; he knew – both about the past deaths, and the upcoming ones. Able-bodied acolytes of socialism were working all around, but he was already planning the times of their deaths. There was a list – and now the young commanders' breach of the security at the podium had taken place! Why? The Leader knew no mercy and wasn't waiting for it, preparing that which he had planned. However, the security breach on the podium occurred at a time when the army was in the hands of one of his own men, Voroshilov!?....

With strengthened security, a certain period of tranquility arrived, and he with his characteristic cold fury told himself: "You need military commanders who are dumber and more obedient. So, give the appearance that you believe that departmental confusion was behind the security breach, smile and wait. Wait until it will be possible not just to cage, but to kill! Kill anyone who interferes with your absolute power, so that those remaining tremble from your name alone!"

Had he started to think then about killing the one among his close associates, who would become more popular than the others? Here's a dandy idea: get close to a rival, present yourself as his best friend, then after his murder lament his death using exactly the same template, thereby creating from his death a pretext for the cruelest terror. Likely, that's just what Stalin was thinking then. It is a monstrous notion – and logical. He needed not simply power, but absolute power. The army commanders must be just as obedient as couriers were to Ghengis-Khan, as the Sardars were to Shah Abbas. Stand at attention!

Meanwhile the military men, who disliked Stalin, rejoiced over his unexpected good nature after the 7 November incident. They rejoiced that there had been no repercussions, that Okhotnikov, Petenko and Geller completed their studies at the Academy, assumed command posts, and were now working for the sake of the RKKA and the common good. The military commanders were human after all. They'd grown tired of hostility.

Not Stalin – he knew where he was headed and had precisely determined the sequence. First – take complete control of the Cheka-NKVD apparatus – at any cost. Of its own accord, in front of everyone's eyes, Dzerzhinsky's death suggested the organization of the quiet poisoning of the incorruptible intellectual Menzhinsky, Dzerzhinsky's deputy, by the "pharmacist" Iagoda (G. G. Iagoda would become chief of the People's Commissariat of Internal Affairs in July 1934, two months after Menzhinsky's death). Then liquidate Iagoda, once he had dealt with Menzhinsky, should he happen to pause in front of the army commanders (Did Iagoda hesitate? Or worse – did he reveal to them a little glimpse of the fate awaiting them?). It would have to be done in such a routine way that the liquidation of enemies wouldn't need to be justified by ideology; so that the elimination of any person need not be justified in any way. There was no need to hurry with the army; fortunately, it was being headed by his own man, Klim Voroshilov. Create some military glory for yourself; gradually make it equal to and then superior to that of all these commanders, who became legendary for their deeds in the Civil War. Klim would write the first article, others who were a little shrewder would follow with their laudatory fiction about the Boss, and from them a reliable circle would form, primarily from cadres of the Moscow District.

A myth began to be created: Tsaritsyn was where the outcome of the Civil War was decided![1] With heroes of that war still living, the myth still couldn't have wide circulation, and so it smoldered on the periphery, waiting for their death. In the meantime, Stalin was flirting with the army commanders and destroying his political opponents. The situation didn't give him much time and he hurried, and of course, made mistakes. He got away with them, though. Why?

The reasons have already been mentioned. We'll repeat the main one: While the military commanders were weighed down by their memories of the bloody Civil War and reluctant to trigger a new one potentially, the General Secretary wasn't burdened at all by any similar feelings and was able to develop a cult around himself. Indeed, the cult blossomed into a regime of personal power with the willingness of the Party majority. Through the efforts of the press, which was wholly subordinate to the Party apparatus, Stalin presented himself, at the very least, as the faithful pupil and successor to Lenin. The cult of Lenin became the focus of propaganda.

Precisely for this reason, an enormously expensive radio broadcast network was deployed

---

1   Editor's note: Tsaritsyn, which would later become renamed as Stalingrad, was the site of a relatively minor battle of the Russian Civil War, where White Cossack forces under General Krasnov were badly pressing the Bolshevik defenders. According to the legend that artificially grew up around the battle, the town was saved for the Bolsheviks by the resolute actions of the chairman of the local military committee, Josef Stalin.

throughout the country, which later justified itself, having extended its lines with their daily brain-washing broadcasts into every out-of-the-way corner, to wherever any footpath or trail led. People of my generation still recall the bitter saying, "We are all directed by radio." A decisive role in this process was played by the creation of *oblast'* [district] radio committees, which worked under the supervision of the Party apparatus and repeatedly and frequently broadcast in the course of each blessed day the name of Stalin in conjunction with the founder of the Soviet state, Lenin, in monotonous incantations like "... under the banner of Lenin and the leadership of Stalin" or "the Leninist-Stalinist practice". After the vainglorious Stalin's work *Voprosy Leninizma* [*Problems of Leninism*] was published in 1938 (not before the country's best people had been eliminated), the expression "Leninist-Stalinist theory" appeared. Unsurprising and related to this is Bukharin's[2] remark back in 1928, which clarified the aim of this outpouring of propaganda: "This is Ghengis-Khan. He'll strangle all of us."

It is possible to understand the sense of doom of Stalin's opponents in the face of the million-member Party, which devotedly chanted Stalin's name, and to understand the dejection of the politicians and military commanders. This feeling was strengthened by the recognition that the Tsarist *Okhranka* was like a school for troubled adolescents in comparison with the institution of the Cheka, while the revolution after all the bloody sacrifices was tamely ending in a counter-revolution. Honorable people could find no footing in order to oppose this process. An act of personal terror? Then what? (Oh, how they needed not think then about what might happen afterward!)

However, the military commanders, in addition to the army's traditional reluctance under legitimate regimes to intervene in affairs unrelated to national defense, had grown tired of political games and strident revolutionary slogans, of all this *brotherhood of detachments of seething proletarian wrath against the yoke of the exploiters*. They'd become tired of the blood of the Civil War and their part in it. The torments of Iakir's conscience for the "cleansing" in the Don area against the Cossacks are unimaginable. Never again did the regime succeed in sending him to suppress any disturbances. However, I assume that the memory of the "quiet Don" sapped his will, when the time arrived for decisions and inactivity meant death. Likely, he wasn't thinking that as a soldier he could refuse to obey an order, and also not thinking that he would be carrying out a revolutionary duty. The time had come to see that the revolution was turning back, and this stripped him of the will to live. His life had been dedicated to the building of an ideal socialism, for which, clenching his teeth, he had gone through the chaos of the Civil War.

Who then of the commanders was the first to dare to speak out from the military ranks? It was he, Iakir.

The Workers' and Peasants' Army was more peasant, than workers. During the collectivization drive, Iakir, the sole military commander who was a full member of the Party Central Committee, appealed to Stalin with a request to alleviate the situation of the Ukraine's starving peasants. Bliukher from the Far East supported him. It must be

---

2   Editor's note: Nikolai I. Bukharin (1888-1938) was a prominent Bolshevik revolutionary and Marxist theoretician, who rose to become a member of the Party's Politburo and Central Committee, chairman of the Communist International, and chief editor of the major Party newspapers, *Pravda* and *Izvestiia*. He was immensely popular within the Party. Bukharin would be arrested in 1937 and charged with conspiring to overthrow the Soviet state. He was convicted in a major 1938 show trial together with other members of the so-called "Bloc of Rightists" and executed very quickly after the trial ended.

remembered what collectivization was for Stalin. He became enraged. Stalin didn't dare openly refuse Iakir's request, but he told him to stick to military matters.

Iakir spoke out too late. Too late. I will repeat again and again that the peasantry, both economically and in the moral sense, be it primitive or be it battered by the revolution, but still alive, was the basis of the country. Having destroyed it, Stalin left the country without a foundation. With the smashing of the *kulaks* [the hostile name for wealthy farmers]; with the setting of the peasant class against one another; with the collectivization, which corrupted the peasantry morally; with the hunger, which crushed it both physically and with the peasantry's awareness of its impotence, the dictatorship tore out the roots essential for Russian village autonomy. Prior to collectivization, the dictatorship reigned on the level of bureaucracy. Now it had become total, so total that there was no return path. This indeed is what Stalin achieved, and he executed it so intrepidly.

What administrator will take power in a country where the very basis of market relations has been liquidated? This is a path to a criminal society! At this stage, Stalin surely separated himself from his rivals. There was now no other alternative than another criminal, who would be ready to continue the repressions – the dispossessed *kulaks* had still not disappeared entirely, and indeed if the repressions had ceased, they would have swiftly returned, taking revenge for their terrible losses. Only another criminal could desire to follow Stalin and rule through blood. At this point there was no one else prepared to do so. The reversal in the fate of the peasantry changed the fate of the country as well.

The military commanders let the moment pass by, when they would have been supported by tens of millions of people. In just the same fashion, the German generals of the *Reichswehr* missed their moment in 1933-1934, for which the Germans would pay their own price.

Or are the lives of millions not worth the lives of leaders? The lives of workers, their offspring, the old people, who toiled their entire lives from dawn to dusk in the sweltering heat and the icy cold, and who died from hypothermia and hunger in the rail cars and barracks or who were buried under the ruins of their beautiful cities[3] – they were not worth the lives of the Party drones, who never worked a single day and never created anything?

Let's establish some concepts. "History has no subjunctive mood" is a maxim long inculcated by tyrants. Yes, the past is unchangeable. Yet history sometimes offers us a hypothetical mood, and it postulates the future. We not only have the right to thumb through the past. We are obliged to look into it and to insert certain acts there, which would have been desirable to occur – but which didn't. The Red Army commanders fell as victims of their own inactivity. Their fate stings the soul. Fearing losses, they sentenced themselves to be slaughtered. However, any losses resulting from the overthrow of a tyrant are incomparable with the losses resulting from his rule.

Incidentally, where are we now in our journey through early Soviet history and where are we headed? Ahead of us lies the legitimate possibility to depose the uncrowned sovereign and to save the country from his costly services. In front of us is the 1934 XVII Congress of the All-Union Communist Party (Bolsheviks) and the opportunity to get rid of the General Secretary by a vote. For this, only one thing is needed: a sober assessment of the country's accomplishments, an examination of collectivization and industrialization from the point of view of their feasibility, and from the point of view of their costs – in black

---

3   Editor's note: The author is clearly referring to the victims of the Soviet gulag and the future victims of the Second World War from the both sides, Soviet and German.

and white. The chasm between separating Russia from the rest of the world was still not yawning. The cessation of blood-letting in the country and its rehabilitation in the eyes of other countries was still possible. The purges and military losses were still over the horizon, but the man at the helm knows how to peer beyond the horizon, isn't that so?

11

A World Turned Upside Down: The "Congress of Victors"

T he XVII Party Congress was the Communist Party's greatest disgrace of all times. Pluralism and collegiality were not essential to the Party from the very beginning. Excessively concerned with unity, the Party became obsessed with this doctrine, but the removal of a leader has no purpose, wherever there is no pluralism. The XVII Party Congress demonstrated this with full clarity. The Congress took place in January and February 1934, and received the name "Congress of Victors".

The capital's abundance and never-before-seen comforts awaited the delegates, freshly-stamped Party members from the provinces, who had been carefully selected to create an obedient majority. They were greeted, wined and dined, entertained and treated, so that they immediately felt themselves as particularly special contributors to the business, for which they'd been summoned: to celebrate the victory, to endorse the path that had brought them to this victory – under Stalin's leadership, naturally. It was a path already now strewn with the bones of millions of Russia's best people, who had tried to avoid it. Those who weren't perturbed by this sacrifice were carefully selected for the Congress, as well as those who didn't comprehend this and who with an exulting roar – from the scum right up to

Military delegates to the 17th Party Congress. From left to right: Army Commissar 2nd Rank I.E. Slavin, Army Commissar 1st Rank Ia.B. Gamarnik, Army Commander 2nd Rank I.N. Dubovoi, People's Commissar of Defense K.E. Voroshilov, Army Commander 2nd Rank P.E. Dybenko, Army Commander 2nd Rank A.I. Kork, Army Commander 2nd Rank I.A. Khalepsky, and Army Commander 1st Rank I.E. Iakir.

the delegates, the cream of the Party! – drowned out the other voices that sought serious discussions. These voices did not ring out. Stalin made sure that this didn't happen. The selection of delegates from the very beginning doomed to a minority those Party activists that wanted to use the podium for business matters. The Congress was designed as a parade. The majority of delegates were inclined to vote for anything, even without hearing it, as long as it came from Stalin.

We were born and grew up in an atmosphere of worship for the Leader, we knew nothing else; for us this was a given as natural as the blue sky. However, it had all been established prior to us, in the generation which had begun to doubt the belief in God. Stop believing in God, in order to believe in a man! It is senseless to ask how this happened. It still happens, and will happen more than once.

The Congress became the voluntary dissolution of the Party. It revealed that its function had become the glorification of the Leader and a puffery, which in the perspective of history looks humiliating. A subordination to discipline fettered the best people, those who might have affected the course of events.[1] In the stormy sea of the 20th century's political currents, the Helmsman steered the nation, having tossed overboard the navigators with their pilot charts and without listening to the lookouts. Those, whom the course of the Congress didn't convince to get rid of Stalin before he implemented the extraordinary legislation and began to murder openly – they could have foreseen this, had they not had their head stuck in the sand – preordained their own deaths, and not only their own. Recognizing that they were doomed, however, the perspicacious among them looked no further.

The Congress demonstrated that the Party masses were submissive to the will of the General Secretary and full of enthusiasm, ready at his bidding to energize the country in the same way. Even the army, the most authoritative force in the country, was in general obedient to the Leader. The RKKA, however, adhered to the slogan of an indestructible defense, which was odious to the General Secretary. This line of insubordination, however, echoed the line of official Soviet proclamations, so the Boss could not challenge it until a suitable time. The army, the hope of the opposition, had become the last redoubt of independent strategic thought – and integrity, according to the harsh international standards.

One more thing: since Stalin didn't share his aggressive intentions with anyone else, the army in the form of its ideological and strategic leadership could, in full seriousness, pursue the peaceful proclamations of the Stalinist government. I would like to emphasize this point: that the upper echelon of the Red Army, those who were destroyed first, was aware of the irreproachability of their position. In the naïve credulity of the army commanders toward the government's peaceful slogans was the benefit that it could never be denounced

---

1   To the Western reader it is difficult, or even impossible to understand how effectively the principle of a simple majority of voices worked in combination with the cruel regime of a police state. At the time of the XVII Party Congress, Stalin was already enjoying absolute power. He had established a surveillance system over everyone that he feared, and knew their every footstep. He took care to ensure that only a portion of the prominent members of the government apparatus were present at the Congress, and these were for the most part his people. Those few who opposed his policies were already so internally repressed that they avoided meeting each other so that they could not be accused of a plot and in doing so cast a shadow of suspicion over their comrades (see V. V. Katanian, *Vospominaniia o Lile Brik* [*Remembrances of Lilia Brik*] (Primakov's wife). Such disassociation excluded the possibility of an organized appearance at the Congress. The voice of any sort of young careerist from a district committee was weighted just as heavily as the voice of any military district commander or People's Commissar. Moreover, the young careerists were pulled together and organized by the leadership into one common choir.

publicly. The defensive posture was invulnerable from the position of international norms, while the re-equipping of the army was justified by the same stance: if someone comes and shows their teeth at us, we'll knock their teeth out.

Was such an army needed by the Leader? The attempt to export revolution to Europe had failed, but Hitler's appearance in the political arena was obviously a new concern: he was hailing the repartition of Europe and the world. In such a case the Boss would remain on the side with his peace-loving army, led by people who only tolerated him and were waiting for an opportunity to depose him. He had to get rid of them at any price, even at the cost of the entire army, if it held them in such esteem and was so attached to them. Moreover, he had to do it as soon as possible, while the army still didn't realize that it was the last bastion of opposition and hadn't yet begun to operate independently. For a beginning, Stalin would free himself from decent people in the government and from the suppressed oppositionists. Not arrest them; the arrested are freed one day and step into leadership roles. No, kill them! The dead are buried and gone; they can do no practical work and lead no masses.

However, for such a purge, oh what a justification.

12

The Justification

It is in the cards for this chapter to be the briefest. Its essence – and horror – can be expressed in a single phrase: there was not a page in the history of the world more ignoble and bloodier in its consequences, than the murder of Kirov[1] as conceived and implemented by Stalin. Just such a popular figure was needed by the tyrant as a sacrifice, in order to kindle the still damp logs of "nation-wide wrath".[2]

Of course, one cannot expect a political actor to be a conscience of his times or a model of nobility. However, there is a yardstick even with vileness. Not in Stalin's. His vileness was immeasurable.

---

1   Editor's note: S. M. Kirov (1886-1934) was an early Bolshevik leader who rose to become the head of the Leningrad Party organization. Given the political and cultural rivalries between Leningrad (now St. Petersburg) and Moscow, and Kirov's apparent popularity, it was natural for Stalin to view him as a potential rival. Matters came to a boil when Kirov countermanded an order from Stalin NKVD chief Iagoda to replace the head of the Leningrad NKVD office with a close associate of Stalin's. Kirov was murdered in a corridor of his offices at the Smolny Institute on 1 December 1934 after the usual guard post at the entry was left unmanned. It is widely believed that Stalin ordered Kirov's assassination, which was handled by the NKVD, though conclusive evidence for this conjecture is missing.
2   The year 2009 was the 75th year from the day of Kirov's murder. Stalin's role in it is offered as one of the versions of the story behind the crime. However the main version – "murder out of jealousy" – still keeps the Leader free of any suspicion.

13

The Congress as a Prologue

The reader now understands, that the cuckoo bird began to cuckoo[1] at the XVII Party Congress.

Iakir, a member of the Central Committee, at Kirov's request, had once given some attention to the Leningrad Military District. They became friends – a little-known fact, but then everything became known to the Leader. The friendship between the accomplices didn't please him. Iakir and Kirov, eh?

At the XVII Party Congress of Victors, everything went smoothly, but during the vote for Central Committee membership, 17 votes went against Kirov, yet 111 votes went against Stalin – a well-known fact.[2] Kirov was a nice guy, while Stalin was already acquiring the reputation of a terrible man, after the bloody crackdown on several opposition groups and a series of puzzling deaths. Kirov's popularity was growing, despite his acceptance and implementation of several deceitful policy suggestions from Stalin. (The expulsion from the city of noblemen and intellectuals – native citizens of Petersburg – unquestionably didn't add to Kirov's laurels as the Secretary of the District Committee.) At the Congress, a proposal to select Kirov as the General Secretary was introduced by some desperate soul. Kirov decisively rejected it. Stalin understood: an unwitting successor had arisen. With his refusal and the glorification of Stalin, Kirov, who hadn't wanted power, signed a death sentence for himself and for others.

That summer of 1934, a conflict between Stalin and the military arose over some leaks abroad of some important information about the army's reform through the agency of the Boss. The intention was good – to win time for rearmament by intimidating the West. However, the Leader didn't know and didn't ask which information he could use for the intimidation, and which he could not. Civilian leaders were drawn into the dispute – Kuibyshev (Chairman of the Council of People's Commissars) and Ordzhonikidze (People's Commissar of Machine Building Industry), Stalin's personal friend. The issue infuriated Kuibyshev. He condemned the General Secretary for his intrusion into matters in which Stalin had no understanding. Stalin was sharply criticized at a meeting of the Politburo. The General Secretary, who was unable to stomach criticism, interpreted this episode as a step toward his removal.

That same summer, Hitler dealt with his rivals (Ernst Röhm, Gregor Strasser and others). The "Night of the Long Knives" was a barbarous action, but Stalin drew his own conclusions from this massacre of closest rivals. With truly Eastern cunning he began to

---

1   According to a widely-known, old Russian superstition, it is said that a cuckoo bird foretells death: the number of times the bird "cuckoos" symbolizes the number of years one has left to live. Traditionally, as soon as one hears/sees a cuckoo bird, they ask aloud: "Hey, cuckoo, how many years do I have left to live?" Then count the number of "cuckoos".

2   At the Congress, the praising of the delegates for Stalin and the abject repentance of the former oppositionists in front of Stalin were audible. The intelligent Bliukher, a member of the electoral commission, understood what was what and agreed to falsify the record to show that only one vote went against Stalin.

make a great show of friendship with Kirov. He took a trip to Sochi for a rest – and brought Kirov along with him. While there, Stalin dragged him everywhere, drank wine with him, and played checkers with him, though the northerner Kirov was suffering from the heat and tormented by sleeplessness.

In the summer of 1934, Primakov was transferred from his post as deputy commander of the North Caucasus District to the same post in the Leningrad District. An upward move? However, Primakov was not a randomly shifted figure. He was never given a chance to acquire friends. At the Leader's behest he was constantly being thrown from place to place. At one point he was a military adviser to China, then to Afghanistan, and only recently he'd been in Moscow. It is fully possible that the transfer to Leningrad at a time when NKVD men were pushing the neurotic Nikolaev toward the murder of Kirov could signify only one thing: Stalin wanted Primakov to be as close as possible to the scene of Kirov's assassination, and moreover, in a significant post.[3]

On 1 December 1934, Kirov was murdered by Nikolaev in a corridor of the Smolny office. (Let's recall the murder of Kotovsky, supposedly due to a jealous rage ...)[4] Of course, in comparison with the liquidation of Röhm, Kirov's murder was almost gem-like. However, rumors about the disappearance of witnesses circulated even in my school years, which were saturated with the glorification of Stalin.

Kirov's murder enraged the population. The words "enemy of the people" had frequently been heard even prior to this, but now they were being broadcast through every channel of the system of mass information and had acquired a concrete form. Not only the fact that a popular leader had been assassinated was terrifying, but also the ferocious decree that coincided with the murder, "On the measures of the struggle with enemies of the people". It was made public on that very same day, 1 December, and rather incredibly already contained a reference to Kirov's murder. It was a law about the introduction of lawlessness, a stunt not new in history, similar to the Roman proscriptions or Ivan the Terrible's *oprichnina* [a territory totally subject to Ivan the Terrible's personal rule and decrees].

Stalin had hurried and tipped his hand! The higher echelon of power did not greet the fact that the new decree had been prepared beforehand with any complacency. The Party bosses demanded explanations. The normally obedient Kuibyshev again rebelled. Who had prepared this? When? Against whom? Beforehand? Now the Leader began to wield his punitive organs, which he fully controlled after the death of Menzhinsky, without delay and indeed in a completely brazen fashion. On 25 January 1935, Kuibyshev arrived home from the Council of People's Deputies and took some medicine that had been sent

---

3   Information must be sought in the materials of Primakov's interrogation, and more in the questions of the investigators than in Primakov's answers. One of the more likely versions of what his interrogating officers extracted from him was a confession of his complicity in the murder of the popular Party leader.

4   It is curious that the film *Chapaev* prodded Stalin to think about glorifying other heroes. The result is really interesting – more films about Kotovsky, Shchors, Sverdlov, Kirov ... a list of his victims. An exception was, it seems, only the film about Parkhomenko, which slipped through the net in some incomprehensible manner, possibly due to the song about the first and second bullets ... [The author here is making a wry comment about Aleksandr Parkhomenko, a famous Russian Civil War hero who was killed while trying to intercept the Ukrainian anarchist and partisan leader Makhno as he was fleeing the Ukraine. There was a very popular 1942 Soviet film, *Aleksandr Parkhomenko*, which featured a beloved, sentimental wartime song about two bullets: In the song's refrain, the first bullet wounds the protagonist, and the second wounds his steed. Stalin loved films and would pre-screen them, deciding which would be released and which would be banned. It is known that Stalin particularly loved the song about the two bullets.]

to him – and died. As in the case with Kirov, his funeral was opulent. As with Kirov, his remains were cremated and walled up in the Kremlin Wall, so that there could not be any exhumations. In just the same way, a city was given Kuibyshev's name (Samara, a city on the left bank of the Volga, where cities traditionally carried names of the feminine gender: Tver', Kostroma, Kazan'...) and Kuibyshev was similarly extolled as a dedicated Bolshevik, a faithful Leninist, etc. Just as with the assassination of Kirov, Kuibyshev's death was cynically used by the killer to settle scores with his personal rivals. Potential leaders and well-known personalities in the Party, the silver-tongued speakers Zinov'ev and Kamenev and their comrades were first on the list.

What does this mean, though: "well-known in the Party"? The Party was purposefully being revamped – first of all by means of a growth in membership, which gave its leader an immediate superiority during voting. Veteran political figures were being removed from their posts and sent away "for a well-deserved rest", or they were being accused as Trotskyists and expelled from the Party. Their places were taken by young careerists, who recognized the advantages of being an *apparatchik*. The constant recruitment of new members led to a point where the Party in its mass knew only the name of Stalin. Latest history illustrates how quickly the names of once well-known people fade away, once they are no longer part of the daily panorama of events. By the time of the Moscow show trials of first Zinov'ev and Kamenev, and then of Bukharin and Rykov, they were no longer to be brilliant public figures by the majority of the Party members, as they had been viewed at the height of their fame. Now they were allowed to approach a podium only to repent. They knew history, they knew that the counter-revolution had triumphed, that the Tyrant was playing with their lives and the lives of their families, and would not only destroy them, but also extract some benefit from this. He would associate the spectacle of the show trials with the ferment in the workers' hopes for a subsequent improvement in their lives and standard of living, for an uninterrupted supply of food and products, and a reduction in the retail prices of manufactured goods.

Imagine as possible the following conjecture: the pessimism of the helpless politicians weakened the will to resist of the military commanders, who still had power. Zinov'ev and Kamenev were put on trial secretly in 1935 and received only (!) a prison sentence. The poisoning of Kuibyshev and the assassination of Kirov were not imputed to them directly, but were judged somehow to be a consequence of their activities. In this way they were incriminated with the charge of desiring to overthrow the scoundrel, who had usurped power through a vote. They were incriminated by the poisoning-plotter himself. Then they were put on trial a second time in 1936 as the Great Terror gathered pace, and both were sentenced to death.

In February 1937, the remnant of the Leninist guard, Bukharin and Rykov, were arrested. They were the last witnesses of Lenin's real attitude toward his probable successor. For the time being, they weren't shot. If not a single ideological figure remained, the army might advance one of their own. This could not be permitted! The annihilation of potential ideological figures in the army must precede the liquidation of the last political oppositionists.

14

What was happening in Germany?

The Führer of the German people had his own difficulties. He, a rag-tag former corporal, was now commanding generals, men that were not only educated, but in the majority were aristocratic. What constrained Hitler more than anything else was these men's burden of their prejudices – moral dogmas and a variety of foolish principles.

On 5 November 1937, not coincidentally after the bloody threshing in the ranks of the Red Army had begun, Hitler met with the *Wehrmacht* leadership. From 4:30 pm until 8:30 in the evening, Germany's military plans were discussed among a small circle. In addition to the Führer, in attendance were the Deputy Minister of Foreign Affairs von Neurath, Colonel-General Göring, Admiral Raeder, War Minister General-Field Marshal von Blomberg, Commander-in-Chief of the Army [*Oberkommando des Heeres*, or OKH] Colonel-General von Fritsch and the Führer's military adjutant Colonel Hossbach, who kept brief notes at the meeting. It was here that Hitler for the first time revealed his plans for expanding the German people's *Lebensraum*, or living space.

Von Fritsch, an extreme nationalist, was nonetheless no admirer of Hitler; von Blomberg idolized him, but the difference in their feelings for the Führer was not reflected in the shared attitude of the military men for Hitler's plans. Both had comprehended the lessons of the First World War, and both had become proponents of the defense. They did not call the plans for swallowing Austria and Czechoslovakia illegal or criminal. As soldiers, they understood that they'd not been invited in order to evaluate the moral side of the matter. They only warned that not only Czechoslovakia would oppose Germany in a conflict, although it alone should not be underestimated, since it had sufficient strength for the defensive stage of the war. France would intervene and with it, of course, England. Germany lacked the strength and resources for a war with them. Preparation for such a war – and even then with no guarantee of the outcome – would require no less than 10 years.

Hossbach's notes reveal that the discussion became heated, although primarily the disputes were between the military commanders and Göring. Hitler took the position of a listener, but was obviously stricken to find that his broad plans did not have the slightest support in the army. It became clear to him that the military commanders had to be replaced.

Mines were positioned under von Blomberg and von Fritsch, both involving matters of officers' honor and conduct. With the ready assistance of Göring and Himmler (head of all German police and the *Schustzstaffel*, better known by its initials, the SS), Hitler was able to use these affairs to remove the military opponents to his plans.

Von Fritsch was already a target of Himmler, due to his dismissive opposition to Himmler's plans for the SS to have its own combat formations. Back in 1935, Himmler had come across a police file on the case of a lowlife and swindler, who had once tried to blackmail a retired *Reichswehr* captain by the name of von Fritsch with the accusation of homosexuality. The streetwalker was ready to testify that Colonel-General von Fritsch was the man he'd witnessed engaging in sexual acts with another man. The head of the SS offered to use this coincidental discovery to smear von Fritsch, but at the time the Führer had no need for this, and ordered that it be put aside and forgotten.

At the 5 November 1937 conference, at one point during the heated debate Von Fritsch had sharply replied that Göring's was being "dilettantish", which enraged the Reich Minister. Now he was burning with a desire for revenge.

Himmler soon staged a face-to-face confrontation between Colonel-General von Fritsch and the lowlife witness who was prepared to testify against von Fritsch, with the clear intention to embarrass the Army Commander-in-Chief. The witness, Otto Schmidt, asserted that Colonel-General Fritsch was indeed the man he'd witnessed engaging in homosexual acts. Von Fritsch protested that he'd never seen this man before. It was now more convenient for Hitler to believe the words of a small-time criminal than those of the Army's top commander. Von Fritsch demanded a court of honor to hear the case and to clear his reputation, but he also resigned his post on 4 February 1938, ostensibly for "reasons of health".

The parallel von Blomberg affair was simpler, but no less messy. In September 1937, the widower Blomberg had become acquainted with a pleasant lady; coincidentally, of course. Erna Gruen was 30 years younger than the Field Marshal and worked as a typist at the War Ministry. There is nothing strange in the fact that the widower fell in love. Soon after the Hossbach conference, at the funeral of General Ludendorff, Blomberg asked the Reich Chancellor's permission to get married. Hitler not only gave his consent, but offered to be a witness at the marriage ceremony together with Colonel-General Göring. The marriage took place on 12 January 1938.

However, soon phone calls started coming in to the *Wehrmacht's* headquarters. Giggling women were expressing their delight that *one of their own* had become the lady of the home of the War Minister. Erna turned out to be a lady with a past. She had grown up in a massage parlor that had been operated by her mother. Pornographic photographs of Erna had been confiscated and were being held in a police station, where she had been registered as a prostitute. Von Blomberg was clearly now in the position of violating the standard of conduct for officers that he himself had devised.

One could sense the role of Göring behind the unfolding scandal, who dreamed of the post of War Minister. Hitler exploded and sputtered in a rage: it was a set-up, he was being disgraced! This was a provocation, an attempt to undermine him, the Führer of the German people! Blomberg must divorce his wife and go into retirement. As for von Fritsch, let them both go away!

Great actors, these politicians ...

At an audition with the Führer, when Blomberg was presented with the choice of either retiring or divorcing his wife, he categorically refused a divorce. Understanding that Blomberg would be leaving, Hitler dropped his tone and offered the Field Marshal the prospects of a return to the colors, if the Reich ever needed this. With a full pension and 150,000 gold marks, the touched Blomberg left with his wife for Italy, where they lived in quiet obscurity.[1]

---

1   I am correcting an error. Von Blomberg died of cancer in the Nuremberg prison in March 1946. He was not involved in war crimes; at his time of service, the *Wehrmacht* still hadn't managed to commit them. However, he had brilliantly laid the foundations of the *Wehrmacht*, which indeed incurred the wrath of the Allies. His good fortune is that he died before the trial, rather than being hung at the insistence of the Soviet accusers, like they hung the former Chief of the Operations Staff of the OKW [*Oberkommando*

The Fritsch affair was drawn out. In March 1938, the court of honor presided over by Hermann Göring himself discovered that the police file was about someone else with the same name and that von Fritsch was fully innocent, but by that time the successful *Anschluss* of Austria made it safe for Hitler to refuse to return von Fritsch to his post atop the OKH.

Soon after Blomberg and Fritsch had left their posts "for reasons of health", Hitler had named himself the Commmander-in-Chief of the OKH, but soon thereafter turned it over to the unblemished, but spineless von Brauchitsch. The post of War Minister was abrogated. Fourteen higher generals went into retirement or were discharged together with Blomberg and Fritsch. All those who left had carried great authority, so the remaining generals understood that this new Reich Chancellor would brook no opposition from even the highest commanders, that he would show them their places, and that he was indeed the Führer. Younger commanders replaced those who left. They kept in mind what had happened and were not inclined to argue with the new Supreme Commander. That's the way Hitler's take-over in the army concluded.

After von Fritsch's inadequate rehabilitation, more than a few generals revealed their desire to retire. The new head of the OKH, von Brauchitsch, talked them out of this. The invasion of Czechoslovakia was nigh, he told them, and they didn't dare refuse to do their duty. Von Fritsch felt the same way. As the commander of an artillery regiment, he later took part in the Polish campaign and was killed. There are grounds to believe that he was seeking his death.

A few words about the participants in this drama – about those who left, and those who survived to play out their role:

After von Fritsch was removed from command of the OKH, Hitler offered his post to Colonel-General Ludwig Beck. Beck declared that he believed in the innocence of his commander and refused to take the post. In connection with the Sudetan crisis, Beck submitted his resignation, not wishing to take part, as he announced, in the destruction of his country. Subsequently, the oppositionists planned to place him at the head of the government after Hitler's elimination. On 21 July 1944, Colonel-General Beck shot himself after the unsuccessful assassination attempt made by von Stauffenberg.

For comparative biographies of Plutarch's type found in his *Parallel Lives*, two personalities would constitute a suitable pair: Colonel-General of the *Wehrmacht*, Werner Freiherr von Fritsch and Red Army Commander, 1st Rank Iona Emmanuilovich Iakir. Like Iakir, von Fritsch was a man of honor and duty. Honor for a German officer of the old school was more precious than life. Too late, von Fritsch understood the odious role played in his affair by Hitler. It was absurd for Hitler to take the word of a member of the riffraff, who was later murdered[2], and not believe von Fritsch, but von Fritsch believed in the sincerity of the Führer right up to his audition with the Führer. Peter Hoffmann, in his

---

der *Wehrmacht*, or Armed Forces High Command] Colonel-General Jodl, who was just as glittering in a professional sense. It was not for nothing that Jodl was rehabilitated already in 1953. After all, on just the same grounds Vasilevsky, Antonov and Shtemenko on the victorious side could have been punished ....

2   Later, in 1938, at the court of officers' honor Otto Schmidt, a man with a criminal record, who had testified against von Fritsch, declared that he was mistaken in his recognition of the general. Fritsch was vindicated, while Schmidt wound up in Buchenwald. In 1942, Himmler sent a letter seeking the agreement of his "dearest friend" Göring to submit Schmidt's case to the Führer to gain his authorization to execute the unlucky rogue, to which Göring responded in a note written on the margin of the letter, "Ought to have been shot long ago."

book about the German resistance, writes: "This was not mere well-bred reticence; this was naiveté." This is a comment that prompts pain in anyone, who understands the tragedy of the best men of the RKKA, bound to it by duty and honor and who only at the very last perceived the hopelessness of their situation. Surely Iakir after Kirov's murder understood where things were heading ...

Hitler subjugated the *Wehrmacht* already after Stalin had resolved the problem of breaking the Red Army – just as filthily as Hitler, but also bloodily. Both of these criminals moved in lockstep with each other.

15

The RKKA and its Murderer

Zhukov condemned the repression, pointing to the quickly rising number of Party members in the Red Army, and as mentioned previously, the increasing percentage of commanders with a worker or peasant background. The Red Army was actually increasingly becoming the Workers' and Peasants' Red Army. However, from Stalin's position this had little significance. He considered the situation in the army catastrophic not because "... 70 percent of the command staff are workers and peasants", but because 30 percent of the command staff was comprised of men who were not workers or peasants; or alternatively, not because "... more than half of all officers are Communist Party members or Komsomol members," but because almost half were not Party or Komsomol members.

Of course, doubts in the right to use force as a remedy are more characteristic of people who hail from bourgeoisie circles, than from workers and peasants. Of course, communization fettered that element that remains free in the officer after taking the oath of duty: pluralism. However, for the Boss, even this meant little. He considered the situation catastrophic, because the higher echelon of the Red Army's leadership was not dedicated to him personally. Thinking military men served the country, not Stalin, yet these were the most influential men in the Red Army.

Stalin had already acquired power. However, he understood that he could not prod the army commanders to attempt territorial acquisitions. Their mindset had become forged in the course of the Russian Civil War. Naturally, this was a defensive mindset. Possibly, the ambitious Tukhachevsky, who didn't share the ideals of his comrades-in-arms, would not have opposed the Leader's aggressive plans, but indeed likely would have himself determined schedules and the necessary level of the army's readiness; this reason alone would have been sufficient for Stalin to want to eliminate this glittering reformer of the army. The majority of the army commanders, though, who were loved and trusted by their troops, were convinced that socialist construction on their own territory was more productive than annexing someone else's land.

Out of ideological considerations and a concern over international reputation, Stalin was compelled to speak about the collapse of capitalism only as a result of a war that the capitalists themselves would start. In this fashion, his hands were bound, and he couldn't implant an offensive spirit in the army. Political workers were nurturing a spirit of indestructible defense in the army, and Stalin, grinding his teeth, endured this, suspecting that the army commanders were tolerating him as long as he remained faithful to the credo, "We don't want a square foot of someone else's land, but we also won't yield an inch of our own." He realized that the RKKA was still an army of defense, not aggression, and that the doctrine of defense was the decisive factor in the army leadership's obedience. Should he challenge this doctrine, the army commanders would have a formal reason for replacing him, accusing him of an attempt to draw into war a country, where the conflagration of war had only recently died out. Vultures were carving up the world. The Japanese were running riot in Asia, Hitler in Europe, Mussolini in Africa, while the Boss who stood above the heads of all of his peace-loving army commanders was watching the carving-up of the planet from the sidelines. (Prior to the morning of 22 June 1941, Stalin simply didn't understand that Hitler had no intention to share any territory with him.) In order to take part in the land grab, he had to get rid of the humanist-internationalists, and at the same time their friends and all of those who refused to believe in their guilt. It is possible to assume that the disbelief in the guilt of the first eight that had been repressed became for the Leader the strongest argument in favor of large-scale repressions in the army and in the country.

Of the 13,000,000 Communist and Social-Democrat supporters in Germany, Hitler killed about 11,000 activists in his death camps. The remaining supporters didn't besmirch the German valor in the "steel cohorts" of the *Wehrmacht* and served loyally. They died on the battlefields, not in the camps. They didn't even rush to be taken prisoner: the Führer wrapped them with a bloody responsibility, and in the eyes of the Russians, there weren't any differences among the German soldiers. From the very beginning, Hitler deliberately conducted the war in such a way as to make the German people his hostage. Seeing what they had created on the occupied territory of the USSR, the Germans understood: they'd been sentenced to a fight to the death. For all Germans, both the Nazis and their committed opponents, that is the way they fought. No one wanted to allow a Russian soldier, who'd become intoxicated by hatred, into their tidy German towns and cities.

The 11,000 ideological victims of the Führer should not be compared with the millions slain by Stalin. For both tyrants, people were raw material; both killed without remorse, but were guided by different criteria. Having an exaggerated opinion of his own command capabilities (which led Operation Barbarossa to failure), Hitler nevertheless knew that not just anyone could be appointed as a commander, nor could just anyone be taught to become one. Thus he acted circumspectly.[1]

One cannot say this about Stalin. The assortment of riffraff in the leading cadres of the USSR, all this dredging from the bottom of society, speaks rather to just the opposite. The Leader needed submission from his executives, but even complete submissiveness could not save those who were too informed, and they were liquidated with no regard for their rank. The RKKA didn't satisfy the Leader with its insufficient devotion to him. Moreover, the creator of the Red Army (as well as the creator of October, the Treaty of Brest-Litovsk, and of the trade unions) was Trotsky. This alone was to cause Stalin to suspect that the army, other than the partisans of the First Cavalry Army, consisted entirely of Trotsky's henchmen.

The Russian Civil War didn't enrich Stalin with military experience, but corrupted him with self-permissiveness. His bloody commissarship began at Tsaritsyn. For disagreeing with his ignorant decisions, Stalin loaded his military specialists onto prison barges and sank them in the Volga River. They were the first victims of Stalinist terror – former Tsarist officers who were serving the RKKA. The result of the "heroic defense" of Tsaritsyn boiled down to the fact that Voroshilov and Stalin were removed, after which the situation had to

---

1   Incidentally, Hitler would not have had much success, had he set out in the wake of his very first victims. The assassination of his predecessor in the Reich Chancellor post, General von Schleicher, on the "Night of the Long Knives" raised such a storm of anger in the higher echelon of the *Reichswehr* that Hitler was forced to play out a scene of hysterical handwringing in public over the supposed error that had just occurred. The officer corps agreed to take it as an apology, but the case served Hitler as a serious lesson for the future.

be restored through genuinely heroic efforts. The Boss didn't forget Trotsky and Skliansky[2] for this.

The catastrophic loss of cadres in the Russian Civil War forced the Council of People's Commissars to appoint Stalin commissar of the Southern Front once again. There he had the opportunity to learn the basics of the military arts from the former Tsarist colonel and future marshal, Egorov. However, Egorov did not have a strong character, and having served under Stalin's command, he knew first-hand of the fate of the military specialists at Tsaritsyn. Egorov simply feared this monster. When disputes arose between the two, Egorov sent Stalin in front of the Chairman of the Revolutionary War Council Trotsky, who possessed the authority and willpower sufficient to force even Stalin to carry out the orders.

The Leaders spent his final class of military parochial school in the First Cavalry Army, where his petty tyranny reached the point of refusing to submit to orders from the *front*, and where the partisan opportunism of the machinist Voroshilov and the cavalry sergeant-major Budenny magnificently bloomed.[3] About Budenny Zhukov said, "... he knew how to talk with troopers and commanders. Of course, he himself didn't conduct any exercises, training sessions or staff games with the personnel. (*"Of course"*! Doesn't this say a lot?) However, no one blamed him for this." This was written while the distinguished cavalry leader was still alive (and who, incidentally, outlived Zhukov himself), and who would one day acquire the title of Marshal, surpassing Uborevich, Iakir, Vatsetis and Sergei S. Kamenev (the latter two were commanders-in-chief in the Civil War)[4], who never became Marshals.

We'll return to Budenny when the bloody games of the Great Patriotic War begin. The Marshal, who was incapable of directing staff games, commanded *fronts*: the Southwestern and Reserve Fronts in 1941, and the Southern Front in 1942, always with disastrous results.

Let's turn our attention to the acquisition of the first Marshal titles. Why Voroshilov, Budenny, Tukhachevsky, Egorov and Bliukher?

However, first let us recall the stages of Stalin's rise. In contrast to Stalin the Intriguer, Stalin the Politician was not a genius.

There was an awkward pause (like novelists of the past used to write) after Ilia Ehrenburg's memoirs *Liudi, gody, zhizn' [People, Years, Life]* came out. Ehrenburg had in his lifetime numerous contacts with the Leader, and everyone was waiting for the promised revelations about Stalin, or at minimum, assessments of his performance. Ehrenburg, with his enormous talents as a publicist, could do this. He had squeezed clever results even from isolated conversations in his memoirs. However, Ehrenburg didn't do it. He made do with general remarks. It's no wonder. A denunciation of Stalin was possible only in the halls of Party Congresses, but it was still dangerous, especially for one who wanted to publish a summary book of his life's experiences, to touch upon this theme. At the time only

---

2   In 1941, when subordinating Eremenko to Koniev, who at the time held a lower rank, Stalin did not forget to console him by reminding him that he, Stalin, had experienced just the same absurdity when as People's Commissar he'd been subordinated to a certain Skliansky. He told him that in war, all sorts of situations can occur. As you can see, this thorn had become firmly planted in his flesh. He drowned Skliansky – but all the same this didn't quench his rancor over the humiliation.

3   Shaposhnikov, who served in the First Cavalry Army as a staff officer, could not have even a bit of influence over this gang.

4   Between 1919 and 1924 S. S. Kamenev was the Commander-in-Chief of Armed Force of the Republic. He died on 25 August 1936 of a heart attack.

Ernst Genri, the pseudonym of the journalist S. N. Rostovsky, gave as far as he could an evaluation of Stalin. In his "Open Letter to Illia Ehrenburg", which circulated through *samizdat* channels, having reproached Ehrenburg for dodging this subject, he listed nine miscalculations by Stalin the Politician. In a free country, any one of them would have been sufficient to ensure that an actor who committed them would disappear from the stage. Genri sees the fact that Stalin practically brought Hitler to power, by having dubbed the German Social Democrats as "Social Fascists" and by preventing the German Communists from cooperating with them, as the Leader's main guilt. In the election, Hitler received a majority (11,000,000-plus votes against the 7,000,000 votes for the Social Democrats and the 6,000,000 votes for the Communists, which did not form a bloc), and then swept from his path first one party and then the other.

With all due respect to Ernst Genri, it is difficult to agree that the assistance to Hitler on his path to power was unintended and a mistake of Stalin's. I see in this a calculated step in the destabilization of Europe. From the position of the present day, Stalin's shot at democracy doesn't look like a roll of the dice or an oversight, but on the contrary, like an accurate hit of the target. Stalin's blunders were many, but he never overlooked the main thing: the strengthening of his own power. The Great Stalin was a myth that he created himself. The Great Commander, the Luminary of the Sciences and the Genius of Diplomacy ... it is laughable.

However, Incomparable Intriguer – that is the truth and it is *ny smyshno* [isn't amusing].[5] The intriguer rose to the pinnacle of state power and began to wield it in on a scale unknown in European history. An Eastern cunning, combined in an unequal marriage with the broadest social movement, produced a compound unique in its monstrosity. Whatever Stalin did, he did everything for the making of his image as Leader. In needs he was modest, but in means he was Machiavellian. If he needed to make his mark, well, even a *mokroe delo* [literally, "wet job", but a Russian euphemism for any matter settled through murder or assassination] was appropriate. His ascent began with the murder of cash messengers not for his personal gain, but for the needs of the eternally empty Social Democratic Party coffers, by which he in fact caught the attention of the leadership of Party. Admitted to the Central Committee, he was transferred to more serious work, but one now not so fraught with danger to life and limb – the publication of an illegal newspaper. Seemingly, he also informed the Tsarist secret police about a cleverly concealed printing press.

Skipping stages of his ascent, we'll note only his Party alias. Previously he had gone under several different names, but this one he donned no sooner than he had placed his faith in Lenin. Lenin, he scented, Lenin, and not Plekhanov, not Martov, not Axelrod, would become the leader of the Party in power. Djugashvili disappeared, Stalin appeared [Stalin is derived from the Russian word for steel, *stal'*], the faithful pupil, the stalwart Leninist, who wobbled only on the most dangerous curves, like questions regarding the armed seizure of power or the "obscene" Brest-Litovsk peace, when Lenin himself for a time found himself in the minority.

One can imagine the smirks and wicked asides in the back rooms of the Party Congresses on the subject of the similar sound of the teacher's and pupil's names. To the teacher it mattered little, but the pupil had already designated himself as the successor, and never forgot insults; he stored them up – until the right time. He indeed managed to come to

---

5   This was Stalin's favorite expression, spoken by him in his heavy Georgian accent that he was never able to shed, despite his excellent knowledge of the Russian language.

power, because his sophisticated rivals didn't view him as a competitor. He is manipulating us? He'll cling to us, so they thought, if only to keep his place in the secretariat of the Central Committee – and the secretariat is what? Clerks and typists. Stalin was the chief of secretaries and Party archivists. However, Stalin the Archivist boiled his archive-porridge and turned the secretariat into the Secretariat, a menacing organ of power.

Then Stalin delivered an oath of loyalty at Lenin's funeral. How did the others regard it? Well, calmly. As many as they'd already buried, they'd become accustomed to dramatic declarations; they'd themselves sinned in delivering such orations. It was a ritual, ringing words, a revolutionary style. "We swear to you, Comrade Lenin ... ." Note Stalin said "We swear", not "I swear". This in return calmed the people: There would be no change. Lenin – Stalin. A parrot-like similarity, but the criminal wasn't considering intellectuals, he was aiming at the masses. Indeed, he hit the target: Lenin – Stalin! He wanted the word "steel" to resound in the name of Lenin. Lenin had died. Stalin – this was Lenin today! Lenin was murderous, but he hadn't seized power simply to feed his own ego. For him, power was an instrument of policy; in this respect he truly was a genius. A comparison of him with Stalin is hardly fitting. Stalin really did possess a steel will – a will of a person having no affection whatsoever.

When Lenin passed away, Trotsky, the main foe of the coalition which existed at the time between Stalin, Zinov'ev and Kamenev, was ill and vacationing in the Caucasus. The telegram informing him of Lenin's death was late for some reason. Stalin had advised not to interrupt Trotsky's rest: after all, Lenin's death had not been unexpected. Yes, it was not. However, Trotsky left on his vacation – and Lenin immediately up and died; another stroke of good fortune for Stalin. Such a lucky fellow ...

As Leonard Schapiro describes this historical episode in his superb *The Communist Party of the Soviet Union*:

> Lenin's death provided Stalin with the opportunity which he required to inaugurate a new cult of 'Leninism'. Its external trappings were in marked contrast to the genuine lack of ostentation which always characterized Lenin – the hieratical oaths of loyalty to his memory, the embalming of his corpse in a mausoleum in Moscow, the renaming of Petrograd. Trotsky's failure to attend Lenin's funeral, whether, as he says, because he was deceived over the date, or because of paralysis of will, despair and distress, helped Stalin immediately to assume the leadership of the cult. The purpose of the new cult was clear to all: if Lenin was Allah, then Stalin was his prophet. Along with the innumerable portraits and busts of Lenin which the party propaganda machinery flung into circulation, went the familiar photograph (even to the inexpert eye, a composite photograph) of Lenin and Stalin smiling side by side in serene friendship, in the summer of 1922. Those few who knew the true course of relations between Lenin and Stalin wisely kept their peace. But it was indicative of the state of mind of the party that a flood of rumors circulated in Moscow – Lenin had asked for poison, Lenin had revealed before his death that he had been poisoned, Lenin had recovered sufficiently to come to Moscow and pay a visit to his office in October 1923 (this fact at least was true) and had discovered that his papers had been rifled.

The struggle within the Party sharpened, but it was an ideological struggle: which way should the Party go – with the New Economic Policy or without it; with the leading role assumed by the Party or the trade unions; with a regular army or a volunteer army? The identity of the Party leader wasn't considered of primary importance. Collegiality had still not been replaced with iron discipline, and Stalin, after the publication of Lenin's letter (his "testament") at the XIII Party Congress, announced his resignation. He knew what he was doing. The fortunate, coincidental deaths were still isolated in occurrence, his colleagues still perceived him as a "genius of mediocrity" (Trotsky's expression), and the contenders for the Party throne were still gathering supporters. As a transitional figure, Stalin satisfied everyone. Crude? Hardworking, though. They didn't like to work. Chancellor's work, so many petty matters to coordinate ... Meanwhile, Koba had an exceptional memory, was able to store matters in his head and to coordinate everything.

If only they'd known what he was capable of doing, exactly what sort of matters he had in mind and what he was coordinating ... They didn't allow him to resign. Even Trotsky voted for Stalin.

He, though, an arbitrary selection among implacable rivals, now began with their assistance to abolish debate and to eliminate competitors. How their squabbles played into his hands ... and how he fostered them! Under the slogan "Unity!" he began to forge an iron discipline in the Party, which would make it unchanging, to repulse contenders for power. He didn't immediately put them to death. The death of a rival is the peak of satisfaction, the crowning glory of intrigue, when he could smooth his mustache and sip a goblet of fine wine.

First he joined Kamenev and Zinov'ev against Trotsky. Once this main antagonist was out of the way, while in the struggle Zinov'ev and Kamenev had in large measure tousled their own feathers, he turned on them. He was working exclusively in the interests of the Party, of course, acting only for the sake of unity in its ranks, and seemingly staying above the fray, following the precepts of Lenin ... which he himself had singled out in his theatrical oration at Lenin's funeral.

☆ ☆ ☆

Thus, the year is now 1935. The use of military ranks, which had been abolished by the revolution, is being restored. This reclassification is underway in the Red Army.

Why? During the analysis of any of Stalin's maneuvers, this question must come first. What was so annoying to the Leader? Why is he reorganizing the army's ranks? Oh, yes, of course – he is so strong now that he can do even this – place the military commanders under his own personal supervision.

Let's take a look: People's Commissar Voroshilov; First Deputy Tukhachevsky; Deputy for Cavalry Budenny. Under the reform of the Red Army, however, the First Deputy was stripped of his access to the operational handling of the forces, while direction over the most mobile type of force at that time was concentrated in the hands of the Deputy for Cavalry. Cavalry became the genuine bulwark of the throne. The commanders of the military districts were all heroes of the Civil War and simultaneously, as a rule, imaginative tacticians and defenders. However, they're on the periphery, while the head of the Moscow Military District is always occupied by a loyal officer from Stalin's old First Cavalry Army. (The reader must bear in mind that Shaposhnikov and Egorov also served under the banner of that Army ...) Even if not all the military district commanders were brilliant, against their backdrop Voroshilov was a nobody, Budenny a celebrated horse-breeder, and Stalin –

Stalin and B.M. Shaposhnikov.

a commissar.

The title of Marshal of the Soviet Union, which never previously existed in Russia, was established for elevating Stalin's own men and for lowering those who were not. There were too many of those who were not, but naturally it was expected nonetheless that this title would be acquired by the country's most famous and prestigious military commanders. Among their number, in addition to Budenny and Tukhachevsky are the teachers of the army, the commanders of the western border military districts, the exacting Uborevich and the Red Army's top favorite, Iakir.

However, Stalin's aim was not to promote men according to their merits. Moreover, the idea of placing incompatible people together within the framework of one institution is the rule for one who wants to dominate. We, ordinary people, may swallow a lot in order to build harmonious relations among our circle of friends. Those who wish to dominate don't make such a mistake. Divide and conquer! It was according to this principle that men were selected for the key posts of People's Commissars, committees and the like. The chosen Marshals of the Soviet Union were selected in the same way. None of the military district commanders became a Marshal, except Bliukher. Formally, even he didn't command a district, but instead the Special Far Eastern Army, which perhaps for just this reason never became a district, like all the other territorial formations.

Ia. B. Gamarnik.

At the conclusion of the Russian Civil War, the RKKA command staff was extremely diverse. By 1937, despite the removal of Tsarist generals and men of the highest cultural level, like Svechin and Snesnarev, the heterogeneity hadn't lessened. Again, Schapiro notes:

"By May 1937 it was calculated that three-quarters of all officers were such young Red commanders, who owed their position and new prestige entirely to Stalin and his policy. The remainder consisted of veteran officers of civil war experience, and all mainly occupying the higher commands. It is easy to imagine the pressure for promotion which this situation created.

"Apart from pressure from below there was also friction at the top. This was due to the system of control ... From 1929 to 1937 the Political Directorate of the army was headed by Jan Gamarnik. Gamarnik had every quality likely to render him unfit for the generation of communists which Stalin was seeking to elevate – Jewish origin, intelligence, internationalism, honesty, and sincere belief in the communist mission. The humdrum junior political instructors whom his machine turned out in large numbers rubbed along well enough with the Red commanders at the lower levels. But at the higher levels, where the civil war veterans were mostly in command, the senior and more intellectual political officers consorted ill with the often uneducated, if militarily distinguished, civil war veterans."

This description is not all-inclusive. Even the veterans were not homogenous; Zhukov is proof of that. Geller and Rapoport note that intelligent "General Staff" types, who continued to track the developments in military thought and were in essence moving toward its forefront, like Bliukher, Gamarnik, Egorov, Primakov, Kork, Tukhachevsky, Uborevich, Shaposhnikov and Iakir were serving alongside former "partisan" cavalrymen. The situation was essentially the same on all the levels of the military hierarchy.

Before the purge of the military, the Red Army command staff consisted of:

- Officers of the old Tsarist army, but now with a new military: a Marshal from among the workers and a former colonel in the service of the Tsar, Egorov; a Marshal from among the gentry, the former lieutenant Tukhachevsky; and army commanders Shaposhnikov (a former Moscow military intellectual) and the former Lithuanian peasant Uborevich;
- Officers who were graduates of military academies, like corps commander Kovtiukh, a former staff captain of the Tsarist army who graduated from the Frunze Military Academy and was now deputy commander of forces in the Belorussian Military District;
- University and gymnasium students who joined the Revolution, and who with standout capabilities for self-study, acquired a military knowledge (like Army Commander, 1st Rank Iakir and Corps Commander Primakov);
- Eminent men, who were practically without any regular education (Marshal Bliukher attended a course of lectures in the German General Staff Academy);
- Recent commissars, who understood the brighter prospects of those who switched from the political staff to the military ranks (division commander and future Marshal I. S. Konev);
- Random individuals, of which there were more than a few in the army.

Stalin created, strengthened and kept track of the congestion on the career ladder through performance reviews. He was already so powerful that no one disputed his recommendations; so omnipotent that he dispensed ranks without regard for the recipient's merits. The distribution was calculated in a way to provoke even greater discord in the army. Five men entered the caste of Marshals, in which Stalin held a concealed majority. Formally, it was not a majority: only two of the five were Stalin's men. However, those two were former officers of the First Cavalry Army and were joined at the hip (though after the purge, when the army had to be administered in practice, even this friendship fell apart), while there were no connections between the other three. Only Tukhachevsky was audacious, a quality Stalin didn't admire in subordinates, but a failure to promote Tukhachevsky, a First Deputy of the People's Commissariat and the Army's chief reformer, would have made the title of Marshal from the very beginning a title for courtiers. So let even Tukhachevsky serve as Marshal; the fame of his name would enhance the prestige of the Marshal of the Soviet Union title. Then just polish off Marshal Tukhachevsky, when the right time comes.

An intriguer with a criminal disposition, Stalin was a fine psychologist, who studied the characters of his appointees and the nuances of their relations. (If there was an absence of conflicts, he would instigate them. The longer he spent in power, the more he excelled in playing these games; his skills blossomed during the Great Patriotic War.) If he had no concerns about elevating two regular officers of the Tsarist army to be among the Marshals, like Egorov and Tukhachevsky, then it must be concluded that these two had nothing between them to draw them together.

Everything looked if not flawlessly, then at least decently. I will remind you: the title was granted seemingly according to position, but not one of the military district commanders received the title of Marshal. Shaposhnikov, who had graduated from the Tsarist General Staff Academy in 1910, didn't become a Marshal. He, having recently received a promotion that put him on the same level with Uborevich and Iakir as an Army Commander, 1st Rank, was appointed commander of the Moscow Military District – Stalin's unspoken explanation to Uborevich and Iakir of the criteria he used to select the Marshals, as if to say: "You shouldn't be offended by this. Look at Shaposhnikov ..."

Not knowing all the aspects of the life of the country in those years, it isn't possible to understand the powerful fissures that this bestowing of new ranks and titles had among the Red Army command. I would have to discuss the professional record of each actor in this drama in detail, in order to give the reader an impression of how inadequate was this comparison between Shaposhnikov, who was a theoretician, a military intellect, and a superb staff officer, and the Civil War active heroes Uborevich and Iakir, who were military-pedagogues, great citizens of the country, builders and favorites of the Red Army, and whose concerns extended beyond the army to military industry and even to patronage over the daily lives of the citizens in their military districts. Meanwhile, all three were certified as Army Commanders, 1st Rank. After the purge, Shaposhnikov would become a Marshal, although he never commanded troops in the field; he couldn't be a field commander due to features of his character.

L. Schapiro doesn't assert that Stalin intentionally split the Red Army asunder. However, even he notes that "... the careerist jostling on the service ladder and the friction among the commanders and political workers at the top ... introduced discord." Stalin used this when he decided that the hour of slaughter had arrived. Informing on others had been cultivated in the Party from the very beginning. The massive scale of this internal whistle blowing, which Zhukov described so brusquely, was stimulated to a considerable degree by this crowding and jostling on the career ladder.

The bestowing of new ranks was a calculated step in a fiendish game. At the Higher Military Council meeting of 1-4 June 1937, three Marshals submissively listened to a vituperative critique of their colleagues and honorable comrade army commanders from the lips of the Marshal and People's Commissar Voroshilov. Senior in rank to those sitting in the hall, but junior in position to the Commissar giving the report, with their silence they restrained those who refused to believe in all this rubbish. Of the four Marshals present, two would live for a little more than a year longer

16

The Army Executions Begin

I t is time to tell about Okhotnikov.

According to the so-called "Affair of I. N. Smirnov's Counter-revolutionary Group", Iakov Okhotnikov, the director of the State Institute for the Design of Aircraft Factories, was arrested. In 1933, he was sentenced to three-years of internal exile. An archive certificate bears witness to his further fate, which was typical for those who were considered oppositionists and, in compliance with an NKVD directive from 29 September 1936, were subject to liquidation: Okhotnikov Iakov Osipovich, born 1897, a Jew, Novaia Romanovka village, Bessarabia, non-Party member, higher education, manager of a motor vehicle repair shop in Magadan. Sentenced by the Higher Military Collegium of the Supreme Court of the USSR on 7.03.37 to the highest level of punishment. Shot 8.03.37. Rehabilitated 15.5.55. Rehabilitate in the Party's view 16.05.1990.[1]

(It is interesting that he was rehabilitated in the Party's view only when the Party had indeed stopped breathing. Even so, he was rehabilitated ...)

The author of this record apparently didn't know that Okhotnikov wasn't considered an oppositionist. It should be said, however, to his credit, that Okhotnikov was indeed one.[2] For all that, in the 1950s, in contrast to the 1930s, an appellate court didn't consider the incident on the podium of Lenin's Mausoleum on 7 November 1937 an assassination attempt, nor that Okhotnikov's execution was a suitable punishment for smacking the back of the head of the wisest, and most importantly, kindest Father of All Peoples.

However in the 1930s, what sort of attitude toward the cadres was there? At a most critical time for the country's defensive capabilities, the intelligence of one who was capable of planning its entire aviation industry was considered only suitable to head a car repair shop, in Magadan, remote from Moscow. He returned to the capital after serving his time in Magadan just in time to be arrested again (in July 1936) and this time irrevocably.

Now, as for Shmidt, Primakov's ablest division commander ...

Or first about Primakov? He was arrested after Shmidt was seized. Does this mean Shmidt betrayed him? There was no need for anyone to squeal on Primakov. His attitude toward the General Secretary was well-known. He had been arrested for the first time in 1934 while occupying the post of Deputy Commander of Troops of the Northern Caucasus

---

1   D. Khardin, *"Bol'shoe predatel'stvo"* [Great betrayal], Novyi zhurnal, No. 219.

2   These names cannot be found in Academician O. Suvenirov's "Martyrology of the RKKA, 1936-1941", which he compiled at the very end of the 1990s. It is even stranger that Suvenirov repeatedly cites Geller's and Rapoport's book, which reported the exact dates for the deaths of Geller and Petenko. It is possible to explain the absence of Okhotnikov's name from Suvenirov's "Martyrology" by the fact that when he'd been exiled in 1933, he'd simultaneously been expelled from the Red Army. The absence of Geller's and Petenko's names can probably be explained by the same reason. In many cases, a discharge from the Red Army preceded an arrest.

B.M. Fel'dman.

District – and released supposedly at Voroshilov's personal order. Primakov's transfer to Leningrad was a promotion. Shmidt was arrested as a former division commander in the Chervonnyi Cossack Corps and as a man who was close to Primakov, the Corps' creator and original commander: in this way, the arrest of Primakov appeared more logical.

Fel'dman, who was at a rank of Corps Commander at the time, in the final stage before the liquidation of the military opposition and plainly to keep it complacent, was appointed a month before his arrest, as if in farce, the Deputy Commander of Troops of the Moscow Military District (commanded by Budenny). Boris Fel'dman, who was not a timid man – his name was well-known from the Civil War and had been given to Primorskii Boulevard in Odessa – became alarmed and fell upon Iakir: "He's going to strangle us all like kittens!" (Likely, Iakir told him, "It's too late, Boria. We've let things slide too long.")

Primakov locked up! He was a hero among heroes in the Civil War! Much more so than Chapaev.[3] He conducted fourteen raids through the rear areas of Denikin and the

---

3   In the 1960s in the Ukraine there was a popular story about how the film *Shchors* was created. At a meeting between Stalin and cinematographers, Aleksandr Dovzhenko was highly praising, as it was purported, the Vasil'ev brothers' film *Chapaev*, when Stalin interrupted him: "It is time for you Ukrainian cinematographers to create a film about your own Ukrainian Chapaev." Dovzhenko assured the Leader that this would be done and upon returning to Kiev, rushed to see Iakir: who did Stalin have in mind? Iakir compiled a list of forty equally legitimate names, though he assured his cinematographer friend that Stalin, of course, could not have been thinking of Primakov, who led the list. Dovshenko went with the list to see Kosior, who added Iakir's name to the list, then returned it to Dovshenko with the observation that Stalin could not have anyone still living in mind, but that he, Kosior, would not give preference to anyone's name on the list. Dovzhenko ultimately had to clarify the question about the Ukrainian Chapaev with the Leader.

Polish forces, and lost not even a single battle.

Primakov the theoretician – he was the author of articles in military journals and a book, *Germanskii general'nyi shtab* [German General Staff]. It was not for nothing that the German General Staff already had so much of the attention of Red Army commanders ...

Primakov the diplomat – he was a military attaché in China, Japan and Afghanistan.

Primakov the man of letters – *"Zapiski volontera"* [*Reminiscences of a volunteer*], *"Po Iaponii"* [*On Japan*], *"Afghanistan v ogne"* [*Afghanistan on fire*] (which they didn't recall in 1979 ...) By the way, Primakov was the husband of Liliia Brik; we'll note this fact – it will prove useful.

Primakov, a leading state figure, was not ready to stand by quietly and watch the liquidation of the state's most worthy people, simply because they didn't consider the criminal who had seized power to be the luminary of thought and the father of mankind. A legendary corps commander (or even more, Army Commander, 2nd Rank?), three-time Order of the Red Banner recipient, deputy chief of the Leningrad Military District, writer, Adonis, cavalryman ... In those days, military men were regarded more kindly than even the most free-wheeling poets. Liliia Brik left Maiakovsky and after his death married the Corps Commander and hero.

This acquaintanceship, this marriage: Were they not another one of Stalin's strokes of luck? Did not a union between the racy Liliia Iur'evna and the gallant Corps Commander suggest itself? Knowing feminine ambitions and how the left wing artists had nestled up to the new power, knowing Brik's influence on many fates, is this speculation really so absurd? A confirmation of it will not surprise me; its refutation will make me happy. Liliia Iur'evna was a strong and cynical woman, and she loved only her first husband Osip Brik and the beautiful life. The role of women in history is well-known. Do not let the trivial nature of this comment prevent thinking about how transparent Primakov's life became in the parlor of his wife after entering into this marriage. (Incidentally, Liliia Iur'evna's younger sister, El'za, known as the French writer Elza Triole, also didn't suffer from a weak spirit and degraded the author Louis Aragon, who began as an outstanding surrealist on par with Paul Eluard, but finished as a realist of a fully drab nature.)

The fate of Primakov had been determined long before by Stalin. Then there was Shmidt, a Chevalier who stood out even among the courageous men of the Chervonnyi Cossacks; a friend of Primakov and comrade-in-arms to Iakir; the Shmidt who had always led from in front, and the commander of the Red Army's first heavy tank battalion. Did Iakir believe in his guilt? What guilt? Being a Trotskyist? Trotsky had long ago been exiled from the country, and Shmidt long ago lost any interest in politics. Iakir called upon Shmidt in the prison where he was being held. It is almost beyond belief, but somehow Iakir managed to meet with him. Yet the hero of heroes Shmidt, a full cavalier with all four Tsarist Orders of St. George, two Orders of the Red Banner, not at all timid in life, didn't say a word to his friend Ion?!

It is easier to get into Gutman-Schmidt's shoes than it is to get into the shoes of the Leader. So you're a three-time Hero; where is that getting you? You have a mother, a wife,

---

Shchors was killed during the Russian Civil War under obscure circumstances at his command post, about 3 *versts* [a little more than 3 kilometers] from the fighting. Cherniak was even shot during an interval in the fighting. Bozhenko was poisoned. All these Ukrainians were supporters of an independent Ukraine. At the time, Stalin was a People's Commissar and Trotsky was the Chairman of the Revolutionary War Council ... Were these acts a sign of collaboration between these two People's Commissars?

a married sister with a clutch of children ... or perhaps they had simply told him, "Utter a peep, and your last-hope friend will stay right here with you, and you'll taken away for interrogation in turns." What, impossible? Shmidt, wounded three times on the battlefields of the Civil War, the legendary hero, didn't break. Shmidt remained silent,[4] and thought: "My last-hope friend, you're no fool. Here I am in front of you, covered with carefully powdered bruises. You yourself can see with whom we're dealing here. Take a stand, while you still have a district under your command!"

Iakir did nothing. It's a long way from Kiev to Moscow. Likely, he already knew about Okhotnikov's second arrest and no longer hoped for anything more. You move – and your friends become expendable. Besides, you can't shake up the Moscow District; it's not military, it's a police district, and everything there had been snatched up a long

---

4   The tortured Shmidt incriminated himself, but he never gave them a single other name.

17

On the Matter of a Plot

"The one who eliminates Stalin will be doing a noble deed."[1] These words almost became the epigraph to this book, yet it is frightening even to utter them. Today, though, they are glorifying the German officers who unfortunately decided too late upon the elimination of a different villain of history. Well then, were Soviet military commanders in fact conspiring against Stalin?[2]

The most notable of those who became victims of Stalin initially had no reasons for concern. Such was the case with Egorov. The Marshal was Stalin's man. Ultimately perhaps a competent commander, brave in battle, but then were any of the Marshals of the weak-kneed sort? In peace time, military men become bureaucrats. They work, prepare the army for future tests, but now with no real thought toward actually leading it in battle. They have played their role; now they can live and enjoy a life of respect and satisfaction. Why go looking for trouble? Especially given that Stalin by the start of the repressions had already managed to score a lot of points in the political game. Had some trouble brewed up, Marshal Egorov likely would have stood by the Leader's side. Perhaps not without some sympathy for the insurrectionists, but after all, military discipline isn't just a hollow concept ... Who of them were so far-sighted, so as to be ready to violate this discipline?

The Boss wasn't mistaken: the first eight victims indeed consisted of men who remembered that they had taken the oath not to Stalin, but to the country. Possibly, they were men who understood that they were *persona non grata* to Stalin. However, rumors of

---

1   Artur Khristianovich Artuzov (Frauchi), a corps commissar and deputy chief of intelligence of the RKKA (arrested 13 May 1937), opened a vein and scratched out this condemnation of Stalin with his blood on the wall of his prison cell. The purge of the RKKA indeed began with arrests in the Red Army's intelligence branch, and the arrested were often immediately executed (in secret, from the summer of 1936). Word is circulating that Frauchi-Artuzov, the creator of the legendary Operation Trust [a Soviet counter-intelligence operation in the 1920s designed to reveal Tsarist loyalists and anti-Bolsheviks at home and abroad], opposed the Leader on the matter of the fate of the Polish officers at Katyn. If so, then this tale originates in the Great Soviet Encyclopedia, which falsely dates Artuzov's death to July 1943. It would be nice, of course, if like the Germans, who cast their lives against the life of Hitler, Artuzov was that dedicated Soviet citizen, who would stand up between Stalin and the victims of Katyn, at the cost of his life separating the crimes of the Leader from the will of the people. Alas, it is possible to falsify history, but not to change it. Artuzov did not live to see the 1939 occupation of Poland; he was executed on 21 August 1937. The motives behind his early arrest (prior to Iakir and his comrades) now seem clear: Artuzov, who had led a network of agents in Europe, was aware of the Gestapo order to compile compromising material on military commanders standing in opposition to Stalin. He even sent a dispatch about this to Ezhov. Who, though, did he tell about this besides Ezhov?

2   The Boss certainly wanted to believe so, and through his agents in Europe, he conveyed these suspicions to the Germans. The Gestapo, under Heidrich's direction, willingly began to fabricate documents designed to lend credence to the belief that the Red Army commanders were behaving treasonously. Eventually, these forgeries were passed back to Stalin in so-called Red Packets. Interestingly, the German generals (and Von Fritsch personally) rejected this project and bluntly refused to give Heidrich a sample of Tukhachevsky's signature from the intercommunications that passed between the *Reichswehr* and the Red Army. The Red Packets were a Gestapo matter.

a conspiracy ... and what can be considered a conspiracy? Many contemporaries, including me, would have been happy to find proof of a commanders' plot against Stalin. This would constitute their genuine rehabilitation before the country and civilization.

Alas, there is no proof, much less any evidence of a plot, either written (of course, there were indeed no documents) or word-of-mouth, even though Stalin's replacement by any other Party figure was a doubtless desire of each of the first eight victims. Moreover, nothing is even known of such a conspiracy. There are only hints, and this is in a case where the first victims were surrounded by a multitude of people, while after their deaths an entire multitude of valuable human beings passed through the hands of the Lubianka [the infamous political prison in Moscow, lying within the NKVD's headquarters] inquisitors, leaving behind only the most general expressions about the desirability of Stalin's and Voroshilov's replacement. Then the inquisitors themselves disappeared, without revealing anything substantial even in the interrogation transcripts.

There is something intentional in this deathly silence. However, the silence continues even to the present day. So, it is possible to speak only hypothetically about how a situation, similar to that which took shape at the start of the war, might have been handled otherwise, if the purge had not occurred. If, even after the rolling of heads between 1937 and up to the war's beginning, certain commanders on the eve of the war paid no regard to Stalin's ban on raising the level of combat alert,[3] then one can imagine how Iakir and Uborevich, the commanders of border districts, would have behaved. Without entering into disputes with the *Kremlin mountaineer* [the celebrated Russian poet Osip Mandelshtam's veiled reference to Stalin] and without bothering to request instructions, they would have issued orders to their available forces according to the situation, while coordinating their actions. Only the role of observer would have been given to the Leader. The emergency situation would have *de facto* left him with no freedom of action. Indeed, here lies the miscalculation of conscientious Western scholars, like John Erickson, who believe that even the army commanders could not have altered the tragic events at the start of the war, since, as they say, all the same Stalin would have remained at the helm. Western historians with their law-abiding mindsets cannot even begin to think about recalcitrance. However, had the purged commanders been present, the events in the Soviet-German theater of the war – if it had even erupted at all – could not have developed in the same way as it did in their absence.

A certain semblance of an effort – not of a conspiracy, but of an overture – has been more fully described by Geller and Rapoport. Even the location of the activity (Kiev) speaks to the fact that from some moment (the Ukrainian famine or Kirov's assassination?), Iakir became a sustained opponent of the dictator. Historians note that Stalin was benevolent toward Iakir, but base this observation on superficial aspects of their relationship. No one was ever in greater danger than the one toward whom Stalin was smiling. He smiled – and it didn't signify that he favored you. If with respect to Iakir the Leader didn't show such loutish conduct, that he displayed in his treatment of Tukhachevsky,[4] this says only that

---

3   This ban was issued to the Kiev and, especially, the Odessa District, as well as the fleets. The fleet gave more consideration to its own intelligence than to intelligence from Moscow. People's Commissar of the Navy N. G. Kuznetsov disobeyed Stalin and, not fearing the wrath of his master, issued a warning about a possible attack on the fleet. There are more than a few such examples, and nests of combat readiness all the same played their own role in the start of the war.

4   In one speech, Stalin had called Tukhachevsky the "Demon of the Civil War", which sounds equivocal.

Stalin took Iakir seriously. The very list of names of the men who were close to Iakir, and who were ready to give their lives for him, was abhorrent to Stalin: Okhotnikov, Shmidt, Primakov, Kotovsky ...

As it happened, in the annals of history the name of Tukhachevsky has become the symbol of opposition to Stalin. By his position Tukhachevsky – a Marshal and the First Deputy People's Commissar of Defense – had occasion to express objections personally to both Stalin and Voroshilov over their incompetent interference in the reform of the army. In a formal sense, the domination of his name is understandable, but hardly correct. The acquisition of such a reputation in history happens as if of its own accord, hot on the heels of the events, although frequently without sufficient justification, while a shift in social opinion, if one even happens, requires decades or even hundreds of years. It is impossible to foretell whether or not this will even happen and when. The inertia of historiography is persistent and hard to overcome. Of course, the diversely gifted Marshal was a leading figure in the Red Army – he gave speeches, wrote articles and books, traveled abroad as a visible member or head of delegations, and in foreign contacts conducted himself with demonstrable independence. In the so-called "Tukhachevsky Affair" he was the key figure, naturally. However, being a military fanatic and the main contributor to the re-equipping of the army (of course, together with the apparatus of the People's Commissariat of Defense and the commanders of the western military districts, which had an enormous influence on the process), he was not an ideological figure. This doesn't detract from his military talents, but it makes clear that he opposed Stalin for being an amateur in military matters, not for being a despot. It still remains for history to crown the modest Iakir in the role as head of the Soviet military opposition, and possibly not only in the military.[5]

No one has been smeared more than Iakir. His name just recently has been cleared from the accusation of having a role in the Ukrainian famine: well, after all he was the commander of the Ukrainian Military District! Not Stalin, not the VKP(b), not the NKVD – Iakir was blamed. Meanwhile, it was the NKVD apparatus that was activated to cordon off the starving areas – the Workers' and Peasants' Army wasn't trusted for the task. The Red Army men, bound by their discipline and oath, were compelled to obedience, but in the famished areas, directly confronted with the horrible images of mass starvation, cannibalism, and the devouring of carrion, their obedience might have collapsed.

Such is the sarcasm of history! The sole man, who dared appeal to the already all-powerful Leader with the proposal to take measures against the famine, stood accused of perpetrating it!

I will outline the events in Kiev:

Stalin didn't let slip such ambiguities with Iakir. In Soviet military parades, officers traditionally rode on horseback. Iakir had a bad back and could not ride comfortably in a saddle. For him, the Leader made the single exception in the RKKA. A luxurious convertible, a Packard it seems, was purchased for him, and at parades the commander of the Kiev Special Military District would drive around the troops while standing in the car. In February 1937, the Leader in a fatherly fashion impressed upon Sarra Lazarevna, Iakir's wife, to take care of her husband; "he's an extremely valuable man for us." (Geller, Rapoport) Probably, this is what engendered the legend about the Leader's benevolence toward Iakir.

5   Iakir was the sole person who opposed the Boss in the Bukharin-Rykov case. "I learned about the courageous conduct of I. E. Iakir, who was a member of the commission that would decide Bukharin's and Rykov's fate and who refrained from voting, from the wives of Iakir and Uborevich (Iakir himself informed Ieronim Petrovich [Uborevich] about this), and finally Chudov's wife told me the same thing. Considering the situation, Iakir's decision could be considered equivalent to a defense of Bukharin and Rykov." Source: A. M. Larina (Bukharin), *Nezabyvaemoe* [The Unforgettable] (Moscow, 1989).

Stalin ordered Iagoda to prepare damaging information against the opponents; let us say to smear them with the charge of collaborating with the Tsar's secret police. (This instruction doomed Iagoda to his own liquidation. Did he realize it?) Fabrications are a risky matter for falsifiers: you need to know completely both the format requirements of the documentation and a multitude of names and circumstances. Iagoda decided first to dig through the Tsarist archives. When looking into the files of a deputy director of a Tsarist police department, NKVD staffer Isaak Shtein discovered in among the files of the Vice-Director of the Police Department Vissarionov[6] an elegant gray portfolio containing a number of reports. Familiarizing himself with the contents, he saw documents about Stalin and decided that he had found new pages on the heroic life of the Boss – but then froze in horror: they were not Tsarist-era accusations against Stalin; they were dispatches from Stalin to the Tsarist police.[7] Saying nothing to anyone, Shtein traveled to Kiev and presented the documents to his friend and former chief, V. A. Balitsky, the head of the Ukraine's NKVD. Balitsky showed the papers in turn to his deputy, Katsnel'son. The papers were subjected to private analysis, which confirmed that they were written by Stalin's hand, the penmanship of which was by that time quite familiar to the NKVD workers.

Then Balitsky presented the portfolio to Iakir and Kosior. In this fashion, five men knew about the portfolio: Kosior, Iakir, Balitsky, Katsnel'son and Shtein.

The gray document case changed the situation. More accurately, it might have changed the situation, had the Party supported the army. Iakir's prominence suggests why the papers were brought to Kiev, even though Kosior was a Stalinist. It means that there must have been a counterweight to Kosior in Kiev, otherwise Shtein and his comrades would have to be considered crazy. However, as employees of a cunning agency not known for naiveté, these were sober men who understood that it was safer to burn such papers. The decision to show the gray portfolio to Kosior was doubtlessly the result of Iakir's preceding familiarity with it and the confidence that Iakir's authority would attract Kosior to the matter. (In this case the Belorussian Military District would have joined up with the Kiev Military District. Kosior, of course, was aware of this.)

That's what prompts one to think about Iakir as a man who saw further ahead than others and was ready to act, should the Party and the NKVD support the army, if only in the Ukraine at least. I understand that there is little evidence for such a conclusion. However, the fate of Iakir, who was the very first to be killed and had shouted right into the muzzle of the firing gun "Long live Stalin!" an instant before his execution (plainly to protect his family), as well as Stalin's furious reaction to these words ("Whore!") support such a supposition.

Stanislav Kosior was a prominent Party activist even in the Civil War. He knew Iakir directly. Iakir was a living legend and an icon to the troops; it was impossible not to admire him, and Kosior was just such an admirer of "the army's first *matershchinnik*

---

6   Sergei Evlampievich Vissarionov (1867–1918) – from 1889 served in a judicial agency; from 1906 he was the procurator of the Iaroslavl' district court. In 1908, Vissarionov became an ad hoc official under the Minister of Internal Affairs and simultaneously the vice-director of the Department of Police. Also serve as a Counsellor of State. In 1913 Vissarionov became a member of the council of the Main Department for Press Affaris, and in 1915, a member of the council of the Ministry of Internal Affairs (http://www.hrono.ru/bio_we/vissarionov.html).

7   Now, when Stalin's collaboration with the Tsarist secret police has been established, as well as his striking luck in dodging a multitude of arrests, justification for him is offered in the explanation that he supposedly was directing an underground revolutionary counter-intelligence group.

[a foul-mouthed person],"[8] just like any other soldier and commander of the RKKA. Not "just such" – even more so. In his work, Kosior associated with Iakir and knew that he was a selfless statesman, who had complete integrity and an enormous capacity for work. Iakir was a model of responsibility, toward which one could only aspire, never reach. Such people in any era in any country of the world are considered singular human beings, and Kosior also knew this.

But Stalin! To declare that Stalin had collaborated with the Tsarist secret police – this would be nothing less than a mortal wound to communism. A secret police provocateur at the head of a country, which is demonstrating energy and strength at a time when the rest of the world is wallowing in economic crisis … That's farce upon farce!

The NKVD agents carried these goods in the gray portfolio to the most authoritative men in the Ukraine, bypassing the Moscow authorities, with one aim: to find out what to do with the documents. (Everyone other than Balitsky perished. He reported to Stalin. Not right away. He played a waiting game: they might suddenly come to an agreement …) The NKVD men didn't raise the question of the Leader's credibility; they limited themselves to the presentation of the documents and the results of the expert analysis. The question of Stalin's complicity arose of its own accord. In the interests of the Soviet state and the ideals of communism, the suspicions were rejected by Kosior. There are no records to reconstruct their conversations. Only two allegedly reliable phrases have been preserved. Iakir purportedly declared: "We will follow Stalin with closed eyes." That's what is said in the darkness, when nothing is visible. Kosior retorted: "Why, we will follow Stalin with opened eyes." That's something that is said, when there is no desire to see anything. Supposedly, Iakir's statement was made after the cautious Kosior had refused even to look at the delivered papers.[9]

Now, when Kosior, without glancing at them, declared the portfolio to be a fabrication, nothing else remained but to report about its contents to Iagoda, which meant – to Stalin. The fate of the participants in the Kiev meeting was decided. (Shtein hurled himself – or was hurled – out of a window; Katsnel'son was executed.) Stalin took the news about the documents with the restraint of an experienced provocateur, as if to say: "Here's another attempt to undermine the Party." He sensibly didn't withhold facts and just as sensibly didn't enlarge upon them. For example, just in case, he let slip something about the documents to Khrushchev. Khrushchev, who was being dispatched to the Ukraine (in order to replace Kosior before long) might find out about the scandalous portfolio from survivors or from third-parties who could have heard something about it. Better if Khrushchev learns about it from the Boss himself …

Another important consideration arises in connection with this matter. Even before it emerged, Stalin knew that somewhere in the archives there were some papers that were deadly for him, but were inaccessible to him due to his high position and the impossibility for him to undertake a personal search for them. He was afraid that they might surface, perhaps not during his lifetime, but even after his death, which was equally frightening, because you see then these highly damaging papers would become part of the historical

---

8   In his book *Stalin*, this was all that the writer Radzinsky found to say about Iakir.

9   Stanislav Vikent'evich Kosior was born in Vengruv, Poland in 1889. On 15 October 1917 he presided over a meeting of the Petrograd Russian Social Democratic Workers Party (Bolsheviks) that discussed questions of preparing for the armed uprising that led to the October Revolution. In 1918 he directed illegal underground work in German-occupied Poland. Kosior survived Iakir by 18 months.

record. Of course, it would be absurd to accuse him of having the intention to restore the Romanov dynasty in Russia. The papers would not change anything, much less the type of government, but they laid bare the Leader's moral character. Who after his death would be interested in declaring these sensational papers a forgery? He had to think about these matters while he was still living. That meant he had to eliminate the witnesses of the past, these old revolutionaries; all of their knowledge might re-introduce a ghost from the past, his old friend, the stoolpigeon Malinovsky,[10] and much would be revealed about the conspiratorial failures prior to 1917, which no excuses or justifications would be able to explain away. Simultaneously, the forgeries were undermining the credibility of the Tsarist archives.

The thoughts of the Leader could be read by his minions. So why not inspire them to concoct falsehoods against other party functionaries? Then the surfacing of his clandestine work for the *Okhranka* could be adjudged as a fabrication. Even a verbal instruction would be sufficient. Scatter so much filth, that his own misdeeds would become lost in the midst of it.

Iagoda didn't dare to cook up false documents.[11] In order to falsify history, one must know it superbly. There were quite a lot of genuine archival files he could use; Iagoda couldn't expect for the comprising material against the Leader to be found among them. If Dzerzhinsky was still alive, if Trotsky still remained in the country, and Tomsky, Kamenev and Zinov'ev could still climb upon a podium, the gray portfolio would have meant a death sentence for Stalin: the matter of his friend, Malinovsky, who had been executed in 1918 upon the verdict of the Central Committee, was still in the recent past.

However, times were changing. The political stage was emptying, and Stalin was too smart to show any concern over the portfolio. He had learned his lesson, though, and in the trial of the army commanders he didn't present any of the false documents created by Heidrich. Not everyone who knew about the portfolio was eliminated during the trials of the army commanders. Kosior remained in his post (apparently he had cursed himself for his loyalty to the Boss), and the connections between the army commanders' executions

---

10   Editor's note: Roman Vatslavovich Malinovsky (1876-1918) was a Bolshevik activist, Duma deputy and Party Central Committee member prior to the First World War, who began to cooperate with the Tsarist *Okhranka* in 1910. In 1914, he unexpectedly fled the country and was expelled from the Party for desertion. He was in Germany when the First World War broke out and was interred for the duration of the war as a subject of the Russian Empire. In 1917, after the February Revolution and the revealing of the Tsar's secret archives, he was accused of being a provocateur. After being freed from internment in 1918, Malinovsky returned to Russia to defend himself against these accusations. However, he was convicted by a tribunal of the All-Russian Central Executive Committee and executed on 5 November 1918 for being a Tsarist spy, even though Lenin was not convinced of his guilt.

11   One forgery was fabricated abroad, wherever cadres of the former Tsarist *Okhranka* were circulating – the so-called Eremin letter. [The letter, purportedly written by Colonel Eremin, a high-ranking official of the *Okhranka*, describes Stalin's work as an *Okhranka* agent during the years 1906-1912] The work was – at any rate – crude; it strongly smelled of an attempt to rehabilitate Stalin. There was no attempt to conceal the fact of the collaboration with the *Okhranka* in the letter, otherwise there would be nothing to discuss in it, but it does stress that Stalin (in the document, which dates to 1913, he is only named once as Dzhugashvili; elsewhere he is referred to as Stalin – a name he didn't acquire until years later) broke off all relations with the *Okhranka*. The ambiguity of the Eremin letter would give Stalin, in case of its publication, excellent chances to defend himself against the presenters of it, and even deflect guilt back upon them. Now the numerous versions of this letter and the commentaries on its origin (both pro-Stalinist and anti-Stalinist) make it impossible today to identify the original and to subject the Eremin letter to expert and independent analysis, and makes any attempt to investigate the matter hopeless.

and the dangerous gray portfolio were way too obvious.

At the start of 1937, the deaths of Kuibyshev and Ordzhonikidze,[12] and the arrests of Bukharin and Rykov, shocked and concerned everyone who read the newspapers. At the moment of dealing with the army commanders, Stalin didn't want to be left standing face-to-face with the army. Let the army know that the last political Mohicans are still alive, and some Party pillars are still standing.

The pillars, who had polluted themselves with oratorical pig-swill at the recently concluded XVII Party Congress and were now isolated from the podiums, those who became no longer the object of compassion, but of derision, those sitting behind their bars with no hope to be heard, even when uttering their final words ...

The interrogators were beating the names out of Shmidt, which they themselves had given him. Unsuccessfully; Shmidt wasn't just beaten; he was disfigured so badly that it was extremely useless to bring him into a courtroom, so they decided the fate of the hero of two wars in a closed, 30-minute session and executed him on 19 June, soon after the killing of his comrades. (Confessions to having ties with those abroad who sought the restoration of capitalism had been demanded of them.) Shmidt was accused of plotting to take the precious life of People's Commissar Voroshilov. There was no charge of intending to murder the Leader, despite the old threat of "I'll cut off your ears!" Stalin didn't encourage such accusations even while the charges were being cooked up – at least in 1937.

Primakov endured torture and refused to sign the transcripts of his interrogation, while his friend Iakir, one of the most powerful men in the country and the commander of the Kiev District, remained free. Primakov only began to confess and to sign everything after his inquisitors told him Iakir had been arrested. Alas, he overestimated both Iakir's power and, more importantly, his willingness to use it. Iakir and Gamarnik, who had enormous influence on Iakir, looked at things soberly. They refused to trigger a possible upheaval simply for the sake of saving their own lives, if it might mean strife and bloodletting in the country, which had been bled white and was enmeshed in the NKVD-OGPU net – is that how they differed then from Stalin?

Yes, that is how they differed.

Nothing happened. Under the thunder of nationwide celebrations dedicated to the epochal triumphs of socialism and the bestowing of the Stalinist Constitution to the people, under the loud imprecations against the enemies of the workers that were encroaching upon the people's happiness and offending their beloved Leader, the villainous cut-throat was quietly mopping up the flower of the country. The military commanders were scattered. They hadn't met for years, fearing to cast a shadow upon each other and to be accused of plotting against the Boss. Their entire life had been in the public eye. They had been transferred from place to place, except for the most key, irreplaceable figures. Tukhachevsky

---

12 The black humor of the situation consists in the fact that Kuibyshev and Ordzhonikidze themselves had cut down a lot of trees, and had fallen far from the level of competence, each in his own sphere – Kuibyshev in the State Planning Agency, Ordzhonikidze in heavy industry. There was no one to criticize them in either place, though. The critics by that time had all been destroyed as enemies of the people and the wise people in the Commissariats kept silent. What else was there for Ordzhonikidze to expect? However, he remained silent too, which again brings a parallelism with Germans.

According to the testimony of contemporaries, von Fritsch, disappointed in Hitler, nevertheless refused to ponder the use of force to overthrow him. This might have led to a bloodbath, which he wanted to avoid even at the expense of his own honor – as if his General's honor was the main problem of his German compatriots!

was either being notified of a trip to England to attend the coronation ceremony of the new monarch, or warned about a possible attempt on his life (devilish humor, is it not?) and forbidden to travel, but he was constantly being requested, and seemingly had no reasons for alarm.

He knew that he was doomed, just as were the commanders of the two main military districts, although they were being summoned to the People's Commissariat of Defense and the Central Committee for consultations on various matters and selected (not without regard for the subsequent shock of the population) to honorable presidiums of congresses. In the final stage, Tukhachevsky was transferred from his post as First Deputy of the People's Commissariat of Defense to take command of the Volga Military District, allegedly to take direct control over the forces and to oversee their training, but was arrested upon arrival, before he could meet with the troops. Iakir was informed about his transfer from the Kiev Military District to the equally important Leningrad Military District, where he immediately lost his important post on the Ukraine's Central Committee, but first he was summoned to Moscow, where he turned himself in for arrest, knowing that everything was over: his friend, deputy commander of the Moscow Military District Fel'dman, had already been arrested two weeks before. Gamarnik learned of Iakir's arrest and shot himself even as Stalin's falcons were scratching at the door for him.

I do not exclude the possibility that Gamarnik was planning to denounce Stalin's insinuations as a lie at a meeting of the Higher Military Council, and to call the military commanders to resistance. He was the conscience of not only the army, and they would have trusted him. However, he understood that he would not be allowed into a meeting of the Council. The Leader was in complete control of the situation. Facts became known to him, even as they were in the process of becoming facts, while they were still only tendencies. In his game with the army commanders, Stalin was ahead not by a pace, but by a horse stride. The Hamlet-like doubts and desire to obtain as much approval as possible killed an intention, rejected at the stage of discussions. Can this intention be considered a plot? As if even a conspiracy would have justified the tragedy of the purge and the war that followed it ...

Pity the army commanders. To tears. However Stalin, who was not overthrown, did so much damage! It is difficult to put aside this reproach, very difficult indeed. Even so, there are still two arguments in favor of the army commanders.

Firstly, they were not politicians; they were soldiers and patriots, who worked 16 to 18 hours a day, often with no days off, to strengthen the country's military capabilities. They worked in conditions of a deficit of everything – from metal to meet the demand of the armaments industry to accommodations for tolerable working conditions for the designers and engineers. Moreover, they worked in the face of the incomprehension and disavowal of the army's needs on the part of dilettantes like the Leader and his cavalry accomplices. They exerted their strength and time, though they never had enough of the latter, to train the army, equip it, and to support the Red Army's ever growing arsenal. The army commanders clearly saw the threat of Nazism and the need to counter it with a military superiority. They achieved this, which they in fact demonstrated at the 1935-36 maneuvers. They were able to devote only fragments of their leisure time – if they did it at all! – to the discussion of Stalin's intrigues and the political situation in the country, even at the times when they dared meet, whereas the Leader, liberated from work in the sphere of defense through their efforts, gave all his time to planning the liquidation of the patriots.[13] Those who are quick to disparage the army commanders need to remember this.

The second argument is the wave of anti-Semitism that had been stirred up by Hitler and was sweeping across the planet. The purge of the Red Army did not carry an ethnic tinge. Incidentally, as Geller and Rapoport note, in order to calm the majority, the first seized were military men with unusual surnames. Primakov, the single one with a Russian name, was not Russian. Jews, like Latvians and Poles, played a visible role in the highest ranks of the RKKA. We've already discussed Iakir. In addition to him, there were Jews in the posts of commanders, deputy commanders and chiefs of staffs of the military districts, chiefs of departments in the People's Commissariat of Defense, instructors at military academies, military advisers – Turovsky, Fel'dman, Aronshtam, Slavin, Shifres, Vainer ... the list goes on. Gamarnik, the chief of the Main Political Directorate of the RKKA and an Army Commissar, 1st Rank, had an exceptionally high reputation and popularity in the country. No military matter could even be examined without his prior agreement.[14] He was the ideological leader of the RKKA in more than a formal sense. His authority in the country was great; in the army it was limitless.

Could he have stirred the army to interfere in the political life given the hysterical anti-Semitism rising in the world and the presence of prominent Jews in the command cadres? He understood how Hitler's propaganda would exploit this, how it would begin to howl with the overthrow of Stalin, and how it would launch the old bogey into worldwide circulation – now in hyperbolic fashion: the Jewish RKKA was stirring up trouble, the Nazis were not idly calling upon the world to struggle against this sinister threat, this global conspiracy, and against the intervention of Jews into the lives of nations, led by their beloved leaders! Hitler, in his opposition to the *Wehrmacht* had reason to fear that the Soviet military would serve as a dangerous example to his defensive-minded generals, who were also convinced that peace had to be preserved, not destroyed. There was no need to doubt in what the intensity of the international reaction would be to Stalin's overthrow. They would be reminded of the participation of Jews in revolutionary agitation and all of the now somehow abated blood of the Civil War, about which the army commanders were trying to forget. That war had been the shame of their lives. In their eyes, the rationales of discipline and revolutionary fervor no longer justified the acts that had been perpetrated in those terrible years, especially in view of what had become of the revolution. They could not shut their eyes to this – the fate of the peasantry did not allow them to do it.

Of course, the second argument amounts only to the level of more or less plausible conjectures. However, when speaking of personal motives, all of history is nothing but guesses and conjectures ...

---

13 Once again a parallel with the German martyrs. They are reproached today for their tardy and too careless preparation of the assassination attempt against Hitler, which, as is said, led to the prolonging of the war, to the sacrifices of hundreds of thousands more Germans, and to the devastation of 1944-45. As if the participants in the plot themselves didn't understand how thoroughly it had to be prepared! As if the one-armed, three-fingered von Stauffenberg wasn't restricted by the conditions for the assassination attempt that had developed and his own service duties, which he continued to carry out so ably and meticulously.

14 When Mekhlis, who had taken Gamarnik's place at head of the Main Political Directorate, arrived in the Far East in 1938 with enormous powers and authority, Bliukher, who already sensed the coming axe, not only failed to show the new Chief of the Main Political Directorate those signs of attention, which he had so deferentially and happily showed to Gamarnik, but even knowing the risks, refused to socialize with him.

18

The Purge

It must be noted that a purge of the Party apparatus preceded the purge of the military commanders. By 1937, nowhere, even at the district committee level, not to mention the republics, were links between the Party and military leadership possible.

Honestly, the Leader was devilishly prudent ...

Arrests in the Red Army had always been going on, but the arrests of commanders of a proletarian origin began in 1936: with one exception. In July 1935, a year prior to Shmidt's arrest, Corps Commander Gai (Zhukov's first commander) was arrested. At the time, he was teaching military history in the Air Force Academy.

Prior to this only former Tsarist officers had been seized: Snesarev (who'd been a witness to "Soso's" exploits at Tsaritsyn, including the sinking of the barge together with the officers), Svechin, Verkhovsky, Kakurin and thousands of others. In 1930-31, approximately 10,000 officers and generals of the Tsarist Army had been expelled from the Army and arrested, accused of whatever came to mind, though the real reason for their arrest was in fact their social origin (according to Geller and Rapoport). Naturally, the matter was not their origins, but instead their mindsets as regular army officers, their independence in thinking and their sober evaluation of the Leader and his handling of the army. The total number of repressed higher officers of the Tsarist Army is estimated at 16,000 men, and this Bacchanalia of arrests was occurring at the same time when Germany was feverishly ferreting out and returning their own officers, generals and soldiers of fortune, who had become scattered around the globe after Germany's defeat in the First World War.

A pause in the arrests ensued after 1932. They even took some military specialists back into the Red Army, but a terrible fate caught up with them in the purges. In 1936, the wave of arrests resumed, but this time it was focused on officers of a proletarian origin. Key figures were picked up, those who were able to kill the tyrant even at the cost of their own life. It started in the Intelligence Branch of the RKKA – possibly in connection with its resistance to the requisitioning of the false documents from the German S.S.: Stalin feared the leak of intelligence information from within the Red Army. Some key figures were picked up by the NKVD selectively at first: one of those to be arrested, in August 1936 – for the second time! – was Primakov, the deputy commander of the Leningrad Military District. Intelligence is traditionally subordinate to the district Deputy Commander. Had Primakov carried out his own investigation into the circumstances surrounding Kirov's assassination and the disappearance of witnesses? If he didn't, still materials related to the matter would have come to him through the channels of military intelligence. This alone was enough for Stalin.

History knows nothing about this. That's a pity. As a witness of those times, I will remind you that all this was taking place under conditions of a continuing hysteria over the matter of the "dastardly, villainous murder" of Kirov. (The hysteria hadn't died out even decades later – the anniversary of Kirov's assassination was marked in the 1940s and even the 1950s, until Stalin's death, before it subsided.) This phrase – the dastardly, villainous murder of the ardent orator of the Revolution – was repeated continuously over the radio and spread over all the pages of newspapers. (Nothing was mentioned about jealousy, which has now come to the surface as a motive for this murder all of a sudden and so advantageously for the revitalization of the Leader's cult.) In the country, unfocused – so far! Suspicion and hatred were seething toward any unknown powers standing behind the "hired killer" Nikolaev. Who was standing behind him? They must face trial! Such was the emotional atmosphere, and it was sharply heating up.

Immediately after Primakov, Corps Commander Putna, the Soviet military attaché in Great Britain, was seized. At the beginning of September, Corps Commander Turovsky, deputy commander of the Khar'kov Military District, was arrested. The Military Political Academy in Leningrad was completely eviscerated. (Leningrad … contacts with Primakov?)

Meanwhile, many events were taking place across the country. In February 1937, Sergo Ordzhonikidze, a friend of the Leader, died in his Kremlin office.[1] A gunshot cut him down just days before the opening of a most important plenary session of the Central Committee. A Central Committee plenary session is not a Party Congress; there are no rapturous delegates present at a plenary meeting and no bursts of stormy applause. A plenary session is a business meeting, and at it, Sergo was intending to reveal unpleasant truths about Stalin. Any sort of speech had long since stopped frightening the Leader: they could be noted as manifestations of personal hostility toward him, a man who had long ago seemingly placed the Party's interests above his own. However, Sergo was a friend, and moreover, Stalin's oldest and most trustworthy friend, and everybody knew this. The Army still had not been touched. Had Sergo confronted Stalin at the plenary meeting, some in the Army command would have supported him, and not only morally. Whether Sergo was shot by a "best friend" or a trusted Chekist is not really important. The Party leaders were informed that Sergo couldn't endure the stresses of the struggle. The explanation's semantics didn't bode well for an unclouded future for the other prominent people in positions of power. There was no mention of the bullet in the official announcement of Ordzhonikidze's death, as if not to rouse the masses. The official explanation was a heart attack. After his death, there was more of the same: cremation, interment in the Kremlin wall, grief, a true Leninist, the best friend of Comrade Stalin, the renaming of cities, books, portraits …

Well, at least he was not tortured.

The timetable of transfers and arrests (and executions) was thought out and carried out with precision down to the hours and minutes. In such matters Stalin was superior to a computer and still remains unsurpassed.

The military district commanders were arrested with exceptional caution. Iakir was the first. Uborevich too was dangerous, but Iakir was a father to the troops, the favorite of the RKKA, and the commander of a district, which – theoretically – was capable of

---

1   On 18 February 1937, the deputy chief editor of the journal *"Rossiia na stroikakh"* [Russia under construction] M. S. Kusil'man, a man who had frequent contact with the People's Commissar of Heavy Industry, was the first to run into Ordzhonikidze's office following the sound of a gunshot. He dropped a gentle hint to me about his great suspicion, when he was talking with me once as I gathered material for my book about Hero of the Soviet Union Tsezar Kunikov [a naval infantry officer who commanded the landing party at Malaia Zemlia during the Great Patriotic War]. In 1974, it was still a long way until perestroika and glasnost', so I can't really fault Kusi'man for not telling me more. Geller and Rapoport connect Ordzhonikidze's death with the Kamenev and Zinov'ev case. Stalin had promised them their lives in exchange for their loyal conduct at the trial. After their execution, Sergo rose on his hind legs, which puts him in the best light: he didn't hide his feelings, as Stalin had been hiding them for years.

arranging a paratroop landing in Moscow. Iakir had to be arrested very delicately; there was nowhere to transfer him where he was not known and loved. Nevertheless, a transfer was announced, to Leningrad – so as to hang him out to dry prior to the arrest: now he no longer commanded the Kiev Special Military District, and now he no longer had the legal authority to issue orders to the troops. Comrade Stalin couldn't even allow him to reach Leningrad, though,

The commanders were arrested by the "rail car method", which had first been tested on Primakov. He, it is true, had driven off the Chekists and with his personal security guard had barricaded himself in the rail car until receiving the guarantee from Voroshilov. Already once before, the People's Commissar had ordered him to be released ...

Just imagine with what calculated scheming everything had been prepared! ... Primakov had been released back in 1934, when he was first arrested, under Voroshilov's personal guarantee, and, I assume that rumors about the case were deliberately circulated by the NKVD in order to give any arrested person a hope that arrest didn't really mean an end, that by his authority the People's Commissar was capable of having someone released and returned to his post. A far-sighted approach. Of course, it wasn't Voroshilov's; over his whole life he couldn't have thought up such a tactic. Over the years, the stage direction had been rehearsed down to the tiniest details prior to the production.

Iakir was arrested en route, in Briansk, while he was asleep, in the early morning hours of 29 May. He was expecting no guarantee. Uborevich was seized by Chekists later that same morning, just as the train reached the platform in Moscow.

The Boss had recovered his wind. Some troop commanders were sitting in isolation cells without belts or any signs of rank, under the guard of such brainless dogs as don't exist even in hell. Others had been summoned to the Military Council and were also separated from their troops.

The Higher Military Council convened on 1 June 1937. Thus, out of the blue, the Army was given a chance.

According to Geller and Rapoport, the greatest confusion was apparent in those who were organizing the Council meeting. The session, despite the exceptional circumstance, was being held in its customary place, in Building No. 2 at the People's Commissariat of Defense, which meant, on army turf. So what if these grounds were being controlled by men of the NKVD? For several hours, the Leader would be alone with the military men. Even having turned in their side arms, they could kill him with their bare hands. The Red Army in the form of district commanders, chiefs of the departments of the People's Commissariat of Defense, and chiefs of the military academies had been given the last possibility to realize that it was being destroyed, that the process had already started, and that it would be implemented according to the principle of removing the best. A choice between the Boss and their comrades had been granted. A choice on one side between a betrayer of the Motherland, who was undermining the defensive strength of the country, and a destroyer of nations, who had called himself their father; and on the other, honorable servants of the homeland, whom Stalin had selected for the start of his bloody game and whom he had accused of treason. Moreover, the possibility of making this selection didn't last for a few fleeting minutes, but for hours: a report by Voroshilov and only then the appearance of Stalin, who directly confronted the gathered commanders with audacious, absurd accusations.

The course of this Higher Military Council meeting is even more painful than that of the XVII Party Congress. Stalin's remarks were vile and deeply derogating the Council participants, few of whom would live another year, but the audience just sat there, listening submissively. How did they tolerate it? A person who can endure such vilification is worthless. Why did army commander Dubovoi, who didn't believe in Iakir's guilt and who opposed Stalin, not rush him? He was arrested during a break in the session. Why didn't Krivoruchko strangle the Leader who had approached him with such slanders, as he would do one day in confinement to the interrogator who had struck him?[2] Why did the commanders, who were strong men, not leap to their feet and seize the Stalinist clique, without a thought about what might happen next? Something would have happened, but better than what did happen. Can it be true that something still wasn't clear, if the Kotovskys were being killed, the Uboreviches arrested and the Gamarniks were shooting themselves, then it was best not to expect anything good in the country and it was necessary to act, without pondering the consequences?

Why? ... They had been beheaded. The best had been arrested. The rest, in comparison with the commanders now gone, did not dare to utter a peep; not even two Marshals, who would perish a year later.

Oh, Gamarnik should not have shot himself! One false step in his splendid life – but such a fatal one! The arrest of this irreproachable authority figure would have alerted all the military commanders to be much more wary of the rubbish that the Boss was feeding them. In contrast, his suicide was presented to his fellow military commanders as a cowardly avoidance of his unmasking and responsibility. They were stunned, and trying to think, but now there was no time to think, they had to act. The military commanders let the moment pass ...

So went Stalin's 18 Brumaire [a reference to the *coup d'état* by which Napoleon overthrew the French Directory]. He didn't anticipate that everything would go so smoothly. A motley crowd was sitting in the hall, all for naught; fate would have gone the same way. At the time of the meeting, though, who might foresee his fate with the Leader standing in front of them, the head of a power, donned in his newspaper armor of nationwide hysterical adoration? At first they were dispiritedly quiet; then they began to deliver speeches. Of the forty-two who spoke with wrathful condemnation of the "traitors", thirty-four soon went the way of those "traitors". Situations like that are so commonly known ...

"That's just what they deserved!" contemporaries say; "They were all previous members of punitive expeditions! All scabs covered with the blood of the people!"

Well, yes, let's tar them all with the same brush. Those who perished must have been scabs, while those favored by Stalin must have been innocent lambs.

Everyone took part in the suppression of national uprisings. It was an order! However, their consciences ate away at some of the commanders, while pride over the very same matter strutted in others. Budenny was proud of his suppression of the Basmachis, and considered it on par with the raid into Denikin's rear area. The crushing of the Basmachi[3] uprising

---

2   Geller and Rapoport write, "The giant Krivoruchko, who commanded the 2nd Cossack Corps after Kotovsky, was distinguished by his spontaneity and unruly nature. He worshipped Iakir, who treated Krivoruchko's cavalier excesses very gently, like a father. In other circumstances, Krivoruchko would have given his life for the Army commander without hesitation. Here [at the Higher Military Council session] he kept his peace. ... Only later in prison did Krivoruchko's nature come through. He grabbed an investigator and throttled him, and then using his body as a club beat back his guards – until they shot him."

3   The Basmachi were anti-Soviet rebels in Turkestan active in the period between the Russian Revolution

was in the 1930s, though, not in the furnace of 1919, when father killed son, brother killed brother, and the time was such that it cannot be judged by present-day measures.

No, on the contrary, the very best were arrested, those who really personified the RKKA mind, honor and conscience. Even tendentious historians dare not try to assert that the purge bore a professional character. Whatever might be said against the army commanders, they could not be faulted for a lack of professionalism.

Here's a story, as told by G. Isserson:

In the Central Hall of the Red Army, the previously mentioned work by Triandafillov, *Kharakter operatsii sovremennykh armii* [Character of operations of modern armies] was being analyzed. Gamarnik presided over the discussion. Egorov, Tukhachevsky, Budenny, Uborevich, members of the General Staff of the RKKA, pedagogues and attendees of the military academies were taking part. The nearly unanimous evaluation of the book was that it had a great practical significance for the development of the Red Army's operational art. Budenny, in a sharp retort, declared the book harmful and contrary to the spirit of the Red Army, which prompted general mirth in the hall. Tukhachevsky spoke up, seriously analyzed Triandafillov's main points and agreed with his conclusions about the need for the Red Army's transition to armor. The horse cavalry, he asserted, didn't justify itself back in the First World War, so all the more so it couldn't play an important role in the next war. This conclusion provoked an outburst from Budenny, who declared that Tukhachevsky was "wrecking the Red Army." Tukhachevsky, turning toward Budenny, said with a smile, "Apparently, it is not possible to explain everything to you, Semen Mikhailovich!" and the hall reacted with laughter.

When Pythagoras proved his theorem, he sacrificed 100 bulls to the gods. Since then, if a great discovery is being made ...

In this case, the discovery consisted of the fact that the horse cavalry had ceased being the main shock force of the contemporary army. Steel steeds had arrived to replace the horse. What then of Budenny and his friend Voroshilov? Well, for the meantime the Main Cavalry Inspectorate was not subordinated to the Red Army General Staff. However, it is clear that this was only a temporary arrangement, and the position of the friends remained unenviable; they couldn't compete with the educated and gifted colleagues on the

---

and the early 1930s. The term, derived from the Turkic word basmak (to attack or raid), connotes banditry and was originally a pejorative term used by Russians. Soviet scholarship characterized the Basmachi as mere brigands and counterrevolutionaries in the pay of British imperialists. The military humiliation and massacres that accompanied the Russian conquest and occupation of Central Asia from the 1860s to the 1880s were still living memories in the region as Russia moved toward the revolution. Tsarist policies enforced cotton cultivation at the expense of food crops. All this contributed to dissatisfaction and fueled several major revolts.

Despite the imposition of martial law, summary executions, and the arming of Russian settlers, this unrest still simmered when the Bolshevik revolution broke out in 1917. Russian settlers completely dominated the Tashkent Soviet and other local soviets, so that Soviet power was largely identified as Russian power and fueled continued intercommunal violence.

The Basmachi rebellion was never a unified movement. The Soviet campaign against the Basmachi was largely successful by 1924, although some groups remained active in the mountainous border regions near Afghanistan until the early 1930s. The Soviets coopted Central Asians into state institutions, reopened closed markets, promised land reform, granted food and tax relief, relaxed anti-Islamic measures, and generally promoted the return of stability and prosperity under the New Economic Policy reforms. Eventually, Russian cultivation of good relations with Afghanistan denied the Basmachis a cross-border refuge.

RKKA General Staff. Just in the nick of time, higher officers of the RKKA General Staff, responsible for the mechanization of the Red Army would perish in a plane crash. Among them was the instigator of this entire mess, the main theoretician of the new strategy and tactics, Triandafillov. Wasn't this a purge, only in a concealed form?

By the number of coincidences and the sum of Stalin's criminal acts, by the cold-bloodedness and his sprawling, hand-written "FOR" on thousands of execution lists containing hundreds of family names comes the right to start with the *presumption of guilt*. Let Stalin's adherents prove that the air crash, in which the friend of Tukhachevsky,[4] Corps Commander Triandafillov, Chief of the RKKA General Staff's Operations Department, perished, was not arranged with the Leader's approval. Let them show that there wasn't partying in the Kremlin after the execution of the first eight commanders and that the wooden-headed Budenny, choking back his laughter, didn't excitedly say to his Boss, "Well, didn't you just explain everything to him, that high-brow? Did he grasp it all?" Meanwhile, the Boss "hides a smile behind his whiskers ..." [This is a line from a famous metaphorical song by Bulat Okudzhava, which compared Stalin to a black cat].

The best were arrested – those, whose intellect the Leader feared;[5] those, who guessed at what really lay behind what was happening, hidden under absurd accusations of betraying the Motherland and collaborating with foreign intelligence agents. The Leader surpassed those that he liquidated, not in intelligence, but in cunning, sanctimony and cagey decisiveness. In these qualities he was beyond compare.

The high-browed intellectuals were liquidated.

The nitwits promoted into the vacant posts remained nitwits.

With them, the country entered into feverish preparation for war.

With them, the country also entered into war.

Geller and Rapoport in their book High Treason [*Izmena Rodine*] write:

> In its consequences, the destruction of the Red Army by forces of the NKVD is the largest of Stalin's criminal acts. It still remains little, very little investigated ... Deprived of the most important documents, we cannot discuss this problem in sufficient depth. To attempt to reconstruct the course of events while naming its likely causes – that, if you will, is all that today can be counted upon as possible.

---

4   In his sensational *Ledokol* [*Icebreaker*], Victor Suvorov, among other findings made the following one: Tukhachevsky hated Triandafillov. That conclusion likely laid the groundwork for one of Suvorov's future books with the argument that Triandafillov's death was a diversion by Tukhachevsky. The source for this shocking discovery, as always, has not been named. Incidentally, *pseudo-historians* often cite documentary files or materials from investigative cases which do not in fact support what they are asserting. They believe that if the assertion gets through – fine; if not – oh well. Based upon how many of their books are printed, the assertions usually slip through. Geller and Rapoport add a note to one of their chapters: "Everyone who needed to know was aware that Stalin was hostile to Tukhachevsky and all of his proposals. Once, when it was necessary to have the Politburo approve an increase in Army manpower, Tukhachevsky and his friend Triandafillov resorted to military cunning. Tukhachevsky cited incorrect figures in his report, not those he desired. Triandafillov objected and introduced the correct figures. Stalin was glad of a chance to spite Tukhachevsky and sided with Triandafillov. The proposal was accepted as Stalin's and Triandafillov's." Was it this little joke that cost Triandafillov his life?

5   When the luxuriantly mustachioed cavalry general Oka Gorodovikov complained to his buddy Budenny about the scale of the arrests and expressed a concern that they would similarly soon arrest him, his friend told him, smoothing his mustache, "Don't worry, Oka, they're taking only the smart ones."

As the Genius of all times and peoples, the Great Leader and Teacher, the Father of workers of the entire world, that is how Stalin now stands before us upon completing the greatest act of his life: the destruction of his own armed forces.

The Russian authors cited above, who were shaken by the emotion-filled facts that they had been able to gather in those desolate times for scholars, completed their book in 1977. It has cost them dearly. Since then, the Soviet Union has collapsed and once-secret archives opened. Investigative files, often retroactively fabricated over the bodies of the army commanders, in order to justify their liquidation, which had been previously approved or even demanded by the Leader. To be sure, it is amusing to search for documents from those times, when the Boss restricted himself to a meaningful glance, obsequiously caught by the executors of his will, or gave only the notorious "verbal instructions". However, some documents have been published. Books have emerged, which described the apparatus of destruction, starting with the arrest and leading to the shot to the back of the head, only separated by minutes from the pronouncement of the sentence, which was always "not subject to appeal". (I'm referring first of all to Suvenirov's book, *Tragediia RKKA: 1937-1938* [*Tragedy of the RKKA: 1937-1938*]) Is Russian historiography enriched by an explanation of the causes of the purge? The military historian and academician Suvenirov restricts himself to a description of the terror and laments the army's destruction, pointing to the terrible experience of the Great Patriotic War. He doesn't attempt to explain, however, why the army became the object of such cruel animosity from the Leader.

Attesting to the purge as "the largest of Stalin's criminal acts", Geller and Rapoport note that even if historians in their heated polemics never in fact come to a unanimous opinion, then all the same our understanding of history is enriched with new views.

There is one more conception of the purge of the RKKA: The high command of the RKKA was so irreproachable and possessed such authority, so towering in its human qualities and its dedication to work, that the army could not believe in the guilt of the eight commanders and simply could not digest it. However, the army did not get rid of the Leader. Then in the wake of the first eight, thousands of others were finished off, practically the entire upper command staff of the army, and the flower of the mid-echelon commanders and the rank and file.

If it hasn't been formulated in this exact way by Russian historians, it is only because they (Geller and Rapoport in particular) wanted, as if in vindication of the victims of the terror, to present the RKKA as prostrate before Stalin. However, the obedient aren't destroyed; this is the fate of the obstinate. Hitler dismissed those in the military who opposed him – Stalin eliminated army commanders who were not malleable. The resistance to Stalin was passive, but it was there. The Führer got rid of headstrong military commanders in his own way. Hitler could not kill; he would have gone the same way as his very first victim. The removal of two key figures was sufficient for him. Those dissatisfied with Hitler then left, and the army became obedient to the Führer.

The Leader found his own way to rid himself of independent thinkers in the military. Stalin didn't allow resignations, and he wasn't spooked by ghosts. So he killed the army commanders, whose ethics didn't permit wars of aggression and terror against their own population. Once they were eliminated, he could conduct any domestic or foreign policy he wished. The Red Army had ceased to be a bearer of virtues.

It remains to be added that this additional conception is not new. In brief, without a detailed explanation of the causes, which perhaps were not even known to the English historian, approximately this same view was also expressed by John Erickson in his book *The Soviet High Command* back in 1962, 15 years before Geller and Rapoport wrote their book. This great work at the time was inaccessible to them. Now, however, any literature is accessible to all, and all that is required of the scholar is to stop seeing the RKKA prior to the purge as a passive instrument of the Leader. If it had been such, the purge would not have been necessary.

Yes, facts do not permit us to assert that the military commanders were plotting against Stalin, and facts are a stubborn thing. However, are all the facts known to us? If to the present day there are British archives that are closed to the public in that ultra-free country is it so absurd to assume that certain sections of the Russian archives also remain classified? In just those, where there might be uncovered the intentions of the most worthy people of power to implement an illegal overthrow of the ruler, potentially resides a breakthrough in understanding – even if there is only an outline of a plan.

Was there nothing like a conspiracy unveiled during the trials? I should say so! Why, though, divulge a scenario that is enticing to the judges, who at the time were still walking around freely without escort guards, but were capable after the trial of seeing the light and of seeing the essence of what was happening in the country ... Even after the Master's replacement was it not in the interests of power to promulgate a process for an orderly change in government, developed by the best military minds in a country with a strong army, rather than suffer under a cruel ruler and a pervasive surveillance apparatus subordinate to him? Was it not better to keep such plans concealed? (This is speculation, of course ...)

In the years of perestroika, books began to come out which revealed much. The international foundation "Democracy" published volumes of previously classified documents. (In 2001 there was also a volume published under the title *Georgii Zhukov: Stenogramma Oktiabr'skogo (1957) plenuma TsK KPSS i drugie dokumenty* [*Georgii Zhukov: Stenogram of the October (1957) plenary session of the CC CPSU and other documents*]. I cannot deny myself the pure satisfaction of citing here the short abstract from this volume, which was compiled by A. N. Iakovlev, the father of perestroika: "This collection of documents reflects the post-war fate of Marshal Zhukov. Already in 1946 he fell under Stalin's disfavor, and in 1957, *at the height of his creative work in the post of Minister of Defense*, became the victim of a Party-nomenclature conspiracy" (author's emphasis).

In that same series (Russia: XX Century), a volume of documents was published in 1999 under the title *Vlast' i khudozhestvennaia intelligentsia, 1917-1953* [*The regime and the artistic intelligentsia, 1917-1953*], which contained abundant memorandums, special communications and briefing papers from the Special Department of the NKVD's Main Directorate for State Security about the moods among the artists and writers with verbatim records of their utterances. It would be the utmost naiveté – not to say *stupidity* – to assume that similar records of the verbatim statements of the military commanders regarding the situation in the army and the country don't exist alongside those of the artists and writers. However, until now nothing about the attitudes of the commanders toward Stalin and political situation in the country has leaked out.

Leaks of information from the "war room" provide a few tidbits only about Voroshilov. Stalin seemingly encouraged criticism of his untalented, but personally loyal People's Commissar of Defense, calling it "constructive". We can place faith in this: the professional provocateur was in his element. He however knew that he could not remain *tet-a-tet* with the army. They wouldn't forgive him the famine and repressions. Stalin used attitudes toward

Voroshilov as a litmus test of the attitudes toward him. He winnowed out the military commanders according to their utterances about Voroshilov, and indeed the arguments over the technical re-equipping of the army served for him only as an instrument for checking the loyalty of the army commanders. Questions about strategy were even deeper, although indeed they were not subject to discussion. The aiding and abetting given the Germans was not welcomed by the army commanders, even if it did bring technological secrets from Germany in return, especially in the area of chemical weapons (though these found no application in the war). The unspoken disagreements were profound. It is possible to assume that the army commanders were guessing that the Leader wasn't interested in a weak and peaceful Germany. He didn't need peace in Europe; he desired conflict, even if it was global, in order to remain outside it until the right time, to exploit all the advantages of neutrality until the decisive stage.

Was this all? Or did one or another of the military commanders go further? Did he understand that the wise leader Comrade Stalin, the faithful pupil and continuer of Lenin's work, had in fact long ago betrayed this work, which meant also the ideals which they all were serving? That he was now not building socialism, even if in only one country, but despotism, his personal and boundless dictatorship? That Stalin was no longer the Party's leader, but a monarch, occupied with expanding the boundaries of his kingdom? Was it so difficult for Iakir to grasp this after his familiarization with the documents in the gray portfolio against the backdrop of all that had happened and was still happening in the country?

However, then the verbatim transcripts of any such conversations would no longer incriminate the army commanders, but the Leader. They possibly contain facts – with details about the elimination of Kirov, Kuibyshev and Ordzhonikidze, about the cruelties committed at the time of collectivization .... Well, such a line of speculation does a good job of explaining the solid wall of silence around the army commanders, the lack of any word from them, even if only against their incriminators. It explains as well the impenetrably tight hermetic seal around the archives of "the military room".

Stalin's destruction of the RKKA became the sole cause of our military losses – and even of the war itself. That's what Marshal Vasilevsky, the most authoritative military chief in the Soviet army and a man who was more than loyal to Stalin, himself believed. A student of Shaposhnikov, he was expressing the views of the teacher, who survived, but whose personality was crushed by the purge and who never recovered from it, and in return knew better than anyone else the strength of the liquidated talents, and, in counterbalance to himself, the strength of their characters. The fate of one of them will serve as an illustration.

19

The Fate of Marshal Bliukher

More than seventy years have passed since the tragic deaths of the army commanders. How their lives and deaths are being treated in literature today is apparent from the description of Marshal Bliukher's fate, which was terrible, even by the standards of the purge. One spirited and apparently popular Russian journalist wrote the following about the Marshal's military talent: "So much has been said about the actions of Bliukher in the years of the Russian Civil War, that there is no sense in repeating it." He then provides a unique list of the Marshal's awards and honors, among which were Orders of the Red Banner and the Red Star, both of which Bliukher was the very first to receive, but then in contrast to these decorations, the journalist makes the following observation: "It would seem that all this speaks to Bliukher's undoubted military talent. However, it must be noted that the entire time, Bliukher was fighting against a relatively weak opponent."[1] In short, Bliukher was managing it like a father against a child ... and who regards that as some sort of military expertise?

For journalism, which has a great influence on public opinion, the following technique is typical: they say that so much has already been said about the person ... and then make an observation that reduces a hero's merits to nothing. They do this out of the desire to turn the well-known into a sensation, or they're just doing what they've been told to do. Whatever a journalist's motives, the ordinary newspaper reader, as he reads a journalistic investigation (it's not important, whether it was ordered or suggested with fame in mind) doesn't recall the subject's activities. In the best case, he or she might recall only the person's name and his or her profession: government minister, academician, marshal ... but indeed, in this particular case where has so much been already said about Bliukher's activities in the Russian Civil War? There is no demand for books about the repressed commanders and such books are not published in great quantities. Certainly, it wouldn't have been bad to provide some sort of summary about Bliukher's opponents and to give the reader himself the chance to assess their strengths and weaknesses, as well as the merits of Bliukher's awards. Indeed, the Revolutionary War Council decided who to award – and this was to be Trotsky and his deputy Skliansky. It is hard to believe that they would have twice awarded the newly instituted Orders to this very man for no reason.

In 1918, Bliukher's opponent in the Urals was the ataman Dutov. The Czechoslovakian insurrection had trapped the Red forces in Beloretsk between the Czechs and Dutov's forces. Kashirin (who later became a reputable commander of the RKKA and an Army Commander, 2nd Rank; like Bliukher he was a member of the tribunal at the trial of Iakir and Tukhachevsky in June 1937, but already in August he was arrested, and like Bliukher, he lost his life in 1938) was elected to lead the unified Red detachments.[2] This was still

---

1   This article was from the weekly *Kur'er* [*Courier*], which is published in New York and reprints the most scandalous materials from Russian newspapers and journals.

2   During this stage, when partisan Red formations gathered spontaneously, commanders were directly voted upon within the formation. It was only after the units became regular Red Army formations and

V.K. Bliukher.

partisan warfare, but it is notable that Bliukher was elected as Kashirin's deputy. The combined unit, numbering around 6,000 troops, in July 1918 reached as far as Iuriuzan' with heavy fighting, but was then compelled to return to its jumping-off area. Bliukher took the place of the wounded Kashirin, reorganized the detachments into battalions and regiments, and proposed a new campaign plan for a march toward Krasnoufimsk, through the industrial regions, where the encircled force could replenish its ranks. During this campaign, the unit grew into a disciplined army, organized into rifle and cavalry regiments, with artillery and auxiliary elements. This army smashed the opposing White forces in the area of Zimino and for a week critical for the Whites, blocked their communications with Siberia. Marching for 500 kilometers across mountains and swamps while engaging in more than twenty battles and destroying seven White Guard regiments in the process, Bliukher's army inflicted a defeat upon the White forces on the Ufa River and linked up with forces of the Eastern Front. Here Bliukher in the role of commander of the 30th (later to become a legendary unit) and 51st Divisions and deputy commander of the same 3rd Army took part in the successful effort to destroy Admiral Kolchak's forces. In his post as commander of the 51st Division, Bliukher gained prominence during the assault on Perekop.

As War Minister and Commander-in-Chief of the People's Revolutionary Army of the Far Eastern People's Republic, he reformed the army and led the destruction of the Whites at Volochaevka, displaying simultaneously uncommon capabilities in the diplomatic game with the countries involved in the Allied Intervention in the Russian Civil War.

Who was the weak opponent? The Czechs? The Cossacks? The Russian hero Admiral

reported to the Revolutionary Military Council that they would higher orders and commanders would be appointed.

Kolchak? Wrangel? Even if the best armies weren't opposing Bliukher, he also didn't exactly have Guards troops under his command. Perhaps the matter is not the opponent's weakness, but that Bliukher knew how to concentrate more strength at the needed place at the needed time, which is not coincidentally an essence of the military art. Perhaps Bliukher wasn't solid on the defense? However, it was he that defended the legendary Kakhovka bridgehead, which was one of the hottest places of the Russian Civil War.

Yes, the reader might say, but he fought poorly against the Japanese at Lake Khasan in 1938. Voroshilov's well-known order, filled with accusations, falls upon Bliukher like an axe:

> The leadership of KD Front Commander Bliukher ... at Lake Khasan was completely unsatisfactory and bordered upon willful defeatism. His entire conduct over the time preceding combat operations, and during the fighting itself was a combination of a lack of discipline, duplicity and sabotage of the resistance against the Japanese forces, which seized part of our territory ... Marshal Bliukher removed himself from any type of leadership over the combat operations, concealing this self-abnegation by the sending of the *front*'s chief-of-staff Comrade Shtern to the area of combat operations ...

Such expressions are used to smear traitors. This is concomitantly a charge of confusion in the use of combat arms and materiel, and an accusation against the troops' poor training and lack of readiness to respond to an alarm to defend the border against the enemy's incursion. For such a military commander like the Marshal, such crude shortcomings are inexcusable.

However, "Stop the camera!" Let's take a break. In 1938, it wasn't the incursion of Japanese forces into Soviet territory; instead it was the master of provocations Stalin and the intrusion of Soviet forces into Japanese territory. A year later, Stalin would use this same approach on the Finnish border, but this time there was no-one left in the RKKA who, against the Leader's will, could try to tamp down the conflict. Thus the shameful Finnish War resulted.

We're getting ahead of ourselves, however ...

The first wave of repressions in the Red Army barely touched the Far East. The year of 1937 and the first half of 1938 passed relatively quietly for the Special Red Banner Far Eastern Army. In July 1938, however, the new chief of the Main Political Directorate of the RKKA Mekhlis and the Deputy People's Commissar of Internal Affairs Frinovsky arrived aboard separate trains. Here I will cite from Geller and Rapoport's work, with some abridgements:

> Soon thereafter commanders were seized by the hundreds.[3] It cannot be said that the

---

3   Including the commander of the so-called "Kolkhoz Corps" Rokossovsky. He was serving under the command of Uborevich, who highly regarded him, and he himself had a very high opinion of his superior. It is a miracle that Rokossovsky wasn't executed. Perhaps it was his own personal charm that was working for him here. Even this played a role at times. Everything played a role, as long as there were no directions from the Leader, and if there were instructions, then nothing else mattered. On the matter of Rokossovsky, there could hardly have been instructions. Nevertheless, we need to find the name of the investigator in charge of his case, and give him a medal, albeit a posthumous decoration – as a positive example of the entire fellowship of investigators, who shun excessive zeal in their work.

     Some data on the magnitude of the repressions, all from the Central Committee of the CPSU report, moment was well chosen. The situation along the border was extremely tense, thanks to Stalin. The great leader had gotten the idea that the Far East was a powder keg, and that the Chinese and Koreans, living under the heel of Japan, were only waiting for a spark to set off the flame of wars of national liberation..."

... There were sectors where the border was not demarcated; however, border patrols from both sides walked specified routes daily and no confrontations had taken place. Late in July Frinovsky and the Assistant Chief of Administration of the NKVD in the Far East Goglidze visited the border. They took with them fresh border troops not familiar with local conditions, and gave them new maps on which several sectors actually controlled by the Japanese were marked as Soviet. ..."

On 29 July, an incident occurred near Lake Khasan in one of the improperly marked sectors. Soviet border guards brought back a captured Japanese officer[4] as proof that the border had been violated. Zaozernaia and Bezymiannaia Heights, where the capture took place, were considered by tacit agreement to be no one's. Our guys immediately occupied them. The Japanese drove the Soviet units out of the area and reinforced their own. Large-scale military hostilities began...

The Soviet troops' situation was complicated by a foolish order from Stalin. They were to make sure that not one bullet landed in Japanese territory. Because of that they tried to regain the heights almost solely on the strength of bayonet charges. ... When Soviet units charged, the Japanese positions opened up at full strength. Soviet losses were heavy. Finally, at the cost of large sacrifices, Soviet troops took the disputed heights. Military action was halted on 11 August. The border was clearly demarcated and confirmed in a peaceful agreement. Wars of national liberation did not break out.

Perhaps, even in this skirmish the losses would have been fewer, if the companies weren't being commanded by former sergeants and sergeant majors, but by the commanders that had trained them and who were "arrested by the hundreds". Then everyone would have known where the stockpiles of weapons and combat equipment were located, and they would have been put into the troops' hands in a timely fashion. The units would have followed the proper regimen for deploying into position, and the types of forces would have cooperated as before.

It is difficult to believe that Bliukher wasn't in command. From Stalin's point of view, Bliukher was too indecisive. Why?

The years 1938 and 1941 present a biting irony, when Stalin, having learned of an attack, failed to issue an order to resist. An excellent strategist, Bliukher knew that the real danger for the country was coming from the west. The conflict in the east was not decisive in any way. It never entered Bliukher's mind (and if it did, he banished the thought) that Stalin was provoking the Japanese. It is also not excluded that the elimination of the Red Army's best people had prompted Bliukher to think: "The Boss provokes the enemy

---

"Ob antikonstitutsionnoi praktike 30-40-x i nachala 50-x godov" ["On the unconstitutional practices of the 1930s, 1940s and beginning of the 1950s"], dated 28 December 1988.

Over the years of 1935 and 1936, 190, 246 individuals were arrested, of which 2,347 were shot.

Over the years 1937 and 1938, 1,372,392 individuals were arrested, of which 631,897 were shot, including 631,692 according to the decisions of extrajudicial organs.

4   The authors' full description of this incident was written before *perestroika* and *glasnost* and is marred with inaccuracies. The prelude to the Khasan incident has been described more accurately in Boris Sokolov's book *Sto velikikh voin* [*One hundred great wars*] (Moscow: Veche, 2001).

personally, only to turn around and make an immediate peace, but will then heap all the blame on me, Bliukher, and thereby justify my liquidation." So the Marshal remained on the sideline. Three years later the Leader and Father, the force behind Voroshilov's scathing order, behaved in a truly disgraceful fashion and treated an invasion along the entire western border as a provocation, about which the Führer was ignorant, and froze in fear. The army was dying, yet an order to resist did not arrive! There's the man, who at a time when not days or hours, but minutes counted, sabotaged resistance to the aggressor. There's why there were losses. There's why there was such confusion. There's why the material-technical base simply was not only not deployed, but disgracefully turned over to the enemy and significantly supplemented his arsenal.[5]

Back to 1938; dismissed from command and sent away for a compulsory rest, the Marshal did a lot of thinking. Indeed, to his misfortune he came up with something. At the beginning of October he wrote a letter to Stalin: "All that happened was the result of provocation ... My boys walked right into the Japanese machine guns ... Frinovsky and Goglidze should be removed from the Far East and punished ..."

Indeed, but their punishment would come later. They were punished for their clumsiness.

With his letter, Bliukher revealed, in addition to his passivity, that he had figured out the reason for the conflict. (Soviet forces were moved to Lake Khasan ahead of time ...) Did this mean he had also figured out the one behind it? Bliukher was summoned to Moscow and on 22 October 1938, he was arrested.

In the *Kur'er* article, a tender version of the Marshal's death is presented. Broken by torture, Bliukher (An accomplishment – tortures were mentioned!) on 6 November confessed his guilt and two days later at an interrogation fell ill and ... "Death came suddenly from *pathogenic* (author's emphasis) causes: from blockage of a pulmonary artery by a clot, created in veins of the pelvis. The clot was formed as a result of insufficient coronary activity against a background of general arteriosclerosis." This about a Marshal, with the fitness of a sturdy 48-year-old man! Clots caused not by beatings, but by arteriosclerosis!

The article comes to an end in a totally pompous fashion – not with a quote from the death certificate, but instead, so to speak, with a creation from the journalist himself: "All remaining organs – the skin, bones, neck, sternum and ribs – were intact according to the examining doctor." There, they didn't break all his bones into pieces. Seemingly we must be giving a full-throated roar, "Glory to the Great Stalin!"

Well, let's check what an alternative source, Geller and Rapoport, have to say about Bliukher's end:

The Marshal was being held in the Lefortovo Prison. The first interrogation was done by the brand-new Deputy People's Commissar Beria. The charges were major: connections with the Japanese dating back to 1921, and the intention to desert to them with the help of a brother-pilot. Bliukher denied everything. His death arrived on 9 November 1938. By the testimony of the witness Dushen'kin, chief of the Central Archives of the Soviet Army, it has been established that Ezhov with his own hand shot Bliukher in his office. The death certificate was composed over his corpse.

---

5   In 1942 Rommel's Afrika Army was destroying British "Matildas" by employing captured Soviet 76mm anti-tank guns against them. (Von Mellenthin)

If the conscience isn't a censor, then anything can be written. The reader of such publications as *Kur'er* is placed in a position where he or she must undertake their own research, since they have not facts, but only the claim of biased journalists that the facts are commonly known. No, they are not commonly known.

This chapter is not an apology for Bliukher. The Marshal was not without sin. As a strategist, he understood early on what was what. Having agreed at the XVII Party Congress to falsify the tabulations of the electoral commission, where it was registered that only one voice was raised against Stalin, he made his choice. He could not then imagine that his friendship with Iakir and Gamarnik would condemn him to death. Tarnished by his acquiescence, he was conferred the status as Marshal of the Soviet Union – and two years later was a member of the tribunal that sat in judgment of his best friends.

We cannot imagine the degree of shock that Bliukher experienced over the suicide of his idol Gamarnik and the liquidation of the first eight army commanders – the flower and conscience of the Red Army. We can only guess at the strength and depth of the shock, and what those who still remained free were thinking. Those, who had been incautious enough to speak out about the Leader somewhere, now knew: the same fate was awaiting them. The thought that they would be disgraced, that frightened over the fate of their children, wives and mothers, they would be lying and smearing themselves with filthy confessions, led them to despair.

There is another version of Bliukher's death, a tragedy which in its force rivals Biblical and Ancient Greek stories. An eye, knocked out of the Marshal, for a long time figured almost symbolically in Bliukher's torments. However, a meaningful version of this symbol became known. At the interrogation following his labored confession, when inquisitors were seeking new names and new confessions from the Marshal, he grabbed a sharpened pencil from his inquisitor's desk and poked out his own eye, so that now mutilated, he could not be presented in front of the gullible public at the next show trial. On the spot, he was then gunned down by Ezhov.

Such is the seamy side of the Marshal's tragedy.

In England, Thomas More calmly went to his execution, in order to preserve his honor. He knew no hesitations. He almost went happily: after all, we must all die some time! In the USSR, though, sycophantism led the honorable war dog Bliukher to the point of a horrifying act, which with his last remaining strength he defended his own dignity.

20

Khalkhin-Gol

The striking of sparks in the Far East didn't proceed without consequences. The emboldened Japanese decided to probe the northern approaches to the USSR in a different place.[1]

There was no horse cavalry at Khalkhin-Gol. The cavalry general Zhukov personally reported to Stalin after Khalkhin-Gol: "If I had not had two tank and three motorized armored brigades, we would not have been able so quickly to surround and defeat the Japanese 6th Army. I believe we should greatly increase the number of armored and mechanized units in our armed forces."

Field experience teaches a fail-safe rule: that which isn't done quickly is never done at all. If in peace time this sounds radical, in war it becomes an imperative. It is impossible to encircle and crush slowly.

Zhukov conducted the operation in a hard-nosed fashion. Yet it would have been senseless for the Marshal to attempt to defend his aggressiveness (and severity!) while writing his memoirs following the brutal purge and the bitter war: the country was sick with denunciations and seething with outrage. At the same time, however, it is nonsense to pass judgment on a commander for sacrificing a battalion in order to save a regiment. Kutuzov wasn't judged for the Schöngraben matter.[2] He was praised. Sometimes it is necessary to set up a blocking detachment, in order to wear down the opponent and then with fresh reserves, defeat him in his now worn condition. One can imagine, however, in what condition the sacrificial lambs will be found after the battle is over.

Here's what General Grigorenko has written about Zhukov's severity at Khalkhin-Gol in his retelling of the battle: "Zhukov was appointing commanders to the units and subunits, and they were supposed to reach them without escort before daybreak. Those who arrived in time assumed their commands and went into battle. Those who arrived late went before a tribunal."

Picture it, a barren steppe, no one to ask for directions, the operation is being prepared in secrecy, there are no signposts on the roads, and indeed there are not even any roads: it was steppe! Imagine, one such new appointee is driving along; they didn't even ask his agreement when he was being appointed. Perhaps he wasn't even eager, but answered a recommendation of the command or was considered suitable because of his dashing appearance, or perhaps he came under the new commanding general's eye and received an appointment on the spot. By daybreak he had to reach his unit. He loses his bearings, though, and winds up at a different unit. For this he goes before a tribunal?

---

1   The conflicts on the border intensified after the destruction of the Red Army's high command not only because the Japanese became less reticent, but also because, having eliminated the conscience of the army and the country, Stalin became bolder.

2   Editor's note: In November 1805, the Russian general P. I. Bagration had been forced to conduct a desperate rearguard action at Schöngraben against the French General Murat in order to save much of Kutuzov's retreating army.

However, war is war. Zhukov wasn't over-intellectualizing: "Don't bark if you can't bite." You're making an impression; that means, you wanted to make it. Zhukov himself not only appeared brave, he answered to this bravery. If you don't answer to it; that means you're bluffing. A war dog also finds his way at night, just like Zhukov always found it. If you can't find it, what sort of commander are you? You'll lead your troops in battle in the wrong direction too. (In the Great Patriotic War, this happened all too often, and turned out tragically all too often.)

Zhukov's method of appointing commanders was a concealed competitive examination for command posts. Was it harsh? Isn't it also harsh with respect to the troops to appoint groveling yes-men as commanders, who don't know how to lead but do desire to command?

It is absurd to idealize Zhukov. It is still more absurd to depict him as primitive. Behind his insular shell, he was a complex man. Of course, he was not a humanist. He was a military commander; moreover, in a country where thousands of crack commanders were liquidated in peace time without any fault other than the fact that they were smart. Was it for him, a son of the era, with his (nonetheless!) rather narrow outlook, to stand on ceremony with loafers and bush-leaguers at a time of war? War! Zhukov fought. Moreover, he understood that a time had come when the question of cost isn't asked, only whether or not an order has been fulfilled. From 22 June 1941, nothing else mattered than to knock the attacking *Wehrmacht's* timetable off-schedule by any possible means. Since Stalin wouldn't even hear of plans of maneuver that were connected with even a temporary loss of territory, it no longer made any sense to reckon with losses or even to count them.

Khalkhin-Gol has become synonymous with the concept of "military art". However, art is not quite equivalent to mastery. Art = Mastery + Inspiration.

Khalkhin-Gol was an inspired operation from beginning to end – from the moment when Zhukov arrived in Tamtsak-Bulak[3] and not without acidity inquired of the commander of the 57th Special Corps Feklenko (who fought later to the level of his capabilities in the Great Patriotic War) whether he thought it was possible to direct his forces from a post over 120 kilometers from the battlefield, right up to the summary report to the Leader on the completion of the operation. In that report, he placed emphasis upon the difficulties of supplying the troops given the thousand-kilometer shuttling of the trucks and the colossal amount of fuel they consumed, which also had to be supplied from the USSR.[4]

---

3   This is my note in the margins of Zhukov's memoir – "Tsatsa and Barmantsak" (the names of lakes, around which Red Army forces for the Stalingrad operation concentrated). The eerie similarity to "Tamtsak-Bulak" and their closely parallel pronunciation are almost mystical. A 6th Army was also encircled during the Stalingrad operation. However, the main protagonist of this victory was another man...

4   The Khalkhin-Gol River, along which unfolded the operation to liquidate the Japanese 6th Army, flows through the territory of the Mongolian People's Republic. Here's a description of the terrain from a novel by the Japanese novelist Haruki Murakami, *The Wind-up Bird Chronicle*:

"The region was an empty wilderness, with literally nothing as far as the eye could see. My work required me to keep checking my map against the actual landforms, but there was nothing out there for me to check against, nothing that one could call a landmark. All I could see were shaggy, grass-covered mounds stretching on and on, the unbroken horizon, and clouds floating in the sky. ... We and our horses struggled across to the far shore of the Khalkha River. The land rose up much higher on the far side, and standing there, we could see for miles across the desert expanse from which we had come. This was one reason the Soviet Army would always be in the more advantageous position when the battle for Nomonhan (the largest village in the area of the fighting) eventually broke out. The difference in elevation would also make for a huge difference in the accuracy of artillery fire. In any case, I remember being struck by how different the view was on either side of the river."

G.M. Shtern.

At this place in his memoirs, Zhukov recalls his chief at Khalkhin-Gol, army commander Shtern, who was commanding the Trans-Baikal Front that had been created for the operation. The mention is worth citing in full:

> In overcoming these difficulties we were greatly assisted by the Military Council of the Trans-Baikal Military District and Colonel-General Shtern with his personnel. Our troops suffered badly from mosquitoes, of which there is a teeming multitude on the Khalkhin-Gol. At dusk they simply ate us alive. The Japanese had special mosquito nets. We had none, and had them made after great delays.

There you have it: One paragraph about Shtern's role in the operation, and only about mosquitoes. Commensurate, so to say, factors.

With all due respect to the Marshal, allow me to note that this place in Zhukov's memoirs is so far from the truth as to be a caricature. Mosquitoes were truly eating them alive, but army commander Shtern, in addition to being eaten alive by mosquitoes, commanded not only truck drivers, but also the air force and ultimately Zhukov's entire *front* grouping.

Colonel Nikitin, who taught one of our military courses called "Motorized Transportation" at our Polytechnic Institute, enthusiastically shared with us details which today are largely forgotten. Having arrived, as the first order of business Zhukov ordered sharpened stakes to be hammered noisily into the ground in front of the lines at night, giving the enemy the impression that the Soviet side was settling into a defensive posture. (The art of war ...) He then sent out a radio dispatch, calculating that the Japanese would intercept it: "Send felt boots, mittens and fur coats." Then – he struck.

Yes, but he struck only after presenting the operational plan to his superior (G. M. Shtern), and only after it was examined and approved. Shtern had planned and conducted a similar operation a year before Khalkhin-Gol at Lake Khasan as chief of staff of the Special Far Eastern Army. Zhukov might have informed us about Shtern's contribution to the plan at Khalkhin-Gol. He didn't do this. Instead he grumbled to Konstantin Simonov, the Soviet author, about an episode during the engagement: the losses were troubling Shtern, he was wavering, but offered to Zhukov the freedom to act as he thought best. (Likely, Shtern also understood that losses were no longer given any attention, if a victory was looming ...) That's all Zhukov had to say about Shtern. The mosquitoes, you see, were annoying, and they didn't have enough fuel. Well, Shtern lent a hand with the fuel supply. Jostling on the career ladder ...

The fierceness of the fighting at Khalkhin-Gol was equal to the battles of the Great Patriotic War, but the attitude toward prisoners was still different. The best description of the fighting, vivid and brief, has been left behind by a witness to the events, Konstantin Simonov, in several short poems:

Towering eruptions of earth and logs; *anyone who wasn't dead we took prisoner.* (from "*Kukla*" ["*The Puppet*"]; emphasis the author's)

The bravest is not he, who, tormented by thirst, scrambled past us in the daytime, and not he, who, trained to be indifferent in the fighting, *withstood seven nights under our fire.* (from "*Samyi khrabryi*" ["*The Most Brave*"])

There they lay dead, where the commanders had ordered them, in their uniforms and their clumsy foreign boots, with empty carbines in their hands ... Awaiting burial they looked sightlessly at the sky; at least those, whose eyes were not being pecked out by birds. The evening before, like in artists' battle paintings of old, their corpses were inscribing the twilight flatlands while birds swarmed overhead. We, humans, can become accustomed to anything, but the battlefield was too horrifying: the eagles were afraid to settle on it. (from "*Orly*" ["*Eagles*"])

Yes, victory did not come easily for us. Yes, the foe was brave. All the greater is our glory. (from "*Tank*" ["*Tank*"])

Already at Khalkhin-Gol there were not enough commanders, but the soldiers and sergeant majors had learned under Bliukher. Select Japanese troops opposed them.

Zhukov's report after the battle was the report of a military leader. The corps commander was summoned to present this report personally to Stalin. Stalin received the report and did not forget the man. Zhukov on his part was deeply impressed by Stalin: "his soft voice, the depth and concreteness of his judgment, *his knowledge of military matters* (Zhukov didn't actually write this. See *Vospominaniia i razmyshleniia*, 10th edition, 1993, p. 287), the attention with which he listened to my report." However, he was struck most of all by the whispering around Stalin. Sardar! Yet here is a soldier, in front of the eyes of which the Great Sardar slaughtered the army commanders, whose operations the soldier most admired. The more so, the Sardar could lock up a soldier; for awhile his fate also was hanging by a thread. How could one not lose courage? However, everything turned out in the best way possible ...

Completing the reception, Stalin said: "Now that you have combat experience, assume command of the Kiev Military District and use this experience for training the troops."

The Kiev District? The Kiev Special District? Iakir's District! So Stalin handed it to Zhukov. Not to Shtern, who commanded the Trans-Baikal Front, which had been specially created to handle the operations. Stalin simply returned Shtern to his duties as chief of staff of the Special Far Eastern Army.

Well, possibly Shtern couldn't be as good as Zhukov in 1941. The losses would have troubled him. However, on a lower level he could be much better than Konev, Kirponos and Eremenko.

Stalin received Shtern as well, whom by that time he knew as the victor over the Japanese at Lake Khasan, and as the main Soviet military adviser in Spain. For Khalkhin-Gol, Zhukov and Shtern were both conferred (following the Communist Party phraseology) the title Hero of the Soviet Union.

Shtern left behind no recollections of his reception in front of Stalin ...

So far so good, right? It doesn't matter that Gamarnik and Goriachev shot themselves; it doesn't matter that Iakir, Tukhachevsky, Uborevich, the legendary raider Primakov and the teacher of Heroes Vainer had been shot. Zhukov had been discovered; he had defeated the Japanese and become the commander of the Kiev Special Military District. Shtern didn't disappear; he was in the Far East ...

The fearful story of Stalingrad still lay ahead.

21

The Kiev Special Military District

G. K. Zhukov and I spent the summer of 1940 in Kiev: He at Pechersk, on Bankovaia Street, in the headquarters of the Kiev Special Military District; I, a dozen residential blocks away in a tiny communal apartment on the corner of Artem (L'vov) Street and Observatornaia Street, "on the western strategic axis". June was sunny and uneasy. The annexation of the "fraternal" Baltic republics was underway, proceeding quietly and peacefully, when suddenly a mess erupted with Romania over Bessarabia and Bucovina. Alarm drills began again. Blue lights began to burn in the buildings. Covers appeared on the headlights of the few vehicles back then. There were sirens. I couldn't stand all of this. The blue lights the previous winter, during the war with Finland, had put me in frenzy. (Later, as an adult, I learned about the magical properties of blue light: I wasn't the only person it drove to agitation.) I was sick with whooping cough. Mama, returning early from work every day, used to take me to the Trukhanov Island to breathe some of the clean, Dnepr River air – as Doctor Veksler had recommended, who, like many citizens of Kiev, had only a little more than a year left to live, until the Red Army abandoned the city. The whooping cough allowed me to miss the majority of alarm drills. In the beginning of July, however, everything quieted down, and we, as we did each year, drove out to the *dacha* we rented that summer in Pushcha-Voditsa.

Georgii Konstantinovich also didn't linger in the city. In June, during the air raid drills, he toured the reintegrated territory of the western Ukraine. As Zhukov writes, "together with the staff of the District Headquarters we conducted a large-scale exercise tour with signal communications support to the Ternopol' – L'vov – Vladimir-Volynsk – Dubno area", which in translation from the military jargon into conversational speech means a "headquarters maneuvers". Zhukov continues: "The exercise proved that the armies, formations and staffs were commanded by highly capable *young* officers and generals. True, since they had only *recently been promoted from less important duties,* they did need some serious operational and tactical training (author's emphasis)."

Here, unfortunately, there is nothing to explain. A year before the start of a great war, the armies were headed by sturdy lads, not fools, but also not commanders, since they needed operational-tactical training, and serious training at that.

Incidentally, work wasn't limited to training. In July, the Southern Front was created, consisting of *three armies* (!), for the occupation of Bessarabia and Northern Bucovina. The Romanians were given cruel terms: "... leave untouched all rail transport, factory equipment and material supplies" (and leave, consequently, on foot in the expectation of handouts ...). In order not to allow the "cornhuskers" (such was the derogatory nickname for Romanians) to leave the evacuated territory with property that legally belonged to them, the District Commander order two brigades to be airlifted across the border to the Prut River. Meanwhile two tank brigades were sent in pursuit of the Romanians toward the river crossings, which they were ordered to reach at the same time as the air drop. Everything ordered was done. The airborne drop occurred at the crossings just as the tanks

E.S. Ptukhin

were approaching them, by which the Kiev Special Military District confirmed that the RKKA hadn't forgotten all that it had learned to do, and not all the Red Army's standouts had disappeared. Therefore, the commander of the air force of the District (no, now the Southwestern Front!), Hero of the Soviet Union (before the war) Lieutenant General Evgenii Savvich Ptukhin was arrested on 27 June 1941, and in the middle of the war, on 23 February 1942, on Soviet Red Army and Navy Day, when there were not enough pilots at the front, especially Heroes, especially generals, he was sent on a flight to the stars. Why? Just to prevent him from talking too much and divulging whose wise instructions allowed the Luftwaffe to wipe out the District's entire air force in 30 minutes at dawn on 22 June 1941.

The Romanians were running, of course, from the tanks that literally dropped directly from the sky upon the panicked confusion of rattletraps and sedans, fleeing to the west, and of course, leaving behind both the transport and the equipment of plants and factories. Indeed, not only all this, but also much of the Romanian army's vehicles and equipment was abandoned, so that two years later, at Stalingrad, the Red Army's Supreme Command wouldn't have to guess where to strike.

However, it was necessary first to allow the enemy to reach Stalingrad ...

Meanwhile, at just this same time the good friend Germany was overwhelming it's natural, non-communist ally, sending its panzer wedges around the Maginot Line – just like Zhukov did at Khalkhin-Gol, but on a much larger scale. Now would have been the time indeed to strike the potential German adversary from the rear!

The arms were too short to reach that far and were also too busy; especially after the just-completed shameful war with Finland ... Stalin underestimated Hitler.

After all, it didn't take a genius to understand that Hitler could not just sit there, like a kernel of grain between two millstones, between Great Britain and the Soviet Union. But no, the Leader frittered away time on territorial hair-splitting, instead of solving the problem radically to spare the country from a war, the horrors of which would never be erased from memory.

Yet to assume that Stalin cared about defense means one has to interpret the military parades as telling the world "Don't touch me!", and not "Prostrate yourselves!" It means one must still assume that the Boss was proceeding from a defensive strategy, and still assume that Stalin's USSR was a peace-loving power, building its socialism.

How naïve ...

A defense to secure the building of socialism in his country didn't concern Stalin. His mind was filled with other plans. To explain them, in the first edition of this book I referred to the author Rezun-Suvorov, who had become fashionable at that time. This was naiveté on my part. I should have figured out the slant of this author. After his trashy book *Ochishchenie* [*The Cleanup*] (as Mr. Rezun appraises the purge), I must explain everything to my own reader by myself as much as I can – because the discussion of the secret protocols of the Russian-German (Molotov-von Ribbentrop) Non-Aggression Pact is nigh.

However, we're still in 1940 in this narrative. The protocols are already in full scale operation, but they are not publicly known. Even for Zhukov, when working on his memoirs, it was forbidden to mention the protocols. Even in the 1960s the country was formally repudiating them, and we, its citizens, were indignant over the slanderous fabrications of the bourgeois West. Poland was colluding with Germany against the USSR – that's what we had learned by heart and insisted upon in answer to the well-grounded admonitions.

Why? By doing so, we were hanging responsibility for the consequences of the protocols on ourselves as well. In this way Stalin's aggression turned into Soviet aggression. It wasn't that way, though! Or was it? Did we desire forcible acquisitions? Subconsciously? Consciously? Did we desire new Soviet republics? Who among us replies to such questions sincerely? Children do. At our Kindergarten No. 31 on Vorovsky Street in the city of Kiev, we rejoiced over the matter of the reunification of fraternal peoples and, I believe, would have exulted even more over a reunification with the proletarian brotherhood of all countries. The children can't be judged; they absorbed this attitude from the atmosphere of their times. Whom do we blame for bringing up such politically mature children?

However, was there an alternative? Who could educate us politically after the deaths of the country's best people? Parents? So as to become victims of the purge after their children spill the beans in their kindergartens about the oppositionist sentiments in the family? Thousands and thousands perished because of children's indiscretions, when they revealed family conversations in their schools and kindergartens. The parents hushed up. They no longer conducted any political discussions within earshot of their own children.

In 1939, my quiet Papa was extended an invitation to join the Party. Could he decline? After they had murdered Iakir, who had been well-known for his goodness and his accessibility to the simple people to hear their needs for the three years he had been in Kiev? (Before this, the district had been called the Ukrainian Military District, with its headquarters in Khar'kov, but Iakir's reputation as a warm-hearted man had followed him from there.) After the disappearance of the best people of the Rosa Luxemburg Textile Factory, where my father had worked for many years, and knew both the value of the people who had been arrested, and the value of those who took their place? He could, of course. If he was ready to stop sleeping at night, listening for footsteps on the staircase, like others who had been invited to join the Party and refused. Like those who were never invited to join. Like those who did join the Party, but even this didn't save them. He decided to accept the offer. He preferred a deferment. My father was never touched. So he indeed remained a passive member of the Communist Party of the Soviet Union until his emigration in 1979 ...

Let's return to Zhukov. Not in 1940, but two years earlier, when "... We were prepared to come to the aid of Czechoslovakia: our aviation and tanks were alerted; up to 40 divisions were massed in regions adjacent to the western border. But the Czechoslovak rulers of that time declined this aid and preferred abject surrender."

A rather forceful statement; but really, to invite the Red Army into Czechoslovakia to defend the Czech citizens – isn't that a surrender? This was when the sounds of the broken glass of *Krystallnacht* [Crystal Night, or Night of Broken Glass was an anti-Jewish pogrom in Germany and Austria on the night of 9-10 November 1938] still weren't heard, and for sundry reasons Germany was still considered a civilized country, while Stalin's barbarism and thirst for expansion was known to the whole world, the purge was in full-motion, and the Leader was destroying anyone of his own people who opposed him. Indeed, it had been precisely through Mr. Benes, the president of Czechoslovakia, that the portfolio of compromising Gestapo documents against the Red Army commanders had been passed to Stalin, after which the bacchanalia of repressions in the Red Army developed. Benes didn't know that these were false documents or that at the trial of the Red Army commanders Stalin wouldn't even present them. It is possible that the Gestapo fabricated the documents only with the Western democracies in mind, thereby killing two birds with only one stone: an attempt simultaneously to behead the intimidating Red Army and to serve notice to the West that it could not rely upon the USSR militarily, by doing it through a reputable European leader. Just to let him know that the RKKA and Stalin were foes, and that neither Czechoslovakia nor its protectors would have reason to count upon the RKKA's assistance in the confrontation with Germany.

It is a great riddle: Before Munich, did the purge influence the Allies' assessment of the balance of power in a possible conflict with Germany, should the Allies not yield to German pressure and refuse to make a deal at Czechoslovakia's expense? The method that they selected for resolving the Czechoslovakian dispute clearly testifies: the purge of the Red Army had a decisive influence on the Allies' decision.

Yes, Hitler effectively used Stalin when fabricating the false documents. Is this not provable? The question is an obvious one. How obliging was the Gestapo's readiness to concoct something desirable for Stalin, if only to inflict a slash upon the RKKA – and while it was being cut, to seize Czechoslovakia! The devilish plan achieved its aim in every respect. After seeing the Gestapo's forged files, Benes couldn't really count upon Soviet divisions coming to his aid. Much less could its allies: "Rely upon such a country? Such an army?" Meanwhile, Hitler already in May 1938, after receiving a dispatch from Ernst Koestring, Germany's military attaché in the Soviet Union, was no longer apprehensive about the Red Army. Perhaps he even let the West know of this dispatch. Further, really might not the military attaché of England and of France have reported the same thing, only in not such open language?

Zhukov's *Vospominaniia i razmyshleniia* was published in 1969, after the Soviet invasion of Czechoslovakia and the crushing of the "Prague Spring". It is difficult to discern where Zhukov's voice is in this section of his memoirs, and where is the voice of his political censors; they plastered both the holy and the sinful with the same color.

However, I digress. As it happened, the Czechs agreed all the same to accept Soviet divisions, but at the last moment, the Soviet offer of assistance was withdrawn. Whether the Marshal knew about this or not is difficult to determine. At the end of the 1930s, he wasn't yet in those posts that would allow him to know the government's diplomatic moves. It would have been most appropriate of all not to touch upon the question of assistance to Czechoslovakia ...

> Throughout the summer and autumn of 1940, the troops of the Kiev Special Military District were engaged in intense combat training ... Due account was also taken of the combat experience of the Nazi troops against several European states.
>
> By that time, World War II was in full swing ...

22

Interlude: The Second World War ...

... began, as is considered, with the signing of the Molotov-von Ribbentrop Pact – as it is known throughout the world – the Non-Aggression Pact. The point of the Pact was clear both to its signees and to its victims.

Germany's rear now appeared to be secure. The USSR's rear not fully so: in the Far East, the situation was still tense. Japan, known for its stubbornness in pursuing its goals, was making headway in China (which indeed subsequently spared Stalin from a second front with Japan).

England and France understood that Poland now lay spread-eagled before Germany like a sacrificial calf.

The USSR remained only a potential threat to Germany. The Red Army couldn't even think about taking on the *Wehrmacht* now, but a stab into Poland's back wouldn't require much. Hitler had decided that it would take too long to seize all of Poland. The campaign would become drawn out, and England and France would intervene ... Germany couldn't sustain a war on two fronts. A war on two fronts had been possible, but after the Pact it would be no longer: France was decaying and England wouldn't defend Poland. Germany's pact with Stalin may have been a sobering factor for the English and French. There would not be even any thoughts about the former Triple Entente! Without Russian resources, human and natural, it is a sure thing that they wouldn't intervene on Poland's behalf. The avaricious Stalin wouldn't be able to resist a temptation; he would be seduced by a portion of the *Rzeczpospolita* [a Polish word for "republic" or "commonwealth"] and would decide to annex it, freeing Germany of the need to fight in forests and hills. Let Stalin swallow the agrarian eastern territories as a reward for his assistance in the liquidation of Poland. It was important to tear that country apart before its allies could even blink. Hitler would see what to do next. It was with these thoughts that Hitler concluded the Non-Aggression Pact with its secret protocols.

At the Anglo-French-Soviet military negotiations in Moscow in July-August 1939, the question about the passage of Soviet forces across Polish territory in case of a war with Germany became a genuine obstruction. Poland was no more inclined toward Soviet assistance than Czechoslovakia had been, even in view of the impending German threat! Everyone feared everyone else.[1] A game of setting a cat loose among pigeons was going

---

1   I recommend to the reader Valentin Falin's book *Vtoroi front: Antigitlerovskaia koalitsiia. Konflikt interesov* [*Second front: Anti-Hitler coalition. Conflict of interests*]. In a superb style, even too lavishly florid for the chosen theme, the book conveys the suspicions in the relations between countries on the eve of and during the war. It is informative not only about the conflicts of interests within the anti-Hitler coalition, but also about the tensions within the Axis bloc. There is only one reproach to which this book is vulnerable: When dealing with an enormous quantity of the most interesting material about the attempts of the Allies to come to an arrangement with Germany before and even during the war, the author in the wealth of facts buries the essence of the matter – the sharpest conflict between *all* the involved ideological systems, the struggle between which didn't cease right up to the collapse of the USSR (and which in a strange manner continues even today). It is disadvantageous for the book's author to contrast the detailed

on. Historians search for the guilty party, but in truth there wasn't one; everyone was acting in their own interests, and everybody wanted to pass the hot potato into someone else's hands. Both the great powers and the fringe states were behaving this way. Nevertheless, Poland in the spring and even the summer of that fatal year for it refused to cooperate with Germany in a war against the USSR, which was a tasty option for Hitler – to pass military units through Polish territory to the Soviet borders untouched. This would simultaneously signify an end to Poland as well. Poland refused to capitulate. It didn't believe in Hitler's ability to crush Russia, and it didn't believe in his adherence to agreements. Poland simply had no choice.

In the late 1930s, England and France were also not in agreement over everything. Italy and Japan were grabbing for everything within reach. Stalin was preparing a global revolution (which was his term for global supremacy), and was carnivorously eyeing the Western Ukraine and Belorussia, the Baltic republics, the Dardanelles, the Balkans, Iran and the Persian Gulf through narrowed eyes.

Hitler, on his path to global domination, relabeled his putative allies as victims. The USSR was intended to be among the first; the Führer hadn't been dissembling while writing *Mein Kampf.* Yet now England and France were getting involved in the war ... because of what? Because of Poland! Hitler became petrified when he received the news. He had prepared for a campaign in Poland, not for a world war involving the entire British Empire.

Poor fellow, Chamberlain; he made only one mistake, and for it he was not forgiven. Meanwhile Stalin screwed up repeatedly, but – a tyrant! – he remained in power.

I'm of the opinion that in the political scheme of things, Chamberlain *did not blunder when signing the Munich Agreement.* I know that this thesis finds no sympathy among the Czech people, whom I cherish. Indeed, I dislike my own evaluation of the Munich Agreement. A price still had to be paid for this act of collusion, though not immediately, but one much more costly. However, that would come later, and in the meantime there was a grace period, which politicians so love to have. If only to gain time, in order to gather strength and to have a bit more time to think. Time solves all problems ...

Indeed, this problem can be viewed from a different angle. England was an ideological foe of the USSR. It had nothing like the French Communist Party. In England a prejudice against communism held sway. The ruling family there was related by blood to the destroyed House of Romanovs. Chamberlain also, naturally, was a foe of communism. Heck, what clear-headed politician wasn't? Churchill? He in 1918 had been raving against it more than anyone. The choice between forming an alliance with Hitler's Germany or Stalin's USSR was a ghastly choice to make. Didn't it make more sense to let one of the monsters devour the other? So Chamberlain didn't stand in the way of Germany's turn toward the east.

Not France, however. Even today, France hasn't forgotten its own revolution and still

description of the diplomatic pirouettes against the demonstrative silence over Stalin's pre-war territorial seizures: the lacerated Poland, the plundered Romania and the annexed Baltic republics. The West's unease with Soviet aggression is mentioned only in connection with the war against Finland, and even then in a peeved tone: the obdurate Finns took no heed of the peace-loving persuasion of the Soviet government to exchange Finnish ports for Soviet tundra. In general, the author uses the concept of "Soviet Union" as if the USSR coped in spite of Stalin (even though Falin himself calls Stalin the guilty party in all of the Soviet people's misfortunes). With this qualification in mind, I still recommend this factually rich book to the reader. Written by a patriot of the USSR, it is the book of a diplomat and political scientist, which while unmasking the West, also reveals against the author's will the USSR as an instrument of Stalinist policy.

celebrates Bastille Day. Franco-Russian ties were closer. France, a relative by religion to Catholic Poland, felt responsible for its fate. As an ally of England and its outpost on the continent, France pressed its traditional anti-German attitudes upon British policy.

Chamberlain was a professional politician, but he was inconsistent and lacked the resolve to resist his French partners, British patriots, and opposition within the Conservative Party – and indeed, his own tidy nature as well. Hitler was becoming more loathsome by the day. In the face of all of this, Chamberlain couldn't hold out. He should have suppressed his own sense of tidiness for a time, as he did at Munich ...

The Munich Agreement was a wise step in the interests of the British Crown. They directed German expansion toward the east. How far? If before the purge Hitler could only dream of a campaign against the USSR, it still was not expected that after a clash with its huge neighbor, Germany would emerge any stronger. Meanwhile, Britain could be preparing for a war, for which it wasn't yet ready. Had things turned out this way, it would have been wise. Chamberlain, in distinction from Stalin, was a fine strategist. He would have allowed Germany to expand eastward, and yielding territory after territory, bring the Reich right up to the Soviet borders. This could have taken place at any time after 1935, when England, in circumvention of the Treaty of Versailles, unilaterally signed the Anglo-German Naval Agreement that for all practical purposes allowed Germany to build a fleet. This Agreement created a serious wedge among the Allies, but it would become even worse. The clamoring for peace among the Germans themselves and the German sympathizers in England didn't cease, and even intensified, while German bombs were smashing London and Coventry.

On the very eve of the signing of the Soviet-German Non-Aggression Pact, on 22 August 1939, the details of a secret flight by Göring to England for ultra-secret negotiations with the top leaders of the British government were being discussed. Göring was lamenting his poor knowledge of the English language, which according to him was hindering him from coherently explaining to the Brits all the advantages of an alliance between the two powers. A visit, though, was being prepared, and in such secrecy that it was planned under a plausible pretext to remove even the servants from the villa where the talks would be held. The allegation that the flight didn't take place because Hitler had come to terms with Stalin and there was no longer any reason for Göring to make the flight is not convincing. Any agreement that would spare Germany from having to fight on two fronts served the purpose.

However, the Führer understood with whom he'd be dealing. He knew that a meeting with the British would give Chamberlain an opportunity to convince him not to touch Poland, and without Poland, Hitler couldn't reach the Soviet borders. Suppose even England was ready to carve out spheres of influence, as was the USSR, but without the seizure of Poland, such an agreement would be meaningless. A new lecture on morals from the British on the eve of the agreement with Stalin was worthless to Hitler. So in this way, by signing the pact with Stalin, he would arrive on the border with Russia. The factor of time, the politicians were hurrying ...

Even so, didn't the former proposal about spheres of influence inspire Hess to make a desperate flight to England on the eve of Operation Barbarossa? Poland by this time had already been wiped from the map and this obstacle no longer existed .... The archives of Great Britain will one day open, when those of us who were contemporaries of the events are no longer living. That is a pity. It would be useful to find out the degree of cynicism, with which we were bought and sold.

One cannot but be skeptical about the consistency of human activity on the whole and of each person in particular. Some people who commit suicide start their final day with morning exercise and taking their medicine. However, even in such absurd combinations one can discern guiding motifs – as long as full information on the question is accessible. In the case of British decision-making in 1939, it is not accessible, and historians cannot make sense of what was going on in the British government on those days at the end of August 1939, which were so fatal and happy, as it turned out, for mankind.

At the last moment, something seized up. It is assumed that on these decisive days, government "... lost control over events."[2] The phrase is both significant and enigmatic. Did revulsion toward Hitler overwhelm the distaste for Stalin? Did France sweep England along? Did America, with its antagonism toward Hitler, have an influence on England? Did England become alarmed by the Soviet-German bloc and the prospects of its consolidation? After all the location of the Soviet factories, which in the 1920s produced the weapons that Germany was brandishing, was no secret to the British Intelligence Service ... [3] Yes, Hitler had eroded communism in Germany. He had closed to communism the path into Western Europe ... but his continued forcible seizures of territory?

It cannot be excluded that in the ideological fog of the 1930s, the politicians of the West ceased to understand: Who was for and against whom. It could have seemed to them that Germany and the USSR could get on well with each other, in view of the similarity of their regimes, and that the just concluded Non-Aggression Pact in Moscow was inaugurating the creation of a super-alliance – of a new and harsh geopolitical type. Having carved up Poland, Hitler and Stalin might next move south, toward Iran, India, and Indochina! To link up with Japan! Together, these monsters would become overlords of the earth! What, too, of the Communist International? The USSR had prepared workers' governments ready to assume power in every European country. The involvement of the international proletariat in politics makes forecasting the course of future events murky: a fifth column! In everyone's memory was the emergence of the People's Front in France in 1936. What about Spain? The International Brigades and Soviet military advisers with weapons in the bargain! The task truly wasn't the simplest.

Perhaps Chamberlain merely lacked time. He plainly would have preferred not to have any obligations which might involve England in a war between Germany and Poland. But he ran out of time, it may happen that his name, in the future, will not ring out as the name of the one who went to Munich, but of the one who couldn't go any farther.

As for Hitler, he simply wanted to secure Germany's rear, and considered any potential partner equally suitable for that purpose. He would rather have got closer to the Anglo-Saxons and would have taken them into his Aryan family; he adored the Anglo-Saxon genes. However, genetics is genetics and politics is politics, so he sounded out the East. No one desired to collaborate with Nazism, and Communism was in the same situation. Which was the lesser of two evils?

While Chamberlain danced his *pas de deux* in the hope of moderating Hitler's appetite, Stalin said "Yes!" which indeed led the world to the noblest page in the history of our civilization: to the declaration of an Anglo-French coalition in defense of Poland without

---

2   *Voprosy istorii* [*Questions of history*], no. 6, 1989.

3   Editor's note: This is a reference to the weapons factories that the Soviet government by secret agreement allowed Germany to set up and operate on Soviet territory, in violation of the Treaty of Versailles.

the slightest benefits for the coalition, simply on principle, and in the condition of complete lack of readiness for war.[4]

Had Hitler reached the Soviet borders in the absence of war with the West, he would have gone further to the East. In order to make this clear, Göring was preparing for the negotiations with the British to let them know: "We're going as far as the Urals, no farther! Not to India!"

What a stroke of luck for Stalin, that Göring's mission to England never took place! Stalin knew that Poland's allies intended to abide by its commitments. It was advantageous for him to believe this piece of intelligence, so he believed it. He was also just a hair's breadth away from a miscalculation. "I've swindled Hitler!" he celebrated upon the signing of the Pact. He had won time for preparing the army! However, he had gained less than two years, while he had lost much more ...

Hitler also reveled in his success. He had feared an alliance of England and France with Poland and the Soviet Union; had that happened, he would have had nowhere to move. Göring, who was prepared to fly to England for negotiations, triumphantly danced a jig on a table top on the occasion of the agreement with Stalin.

The Pact was signed on 23 August 1939. The debates still continue: who swindled whom? Stalin, Hitler or Hitler, Stalin? This obscene balance amounts to over tens of millions of war casualties. To the present day, writer-historians maintain that "Germany demonstrated a will to return to the number of great nations ..." or that "the USSR demonstrated to all that it did not intend to be an 'object' of foreign designs and is in the condition to defend its interests."[5] We sometimes hear such empty words like these even today in Russia from political analysts and even politicians. One may also use these expressions about the democratic England and America. However, such language is unjustified when speaking about Germany and the USSR. In those places, it was only possible to speak about Hitler and Stalin: "Hitler demonstrated a will to return to the number of great nations ..." and so forth. The two leaders deceived their respective nations, these millions of stalked, slain, and physically and spiritually maimed people. The summer of 1941 was marked by a record number of suicides among soldiers of the victorious *Wehrmacht*, who'd been involved in the liquidation of children and elderly people in the occupied territory. From the Soviet side in response to the brutalities emerged an indescribable hatred, damaging to the conscience. War in general is an evil time for mankind, but *that* war elicited such a shameful hatred for a neighboring nation, the recollection of which even today, decades later, causes a painful reaction.

On 1 September 1939, Germany invaded Poland. This date has been accepted as the start of the Second World War, but this isn't true. Even then the rest of Europe might have slept peacefully, had Chamberlain declared: "Let them dismember Poland. We have nothing to do with it. Let them lock horns together. Let the two demons destroy each other. We'll emerge at the end." However, the Western democracies didn't believe that the demons were incompatible and that they would lock horns.

On 3 September 1939, England and France declared war on Germany, a great step in

---

4   I think that it was precisely the British adherence to principles that restrained Stalin from a campaign against post-war Europe. The experience of the war forced him to believe in the obduracy of the British, and that they would fire their atomic shot even under the threat of their own certain death.

5   These phrases are from Molotov's report "On the government's foreign policy" presented at the Extraordinary Fifth Session of the Supreme Soviet of the USSR on 31 October 1939.

human history. Now the Second World War had begun – and with no combat operations in the Western theater. So Chamberlain earned the reputation of a simpleton. Englishmen, of course, are not simpletons and never have been. However, they have been reflecting intellectuals, an endearing trait. When you think how history might have gone, if they had been a bit looser in their principles, it gives you the shakes.

A strange war ... but what is strange in it? Zhukov cites the testimony of General Jodl, the *Wehrmacht*'s Chief of the Operations Staff, at the Nuremberg trial: "If we did not collapse already in the year 1939 that was due only to the fact that approximately 110 French and British divisions in the West were held completely inactive against the 23 German divisions."

Inactive? I should say so! The declaration of war against Germany by the Western allies was a political maneuver. It was assumed that the sobered Hitler would recall his forces. Neither France nor England was ready for military operations against the mobilized Germans. They didn't even have any plans. The combat readiness of these 110 divisions is dubious. Were they to attack the well-trained and seasoned *Wehrmacht* off the cuff?

However, a year later the situation was repeated. Jodl could easily have said, "If we did not collapse during the campaign in Europe in 1940 that was due only to the fact that 110 Soviet divisions were held completely inactive during the war with France against 30 German divisions." I cannot vouch for those numbers, but this doesn't change the essence of the matter. Possibly even such a phrase was in fact uttered by Jodl, if not in the courtroom, then in the lobbies of the Nuremberg tribunal.

Is it proper to reproach the Soviet military commanders for letting slip the moment in 1940, given the ephemeral agreement with Hitler? It is not the military commanders that choose the time to strike. That's a decision for politicians. In 1940, this possibility didn't tempt Stalin. He needed *all* of Europe. Remain face to face with the Allies over a defeated Germany? This had already happened in 1918, and would be repeated again in 1945 – but at what an awful price!

The Second World War, given the disproportion of forces between the opposing powers with which it began, would not have resulted in such human losses, had the Allies struck Germany in the summer of 1939 or had the USSR attacked Germany in the summer of 1940. The Allies didn't do this because they feared the losses. Stalin didn't do it out of strategic considerations. Losses didn't perturb him. He was anticipating a positional struggle in the West, and didn't have time to re-orient his policy when France fell so quickly. He understood too late that his turn was next

23

Cadres and People

From Zhukov's memoirs:

> Towards the end of September 1940 the General Staff notified us that a conference of the top echelons of the Army Command would be held *on the instructions of the Central Committee of the Party* (author's emphasis, reminding the reader of Zhukov's barbed remark about the Tsarist Army, the brain of which was not the Central Committee nor even the Tsar, but the General Staff). I was to prepare to speak on the nature of modern offensive operations.

Gracious me – that was Triandafillov's subject!

A large-scale strategic war game was also planned, and Zhukov notes, albeit in passing, that all the material prepared by the General Staff for the game reflected the latest German combat operations in Europe. The war game itself was based upon a probable attack on the Soviet Union in the western frontier zone (Belorussia), and Zhukov was entrusted with handling the attacking "Blue" side (the Germans). The "Blue" side was to hurl 60 divisions into an offensive against over 50 defending "Red" divisions; Zhukov was, of course, supposed to lose. However, he won ...

Zhukov notes: "The game abounded in dramatic situations for the eastern side. They proved to be in many ways similar to what really happened after June 22, 1941, when Nazi Germany attacked the Soviet Union ...."

The meaningful ellipses at the end of the last statement are Zhukov's, not mine. When writing his memoirs, Zhukov knew that the "dramatic moments" had been foretold by Tukhachevsky in his false confession, known today as "Marshal Tukhachevsky's final testament." Perhaps, it was precisely this "final testament" (without referring to it by name) that was played out on the maps of the war game. That the game ended with the defeat of the "Red" forces, which were being handled by Colonel-General Pavlov[1], infuriated the Leader who was familiar with Tukhachevsky's testament. He was in a silent rage, and the silence of his fury was all the more dangerous. After the game, a number of the assembled commanders gave reports on the results; the sharpest remarks were given by General Rychagov, the Air Force Commander-in-Chief. These reports, which exposed the depth of the failures in re-equipping and training the armed forces added to Stalin's wrath. The Leader understood that he himself was responsible for the lost time. Incidentally, in his memoirs the Marshal says nothing about the causes of Stalin's anger; these are my own conjectures.

Tearing away from the Marshal's memoirs, we'll note that not only the reports, but

---

1   There is a suspicion that this portion of Zhukov's memoirs is not quite accurate. However by no means could Zhukov admit in his writings that it was not a defensive, but an offensive game being played at those maneuvers... I dare to suggest that the defensive alternative was also discussed – at least in lobby of the maneuvers.

P.V. Rychagov

also the on-the-spot remarks, went contrary to Zhukov's views, but were instructive to him, although he never recognized that he had ever learned anything from someone junior or even equal to him in rank. Due to his incomplete education he, like the overwhelming majority of Stalin's military leaders, had to learn at the expense of his soldiers' blood. At the risk of repeating myself, I will once again note the wrongfulness of reproaching Zhukov regarding the gaps in his education and the ignorance of his colleague-generals, who fought the war. It is not their fault that they wound up in high posts, for which they may have been unsuited.

The remark by Lieutenant General Romanenko, Commander of the 1st Mechanized Corps, became a menacing warning to the assembled generals. This student of Triandafillov's, who graduated from two military academies (including the prestigious Frunze Military Academy back in 1933, at the time it was flourishing), in essence gave a brief, critical lecture to the gathered commanders on the use of tanks in massed formations and the cooperation among different types of forces. Romanenko called attention to the vulnerability of tanks to attack from the air and their need for reliable cover as they moved toward their assembly areas. There were neither questions nor comments after his remarks. It was just another topic. What, though, could Romanenko do by himself? He would have been heard, had he been speaking to disciples of the massed use of tanks, to those who shared his views, who had already been repressed. However, in that case there would have been no need for his presentation. At the same time, Romanenko, a learned commander, who sparklingly played his part later in the Stalingrad offensive, would not have had to witness with horror, at a conference at the highest military level, while recently promoted generals zealously defended their institutional interests, but gave no thought at all about cooperation among the different types of forces, which would become decisive in the war.

Zhukov's presentation after the war game contained a mention about establishing cooperation between the tanks and aviation during the rear-area training sessions prior to the Khalkhin-Gol operation. However, at Khalkhin-Gol the air force covered the tanks only on the battlefield. This was before the campaign in the West began to thunder. No-one at the conference even began to discuss the need to cover tanks while on their march to the battlefield.

Romanenko had a reason to be agitated at the conference. In the summer of 1941, all attempts to parry the thrusts of the German panzer wedges with the numerically vastly superior Soviet tanks corps were disrupted by the German Luftwaffe. Thanks to the "sagacity" of Comrade Stalin, the Soviet Air Force was destroyed on the ground at its airfields in the very first hours of the war, while the German air force simply didn't allow the Soviet tank columns, deprived of their air cover, to reach the battlefield. It was possible to conduct marches only at night. Was the level of training of the tank crews of the time adequate for night marches, however?

After the analysis of the war game ended, Stalin summoned Zhukov and informed him that he was being appointed Chief of the General Staff in Meretskov's place. Meretskov was later arrested – amazingly, on 23 June 1941. The Boss had remembered that Meretskov had been Uborevich's Chief of Staff. Meretskov wasn't the only one arrested in that troubled June – many others of the very best were seized. Let's give the Leader his due: on the eve of the war, to accuse and imprison is an excellent way to shift the blame onto someone else's shoulders.

Zhukov continues: "I left for Kiev the same night, to be back in Moscow as soon as possible. To be frank, I was leaving with a heavy heart."

He had not forgotten his mood after the appointment even decades later. One should think so! The appointment was similar to the way Zhukov himself had handed them out at Khalkhin-Gol. Moreover he knew what was waiting for him in the action plan, and he'd always be under observation. Whose observation?! Likely, he would be the next candidate to take the fall. All the responsibility and none of the authority: the General Staff wasn't the brain of the Red Army!

Thinking about Zhukov's successful military career, eventually one can't help but think – especially after seeing the catastrophic course of the border battles at the start of the war – about Meretskov, his predecessor in the post of Chief of the General Staff.

Kirill Afanas'evich Meretskov completed the Academy of the RKKA in 1921, when the genuine lights of military science Svechin and Snesarev were teaching the military craft in its classrooms. After graduating and before his assignment to the post of Chief of Staff, Meretskov, a staff officer by calling, had spent time in more than one staff position, including Chief of Staff of the Special Far Eastern Army and Deputy Chief of Staff of the RKKA. Together with his chief Shaposhnikov, he had twice proposed to the Leader a plan of strategic deployment in case of an attack, based upon the expectations of the main blow landing where Tukhachevsky had been predicting (and where it indeed occurred). Both times the plan was rejected by Stalin, who wanted to concentrate forces on the southwestern axis, not the western axis: Stalin believed a quick strike into Romania and the seizure of its oil resources would instantly paralyze the German Army.

Zhukov, who'd been born to be a commander in the field, couldn't stand staff work. However, a powerful competitor, with the force of his temperament he subconsciously shouldered aside his closest rivals. His vigor enabled him to offer stiff competition to other commanders in any arena, even one in which Zhukov wasn't fully competent: after the devastation of the purge, he was the strongest personality left in the RKKA. It was for this aspect of his nature that Stalin indeed selected him for the post of Chief of General Staff. Zhukov had defeated Pavlov in the war game using the materials, which had been prepared by staff officers, including General Staff officer Bagramian (though Bagramian himself modestly says not a word about it in his memoirs), who of course was familiar with Tukhachevsky's "final testament". The next day, during the assessment of the war game, Zhukov capably analyzed his success. The victory of the "Blues" decided the fate of Meretskov, who by some miracle emerged alive from the torture chambers, deprived of his teeth and his ability to raise objections to the high command: A General of the Army and Hero of the Soviet Union in 1940!

Colonel-General Kirponos replaced Zhukov in the post of commander of the Kiev Special Military District. Entering his office at the District Headquarters, he reportedly made a slashing gesture across his throat and said "Just a division would be to handle right now." This is an honest acknowledgement of a military man, who was comparing himself with those who had taught him. Prior to 1939, Colonel Kirponos had been the superintendent at an infantry school, but he asked for a line command. His request was honored. For the actions of his 70th Rifle Division in the war with Finland, Kirponos earned the title of Hero and the rank of Major-General. Less than a year later, the division commander became the commander of a special military district.[2] Not a single other contemporary army witnessed such rapid career rises. In the Red Army of 1940, such careers trajectories were normal.

Captain Matykin, a battalion commander, was given command of a division, as was Captain Neskubo, the chief of a regimental school. Major Gusev, an aviation squadron commander, received command of an aviation division and was appointed commander of the Belorussian Military District's air force. Senior Lieutenant Kopets became a Colonel and was appointed deputy commander of the Leningrad Military District's air force. By the start of the war, he was now a general and commanding the Western Military District's air force. Having learned of the destruction of his air force as the aircraft stood parked at their airfields on 22 June 1941, Kopets couldn't withstand the shock and shot himself.

Then there's Budenny's orderly, V. I. Kniga, who withstood the shock and didn't shoot himself. As a reward for carrying out delicate orderly assignments, he was made a major general and wangled command of a cavalry division, which he unhesitatingly hurled with their sword blades against German armor. He wasn't punished for the death of 17,000 men along with their steeds, since "he didn't deliberate; he carried out."

We'll return to Kirponos, when the situation on the Southwestern Front becomes inextricably complicated.

So, a half-year before the outbreak of the war, on 31 January 1941, General of the Army Zhukov assumed command of the General Staff of the RKKA. Yet there were Marshals

---

2   Marshal Rokossovsky, a reliable source of information, who in 1941 was a subordinate to Kirponos, said about the commander: "I was utterly surprised by his striking bewilderment … There was the impression that he either didn't know the situation, or he didn't want to know it. In these minutes I definitively concluded that this was not the man for such enormous, complex and crucial responsibilities, and that a bad fate awaited the troops entrusted to him." It is a pity that Rokossovsky didn't see other commanders in similar circumstances, and couldn't leave his impressions of them with us.

above him: Voroshilov, Timoshenko, Budenny, the broken Shaposhnikov and a certain Kulik. We small-fry knew each and all of the Marshals. We remembered by heart all their Orders and medals. We just didn't know what each one was worth.

There remained 141 days until the start of the war.

24

The Wise Strategist Comrade Stalin ...

... had brought his USSR to the most dramatic moment of Soviet history. However, it began not on 31 January 1941. It began immediately upon the signing of the Molotov-von Ribbentrop Non-Aggression Pact, the secret protocols to which I present below:

Secret Additional Protocols

On the occasion of the signature of the Non-Aggression Pact between the German Reich and the Union of Soviet Socialist Republics, the undersigned plenipotentiaries of each of the two parties discussed *in strictly confidential conversations* the question of the boundary of their respective spheres of influence in Eastern Europe. These conversations led to the following conclusions:

1. In the event of a territorial and political rearrangement in the areas belonging to the Baltic States (Finland, Estonia, Latvia, Lithuania), the northern boundary of Lithuania shall represent the boundary of the spheres of influence of Germany and the USSR. In this connection the interest of Lithuania in the Vilna area is recognized by both sides.

2. In the event of a territorial and political rearrangement of the areas belonging to the Polish state, the spheres of Germany and the USSR shall be bounded approximately by the line of the rivers Narev, Vistula and Stan.

The question of whether the interests of both parties' makes desirable the maintenance of an independent Polish state and how such a state should be bounded can only be definitely determined in the course of further political developments.

In any event both Governments will resolve this question by means of a friendly agreement.

With regard to Southeastern Europe, the Soviet side calls attention to its interes in Bessarabia. The German side declares its complete political disinterest in the area.

This protocol shall be treated by both parties *as strictly secret*. (! – author)

Moscow, 23 August 1939

For the Government of the German Reich – (signature) Ribbentrop

Plenipotentiary of the Government of the USSR – (signature) Molotov[1]

The way Finland wound up in the list – with an absurd boundary with northern Lithuania – it is as if blind men were looking at the map! A month later, the two governments refined the respective spheres of influence of the two countries in addenda to the secret protocols:

---

1   Editor's note: English translations of this and the other documents of the German Foreign Service cited in this chapter can be found on the Internet as part of Yale Law School's Lillian Goldman Law Library's Avalon Project at the following web address: http://avalon.law.yale.edu/subject_menus/nazsov.asp (as of 10 January 2010).

Secret Supplementary Protocol

The undersigned plenipotentiaries declare the agreement of the Government of the German Reich and the Government of the USSR upon the following:

The Secret Supplementary Protocol signed on 23 August 1939 shall be amended in Item 1 to the effect that the territory of the Lithuanian State falls to the sphere of influence of the USSR, while, on the other hand, the province of Lublin and parts of the province of Warsaw fall to the sphere of influence of Germany ... the present German-Lithuanian border, for the purpose of a natural and simple boundary delineation, shall be rectified in such a way that the Lithuanian territory situated to the southwest of the line marked on the attached map should fall to Germany. ...

28 September 1939, Molotov Ribbentrop

Secret Supplementary Protocol

The undersigned plenipotentiaries (the same intrepid fellows Molotov and Ribbentrop; only one of them was eventually hung ... the author) on concluding the German-Russian Boundary and Friendship Treaty have declared agreement upon the following:

Both parties will tolerate in their territories no Polish agitation which affects the territories of the other party. They will suppress in their territories all beginnings of such agitation and inform each other concerning suitable measures for this purpose.

28 August 1939 ...

At Katyn, the Soviet government was so zealous in liquidating the beginnings of Polish agitation in the form of captured Polish officers! Did it inform the German government, out of its touching friendship with it, about this action? Or did it perpetrate Katyn at its own initiative, as a pleasant surprise for its dear ally? However, it was Stalin who had no need for the Polish officers ...

Even the above amendments didn't stop the two sides from making further adjustments. On 10 January 1941, People's Commissar of Foreign Affairs Molotov and the German ambassador to the Soviet Union Count von der Schulenburg agreed to remake the secret protocols from the beginning. Germany dropped all claims over that part of Lithuania, which had been specified in the Protocol of 28 September 1939. Not without compensation, of course, but for $7,500,000 worth of gold. The Soviet side would pay part of this sum in the shining metal in the course of three months from the signing of the new Protocol, the rest "... by means of a deduction in the German payments of gold, which Germany has to produce *before 11 February 1941* (emphasis the author's)."

Therefore, it seems, significant benefits in raw materials had to be going to the German side, if $7,500,000, not a trifling sum at the time, represented only a portion of the German payments, which had to be counted out within a month! However, even this is just an introduction. The main tale lies ahead. Which one? The Tale of the White Calf.[2]

---

2   Editor's note: This is a joke in the Russian language. The Tale of the White Calf is essentially a tale that never ends, in no small part because it never really begins: "Do you want me to tell you the Tale of the White Calf?" "Go ahead." So I'm saying, that you're saying, that you want me to tell you the Tale of the White Calf?" "Tell me." So you're telling me to tell you what you're going to get, and that's a tale about a white calf. Shall I tell it to you?" etc. Mezhiritsky's point here is that to begin to talk about Stalin's mistakes and crimes leads to a potentially endless tale, because they were so numerous.

As discussed above, immediately after concluding the Non-Aggression Pact with Germany, the voracious Comrade Stalin, whose cerebral abilities were always overestimated, lashed out at his neighbors, provoking their – and not only their – hatred and fear. Finland stood first on the list – and she was attacked first. This campaign placed the Red Army in a highly unflattering light, and served as a stimulus to Hitler in favor of the soonest possible invasion of the USSR. The helpless floundering in the Finnish snows encouraged a war against a giant, which had fought so awkwardly against a runt.

Next the calendar of acquisitions of the year 1940, even in the gentle terminology of Soviet ideology, acquired a feverish appearance:

12 March – the signing of the Soviet-Finnish peace agreement;

15-17 June – the overthrow of the *fascist dictatorship* in Lithuania and the re-establishment of Soviet authority;

20 June – the overthrow of the *fascist dictatorship* in Latvia and the re-establishment of Soviet authority;

21 June – the overthrow of the *fascist dictatorship* in Estonia and the re-establishment of Soviet authority;

Fascist? Dictatorship? Rubbish! These were republics. "Re-establishment" ... just when had there been Soviet authority there? Tsarist, yes, but Soviet?

Let us not forget the simultaneous step in Soviet military preparations – the 7 May decree of the USSR Presidium of the Supreme Soviet about the restoration of generals' and admirals' ranks for the higher command of the Army and Navy. (Here, Zhukov became a General of the Army, leaping over many of his peers.)

22 June – France capitulates to Germany

23 June -- ...

Let's take a break and return to the documents.

Ambassador Schulenburg to the German Foreign Office, 23 June 1940
Telegram
VERY URGENT
Molotov made the following statement to me today: The solution of the Bessarabian question brooked no further delay. The Soviet Government was still striving for a peaceful solution, but it was determined to use force, should the Rumanian Government decline a peaceful agreement. The Soviet claim likewise extended to Bucovina, which had a Ukrainian population...

I stated to Molotov that this decision of the Soviet Government had not been expected by me. I had been of the opinion that the Soviet Government would maintain its claims to Bessarabia – not contested by us – but would not itself take the initiative toward their realization. I feared that difficulties in the foreign relations of Rumania, which was at present supplying us with very large amounts of essential military and civilian raw materials, would lead to a serious encroachment on German interests.

Ambassador Schulenburg to Ribbentrop, 26 June 1940
VERY URGENT
For the Reich Foreign Minister personally.
Molotov summoned me this afternoon and declared that the Soviet Government ... had decided to limit its demands to the northern part of Bucovina and the city of

Czernowitz.

Regarding further treatment of the matter Molotov has the following idea: The Soviet Government will submit its demand to the Rumanian Minister here within the next few days and expects the German Reich Government at the same time urgently to advise the Rumanian Government in Bucharest to comply with the Soviet demands, since war would otherwise be unavoidable ...

Ambassador Schulenburg to the German Foreign Office, 27 June 1940
Telegram
VERY URGENT
Molotov just informed me by telephone that he had summoned the Rumanian Minister at 10 o'clock this evening, had informed him of the Soviet Government's demand regarding the cession of Bessarabia and the northern part of Bucovina, and had demanded a reply from the Rumanian Government not later than tomorrow, i. e., on July [June] 27.

Ribbentrop to Counselor Shmidt, 27 June 1940
The following instructions must be immediately transmitted over the telephone in open text (! – author) to Envoy Fabritsius:
"You are instructed to visit the Minister of Foreign Affairs immediately and inform him of the following:
'The Soviet government has informed us that it is demanding the transfer of Bessarabia and the northern part of Bucovina to the USSR from the Romanian government. In the avoidance of war between Romania and the Soviet Union we can only advise the Romanian government to yield to the demands of the Soviet government ...'

France had fallen, but England continued to fight with unshakeable resolve. The war in the west was continuing, and Hitler's hands were tied. So, in your opinion, my reader, who was asking for trouble here? And how transparent are the threats (not addressed toward Romania!) contained in Ribbentrop's instruction to Counselor Shmidt?

The acquisitions continued:

28 June – the return (!!) of Bessarabia and Northern Bucovina by Romania to the Soviet Union.

That explains why the "large-scale field exercise with signals communications support" of the command staff of the Kiev Special Military District in the area of Ternopol' and L'vov had taken place. That's what the maneuvers on the northern borders of Bucovina signified. Still one more planned coincidental occurrence ...

Ahead lay the effective assault on the border of Romania. With that – Hurrrrrrah! We had now turned the enemy's gaze toward us!

On 22 July Hitler demanded, and on 27 July received the first draft of a plan for a preventative war against the USSR. On 31 July he announced his intentions to his immediate circle. The plan subsequently became called "Barbarossa".

LONG LIVE THE WISE LEADER COMRADE STALIN!

25

Great Expectations

As is befitting on the eve of great events, Zhukov draws up the balance of forces that existed prior to Barbarossa. The reliability of Soviet statistics is doubtful. Only the following statement by Zhukov carries weight historically: "Recalling what we military leaders had demanded of industry in the last few months of peace, I can see that we did not always take full stock of the country's economic possibilities. Although, perhaps, from our departmental point of view, so to speak, we were right."

Indeed, they were right. However, industry is equal to tasks of such magnitude, only when the economy has been totally mobilized for war. These are tasks resulting from extraordinary circumstances.

Given the impressive demonstration of the *Wehrmacht's* power, and the Red Army's own pitiful travails in Finland in comparison, it was natural to expect more restraint in Soviet foreign policy, or at least a suppression of appetite. Alas, this didn't happen. In November 1940, People's Commissar of Foreign Affairs Molotov made a visit to Berlin. One of the gravest failures in the history of diplomacy was regarded by the Soviet side as a triumph.

Hitler's stomach was still turning over (an expression, probably, favored by the Führer even before it became known in connection with the forthcoming Kursk operation in 1943) with the thought of war with the Soviet Union. No matter how much he was declaring his hatred for the USSR in comparison with the British, he was nevertheless currently embroiled in a war with England. However, while waging war against it, he was also sounding it out. Rumors about the island country's difficult situation, about the population's dejection under the terror campaign from the sky, about the plausible possibility of the replacement of Churchill's cabinet by a different one with a more pro-German tilt nevertheless did not lead to the establishment of contacts with the British government even through Hess's audacious flight and did not eliminate the concerns regarding the British walnut and its suitability for launching a landing on the Continent. Gazing at the maps and comparing the dimensions of England and the USSR, it is possible to understand the Führer's hesitations.

For some reason it is considered that the invitation for Molotov to come to Berlin was just a show, that the decision to invade had already been made, and that Hitler was putting on an act designed to lull Stalin's vigilance. However, if Hitler's proposals at the meeting are judged against Stalin's counter-proposals, one must come to a different conclusion: the sides were not in agreement. This has been clearly demonstrated in Lev Bezymensky's superb book *Gitler i Stalin pered skhvatkoi* [*Hitler and Stalin before the struggle*].

Hitler offered Stalin participation in the Axis bloc, and not the partitioning of Europe, but a partitioning of the world, with one condition: that Stalin make no effort to strive to the west or southwest. The south (Iran, India) was open to him. Stalin could reach an agreement with a potential Axis ally, Japan, over the carving-up of Asia. Hitler's desire was obvious through the efforts of the Soviet Union to penetrate into India and get rid of the British Commonwealth. Meanwhile, he would tackle Great Britain and liquidate that bridgehead, which gave the Americans the opportunity at any moment to intervene in European affairs. However, a Führer directive dated 12 November 1940, the day of Molotov's arrival in Berlin, ordered that all preparations in the East be continued, independently of the results of the negotiations. The Führer wasn't expecting much from the talks.

However, the results proved to be even paltrier. Stalin, plainly, still assumed that Hitler was elated by the Non-Aggression Pact and valued it highly. He was at war with Great Britain, a powerful foe, and the Berlin talks were held in a bomb shelter, while British were pounding Berlin. It was the proper time to put forward demands! Hitler had nowhere to turn, and was in no position to fight a two-front war! (These assumptions were the starting point for Stalin's diplomacy ...)

So Molotov, following instructions, presented demands from the Soviet side and made no effort even to hide the fact (though he should have!) that these were not his, Molotov's, preliminary blueprints, but the desire of Stalin himself, and that Stalin in fact was speaking through him.

So it became clear to Hitler that:

(a) the USSR would not take part in a war against England, but wished Germany success;

(b) the USSR was not against dividing up the British Empire and, so to speak, would be grateful for the access to the Indian Ocean in the area of the Persian Gulf, but

(c) ... also wanted control over Spitsbergen (and its iron ore!) and the straits of the Bosporus and Dardanelles, and was demanding (!?) the withdrawal of German forces from Bulgaria (yes!) and Romania (oil!).

Russia, traditionally strong in diplomacy, had gone wrong only under Nicholas I, in the episode that led to the Crimean War: imperial fantasy won out over common sense. If Stalin's demands aren't the apotheosis of imperial whim, then the reader will have to rake his or her memory for another example that befits both Stalin's demands and failure. Hitler's invitation to join the Axis was, of course, an attempt to bury the USSR with its own hands. However, if Stalin was striving to delay the outbreak of war, wasn't there really some other tactic than issuing counter demands? Wouldn't it have been more sensible to stall for time and preserve Hitler's hopes for Russia to join the Axis? British bombers indeed were striking Berlin. Hitler urgently needed both Soviet divisions and Soviet petroleum.

The writer ought not to adopt a didactic tone, and Western authors easily avoid this. We, though, who have been beaten down by censorship, are destined to engage in fervent polemics, offending against notions of style. I have invoked this confession to soften the following sermon:

History must be clear. It is unseemly to hide it behind pseudo-scientific phrases. Its lesson here is that long before 22 June 1941, an aggressive Stalinist state with its maneuvers and threats brought on a diplomatic war, gathering what seemed to it to be the important crumbs from the table of a war-waging, aggressive Nazi state. Obscuring this with phrases about a peace-loving Soviet people transposes responsibility from the Leader to the people, as if the law-abiding citizens of the USSR (or Germany), conscripted into the army or recruited to work for the war effort, had any free will and could direct events according to their own beliefs. The regime is responsible for poisoning the children with propaganda.

Heroes, who chose a path of resistance, have been noted by history.[1] However, the historian dare not ignore the restrictions on the freedom of citizens under totalitarian regimes and, correspondingly, the insignificance of their influence on the course of history. Arguments about the role of the personality have no clear end, but it looks like history is fated to remain a collection of biographies of the worst representatives of Homo sapiens. These Herostratuses, concerned only with the immortalization of their own names, provoke outbursts of warfare, which otherwise given the xenophobia inherent among peoples and nations would peacefully smolder among them for another thousand years.

Although the following conclusion goes beyond the boundaries of this theme, I will note that the Soviet regime, which in general was not favorable to mankind, complicated its fate even more by concealing Stalin's machinations. Had it formally acknowledged the existence of the Secret Protocols to the Non-Aggression Pact after Stalin's death or at least after the CPSU's 1956 XX Party Congress, where Stalin's "cult of personality" was denounced, the attitude of the West toward the USSR could have been much warmer, and the picture of the contemporary world much more secure.

By the way, it was precisely on the concealment of the Protocols that indeed the Leader's apologists made a comeback. In their opinion, the revelation of the Secret Protocols didn't in the least tarnish Stalin; on the contrary, it rehabilitated him. You see, he wasn't a simpleton! He just stole a march on Hitler. The devil-may-care admirers even designated a precise date, 6 July, in order to convince others.

Western historians, with whom I've had the honor and pleasure to communicate, don't take such blather seriously – which indeed allows some people to this very day to speculate successfully with their revisionist books, and historians don't bother to dignify them with refutations. That's a pity. Every person must earn their keep, and I'm not against the fact that some successful hucksters built their prosperity on the editions of their books. However, the absence of a rebuff to their deceptive arguments keeps alive legends about the wisdom and omniscience of the Leader.

Of course, not all plans are itemized in meeting minutes. On his preparations for the campaign in the East, Hitler also gave at first only verbal instructions. However, as the plan developed, papers were generated. Such measures as an offensive by one enormous country against another – well, you just can't get by without papers; without piles of papers. The forces must be supplied with written instructions, without which they'll mix up both the their designated staging areas and their march routes, and this will create a real muddle, in comparison with which the Soviet defensive mess of 1941 will look like an orderly handling of the fighting (which, to our surprise, did to a significant degree exist, but about this later).

The ardent desire of some writers to rehabilitate Stalin is revealed by a reference to a concrete date, which can only be verified from paper documents. The absence of supporting documents[2] scatters their assertions just as easily as an ocean wave washes away children's

---

1   Historians have done much to preserve the memories of Resistance heroes, but so far remain in hopeless debt with respect to those who weren't even conscious of their heroic act. I am speaking of those Soviet military prisoners who died in the camps, having refused to cooperate with the Nazis – the most long-suffering group, in numbers comparable only to the victims of the Holocaust.

2   If the absence in the archives in the Ministry of Defense of at least some supporting documents doesn't convince the followers of Suvorov that there were not any prepared plans for an immediate invasion of the Reich, then let them give a thought to at least this: With a developed network of railroads and highways and the excellent mechanization of the *Wehrmacht*, the preparation for the invasion of the USSR began with the transfer of forces over a period of six months prior to the attack. With the condition of the road

sand castles. However, although the legend of '6 July' has been dispelled, the inadvertent service of its adherents in exposing Stalin should be noted. In his time V. Suvorov loudly proclaimed (with sensational aims in mind, of course) as news something that was at the time only the property of scholars – Stalin's aggressiveness and the wait-and-see character of his foreign policy: Let the West exhaust itself with a war, like the First World War! The blatancy and mass circulation of Suvorov's books did something that the dry and small editions of scholarly research could never do – their scandalous tone focused attention on the pre-war period and made it a subject of fervent study by many. The bitter arguments between Stalin's supporters and opponents over this slender hypothesis, which had been promoted to a truth, attracted so many readers that it made the history a topic of mass interest.

The confidence in an unavoidable, prolonged trench war in the West became a fatal miscalculation of Stalin, even though the *Blitzkrieg* campaign of 1940 in France directly followed the similar 1939 campaign in Poland. However, Stalin wasn't interested in the military side of matters; he only grasped the political, or more accurately, the geographical – the change of boundaries. He couldn't see any farther than this. The denseness of the Leader, who understood nothing of the patient explanations of his army commanders, or of Tukhachevsky's "final testament", or even of the campaign lessons on the fields of Flanders and France in the summer of 1940, is beyond belief. Yet how hard his generals had tried to make him understand that aviation and tanks were fundamentally altering the nature of combat operations ...

"Fatal miscalculation" is not a misstatement. Personally for Stalin, the blunder wasn't such. Whereas the tens of millions of those who fell in the war, bailing out the regime with their lives – how tragically these losses affected Russia's demographic profile and its present-day fate.

Thus, if one is to call it wise, or at least shrewd, then with the fall of France, Stalin had to encourage his powerful neighbor to launch an invasion of England, without raising any suspicions. The French roll of the dice had failed – now it was England's turn. The Potentate, not bound by any morals or opposition, should have turned all his efforts to helping his fearsome friend Hitler get tangled in a new campaign, one which would inevitably draw in America. And then ...!

However, if the avarice of the Potentate is so plainly visible, what sort of politician is he? The seizure of Bessarabia and his plain interest in Romania alarmed the Führer. It is amusing that Stalin has earned a reputation as a cautious politician. I believe that the assessment of his political skills will be re-examined, just as was his genius, but this will still take a lot of time. Hitler, on the other hand, a Western diplomat, set the hook into Stalin via Molotov with a tempting lure. I don't know what talents the composer Skriabin's nephew possessed.[3] Sagacity, if it indeed was part of the family line, must have passed backwards, from the future to the past. As the Berlin talks were coming to a conclusion, Hitler, hiding

---

network in the USSR, the meagerness of the Red Army's motor vehicle park and the incredible load on the railroads, when could it have really been possible to mass forces on the border for an attack upon Germany, when the shift of armies to the western regions began in April? What would have been the condition of the Red Army's formations after marching to the border frontiers on foot?

3   Editor's note: Because Molotov was born as Viacheslav Mikhailovich Skriabin, it has been asserted that he was the famous composer's nephew, or at least some other distant relation. There is no strong evidence to this, however, although as a young boy Viacheslav played a lot of music with his violin, mainly Beethoven's quartets, together with his brothers.

his disappointment, escorted Molotov to the massive doors of the Imperial Chancellery, and affably gripping his hand, pronounced: "History will remember Stalin's name forever. I believe it will remember mine too. Therefore it is natural that two such political figures, as we are, would meet. I ask you, Mister Molotov, to pass my greetings to Mister Stalin and my expectations for such a meeting in the near future."

An excellent move! Molotov carried this flattering remark back to Moscow, like a torte, and in the future the Leader would lull himself with it: he was too great a personage for Hitler to start a war without meeting with him first. So he waited, while not proposing a meeting in return: Could the Sardar, the Eastern Grandee, really be first to offer? The little Hitler would make the request! However, the little Hitler didn't request, and continuing to smile at the Soviet emissary, confirmed the plan for Operation Barbarossa on 18 December 1940. Stalin came to know about this. Moreover, German exports to the Soviet Union halted. A cold wind began to blow ...

The XVII Communist Party Conference was convened. It lasted from 15 to 20 February 1941 and confirmed the draconian disciplinary measures in industry and transportation. Workers were practically nailed to their factories. The task was to increase sharply the volume of shipments, and sharply (everything sharply!) to boost the pace of industrialization beyond the Ural Mountains. The volume of military production in 1941 in comparison with 1940 was to rise by 16 to 18 percent.

This was sheer voluntarism.[4] What wasn't voluntarism, though? The strangling of the New Economic Policies? Industrialization with over fulfillment of plan norms on paper? The horror of collectivization? The liquidation of the best people? The strategic adventurism?

The very convening of the XVII Party Conference, when the *Wehrmacht* had already begun to gather its forces to the Soviet borders, testified to Stalin's agitation. The hysteria around industrialization and transportation aimed for a total mobilization of resources – organizational, industrial and labor. The country was now urgently and frantically preparing for war!

For external consumption, Stalin made a pointless maneuver and expelled "anti-Germans" from the Central Committee: Litvinov, Likhachev and Vannikov. These were human sacrifices. Likhachev was the legendary Ivan Alekseevich Likhachev, the creator and director of a Moscow automobile factory that would later bear his name, while Vannikov was Boris L'vovich Vannikov, who later became the People's Commissar for Ammunition, thrice Hero of the Socialist Labor, and father of the Soviet atomic and hydrogen bombs. Chekists beat a confession out of him, of course, but later threw him back to his work office, desk and telephones immediately after the start of the war, and without any explanations: he was much needed.

Of course, economic administrators fell into disfavor not over their possible anti-German sentiments (in their posts, their sympathies and antipathies had no bearing on anything), but as opponents of the dictated timetable for war readiness. Stalin demanded that the country be ready by the winter of 1942. Vannikov and Likhachev advocated by the winter of 1943 (Back in 1937, when Hitler had revealed his plans to his generals, Blomberg and Fritsch had argued that Germany still wouldn't be ready for a full-scale war by 1944) ....

Events were overtaking the leaders and dragging them along in their wake. Iakir at the Kiev maneuvers had said in a speech before the troops, "We must win two or three years ..."

4　This was a frequently-made charge against "wreckers" and other loose cannons in the Soviet regime.

He, the organizer of the assembly line method for producing tanks in the country, knew the difficulties in manufacturing and moved realistically, step by step. Now these years had passed. The years 1937-1939 had been spent executing those, who had gained that time.

The country was lacking administrators. Anyone smart enough preferred to remain invisible and left the apparatus. Tsezar' Kunikov, the future leading light of Soviet naval infantry, left the People's Commissariat of Machine-building, where he was the head of the Technological Department in 1937. The People's Commissariat of Machine-building was later divided into three commissariats – ship-building, medium, and heavy machine-building. Direct the policy of such a Leviathan given the jostling on the career ladder and the voluntarism of the Leader? Kunikov went into science, and from scratch created the Central Scientific Research Institute of Technology and Machine-Building, which today flourishes (without mentioning the founder's name, of course) as the Scientific Research Institute of Standardization and Certification in Machine-building. From there he went into mass media, where he became the editor of two central publications. However, war was breaking out, and the People's Commissar of Ammunition Goremykin requested Kunikov as his deputy. A plum position in a time of war – the Deputy People's Commissar of Ammunition! "What kind of People's Commissar of Ammunition can you make from me? I've never smelled gunpowder!" The formula had been found. Kunikov strayed from his path and departed for the front, where in fact he was killed – not before, incidentally, he had gained fame.[5]

In a word, the composition of the Central Committee at the XVII Party Conference was changed not because of old members' lack of confidence in the prospects for German-Soviet relations – no one, other than Litvinov, expressed this skepticism aloud – but because of their disbelief regarding the feasibility of carrying out such enormous tasks in the amount of time given to complete them.

Then the fate of aviators was decided as well, those who opposed the accelerated training of pilots[6] (and the fate of the pilots too; the Soviet ace Pokryshkin downed 59 enemy aircraft, while the German ace Erich Hartmann shot down 352 ...). To Lieutenant Generals of Aviation Arzhenukhin, Rychagov, Ptukhin, Proskurov, Pumpur and Smushkevich (the latter four were Heroes of the Soviet Union, while Smushkevich was a twice-Hero before

---

5   "We, though, whose wool is being sheared, will be satisfied people with the socialism of trashy booklets and a monument in the 30th century" – Kunikov wrote this in 1929 in some ironic verses on his twentieth birthday. He in time understood that he had to leave prominent posts and courageously, skillfully and actively defended himself and his colleagues of the press agencies, knowing that the arrest of any one of them would also sweep him away. M. Kusil'man passed along these facts about Kunikov to me. However, to write about them in that time was impossible, while now they are uninteresting. From the words of N. V. Sidorova, Kunikov's wife, in the First Edition of this book it was said that Vannikov was the one who requested Kunikov as his Deputy People's Commissar. However, Vannikov replaced Goremykin as the People's Commissar of Ammunition already during the war. I believe that the demand to return Kunikov from the front came from both one and the other repeatedly. I am again mentioning Kunikov because he literally fought with a little blood, even at Malaia Zemlia, the bridgehead created by his marines near Novorosiisk. After the purges, however, how many commanders remained, who were ready to set themselves up to take the fall, in order not to lose valuable human material? Among the Marshals, there was only Tolbukhin.

6   Mystery is still surrounds the question of the situation with the Soviet aviation. Despite terrible losses in the first hours of the war, thousands of aircrafts, including the most modern, were available on remote airfields. What about the pilots for them, though? There is something strange in the passivity of Soviet aviation in these first months of the war, as if the pilots were not entrusted to fly ...

the war!) it was not credible that they could lose their heads over their unwillingness to push students hastily through flight training simply to graduate targets for the vultures of the Luftwaffe. Stalin, though, was too busy to teach the Generals morals. Substantive people were opposing him over the matter, this he knew. He hated them because they were right. He had neither the time nor the desire to change their minds. It was simpler to kill them.[7]

---

7   The massacre of the Generals of Aviation illustrates the general principle of the purge. The composition of the aviators was the most homogenous. Almost all the aviation commanders of the military districts and the deputies of the Commander-in-Chief of the Soviet Air Force were peers, young men (their Commander-in-Chief, Rygachov, the youngest, was not even 30 years of age), aviation fanatics, and friends who knew each other through and through. To them, daredevils like almost all pilots were back then and far removed from politics, there was no reason to suspect that one of them might be a traitor or foreign agent. If that's the way it was, then they were all executed, so as to not leave any witnesses to the crime, or even any potential avengers for their friends. The method of wiping out the entire nest ... The chief of the Red Army Air Force's Command and Navigation Staff Academy Arzhenukhin, Heroes of the Soviet Union Proskurov and Rychagov, twice-Hero of the Soviet Union Smushkevich (a combat comrade of Zhukov's at Khalkhin-Gol and an assistant to the Chief of Staff for Aviation of the Red Army's General Staff) were all shot without trial already after the war had started. The repressions in the Air Force still await its researcher. He or she will have to describe the horrifyingly inadequate ground facilities and equipment of the airfields and their auxiliary services not only for active units during the war, but also for training units. The Leader targeted the aviation commanders to express his dissatisfaction with the country's general backwardness.

26

Politics and Morality, Genius and Villainy

To the global community, Stalin's aggressiveness was no secret. Responding to the Opposition's partisan questions about the slow pace of negotiations with the USSR on the eve of the decisive events of 1939, Chamberlain said: "We don't intend to purchase peace at the cost of such concessions, which will lead to further demands."

Let's mark these words. This is recognition of the miscalculation at Munich: the scoundrel Hitler had deceived the gentleman Chamberlain, when he had announced that the Sudeten problem was Germany's final territorial claim. However, this statement is also an allusion to the USSR's claims. Finland, the Baltic States, Romania and Turkey were apprehensive about any pact between the USSR and the other great powers, knowing that it could be achieved at the expense of their interests. Chamberlain indeed explained to Parliament in all gentility: "Having obtained cooperation with one country, it is necessary at the same time not to push away other countries. Therefore certain difficulties are being encountered in the matter of concluding an agreement with the USSR."

The Secret Protocols to the Hitler-Stalin Non-Aggression Pact (as it should be called in order to separate both the German and Soviet people from it) make clear what sort of difficulties were being met by the British government in its talks with the USSR. Stalin was expecting similar protocols from England, although the British attitude toward such business had already been expressed on the eve of the First World War by the then Minister of Foreign Affairs, Edward Gray: "Great Britain would consider participation in such transactions an eternal shame to itself."[1] However, not everyone adheres to such strict moral norms. It is hardly believable that Stalin knew the statement by Sir Gray, but the Leader didn't consider *such transactions* to be a shame.

While gathering materials for my book about Kunikov,[2] I began to realize that immediately after signing the "Pact with the Devil", the USSR began feverishly preparing for war. This became clear in bits and pieces – from people who were occupying prominent posts before the war, from my senior colleagues, and from publications that slipped through censorship, like the memoirs of Vannikov that was known back then only from excerpts in

---

1   Chamberlain's statement was quoted in *Istoriia diplomatii* [*History of Diplomacy*], Vol. 3, which was published in 1945 immediately after the victory. The book cites no rejoinders to Chamberlain on the matter of certain difficulties in coming to an agreement with the USSR. The box on the ear was taken silently. Citing such a political maxim at that time without any commentary appears to be a heroic deed, and could be one of the reasons for the practically complete destruction of the edition in the publishing warehouses. However, the book generated such little trust in its contents that there were few who actually read it. It was sufficient for the reader of those times to see among the authors the names of Pankratova or Tarle in order to stop believing in the truth, which these authors were trying to express as far as they prudently could (in view of the danger to themselves). Perhaps it was following this substantial work on Soviet diplomacy that the famous Cold War document "*Fal'sifikatory istorii*" ["Falsifiers of history"] was created – it seems, by the very same authors. You see, as has already been noted, in order to falsify history, one must know it well.

2   P. Ia. Mezhiritsky, *Tovarishch Maior* [*Comrade Major*] (Moscow: Politizdat, 1975).

magazines. Stalin did not succeed in making up for the time lost while wiping out the army commanders. The Dispatcher of Evil dedicated three years to the destruction of potential opposition. Where was the time to think about managing the country, about strategy and tactics? (Do historians consider this factor – the time lost by any ruler while strengthening his personal power at the expense of national security?) Now he was nervous and hurrying.

I must confess that, indeed like all of the citizens of the USSR, I was unwilling to acknowledge these facts. Our unwillingness to accept them was caused by the "treacherous invasion". We children suffered through a monstrous war along with the adults, sharing their losses and incurring our own, and had no wish to part from the position that our country was not an aggressive country; it was psychologically comforting. Pity the Germans, they were in ruins, just as we were, but they were the guilty ones. It was *their* Hitler that had started the war.

Their Hitler and *his* initiation of the war; this remained for us a reproach to those who had never bothered to vote, or who had failed to cast their ballots for the right candidate. (Well, how one might know for whom to vote at a critical moment ...) However, is it appropriate to speak about treachery, when in both countries men with criminal minds had risen to power? Both leaders were waiting for a moment to launch a stealthy attack. Hitler's *Mein Kampf* loudly and audibly spoke about the psychological preparation of the Germans. The Soviet side was more restrained; however, the verse *Odnopolchane* [*Brother Soldiers*] by Konstantin Simonov, one of the most ideologically perceptive authors of the era, had been published:

> And we shall use an empty food-can
> To scoop up water for a friend
> And wrap a spare puttee around him
> To help his wounded leg mend.
> At Konigsberg one early morning
> We both shall fall, two wounded men
> And then a month in the hospital
> And we'll survive, and be back again.

At Konigsberg! If the reference to this German city seems strange to someone, just glance at the date of the poem's publication: 1938! Prior to Khalkhin-Gol!

However, ideology was just an intention, but reality had resisted. So then the Leader's malice fell upon the administrators and managers for their stubborn conviction that the USSR could be ready for war no earlier than the winter of 1943.

Who and when has anyone begun a war fully prepared? Hitler hadn't been ready, but this did not prevent him from starting one. What could be expected of Stalin?

The author of the "6 July 1941" scenario explains the tragedy of 22 June 1941 by offering a tale about Stalin's preemptive strike (Stalin was just a bit late, by a matter of days!) and in a rage of epiphany compares the states to bandit gangs, and their heads of state to chieftains. Lo and behold, one of them, Stalin, conceived a genius combination, adequate to bury all the other criminal gangs: Let those in the West fight themselves to exhaustion, and then we'll take them from behind – One! Two! ...

We'll assume that it never occurred to someone that "genius and villainy are two incompatible things", while *genius combinations* are more frightening than comets.

Civilization is not a collection of bandit states. If it was, peace indeed would collapse when bandits with the mindsets of cave-dwellers come to power. Agreements with secret protocols are a trampling of the principles, upon which peace rests. This is a card game between criminals, with the lives of the citizens of their countries as the stakes.

However, in 1941, the reaching of a decision to beat Hitler to the punch didn't require the trampling of moral principles. It is not reprehensible to preempt an enemy, who is coiled to strike. One even wants to believe these tales. In the end, knowing how frequently deadlines for start-ups and completions were delayed (or if it was so directed, accelerated), it is possible to assume that Stalin, convinced in the seriousness of Hitler's intentions, was preparing a preventive, super-urgent attack of his own. Let's make that assumption. However, where is the evidence of a planned attack? Whether or not the documents and papers for one were there, where was the attack? Was Stalin running late? Did he blunder? All that on top of the villainies, conceived for his personal safekeeping? When it came to his own security, he never miscalculated, he was always on time; he killed with no hesitation, well in advance! On time in that case, yet late now? The only time when the situation truly rushed him? A blunder at the expense of the people?

That's it, enough of the lies. "Just a bit late" doesn't matter. The amount of time spent on strengthening his personal security at the cost to the nation's security must be considered. He couldn't miscalculate. He had to win.

He did win, it is true. At what cost, however?

We don't know what might have been. We know what was. Zhukov had proposed a pre-emptive attack, but at the end of his life he let slip that things would have been even worse had they done so. Once the war was underway, there was an attempt to get the jump on a *Wehrmacht* that was prepared to attack, at Khar'kov, where Stalin hoped to rewrite 1941 by striking first in order to seize the initiative in the 1942 summer campaign. It ended with the Germans in the Caucasus and on the Volga. So, speaking about the pre-war pencil pushers with their boisterous combat projections, in reality events would have unfolded directly and precisely in quite the opposite direction. Not to mention the abandonment, if a preemptive attack had been made, of the righteous defensive nature of the Great Patriotic War which became indeed the main factor in our victory, above and beyond the "genius" Stalinist leadership and the enormous material aid from the Allies. It is now possible to compare the positions of the two sides and even find them symmetrical. Even then, only we have the right to claim our war just, because we didn't attack, the Germans did.

We, the people, had no inkling about the designs of the two leaders. They didn't ask our opinions – everything was concealed from us. On one beautiful morning in June, we were bombed, this proved to be a shock, even though our intelligence officers had given their lives obtaining evidence of the Germans' intentions. The Nazis occupied our land and began to kill us – first the Jews and commissars, and then anyone and everyone who refused to conform to the "New Order" and offered shelter to the victims. Whenever the "Holy War Song" might have been composed, in 1914 or in 1941, it sounded from the depths of our souls and shook us to our core. Even now, it squeezes our throat with the remembrance of those who, caught between two fires, gave their lives in obscurity. There were no "ifs". It was as it was. It was a war like history has never known, enormous for the extent of courage and inhumanity; a patriotic war.

Returning to the moment of enlightenment: if the sources, which became accessible to me in emigration, had fallen into my hands in the USSR, the comprehension of all this staggering information would have struck against the nearly insurmountable inner resistance of a contemporary of this war and citizen of my country. Trust in evidence, received from the sources of so-called bourgeois propaganda, was not natural to citizens of the country of Soviets, while the collective consciousness was a tenacious substance. Only having torn yourself from its grasp can you see the logic of Stalin's preparation for a campaign against a Europe that had been bled white. By the autumn of 1940 the moment was unique, and everything seemed feasible. Poland, France and the Benelux countries were being crucified. Knock off Germany, to which they all belonged – and they would then come to belong to the new master, plus Germany itself. What would remain? The Slavic Balkans? Italy, Spain? Crumbs!

Great Britain, though – that was another matter. This was a stubborn and implacable opponent. The Empire could lose battles, but not wars. It was waking up, and the military potential of not just the colonies, but even the mother country, had only begun to deploy, and America behind it ... The Leader would have to wait for the defeat of Germany and the weakening of the British Empire that this would require, and winning the war would give him, Stalin, a favorable position for dictating the peace terms.

The selection of the time for a stab in the back was a matter of particular pride for Stalin. He was accustomed to approaching an adversary, only checking to see that his hands were tied – and that he was looking in a different direction. However, in front of Hitler he blundered. He was so lulled by the thought that Germany would spend two or three years with France, like in the First World War. They'd sit in trenches, inhale poison gasses and start to fraternize. At that point, Stalin must have thought, he'd blanket them with his lads. They're nothing but spring chickens, they don't know how to fly, nor have they been trained to shoot, but there are a lot of them, while at the same time they're highly enthusiastic, and on the plus side, they will come out of the blue ...

Yet the Germans attacked him. Unexpectedly? This after the early warning about Barbarossa, which was confirmed by the arrival of German troops on the Soviet border back in January? After the numerous and wide hostile actions against the Reich, reliably concealed in Stalin's opinion, but in actual fact superbly known to the Gestapo?[3] After the collapse of the talks in Berlin? The Leader's hands held all the strings. He knew the situation better than anyone else, yet he was caught unawares, not by the war, but by the initiation of the *Wehrmacht*'s concentration on his borders. He, like no one else, recognized his lack of readiness and understood everything long before the invasion (just as subsequently, bogged down in front of Moscow, the Führer would understand first among his clique that the war was lost). He understood, but he didn't want to see that the Führer considered the immense USSR a more realistic target than the puny island metropolis that remained independent. Could that really be? The Boss would kill those who tried to poke obvious facts in his eye. Perhaps that is why he had murdered the most persistent of them? Is that why he, before the very outbreak of the war, ordered the arrest and extrajudicial executions of two heroes of Khalkhin-Gol, Colonel-General Shtern (arrested 7 June 1941) and Lieutenant-General Smushkevich (arrested 8 June 1941)? Is that why on 31 May the commander of aviation of the Moscow Military District Lieutenant General Pumpur was arrested, and on 19 (the Nineteenth!) of June, Colonel-General Loktionov, who had been removed from his post as the commander of the Baltic Military District? Traitors?

---

3   See the Appendix for a copy of the 21 June 1941 'Memorandum'.

Ia.V. Smushkevich.

Meanwhile they, who had foreseen the course of events, kept pestering him, and not without reason: "Comrade Stalin, you with your agreements and trust in them are causing you to overlook an attack against you from a formidable adversary!"

He did not believe Hitler just as he had no trust in anyone ... but what would it mean to acknowledge the concentration of the *Wehrmacht* on the borders? He had lost; they had gotten the jump on him! That meant he would either have to give up his claims on Europe, or openly go to war. Neither one nor the other option was suitable. To abandon his designs – that wasn't Stalin. "I'm coming for you" – this a thousand times was also not like Stalin. There remained, as in his game with the army commanders, a smile and show no notice that they don't like you, and in the meantime feverishly prepare for war.

All this talk about the German "surprise attack" is absurd. There was no surprise! Children knew. We, running around our kindergarten like airplanes with our arms outstretched, shouted: "Warning, warning, Germany is coming for you! A brick to their face, that's what we'll do!" My uncles, though, hadn't read the classics of Marxism, had no access to hear the secret speeches of the Leader, and they believed in the peaceful declarations of the government. They almost paddled me, a young kid, when on the evening of 21 June 1941 at a large family celebration, I in my childish misbehavior had asserted – contrary to all of them! – that war was right in front of their noses. "Brat, what do you understand?" They *knew* what war was, while kids weren't afraid of self-fulfilling prophecies and asserted only what they sensed: War was coming; it was hanging in the air.

Later I read something in Clausewitz, and I'm paraphrasing here: "I've spent much time studying the histories of war. All the time, I see the same thing: contemporaries assign war to some unknown future, when it is already standing at the doorstep of their country."

My uncles were referring to a TASS announcement: "Stalin said!"[4] The king was naked. He had run out of time.

He had taken even Bessarabia out of inertia, during the victorious conclusion of Germany's 1940 campaign. The seizure had been planned according to a scenario. The scenario had changed, but the inertia propelled him, even though the Leader couldn't believe his eyes: "So quickly? But where's the trench warfare?" Perhaps, later he lamented to himself: he wasn't like Machiavelli in this case; the occupation of Bessarabia was no attack in the back, but rather just a cuff to the ear, which indeed only infuriated the foe ...

Rumors circulated ... rumors about a "peaceful capitulation" as the last way to prevent war: Stalin would yield control of his military industry to Hitler. Geller and Rapoport write: "This is hardly believable and unconfirmed by documents, but how must one behave, in order to give rise to such humiliating talk?"

Yes, the ignominy was as it had to be! Stalin went toward it deliberately and, who knows, perhaps he therefore supposed that he would outfox Hitler with his debasement, redirect his attention back toward the West and win more time in order to strike first. His collapse at the start of the war was a typical reaction of disillusionment. He had long believed that he had taken advantage of the adversary – and suddenly on 22 June 1941 he discovered that he was the one to have been sold a bad bill of goods.

For some reason, the so-called "depot problem" is the strongest argument that the supporters of the "6 July" hypothesis have. They are perplexed: gigantic stockpiles of weapons, fuel and ammunition in the western regions of the country were left untouched for the *Wehrmacht*! They weren't destroyed? Why? The presence of the depots close to the borders must be proof that a campaign against Germany had been designated for July!

Alas, it isn't so. Supplies had been accumulating for years, but were far from enough to support offensive operations on the giant scale planned by Stalin. The 1st Ukrainian Front was fighting in the Carpathians, but its fuel depots were still located in Sviatoshino, a Kiev suburb. The Front command sent trucks on a one-thousand kilometer roundtrip journey, but as taught by war, they weren't hurrying to shift the depots closer to the front lines. Such was the lesson. By June 1941 however, they weren't going through such terrible lessons, nor fearing any bomber raids, nor expecting an attack. They themselves were preparing for one, for a great war, against all of Europe laid out before Stalin, all the way to Gibraltar! All these preparations for a campaign across all of Europe had to be made under conditions of a deplorable state with transportation, an appalling breakdown and accident rate, and such strain on shipping that it became a subject of constant discussion at Politburo meetings and a subject of bickering at the 18th Party Conference. Although much had been stockpiled, even more had to be delivered. Kiev is closer to the Carpathians than Minsk is to Berlin, but they would have to go even further, to fraternal Spain, where there is the province of Granada, and to where not long ago all sorts of assistance had gone. Moreover, on the eve of the attack, the railroads would be occupied with bringing up troops ...

That's the situation with the "depot problem". Those, who wish to speculate that the Red Army was ready to strike, can declare the stockpiles sufficient; this is a matter up to each

4   Editor's note: On 14 June 1941, the official Soviet news agency TASS had issued a communiqué denouncing rumors of a pending war between the Soviet Union and Germany and claiming that forces hostile to the USSR and Germany (with the strong implication that it was the United Kingdom) were hoping to expand the war by spreading rumors that Germany had presented territorial and economic claims against the USSR.

individual historian's decency. In fact, the stockpiles were still in the process of being filled. Why weren't they liquidated? Because this would have meant that the plan for conquering Europe would have been liquidated as well. Stalin wouldn't have gone for the destruction of the stockpiled supplies even under the threat of what actually did happen. Supplies for a great war can't be restored in a matter of weeks; this work requires years. If you destroy the supplies, you are putting off the war. Such is the inertia of grand projects. Catching the proper time to start the war was a matter of days, but to set one back meant years!? To Stalin, that was preposterous – and that is why there was no order to destroy the stockpiles, even in the unforeseen case that the Germans would beat him to the punch. There was no foresight, Stalin didn't foresee, and he alone had destroyed the cream of the crop of the Soviet nation .. Even while he was in power, for some, alas, short period of time, as strange as it may sound such an international community still existed. Having destroyed it, having smothered its voices, Stalin brought terrible calamities onto the country.

Many are surprised: How could he have done this, if he was so smart?! Was he really? We are inclined to overestimate the capabilities of people who rule us. They all too often are more capable of striking a pose, and have the ability to conduct themselves, rather than actual intelligence. Was Stalin equally smart in everything? Or smart in those machinations, which was really his strong suit?

Judge for yourselves: Since he understood state security to mean the security of his own life and power, the destruction of other lives and state institutions weren't considered to be a security threat. However along with people, doctrines were destroyed as well.

Together with Tukhachevsky and his comrades, the strategic doctrine that held Nazi Germany as the main threat to the USSR was destroyed. The First Deputy People's Commissar of Defense Tukhachevsky had read *Mein Kampf* much more carefully than the Leader.

Together with Iakir, the specific doctrine of an active defense was destroyed. It promised to tie the foe up with a tenacious struggle in a shallow, previously-prepared fortified zone, lying in front of the main line of fortifications and teaming with partisans, with subsequent flank attacks on the weakened aggressor by massed formations of armor. This tactic of the deep battle, which was worked out by the best minds in the RKKA, was polished in a spirit of military comradeship and with careful regard for human lives. It would be a war with little blood on an aggressor's territory. The executed army commanders were the only ones capable of doing this, and it was fated to reveal itself only in September 1945 in the operation against the Japanese Kwantung Army.

Together with Ian Berzin (the 1937-1938 head of Military Intelligence), Stalin destroyed trust in an invaluable spy network, created by the geniuses of military intelligence jointly with the fanatic disciples of socialist internationalism and the true-blue opponents of Nazism. Stalin weeded out this network of agents.

"Banned" ...

Having been outplayed at every turn and having weakened the country by expanding into the defenseless buffer of the western regions of the Ukraine and Belorussia, Stalin paid no heed to warnings. In truth, one must be overly clever to construct a system, in which state security and the security of the head of state contradict each other. However, in that case, one of the two elements must be immediately eliminated!

Young people, who read the first edition of this book, pestered the life out of the author with questions: "Why didn't they get rid of Stalin? How could that be? They knew about the investigative tortures – but didn't kill him?"

They didn't know about the tortures! Everything was kept concealed! Those capable of raising a hand against the Leader weren't capable of being directed by suspicions. They required proof. They received proof via their own flesh.

The past can't be changed, but it is absurd not to extract lessons from history only for the reason that we keep repeating a poisonous bit of sarcasm: "The main lesson of history is that it teaches nothing." The expression is convenient, but false. History does teach the assiduous student (as long as they don't discover that they took it up too late). The circumstances of Stalin's death raise doubt in the grief, which his peers tried so hard to show. They turned out to be diligent students of history. They likely had finally put two and two together and concluded that the potentate, if he falls into lawlessness, proclaims himself beyond the law. As soon as his indifference to the lives of the citizens in contrast to his own welfare was proven, he should have been eliminated, and only a sick country will not find a citizen for this timely act. However, sooner or later this act will occur – even in this case, possibly, the solution was belated, but nevertheless Stalin's death was timely.

Thus, brushing aside common sense, the Boss began to be governed by his own conviction: "Germany wouldn't dare fight a war on two fronts." Awash with this pathetic notion and a frenzied unwillingness to see reality, the Leader didn't even notice that Germany's ground forces in 1941 were not conducting a war on two fronts. The responsibility for this blindness falls totally upon him and the clique of insignificant and fully submissive courtiers that surrounded him. The Party had become the same nonsense – millions of subservient members. What could the Party members do? Just die, wherever they were shown to die; just like the people.

The Leader was demonstrating naiveté: showing lenience toward German reconnaissance flights, ignoring warnings from various sources, inspiring the ignominious refutations from TASS. He also forbade any force movements on the frontier. This was a theatrical indifference to the obvious preparations of a fearsome adversary; moreover, against the backdrop of the secret hostile buildup against him, in truth it was the apotheosis of stupidity. The demonstrative lack of concern fortified Hitler's resolve: "The unsuspecting Stalin! For what sort of dupe has this guise been designed?" The model of suspiciousness, the maniac who had destroyed his own army commanders trusted the Führer! To be true, this is no longer even amusing.

It is painful to think about how Hitler must have been laughing by the end of 22 June 1941, having learned about the Soviet airplanes pulverized while parked openly on the ground, about the commanders taken prisoner in their underwear, and about the bridges seized intact. With all the weakness, to which the Red Army had been reduced, we aren't even speaking about complex maneuvers here. The Army was defending the borders. It was only necessary to deploy the formations on their defense lines. Warn them of a possible attack. Supply them with ammunition. Issue a combat alert order. That's all – and the German summer 1941 campaign would not have gone like forced march.

Geller and Rapoport consider that the mistake lay in the failure of the People's Commissar and the Chief of the General Staff to insist upon a call for mobilization: "It was not too late to do this even at the beginning of June. Such a measure would have unquestionably upset the Germans' plans and might in general have prevented the attack."

In a strange manner, at the end of this anti-Stalinist book the authors lapse into a pathos of hostility for the high brass that survived the purge and even endow it with a free will: as if the People's Commissar and Chief of the General Staff could take a decision independently of the Leader. Doubtlessly while writing the book, Geller and Rapoport, like indeed all Soviet citizens, were not even thinking about Stalin's aggressiveness and were considering the military aspects of the situation only in terms of a peaceful Soviet defense.

However, Hitler knew that time was working against him. He had no way out, other than the destruction of the Stalinist USSR without any delay, while the Anglo-Saxons were still gathering strength and before they made a landing on continental Europe. *The attack upon the USSR was an operational necessity.*[5] Only Stalin himself could not recognize the obviousness of his wait-and-see posture and dwell in the confidence that Hitler couldn't figure out his intentions. The attack could not be averted by even an immediate transfer of Soviet forces to the western border at the first signs of German movements on the borders. The density of the road network on the German side and the *Wehrmacht's* transportation possibilities exceeded the possibilities of the RKKA. Jumping-off first, the *Wehrmacht* would hold the initiative and dictate the pace of operations. However, the authors have a point: if the Army had been poised in a state of high morale and readiness to take the offensive, no bravura procession of the *Wehrmacht* through the expanses of Belorussia and the Ukraine would have been possible. It was not for nothing that Hitler made the element of surprise the cornerstone of his offensive and was personally involved with this – but not alone. Stalin helped him. An intriguer, exceeding in his Eastern cunning, in blind confidence that after all the hostile actions, he would nevertheless trick the Führer with his show of nonchalance, he ordered the maintenance of deathly calm on the borders. He did not rouse his army to prepare to repulse the enemy. He ordered it to sleep.

---

5   At the First Congress of Writers, carbon paper copies of a hand-written leaflet circulated. It addressed the foreign guests of the Congress, and contained the following paragraph:

"You convene your anti-military congresses and organize anti-military demonstrations. You praise Litvinov's peaceful politics. Have you really lost the normal sense of accepting real events? Do you really not see that the entire USSR is a complete military camp, waiting for the moment when flames will flare up in the West, in order to bring to Western Europe on its bayonets a real manifestation of the height of modern culture – the philosophy of Marx, Engels, Lenin and Stalin?"

The dating of this leaflet is no later than 20 August 1934 ... The helmsman of this course was named as "the former dabbler in a Georgian seminary, Iosif Dzhugashvili (Stalin)".

Probably someone will be tempted to interpret the author's persistence in stressing the aggressive Stalinist policy as reflecting hatred toward the country, where he had been born and where he had lived the greater portion of his life. No one is immune to such accusations. However it is useful to note that this book is about the patriots, who paid with their lives for their love of the country. The best of them, the humanist-internationalists, also had inherent the highest patriotism – the patriotism of educated people, who understand that it is impossible to wish good for their country separately from the entire world.

27

On the Eve

Thus, if the goal, established at the XVIII Party Conference was for the country to be prepared for war by the winter of 1942 (or was it 1943? Exact plans were not revealed anyway...), the bitter reaction of the bureaucrats in the People's Commissariats becomes clear: they understood "readiness" as they had become accustomed to discuss it with the executed army commanders. The Leader, however, wouldn't even begin to articulate to them that *his* readiness didn't mean "a war with little blood on aggressor's territory", but "by any mean and at any cost". However, the slogan favored by the murdered military hadn't been retracted, and the bureaucrats were still taking it seriously. The best of them were idealists who had dedicated their lives to the socialist experiment: "A devil may be in charge, but the experiment is holy and the aims pure." So they were horrified, realizing that after the nightmare of the Russian Civil War, the violence against the peasants had been undertaken not for dragging them out of the darkness, but for fixing them in the darkness forever. The idealists understood – and were refusing to understand, wishing to disbelieve their own eyes – that after the "enormous, clumsy, grating turn of the helm" (O. Mandelshtam), the control in the hands of a despot was serving not the experiment, but the despot himself. They saw – and didn't want to see that power for him was not an instrument of progress, but simply a means to pamper his own mania. So on every administrative level he had planted little demons, dedicated to him personally and ready to do anything for the sake of power. We regard those victims of the repressions, who having survived the Gulag camps still remained faithful to the "ideals", as an extreme example. Although they are a bitter reminder of a lack of a desire to see the things in their genuine light, such blindness is sadly not uncommon in humans. To be unable to understand these people is to be unable to understand not only Soviet history, but if you will the human mind as well. It means to be unable to understand the numbness with which thousands of honest, trusting people, or of those who had begun to doubt, greeted their own punishment. (Those who had those doubts, to the extent that they were waiting only for an opportunity to strip the power away from hands of the clique that had so greedily seized it, had been destroyed first, and none of their leaders remained.) To fail to understand these people means to not understand their bright spirit and their naive, from our point of view, idealism. It is to fail to understand their disagreement with the Leader, with his goals and his methods, and with his interpretation of the word "readiness". To him, readiness was only a word found in the last line of the song, "*Esli zavtra voina* ..." ["If tomorrow there is war ... Soviet people will stand up as one for the defense..."].

Combat readiness involves the training of soldiers, the schooling of commanders, and the mustering of resources. So, it is a question of time. Here, though, those responsible for ensuring combat readiness would bump into the Leader at every turn. He would agree with a scheduled deadline, but then demand a completion ahead of schedule. The Five-Year Plan – in 4 years and 3 months. Any construction project had to be finished early. Such was the practice in peacetime. It is not too difficult to imagine the consequences of accelerated schedules in war preparations, especially when one considers that so many of the best officers and managers had been disposed, leaving those who remained alive to understand that they would be paying for this lack of readiness with their lives, and possibly with the lives of their families as well.

Before his appointment to the post of Chief of the General Staff of the RKKA in place of Meretskov, who had fallen into disgrace, and while analyzing the staff war game, in which as the commander of the "Blues" he had defeated the "Reds", Zhukov touched upon the construction of the fortified zones in Belorussia, noting that they were "too close to the frontier" and had "an extremely disadvantageous operational configuration, particularly in the Belostok [Bialystok] bulge." He expressed the same notion about the fortified zones in the Ukraine – they should be built more distant from the border. Voroshilov erupted: "Fortified zones are built according to the approved plans of the Chief Military Council." And that was all. Left unsaid was a reminder: "Listen, wise guy, stick to your own business."

Indeed, in the role of military district commander, Zhukov allowed himself this comment on the fortified zone. He never again raised the issue while in the role of Chief of the General Staff. This means that in his new position, he must have learned that the fortified districts were not being built for the defense. It is difficult to explain his silence on the topic in any other way. After all, in December, the commander of the Kiev Special Military District General of the Army G.K. Zhukov, explains that one of the reasons for the defending "Reds'" defeat in the staff war game was the unjustifiable proximity of the fortified areas to the border. A month later the Commander of the General Staff bypasses this issue ...

That means Zhukov, too, was a proponent of the defense ... at least until he assumed his high position. Naturally! He had smashed the Japanese, and while doing so was singing the same song along with the troops: "Don't touch us – and we won't touch you, but if you lay a finger on us, we'll give you no quarter." As commander of the Kiev Special Military District, General of the Army Zhukov, like all the military district commanders, was preparing the USSR for a just defensive war. In such a war, the fortified zones should have been pulled back from the frontier. After an enemy attack, this would allow the troops time to fall back to the fortified regions and there get ready for defense. That's why General Zhukov had interjected his critical comment about the fortified zones when analyzing the war game.

However, Chief of the General Staff G. K. Zhukov was no longer on the same page with the troops. He now knew that the USSR was preparing for an offensive war. The Leader could not keep this hidden from him in his new high post, or else he wouldn't be able to do his duties properly. If the fortified zones had not been designated to wear down the enemy, but instead to support their own attacking forces in case of an enemy counteroffensive, then indeed they had to be placed in the zone of strategic deployment, closer to the borders. Otherwise on the strict defensive, such fortified areas would become traps for the defenders ..

It seems that the Leader didn't confide in Zhukov immediately about his plans. However, the days between his appointment as Chief of General Staff and the Party Conference were enough for an incident, which Zhukov describes in the canonical version of a peace-loving USSR that was anticipating nothing bad:

Saturday night I went to Stalin at his country-cottage, taking along a list of questions I wanted to raise. I found there Marshal Timoshenko, Marshal Kulik and some members of the Politburo.

"After greeting me, Stalin asked if I was familiar with the Katiusha rocket launchers;

'I've only heard about them, but I haven't seen them,' I said.

'Then Timoshenko, Kulik and Aborenkov must take you to the testing grounds in the next few days, so you can see them fired. Now tell us how things are at the General Staff.'

"I briefly repeated what I had already reported to Timoshenko, and said that in view of the gravity of the military and political situation urgent measures must be taken to eliminate the flaws in the defense of the western border and in the armed forces in time.

"Molotov interrupted me.

'So you think we'll have to fight the Germans soon?'

'Just a moment...' – Stalin stopped him.

After listening to what I had to say, Stalin asked us all to the dinner table.

Four months remained until the start of the war. Four months, reader ... for all the "urgent measures to eliminate the flaws in the defense of the western border and in the armed forces in time"! What sort of "in time" could there be, when there were only four months for everything!

The story terminates prematurely. Molotov's indignant interruption hangs in the air. This is not an oversight by the editor; the memoirs were published repeatedly in this same form, only Stalin's "Just a moment ..." was replaced in the 1995 edition by the more expressive "Stalin cut short Molotov". For many years, this question of Molotov confused Soviet citizens. It could be interpreted as a desire to put an overreaching upstart in his place, or at least to let Zhukov know that the political situation was outside his jurisdiction. Perhaps it was ignorance of how much the Master had managed to disclose to the new Chief of the General Staff. I don't exclude the possibility that Molotov himself at the time didn't know of Stalin's intentions: somehow, to be able to act naturally in front of Hitler. I won't even exclude the possibility that Zhukov knew, but Molotov didn't. The Leader was a man of the East, and was greatly governed by maxims of the sort: "Don't reveal to a friend that which you wish to keep concealed from an enemy." In those times, it was possible to disappear even through a slip of the tongue....

However it went, this episode has passed as an example of Stalin's peaceful intentions. Molotov ... a perturbation ... fight the Germans!? ... Indeed! Superb; a masterly performance! May it be that way with Hitler!

Marshal Zhukov, however, was not Marshal Brezhnev. He had no reason to make up stories. The group in power did not let him talk freely – well, he still might at least leave a hint. So after Molotov's indignant question, there followed Stalin's "Just a moment ..."

I dare to presume that the Marshal's *Reminiscences* were not intended for the Soviet people all at once. They were intended for the inner circle of the country's leadership and first of all for his own kind. As he wrote his memoirs, the disgraced Marshal was continuing polemics with his opponents in the army and government. These are our mental discussions with those with whom we would like to joust verbally, if only we weren't gagged. The group in power knew. There weren't many of them, but the Marshal didn't want to look like a liar in their eyes; this wasn't necessary for him. It was also not in his interests to hide the truth. He hid as much as he'd been ordered to conceal. But for his kind ... they doubtlessly understood the significance of Stalin's "Just a moment ..." and the subsequent lapse into silence. I am guessing that the Marshal had to contend with the censor even over this elliptical "Just a moment ..." – at the time, Molotov was still quite well and living! – with the hope that future generations would suddenly be able to decipher the ellipses.

During the writing of Zhukov's memoirs, the issue of the fortified zones suddenly sharpened with the publication of the book *1941, 22 iunia* [*1941, 22 June*] by Aleksandr Nekrich, who was vilified by the authorities for being anti-Soviet right after the book's publication. Zhukov, without mentioning Nekrich, was offering excuses in front of the Soviet public, which had been agitated by the historian. After all, he was the Chief of the General Staff before the war broke out. The country's lack of readiness for the war incriminated him (and continues to do so!). At the time, long before *perestroika* and *glasnost'*, he could not acknowledge that which Russia today will still not acknowledge: Stalin was not preparing for a defense, but for an offense![1] In his otherwise sparsely-detailed memoirs, Zhukov dedicates many pages to the issue of the fortified zones (although his treatment of the issue received only three pages when the memoirs first came out). In particular, he reveals that 140,000 workers were employed daily in fortifying the new borders. Is that a lot? The figure doesn't command much respect. Incidentally, in the 12th edition of Zhukov's memoirs, so much was added about the lack of readiness for war that there is now no need to incriminate the Marshal. The repressions receive mention, as well as the lack of military professionals for the new army formations that he created. Even the name of the only person responsible, Stalin, is given.

At the XVIII Party Conference, such luminaries of political thought as Litvinov and such titans of industry as Vannikov were removed from the Central Committee, while military leaders were brought onto it: Tiulenev, Kirponos (!), Tributs, Oktiabr'skii ... and Zhukov. How can it not be noticed that of the military leaders prior to the purge, only Iakir was a member of the Central Committee?

Was Zhukov a military thinker? He didn't originate any new military doctrines. On the scale of Stalin's Central Committee, likely, he was an intellect.

In Chapter 9 of his *Reminiscences and Reflections* ("Eve of the War") Zhukov summarizes the condition of the Red Army by its types of forces. The summary is convincing. What he has to say about the design and production of weapons has been confirmed by history.

However, there are also laughable places:

> D. F. Ustinov was then People's Commissar for Armaments, B. L. Vannikov People's Commissar for Ammunition, and Generals I. I. Ivanov and V. G. Grabin chief designers of artillery systems. Stalin knew them all personally, often received them, and had full trust in them.

He knew, he knew! He trusted them, incarcerated them, shook the spirit out of them, and then let them go ...

Incidentally, Vannikov was not People's Commissar of Ammunition before the war. He had been arrested in his post as the People's Commissar of Armaments, but became the People's Commissar of Ammunition in the winter of 1943 in place of Goremykin, to whom

---

1   For this reason even Rezun-Suvorov's books are being burned in modern Russia by so-called patriots.

he'd been appointed as deputy after the war started. However, this is by the by, the details of command leap frog.

Here's another quote:

> The General Staff radio net (!!! – the author) had only 39 percent of the required RAT radio sets and 60 percent of the RAF and 11-AK radio sets. There were only 45 percent of the required chargers. The Western Military District on the border had only 27 percent of the required radio sets; ... (This figure elicits a shriek of horror from anyone who understands modern warfare, combat, and military cooperation – the author) ... What came of this at the outset of the war is commonly known.

Oh yes, now this is commonly known. This is the first reason, after the blinding of vigilance (of course, not considering the liquidation of *Komandarm* [Army Commander] Uborevich) for the collapse of the Western Front: the lack of communications. This needs to be written in letters a meter tall: "*Communications! The top concern of the slain army commanders!*" Yet now that they were gone, what?

There is also the following: "Some 30 to 40 RUS-2 radar sets were located in the Leningrad and Moscow air defence zones." Not a word more about radar stations. However, from other sources it is known that several dozen bombers, personally sent into dense cloud cover by Hitler with the order to bomb the belatedly discovered Moscow military parade on 7 November 1941, were intercepted in this cloud cover – it was like finding a needle in a haystack! Plainly, something that Tukhachevsky had left behind had started to work ...

On 13 April 1941, there was a meeting between Zhukov and the Japanese Minister of Foreign Affairs Matsuoka. After the meeting, Zhukov phoned Stalin and reported the details. Stalin was pleased and announced that the Japanese government had agreed to sign a neutrality accord.

There is legitimate pride in Zhukov's telling of the circumstances surrounding the signing of the treaty. There was logic in the visit of Matsuoka to the People's Commissariat of Defense. The Japanese diplomat was an opponent of an agreement with the USSR. So at the very least, he wanted to ascertain whether or not the Red Army's command ranks still had that Zhukov, who ... Many others were no longer present. So if Zhukov was also gone, the neutrality agreement could wait. Here, I think, is the answer to the enigma why Zhukov's co-author at Khalkhin-Gol, Colonel-General Shtern, also still remained free. A German airplane's later appearance over Moscow was the cause of his arrest (if it wasn't a provocation).

Zhukov didn't write – did he not know? – about the fact that the bloody war with Finland had made an impression on the Japanese: the readiness to take such losses for the sake of a clump of land? He also didn't write about the cultivation of political circles and public opinion in Japan, conducted by Richard Sorge in favor of a neutrality agreement.

A strange figure, this Sorge. The great agent, Richard Sorge – he was a defector, homeless alone in the universe. To return to Germany was to be treated kindly. To return to the USSR was to be tortured in the Lubianka. To remain in Japan was to be betrayed. He doomed himself when he passed word of Japan's decision to engage in war with the United States Soviet divisions in the Far East began moving toward Moscow, but Stalin, of course, didn't inform Roosevelt of Sorge's report. Then, feeling uneasy in front of his ally and pathologically distrusting the devotion of his agents, he would cold-bloodedly torpedo Sorge ...

However, in the meantime Sorge, from Tokyo, was pounding Moscow with dispatches about the preparation of a German invasion; in vain. He reported the exact date; uselessly. Stalin ignored that which he could not shackle. The Leader remained confident that in this critical situation, he would suitably exert his will, and the circumstances would yield.

The circumstances didn't yield.

Zhukov writes:

Comparing and analyzing Stalin's conversations with people close to him in my presence I have come to the firm conclusion that all his thoughts and deeds were prompted by the desire to avoid war *or delay its start* (author's emphasis)[2], and that he was confident in succeeding.

Zhukov could not say more. However, even this phrase allows us to retain respect for the Marshal. It isn't at variance with the offensive war that the Chief of the General Staff of the RKKA and General of the Army Zhukov were preparing for 1942-1943, had the Germans not preempted it.

---

2   Editor's note: This key phrase is not found in the earliest editions of Zhukov's memoirs.

28

Interlude: The War of Ideas ...

... had been going on for a long time and with ever increasing fervor. Everything was getting stirred together in the ideological kitchen. In the 1920s, there weren't many who could distinguish between allies and opponents. But by the 1940s, everything had fallen into place.

I am citing from Louis Pauwels' and Jacques Bergier's book *The Morning of the Magicians*, which was published in France in the 1950s and later translated into English by Rollo Meyers in 1960 for an American publisher, Destiny Books:

> The S.S. Colonel Wolfram Sievers, who had put up a purely rational defense asked, before his execution, to be allowed for the last time to celebrate his rites and say mysterious prayers. He then calmly went to the gallows unperturbed.
>
> He had been the general manager of the Ahnenerbe, and it was for this that he was condemned to death at Nuremberg. The Society for the Study of Ancestral Heritages, the Ahnenerbe, was founded privately by Sievers' spiritual teacher Frederick Hielscher, the mystic and friend of the Swedish explorer Sven Hedin who was himself closely associated with Haushofer.
>
> Sven Hedin, an expert on the Far East, had lived for a long time in Tibet and played an important part in establishing the Nazis' esoteric doctrines. Frederick Hielscher was never a Nazi, and was even friendly with the Jewish philosopher Martin Buber. But his profound theories had something in common with the "magic" doctrines of the Grand Masters of National-Socialism. Himmler, in 1935, two years after its foundation, turned the Ahnenerbe into an official organization, attached to the Black Order. Its declared aims were: *"To make researches into the localization, general characteristics, achievements, and inheritance of the Indo-Germanic race, and to communicate to the people the results of this research. This mission must be accomplished through the use of strictly scientific methods."* In other words, the whole machinery of German rational organization was to be employed in the interests of irrationality.
>
> In January 1939 the Ahnenerbe was purely and simply incorporated into the S.S., and its leaders absorbed into Himmler's personal staff. At that time it had fifty branches under the direction of Professor Wurst, an expert on ancient sacred texts who had taught Sanskrit at Munich University.
>
> "It seems that Germany spent more on the Ahnenerbe's researches than America did on its preparations for the first atomic bomb. These researches ranged from strictly scientific activities to the practice of occultism, and from vivisection practiced on prisoners to espionage on behalf of the secret societies. Negotiations were entered into with Skorzeny with a view to stealing the Holy Grail, and Himmler created a special section for the collection of information 'in the sphere of the supernatural.'
>
> One is astounded at the list of reports drawn up at enormous cost by the Ahnenerbe on such subjects as: the strength of the Rosicrucian confraternity; the

symbolism of the suppression of the Irish harp in Ulster; the occult significance of Gothic towers and of the Etonian top hat, etc. . . .

"During the war, Sievers organized in the camps for deportees the horrible experiments which have since been the subject of several 'black' books. The Ahnenerbe was 'enriched' by an Institute of scientific research for national defense equipped with 'all the facilities available at Dachau.' Professor Hirt, who was in charge of these Institutes, formed a collection of typically Jewish skeletons. Sievers ordered the army in Russia to bring back a number of skulls of Jewish commissars. When reminded of these crimes at Nuremberg, Sievers betrayed no signs of normal human feeling or pity. He was elsewhere. He was listening to other voices.

"Hielscher had no doubt played an important part in the drafting of the secret doctrine. Except in relation to this doctrine, the behavior of Sievers, as of the other principal instigators of these crimes, remains incomprehensible. The expressions 'moral monstrosity', 'mental cruelty' or 'madness' explain nothing. Little is known about Sievers' spiritual mentor. Ernest Jiinger, however, speaks of him in the diary that he kept during the Occupation in Paris. On October 14, 1943, Jiinger wrote in his diary:

> 'In the evening, a visit from Bogo. [1] At a time when strong personalities are so scarce, although he is one of the people I have thought a lot about, I do not seem able to form an opinion about him. I thought once that he would make his mark in the history of our time as one of those people who are little known but are exceptionally intelligent. I think now he will play a more important role. Most of the young intellectuals of the generation, which has grown up since the last war, have come under his influence, and often been through his school. . . . He has confirmed a suspicion I have had for a long time that he has founded a church. He has now gone beyond dogma, and is mainly concerned with liturgy.'

And Jiinger adds, confirming our theory:

> 'I have noticed in Bogo a fundamental change that is characteristic of all our elite: he is throwing himself into metaphysics with all the enthusiasm of a mind brought up on rationalist lines. The same thing had struck me in the case of Spengler, and seems to be a propitious sign. It could be said, roughly, that while the 19th century was the century of reason, the 20th is the century of cults. Kniebolo (Hitler) lives on them, which accounts for the total incapacity of liberal-minded people to see even where he stands.

Hielscher, who had not been disturbed by prosecutors, came to give evidence on Sievers' behalf at Nuremberg. He confined himself at the trial to political matters and to intentionally absurd statements about races and ancestral tribes. He asked as a favor to be allowed to accompany Sievers to the gallows, and it was with him that the condemned man said the prayers peculiar to a cult which was never mentioned throughout the trial. He then returned to obscurity.

---

1   As a precaution Jiinger used pseudonyms to refer to all important persons. "Bogo" was Hielscher; "Kniebolo," Hitler

I assume that there is no reason to ask the reader's forgiveness for offering this long extract from *The Morning of the Magicians*. This reading is more captivating than that which I'm able to offer with my own clipped, rational Cartesianism. We're all like that. The authors of the book, without excluding themselves, note with regret our stubborn determinism. It is not simply that we like it, we need it. We demand a flow of events along a direct path, from the cause to the measurable effect. Unfortunately, the determinism of historical events is more complicated.

Turning to the history of religions, we see that they required centuries for the cult to adopt a clear form, yet even today in any of the religions there remain more than a few contradictions. Nazism had only a few years to develop, but the successes of Nazism, as a cult, as a new civilization, surpassed anything that had ever occurred before in history. This is a horrifying fact, and we need to be aware of its special significance and perceive it as a deplorable and menacing precautionary symbol.

Again, I cite from Pauwels' and Bergier's book about the esoteric Nazi doctrines:

> The terrestrial and cosmic period in which we are living while waiting for the advent of a new cycle, which will bring about mutations on the Earth, a reclassification of species and the return of the giant magician, the demigod, is characterized by the coexistence on this globe of forms of life originating in the various phases of the secondary, tertiary, and quaternary periods. There have been phases of upward and downward movements. Certain species are degenerating; others are forward-looking and bear within them the seeds of the future. Man is not a unity. Nor are men the descendants of the giants, only their successors—and they, too, were created by mutation. But this intermediate species of humanity is not itself a unity. There is a true race of humans, which will come with the next cycle, endowed with the psychic organs that will enable it to assist in maintaining the equilibrium of the cosmic forces, and destined to play its part in a heroic adventure under the guidance of the Unknown Superior Beings of the future.

Well, what of that? The essence of Marxism can be expressed in a nutshell: "We'll take from the rich and give to the poor." It seems that a few words about Nazism before the war will also not be a hindrance. Once more, let us turn to Pauwels and Bergier regarding the Nazi's beliefs:

> ...There is also another species of humanity which does not deserve the name and no doubt came into being on the globe during some dark and dismal epoch when, after one of the Moons had descended on the Earth, vast portions of the Earth's surface were nothing but a desolate swamp. It was probably created along with other crawling and hideous creatures, the relics of a baser form of life. The Gypsies, Negroes, and Jews are not human, in the true sense of the term... a kind of unfortunate lapse on the part of an enfeebled creative force, these 'modern' creatures (particularly the Jews) imitate man and are envious of him, but do not belong to the same species. 'They are as far removed from us as animals are from humans,' said Hitler (these were his very words) to a terrified Rauschning who then realized that Hitler's views were crazier even than those of Rosenberg and all the racial theoreticians. 'I do not mean,' Hitler was careful to explain, 'that I look upon Jews as animals; they are much further removed from

animals than we are. Therefore, it is not a crime against humanity to exterminate them, since they do not belong to humanity. They are creatures outside nature.'

It is for these reasons that certain sessions of the Nuremberg Trial were meaningless. The judges could not possibly have any kind of communication with those who were really responsible, most of whom, in any case, had disappeared, leaving in the dock only the men who had been their instruments. Two worlds confronted one another, with no means of communication. It was like trying to judge creatures from Mars by the standards of our humanist civilization. They were, indeed, Martians – in the sense that they belonged to a different world from the one we have known for the last six or seven centuries. A civilization totally different from what is generally meant by the word had been established in Germany in the space of a few years, without us having ever properly understood what was going on. Its initiators no longer had any intellectual, moral, or spiritual affinities with ourselves in any basic sense; and despite external resemblances, they were as remote from us as the Australian aborigines. The judges at Nuremberg tried to act as if they were not conscious of this appalling state of things. To a certain extent, indeed, there was a case for concealing the truth so that it could be buried and made to vanish, as in a conjuring trick. *It was important to keep alive the idea of the permanence and universality of our humanist and Cartesian civilization, and somehow or other it was essential that the accused should be integrated in this system.* This was necessary in order not to upset the equilibrium of the Western way of life and conscience. It must not be imagined that we are questioning the benefits that have resulted from the Nuremberg Trial. We merely believe that a world of fantasy was buried there. But this was only right in order to save countless million souls from being corrupted. The exhumation we have been carrying out is only for the benefit of a few amateurs, who have been warned and are equipped with masks. (Emphasis the author's)

I am citing these tenets of Nazism as laid out by Pauwel and Bergier not because their book is credible in all it says. However, the authors – one a chemist, the other a journalist – found the strongest and most succinct words to impart the horror of what *de facto* happened with the world community in the 1930s and 1940s.

In Germany, a different civilization gained a foothold, one that stood in total contrast from the European. It was unique by its unprecedented irreconcilability. Only as a result of the Nuremberg trials was it given to our civilization to realize that it had been standing on the edge of a precipice and had turned away from it only at the last moment. Only at the trials did the difference become clear between our civilization and that which might have happened. Indeed, the present misfortunes of civilization have arisen, not because the prosecutors at the trial when conducting their exhumation of the past, freed a genie from a bottle. Possibly, humans are truly dissimilar genetically and are refugees from other planets and even systems. However, really does either the extermination of wasps by bees or bees by wasps look enticing?

Incidentally, Soviet historians were unflappable even before Nuremberg trials and, I would say, with a professional grasp of the essence of the matter wrote about what it was like in 1933:

... millions of Germans heard the rousing speeches of Nazis about the resurrection of a great Germany, about how there must be war if you want a bright life, that peace should be a product of war, that the German – a people of a higher race – must first subjugate the world, and then establish peace and a new order in it.

Hitler didn't rush to propagandize his ideology. If he didn't keep its essence exactly secret, he also didn't highlight it. The creation of a new world was in the cards, where the blue-eyed blonds would be the only contributor to its genetic fund. Would that mean that others would be shipped to a gas chamber and then sent up a chimney? Let us not frighten the dark-haired prematurely; let them fight for the great Deutschland, and then we'll sort them out later. So Hitler was setting aside the broadcasting of his ideology until the time when the world would be prostrate before him. Not all the high-ranking members of the Third Reich were initiated into the secrets of the Ahnenerbe. It was possible to be a good administrator and a bad mystic. For mystics the Führer had other people. Take Wolfram Sievers, for example. This gave rise to misconceptions. The Gauleiters were not admirers of Jews. However, an enormous distance lies between having distaste for a certain ethnic group and the desire to see it wiped from the face of the earth, which indeed stalled "The Final Solution" of the Jewish question in Belorussia prior to Gauleiter Kube's assassination by partisans.[2]

An Important Narrative Comment: With this excursion into ideology is the author straying from the reading of Marshal Zhukov's memoirs, as expressed in the title of this book? Yes, this excursion is long. However, summarizing the results, any person strives to answer the single question that burns in any life: What is the balance? Has the life contributed to the forces of Good? Or has it represented Evil? What happens as a result? Where will the soul wind up?

Oh, when the matter reached its end, the Marshal felt much more tentative than the most sinful monk. Yet Zhukov didn't have the slightest possibility to discuss these themes.

It is fair to summarize: According to all the knowledge in mankind's possession at the writing of this book, Hitler remains as Satan's servant, and his downfall was a righteous matter. It is also fair to see in the far from angelic face of Marshal Zhukov the St. George who slew the dragon.

---

2   Editor's note: Wilhelm Kube, the *Generalkomissar* for Belorussia, had balked at executing thousands of Jews that had been deported to Minsk from Germany, when he discovered that among the deportees were World War I veterans with combat decorations and other people who were half-Aryan or three-quarters Aryan. He wrote a letter to Hinrich Lohse (the *Reichkomissar* of the *Ostland*) that caused a firestorm of controversy within the SS. This letter said, in part: "I am certainly hard and I am ready to help solve the Jewish question, but people who come from our cultural milieu are certainly something else than the native animalized hordes. Should the Lithuanians and the Latvians – who are disliked here, too, by the population – be charged with the slaughter? I could not do it. I ask you, consider the honor of our Reich and our party, and give clear instructions to take care of what is necessary in a form which is humane." See Raul Hilberg, *The Destruction of the European Jews: Revised and Definitive Edition* (New York: Holmes and Meier, 1985), p. 354. A copy of the letter and a discussion of the controversy is available on the Internet at: http://www.einsatzgruppenarchives.com/trials/profiles/kubeminsk.html.

29

The War of Ideas (Conclusion)

I t is Paris, 1799.

The haute bourgeoisie was dreaming about a dictator, about the re-establishment of commerce, about a man who would secure the development of industry, and bring France a victorious peace and a strong internal 'order'; the petit bourgeoisie ... was desiring the same things ... As for the lumpen proletariat, the day laborers from the villages, for them there was only one slogan: 'We want a regime, under which people can eat.' (Tarle, *Napoleon*)

Already by the summer of 1799, the thought of a 'firm order' had been molded, as they say, into crystalline pure forms. Everything had become clear, and doubts had been cast aside – a *coup d'état* was on the agenda. Joubert's death had momentarily made that option impossible, but didn't in the least shake the idea. After Joubert's death, Sieyès held discussions with Moreau and Macdonald. On their own, Bernadotte and Jourdan were pondering the idea of a coup, while Lafayette, probably Pisegraux and a few of the other generals had their own notions.

When Bonaparte in October, escaping the unavoidably approaching collapse in Egypt, arrived in Paris, he wasn't at all thinking about a government overthrow; he had more important things on his mind. He was preoccupied with the thought of how to escape retribution for his unwarranted flight from an army, which he had abandoned to the whims of fate. (A. Manfred, *Napoleon*)

What's this? Napoleon wasn't the only pretender for the role? Napoleon, with all his uniqueness?

Yes, even Napoleon with all his uniqueness. Had Joubert, who had been abandoned in Egypt not died, the name of Napoleon today would be known only to experts on French military history. Such are the techniques of power: some govern; other own. To the citizens of the USSR, where, according to the expression of the Strugatsky brothers[1] a "group of unknown fathers" governed and ruled, it was difficult to part with a conception of government that united Power and Money. In the meantime, it was only a brief circumstance in a unique century. At all previous times, money was one thing in and of itself, and power was another thing in and of itself. Sometimes, with money you could buy power, as Lucius Licinius Crassus did in Rome. More often, Money purchased acceptable rulers. In addition, those who have Money always had a broad choice.

It shouldn't be thought that the competition for a leading role in history is any different from a contest like the "Miss America" or "Miss Russia" competitions. Those who aspire to the post of dictator are not obliged to be a luminary of thought and an author of ideas. A

---

1   Editor's note: Arkadii (1929-1991) and Boris Strugatsky (1933-) were very popular Soviet science fiction writers.

new platform isn't expected of him – rather, a dependable defense of the here and now is expected. The best candidate does not at all mean the wisest. The best – that is the strongest, but still manageable candidate.

That's the mistake they made in their time with Napoleon. That's also the mistake they made, later and more tragically, with Hitler.

> ... Bonaparte did not have to propose or devise anything – everything came to him in completely ready form. The idea of a *coup d'état* with his participation was served up to him in a fully worked-out, even polished form. It wasn't he that brought to France the idea of renewal. This idea had already been germinating in Parisian political circles for a long time and existed in many variations. It was offered to Napoleon, he consented and accepted it. (A. Manfred)

The replacement of the Weimar Republic had been germinating more fervently than the overhaul of France in the time of the Directory. The Russian Revolution introduced the factor of ideological opposition. In the time of the Directory, anyone could have become a dictator, as long as he wasn't Bourbon. In Germany in the 1920s, it was far from enough not have been a member of the House of Hohenzollern. The revolution was put down, the leaders were killed, but the cause of social-democracy wasn't lost. A revolution was menacingly yawning in the East. The war of ideas blazed up. The streets of German cities became the arenas for bloody street fights between the "Left" and the "Right".

Money sought out weapons in the struggle with Social Democracy, and behind it now stood a strengthening government, which falsely called itself a government of workers and peasants. Like mushrooms, political parties sprouted in Germany. They needed resources. However, resources aren't invested in trifles. The investors must be shown the goods. The commodity in Germany was Nazism, and Hitler was not its originator. He was sought out among others, whipped into shape and subsidized. He was still not a politician, only a superb demagogue. In distinction from Stalin, Hitler started even outside a political party, from nothing.

Stalin was a man of the East: focused on power, absolute power in fact, and not attuned to ideas that didn't relate to power. Although he fully understood the importance of ideas for power he didn't even have to work for it; everything was done for him by the Marx-Engels-Lenin complex of political writers. He acquired the Party already consolidated around Lenin's authoritative precept of strengthening solidarity. His "creativity" was focused on strengthening his personal power. This didn't require any erudition.

The same could not be said about Hitler. Sources have preserved for us Hitler's pathetic origins. In distinction from Stalin, he had to build a party himself, and to build an ideological foundation for his thirst for power. Without that foundation, how would the party attract the masses? The Nazis – or those who later became Nazis – needed their own tale, plausibly promising *much and right away*. From where should the tale be taken; where should a theory be acquired?

We are approaching a question, which I, with perhaps excessive presumptuousness, have undertaken to explain for myself and the reader: the question of the hidden springs of historical processes ...

The socialist idea had already taken hold of the masses. One who wanted to lead the masses had to take regard of this. (Even Great Britain has stirred ...) Stalin sought not to change a word in his ideological inheritance. On Marxism's materialistic basis, he together with his Bolsheviks was building a god's kingdom on earth. This ideology had no subtext.

Hitler ought to have opposed this with something no less alluring. For a start he armed himself with Italian fascism's slogans of a people's government. However, some time was needed before the forces of Evil noticed Mussolini's undistinguished follower ...

There are things about which it is unpleasant to speak. However, the question nevertheless remains: At root, have we humans, God's creations with immortal souls, been meant for Good – or are we the Devil's offspring, doomed to do Evil? (There is a third way between the two; it is also acceptable.)

We live in God's world, thank God. However, it is conceivable – after Hitler no longer theoretically so – that the world is the Devil's domain. The Devil's disciples will be persuasive and will produce a full levy of Hitlerites, and add to it a bouquet of the latest illnesses: overpopulation, pollution, crime, an overabundance of weapons, the coalescence of state and Mafia structures, and a bevy of social, genetic and energy problems.

In God's world the Satanists are underground and compelled to proclaim God, seemingly through their teeth. In the Devil's world they unceremoniously christen Satan with God's name. Evil steps out onto the front of the stage with the support of state institutions. God-bearers go underground and Good is left to do its work in darkness.

Fantasy? All right, in the years 1939-1945 a significant portion of mankind was already living under such morality, and millions were terminated in full accordance with its doctrine.

Bergier and Pauwels use the terms "Satanist" and "demonic" because people are accustomed to link them with something malevolent, ill-intentioned against the conscience, some secret pact against humans in the name of seizing power and doing them harm. The authors of *Morning of Magicians*, using the available terminology, nevertheless pay attention to a satanic cult: it, like God, has its adherents:

In the autumn of 1923 the death took place in Munich of a singular personage – poet, playwright, journalist, and Bohemian – named Dietrich Eckardt. With his lungs injured by mustard gas, he addressed a prayer of a very personal nature, before he died, to a black meteorite which he used to call his 'Mecca Stone' and had left in his will to Professor Oberth, one of the pioneers of astronautics. He had just sent a lengthy manuscript to his friend Haushofer. After his death the Thule Society (such was his prayer) would continue to exist and would soon change the world and all life upon it.

"In 1920 Dietrich Eckardt and another member of the Thule Society, the architect Alfred Rosenberg, had made the acquaintance of Hitler. Their first meeting took place in Wagner's house at Bayreuth, and for the next three years they were to be the constant companions of the little *Reichswehr* corporal, dominating all his thoughts and acts. Konrad Heiden (in his *Adolf Hitler*) wrote that 'Eckardt undertook the spiritual formation of Adolf Hitler.' He also taught him to write and speak. His instruction was given on two levels: one being concerned with the 'secret' doctrine, and the other with the doctrine of propaganda.

Three years of individual instruction – that's the duration. It didn't make an egghead out of Hitler, but he had passed a course in the University of Evil. They had taught the little corporal a love for edelweiss and the music of Wagner.

Bergier and Pauwels continue:

"In July 1923 Eckardt became one of the seven founder-members of the National-Socialist Party.

"Seven: a sacred figure. In the autumn, before he died, he told his colleagues: 'Follow Hitler. He will dance, but it is I who called the tune. We have given him the means of communicating German. . . .'

"The legend of Thule is as old as the Germanic race. It was supposed to be an island that had disappeared somewhere in the extreme North. Off Greenland? Or Labrador? Like Atlantis, Thule was thought to have been the magic center of a vanished civilization. Eckardt and his friends believed that not all the secrets of Thule had perished. Beings intermediate between Man and other intelligent beings from beyond would place at the disposal of the Initiates a reservoir of forces which could be drawn on to enable Germany to dominate the world again and be the cradle of the coming race at Supermen, which would result from mutations of the human species. One day her legions would set out to annihilate everything that had stood in the way of the spiritual destiny of the Earth, and their leaders would be men who knew everything, deriving their strength from the very fountain-head of energy and guided by the Great Ones of the Ancient World. Such were the myths on which the Aryan doctrine of Eckardt and Rosenberg was founded and which these prophets of a 'magic' form of socialism had instilled into the mediumistic mind of Hitler.

"But the Thule Society was at that time, no doubt, nothing more than a fairly powerful little machine or confounding fact and fiction. Under other influences and in the hands of other persons it was soon to become a much stranger instrument – an instrument capable of changing the very nature of reality. It would seem that it was under influence of Karl Haushofer that the group took on its true character of a society of Initiates in communion with the Invisible, and became the magic center of the Nazi movement ... Occultism teaches that, after concluding a pact with hidden forces, the members of the Group cannot evoke these forces save through the intermediary of a magician who, in turn, can do nothing without a medium. It would seem therefore that Hitler must have been the medium, and Haushofer the magician."

Bergier and Pauwels use the worn-out terminology of ancient legends in order to simplify things. However, even Hitler's companions couldn't find other expressions. Hermann Rauschning, the President of the Senate in the Free City of Danzig and a man of aristocratic old German heritage, became a trusted acquaintance of Hitler's. Rauschning fled from Germany prior to its terrible crimes and published a book in London, *Hitler Speaks: A Series of Political Discussions with Adolf Hitler On His Real Aims*. His voice was not heard.[2] Indeed, inertia saves mankind, but at the same time dooms it...

Rauschning, in describing Hitler, wrote as follows:

One cannot help thinking of him as a medium. For most of the time mediums are ordinary, insignificant people. Suddenly they are endowed with what seem to be

---

2   This is what Rauschning himself believed. My opinion is that he was heard in the very best way by key people in England, which consequently generated such strong determination in the British struggle with the Nazi monster.

supernatural powers, which set them apart from the rest of humanity. These powers are something that is outside their true personality – visitors, as it were, from another planet. The medium is possessed. Once the crisis is past, they fall back again into mediocrity. It was in this way, beyond any doubt, that Hitler was possessed by forces outside himself – almost demoniacal forces of which the individual named Hitler was only the temporary vehicle. This mixture of the banal and the supernatural created that insupportable duality of which one was conscious in his presence. This was a Being who might have been invented by Dostoevsky. It was like looking at a bizarre face whose expression seems to reflect an unbalanced state of mind coupled with a disquieting impression of hidden power.

According to Strasser: 'Listening to Hitler one suddenly has a vision of one who will lead mankind to glory ... . A light appears in a dark window. A gentleman with a comic little moustache turns into an archangel. . . . Then the archangel flies away . . . and there is Hitler sitting down, bathed in sweat with glassy eyes. . . .'

Bouchez said: 'I looked into his eyes—the eyes of a medium in a trance. . . Sometimes there seemed to be a sort of ectoplasm; the speaker's body seemed to be inhabited by something . . . fluid. Afterwards he shrank again to insignificance, looking small and even vulgar. He seemed exhausted, his batteries run down.'

Heinz Zollin Höhne also describes Hitler's appearance in his book *The Order of the Death's Head*:

An unwitting midwife at the birth of the National-Socialist Movement was the Munich historian, Karl Alexander von Müller. He was in close touch with the young nationalist officers who were calling the tune in Munich at the time and at a soldiers' rally he was impressed by a man who seemed to have an extraordinarily compelling power of oratory. He says: 'Below locks of hair hanging down in a most unmilitary fashion, I saw a pale thin face with a close-cropped moustache and strikingly large light-blue eyes with a cold fanatical stare.' Müller nudged his school-friend Mayr, who was sitting next him: 'Do you know you have got a "natural" orator among your pupils?'

Captain Karl Mayr was head of Abteilung Ib/P (Press and Propaganda) in *Reichswehr* Group Headquarters No. 4 (Bavaria). He knew the man: 'That's Hitler from the List Regiment. You, Hitler, come here a moment.' Müller remembers that Hitler 'did as he was told, moving awkwardly, half defiant, half embarrassed.' The scene typifies Adolf Hitler's dependence upon the officers of the Bavarian *Reichswehr* and the sense of inferiority which the future Führer of the Great German Reich took years to overcome.

Mayr was quick to recognize Corporal Hitler's propagandist ability. In July 1919 Mayr's section in the Bavarian War Ministry drew up a confidential list of their contact men in individual units: the list included one 'Hitler, Adolf.' Mayr found Hitler only too ready to use his oratory wherever the ideological front was threatened.

The corporal gradually proved himself so useful that Mayr dropped his parade-ground manner, and began to address his letters politely 'Dear Herr Hitler.' Hitler was a frequent visitor to the War Ministry and ranked as a member of Mayr's political staff. One day in the demobilization camp at Lechfeld it looked as if the officers were losing control of their men; Hitler moved in at once and restored the situation. Another contact man, Lorenz Frank, reported on 23 August 1919: 'Hitler particularly is a born demagogue; at a meeting his fanaticism and popular appeal compel his audience to listen to him.'

Mayr decided to use his discovery for greater things. One of his duties was to watch political parties in Bavaria; in September 1919 he accordingly dispatched Hitler to a meeting of the German Workers Party (*Deutsche Arbeiter Partei* – DAP) – a collection of nationalist sectarians who, in addition to hatred of the Jews and the Republic, preached an emotional lower-middle-class socialism using such phrases as 'breaking the yoke of the usurer.' Hitler soon became the star speaker at the DAP meetings and had little difficulty in shouting down the more discreet among his competitors in the beer cellars. In January 1920, the party, then 64 strong, elected him Head of Propaganda and accepted the party programme which he drew up. It later re-named itself National-Socialist German Workers Party (NSDAP).

With the exception of his pathological hatred of Jews, Hitler started his path marching side by side with social democracy: the same envy toward wealth and the confidence that its redistribution would lead to a life of happiness and prosperity for all. However, the chauvinistic lurch in Germany gave him the chance to create his own party. He didn't have the idea, but the socialist charge of fiery slogans about "the yoke of the usurer" was enough for "that Hitler" to quench his thirst for at least some sort of power. Indeed, he would have remained there. That Hitler, the former corporal and political novice, could not have achieved power over Germany had he remained alone. He lacked a fuel capable of igniting a nation, which was suffering bitterly the humiliation of defeat. However, at this stage of his incomplete education, the novice Hitler was spotted by the intellectual Eckhardt, and he with his Thule Society endowed the amateur painter with a mystical idea, which could not be proven, but in which one could only believe: "Follow Hitler. He will dance, but it is I who called the tune."

Again the word to Bergier and Pauwels:

The medium represented, no doubt, not just one man, but a group, a collectivity of forces, a sort of magic powerhouse. What seems certain to us is that Hitler was animated by something other than what he was preaching: by forces and doctrines badly coordinated, no doubt, but infinitely more dangerous than the mere theory of National-Socialism – an idea far greater than anything he had thought of himself, which was more than he could grasp and of which he could only convey to his people and his collaborators in a much vulgarized and fragmentary form. In the words of Dr. Delmas:

'A powerful resonator, Hitler had always been the "sounding board" he claimed to be at the Munich Trial, and remained so until the end. Nevertheless, he only retained and used what at any given moment could satisfy his ambition and lust for power, his dreams of conquering the-world and his crazy obsession: the biological selection of a species that would be half man, half god.'

Another of his dreams, which was also an obsession, was to change life on Earth everywhere. He sometimes alluded to it or, rather, was unable to prevent what he was thinking from escaping now and then in some casual remark. He once said to

Hermann Rauschning: 'Our revolution is a new stage or, rather, the final stage in an evolution which will end by abolishing history. ... '

Abolishing history? That sounds topical even today, does it not?
Yet there was still more that Hitler said to the same conversation partner:

You know nothing about me; my party comrades have no conception of the dreams which haunt me or of the grandiose edifice of the foundations, at least, will have been laid before I die ... The world has reached a turning point: we are now at a time hinge ... The planet will undergo an upheaval, which you uninitiated people cannot understand ... What is happening is something more than the advent of a new religion ...[3]

Here, every letter of this passage needs to be emphasized in thick italics. It is not the caliber of Corporal Hitler and his wretched eloquence in the primitive concepts like "yoke of the exploitators" or "cult of power".

A new religion ... a time hinge... where does this come from? From Dietrich Eckhardt. From Karl Haushofer.

Haushofer held a professorship at Munich University. One of his students and, like the professor, a member of the Thule Society, introduced Hitler to him. The assistant's name was Rudolf Hess. He had found a leader! He had found the one, by whose hand the sissy members of the Thule Society could do dirty work.

At Hess's later trial,[4] he indicated that Haushofer was a secret master of the Thule Sosiety. Hess had resolved upon his flight to England, after Haushofer told him that in a dream he had seen him flying. Hess was the last surviving member of the Thule Society.

After the Beer Hall Putsch (8-9 November 1923), Hitler and Hess served time together in Landsberg Prison. Haushofer visited his pupil almost daily. There he also had conversations with the future Führer. Meanwhile, Hess at this time was manufacturing an ideology for the Party leader. Hitler's *Mein Kampf* was being written. A trusted person of Haushofer's, Hess ensured that the secret teachings would not be revealed in the book. Hitler himself wasn't pressing for this. Why prematurely frighten people who weren't blue-eyed blonds prematurely?

Karl Haushofer was born in 1869. He often spent time in Japan, learned the Japanese language, and joined an elite secret society, "The Black Dragon", the membership of which demanded that any unsuccessful activity of a member of the society should necessitate seppuku, or ritualistic suicide. During the First World War, General Haushofer drew attention for his gift of prophesy. He often correctly predicted the hour of an enemy attack, where heavy artillery shells would fall, and forecast the weather. He even foretold political changes among the enemies of Germany. (Likely, he was speaking about the Russian Revolution, in which the German Kaiser invested a lot of means to bring it about.) At the

---

3   Despite some doubts today that the Führer would speak so openly with the former mayor of Danzig, just these brief and offhand haughty comments sound credible. They are just like something Hitler would have said.

4   Some historians suspect that at the Nuremberg trial, it was not the genuine Hess that the English brought before the court, but a double. The strange story of Hess and his suicide at an age beyond 80 is indeed suspicious, even more so because the government of the United Kingdom declared that his files be sealed until the year 2041. Something is compromising the Brits. No one's hands are fully clean ...

time of his acquaintanceship with Hitler, Haushofer was about 50-years-old. He was a charming, high-browed aristocrat with a well-groomed mustache and a cheerful, imperious gaze.

In the future, the Führer would take on the role of soothsayer himself. When he decided to occupy the Rhineland, experts considered an armed conflict unavoidable. Hitler foresaw a different outcome and wasn't mistaken. He foretold the date when his troops would enter Paris, and when President Roosevelt would die. Some say that Haushofer was advising him. (This is doubtful. Haushofer's wife was not Aryan, and with Hitler's accession to power, the formerly close teacher and the pupil drifted apart.) Judging by his inspired dream about Hess's mission to England, Haushofer was one of those who were warning Hitler about an unavoidable collision with Russia. Was he warning against the unavoidability or the fatal outcome? Incidentally, here one is the same as the other. In 1938, a final breach occurred in the relationship, and Haushofer returned to academia, immersed himself in political geography, and through the journal *Geopolitika*, which he founded, published a number of articles, notable for their narrow materialistic realism. Members of the Thule Society strictly adhered to a materialistic terminology, which provided cover for their pseudo-scientific concepts.

An aristocrat, officer, ascetic, and the creator of a mystic, militant ideology had shut himself off from the world under the guise of a professor of geopolitics. Through Schopenhauer he came to discover Buddhism, gathering secrets adaptable for controlling people from everywhere. There is reason to believe that Haushofer is the one who chose the swastika as the Nazi's symbol.

Here's one more legend, one more component of Nazism; with a glance at the present day, not only of Nazism. It, likely, has been designated to still play a role, which for mankind is hardly propitious ...

According to the legend, 340,000 years ago, an advanced civilization was flourishing in the Gobi. A cataclysm turned the Gobi into a desert. The survivors fled to the north. Thor, the god of Nordic legend, was one of the heroes of the migration. The members of the Thule Society believed these refugees were the roots of the Aryan people, the "primary race". Haushofer's notion of a "return to origins" meant the conquest of Europe and the Asian Pamirs, including Tibet and the Gobi Desert. This, according to this thinking, was the heart of the planet, and its possessor would rule the world. In the schedule of the Ahnenerbe's work, there appeared the delivery of Aryan horses for scientific study and Aryan bees, which produced a special type of honey. Those, who were repulsed by vivisection, studied the horses and honey, while other "scientists" of the Ahnenerbe with a smile on their lips performed bizarre experiments on children, while simultaneously treating them with candy.

This legend, with which Haushofer became acquainted in 1905, holds that the sons of the "Intelligence from beyond", the ancient civilization's teacher, after the cataclysm took shelter in Himalayan caves. There they took alternative paths. One of them created the Kingdom of Agharti, a subterranean world of Good dedicated to meditation which rejected involvement in worldy matters. The other one founded Shambala, a center of power that governs verses (and peoples) and accelerates the path of mankind toward a turning point in time. (That's the origin of Hitler's "time hinge" in his ravings to *Rauschning*.) Seven of those dedicated to the Thule Society were preparing to rule the planet. Each swore an oath to kill himself in case of the failure of his mission, and each was obliged to offer human sacrifices. The practices of Nazism pushed Haushofer away from his godson Hitler. After the assassination attempt on Hitler, Haushofer was imprisoned in a concentration camp and emerged alive only by happenstance.

In March 1946, Karl Haushofer, at the age of 77, committed suicide together with his wife. Some say he committed hara-kari, while she drank poison. Failure was directly at hand. In connection with the Nuremberg trials, Haushofer had been summoned for questioning and was interrogated about his ties with Hess and Hitler. The facts revealed before the Nuremberg tribunal were horrifying to him.

Haushofer's own son, Albrecht, a prominent staff member of the German Foreign Ministry and a specialist on England, was killed. A poet, a playwright, and a person even more brilliant than his father, Albrecht was an advisor to Hess on questions of foreign policy – and one of the key figures of the German opposition. Hess used Albrecht's British connections for his leap to Scotland, but the failure of his mission forced Hitler to curse and condemn the Deputy Führer (Hess), which complicated the Haushofers' position. After the 20 July 1944 assassination attempt, Albrecht attempted to hide, but he was arrested at the end of 1944. On 23 April 1945, the administration of the Moabit prison freed its prisoners, but S.S. troops seized them at the entrance, led them away to the nearest abandoned lot, and executed them with shots to the back of the head. Albrecht's body was found three weeks later by his younger brother. The dead man's hands were clenching pages of his Moabit Sonnets to his chest. One sonnet says:

> That fate had been decreed to my father.
> It once lay within the strength of his will
> to plunge the daemon back into its durance.
> But my father broke away the seal.
> He did not see the rising breath of evil.
> He let the daemon soar into the world.

The formidable name of the Supreme Wizard Haushofer prompted Hitler to delay with the execution of his son. Albrecht sensed the approaching retribution. However, when Russian shells were ripping apart the Berlin sky, the fate of the intellectual, one of those who defended the honor of the German people, was decided. Here is one of his sonnets:

XLIII: Burned Books

> When China's great despot Shi Hwang Ti
> came to feel the spiritual past
> offering resistance to his will
> he simply ordered: Let them be destroyed!
> He had the books collected and done away with,
>   wise men put to death. Through the whole land
> imperial power drove murder and conflagration.
> Eleven years of burning and condemning.
> In the twelfth year the great despot was dead.
> The old books were then written anew
> by those who had nonetheless survived.

The next emperor who ruled in the land
looked in a friendly manner on all thinking:
did not burn books, did not burn wise men.[5]

Klaus Haushofer, gifted with a strong psyche, was a man of enormous culture and set out on an inhuman path, which seemed to him to be superior. The everyday world often gives rise to abominations. However the correction of human abominable deeds by means of an inhuman path leads to villainy on a cosmic scale. Playing with toys unknown to him, Haushofer didn't know that they were dangerous to him as well. The dearest people to him, his wife and son, who like himself, evoked the admiration of his pupil, the second man in the Nazi Party, proved to be incompatible with the goals and means of this Party and with the "New Order", which it inculcated. His gift as a soothsayer couldn't help Haushofer see the consequences of his activities or his own fate. Such little people we turn out to be, when fancying ourselves as equal to gods ...

It is time to end this topic. If we could only put an end to it in reality ...

One thing is clear: Nazism in Germany arose on the corpse of a deceased monarchy as an ideological balance to communism after the German revolution on 9 November 1918. Inspiring slogans were found for the masses that were distinct from the Russians', a notorious soup for the paupers, while the ideologues were inspired with Evil, which they kept under wraps until the right time. From the outside, everything looked like socialism with a strong personality. Over the personality they draped a cloak, fabricated by the best tailors, experts on mass psychology:

1. I understand your needs.
2. Personally I need nothing, other than your well-being.

Communism, as a doctrine, had no subtext. Nazism was born with an evil, demonic subtext.

Was the Evil a secret to the rulers who brought Hitler to power? No. Just as Napoleon's ambition wasn't a secret in his own time. "Children's playthings; let them play, as long as they've done their chore." The rulers hoped to manage with this. I'm not speaking about Eckhardt and Haushofer. They were convinced and, so to speak, pure apostles of Evil. Here I have in mind the good congregations, who donated money out of impulses for upholding law and order.

Soviet propaganda had brought so much scandal upon itself, that it wasn't believed even with respect to the obvious. There was once a popular writer in his time named Nikolai Shpanov, who before the war wrote about how events would unfold after an attack upon us by the fascists to the exact contrary of what really did happen. According to him, we would smash the fascist swine like nobody's business (socialist realism!), and they would flee all sniveling and, excuse me, losing their trousers. After the war Shpanov, a patriarch of a highly successful genre, wrote quasi-historical, thick novels, many of which even today are remembered, if not as novels, then for their voluptuous size, like *Podzhigateli* [*The Arsonists*] and *Zagovorshchiki* [*The Conspirators*]. They were published in such large editions that they made other authors's mouths water, including mine. These volumes could be found in any

---

5   Retranslated from Russian by Valentina Kucher.

home. The CPSU encouraged the justification of its Non-Aggression Pact with Germany through literature: "If we hadn't signed it, then one would have been signed against us. The capitalists had funded Hitler, brought him to power and were shoving him toward the East."

Regarding the shoves – alas; the capitalists didn't love the USSR. Indeed, why should they have? So they provided money, with no conditions. Hitler didn't bind himself with obligations. It is simple – they gave him money, throwing a glance to the east. They were prominent monopolists – Voegler, Krupp, von Renteln, Shacht, even Henry Ford. They were confident in their ability to hold the dog on the leash and to control events ...

... until one beautiful morning they woke up suddenly to the reality of the Gestapo, in a world where even their money had no influence.

On 20 April 1939 under the new Nazi banners, the *Wehrmacht* revealed to the world its daunting power in honor of the Führer's 50th birthday. Six years later, these very same banners were tossed into the slush on Red Square in Moscow -- but at what a price ...

30

The Eve

The commanders had been feverishly preparing on the precipice of war for a half-year, but dutifully following the Leader's orders, the Red Army turned out to be not ready for it. They pestered Stalin with requests for permission to shoot down, or at least chase off, the brazen German airplanes overflying Soviet territory, beseeched the Leader to strengthen the border with reinforcements and fortifications and to heighten combat readiness, and were extremely busy with something. With what? War-game scenarios? Defensive? Offensive? On the north, the west, the southwest? *Die erste Kolonna marschiert, die zweite Kolonna marschiert ...* (The first column is marching; the second column is marching ...)[1]

Zhukov writes:

> Tension kept mounting. And the greater loomed the threat of war, the more tensely the leadership of the People's Commissariat of Defense worked. Indeed, the leading members of the Commissariat and the General Staff, and especially Marshal Timoshenko, worked 18 or 19 hours a day at that time, and often remained in their offices all night.
>
> On June 13, Timoshenko phoned Stalin in my presence and asked permission to alert the troops of the border districts, and to deploy the first echelons according to the cover plans.
>
> 'We will think it over,' Stalin replied.

What was there to think about? The People's Commissariat of Defense was working for 18 to 19 hours a day. It was already at war! One definitely doesn't envy the People's Commissar and the Chief of the General Staff in their positions. They understood the advantage of the adversary's situation and were suspecting that war was looming right in front of them, but they could do nothing, lest they be killed for nothing, like the recently arrested air force commanders, and before them the thousands of best military commanders, who had taught the People's Commissar and the Chief of the General Staff the skill to forestall the enemy ...

Only 168 hours remained until the start of the Great Patriotic War.

One evening shortly before the fatal hour, the darling Z. Rybkina, who was an employee of the People's Commissariat of Foreign Affairs and also an NKVD agent (and who later, after an unavoidable stint in prison, became the children's book author Zoia Voskresenskaia), was at the German Embassy in Moscow, quietly poking around the

---

1   Editor's note: This is a line from Leo Tolstoy's *War and Peace*, a mocking generalization from the example of a Prussian-trained Austrian general at Austerlitz who was so meticulously following orders that he was ignoring the sudden turns in the battle that rendered the orders no longer relevant to the situation. Tolstoy extended this to anyone who commands blindly, and now the author is applying it to Stalin and the Red Army high command.

Embassy building for suitable locations for listening devices. She noticed the disappearance of several paintings and decorative pieces and through an opened door saw with horror that Embassy workers were packing suitcases. Her observations immediately reported up the chain of command.

There was no reaction. Now there was less than 54 hours until the start of the Great Patriotic War.

Trains were rolling into Germany. Even though the railroads couldn't handle the domestic demands on transportation, strings of trains, one after the other, loaded with timber, grain, oil, and steel, were still punctiliously delivering everything to the Germans as had been agreed. This has caused quasi-historians to see an underlying design in this, and they have set forth the aforementioned not as a hypothesis, but as a plan that really existed: to smother the Germans with trains, jam their rail network, and then give them a whack from above – and they'd be dead meat.

It is bad if a scholar lacks imagination. However, such a surfeit of it is simply a calamity. After all, if you even agree with something like this, then it is possible to conclude as well that the masses of prisoners at the start of the war were not captured by the *Wehrmacht*, but deliberately sent into the enemy rear, in order to distract him with the need to escort these prisoners, clog the roads, sow confusion, then give them a whack and ... And the good whacks didn't come for a long time.

Now there was no longer time. Not two or three years, or even two or three days. Not even an hour. The bread had reached the soldiers' stomachs, the fuel had filled the tanks in the airplanes, the steel had been turned into gun barrels, and the timber converted into carbine butts, which would be crushing the heads of captured commissars.

The war had begun.

At 3:00 am on 22 June, the People's Commissar of State Security Merkulov gathered his key colleagues and announced that the USSR had been attacked by German forces along the entire length of the western frontier. The Leader only learned about this 45 minutes later, though he didn't find out from those who were the first to receive this terrible news, not from his experienced courtiers, who only brought their Master exultant news. Zhukov woke up Stalin.

At the same time, the sons of the Motherland in the border garrisons and manning the frontier outposts, who weren't warned about anything and who suspected nothing, were peacefully sleeping in their barracks.

Death woke them up.

31

The War Begins

The cadres of the 1941 May Day parade were struck by the apparent agitation which the leadership of the country, who had destroyed the flower of its Army, was displaying in that alarming time. Under a gloomy sky – the spring had been cold and late in arriving – columns of troops were freezing at attention on the broad Red Square. On the podium of Lenin's Mausoleum, Marshal Timoshenko, in a high voice that was cracking with strain, was elucidating the peacefulness of our nation, of the Red Army, and its readiness to repel an attack – the entire holiday repertoire. Meanwhile behind him, the Boss was pacing back and forth like a caged animal. The Leader, who knew how to handle himself in public, who was normally so inscrutable! Now he was restless, his eyes downcast, slouching, and there was so much worry in this wandering around behind the back of the People's Commissar of Defense, who was straining mightily to shout out the words of his script, that it was clear: Stalin understood everything; he already knew that he had lost the game.

Late in the evening, on Saturday, 21 June 1941, I, with my parents and grandmother, was returning from our family celebration, marking the 25th birthday of my cousin, a lieutenant who had returned wounded and frostbitten from the war with Finland. We had gathered in an apartment in the center of Kiev with the address Malo-Podvol'naia Street No. 6, which at one time had fully belonged to my mother's older brother, a well-to-do Kiev merchant, and had at one time held my own cradle. Our entire family and the brothers and sisters of my mother and father were present. My cousin was dressed in civilian clothes, but his tunic with an Order and its lieutenant's insignia of two little squares was hanging on a chair in the bedroom. Everyone went to take a look at it, while the youngest son of my uncle and aunt, who was shot in 1944 for refusing to lead into an attack a platoon of soldiers who didn't understand the Russian language, was re-telling with admiration the war stories he had heard from his brother. The table was spread with my aunt's home-cooked dishes, including a special goulash and tasty blintzes; the adults in the family drank cherry liqueur by the shot glass and there was a great deal of conversation, but they didn't forget about us little ones. We were constantly hovering underfoot, and we were all ears. They weren't saying any names, and even the name of the Leader was spoken only once in a discussion among the men – when my father's older brother, a writer, who would meet his death in 1951 in connection with the so called "Case of the Jewish Anti-fascist Committee", shouted at me, the little brat who had broadcast that war was coming, and had shut my mouth with the authoritative word of Stalin, who had said just a week before that there would be no war.

On Duma Square, by the fountain – where four and a half years hence they would erect gallows and hang German officers, who had taken part in the murder of the peaceful residents of Kiev, in front of a large gathering of people and leave their bodies hanging for public display – we boarded Trolley No. 4 and traveled three stops to Sennaia Market (L'vov) Square. It was a warm summer evening, calm and clear. The sky was silent and full of stars. It seems that the night sky was bluer then, than it is now. From the Sennaia Market Square we walked along the even-numbered side of Artem (L'vov) Street as far as Observatornaia Street, but we couldn't cross to our apartment building's side: a column of covered Army trucks was moving down L'vov Street to the west. Little shields were dimming the trucks' head lights. In my childhood, automobiles were a rare sight, even in Kiev. Yet here was a whole column of vehicles, which seemed endless. I was squirming, and my mother and father were holding me by the hands. We stood there as the quiet and dark trucks rolled by. This silent, alarming parade lasted for quite awhile. As we entered the building and climbed the four flights of stairs to our apartment, I pestered my mother and father with inquiries, but my parents were sullenly silent.

On the blindingly bright next morning of 22 June, I awoke around 9:00 am, and as I was stretching in bed, my grandmother walked up to me: "Peten'ka [an affectionate diminutive of Peter], it is war." "With the Germans!?" – I cried out. I had slept through a night-time bombing raid. There was not a cloud in the sky. My mother was at work, while my father and sister had gone somewhere. I rushed to a network loudspeaker. It was transmitting light music. Then there were songs: *"Our step is firm, and the foe will never set foot on our republics."* No one approached the microphone. The fear to say something inappropriate was immobilizing the country.

The outbreak of war ... it caught him in bed. The news of war woke the Leader from his sleep, while in the People's Commissariat of Defense, which had finally extracted from the Boss the authorization for the transmission of Directive No. 1 on bringing the border forces and outposts to combat alert, no one had gone to sleep that night. The People's Commissar couldn't make up his mind to call Stalin. Zhukov phoned him and didn't get rattled when Stalin's security chief informed him that Comrade Stalin was sleeping.

"Wake him at once. The Germans are bombing our towns!"

It was 3:45 am. Of course, Directive No. 1 didn't go anywhere. War was already underway, and German saboteurs were cutting the lines of communication and killing the unaware, isolated Red Army commanders. Only at 7:15 am. was Directive No. 2 transmitted, directing the available forces in the border zone to engage the enemy and to block his further advance – to the military district commands! God knows whether it reached the forward units and when it arrived, if it did. God knows what the commanders were thinking and what they did, frightened as they were by the bogeyman of "anti-German tendencies", confused as they were by the recent TASS denunciation of rumor-mongering and the strict orders "Don't open fire, don't yield to provocations!" and then suddenly the arriving Directive – "Attack!"

Attack ... but the initiative was entirely in the hands of the *Wehrmacht*, which was attacking energetically and with enthusiasm.

The word to Khruschchev:

Later, after the war, I found out that in the first hours of the war, Stalin was at the Kremlin. Beria and Malenkov told me this. Beria relayed the following. When the war started, Stalin gathered the members of the Politburo. I don't know whether it was the entire Politburo, or just a certain group that met with Stalin the most often. Stalin was completely depressed. He made an announcement approximately like this: 'War has broken out and it is unfolding catastrophically. Lenin left a proletarian Soviet state to us, but we're pissing it away.' That is just how he put it, according to Beria. Then Stalin said, 'I'm abdicating my leadership.' With that, he walked out of the room.

He left, climbed into his car, and drove off to his nearest dacha.

What sort of gesture was this? WE'RE pissing ...?! It is as if he's beside the point!

That's how historical catastrophes happen – in a single moment. That is also how death arrives. That was a moment about which the army commanders had been dreaming. A moment in which the Leader himself, startled by his own stupidities, voluntarily let go of the reins and the government of the country could bloodlessly pass to more sober minds and the leadership of the war into steadier hands. At least the cruel consequences of Stalin's wartime command might be avoided, even if the consequences of Stalin's diplomacy could not be averted.

Beria described to Khrushchev what happened next:

> We remained behind. What next? A certain time passed after Stalin's performance. Molotov, Kaganovich, Voroshilov and I talked it over. We discussed the situation and decided to go to Stalin and return him to power. As we tried to convince him that our country was enormous, that we still had a chance to get organized, to mobilize industry and people, in a word, to do everything necessary to rouse the people and put them back on their feet in the struggle against Hitler, only then did Stalin seem to come back to himself a bit. We determined who would do what to organize the defense, industry, and so forth.

Perhaps they'd dropped a hint, of course, with complete respect to Leader, that the hallowed seat could not be left empty, that power could not wallow on the floor, and that someone would pick it up. Perhaps they added, "What would that person do with us, your loyal servants, and with you yourself, our great and wise Comrade Stalin?"[1]

The Leader's behavior suggests that he really believed in his own ability to control events and really counted upon his iron will to influence them – and that the war had caught him with his pants down. He was lost, stunned. It was as if the cards he'd been holding in his game with his international partners had suddenly at a critical moment turned into palm leaves or newspaper galley proofs. The chit-chat about Hitler's masking of his invasion of England by concentrating the *Wehrmacht* on the Soviet borders was just as absurd as the alternative explanation that the concentration of forces had been conceived as a way to put pressure on Stalin, to make him more accommodating in negotiations.

There are astronomers, who observe the cosmos for years and make direct discoveries of objects by spotting something that others have so far missed. There is also another method, searching for heavenly bodies by the influence they have on the trajectories of other heavenly bodies. There are facts, each of which taken alone may not explain a phenomenon, but an aggregation of facts sometimes permits one to speculate about the presence of an as yet unknown fact, which might. The vulnerabilities of this method are indisputable. William of Ockham back in the 14th century expressed a fundamental principle of science, today known as Occam's razor: "*Entia non sunt multiplicanda sine necessitate.*" ["One should not multiply entities beyond necessity." In other words, don't look for more complex explanations when a simpler explanation exists.] A method of filling voids cannot be convincing. I repeat and emphasize: many of the suppositions in this book are in need of

---

1   Later the memoirs of Mikoian became published, which deserve greater trust and which dates this episode described by Beria to the end of June.

supplementary research! In this version, bricks have been fitted into the mosaic of history. However this particular interpretation of history rests upon them.

Such a method leads to the conjecture that Stalin was genuinely expecting a German ultimatum before any war erupted, which means that Hitler's subterfuge had worked. He had truly outfoxed the Leader, who had considered himself to be the ultimate trickster. You see, an ultimatum would have given him some time. Well, at least until the ultimatum expired. Fully enough time to blow up the bridges (which the Germans particularly feared) and at least for issuing a combat alert order. The Boss didn't think that Hitler's own brain was capable of coming up with such a rationale against issuing an ultimatum, and he shrank from even thinking about this possibility. But what if Hitler was suddenly reading his thoughts? The Leader's close associates effortlessly read his mind, but the Führer might have to exert himself a bit. He possessed the same qualities, let us say, as Molotov, or even greater. The Führer, they said, was a mystic, a mage, which meant it was better not to think, in order not to have these thoughts intercepted, which could leave Stalin helpless.

He left his border troops helpless.

Germany wasn't capable of fighting on two fronts! Its preparations were a bluff and being conducted only to give weight to the issuing of an ultimatum. Once issued, he and the Führer would meet face to face – the planet's great leaders. They would meet and decide the planet's fate!

Hypnotized by his greatness, lulled by his sycophantic circle of associates, Stalin was expecting even Hitler's respect. Allegedly, "At least Hitler esteems me so highly as to let me know directly in case I overindulged my appetite." Stalin had no doubt that there would be direct negotiations. So the rumors about a "war of nerves" coming from circles close to Göring – in order to demoralize the USSR leadership – were preceding the ultimatum. In a word, sleep, Soso. There will be an ultimatum.

He in fact overslept. He had believed that this wasn't war, but simply a "war of nerves", and gave his nerves a rest.

However, there was the TASS denunciation.[2] It was issued not without a reason. On the eve of the war Anthony Eden had announced to the Soviet ambassador in London that in case of a German attack on the Soviet Union, Great Britain was ready to send a military mission and "urgently examine the question of rendering economic assistance to Russia." Yes, the entry of the USSR into the war as an ally was a rosy dream of the English. Yes, the forewarning was also a wish. Yes, the information of the Brits had to be regarded cautiously. J. R. M. Butler in his authoritative book *Grand Strategy: A History of the Second World War* writes that an answer to this British offer, as usual, did not come. Yet that is an answer! The TASS denunciation of the possibility of war was in fact a reply – in case the English revealed the diplomatic demarche to the public. It was also a query to the Germans: a humiliating one, but not stupid. Yet you, Leader, had previously been receiving responses to similar queries from the very same partner within a matter of hours; at the very least, in the case of the annexation of Bucovina. Yet here seven full days had passed. This would have been sufficient time not only to issue a combat alert order, but also for bringing the frontier to higher readiness as well. In fact, you didn't raise the alarm, and you didn't raise the country to arms!

---

2   But who today remembers that it wasn't the first? An analogous denunciation had been published on 9 May 1941 in Soviet newspapers – without the least diplomatic reaction from the German side. Wasn't that an ominous sign? Didn't that demand some action?

There is no excuse for this. Whether a preemptive attack in July 1941 or an invasion of Germany in May 1942 was in preparation or not, there is no justification for the Leader's cowardly inaction and his awakening from sleep by the terrible roar of war.

The description of events in the pre-war 1941 period is credible only in the memoirs of eyewitnesses to them. German sources are more reliable than the Soviet ones. Zhukov delved into the Soviet archives and made a significant announcement: "Sometimes, very important documents are disappearing from our historical research circulation." (? – I don't know. I think this is an archival excerpt authorized for citation.)

Indeed, a document has disappeared, one which should absolve Zhukov of blame. Of course, not everything is preserved. Indeed, who is interested in the eternal preservation of evidence? Incidentally, the document, a photocopy of which appears in L. Bezymensky's book *Gitler i Stalin nakanune skhvatki*, is likely the one for which the Marshal was searching and which the leadership at that time was keeping concealed from him. After the Marshal's death, the document turned up – the so-called "Zhukov Plan". It recapitulates that more than 100 German divisions had been concentrated on the Soviet border. A sudden attack upon the Red Army was possible, which must be forestalled by our own attack with the forces of the Kiev and Western Military Districts in order not to give the initiative to the German command and to destroy (This word was crossed out! This likely meant at least *to catch*) the German Army while it was still deploying. The document, handwritten by A.M.Vasilevsky, has not been signed by those whose names it bears (People's Commissar of War Timoshenko and Chief of the General Staff Zhukov), not to mention it lacks Stalin's endorsement. Even though Zhukov toward the end of his life unambiguously expressed the opinion that such an attack would have led to an even greater disaster, the drastic document amply illustrates recognition of the gravity of the situation that had developed.

The motives of ostrich-like behavior of the Boss himself are inexplicable. Either attack or withdraw, but just don't sit there and wait for it! Why not deploy the first echelon to cover the frontier? This is elementary.

Any guess is as good as another. Those I am putting forward are no better and no worse than any others.

I will repeat again: Stalin was mesmerized by the dogma that Germany wouldn't undertake a war on two fronts. Having indicated a deadline for the Red Army to be ready for war – apparently, by May 1942, although the civilian leaders were insisting upon the winter of 1943 – he clung to this deadline. So, being illiterate in military matters, he didn't know what to do when Hitler reached his decision about a preventive war and began to implement it. The *Wehrmacht*'s concentration on the Soviet border caught Stalin off guard. Being a genius, as he was described, and stunned by the first reports of war, he would not trouble himself with making evasions.

He understood immediately that he was late. Had he started moving forces up to the border, the Germans would have dropped their concealment and beaten him to the punch. That the Germans would lose the factor of surprise, to which they had given the primary role – this he didn't even understand and didn't consider – and he flinched. After the Finnish muddle he felt so weak! He didn't dare advance the forces to meet Hitler. The time for this had been missed in January, and not in May-June. Between May and June he had reached the point that would come to Hitler later. When nothing else remains, maniacs resort to willpower: "I'll flex – and it won't happen."

The dispatches about the *Wehrmacht*'s concentration contained the exact identities and strength of the German formations. Stalin could not oppose this methodical implantation with anything commensurate in quantity (or quality!), so he decided to present an air of nonchalance to Hitler: "Look, they say you're preparing for war and your explanations aren't entirely convincing in the face of England's massive disinformation (although rumors are circulating that you are intimidating us before issuing an ultimatum), but we trust you. The Germans are people well-known for their integrity. You are fighting with England – and may you enjoy success. We, though, are content with the Pact and not preparing for any war, nor even giving that a thought." (Then there was really nothing else to do, but to maintain that deathly silence on the borders!)

The senselessness of such behavior can be further argued by the fact that receiving intelligence information about the Reich's military plans from its very core, the *Wehrmacht's* General Staff, Stalin was simply obliged to suspect that some sort of similar leak of information was possible from his General Staff as well. If so, then Hitler had to know something about the Red Army's own worked up attack plans, or else at a minimum, that the Red Army General Staff was not developing defense plans. Perhaps instead the Boss was assuming that having destroyed anyone who thought differently, having executed the top brass, and having weeded out the German intelligence service (which knew about the innocence of the high command, and for which it indeed perished), he had at the same time completely uprooted a fascist espionage network? So he believed in the effectiveness of his repressions? So he didn't think that with the brutalities he was creating new foes? If so, his stupidity was immeasurable.

In contrast to Stalin, though, Hitler believed in the intelligence reports he was receiving. Besides, he was able to find confirmation for them with his own eyes. The USSR's preparation for a war on an unprecedented scale had become a fact, which had not been hidden. The cruel strengthening of discipline at factories, which punished tardiness with prison time, the new huge army supply depots in the border districts, the moving up of second echelon forces ... Meanwhile we're outstripping the Russians, Hitler explained to his close associates. They're not even beginning to think about an attack? Yes, not just yet. They're not ready. The Red Army is in the process of re-equipping. We must take advantage of this. In the meantime, to restrain Stalin from launching a preemptive attack, we'll give him some hope – a rumor of an ultimatum.

Stalin wanted to deceive Hitler. He wanted this, he hoped for it, and he was confident that he would put one over Hitler. He would stall and win time. This confidence was a cut-and-dried miscalculation. Hitler had the measure of Stalin as a politician who would shoot without warning. With his fawning credulity, Stalin only strengthened the Führer's suspicions. Stalin had also smiled at the army commanders. Hitler understood this; he had mastered the lesson and outplayed Stalin. The Leader's collapse at the start of the war was signifying a defeat in single combat. This was stinging.

Hitler's complacency in triumph is easy to imagine: he had deceived an enemy, who for a half-decade had been insidiously deceiving his own Party comrades! Of course, the Führer watched with gleeful malice as Stalin, as if in alliance with the Führer – who knows, even that might be lurking in the Leader's background! – kept destroying his own army. So with the sudden blow in 1941, the Führer might well consider himself a personification of retribution on behalf of the deceased commanders. Now, looking at the film footage on the frozen fields around Moscow and on the steppes near Stalingrad, we shrug our shoulders: How could Hitler have thought he could stick his nose into Russia, how could he have dared believe that he would overcome it? Temporarily putting aside the question of the believability of overcoming Russia, with its repeatedly and thoroughly considered aspects of territorial expanse, Russian fatalism, and the Russian will to resist, offset by the cost of that resistance and all the other factors (including the devastation inflicted on the RKKA by Stalin), let's turn to the decisive factor, which prodded Hitler to act. This was Great Britain.

Hitler knew that an invasion of England would lead to a war with an empire that had never yet lost a war. It is not in vain that Directive No. 17, known as the plan for Operation Sea Lion, contains so much diplomatic rhetoric:

> As England, despite her hopeless military situation, still shows no sign of *willingness to come to terms* (Suggesting that it should have already!), I have decided to prepare, and *if necessary* (That is to say that there is still time to come to one's senses) to carry out, a landing operation against her. The aim of this operation is to eliminate the English motherland as a base from which war against Germany can be continued, and if necessary (!! Suggesting that it will not be too late to capitulate even after an invasion, in which case I, the Führer, won't even begin to occupy any part of your islands), to occupy completely. (Parenthetical expressions are the author's.)

However, diplomatic pirouettes are one thing, and war is another. The latter is full of surprises. By accident, the Luftwaffe scattered some bombs on London. A childlike mentality holds sway in so-called "Grand Policy". The Brits didn't even begin to investigate the incident and responded with a massed – according to their understanding of the term – bombing raid on Berlin. Hitler went into frenzy and committed a massed – according to the Luftwaffe's capabilities – raid on London. With that it all started! At the moment of confirming the plan for Barbarossa, the Führer was converting a lot of British cities and towns to ruin, and war was blazing everywhere. Thus it is surprising that the English a half year later were still taking seriously a document, Directive No. 17, dated 16 July 1940, when the Führer was at the zenith of his vile vainglory, especially when you consider that this document was never supplemented nor re-examined, while the *Wehrmacht* was concentrating in eastern Poland, a thousand miles from the supposed battlefield. Moreover, the invasion was contingent upon several conditions: Great Britain's Royal Air Force must first be worn down and unable to hinder the landing operation; the sea corridors leading to the invasion sites along the southern coast of England had to be swept clear of mines; the entrances to the La Manche [English Channel] must be densely mined to prevent external assistance to England through the channel; powerful long-range artillery must be able to support the invasion from the continent; and the Royal Navy, weakened by attacks from the air and the sea, must further be distracted by naval operations in the North Sea and the Mediterranean theaters.

Not a single one of these conditions deemed necessary for the invasion was ever achieved. An attempt to realize the first of them was foiled in the Battle of Britain, in which Germany suffered its first defeat in the war. Moreover, what would have awaited the Führer in the case of an invasion, even a successful one? Despite its small size, the Nazi leadership understood that the island would never be an easy prey. It understood that to subjugate England was not the same as conquering France. The government of France had capitulated, and with it, the people. The English King would definitely go into exile, and the people would not acquiesce. Would America simply wait, while the King mobilized the resources of an empire that stretched across four continents to come to the aid of the home island? For how many years would such a war go on? What would the USSR be doing during this time?

With the defeat in the Battle of Britain, the Führer already sensed that time was now working against him; he knew this and was laboring under no delusions about Stalin. The negotiations in Berlin in the autumn of 1940 might have turned out completely differently, if Stalin had directly expressed a desire to join the Axis; Hitler would have granted it. A change of heart preceded man's first friendly gesture toward a wolf, the ancient progenitor of the first dog. Hitler didn't sense anything like this in Stalin. Ribbentrop might melt over the fact that in the Kremlin, he felt as if he was greeting old party comrades. The Devil, more perspicacious than his Minister of Foreign Affairs, scented something else. Within the Axis bloc, Stalin would have played a secondary role; he understood this, and this didn't satisfy him. He was lying low and he was getting ready. The threat from the direction of the USSR had to be eliminated immediately, before active operations in the West resumed. Hitler simply had no way out of this dilemma. Choosing between two adversaries, he selected the USSR first. Had he taken on England, he would have wound up in a worse situation, confronting not a "Colossus with clay feet", but the monolithic England, supported by America, and with a Red Army behind his back that was preparing for an invasion, in which case it would have possessed the initiative.

Winston Churchill wrote in Volume 3 of his book *The Grand Alliance*:

> War is primarily a catalogue of blunders, but it may be doubted that any mistake in history has equaled that of which Stalin and the Communist chiefs were guilty when they cast away all possibilities in the Balkans[3] and supinely awaited, or were incapable of realising, the fearful onslaught which impended on Russia. We have hitherto rated them as selfish calculators. In this period they were proved simpletons as well. The force, the mass, the bravery and endurance of Mother Russia had still to be thrown into the scales. But so far as strategy, policy, foresight, and competence are arbiters Stalin and his commissars showed themselves at this moment the most completely outwitted bunglers of the Second World War.

Nonsense. In March-April 1941 it was already too late. If the criteria of foresight is the arbiter, it is a pity that a plot by the Red Army commanders never occurred and that the criminal with the low forehead remained at the helm of Russia. Indeed, one feels completely awful when one thinks that after the Victory, the Ruler, who continued all the same to exterminate and to give the people the run around, offered only a cold toast "to the great Russian people", while the words about the bravery and endurance of Mother Russia were uttered not by its ruler, but by a British Lord, a cynical politician, to whom Russia was not sort of any mother, but only a much-suffering ally in a terrible war on its territory.

On 23 June 1941, the Russian newspaper *Pravda* published the following communiqué from the Red Army's Main Command:

> At dawn on 22 June 1941, regular forces of the German Army attacked our border units on a front from the Baltic to the Black Sea and in the course of the first half of

---

3   In reference to March and April 1941 when Hitler invaded Yugoslavia and Greece

the day were held back by them. With the second half of the day the German forces were met by the forward units of the Red Army's field forces. After savage fighting the adversary was repulsed with great losses. Only on the Grodno and Krystynopol directions did the enemy manage to achieve insignificant tactical successes and to occupy the towns Kal'variia, Stoiianuv and Chekhanovets, the first two located 15 kilometers and the latter 10 kilometers from the border.

Enemy aviation attacked a number of our air bases and populated locations, but everywhere it encountered a decisive repulse from our fighters and anti-aircraft artillery, which inflicted heavy losses on the foe. Sixty-five enemy aircraft were shot down.

The English also didn't confide everything in their communiqués. This, however .... I don't think that Nazi propaganda even by the final days of the war had learned everything that Soviet propaganda knew on its first day. Had the population known about the real pace of the *Wehrmacht's* advance, about the losses, about the absence of contact between the forces, about the reaction of the Leader himself to the news coming from the battlefields, instead of a nation, there would have remained only a panic-stricken herd.

Glory to Soviet censorship! If the End of Days will be censored in the Soviet manner, a decorous exit from the stage is prepared for mankind. Censorship didn't allow the effect of the surprise to spread among the general population. The testimony of refugees was silenced by the threat to punish fear-mongers as subversives. Eyewitnesses, fearing to be regarded as fear-mongers and hence as subversives, preferred not to trust their own testimony, considering what they had seen to be limited to their own experience, while in other places ...

Glory to Soviet propaganda! The country, which had been blinded by the TASS denunciation of rumors of war, through the efforts of propaganda quickly came out of its shock from the surprise attack and proved to be ready to resist. This people had been educated through the ages to be ready for a struggle at any cost. Propaganda did not overlook this experience; it exploited it, creating immortal works of art, marvels of song and great films.

The spirit of the population didn't buckle, but this didn't improve the situation on the various fronts. Zhukov headed to the Southwestern Front as a *Stavka* representative, Shaposhnikov and Kulik were sent to the Western Front.

On the Western Front, nothing could be done. Kulik, feigning fearless activity, flew into the forming Suwalki pocket for a few minutes. Shaposhnikov became ill – he in fact was a seriously unhealthy man, and the stream of terrible news knocked him off his feet.

The course of the border fighting on the Western Front causes one to think that Meretskov's replacement by Zhukov as Chief of the General Staff was not a result of the defeat of the "Reds" in the command staff game, but was because Meretskov was blamed for the disastrous war on Finland, which he, of course, hadn't wanted. Meretskov, a protégé of Svechin and a secret supporter of Iakir's defensive doctrine, became frightened and timid, and provoked the ire of the Leader, who was impressed by Zhukov's aggressiveness. Meanwhile, because of the insuperable need to win, the post of Chief of the General Staff fell to Zhukov, which he didn't want, and in which he displayed the weakest aspects of his giftedness. His blunders were the poor arrangement of forces along the northern face of the Belorussian District's border[4] and, most importantly, the absence of a clear instruction, which the troops could follow in case of an attack. As a result, the competently led and elite 6th Mechanized Corps in the Suwalki salient, which was advantageously positioned for a counterstroke, despite its offensive élan turned out to be short of ammunition and fuel, and immobilized by contradictory orders, at a time when minutes decided everything and there was no time to wait for orders. Its tanks were blown up or abandoned, and its commander General Khatskilevich was killed ...

On the Southwestern Front, Zhukov did everything possible in his role as *Stavka* representative. He accurately assessed the situation, but could not regain the initiative, despite the significant numerical superiority of his forces. After all, this was no longer Iakir's *front*, in which a partisan network would have remained intact and been operating from the first days, the soldiers would have been fully trained, while Timoshenko would be commanding only cavalry ...[5]

In view of the alarming situation on the Western Front, Zhukov was summoned back to Moscow. A catastrophe could not be prevented. Credit in the further measures to prevent the military catastrophe from leading to disintegration of the nation belongs first of all to the Red Army soldiers, who stubbornly continued to fight even in encirclement, next to the lack of roads, and only then to the *Stavka* of the Supreme High Command.

The course of the Red Army's combat operations on the Soviet-German front for the duration of 1941 was nothing other than an effort to scuttle the attacking *Wehrmacht*'s offensive timetable. (It is in this sense that in connection with the potential chaos likely to result from the mythical Soviet attack plans for 6 July, I made the observation that the real situation seemed nevertheless to be "an orderly handling of the fighting.") In counterattacks in the Ukraine, in Belorussia, at Odessa, Smolensk and Briansk, human meat, often without weapons, was hurled under the wheels of the German military machine in order to slow it down.[6] The lack of readiness for war forced the use of this tactic. However, the same

---

4   Nevertheless it is hardly fair to blame Zhukov for this. The victory of the "Blues" over the "Reds" in the 1940 command staff game convinced him of the danger of a German attack north of the Pripiat' Marshes. A warning of this was the essence of Marshal Tukhachevsky's "Last will and testament", which had the full attention of Shaposhnikov. However, even before the Purge the right to conduct strategic planning was stripped from the military commanders and became Comrade Stalin's personal possession. Under the Leader's doctrine, it was easier to mask the concentration of Red Army forces on the axis of attack planned by Stalin for his own aggression. It is hard to believe that after the command staff game, now in his role as Chief of the General Staff, Zhukov didn't challenge this plan – unless his attention was focused not on defense, but attack. Then there would be no reason to challenge it ...

5   Iakir once joked about Timoshenko, "I have a fine deputy for the cavalry – if he would also only think a bit ... " However, the war would later show that Timoshenko had learned a lot from his outstanding commander. Incidentally, the liquidation by Stalin's order of the partisan bases in the eastern Ukraine after Iakir's execution had an effect on the initial stage of the war, just as did the purge in the Red Army itself. The Army commanders were accused of creating these bases as "secret weapon stocks for bandits". It is horrifying even today to read this ... After all, it isn't difficult to imagine the difficulties that lay in wait for the *Wehrmacht,* had sabotage against the railroads started already in July-August 1941. Had the Germans been reading Soviet literature, the partisan war would not have been such a surprise for them. The children's book author Arkadii Gaidar had almost betrayed a military secret to them. His tale, "*Timur i ego komanda*" ["Timur and his detachment"] was undoubtedly inspired by the ideas of partisan warfare against an aggressor. A Russian Civil War veteran, Gaidar was close to the repressed Army commanders, and the organization of partisan bases was not kept secret from him. Gaidar was in fact killed in the German rear, while serving with a partisan band.

6   See the book by Vice Admiral I. I. Azarov, *Osazhdennaya Odessa [Besieged Odessa]* (Odessa: Maiak, 1975). It is a clamor for the delivery of rifles and hemp-wrapped Molotov cocktails.

tactic was possible in 1940, if the Soviet Union had attacked Germany when the hands of the Führer were tied in the West. The deficit in training over the year would have been compensated by having the initiative, supported by 10,000 tanks and the largest air force in the world, and the losses would not have been so terrible, as they turned out to be as a result of Stalin's display of a pacific lack of concern.

By 1941 the situation had changed. Now the Red Army would have to strike not when Germany's back was turned, but head on. In desperation, Zhukov had proposed a preemptive attack on the armies of the *Wehrmacht* that had assembled for the invasion. However, the Marshal should be trusted, when toward the end of his life in a conversation with Simonov, he said that such an attack would have had even more grave consequences.[7]

What could be graver than the loss of Minsk, Kiev, Odessa, the siege of Leningrad, and the near loss of Moscow? An immediate defeat in the war.

Bracing for an invasion, Great Britain intensely followed Hitler's preparations in the East. On 14 June, the same day of the TASS denunciations, the British Intelligence Committee presented a report on aspects of a possible Soviet-German war. The report noted that the USSR possessed significantly larger formations than Germany, but the Red Army was in the process of rearming, lacked adequate signals capabilities, and its command was of low competence. The Committee believed that the first phase of an invasion, including the occupation of the central Ukraine and Moscow, would take 3-4, at the most, 6 weeks. According to the report, the primary consequences of such a war would be that one-third to one-half of the *Wehrmacht* and Luftwaffe over this time period would be occupied in the East, and it would require additional time to rest and refit them before returning them again to the West. This meant that Hitler would have to postpone the invasion of the British Isles.

There was no talk that the resistance of the USSR might stop the *Wehrmacht*. The Red Army had been plainly weakened by the bloodletting of the purge. As for the people – well, who could expect such sacrifices from a deceived and downtrodden people?

The most important problem in the life of an individual is the problem of choice ... To attach to it the designation "fatal" makes trivial both the word "choice" and the problem itself. Each of us knows this for ourselves, each choice we have made has shaped our lives, each of us must make choices daily, and once every four years in our democracy the choice becomes nagging. That we do not know the eventual costs of a choice when we make it is clearly illustrated by the example of Germany in 1933. The problem of choice stood before the public figures of the 1917 Russian Revolution as well.

The politicians were luckier; they were at the center of an ideological struggle and were gripped by fundamental questions, their attitude toward which would determine the further course of the ship of state – whether it would go in the direction of the people's interests or in the direction of the party clique that had seized power. As a result of these

---

7   It cannot be excluded that this document, written by Vasilevsky, was a means to cover the General Staff on the eve of the invasion with at least some type of excuse in Stalin's eyes. It must be kept in mind that repressions were intensifying at that very time, and none of the generals felt secure.

bitter arguments and their impotence in the face of a majority to alter the course of the nation in a favorable direction, Martov, Dan, Schwartz, Axelrod, and Plekhanov jumped overboard and remained clean in the view of history ... Others – Tomsky, Shliapnikov, Sukhanov, Sokol'nikov – although they didn't leave the captain's bridge and continued to serve the state, they later paid with their lives for their former views that were displeasing to the Leader, but they also remained clean.

Only the military commanders turned out to be damned. In their posts, far removed from political discussions, they knew almost nothing about where the country was heading in 1917; they were preoccupied with the current military situation, with carrying out orders from the center, and were caught completely unawares by the orders to shoot hostages from among the civilian population during the Civil War. Military discipline leaves little room for discussion; during that struggle, such deliberations frequently ended with a shot from a Mauser only several minutes after they started. The slogans were appealing, but the cruelty of the civil conflict, which drew in both women and adolescents, didn't contribute to a lucid view of things. Later, when the Civil War ended, the best among the military men gripped their heads: How could this have happened??

As it turned out, however, this wasn't the end of it. Collectivization followed the Civil War. The Red Army didn't take part in the process, but after all at that time it was almost exclusively of peasant-origin ...

The main factor behind the stratification of the military milieu in the 1920s and 1930s, I believe, was not the jostling on the career ladder, but that which occurred in the consciences of the military commanders. Collectivization, the conversion of the peasants into slaves, became decisive in the ideological disillusionment of the Army – or at least its better part. It is they who were simply executed. Those, who didn't suffer anguish over this matter and those who managed to hide their suffering, survived and more or less successfully won the Great Patriotic War. There are no grievances against them – neither for their participation in the Civil War or for their suppression of national uprisings.

With a strange coyness, only a few authors mention that the Party and Army public figures that were liquidated were the best in the Soviet leadership. It was precisely those who, with a few exceptions, hadn't become cynics and who had kept their faith that they might still succeed in raising the people's well-being. These people embodied a public spirit – social justice, accomplishment, education. With the magnitude of their thinking, they knew how to value matters fairly. They were notable for their sense of humor; their ability to spend their leisure time in ways other than drinking bouts; their manner of moving, speaking and greeting; their appreciation of art and ability to play musical instruments. These were people, not puppets. In no way were they merely cogs in a machine. They were individuals.

However, as Boris Pankin wrote in *Chetyre Ia Konstantina Simonova* [*The Four "I" of Konstantin Simonov*]:

> ... beside the main, obvious, immeasurably terrible calamity, understood and explainable to everyone, which struck the country in June 1941 ... beside this mortal danger, there existed another devilish affliction, unseen and omnipresent. Even before the obvious and explainable drama arrived, it was sucking the life-giving blood from the country; carrying away people, like a thief in the night, depopulating cities and communities; parching the fertile fields and causing such a blight, that a cruel foe

seemed to people to be the most dear and great friend, and friends – enemies of the people.

It was with this cruel foe at the head of the country that the Soviet people in fact entered the war.

Alongside such glittering tacticians as Tukhachevsky and Uborevich, next to such virtuoso strategists as Iakir and Bliukher, Zhukov was not a sparkling prodigy, but a superbly prepared general of the Red Army who was not without his own gifts. The purge of the RKKA made him the only general who combined optimal skill with an uncompromising resolve. His uniqueness made him a genius.

Part Two

32

The "Barbarossa" Plan

H itler's attack on the USSR could be compared to a murder attempt against a
sleeping man. The sleeping man woke up, though. Hitler had assumed that the
USSR would not manage to deploy for resistance. He badly miscalculated not
his own forces, but natural conditions – and the opponent. Not so much the opponent's
leader, but the people. Importantly, he himself in the course of combat operations helped
the adversary get back on his feet.

However, the beginning of the war was dazzling. German General Hoth, commander
of the Third Panzer Group, summarized the first day of the invasion: "As a result of the
unexpectedly rapid seizure of bridges, a completely new situation was created."

Lightly rephrasing the General's words: as a result of Stalin's display of nonchalance,
the "unexpectedly rapid seizure of bridges" allowed the panzer columns simply to drive
across the bordering rivers. Breathtaking prospects arose. The advance proceeded ahead of
schedule.

V. Suvorov rebukes the Red Army for the defeats at the start of the war. He and his
supporters interpret the 3,000,000 Soviet prisoners by the spring of 1942 as an indication
of the Army's refusal to defend the country. Neither the shock of the sudden attack, nor
the lack of communications between the armies and the *fronts*, not the helplessness of the
command at all levels, nor the poor training of the troops and the weak, disorganized fire,
not even the river crossings captured intact by the Germans – not one of these factors do
they mention. Nor do they note the 2,500,000 Red Army soldiers killed in action in the
first six months of the war. Then there are those writers that know the real worth of Stalin's
strategic talents and who, like I do, merely stay within the framework of normal lexicon
when describing him, but even they depict the matter as if Stalin had nothing to do with
it. In their view, if you will, it was the General Staff that prepared poorly to repulse the
German offensive.

Zhukov doesn't even offer a hint as to what the General Staff and the People's
Commissariat of Defense were working on so intensively on the eve of the war. One
can only assume that after Stalin's outcry over the preemptive attack proposal compiled
by Vasilevsky, the General Staff no longer dared show any initiative and was busy with
only whatever it was that the Leader ordered. What it was – that's the question! Evidently,
they weren't busy with defensive preparations against an attack, or else the General Staff
officers would have shared at least a few of their mistakes, if only to avoid accusations of
inactivity. Obviously, defensive planning had been forbidden by the Leader! This is the only
explanation for what happened. The military commanders had been ordered to think that
the Non-Aggression Pact with Germany would protect the country. Zhukov indeed offers
evidence to this when he wrote that Stalin was confident that he could: "...avoid war, or win
time before it started." As a result, the Red Army turned out to be unprepared for defense
in every respect: tactically, psychologically, and materially.

However, all German authors without exception note the resistance encountered

German-Soviet Frontier, 22 June 1941

already in the border areas. In the majority of cases, it was easily overcome. Indeed, there were also cases of panicked flight, unavoidably so given that even thinking about a possible German attack was a punishable offence – and then suddenly the earth and sky were exploding around the troops. In those places, though, where in circumvention of the Boss, the garrisons were allowed to consider the tenseness of the situation, things were much tougher for the *Wehrmacht*. The Northern Fleet and the Black Sea Fleet were led by commanders who saw things clearly, and on the extreme northern and extreme southern flanks, the *Wehrmacht*'s success could be measured in tens of meters. In contrast, in the center of the offensive, Army Group Center already in the course of 22 June had broken into operational space. The first 24 hours, everything went exceedingly well, and Halder put together a timetable for the next stage after crossing the border. Any complication, which held up the forces for two or three hours, exasperated the Chief of the OKH.

Already on the second day, though, the Third Panzer Group of Army Group Center was struggling not with enemy reserves or the second echelons of the Red Army, but with the roads. Hoth observed that the roads, depicted on the maps, were unpaved. The roads ran through pine-covered sand hills. The sand bogged down the tanks, but to bypass the bogged machines by going through the woods turned out to be not a simple task. The day was lost, and on the next day troops now had to overcome Soviet screening forces. These were swept away. However, in order to brush them aside, they had to be attacked. To assess the situation, deploy, sweep aside the blocking force, limber up and reassemble into column all required time and this complicated the task of seizing the European territory of the USSR before winter.

That was the point of Operation Barbarossa. However any plan is inseparable from the manner of its execution, and while conducting Barbarossa, the Führer made changes to its implementation ...

Upon familiarity with the war plan bearing the ringing code name "Barbarossa", which is unrivalled for its notoriety in military history, an ambivalent feeling rises among native sons of the USSR, who knew first-hand their country and its patterns of life. In the first edition of this book, I had the following to say about "Barbarossa": "Scholars of the war and many writers exhibit a certain fixation with this plan. Numerous books in every language have been dedicated to it. But the plan was more a wish than a reality."

This is indeed true. However, the longer one lives, the more clearly one realizes that directly contrary things can be said about one and the same thing – and both assertions can seem correct. Take for example: "We're all the same, like two drops of water" and "We're all different and guided by various motivations". My uncle's wife, a suffragette at one time and always an original woman, liked to imitate a brainless quasi-intellectual with a thirst to be heard: "On the one hand, yes, of course ... on the other, taking into account certain points, yes, but just generally – at least that's it!" Think about Barbarossa, and you can't help but recall my aunt's remark. From one perspective, the plan is a typical "Well, it was flat on the map, but where did all this rough terrain come from?" On the other hand, it directly strikes the viewer as a combination of pinning attacks along the entire national border (Russian generals will not forget the lesson!) and an accurate thrust at the heart – toward Moscow. Yes, there were Russian gullies, Russian roads and, of course, the black earth that even after just a good summer cloud-burst becomes a gooey, viscous muck on the wheels. However, we contemporaries of the war cannot shake off the thought – especially after the dizzying, momentary breakup of the Soviet Union in one Belovezhskaia Pushcha drinking spree![1] – that perhaps just a single rainy day or just one decision by a single German division commander kept the plan from becoming the realization of a victory over us. Such a plan could be conceived only by one who understood how centralized power had become in Russia, and how fatal would be the seizure of the country's administrative center. It is as if the plan was conceived not by a German, but by a Russian.

He wasn't a Russian. At an instruction from Halder, the Chief of the OKH, the plan was outlined by the Chief of Staff of the 18th Army, Major-General Erich Marcks.

The *Wehrmacht* of 1941 was magnificent. The training of the soldiers was being directed by a disciplined and well-schooled officer corps. The profundity of the general officers' gambling mentality was nurtured by the fruits of Hitler's political gambles, which gained for the *Wehrmacht* the element of surprise and, subsequently, the unchallenged possession of the initiative. One must not discount as well the love of the soldiers for the Führer, who put a chicken into every pot and who had turned the vanquished into victors. The *Wehrmacht* in combination with the Luftwaffe was a military machine capable of crushing the numerically superior forces of any army of the world of that time.

Departing from this, Major-General Marcks proposed an attack along the entire border in order to strip the Red Army of the freedom to maneuver. The main attack, a double-pronged armored assault with highly concentrated forces would be launched from Prussia and Galicia on a narrow front north and south of the Pripiat' Marshes. The prongs would then come together in the flat country beyond them. The goal was to encircle the Soviet armies on the way to the capital. The armored fist, untroubled by its flanks, which would be secured by Army Group North and Army Group South, not being distracted by opportunities that would arise along the way – with the surprise attack a lot of them would appear! – and refusing to be drawn into fighting with the encircled Red Army formations, was to slice through the intercepting Soviet divisions hurled against it, and continue to advance in order to encircle Moscow and to seize the industrial area of Gor'kii.[2] The rapid pace of the offensive would not leave the USSR time to mobilize and organize a defense. The fall (or the isolation) of Moscow and the capture of the industrial region, under Marck's draft, would be completed by the end of August (or in the worst case, by the middle of September). Then, if the system of government hadn't collapsed, an attack on the Baku oil fields would be launched from the north and the west.

With the implementation of this plan, the European territory of the USSR would

---

1   Editor's note: The Belovezhskaia Pushcha [Woods] in Belorussia are a famous destination that served as a well-known gathering place for top Soviet officials, where they would confer, hunt, and especially engage in heavy drinking. There, on the night of 29 December 1991, the heads of the various Soviet republics signed an agreement that formalized the termination of the Union of Soviet Socialist Republics. A lot of alcohol was consumed on the occasion.

2   Seemingly, Hitler wasn't directly planning to enter Leningrad or Moscow, but only to isolate them from the transportation network and the system of defense. It is costly to take such cities by storm. It is even difficult to occupy them because of the drain on resources caused by the need to police the city to keep the population in line and ensure security. Large cities undermine the discipline of the occupying garrisons; this should also be taken into consideration. Also, after the horror of the explosions and conflagrations in Kiev, there could not be even any talk about stationing troops in the deliberately mined cities of Leningrad and Moscow.

be carved into pieces. These, in turn, would be further cut up by mobile spearheads. (In our present time, it is impossible for the reader to imagine or for me to explain the panic generated by the sudden appearance of two German motorcyclists with machine guns in settlements or at crossroads deep in the rear of the defending Soviet forces.) Once seized, the Moscow communication hub would allow the *Wehrmacht* to shift forces rapidly in any direction by rail, avoiding Russian messy roads – an argument of fundamental importance. The Leningrad area would be turned over to the Finns. The Ukrainian region, if it hadn't capitulated with its remaining forces, would be compelled to defend with a reversed front. Such a defense alone is an exceedingly difficult task, but when the defenders must cope with pressure from two directions simultaneously, it becomes hopeless. Execution of this plan would lead to the fall of a multi-national state, and subsequently there would be the sharing of conquered territories with border neighbors, as was the case with Czechoslovakia and Poland.

Let us note a principal consideration in Marcks' draft plan: Do not get distracted by opportunities that present themselves! The goal was Moscow!

Von Manstein, who had no authorization at that time to discuss the plan (he was still only a corps commander), observes in his memoirs that Hitler underestimated both the Red Army and the strength of the USSR, the destruction of the government of which in the course of one summer campaign would be impossible without assistance from within. Although von Manstein expressed this view after the war, it is in general an echo of von Rundstedt's thoughts, who in May 1941 had said:

> This war with Russia is a nonsensical idea, to which I can see no happy ending. But if, for political reasons, the war is unavoidable, then we must face the fact that it can't be won in a single summer campaign. Just look at the distances involved. We cannot possibly defeat the enemy and occupy the whole of western Russia, from the Baltic to the Black Sea, within a few short months. We should prepare for a long war and go for our objectives step by step.

Von Rundstedt opposed the war.[3] Von Manstein expressed no fundamental objections,

---

3   Plainly, there was a leak of information about the preparation of a campaign against Russia through such military commanders as von Rundstedt and such diplomats as von der Schulenberg, which confirmed American intelligence data and allowed the American government to warn the Russians. I'll sketch it out for you:

In view of the Soviet aggression against Finland, relations between the United States and the Soviet Union had cooled. The Soviet Ambassador to the United States was K. A. Umansky. After a routine visit by him to the State Department, there occurred a thaw in the attitude toward the USSR, which was dictated, incidentally, by US national interests. On 30 March 1941, the US Deputy Secretary of State Sumner Wallace summoned Umansky and told him face to face about the German plan of attack against the USSR. Umansky turned deathly pale. Composing himself, he assured the Deputy Secretary of State that he highly valued the credibility of the USA and that he would make the top Soviet officials aware of this news. He, of course, carried out his promise. Umansky's report was as authoritative as Richard Sorge's intelligence.

In June 1943, the Umansky's only daughter Nina was killed under mysterious circumstances. At the end of the war, Umansky, who was at the time the Soviet Ambassador to Mexico, was also appointed to be the Soviet Ambassador to Costa Rica at the same time. He was to fly to Costa Rica with his wife; at the airport in Mexico the airplane took off and immediately plummeted back to the ground, killing everyone aboard. Perhaps it was an accident; perhaps not. Stalin did not tolerate witnesses.

but he also wanted help from within. A glittering tactician, but not a politician, he made the same mistake that Hitler made: the taking of Moscow soon after the start of the campaign indeed would have been a blow as decisive as help from within.

General Marcks completed his genius draft by 5 August 1940. The draft became the basis of the plan presented to Hitler on 5 December 1940.

We will not go into the details, leaving it to the competence of military analysts. They will not stop debating over Barbarossa for a long time to come, modeling the situation with computers and criticizing the plan for giving too much credence to inaccurate intelligence reports, for its lack of familiarity with the roads, for failing to take into account the wider gauge of the Soviet railroad tracks, and for underestimating the numerical strength of the Soviet armies. Yes, according to understated Soviet statistics, 4,500 German tanks were opposed by 10,000 Soviet tanks. Yes, the Germans weren't expecting such a large numerical superiority on the Soviet side. So what? Wouldn't they grind them all anyway? Even if one acknowledges that the reliability of the Soviet tanks (on average) was lower than the German tanks, the Soviet command would hardly have agreed to a swap.[4] One T-34 from a distance beyond return firing range could smash dozens of German "Marks". The real ratio of losses, however, would be determined by the skill in using the tanks. We already grieved over this in the first part of the book, but now – well now, there was no choice but to go to war with what was left after the purge.

Something else is more important: while developing his draft plan, Marcks bound himself to a central point – the idea of a two-pronged attack, which in concert (! – an important limitation!) were to outflank the Pinsk swamps and link up on the left bank of the Dnepr River for the assault on Moscow, leaving behind the mass of encircled Red Army troops and Kiev, once it had been taken.

Halder went further: he would *leave behind the mass of enemy troops defending Kiev.* The cautious Chief of the OKH proved to be the best assessor of the plan. He considered directing the attacking prongs toward two divergent goals, Kiev and Moscow, to be risky. He understood that Moscow alone would be sufficient. However, the Führer regarded Marcks' plan to be venturesome.

Really? Perhaps quite the contrary – more feasible? It depends upon how you look at it.

The plan was a gamble, but then isn't any campaign something of a risky undertaking? Especially one against Russia! Deputy Chief of the OKW (*Oberkommando der Wehrmacht*, or High Command of the Armed Forces) Operations Staff, General Warlimont later wrote: "There was no carefully thought-out plan as a basis for action against Russia such as would have been made in the old days by the Prussian-German General Staff; moreover as opposed to his procedure during the period prior to the western campaign, Hitler's views on the conduct of operations were confined merely to a few passing remarks."

A gamble, yes. Still ...

To the present day the questions linger: How did Hitler dare to go to war with Russia?

---

4   Even by Soviet sources, at the moment of the invasion the Red Army had 10,394 tanks against the 4,642 tanks possessed by Germany and its satellite allies; 1,475 Soviet tanks had a main gun with a caliber of 76.2mm or greater, versus 479 German tanks. Against the qualitative superiority of the German aircraft, the Soviets could put up twice as many. This numerical superiority on the Soviet side was parried by the German early morning attack. In the very first hours of the war, Soviet aircraft losses numbered approximately 2,000, while the Luftwaffe lost only 17 aircraft on 22 June. The *Wehrmacht*'s superiority in the correlation of the number of ground troops to the Red Army's at the moment of the invasion, 1.3:1.0, was also far from the correlation considered necessary for the attacking side.

Why didn't his generals band together against this idea? So what if it was called the USSR, its command staff had been destroyed, and its weapons were outdated? This still was Russia!

The American military analyst Russel Stolfi rightly asks in his book *Hitler's Panzers East: World War II Reintepreted* why Hitler has been considered doomed from the moment he made the decision to invade the Soviet Union. His question undoubtedly relates to the oft-forgotten fact that the British military before Hitler's invasion of Russia estimated that the campaign would last only four to six weeks.   Yes, the Führer was apprehensive. However, with the conquest of Poland, which brought him face to face with Stalin, he left himself with no alternative. This is the truth: He had grabbed hold of a bear! Now nothing would prevent Stalin from attacking Germany from the rear, as soon as operations in Europe had tied it up. To the Führer it seemed – not without justification – that he was choosing the lesser of two evils when he decided to attack Russia. Those German generals, who (like the resigned German commanders) foresaw a catastrophe resulting from any violation of the stability in Europe, and who considered a campaign in the East totally senseless, opposed the plan – but not to the point of submitting their resignations. Von Rundstedt directly expressed his doubts. Von Bock, in contrast, believed that the only possibility to defeat Russia was by a lightning attack. He, of course, was aware of the published writings of division commander Svechin, a former Tsarist general, military theoretician and strategist, who believed even back when the RKKA and the *Reichswehr* had been cooperating that a lightning attack would have been suicidal. However, conflicting opinions are not so simple to judge. Fedor von Bock was no less authoritative than Aleksandr Andreevich Svechin. The one who breaks the rules is the successful one!

The young German generals, though – they enthusiastically trusted the Führer. They believed in the luck of this comical, pompous man. Some of them had even grown to love him. Indeed, given the facts, how could they not? The Führer had always disdained logic, and so far he had always been right, one against all!

Everyone had feared an Allied intervention if Germany reoccupied the demilitarized Rhineland in violation of the Treaty of Versailles. Hitler directed his troops to enter it, and nothing happened. They had warned him against the *anschluss* of Austria, yet the *Wehrmacht's* entry into Austria turned into a jubilant triumph. They had appealed for a show of restraint with Czechoslovakia – Hitler devoured it and nothing occurred. They had prophesied a catastrophic collision with England and France in the case of an invasion of Poland, but the Allies' declaration of war proved to be a bluff, and Poland was dismembered in three weeks. The Allies' bluff ended in a capitulation and the fall of Paris, within a timeframe about which no one had dared dream.

They had achieved all these exploits under Hitler's banner! He had given them elbow-room. He had offered the *Wehrmacht* chances, one after the other. Of course, this couldn't be mentioned aloud, but what military professional's heart wouldn't leap from such possibilities? The *Blitzkrieg* in Poland; the Paris triumph; the lightning seizure of Yugoslavia, Greece, and Norway; why not a *Blitzkrieg* campaign against Russia? Hadn't France once seemed invincible? Moreover, the Führer had called Russia a colossus with clay feet.

Was he convinced of this? More likely, he convinced others. Hitler had no other choice. A Soviet attack on Germany at any moment that Stalin considered suitable – this may be a secret to jaundiced historians, but it was not to Hitler. The opportunity to get the jump on Stalin could not be missed. Yes, the occupation of the European territory of the USSR in the course of a single summer campaign was a gamble. How many previous gambles, however, had ended in triumphs! They'd been seemingly insane undertakings even, yet he had succeeded. In essence, the matter often boils down to this: Is a venture crazy enough to become successful?

The plan, which had been proposed to Hitler on 5 December 1940, was of that nature. Its absence of reason was genius. However, though a genius doesn't like corrections, Hitler confirmed the plan with a correction; with a single, but fatal amendment.

The western areas of the Soviet Union were spread before the *Wehrmacht* like the grand stage for a military show on a scale never before seen in the history of mankind. The illumination was superb and the weather radiant. The one who conceived the drama looked forward to the spectacle and trembled in nervousness and anticipation. Made apprehensive by the experience of Napoleon, he was doomed.

Is this a paradox? No. It isn't simple to turn away from the lessons of great people in history, and the fate of Napoleon, who lost his power in the expanses of Russia, prompted Hitler to plan his campaign differently from Napoleon's. How so – with speed? Napoleon covered the distance between the Neman River and Moscow in three months. The modern means for conducting warfare allowed faster movement. However, Hitler didn't see the difference between his campaign and Napoleon's in speed, but in its scale. He intended to reach a line stretching from Astrakhan' to Arkhangel'sk before winter. The campaign would conclude not with the taking of Moscow, but with the seizure of the entire European territory of USSR. Deprive the country of human resources, its Army, industry, oil and gas resources, and then cut it off from the rest of the world!

Zhukov in his characteristically laconic style told the writer Ehrenburg in 1942: "The ease of its successes has spoiled the German Army." This analysis deserves attention not because it was offered by Zhukov, but because this is the most concise summary of the entire circumstances. The victories at the start of Barbarossa seemed to be an extension of the victorious campaigns in Europe. The German command became dizzy from them. Hitler, bewitched by Napoleon's fate, almost from the very beginning began to push Moscow aside in favor of operations on the flanks. He wanted the same pace of advance across the entire front and paid no regard to the plan that Halder had set down. But in Napoleon's times, Moscow wasn't the capital. Indeed, the role of the capital in the country had grown. Yet Moscow wasn't simply a capital, it was the capital of a totalitarian state, the center of radio communications and all its defensive propaganda. Moscow was at the same time the most important, even unique, hub of communications and transportation in the nation.

Nothing could dissuade the Führer. The glittering start of the campaign led him inevitably to err. He was expecting the fall of the regime from day to day – just as it had been in France! – and was now considering any goal attainable at any moment. As a result he was unable to turn away from his geopolitical view of the campaign.

Napoleon's *Grande Armée* had perished in Russia because the war hadn't fed it, as it had been fed in Europe. In Europe his army had grown fat, but in Russia the foragers couldn't cope with the difficulties caused by the narrow front of the invasion and the *Grande Armée*'s single line of communications, which beyond all other problems was being terrorized by partisans. War must feed itself! Expand the belt of conquered land! Destroy the population! Deprive the enemy of human resources, raw materials, and roads!

Victories are sometimes more dangerous than defeats. Suddenly everything seemed possible. The bravura start of the campaign led the Führer to a decision, taken by him alone and that resulted in a defeat in the war, which might have been won and would have led to an incalculable political change on the planet.

The Führer clearly – and even excessively – recognized the disadvantages of a war with the British Empire, supported by the entire might of the United States. There, a campaign stretching for years would be unavoidable. Resources would be necessary, a lot of resources. Russia had these resources. However, in the war with Russia, Hitler disregarded Russia – despite himself. Mesmerized by the early successes, he even ordered the level of German military production to be lowered, and its output (let us say, tank engines suitable for models under development) not to be turned over to *Wehrmacht*, but to be stockpiled for the future. Seemingly, the Commander-in-Chief in June-July 1941 and even later, up to October, couldn't comprehend one crucial thing: if Germany didn't give its all to this war from the very beginning, there would be no future.

There were also problems with regard to esteem for the Red Army. Napoleon considered Bagration to be Russia's only real general. Having invaded, he discovered that while Russia didn't have any well-known names, it did have generals. The Führer kept this in mind, but forgot that the Tsars didn't purge the Russian Army, and he didn't believe the results of Stalin's radical purge of the Red Army: after all, there had been Khalkhin-Gol! Even after the Red Army's pathetic performance in the war with Finland, the Führer during the implementation of Operation Barbarossa became wary of deep penetrations, which might tempt the Russians to cut them off, and demanded a more uniform advance. Russian counterattacks, though weak and lacking air support, but conducted without regard for losses, had already from the start of the campaign disclosed this wily tendency of the Red Army command – to envelop the prongs of the German pincers with their own pincers. The Fuhrer in 1941 was maniacally fearful of pincers.

Marshal Chuikov believed that the fall of Berlin and an end to the war in February 1945 had been prevented by the cautious overreaction of the *Stavka* to a possibility of a flank attack from the north by the weak *Wehrmacht*. With time, analysis will explore this scenario as well, but the Soviet armies in 1945 doubtlessly fought much more cautiously in large-scale operations than they had in 1941-1942. Even if Chuikov's argument about the matter is correct, the academism of the Soviet command had no effect on the war's final outcome. However, academism cost the Führer the defeat in the war. In summer of 1941 *Wehrmacht* could have waged the war much more boldly...

☆ ☆ ☆

Just a fleeting glance at a map of the USSR is sufficient to raise doubts about the feasibility of reaching the line Volga-Kama-Northern Dvina in the course of a single summer campaign, unless one supposes not a conquest, but an occupation following the collapse of the regime, with no need to grind up the enemy's army, no need to attack, but only the need to expand authority, arrest the top military commanders and liquidate the Communist Party functionaries. That's all!

The German generals spoke out after the war. Below is a lengthy piece of analysis of the situation, given by General Blumentritt in the book *The Fatal Decisions*:

> ...The Siberian, who is partially or completely an Asiatic, is even tougher and has greater powers of resistance than his European compatriot. We had already learned this

when we met the Siberian Army Corps during the First World War. To the Western European, accustomed to small countries, distances in the East seem endless... This is reinforced by the melancholy and monotonous nature of the Russian landscape, which is particularly oppressive during the gloomy days of autumn and the interminable winter darkness. The Russian is much influenced by the country in which he lives, and it is my belief that the landscape is largely responsible for his passivity and monotony.

The psychological effect of the country on the ordinary German soldier was considerable. He felt small and lost in that endless space and he missed the happier life and higher state of civilization to which he was accustomed in his homeland... The Eastern theater of operations became the true testing ground of our troops. It was a hard school: a man who has survived the Russian enemy and the Russian climate has little more to learn about war.

All the wars that Russia has fought have been savage and bloody. Frederick the Great learned to respect the quality of the Russian soldier during the Seven Years War. Napoleon considered the Battle of Borodino to be the bloodiest he ever fought. The Russo-Turkish War of 1877-78 was ferocious, as was the Russo-Japanese one at the beginning of our century. In both these wars casualties were on a very heavy scale. During the First World War we learned to know the Imperial Russian Army at first hand. It is a significant and little-known fact that our casualties on the Eastern Front were greater than those suffered in the West during the 1914-18 war. In that war Russian leadership was certainly inferior to our own and the tactics of their massive armies clumsy. But in defense the Imperial Russian Army was stubborn and tenacious and they were masters at constructing defensive positions with great speed. The Russian soldier showed great skill in night operations and in forest fighting, and he preferred hand-to-hand combat. His physical needs were slight and his ability to stand up to punishment unshaken truly astounding. Such was the soldier whom we had learned to know and respect a quarter of a century ago. Since then the Bolshevists had systematically re-educated the youth of their country. It was logical to assume that the Red Army would prove an even tougher nut to crack than had been its Imperial predecessor.

... It was extremely difficult to form any clear picture of the Red Army's equipment. Their security had been both thorough and effective. Hitler refused to believe that Russia's industrial production could equal Germany's. Our greatest single lack of intelligence concerned Russian tanks. We had no idea what their monthly tank production figures might be. Even maps were hard to come by, since the Russians regarded their geography as a military secret and safeguarded their maps accordingly. Those that we did have were not infrequently entirely incorrect and misleading.

As for Russian strength as a whole, no assessment was uniformly acceptable. In general those of us who had fought in Russia during the First World War regarded it as high, while those who did not know the new enemy tended to underestimate his powers.

The attitude to be expected from the civilian population was also largely unknown. In the 1914-18 war we had found them affectionate, loyal and good-natured. How they had changed in the intervening years no one could say. Those of us who knew them of old, however, believed that **that amicable nation deserved a better government than the one under which they had been compelled to live for**

a quarter of century. (Emphasis the author's)

This piece of the General's commentary especially touched me, bringing me to the point of tears. I believe I am not alone in my reaction. The fox felt sorry for the hen. The General was wishing a better government for the people than the one that had ruled them for a quarter of a century ... This after Nuremberg and the public disclosure of all the evil acts under the German occupation and the "scorched earth" policy during the *Wehrmacht*'s retreat.

Of course, these comments are beside the point. Most importantly, Blumentritt's comments are fundamentally an expression of sorrow that the German generals had obeyed the Führer, even though they had foreseen a campaign on an expansive territory with a harsh climate, a poorly developed road network, and a large population that loved their motherland. From where, though, does the worry over the roads come, if scouts had not taken the time to travel along them? (Despite Blumentritt's assertions, there were such possibilities!) From where does this expression "population that loved their motherland" come from, when one constantly runs into such terms as "colossus with clay feet" and "conglomeration" in reference to the USSR? Any empire is a conglomeration, though their collapses rarely come from war. On the contrary, war unifies empires; Rome is an example of that. Did Hitler take this paradox into account? How did he intend to deal with it? By terrorizing the population? By liquidating the Jews? Labeling the Slavs as non-humans?

What of the weather conditions? The very first downpour prevented the sealing of the pocket around Minsk, which prompted a migraine in Halder and an hysterical outburst from the Führer. War doesn't unfold on parquet flooring, and the complaints about the climate in the memoirs of the German generals, who had begun to understand the sense of the word *rasputitsa* [the Russian term for the conversion of dirt roads into quagmires during the spring thaw and periods of rain] only when the clinging mud was sucking the boots off their own feet, are pointless. The soldiers, inadequately dressed, were facing winter. The transport system stalled, and the movement of supplies became dependent upon one million horses, the death of which became still another tragedy in the war, though it simply was dwarfed by the death of tens of millions of people.

Was all that taken into consideration? Did Hitler and his top military commanders consider that the Red Army would be learning from its initial defeats, and that the victors would inevitably face a counter blow? Did they pay any attention to this? What about the expenditure of fuel on the poor Russian roads? And the expenditure of fuel to deliver the same fuel over a distance which would constantly grow as the armies advanced?

A *Blitzkrieg*; that's what the plan presented to Hitler rested upon. In the fifth month of the war, at a celebratory gathering dedicated to the anniversary of the "Beer Hall Putsch", the Führer had to make excuses: "I've never used the word '*Blitzkrieg*', because it is a stupid word!"

Nonsense, he did use it, and not without reason. The campaign of three Soviet *fronts* against the Japanese Kwantung Army in Manchuria in August 1945 was a *Blitzkrieg*. So was the 1967 Israeli-Arab Six Day war. The ground campaign in Operation Desert Storm against Iraqi forces lasted for six days in 1991. What about Napoleon's smashing victory over Prussia in a six day war back in 1806? Simply, it didn't behoove the German commanders to complain about the roads and the Russian climate in their post-war memoirs. All of this should have been considered beforehand.

Soviet officials were utmost angry about the British military historian B. Liddell Hart's comment in his book *The German Generals Talk*. Hart wrote:

> Here is the most startling of all. What saved Russia above all was, not her modern progress, but her backwardness. If Soviet regime had given her a road system comparable to that of western countries, she would probably have been overrun in quick time. The German mechanized forces were baulked by the badness of her roads.

Even today, I cite Hart's observation not without some trepidation. It wasn't stated by Hermann Hoth or any of the other German panzer generals with whom Hart spoke. It was expressed by Liddell Hart himself, our ally in the past war.

It isn't hyperbole. If not for the lack of roads, the losses suffered by the USSR in the war would have been even more terrible. As such, the native soil itself, churned up by the treads of German tanks and the wheels of their vehicles, assisted our defenders. Of course, there was also blood and more blood. There were the propitious decision-making pirouettes of the enemy leader as well. The German generals refer to them with full justification: Hitler altered the original war plan.

Of course, war plans can't be worked out in detail; such a utopian possibility doesn't even enter military commanders' minds. War is a choice between arising possibilities. A general plan is sketched out, and all the rest depends upon the circumstances. The glittering tactician von Manstein confessed that the most complex decision he faced in the initial stage of the war was the choice of the direction to take: they were all equally enticing. The selections made were not error-free. The miscalculations of the German generals however, and there were more than a few of them, were not fatal; Hitler's single decision was. A decision that he made at the stage of confirming the plan and which was written into it as an amendment. Many military analysts assert that it was precisely this amendment that decided the outcome not only of the 1941 campaign, but of the entire war.

However, meanwhile everything was going swimmingly well at the start. A stunning success transpired on the Moscow axis, which immediately put von Bock's Army Group Center well ahead of Army Group South. The seizure of intact river crossings was wildly celebrated, but the significance of the roads designated on the maps which proved to be muddy tracks was discounted. The capture of masses of Red Army troops was interpreted as their refusal to fight, and the isolated pockets of resistance was attributed to the presence of fanatic commissars. That's how they explained the heroism of the Brest defenders as well: you see, its commissar was a Jew, that's all, that's why he made sure the defense was so tenacious! To the Führer, and to his military command as well, everything became easy.

As the resistance grew more ferocious, the Führer increasingly became consumed with the idea of destroying the entire Red Army. This goal became first on the list of priorities. The acquisition of territory dropped to second place.

33

Implementing Barbarossa

Troubles for the *Wehrmacht*, as noted earlier, began during the discussion of the plan, which was confirmed by Hitler on 18 December 1940 with one amendment: Army Group Center (von Bock received command of the most powerful army group) upon achieving a position suitable for a subsequent lunge toward Moscow (the highland east of Minsk) should halt and prepare to assist its neighbors – Army Group South (von Rundstedt) and Army Group North (von Leeb).

Halt ...

That wasn't the Führer's first attempt to rein in a dash by his troops. Guderian at Sedan in 1940 had forged ahead, and the Führer became nervous: to fight so nimbly with the French!? He didn't have time to stop *"Der schnelle Heinz"* ("Hurrying Heinz"). Events were moving swiftly. The motorized war had disclosed the tactical possibilities of armored formations. The dizzyingly rapid penetration of cooperating ground and aviation spearheads into the innermost depths of major powers had become possible. The panic effect of combined, swift actions in the air and on the ground upon the adversary's forces and civilian population was revealed. The masses of refugees clogging the roads paralyzed the movement of enemy forces, which confirmed the experience of the Polish campaign. Such a reliable model could be adopted when planning the campaign against Russia.

Halt! A stroke of genius, with which the Führer fleshed out the plan, correcting the mundane thinking of his generals and making his campaign different from Napoleon's: not Moscow, but the entire European territory of the USSR plus Moscow was the objective! Moscow, so to speak, would be the crowning achievement after the seizure of resources.

In his book *The German Generals Talk*, Liddell Hart mentions a discussion he had with von Manteuffel. This superb leader in the autumn of 1943, after Vatutin had seized Kiev, prevented a collapse of the German front with a series of surprise night counterattacks. He was a guest of the Führer in a private meeting, and later testified that it was difficult to oppose Hitler, if the conversation was on the nuts and bolts of the military craft, such as the specifics of various weapons, the influence of terrain and weather, or the morale of the troops, in which Hitler was particularly strong. However, he didn't have any idea about strategy. He knew how a division fights, but had no understanding of an army operation. The diplomatic ability, which allowed Hitler to rise to power and enslave half of Europe, was not combined – fortunately! – with a gift in military command. By analogy, his generals, who were strategically gifted, didn't know how to choose the best moment for an invasion. The difference is that lacking such a gift, they made no attempt to influence Germany's politics, while Hitler, a neophyte in military matters, imagined himself a genius, and his opinion was decisive.

The generals stomached the amendment to Barbarossa, which converted the planned *Blitzkrieg* into a conventional war. They made protests, but only moderately so. Indeed, only Halder and von Bock were supporters of the original plan. A thrust toward Moscow, bypassing Kiev, didn't entice the others at all. The gift of persuasion is a special gift. The person who is correct isn't always convincing. Von Bock and Halder, who were in the minority and soberly evaluated their diplomatic charms, didn't lock horns over the amendment. Maybe von Rundstedt would move through the Ukraine more vigorously than von Bock would push through Belorussia. Maybe they would both get around the Pripiat Marshes at the same time. Perhaps the Bolshevik regime would collapse before the fall of Kiev. In a word, actual events might obviate any disagreement, and a successful course of the war might shift the Führer in favor of the Moscow variant, the incontrovertible advantages of which would be no easier to prove than a postulate. Simple truths are the most difficult to prove ...

By the time of Plan Barbarossa's development, Poland and France had already fallen, and the British Expeditionary Force had barely been saved, and not without the Führer's benevolence. (The success of these campaigns would be reflected in the Plan's scale and daring.) Although it sounds strange, having wound up in a war with the English and French, neither Hitler nor the *Wehrmacht* leadership dared even plan their destruction. On 9 October 1939 the Führer issued a directive to launch an attack in the West no later than 12 November. As stated in Hitler's Directive No. 6, the goal was "... to defeat as much as possible of the French Army and of the forces of the allies fighting on their side, and at the same time to win as much territory as possible in Holland, Belgium and Northern France to serve as a base for the successful prosecution of the air and sea war against England and as a wide protective area for the economically vital Ruhr."

The phrase about the creation of "a wide protective area" doesn't ring victoriously at all. Success offered the prospects of seizing some 40 miles of coastline along the English Channel to serve as a staging area for a possible landing in England. If unsuccessful – war doesn't always go as planned – the autumn invasion would lead to a positional struggle, to a repeat of what had occurred on the fields of the First World War. The directive reflected the Führer's apprehension that France would occupy Belgium and strengthen its borders.

Halder and von Brauchitsch were troubled by this plan, but remembering the fate of their predecessors, they kept quiet. Unfortunately for civilization, poor weather, suspicions about the leak of information about the plan, and the resistance of those higher German officers, who unlike the Commander of the Ground Forces and the Chief of Staff, were not worried about their posts, led to the plan's cancellation. At the same time, Major-General von Manstein proposed a more focused plan, which was approved by his colleague Guderian, though rejected by the OKW, but which reached the Führer's desk and was approved by him: an offensive through the Ardennes, where it indeed took place in May 1940, leading to Hitler's supremacy over Europe.

The timid plan, which reflected the Führer's fear of allowing the Allies into Belgium, disclosed the nervous nature of his personality. However, in the course of the campaign in the West fortunately for himself, he managed to interfere only once, when with a political aim (which was unjustified) he allowed the British Expeditionary Corps to escape at Dunkirk. Nevertheless, owing to his generals, Hitler received the opportunity to go into a jig – a famous scene![1] – next to the railroad car in Compiegne, France, where he received the surrender of the French government.

Dunkirk wasn't the final act of the Führer's military creativity. (The next decisive interference in the leadership of the forces in a theater of combat operations would cost

---

1   Editor's note: This "jig" was a successful artifice made by looping several frames of film in which Hitler had stepped back and then lifted his leg after receiving the surrender. It was designed to provoke popular outrage against Hitler and received wide circulation during the war.

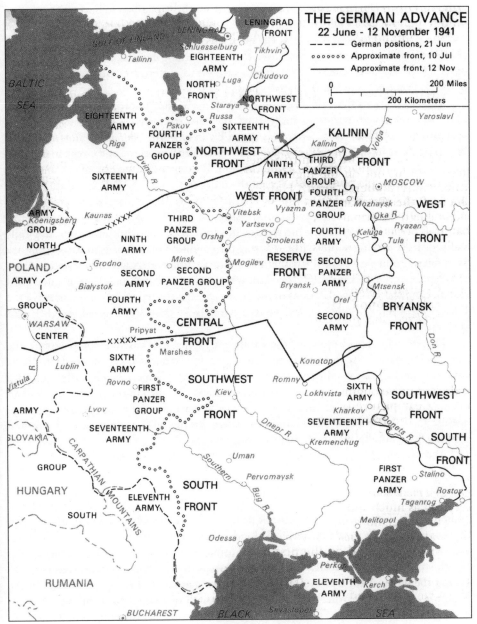

The German Advance, 22 June-12 November 1941

him far more dearly ...) However, a victory is a victory. Only by accepting von Manstein's plan, the Führer had earned the right – the sordid advantage of authority! – not simply to claim co-authorship, but to bask in a victory that was fully ascribed to him. His authority became untouchable. After the fall of France it became awkward even to contradict him, and before the invasion of the USSR the question of the amendment to the plan, made by the Führer, didn't even surface. Moreover, the Russian campaign was preceded by a series of dazzling operations that must be taken into account to capture accurately the atmosphere of the *Wehrmacht's* intoxication with its power.

These operations from the beginning of 1941 were truly implemented with machine-like precision. Their relentless energy and pressure stunned the world. Norway was occupied almost bloodlessly. Crete was seized by an airborne operation. Thrusting from Bulgaria, Hungary and Austria, the *Wehrmacht* subdued Yugoslavia and Greek in eighteen days; losses in killed and wounded number 5,500. The opponents were small in comparison with the Reich, and Hitler, having issued the order to occupy the Balkans, didn't bother going into details. He was busy with the forthcoming invasion of Russia. The preparations in the East placed particular emphasis on surprise, which yielded immense advantages to the *Wehrmacht*. Hitler was personally involved with the disinformation and fully succeeded. (In trifling matters, like assessing the condition of the roads in Russia, he took no interest. So he never asked whether his military commanders were interested in them ...) Whereas in the Balkans the *Wehrmacht* was given a free hand, and demonstrated great skill in conducting deep operations of the same type that the repressed commanders of the RKKA had been working out, for the Red Army these skills were buried together with their creators.

Despite widespread opinion, the campaign in the Balkans did not postpone the initiation of Barbarossa (because of the late spring and frequent rains, the roads in Russia were still drying, the conditions of which the German planners incidentally took into consideration) and didn't weaken the initial attack. On the contrary, after the Balkan workout the *Wehrmacht* was like a super powerful machine at the start of the campaign against the USSR, its personnel and equipment having gone through a trial run and training in conditions maximally approaching real ones.

At dawn on 22 June, the hellish machine began moving to the east.

Although the *Wehrmacht's* errors are not mentioned here in view of the insignificance (in my opinion) of the generals' operational blunders in comparison with the Führer's strategic blunder, it must be noted: Hoepner, von Manstein and the commander of Army Group North von Leeb, and indeed the entire leadership of the German ground forces, failed to exploit the fall of Daugavpils to capture Pskov, the gateway to Leningrad, already in the beginning of July. Everyone understands that the fall of Leningrad in July would have sharply upset the stability of the Soviet front, which was already tottering even without it.

The success of Army Group Center in Belorussia on the axis of the main attack opened a path to Smolensk and Moscow for the *Wehrmacht*. On 2 July, just ten days after the start of the war, von Bock's panzer spearhead reached the designated staging area for the subsequent attack toward Moscow in the area of Iartsevo, east of Smolensk, on the highland beyond the Pripiat' Swamps, where General Marcks had intended the link-up between Army Group Center and Army Group South. The superb panzer leaders Hoth and Guderian were targeting Moscow and Gor'kii – the heart of the country and the country's industrial heart. They fully sensed the panic and terror they were spreading together with the Luftwaffe, which was covering them from the air. They left burning fields and villages behind them to mark their progress for air support, using fires crudely to designate the front line and to indicate targets along the front for the arriving Stukas. The experience of past victories infused them with self-confidence. They weren't concerned with their flanks and trusted the infantry. The expenditure of fuel didn't bother them; the war had only started, and there was plenty of fuel. They were moving day and night, cutting lines of communication and smashing garrisons, while the main body of Soviet forces, isolated in semi-encirclement in the area of Smolensk, was spilling its blood in poorly coordinated counterattacks that failed to slow down the attacking panzer spearhead. Had it broken through to the Moscow area with its developed network of roads in July-August, when the weather was excellent, the *Wehrmacht* still fresh and the Red Army in tatters and the mobilization effort only starting, while the stripping of forces from the Far East was still under discussion – the situation would have been beyond retrieval.

The Führer, however, intervened. On 2 July, still not categorically, he tried to stop von Bock, who for the sake of a further advance toward Moscow was sweating out a furious dispute with him and Halder (?!), who were worried about the flanks. Hitler was measuring military success by the number of prisoners taken, something which had not interested him in the Balkans, and the number of Soviet prisoners was not satisfying him. Von Bock on the other hand sensed the enemy's confusion, but knew that this was a fleeting factor and precisely therefore understood the need for exploiting it with maximum energy in order to achieve the main goal – the winning of the war. The Red Army mustn't be given an hour of rest, blows must rain down upon it like a hail storm, and the *Wehrmacht* was capable of this – it was mobile!

However, rulers are not to be taught axioms. The appearance must be given that the leaders understand everything as it is. The chain of command was compelling, the subordinate status of a true soldier before the supreme commander. The enraged von Bock managed nevertheless to defend his opinion. Not for long, though.

The shift in Halder's position in this episode is interesting. After the war, discussing the reasons of the *Blitzkrieg's* failure with Liddell Hart, Halder and von Rundstedt named the unexpectedly large number of Soviet troops in the Ukraine as one of the main reasons. In Hart's original, there is the word "awkward". It is hard to believe that the large number of Soviet troops was truly unexpected for the *Wehrmacht* leadership. Then, what? The assumption that because there were so many troops in the Ukraine, there had to be more on the Moscow axis?

However it was, when allocating the strength among the armies, preference had been given to Army Group Center. So the *Wehrmacht's* forces turned out to be distributed in reverse proportion to the distribution of Soviet strength along the front. As a result, Army Group Center forged ahead, while Army Group South lagged behind, even more than Halder was ready to admit, while repulsing hopeless, desperate counterattacks by Soviet tank corps that were unsupported from the air. An equal advance across the front did not result, and Halder lost his nerve. To head toward Moscow with Army Group Center alone, past Kiev and its Southwestern Front which was continuing to resist Army Group South, even if von Bock had both Hoth's and Guderian's panzer armies? Halder backtracked away from von Bock, and the Führer's amendment to the Barbarossa plan became a reality. (Halder soon recollected himself, but it was too late!)

Von Bock in contrast, taking into account the level of the enemy's command, the inexperience of the troops, the lack of coordination between different types of forces and of communication between the formations, was confident that the enemy's confusion – temporary! – was the *Wehrmacht's* only chance. He understood that to win this war was possible only by acting ceaselessly and overwhelmingly.[2] So the fateful moment was now, while the Russians hadn't yet come to their senses. (Let us recall: this was occurring when the Leader still hadn't dragged himself up to the microphone to speak to the country. Had he waited a bit longer, the speech might never have taken place ...) Any delay would lead to a defeat! Simple truths are the most difficult of all to prove ...

The drama of von Bock is a common one for military commanders. They are used to command and don't know how to persuade. Indeed, just whom was von Bock trying to convince? Hitler? Who is able to convince a maniac?

Seemingly, Halder himself refused to see that by siding with Hitler and against von Bock, he had knocked together Nazism's coffin. Yet the honorable soldier von Bock, who like Halder was no admirer of the Nazis, almost led Nazism to a triumph. The ironies of History ...

Meanwhile, the *Wehrmacht* continued to improve its jumping-off positions for a thrust toward Moscow. Halder in his military diary seethed with wrath at von Bock for his "devil may care" attack toward Roslavl', but von Bock needed only five days to bring his forces back to order after Roslavl', which had become yet another of his victories – and still one more tragedy for the Red Army.[3] Incidentally, it cannot be excluded that Halder had reason to seethe, having lost those five days, which changed the course of the war ...[4]

---

2   Our own tank spearheads operated just as boldly at the end of the war. One veteran serviceman, a major in the tank arm, told me in 1975 how back in 1945 Soviet tank battalions, mounting submachine gunners on their armor, had rushed along German roads with burning headlights, scattering German columns, seizing towns and river crossings and demoralizing the German resistance. In 1986 I discovered that these assault forces even rolled into Holland in a few places. The soldiers didn't recognize the border, while a tank needed no visa. The most recent story revealed on the 65th Victory Anniversary tells about the Soviet prominent biologist, candidate for a Nobel Prize and a Lenin prize winner, Iosif Rapoport, a battalion commander in the war, who during one such impetuous advance at the head of his column bumped into three Tigers that were blocking the road. The battalion was advancing without any artillery, so these three Tigers could easily smash the entire column. Nevertheless, the Soviet commander approached the first Tiger on foot, pulled out his pistol, knocked on its armor, and in German demanded that German tanks clear the road and allow his battalion through, informing the Tiger crew that he was being followed by the main forces which had tanks and guns. Amazingly, the Tigers complied and freed the road. Such was a victor's confidence and vigor and such was the defeated side's perplexity and dejection – on the German army's own territory! (This story can be found at: http://www.zn.ua/3000/3760/69349/)

3   In the summer of 1975, when I was a member of a team of test-drivers for the L'vov Motor Factory, I happened to be a guest at a gathering put together by Smolensk Komsomol members. They arranged a regal picnic on the banks of the Oster River and treated us to crawfish, which were teeming in the river, and in passing mentioned the bountiful numbers of the local fauna after the bloody harvest of 1941.

4   In a recently released book written on the basis of his Ph.D. dissertation, David Stahel stresses that the German *Blitzkrieg* in Russia depended almost entirely upon the motorized Panzer Groups. Using previously unpublished archival records, Stahel presents a new view of Germany's summer campaign, focusing on the two largest and most powerful Panzer Groups on the Eastern Front. Stahel's research provides a fundamental reassessment of Germany's war against the Soviet Union, highlighting the prodigious internal problems and stresses within the *Wehrmacht* and its vital panzer forces, and arguing that their failures in the earliest phase of the war undermined the whole German invasion. His thesis rests

On 16 July, Smolensk fell. The *Wehrmacht* losses were moderate, but their correlation between the two sides was terrible: for each *Wehrmacht* soldier killed in action, 22 Red Army soldiers perished. Red Army men in dense chains launched bayonet attacks, suffering enormous losses in order to achieve modest tactical aims. Pinned in place by the *Wehrmacht's* infantry, they were screened from the panzer spearheads' advance toward Moscow and were unable to break out in order to hinder them. However, the victories strengthened Hitler's conviction that he was succeeding in grinding up the Red Army and would still be able to enter Moscow before winter set in. So, instead of repelling these flank attacks while continuing to push on to Moscow and Gor'kii and bypassing the trapped Soviets, he accepted the challenge. Thus the battle for the Smolensk pocket flared up. In the ensuing fighting, the correlation of losses between the two sides was more equivalent, and the *Wehrmacht* also became battered. The battle ended on 27 July. The results were for the *Wehrmacht* a loss of time; for the Red Army, they were more colossal losses, but hand-in-hand with the same military incompetence, there was also growing ferocity in the counterattacks and an increase in morale.

Also – time gained for mobilization. Perhaps this indeed was the main outcome of the battle: the entire country was drawn into the war. Yet there was even more: After the Japanese envoy to Germany General Oshima visited the battlefields around Smolensk, he became convinced that the pace of the *Wehrmacht's* advance was slowing down and that the Red Army's resistance was growing, so Japan decided to direct its efforts to the south. Incidentally, even now it was still not too late to attack Moscow; and indeed, Japan would also not have been forbidden, in the event of a collapse of the USSR, to seize the Far East.

---

on the idea that the fighting around Smolensk broke the *Wehrmacht's* back, and thus the choice between Kiev and Moscow was a moot point – the war was lost no matter which objective was to be pursued. This opinion rests strictly on a military standpoint and ignores the damage to the morale of the Soviet population, if Moscow had fallen into enemy hands. See Stahel, *Operation Barbarossa and Germany's Defeat in the East* (Cambridge: Cambridge University Press, 2009).

34

"Separate and finish off!"

O n 6 June 1941, on the eve of the invasion Hitler, from his Führer Headquarters, issued an order about how the commissars should be handled. This is the main part of the text of this order:

Directives for the Treatment of Political Commissars:
In the battle against Bolshevism one cannot count on the enemy acting in accordance with the principles of humanity or international law. In particular it must be expected that the treatment of our prisoners by the political commissars of all types who are the true pillars of resistance, will be cruel, inhumane, and full of hatred.

The troops must realize:

1. That in this fight it is wrong to treat such elements with mercy, and consideration in accordance with international law with regard to these elements is false. They are a menace to our own safety and to the rapid pacification of the conquered territories.

2. That the originators of the Asiatic-barbaric methods of fighting are the political commissars. They must be dealt with promptly and with the utmost severity.

Therefore if taken while fighting or offering resistance, they must, on principle, be shot immediately.

For the rest, the following provisions also apply:

2. ... Political commissars as agents of the enemy troops are recognizable from their special badge—a red star with a golden woven hammer and sickle on the sleeves ... . They are to be separated from the prisoners of war immediately, i.e. already on the battlefield. This is necessary, in order to remove from them any possibility of influencing the captured soldiers. These commissars are not to be recognized as soldiers; the protection due to prisoners of war under international law does not apply to them. When they have been separated, they are to be finished off.

3. Political commissars who have not made themselves guilty of any enemy action, nor are suspected of such, should be left unmolested for the time being. It will only be possible after further penetration of the country to decide whether remaining functionaries may be left in place or are to be handed over to the Sonderkommandos. The aim should be for the latter to carry out the assessment.

In judging the question 'guilty or not guilty', the personal impression of the attitude and bearing of the commissar should as a matter of principle count for more than the facts of the case which it may not be possible to prove."[1]

---

1   Editor's note: A translation of this document can be found at http://germanhistorydocs.ghi-dc.org. I have adjusted this translation slightly in order to conform to the author's use of some of the terminology found therein.

This Directive had a preamble: "You are requested to limit the distribution to Commanders in Chief of Armies or of Air Commands respectively and to inform the junior commanders by word of mouth."

How to keep secret, though, by limiting the circulation of copies of this directive, if German soldiers witnessed the execution of regiment commissar Fomin, the leader of the astounding defense of Brest, there, on the border of his Motherland, by the Kholm Gates of the fortress, on the banks of the bordering Mukhavets River, where the victors should have saluted his military valor?

In the 2nd edition of this book, I noted that the OKH knew in advance about this order and tried to parry it by Brauchitsch's 24 May 1941 directive, which stressed that "... the duty of the troops was fighting and that this would usually allow no time for special search or mopping-up operations; under no circumstances were individual soldiers to act arbitrarily. They must always act under the order of an officer." I commented upon it, comparing the naiveté of the German officers to the guilelessness of the Red Army commanders: both one group and the other adhered to a code of honor, overestimated their ability to control events, and assumed that they were carrying the flag staff, when it was actually in the paws of their leaders. I even excused the *Wehrmacht*'s leadership by citing the above passage from P. Hoffman's book, *The History of the German Resistance, 1933-1945*.

However, the traffic is heavy on the thoroughfare of History, and the picture is changing incessantly. Approaching the next edition of my book, while examining new discoveries about the Second World War, I stumbled upon the work of Wolfram Wette, *The Wehrmacht: History, Myth, Reality* – and I was delighted that the author didn't yield to Hoffman's charms and didn't forget to emphasize that the protest from the German officers was weaker, the higher their position in the chain of command. The strictly terse writing in Wette's book makes its findings all the more shocking. The book discloses the fact that the *Wehrmacht* command only formally protested against Nazi ideology, or else didn't protest at all. It isn't surprising that at the war's finish, many of the higher officers found themselves on trial.

Incidentally, the generals who did protest were not mistaken in their understanding: an order which gives no choice to an adversary complicates a war immeasurably. For this reason, in 1942 this order was officially cancelled, and captured commissars were exhibited in German propaganda films. The Führer at first, however, was not troubled in the least about the absence of even a minimal humaneness in the implementation of combat operations. On the contrary ...

Zhukov's driver A. Buchin notes:

The German Army of 1941 made a strong impression, first of all by its ruthlessness. It was a cool day toward the end of summer. Some of our I-15 and I-16 fighters were returning from the west in a disordered formation. There were about ten of them. Likely, they had gone out to make ground attacks and had expended all their ammunition. A couple of 'Messers' were buzzing around them, firing at our guys in turn from their cannons and machine guns. Our I-15 biplanes looked particularly pathetic. Having received a burst, the plane would dip, go into a spin, and plummet toward the ground like a falling leaf. A pilot managed to bail out of one I-15. A parachute blossomed above him. Georgii Konstantinovich [Zhukov] and I, witnesses to what was happening, sighed with relief: at least this guy would safely come to ground. That same second a 'Messer' flashed by, fired a point-blank burst into the fellow helplessly dangling in the straps and flew away. The parachute seemingly tenderly lowered the body of the pilot to the ground not far from us. We approached him. He was still a lad, dressed in a blue jumpsuit and a leather helmet, entirely drenched in blood. Zhukov curtly ordered: 'Bury him with honors.' Then he turned and quickly stalked off. It was rare for me to see such wrath on the face of the general; his eyes were narrowed and he was literally ashen-faced.

After a couple of days, General Kokorev, who was Zhukov's assistant, for some reason set off in my vehicle to visit the troops on the front line. We were driving along a secondary road through a forest and suddenly emerged in a clearing and encountered a scene of panic – dozens of crazed Red Army soldiers were rushing in every direction, and above them a 'Messer' was frolicking at low altitude, strafing the frightened fellows. My MK vehicle was camouflaged, and the German, plainly, didn't notice our arrival. In a flash I drove the car into the bushes and parked it under a tree. Kokorev left, and for some time I had to watch further the bloody escapades of the scoundrel. I even recall the mug of the grinning killer; the swine was a skilled pilot and was flying so low that he almost ran into the ground, so I could see him through the Me-109's canopy.

The burning towns and villages left the population with no hope, but news reporters had no shortage of facts, and the newspapers from the first days of the war were splashed with photographs of elderly people and children, who'd been killed on the roads by Luftwaffe pilots. In September near the village of Chuvakhley in Gor'kii Oblast, one such hunter, flying so low that the belly of his plane almost scraped the ground, casually strafed a kid, who was strolling through a field in the middle of a bright day – the only single person in the rye field. He muffed the shot. Perhaps he took pity on the kid and spared him. However, thousands of those, who were not spared, appealed for revenge from their graves.

Was it useless to prepare ideologically for a *Blitzkrieg*? Let's assume so. However, this war dragged on. Hitler lost it ideologically from the very beginning. He hardened the war with his order about the commissars and made no correction. The course which Hitler followed was an ideological winning ace for the Soviet Union. The war from the beginning became a people's war. It could not help but become a patriotic war.

35

The Brief Rule of the People's Commissariat of Defense

Thus, already at midday on 22 June, Zhukov flew off to the Southwestern Front as a *Stavka* representative. On 26 June, he was summoned back to Moscow. What did he accomplish over those four days?

Oh, he managed to do a lot. He was able to impress upon the *front's* staff commanders the proper tactics to use against an adversary that was dominant in skill and mobility, had air superiority, possessed the initiative, and was lunging toward the country's vital centers in the face of its unprepared defense.

In their description, Zhukov's defensive measures were primitive: counterattack advancing enemy wedges everywhere at their base, seize the initiative at any cost, regardless of losses and without waiting for the complete concentration of the forces designated for the counterattack, because with the enemy's air superiority such a concentration couldn't be achieved anyway. Attack, and attack again! Attack ceaselessly, in order to disrupt the enemy's coordination and timetable, and never in any event allow him to penetrate and outflank. If such a danger arises anyway, withdraw the troops to the nearest suitable defense line and attack again, precluding any possible movement by the *Wehrmacht*, trying to envelop his attacking spearheads, no matter how weak your effort.

One can imagine both the difficulty of carrying out these simple instructions and what losses such maneuvers foretold when applied against the German war machine. What of the losses from the Luftwaffe's activities alone during the stage of assembling the forces for the counterattack as well? However, nothing like the Bialystok and Minsk encirclements occurred on the Southwestern Front until the end of July, and this is undoubtedly a tribute to both Zhukov and the *front* command. Armies maneuvered their forces at least in some fashion, and the Red Army troops continued to struggle even when encircled. As for the losses – well, the Leader had preordained them for the country from the beginning, and now there was no other way left to slow down the *Wehrmacht's* panzers. Already on 1 July, however, von Rundstedt requested assistance from von Bock, since like Hitler, the former was a supporter of maintaining an equal rate of advance across the entire front.

Returning to Moscow, Zhukov left his former district, which was now a *front*, not in the best shape, but at least it had been instructed about the way of conducting combat operations. Who had called him back to Moscow? That is a good question. Khrushchev claims that Stalin was hunkered down in his dacha. However, Zhukov was called back by Stalin over the telephone with a specific assignment: to look into the situation with the Western Front.

The Leader had removed himself from power, but had reasons to expect that his little henchmen, who had remained in the Kremlin with gaping mouths, would call him back.[1]

---

1   There are still arguments about Stalin's behavior in these first days of war and whether he was still really in command. Those who argue he was still in control refer to his daily journal of visitors. Yes, he was

He needed to be called back. That would be an open acknowledgment of their insignificance (which is indeed why Stalin had brought them into his inner circle). That would also mean that they would forget that in the rivalry with Hitler, their far-seeing patron had proved to be a klutz, who, when dragged out of bed by the war, had even ventured that the Führer didn't know about the attack. He was hoping that they would come crawling back to him, their tails tucked between their legs and feeling guilty that they hadn't delivered the truth to the Leader, which he hadn't wanted to hear, while they, cowering before the one who had destroyed men who had spoken the truth and who were incomparably more worthy for power, had fawningly withheld the real situation of affairs from him.

Now at the dacha Stalin was trembling in front of both Hitler and his own personal minions. He was encouraged only by the fact that there was no one else in the country to assume responsibilities. With his purges, Stalin had guaranteed this. Again and again he had persecuted everyone that he imagined might be able to say "I'm taking full authority." There had been no such people. Perhaps he was even smirking: what foresight! Perhaps he'd been consternated: What a tremendous amount of work had been accomplished in an enormous country! A succession of politicians and state thinkers went by, culminating in those Marshals and army commanders, whose military capabilities were combined with administrative skills. Some were sent off with bullets to the back of the head, some with accidents or poison, and some with trials or without...

He had abdicated, and now he was biding his time. He was drinking a little wine, just enough to calm his nerves. He knew the defects of his psyche and had long ago learned to manage them. He was smoking a lot of cigarettes; he didn't have the patience to fuss with his pipe. Having the jitters, picturing the Führer's exuberance and the fate that had been prepared for him, he was also likely dreaming: The Führer would suddenly understand that it wasn't easy to reach Moscow over such roads, and he would stoop to making contact ... than at least he, Stalin, would be able to negotiate his fate ... Well, who could have known that Hitler would defy the Non-Aggression Pact – without an ultimatum, without negotiations!? He, Stalin, would have agreed to anything, even to go to war with England. It would have been scary, of course, but not as much as it was now. England was distant. Such a war was feasible. Even if the losses were equivalent to what the troops were suffering now, just imagine the benefits. The USSR's population was larger than Germany's. After England, he could take care of Germany – and Europe would be in his pocket. (Through the Bulgarian ambassador he entreated Hitler for peace under any conditions ...)

Yes, he had miscalculated; there was no doubt about that. The underlings would come, however; where else could they go? Although ...

They arrived. At first Stalin was filled with doubts: just why had they come? However, on the basis of those who had perished in the purges, they fully acknowledged their own unworthiness, and they hadn't come to replace him. They began to coax him: Russia was a large country; there were vast ore, oil and coal deposits even in Siberia, and the large population had its role and we would be mustering more divisions – the Germans couldn't even dream about having that many, and the British would give us rifles with cartridges, they had promised... We have just now organized the GKO[2] under your leadership... Come

---

receiving visitors, but he made no decisions. The first decisions, which may be considered as taking steps to organize the state's defense, were made on 30 June 1941 in his absence.

2   GKO is the Russian abbreviation for the State Defense Committee, which was created on 30 June 1941. The idea had been proposed by Beria at a meeting in Molotov's office in the Kremlin, which was also

back, our Father and Teacher.

The Red Army commanders didn't live to witness this hour. They knew that the Leader was bankrupt. They just didn't realize that he would make himself secure even in bankruptcy ...

So his underlings persuaded him to come back. He returned. On 26 June he phoned Zhukov. He met with him twice in the Kremlin, on that very same day – between 15:00-16:10 and between 21:00 and 22:00. Then what? Perhaps he stepped aside a second time, upon finding out the magnitude of the disaster on the Western Front and having previously driven Zhukov into a teary fit at the General Staff headquarters? (That did happen!) Was it then that Voznesensky told Molotov something that would later cost Voznesensky his life: Viacheslav, lead us ..."?

However, on 2 July, Colonel Ia. Kreizer's 1st Moscow Motorized Rifle Division stopped the *Wehrmacht's* armored spearhead for two complete days on the main axis, at Borisov, and on 3 July, while Germans were involved in heavy fighting, the Leader, having pumped himself with tranquilizers, was courteously dragged by his courtiers up to a microphone, in order at last to say a word to the nation.

He spoke. Every radio station across the Soviet Union was transmitting his speech. I listened to it. Next to me was my cousin, a lieutenant and communication engineer in the Red Army. He had taken a leave of absence for a few hours in order to help us get ready for evacuation, since my parents didn't dare leave work. So, with a bag in his hands, transfixed, he heard the Leader's entire speech, which began with words which had never appeared in the press and would never fade from memory: "... Brothers and sisters, I am addressing you, my friends, at this difficult hour for our Motherland."

His voice was unsteady, his teeth were clattering against his drinking glass, and when he swallowed it was just as audible as his words, and millions of us, who for two long weeks of war had been waiting for the Teacher and Genius to speak, were listening to all of that in dead silence.

What a country ... What a people ... What patience ...

Moreover, this day is remarkable for the little known fact that having taken courage in the menacing company of Beria and his retinue, the Leader again appeared at the General Staff headquarters on Kirov Street in order to head the Army, which seemed to him to have no head. Yes, the Army, beheaded by his efforts, was being led in so far as the commanding positions were occupied. The occupants, though, were often inadequate for their posts, and this did not lend itself to a quick fix. However, the General Staff did have a handful of men, whose understanding of the situation and military capabilities were not inferior to the Germans'. Unfortunately, there was a sharp lack of such men in the field, and all capable officers of the General Staff were sent to assist the inexperienced and bewildered *front* commanders. In the long-term view the re-appearance of the Leader on Kirov Street alas had a lingering effect, although little by little the selection of men for command posts began to be based only upon their professional qualities, without a scrupulous background check to assess their personal dedication to the Leader. It is not superfluous to mention that without the Leader, the General Staff would have selected cadres more quickly, and better

---

attended by Malenkov, Voroshilov, Mikoian and Voznesensky. It was decided to place Stalin at the head of the GKO, in view of his indisputable authority in the country. Having made the decision, the sextet that afternoon (after 4 pm) headed to Stalin's nearest dacha, where they persuaded Stalin again to assume the functions of head of state and allocated the duties in the newly-created Committee.

ones at that.

Zhukov let something slip in his memoirs about the changes in the leadership supposedly implemented by Stalin: the resolute Vatutin was appointed Chief of Staff of the Northwestern Front; the analytical Vasilevsky was appointed Zhukov's deputy ... However besides the elliptical evidence in Zhukov's memoirs, other signs suggest that the Army for a brief period was controlling itself, and so far as its beggarly possibilities allowed – only a handful of people remained! – it was managing itself sensibly. The General Staff was making the appointments, and the Leader was only confirming them.

Stalin's visit to the General Staff headquarters didn't go smoothly. The military commanders – the People's Commissar and the Chief of the General Staff – bristled. They lashed out at the Leader, who had to hear out the impudence, for which not all that long ago men had paid for with their lives. Now he showed leniency. At this stage the military commanders, plainly, had managed to get back a number of friends, who'd been checked into Beria's agency and were still alive. The military men even managed to insist on a more or less orderly withdrawal to the next line of defense. Incidentally, both the orderly withdrawal and all this "military democracy" came to an end in just a few days. The summary execution of the leadership of the Western Front showed everyone who was the boss of the Red Army and the country.

With that, everyone simmered down. The General Staff understood much better than the Leader both the situation and how to get out of it – or at least, how to try to get out of it. No one coveted the role, for which the Leader had recommended himself. Now, when Stalin had allowed himself to be persuaded to return, it was the most inopportune time for a coup. Indeed, there was no one to enact it.

36

The Finest Hour

Counterattacks remained the only way to slow down the *Wehrmacht*. The Leader wasn't troubled by any losses (as long as they weren't prisoners!), and for a time peace was established between him and the General Staff. The Smolensk battle combined with the solid support of England and the USA inspired hope in the Leader for a successful outcome to his bloody game. The degree of his anxiety can be measured by the nature of the proposals he presented to his foreign partners: to open simultaneously two second fronts, one in northern France through the efforts of England alone (this in the summer of 1941), the other a joint venture by the Red Army and the Royal Navy in the Arctic. Both suggestions were declined. ("You see, Semen Mikhailovich [Budenny], it isn't possible to explain everything to you ...") Then the Leader requested 30 (thirty!) British divisions, and allowed that they could even remain subordinated to the British High Command. I can't imagine the reaction of the War Cabinet, which at the time was operating with battalions and companies. The reserved Brits didn't laugh – at least not aloud.

However, a collapse didn't happen. The country was fighting, expending not companies, not battalions, but entire divisions and shedding an enormous amount of blood. After the Smolensk battle, the Father of the working people of the earth was so confident of a successful outcome that in a discussion with President Roosevelt's emissary Harry Hopkins on 31 July, he designated the line Odessa-Kiev-Leningrad as a stable holding line. He added that in October, the poor weather would paralyze the German tanks and the Luftwaffe, and then, supported by the cities of Kiev, Moscow and Leningrad, where three-fourths of the military industry was located ... (? I don't know; this is what Stalin told Hopkins in their discussion) ... the Red Army would begin to push the Germans back!

Regarding October, he wasn't mistaken; the weather didn't betray him. However, how did he get the idea that the line Odessa-Kiev-Leningrad would be firm? It is now when Zhukov's finest hour arrived.

Stalin was preparing for Hopkin's pending visit. Zhukov, likely, didn't know about it. Moreover, he wasn't aware of the evidence that Stalin had prepared for the American president's emissary to muster support for sending assistance to the USSR.

Marshal Zhukov's life was rich with accomplishments. At critical moments he changed the course of events, which had seemed hopeless. He planned and conducted gigantic operations to their completion. He signed Germany's act of surrender. He reviewed the Victory Parade in Moscow mounted on a white steed[1] (and, perhaps, paying silent tribute to his teachers, Marshal Egorov and Army Commander Uborevich). He took part in festivities, like the one described in the Foreword to this book. He met with peers around a table, where events are assessed, as it is called, according to objective criteria. Such events could also be called an achievement.

Zhukov's genuine finest hour arrived on 29 July 1941, and stretched on for days (at

---

1 The parade commander was Marshal Rokossovsky, his former superior, who was now reporting to him about troops' readiness for ceremonial march.

least until 19 August 1941). Seemingly, the Marshal knew that this was his hour of glory and described it in detail, and despite the unceasing efforts of numerous contemporary interpreters, you cannot find a better description than the one Zhukov offers himself:

> Having discussed the existing situation on the fronts with chief of the General Staff's operations division, V. M. Zlobin, his deputy General A. M. Vasilevsky and other leading officers ... we reached, as it seemed to us, the only correct conclusion. Essentially it went as follows: the Nazi command apparently did not dare leave a sector dangerous for Army Group Center – the grouping's right wing – without attention and would attempt to crush our Central Front in the nearest time.
>
> Were this to happen, the German troops would gain an opportunity to come out on the flank and in the rear of our Southwestern Front, rout it, and obtain a free hand on the left bank of the Dnepr after capturing Kiev. Therefore the Nazis would be able to begin an offensive against Moscow only after the threat to their central force's flank would be eliminated.

In later editions, this paragraph was expanded to the length of a page, which contained, in addition to similar details, the assertion that at the moment of evaluating the situation, the adversary wasn't ready to attack Moscow, "... because he lacked the required shock troops of the necessary quality."

Comparing this report with von Bock's plan, one understands who has the right to contend for the title of the greatest commander of the war. Zhukov on 29 July didn't give any thought to the notion that the Germans would dare head toward Moscow, leaving the Kiev Fortified District in their rear. He even took upon himself the assessment of the condition of the German forces and dismissed their capability to attack Moscow.[2] Von Bock, in contrast, hoped to the end to obtain permission for a lunge past Kiev in the direction of Moscow and Gor'kii, until the Führer turned his panzers toward Kiev. What if his opinion had prevailed? He knew the condition of his troops better than Zhukov. The tenacity of the *Wehrmacht* in front of Moscow in the winter of 1941-1942 demonstrates that it was beyond

---

2   Today authoritative military historians (Glantz, Stahel and others) argue against Zhukov's confidence and believe that the decisive damage to the *Wehrmacht*'s Ninth Army, which was attacking Moscow, was inflicted not in the Battle of Smolensk, but in the counteroffensive launched by Timoshenko with the forces of the Western (according to Zhukov, the Reserve) Front between 15 August and 5 September. Zhukov devotes only one short paragraph to this in his memoirs, possibly not suspecting the importance of this operation in the overall picture of the 1941 campaign. Curiously, though, Guderian also doesn't even mention it. However, perhaps both of them were uninformed about the Ninth Army's tribulations, since at the time Guderian was preoccupied with the Kiev pocket, and Zhukov with his operation at El'nia. An additional strange thing: von Bock, who possessed all the available information, nevertheless was insisting on a thrust toward Moscow and Gor'kii, bypassing Kiev. Apparently, having repelled Timoshenko's counteroffensive and soberly evaluating the Army Group's condition and the amount of time remaining until winter, von Bock understood what Hitler already understood: the blitz campaign in the East had failed. Von Bock, plainly, also understood even more, but that was impossible to state aloud: since the war with Russia would be lost all the same, the only chance to avoid eventual destruction was to attempt to seize the Moscow-Gor'kii region. The undertaking was dubious, but total defeat in a lengthy war was doubtless. However Hitler, fearing to get tied up in fighting for Moscow and in the city itself – all of that was Napoleon's experience! – preferred to go after the resources in the south of the USSR and to take his chances with a long war, ignoring the prospects that von Bock was setting forth: the demoralization of the Soviet population in the event of the capital's fall, the collapse of the communications network, and a political collapse.

the strength of the Red Army to break its defense, even though the German defenders had been weakened by the severe cold and were under assault by vastly numerically superior forces. At Stalingrad a year later, this would be accomplished with difficulty on sectors held by the Romanians. There were no Romanians around Rzhev, and there was no breakthrough. (A reader may ask why we're discussing Rzhev and Stalingrad in the same breath here. All will become clear soon enough ...) The armies of the Kiev Fortified District, suffering losses, might have pounded against the *Wehrmacht's* flank defenses, but in the meantime the German Panzer spearheads would have encircled Moscow and taken control of Gor'kii – over the dry ground in July and August, without overconsumption of fuel. After which the panzers could have been transported to the Ukraine over the captured railroads for the culmination of General Marcks' absurd and brilliant plan.

With all respect to the role that Zhukov played in the war, again one bitterly regrets the absence of the RKKA's executed army commanders. Their strategic imagination was akin to von Bock's. They would have foreseen the likelihood of a direct thrust toward Moscow. Such an alternative was not foreseen by the General Staff. Just what might have been, had the Führer not struck toward Kiev? (It might also be the case that the Soviet military did foresee such a move, but could not do much to beat it back ....)

Kiev, a city with a large population and industrial resources, and a transportation hub located on the bend of the Dnepr River, was a natural fortress on the path of the German offensive to the east. It was like a boulder hanging over von Bock's right flank. The further his forces would have pushed on toward Moscow, the more dangerous Kiev would have become as a launching point for a deep attack into the German rear, allowing a greater number of German troops to be cut-off by such a likely attack.

One doesn't have to be a genius to see that this danger looked menacing on the map only. In reality with the initiative in the hands of the *Wehrmacht* and given the Luftwaffe's supremacy in the air, the battered and blockaded armies of the Kiev Fortified District would have seemed similar to the previously mentioned German army in February 1945 on the Berlin axis. They were not in fit to take the offensive. Well, they might have been able to push back the enemy by 5 to 10 kilometers at the cost of frightening losses ... while the fall of Moscow would have killed hopes for assistance from abroad – and with them further resistance, no matter how much propaganda tried to assert that "the fall of Moscow is not the fall of Russia." Not everyone knew Kutuzov's slogan, nor was the Moscow of 1941 anything like the Moscow of 1812.

One also doesn't need to be a genius to grasp this, or to understand that Kiev could not be held. Or that the seasoned armies of the Kiev Fortified District, withdrawn in a timely manner across the Dnepr River, on the defense might become a genuine barrier on the path to the capital, or else even totally stop the *Wehrmacht*'s march. Thus, the loss of Kiev had two alternate paths – one leading to a catastrophe and the other not.

However, the Leader had already shown the Red Army his teeth and was once again dictating the decisions. No one dared oppose them.

Zhukov dared. Incidentally, it must be noted that the list of General Staff officers who shared Zhukov's assessment of the situation in the area of Kiev doesn't include the most authoritative name of those times – Marshal Shaposhnikov.[3]

---

3   Shaposhnikov, apparently, was ill at this time, but it is difficult to believe that his close associate Vasilevsky didn't visit with him and consult with him on this subject. Likely, the Marshal replied with his inherent gentleness: "I fully agree with you, my dear friend, but let me go and get along without me ..."

Zhukov continues:

... being convinced that our forecasts were correct, I decided to report urgently to the Supreme Commander-in-Chief. We had to act immediately. All of us believed that any delay in preparing and carrying out counter-measures would be used by the enemy in whose hands the operational and strategic initiative was at the time. On July 29 I called Stalin and requested to be received to deliver an urgent report.

'You can come,' said the Supreme Commander-in-Chief.

Taking along a map of the strategic situation, a map showing the deployment of German forces, references on the condition of our troops and logistics and equipment at the Fronts and the center, I entered Stalin's reception office where A. N. Poskrebyshev was and asked him to announce my arrival.

'Have a seat. Orders are to wait for Mekhlis.'

About ten minutes later I was invited to come into Stalin's office. L. Z. Mekhlis was already there.

'Well, report what you've got,' said Stalin.

Mekhlis? His presence alone signaled that Zhukov was close to a fall from grace. This was also an opportunity to embroil Zhukov in a dispute with Mekhlis. (They had no taste for each other's presence. Mekhlis, incidentally, was a rough-hewn man and was very strong physically; a guard dog!)

More from Zhukov:

... spreading my maps on the table I described the situation in detail beginning with the Northwestern and ending with the Southwestern Direction. I gave the figures of our main losses on the Fronts and described how our reserves were being formed. I showed the deployment of enemy troops at length, talked about the German army groups and set forth the nearest expected enemy actions.

"Stalin listened attentively. He stopped pacing back and forth, came up to the table and stooping slightly began to examine the map closely down to the finest print.

The Master was attentive; that's a good sign. The dog, though, was inclined to bite. Incidentally, Stalin had no wish to liquidate Zhukov, only to distance him from Moscow. He'd be more useful in the field, and things would be more peaceful for the Master. Given the military failures, why keep a man with a strong character here, close to home? What might he suddenly think up ... he's best friends with Timoshenko ... They had blossomed here, after a not very successful start of the war, truth be told. To dispose of such an authoritative figure now? Just send him away – and another day you may find yourself disposed in the same way!

One can easily imagine what the Master might have said to his chained dog before Zhukov entered the office. This is strictly my conjecture, of course, but it was probably something like this:

This Zhukov here ... What do we do with him? Stubborn like no one else I know. He keeps pounding on military science, and the Germans are pressing hard. Could it be said that the Politburo had discussed his work as Chief of the General Staff and had decided to give him other responsibilities? Who'll replace him? Have a seat, take a listen. Bark, if you sense something.

Perhaps that is why it was at this point in Zhukov's presentation that Mekhlis suddenly spoke up: "How do you know future German actions?' Mekhlis put in abruptly."

It is striking, how ignoramuses ask sensible questions; of course, without expecting a reply. The Führer really did have a choice. Amusingly, Zhukov was thinking in tune with the Führer! However, von Bock wasn't. His war was not only a war of maneuver, but also one of nerves. Tactically – the deep operation, that stunning war "of little blood on an aggressor's territory", which in case of an enemy attack was being developed by the best brains of the RKKA, who did not survive to the time of its implementation. Psychologically – a wager upon the panic and the collapse of authority, something similar to the hopes of modern-day terrorists; something fully real for warfare. However Mekhlis, had he lived a hundred prior lives, would never have risen as highly as in this one, and, asking a question, had never thought about anything similar. He wasn't a military man; he was an executioner. He, seemingly, was intentionally trying to provoke Zhukov in the hope that he might blurt out: "Hitler himself reports to me!" And after such a retort just go and handcuff him!

Zhukov continues (the parenthetical comments inserted throughout are mine):

> 'I don't know the plans according to which the Germans will operate,' I answered, 'but proceeding from an analysis of the situation, they can act in this way and in no other way. (But of course they could!) Our assumptions are based on an analysis of the state and location of large groupings and armored and mechanized troops, above all.' (Even this was not a sure thing ...)
>
> 'Continue the report,' said Stalin.

He was listening, while Mekhlis wasn't even trying; the substance was beyond his comprehension. Indeed, why bother? Regardless, Zhukov would be subject to removal. *What* he was saying wasn't important. *How* he was addressing the Boss – that was the important thing. As well as how he, Mekhlis, should react. There had to be some reason he'd been invited to see the Holy of Holies. If he couldn't grasp the essence of what was going on, then he'd at least give some pepper to this Zhukov, in the Bolshevik style ...

Here the Boss ordered him to be quiet, nodding to Zhukov: "Continue the report."

> ... The Central Front is the weakest and most dangerous place in our defences ... The Germans may take advantage of this weak spot and attack the flank and rear of the Southwestern Front's troops holding the Kiev area.
>
> 'What do you suggest?' Stalin became tense.
>
> 'To begin with we should strengthen the Central Front transferring at least three armies reinforced with artillery there. One army may be obtained from the Western Direction, another from the Southwestern Front, and the third from the Supreme Command reserve. An experienced and energetic commander should be put at the head of the Front. I specifically suggest Vatutin.'
>
> 'Do you mean to say that it's possible to weaken the Moscow sector?' asked Stalin.
>
> 'No, I don't. But in our opinion the enemy won't advance here yet ...

(Yes, that's exactly what the German command was stewing over at the time! It was just such a move that the enemy was debating. Moreover, that is the direction they were preparing to move! The Führer prevented it. He was thinking like Zhukov, though at the time under discussion, Zhukov still had no understanding of Hitler and his thinking.)

> '... and in 12 to 15 days we can bring up not less than eight completely combat-worthy divisions from the Far East, including one tank division.'
>> 'And we'll give the Far East up to the Japanese?' Mekhlis made a caustic remark.
>> (This to the victor at Khalkhin-Gol ... such tact!)
>> I did not answer and went on: 'The Southwestern Front should be withdrawn right away completely beyond the Dnepr.'

Bravo, General Zhukov! The radical nature of your conclusions, even more considering to whom you were proposing them, is a high honor to you. If in your life you managed to do nothing else, if you had been executed for your impudence, like hundreds of others of your co-equals and more capable military commanders (about which, incidentally, you were more aware than anyone else – and which makes your step particularly dramatic!) – this deed already gives you the right to be inducted into the pantheon of war heroes. Bravo!

> 'Reserves of not less than five reinforced divisions should be deployed behind the junction between the Central and the Southwestern Fronts. They will be our shock force and operate according to the situation.'
>> 'What about Kiev?' said Stalin looking me straight in the eye....
>> 'We shall have to leave Kiev,' I said firmly.
>> An oppressive silence settled in. I continued to report, trying to remain calm.
>> 'A counterblow should immediately be organized on the western direction with the aim of eliminating the Yel'nya [El'nia] salient in the enemy front. The Nazis may later use the Yel'nya bulge as a springboard for an offensive on Moscow.'
>> 'What counterblows? It's nonsense!' Stalin flew into a rage and suddenly asked in a high voice: 'How could you hit upon the idea of surrendering Kiev to the enemy?'

He had prepared optimistic talking points for Hopkins about the solid configuration of the front along the line Odessa-Kiev-Leningrad, about industry, and about a counteroffensive, but his Chief of the General Staff was turning all of this into a mirage! Zhukov could hardly have ever imagined the juxtaposition of these two events: Hopkins arrival for discussions with the Leader and his suggestion to abandon Kiev in exchange for a firm line of defense along the eastern bank of the Dnepr.

Zhukov continues:

> I was unable to restrain myself and retorted:
>> 'If you think that as Chief of General Staff I'm only capable of talking nonsense, I've got nothing more to do here. I request to be relieved of the duties of Chief of General Staff and sent to the front. Apparently I'll be better use to my country there.'

In his posthumous memoirs *Glazami cheloveka moego pokoleniya* [*Through the Eyes of a Man of my Generation*] Konstantin Simonov reveals a conversation with Zhukov about this incident. Zhukov observes that on occasion he had to answer Stalin's rudeness with truculence of his own, and relates that his response to the Leader on 29 July was much blunter than as given in his memoirs: "Comrade Stalin, I request that you withdraw your remarks. I am Chief of the General Staff. If you as the Supreme Commander-in-Chief believe that your Chief of the General Staff speaks nonsense, then he must be relieved of his duties, which I am requesting."

In general, the tone of Zhukov's comments about the Leader in his memoirs are forcedly (and strikingly) different from the tone of his remarks in his conversation with Simonov, who was perceptive and now understood that Stalin was not great and fearsome, just simply fearsome. Zhukov until the end of his days, when speaking about Stalin in one way or another, continued to be proud of his close association with the tyrant and, to put it crudely, to suffer from unreciprocated love. "Everything has a duality, even virtue." Who said this? Balzac, it seems. This duality is not a desire to imitate a companion. This is a duality of thought. Not only Zhukov's; in all of us. On one hand, we understand. On the other hand, we continue to believe in rubbish, in which it would seem we long ago should have stopped believing.

Let us return, however, to 29 July. If Zhukov truly did reply in this fashion, then he did it because he knew that the forest of cadres behind him had been burned to the ground, and the Leader now had no other choice but to yap at him, send him away – and bring him back. There was no one to replace him. This is a partial explanation for Zhukov's audacity. There may have been no substitutes, but Stalin was still Stalin, a deadly animal. Zhukov knew this. This indeed was the implication, when at the start of the book I said of the commander that in the initial phase of the war, he demonstrated a courage bordering on madness.

In the painful labors to stabilize the front and to delay the German advance (and in that situation there was no other solution than to delay the *Wehrmacht*, which was obviously unready for winter), Zhukov proposed a maneuver to trade territory in order to hold the *Wehrmacht* here, on the Dnepr River line. Whether this was the correct decision in a strategic sense or not – at present this cannot be established with complete certainty. What is important is that Zhukov dared to express his point of view in front of such an antagonistic audience, since he believed that time was running out! Delay was akin to death! So he didn't permit the tyrant to get nasty with him again.

Yes, he had a high regard for himself in that bloody game, which had been going on for more than a month, and understood that he was up to the forthcoming tasks. The professional within him erupted and he couldn't remain silent in front of the Leader, though he was aware that this was fraught with risk.

Zhukov continues his narrative of this episode:

An oppressive pause set in again.

'No need to get excited,' remarked Stalin. 'However ... if that's how you put it, we'll be able to do without you ...'

(In the 1995 edition of Zhukov's memoirs, Stalin's statement is "We got along without Lenin, and we can get by even more without you." This version is completely in the style of Stalin. As it was, he'd already, for a long time, been trying to get by without needed people – with obvious results!)

'I'm a military man and ready to carry out any orders, but I have a firm idea of the situation and ways of waging the war, believe that my idea is correct, and reported what the General Staff and I myself believe.'

This was a calculated move, as if saying to Stalin, "You can grind me into dust, but the General Staff believes the same thing. And if you shoot me – the situation at the front won't get any better because of this!" If Zhukov is laying out the entire episode with accuracy, from a sort of affair in which only separate phrases are accessible, then subsequent events with his successor, the factual Chief of Staff Vasilevsky, provide a basis to trust his words on the main point: The General Staff believed the same thing! Stalin rejected the proposal, but not Zhukov. The obstinate subordinate would be punished, but lightly so. He had to remain around. There was no one else.

More from Zhukov:

Stalin no longer interrupted me but listened to me now without anger and remarked in a calmer tone:
'Go and do your work, we'll send for you.'
Collecting the maps I went out of the office with a heavy heart. I was invited to the Supreme Commander-in-Chief in about half an hour.
'You know what,' said Stalin, 'we've sought each other's advice and decided to relieve you of the duties of Chief of the General Staff. We'll appoint Shaposhnikov to the post. It's true, his health is rather poor, but we'll help him alright.'

We'll, Lord God, help out the seriously ill Shaposhnikov ...

No, the Leader wasn't stupid. His penetrating gaze noted young officers in the People's Commissariat of Defense – without merits, not long in grade, but educated, capable and most importantly, manageable. Among them was Major-General Aleksandr Mikhailovich Vasilevsky,[4] an intelligent son of a priest, a man with an attentive gaze, pleasant manners, a soft voice and astonishing memory. The Leader was an old hand in cadre matters, but in military matters? Well, the military commanders themselves would give him a boost. The fee for this training would be told on the battlefields, but who would do the paying? Mothers, wives ... Stalin's unloved son Iakov was a propitiatory sacrifice[5], so that it couldn't be said that the Leader himself hadn't lost anyone in the war. His son Vasilii flew for the same reason, though it is true, under solid personal security.

Stalin again, through Zhukov's memoirs (the parenthetical comments are mine):

'We'll use you in practical work. You have extensive experience in commanding troops in field conditions. You will be of undoubtable use for the army in the field. Of course, you will remain deputy People's Commissar for Defense and member of the *Stavka*.'
'Where would you order me to go?'
'Where would you like to go?'
(Wow, is this Stalin??)
'I can do any work. I can command a division, a corps, an army, a Front.'

---

4   On the day following Zhukov's removal, 30 July 1941, Shaposhnikov was appointed Chief of the General Staff, while chief of the Operations Branch Major-General Vasilevsky was made his deputy.

5   Iakov Djugashvili was a captain and commanded an artillery battalion. He was taken prisoner in the town of Liozno on 16 July 1941 when trying to make his way out of encirclement. Stalin purportedly said in response to an offer to exchange Paulus for his son Iakov, "I don't trade field marshals for lieutenants."

(A General of the Army, Deputy People's Commissar, and member of the *Stavka* is saying this! You were angry, Georgii Konstantinovich. You were also demonstrating your character, however: "You're the boss, but I'm right!" Your finest hour ...)'

'Don't get excited, don't get excited! (As if to say: 'Listen, jackass, calm down, eh? Or else, you know ... we'll have to shoot you, right? You don't want that – and I don't want it either! So, calm down, right?') You reported here about organizing an operation at Yel'nya. Well, take it into your hands.'

Then, pausing a while, Stalin added:

'Operations of the reserve armies along the Rzhev-Vyazma defense line must be unified. (One can plainly sense in this decision the hands of Zhukov's colleagues in the General Staff ...) We'll appoint you Commander of the Reserve Front. When can you leave?'

'In an hour.'

'Shaposhnikov will arrive soon in the General Staff. (Really ... the ill Shaposhnikov was at home even in these terrible days. A fitting replacement for Zhukov ...) Turn over you duties to him and set out.' (Yes, yes, dear fellow, set out, all the sooner! Get out of Moscow! Return when you're called ... only when you're called!)

'Do I have your permission to leave?' (Do you sense the nerve, reader? This in a conversation with a tyrant, the murderer of your instructor-commanders! The finest hour!)

'Sit down and have some tea with us,' now smiling, said Stalin, 'we'd like to talk about some other matters.'

We sat at the table and began to drink tea, but the conversation didn't shape up.

With whom? With the executioner Mekhlis? The combat general Zhukov could not have had any conversation with him. However, the Leader couldn't send Mekhlis away upon his fulfillment of his dog's functions as a witness and bodyguard: after such heated conversation he couldn't remain alone, eye to eye, with Zhukov!

Stalin's supporters have scrubbed the Leader of complicity in the enormous losses suffered by the Red Army, pointing a finger at Zhukov instead, and today various opinions prevail regarding whether the Zhukov's meeting with Stalin and Mekhlis on 29 July actually occurred. Alas, mistrust has reached that far. Doubts are strengthened by the fact that in Stalin's visitor log for this date, the Marshal's name does not appear. Those who wish to be so can be convinced: Zhukov's name is not the only one missing from the list of visitors; not a single leader of the General Staff or the People's Commissariat of Defense (other than Kulik) appears on it.[6] Why? Because the time of the military commanders during those terrible days and nights was valued more highly than the time of the Leader with all his Politburo members taken together. With his sleepless nights, Zhukov had no time to wait in reception rooms. The name of the Marshal isn't in the visitors' logbook because Stalin himself, together with his loyal hell-hound Poskrebyshev was on that day a visitor to the General Staff. Though indeed he wasn't a visitor; he had migrated to the General Staff headquarters on Kirov Street as a controller and warden. He spent the nights

---

6   A note has been added to the Leader's journal of visitors for this day: "Not received in the Kremlin office." On that night Stalin received nine people elsewhere than in his Kremlin office, between 2:00 am and 3:45 am. Let those who doubt the Marshal's honesty give some thought to where else the Leader could spend the day, other than in the General Staff headquarters ...

at his dacha or in the Kremlin, but whiled away his days at the General Staff headquarters. He even had an office set up there, with a reception room. A lot of premises were available there ... The conversation, relayed by Zhukov and interrupted by Stalin's order "Go and do your work, we'll send for you" (which for some reason has not been called into question) took place there. Where else could Zhukov be working? The General Staff wasn't located in the Kremlin. In those days and nights, the fate of the country was being decided at the General Staff. It was also the location of the telegraph that provided direct contact with lower headquarters .... Given the rapidly changing situation at the front, there was no time for the generals to commute between the General Staff and the Kremlin. The Leader also understood the importance of his presence here. He felt confident there. Here is where he could keep a leash on his army!

Perhaps Zhukov embellished something in his narrative of the discussion, although General of the Army Belov in his memoirs notes the independence in Zhukov's behavior in front of Stalin in the first year of the war. This is explainable. Whatever tyrant and monster you might be, you'd still have to feel guilty, if you had rejected the demands of the military commanders to declare mobilization or at least a higher level of alert, and had permitted the army and the country to be caught off-guard. On this wave of guilt feelings, even the Leader might lower his voice a peg, and the military commanders, Zhukov in particular, might raise theirs.

However, from 29 July 1941 up to 27 August 1942, prior to his summon from the Western Front and appointment to the post of First Deputy of the Supreme Commander, Zhukov was sent out on specific assignments and removed from strategic planning. He was in Moscow only when summoned, and his opinion valued only on matters concerning the military situation around Moscow (about which the Marshal speaks only in passing in his memoirs).

Yes, of course, Zhukov was not a suitable Chief of the General Staff, especially at a time when there was a catastrophic deficit of field commanders at the rank of *front* and direction commanders. However, his removal could have been done with more decorum. Ultimately, it wasn't his fault that Red Army lacked commanders and chiefs of staff.

37

The Kiev Express

This settlement at the confluence of peaceful rivers, where the very first structures from the period of early human history have been discovered, was plainly doomed from the beginning to experience tragedy. How else can it be explained that amidst the tranquility of springtime within the last quarter-century, after the countless bloody raids and sieges of the past thousand years, it has been battered by an enormous mudslide,[1] climactic change caused by the construction of the Kiev Reservoir dam, and Chernobyl'?

However, in 1941 Kiev was an ecological marvel. The view sank into the endless azure depth of the sky, and returning to the transitory earth, from the high right-bank of the Dnepr, one could see the vast Ukrainian plains, green and blue, stretching like a sea into the distance, the pure waters of the river, glittering like a mirror and reflecting the enormous sky. In this ether, barges floated by, and clouds, and fish, and leaves, and birds. A unique breeze flowed, like exists nowhere else on earth today.

Indeed, there are few places like it on the planet. These fertile soils under the caressing sun in the confluence of the Pripiat', Desna and Dnepr Rivers gave life to hundreds of generations. Who hasn't been drawn to it? Everyone longed for this source of water and pure air, this earthly plum with its moderate climate, dry breeze and the radiant sky overhead. People have settled here from time immemorial; settlements have existed on the location of Kiev for 15,000 years. Yet now, after the Polovtsy, the Tatar Mongols, the Poles, the Swedes, the Germans, after the bloody civil internecine war, the Nazis were approaching and – got stuck. Here the Führer's chances for victory crumbled, which were real before his attention was attracted by Kiev, the gateway to the south.

Propaganda at the time was full of expressions about the valiance of Kiev's defenders. The city was one of the first – after the war, however – to acquire the title "Hero City". Yet it was no less worthy of this title than Odessa, which received it during the war after 72 days of defense. Kiev held out for 76 days[2] on the central sector, at the boundary between two

---

1   On 13 March 1961, the so-called Kurenevka tragedy occurred: an enormous volume of sludge, which was being pumped through conduits to Babi Iar, as if to wipe it from the earth and to erase the massacre of Kiev's Jews from memory, burst through a dam and flooded the city district of Kurenevka. Hundreds of people perished, residential buildings and the metro station were destroyed, and several factories were damaged. A. Kuznetsov, the author of a book about Babi Iar and a "defector-tourist", wrote: "The attempt to wipe out Babi Iar ... led to a new wholesale slaughter and even engendered superstitious beliefs. The phrase 'Babi Iar is taking revenge' became popular."

    The Kiev Reservoir with a surface area of around a 1,000 square kilometers, which was constructed in the 1960s at the confluence of the Pripiat', Uzh and Teterev Rivers with the Dnepr River above Kiev in a southern defile of the Pripiat' Marshes, not only made the strategic city, which previously had been relatively impregnable, vulnerable to being swept away by one or two well-placed bombs on the dam. It also significantly altered the city's dry climate and now blesses the city with hordes of mosquitoes in the warm months.

2   Officially, only 71 days. I'm counting from 5 July, when on this day in Kiev the Communists and Komsomol members were mobilized to form militia units and to build fortifications. Air raids on the city were so punctual that one could check the time by them and occurred at 6:30 am. From 3 July (on 2 July

Commander of the 12th Army Major-General P.G. Ponedelin.

fronts. The city continued to stand, fettering the Führer's plans, but setting up a cruel fate for the defenders and the city's civilians.

The tragedy of General Kachalin's 6th Army and General Ponedelin's 12th Army nevertheless assisted to the successful defense of Kiev. At the end of July, these two armies were encircled (at the time when Zhukov was making his proposals) in the area of Uman, but kept 22 German divisions tied up on the southern flank of the Kiev defense until the middle of August. (Unwilling witnesses of the shame of 1941, the valiant generals, who became prisoners through the fault of the Leader and who honorably spurned enticements from the Germans, and later the Allies as well, to switch sides, were shot in 1950.)

Zhukov's memoirs have this to say about the defense of Kiev:

> Different versions now exist concerning the positions of the Stavka, the General Staff, the Command of the South-Western Direction and the Military Council of the South-Western Front regarding Kiev's defense and withdrawal of troops to the Psyol [Psel] River to avoid the threat of encirclement. That is why I deem it necessary to quote excerpts from a conversation between Stalin and the Commander of the South-Western Front M. P. Kirponos on August 8, 1941. They show that the opinions of the

---

strong thunderstorms raged between sunset and midnight, preventing air raids), evening aerial attacks began which included strafing the streets with machine guns. Under an air raid we, several families, were fleeing the city in a truck across a suspension bridge, which was later blown up. It was 6:30 pm. on 4 July. Just a little more than 60 kilometers separated the city from the front lines at the time. Sometimes the *Wehrmacht* covered such a distance in the course of a single day. This time, it required more than two months to travel that distance.

Generals Kirillov and Ponedelin in German captivity. Possibly, the
German cigarettes that they are holding served as incriminating
evidence against them of betrayal and cost them their lives.

Supreme Commander-in-Chief and the Military Council of the South-Western Front
coincided: they were against the withdrawal of Soviet troops from Kiev.

In the memoirs, there follows this exchange by teletype between Stalin and Kirponos:

Stalin: According to information that has reached us the Front has decided to
surrender Kiev to the enemy with a light heart **allegedly due to a shortage of units**
capable of defending Kiev. Is that true?

   Kirponos: ... You have been misinformed. The Military Council and I are taking
all possible measures ... (and so forth). At the same time I must report that **I have no
more reserves on this sector**. (Emphasis the author's)

Zhukov interprets this as a convergence of opinions? Good grief! If the reader had
doubts that a *Wehrmacht* strike toward Moscow was possible while ignoring the Kiev
Fortified District's supposed threat to von Bock's flank, then after this confession by the
Front commander it is time to appreciate the seriousness of the danger hanging over our
Motherland in August 1941, the full correctness of von Bock's position and the full extent
of Hitler's miscalculation.

   Zhukov, an experienced polemicist, duly stipulates that "Different versions now exist ..."
but Kirponos' final phrase completely cuts across the Marshal's rhetoric about the similarity
of views between Stalin and the Southwestern Front command. Indeed, why would the

Leader have sounded so threatening, if the Front command had either indirectly, though its operations department, or else through the Chief of the General Staff himself, not raised the question of withdrawing its forces? But where did the Leader get his information? Front headquarters didn't report to him personally ...

The General Staff supported the idea of withdrawing beyond the Dnepr and creating a new line of defense there. This idea was the basis of the report of the Chief of the General Staff and General of the Army Zhukov to the Leader on 29 July, and didn't disappear after Zhukov's replacement. The author of this plan was primarily the chief of staff of the Southwestern Front Major-General Tupikov. In Kiev, at the quiet intersection of Chkalov Street and Timofeev Street (now, seemingly, Oles' Gonchar Street and Mikhail Kotsiubinsky Street), there stands a building with Doric columns. After the war, the headquarters of the Kiev Military District was located in it. Across the quiet square, there is a gravesite with a modest obelisk. The inscription says that here lies Major-General Vasilii Ivanovich Tupikov, chief of staff of the Southwestern Front. One of the RKKA's remaining operational-tactical thinkers after the purge was buried here by the Germans. In distinction from the way they treated the commissars, they buried commanders who fell with a weapon in their hands with military honors. They knew Tupikov; he'd been the military attaché to Germany on the eve of the war.

On 21 September 1941, Major-General Tupikov, as the senior remaining commander of the Southwestern Front, led a column consisting of hundreds of the Front's staff officers in a night attack in the effort to break out of encirclement. Without firing a shot, they came bursting out of the dark and fell upon the enemy. While the foe was recovering from the shock in the darkness, those who were fortunate broke through – Generals Dobykin, Danilov, Paniukhov.... Tupikov wasn't among them. He fell in an empty field, 2 kilometers from the Shumeikovo grove. On 24 September, the Germans gathered the bodies of the fallen commanders on the battlefield.

This RKKA intellect who had survived the purge was one of those that Stalin despised. The Leader couldn't tolerate people with analytic capabilities and targeted them for liquidation. These analysts, you know, they always might hit upon something ... but you can't kill everyone! Tupikov survived, so that in our time to become one of the prosecutorial witnesses against the Leader. As has already been mentioned, Stalin couldn't tolerate sensible reports that were contrary to his opinion. Tupikov inspired Stalin's dislike long ago with his reports from Berlin about the *Wehrmacht's* preparations. The Leader called Tupikov's dispatches nothing other than alarmism, and refused to take them seriously.

The attitude toward Tupikov hasn't changed even today. The hero, whose merits were honored by the enemy, is ignored by his compatriots. In the last edition of the *Great Soviet Encyclopedia*, there is an entry for "Trotskyist" (though it contains not a word about Trotsky, or even about the rehabilitated Bukharin and Rykov), but not for Tupikov. He's been totally unlucky also in the memoir literature. You can learn something about him only from the memoirs of his subordinate, Marshal Bagramian. Bagramian, though, lets us know that the leak of information to Stalin about the discussions of the Southwestern Front's leadership went through Burmistenko, a member of the Military Council, Secretary of the Kiev District Committee, a solid Party member, and a man of great courage but little understanding of military matters. He had his own line of communication with the Leader, and so the voice of a member of the Front's Military Council had more influence than the voice of the Front commander, not even to mention the voice of the Front's chief of staff.

Meanwhile, events were unwinding catastrophically – for both sides. Yet since the victory at Kiev truly became pyrrhic for the Barbarossa plan, then why is this author chiding Stalin, while in contrast praising Zhukov and Tupikov? From today's perspective, the Leader's determination to hold Kiev looks wise. Given the choice between the loss of a million troops on one hand, and the loss of the war on the other, it is clear which one to choose. Even more, where is the guarantee that a defense along the line of the Psel River would have been stable and would not have shared the same fate that befell the Western, Briansk and Reserve Fronts two weeks later?

As far as guarantees – well, what can be guaranteed, all the more so from the future into the past? The armies of the Kiev Fortified District were elite in the RKKA, seasoned, and had the experience of successful defensive fighting. They couldn't crush von Bock's forces moving past them toward Moscow, but a timely withdrawal to the line indicated by the General Staff truly might have averted the later tragedy of the three fronts defending Moscow. Moreover, having found any evidence that Stalin was deliberately planning to sacrifice the Southwestern Front, then one would have to recognize the presence of military genius in the Leader. However, there is no evidence that he had securely, as he seemed to believe, screened himself and Moscow with three entire fronts. The illusion of security evaporated weeks later, when out of the more than a million troops which were defending the Moscow axis there remained only a thin shield of 90,000 dispersed and badly shaken men.

However (other than the indirect evidence in the form of the arguments presented to Hopkins) there is direct and reliable proof that here, as in all other analogous situations, the Leader's territorial avarice and absence of the slightest understanding of maneuvering were operating: *he did not even order to prepare a plan for a timely withdrawal from Kiev to positions across the Dnepr River*! In that case, the Führer would truly have been left looking the fool, with both the loss of time and the failure to encircle the troops defending the Kiev Military District. He even feared this, reasoning that any direct advance on Moscow leaving Kiev in the wake would allow the divisions of the Southwestern Front to slip out of the city and fall with all their weight on the flank of Army Group Center's advancing armies to cut their lines of supply! No, first of all Kiev had to fall. The Southwestern Front had to be encircled and destroyed!

I've already discussed the prospects for an attack by the weakened Southwestern Front. However, there was no plan for a withdrawal even in the defensive plan variant! As for the military commanders – well, they had proposed a sensible solution, even if they'd erred on the matter of the German intentions.

From the very outset, Army Group South was inferior to the numerical strength of the Southwestern Front by a ratio of 4:5. The city is located on heights, so it was difficult to take through frontal attacks, so the Führer made the decision to remove Guderian's Panzers from von Bock in order to assist von Rundstedt and to commit them to a deep envelopment of the city from the north. The assault on Moscow was to be postponed. The Führer met with von Brauchitsch and Halder over this question on 4 August in Borisov. Von Bock, Hoth and Guderian in turn gained a private hearing, so that they couldn't hear the others' opinion. They all spoke in favor of the Moscow option. Hoth said he would be ready by 20 August and Guderian by 15 August, though he requested the replacement of motors that had been consumed by the dusty Russian roads. Hitler was skeptical and listed his priorities as Leningrad, the Ukraine, and especially the Crimea, from which Soviet bombers threatened the Ploesti oilfields. The meeting concluded with some hope that the Moscow variant would be chosen. The generals got busy with preparations and improving their jumping-off positions.

I turn the words over to Guderian, "Hurry-up Heinz":

> On August 23rd I was ordered to attend a conference at Army Group headquarters, at which the Chief of the Army General Staff was present. The latter informed us that Hitler had now decided that neither the Leningrad nor the Moscow operations would be carried out, but that the immediate objective should be the capture of the Ukraine and the Crimea. The Chief of the General Staff, Colonel-General Halder, seemed deeply upset at this shattering of his hopes, which were based on a resumption of the Moscow offensive. We discussed at length what could still be done to alter Hitler's 'unalterable resolve.' We were all agreed that this new plan to move on Kiev must result in a winter campaign: this in its turn would lead to all those difficulties which the OKH had very good reasons for wishing to avoid.

If the concern had been only about a winter campaign ... The generals understood that the Russians would be gaining critical time for mobilizing people and resources. Then the advantage of surprise, which had been achieved, would be thrown away! However, it is awkward to mention truisms in a presentation to the Supreme Commander. (It was also not very comfortable to write about the factor of surprise achieved by the Germans even years after the war, and, possibly, it is still uncomfortable now.)

Guderian relates what happened next:

> Field-Marshal von Bock... finally suggested that I accompany Colonel-General Halder to the Führer's headquarters; as a General from the front I could lay the relevant facts immediately before Hitler and thus support a last attempt on the part of the OKH to make him agree to their plan. The suggestion was approved. We set off later that afternoon and arrived at the Lotzen airfield, in East Prussia, just as it was getting dark.
>
> I reported at once to the Commander-in-Chief of the Army, Field-Marshal von Brauchitsch, who greeted me with the following words: 'I forbid you to mention the question of Moscow to the Führer. The operation to the south has been ordered. The problem now is simply how it is to be carried out. Discussion is pointless.' I therefore asked permission to fly back to my Panzer Group, since in these circumstances any conversation I might have with Hitler would be simply a waste of time. But Field-Marshal von Brauchitsch would not agree to this. He ordered that I see Hitler and report to him on the state of my Panzer Group, 'but without mentioning Moscow!'
>
> I went in to see Hitler. There was a great many people present, including Keitel, Jodl, Schmundt and others, but neither Brauchitsch nor Halder nor, indeed, any representative of the OKH. I described the state of my Panzer Group, its present condition and that of the terrain. When I had finished Hitler asked: 'In view of their past performance, do you consider that your troops are capable of making another great effort?'

I replied: 'If the troops are given a major objective, the importance of which is apparent to every soldier, yes.'

Hitler then said: 'You mean, of course, Moscow?'

I answered: 'Yes. Since you have broached the subject, let me give you the reasons for my opinions.'

Hitler agreed and I therefore explained basically and in detail all the points that favoured a continuation of the advance on Moscow and that spoke against the Kiev operation... I tried to show how a victory in this decisive direction, and the consequent destruction of the enemy's main forces, would make the capture of the Ukrainian industrial area an easier undertaking: once we had seized the communication hub of Moscow, the Russians would have extraordinary difficulty in moving troops north to south.

I pointed out that the troops of Army Group Centre were now poised for an advance on Moscow; that before they could start on the alternative operation towards Kiev a great deal of time would be wasted in moving to the south-west; that such a move was towards Germany, i.e. in the wrong direction; and that for the subsequent attack on Moscow the troops would have to retrace their steps (from Lochvitsa to Roslavl, that is to say 275 miles), with consequent heavy wear to their strength and to their equipment. I described the condition of the roads over which my Group would have to move, giving example the ones I knew as far as Unecha, and the unending supply problems which would become greater with every day's march toward the Ukraine. Finally, I touched on the enormous difficulties which must arise if the proposed operation were not terminated as fast as was now planned and were to be protracted into the period of bad weather. It would then be too late to strike the final blow for Moscow this year. I ended with the plea that all other considerations, no matter how important they might seem, be subordinated to the one vital necessity – the primary achievement of a military decision. Once that was secured, everything else would be ours for the taking.

Hitler, let me speak to the end without once interrupting me. He then began to talk and described in detail the considerations which had led him to make a different decision. He said that the raw material and agriculture of the Ukraine were vitally necessary for the future prosecution of the war. He spoke once again of the need of neutralizing the Crimea, 'that Soviet aircraft carrier for attacking the Rumanian oilfields.' For the first time I heard him use the phrase: 'My generals know nothing about the economic aspects of war.' Hitler's words led up to this: he had given strict orders that the attack on Kiev was to be the immediate strategic object and all actions were to be carried out with that in mind. I here saw for the first time a spectacle with which I was later to become very familiar: all those present nodded in agreement with every sentence that Hitler uttered, while I was alone with my point of view. Undoubtedly he had already held forth many times on the subject of his reasons that had led him to take a strange decision. I was extremely sorry that neither Field-Marshal von Brauchitsch nor Colonel-General Halder had accompanied me to this conference, on the outcome of which, according to them, so very much depended, perhaps even the result of the war as a whole. In view of the OKW's unanimous opposition to my remarks, I avoided further arguments on that occasion; I did not then think it would be right to make an angry scene with the head of the German State when he was surrounded by his advisers.

Since the decision to attack the Ukraine had now been confirmed, I did my best at least to ensure that it be carried out as well as possible...[3]

It cannot be denied; everything was carried out brilliantly. However, the generals who knew nothing about the economic aspects of war understood strategy. In August, the Kiev Express started to rumble. Prior to this, to secure the move, the *Wehrmacht* had to organize two breakthroughs across the Dnepr, one above and one below Kiev. In return, the area encompassed by the looming envelopment expanded, and with it, correspondingly, the dimensions of the Red Army's catastrophe. What of it? The *Blitzkrieg* was dead.

A general comment: A heavy feeling grips the Russian reader when comparing the awkward, colorless, ghostwritten memoirs of the Soviet Army's military commanders[4] with the concise and expressive memoirs of the *Wehrmacht's* generals. However, this also generally reflects the comparison between the military level of the participants of the huge battles. So, as a result, goes the comparison of the losses ...

One day in November, when the fall of Moscow seemed to be a certain matter of days[5], Hitler, at a meeting, in his characteristically messianic style, made the following declaration:

The epoch of panzers will soon come to an end ... If we successfully complete our European mission, our historical evolution can be considered secure. Then, in defense of our gains, we will use the advantages of the triumph of defense over the panzer to defend against any encroachments.

So much can be found in these words ... the misunderstanding of the nature of contemporary warfare; an inability to recognize that any defense can be overcome. Also now a lack of confidence that the USSR could really be conquered, as if the goal of the war was only to plunder the country, grab the territory containing resources, and to toss away all the rest. To build a wall against the Russian hordes across the continent, like the Romans had done against the untamed Caledonia, and just let the remnants of this USSR rot away on the far side of the Urals with their absurd attempts to shake the Reich's steel wall with their tanks ...

"My generals know nothing about economics" ... It seems like this bourgeois understood less about economics than his generals if he assumed that the population of Russia wouldn't present a danger to the Reich, even if pushed back beyond the Urals. He had inspired his

---

3   By this time under the influence of von Bock's arguments, the Chief of the Army General Staff Colonel-General Halder returned to General Marcks' plan and, angered by what he considered to be the insufficient persistence of Guderian in his presentation to Hitler, he refused to meet with "Hurry-up Heinz" before his departure to the front. There is not anything even to say about von Bock. It would be impossible to call his relationship with Guderian at this time as one of mutual confidence. Guderian didn't hide his grievances. Of course, one can suspect that von Bock preferred to have someone else's hands pull his chestnuts out of the fire, but plainly, of the three Guderian was recognized as the strongest in the art of persuasion, so the mission was laid upon him, and he couldn't cope with it. However can someone really blame Guderian if he was unable to bring a maniac around to his views?

4   Only A. M. Vasilevsky wrote his memoirs himself – and as a result, the Soviet Voenizdat [Military Publisher] refused to publish it.

5   It was precisely on one of these days, 17 November 1941 that the German veteran and ace of the First World War, Ernst Udet, who was the closest person to Göring and the head of the Reich Air Ministry's development branch, committed suicide in despair over the course the war had taken.

generals for the campaign. They had believed him and had implemented his plan with striking success. He didn't believe his generals, though – a paradox! He was like someone who contracts a killing, but at the moment of the assassination attempt grabs the pistol from the hired professional killer to shoot himself.

There's one more thing: Hitler had lost faith in ending the war before winter – yet he didn't allow the *Wehrmacht* to prepare for winter. If you fail to crush the USSR before winter, you'll be laid low by the brutal cold! The *Wehrmacht* might have destroyed the USSR, but Hitler became distracted by opportunities, which given their surprise attack appeared in multitudes! His nervousness and tendency to change plans were fully apparent, and his decisions were unshakeable. It would have been difficult to lay out the arguments of the leadership of Army Group Center any better than Guderian did ...

The exact same can be said about Stalin. He demonstrated his incompetence more than once, just as obdurately. Losses? What were they to him?

Seemingly, at this stage of the war, the clash of personalities was already dominating strategic considerations. Stalin is clinging to Kiev? Then we'll take Kiev! Isn't that just how Hitler flew off the handle in 1942 at Stalingrad?

The word to Marshal Vasilevsky:

A compromise decision was reached. At just the mention of the need to abandon Kiev, Stalin would lose his temper and for a moment (Author's note: Huh? Not forever? He'd calm down? That means the issue must have been discussed even after Zhukov's removal ...) and lose self-control. We, clearly, didn't have the necessary toughness to withstand these outbursts of uncontrollable anger ...

An honest confession. Everything was just like at the Führer's headquarters.

By 9 September it was getting too late to take any measures, but even now the Leader would lose his temper as soon as anyone mentioned the matter. By now even Budenny was urging a withdrawal using almost hysterical expressions, for which on 11 September he was removed from command of the Southwestern Direction and replaced by Timoshenko. The typical command merry-go-round in a panic ...

However, Zhukov was still in time, when, continuing his finest hour, he sent a telegram to the *Stavka* from his El'nia post on 19 August:

Seeing that we had deployed large forces on the way to Moscow, with our Central Front and Velikiye Luki group of troops on his flanks, the enemy has temporarily abandoned the idea of an assault on Moscow and, passing over to an active defense against the Western and Reserve Fronts, has thrown all his mobile and panzer shock units against the Central, South-Western and Southern Fronts.

The possible enemy plan: to crush the Central Front and reaching the Chernigov-Konotop-Priluki area to smash the armies of the South-Western Front. Following this will be the main assault on Moscow, bypassing the Bryansk forests, and a blow at the Donbas ...

I believe that the enemy knows very well the entire system of our defence, the entire operational-strategic grouping of our forces, and knows our nearest possibilities ... I would think it necessary to create a large force in the Glukhov-Chernigov-Konotop area as soon as possible to strike a blow at the enemy flank when he begins to carry through his plans. Immediately send out a screening force to the Desna River to cover the assembly ...

The answer from the *Stavka* arrived that same day:

We consider your assumptions on the possible German advance in the direction of Chernigov, Konotop and Priluki correct. German progress ... will mean that our Kiev group will be bypassed from the Dnepr's eastern bank and our 3rd and 21st Armies encircled. In anticipation of such an undesirable incident and to prevent it the Bryansk Front has been created with Yeremenko at its head. Other measures are also being taken of which we will communicate to you specially. We hope to check the German advance. Stalin, Shaposhnikov.

Zhukov observes, "I knew what the troops of the hastily formed Bryansk Front were worth in combat ..." He knew the troops. He also knew the fellow commander, who had been appointed to command this emergency front. To that hell a sharper fellow needed to be assigned... However, even Eremenko was hauled back from the Far East, and in Chita transferred from his train to a bomber, in order to get him to Moscow more quickly. Did Zhukov need to say why he was in the Far East? Mention it in his memoirs? Mention the purge? That's a matter for descendants. So, the Marshal remained silent about Eremenko, but he spoke up about the troops. It can easily be imagined what his mood was then, in 1941, having just learned about the new front and its commander ...

11 September. By now, a catastrophe was unavoidable. Again, there was a dialogue between the *Stavka* and the headquarters of the Southwestern Front. At the teletype machine in Kiev were Kirponos, Burmistenko and Tupikov. On the line in Moscow were Stalin, Shaposhnikov and Timoshenko.

"Stalin: Your proposal to withdraw the troops beyond the river, you know, seems dangerous to me ..."

Huh? A withdrawal was now impossible. However, the Leader with hindsight still enumerates what to do, in order to execute a withdrawal and to avoid the inescapable. There follows the sensible "First," "Second" and "Third", repeating – with an adjustment for the situation, of course – Zhukov's proposals, although now fully supported by the General Staff. Their single shortcoming was that at the time of this recitation, they were only a poultice for the corpse of the Southwestern Front.

Even at this point, however, when all there was left for Colonel-General Kirponos was to send some strong language to the Leader, he timidly replied: "We had no intention of withdrawing the troops before we were asked to present our considerations ..."

The colonel in the Colonel-General is apparent. There was not enough of the commander's voice in Kirponos. If Iakir had been in his place, who had shouted "Long live Stalin!" into the muzzle of the executioner's gun (a cry that angered the Leader) he would have acted according to the situation and his troops would not have been doomed to die or to become prisoners. The Nazi generals now and then went against their orders. In a real war with its sudden and ominously changing circumstances it is impossible always to follow directions from a leadership distant from the theater of combat operations.

Kirponos, though, was silent. He held his tongue, knowing what was going to happen to him and his Southwestern Front. Indeed, with whom was he speaking? Finally, at the very end of the same 11 September conversation, shortly before the fall of Kiev itself, which happened on 19 September, the Leader tossed out at the end of his list: "Cease, after all, searching for new lines to which to retreat, and search for new ways to resist."

Bravo! A catch phrase, worthy of Mekhlis himself!

Bagramian continues:

Silence settled over the teletype machine. With his iron logic (-- ?! Just where's the logic? – the author), the Supreme [Commander] could disarm anyone he wanted. Even Tupikov was at a loss. Subsequently, he told me ...

(Subsequently? Tupikov had only ten days left to live! He was saying this, on the spot, to his subordinate, the Chief of the Front's Operations Department. Typical carelessness of military commanders and their ghost writers with regard to the wording of their memoirs ...)

... that he had a thought (during the discussion with the *Stavka*): we had to make use of the proposal, for a start by withdrawing five-six divisions and a significant amount of the artillery to the line of the Psel River. This indeed would have initiated the withdrawal of the *front*'s troops to a new line ... But everyone had been stunned by the Supreme Commander's parting words: 'Cease, after all, searching for new lines to which to retreat ...' According to the testimony of Zakhvataev, the ashen-faced Kirponos read this phrase aloud twice. He asked the members of his Military Council:

'Well, what do you have to say, Comrades?'

Burmistenko quietly said: 'Now it's impossible. We will not be insisting upon a withdrawal from the Dnepr.'

Time was passing, and at the other end of the line, Stalin was waiting. Kirponos resolutely turned toward the typist: 'Transmit!'

He spoke slowly, as if filtering every word: 'We had no intention of withdrawing the troops before we were asked to present our considerations.'

Zakhvataev later told me that Tupikov, listening to Kirponos, clutched his head. Again the apparatus started to chatter. The words on the tape were as heavy as ingots: 'Do not leave Kiev and do not blow up the bridges without permission of the Supreme Command. Good-bye!'

Good-bye? Unlikely ... the possibility of meeting again was being excluded.[6] The former colonel didn't have the courage to offer a retort. To whom, the Boss?? One of the most disciplined of those who had been promoted after the purge was now doomed to perish with the troops of his front, on the subject of which Vasilevsky on that same day phlegmatically noted: 'I think withdrawal of the troops beyond the Dnepr is long overdue ...'

Meanwhile in Kiev all was quiet. In the final letter sent to his wife, a staff officer of the Southwestern Front, Major Kanevsky wrote that the schools were starting another academic year. The real situation of affairs was being hidden not only from the citizens, but also from the staff officers.[7]

---

6 Editor's note: the Russian "good-bye", *do svidaniia*, roughly translates as "until we meet again".

7 I remember that on 19 September 1941, I was running from a public loudspeaker, which had been set up in

By fate, Zhukov's finest hour coincided with the hour of the great tragedy of hundreds of thousands of people. But this wasn't Zhukov's fault

front of the village Soviet in Chuvakhlei, toward the hut where we were living, shouting "Heavy fighting near Kiev!" There was no further announcement for three more days while the *Wehrmacht* seized Kiev.

38

El'nia

E l'nia. The *Wehrmacht's* first withdrawal after a direct collision with the Red Army. The first achievement. Bloody, but undisputed.[1] The *Wehrmacht* would launch its final assault toward Moscow not from the El'nia salient, but from a line further west – and later.

At El'nia Zhukov didn't stop thinking about Kiev. The Red Army's activity around El'nia didn't avert the Kiev tragedy. Shaposhnikov didn't insist upon a withdrawal beyond the Dnepr. He couldn't, and in the future he repeatedly could not, would not, and didn't dare, though he understood the situation no worse than Zhukov and perhaps even better, which gives the right to name him – alongside Zhukov – among those who rendered a decisive influence on the course of the war – alas, only by expressing his opinion.

A lot has been said to this point about the timid Shaposhnikov, but we'll need to speak about him again in connection with the summer 1942 campaign.

Zhukov describes the fighting at El'nia more like a war correspondent than as the commander of the operation. There's not even a word here about the tactics. The Marshal goes into side details, and certain episodes appear openly comical, but those who aren't familiar with military matters can't catch this, and Zhukov's description with its ostensible forthrightness achieves its goal of making clear the enormous difference in quality between the Red Army and the *Wehrmacht*.

The art of war has its own aesthetic. To calculate out an operation for two or three moves is the essence of the art of war. However, to attack with untrained troops led by inexperienced commanders who were formerly NKVD officers, to conduct sanguinary battles without air support to gnaw through an enemy defense – this isn't what Zhukov had been taught. A hard man himself, Zhukov was compelled as a result of the productive activity of his bloody patron to fight in this way for such a long time, that he became an example for others to follow. Losses didn't trouble the Leader. In the case of El'nia Zhukov at least may be praised for the right choice of where to strike. It also goes to the Marshal's merits that under his direction, despite the losses that were many times greater than those suffered by the Germans (as Iosif Brodsky said about him, "As a commander, making walls crumble, he held a sword less sharp than his foe's."), the weak Red Army forced the mighty *Wehrmacht* to retreat in a campaign, in which no retreat had been planned.

The Soviet ideological machine rumbled and spat out a new distinction. The best formations acquired the "Guards" title.

In his own memoirs, *170,000 kilometrov s G. K. Zhukovym* [*170,000 kilometers with G. K. Zhukov*] here is how Zhukov's driver, A. N. Buchin, describes the commander at El'nia:

---

1   In light of the research by Glantz and Stahel on the counteroffensive, launched by Timoshenko between 15 August and 5 September 1941, the reason for the *Wehrmacht's* withdrawal from El'nia becomes clear. The *Wehrmacht* had become overextended, even before the operation to encircle Kiev was in full-swing. Zhukov doesn't have a single word to say about this.

"Fighting was going on around the clock the final days before the capture of El'nia, as Zhukov had planned the operation. He was on his feet around the clock. I confess that on these days I sometimes was a little afraid of Zhukov; he was extremely stern and not talkative. He suddenly and magically changed, when under the pressure of our forces the Germans fled from El'nia one night ... Georgii Konstantinovich glanced around at the city, which had been smashed and burned by the Germans before retreating. It was a tragic picture. The only recent construction was a German military cemetery, which civilians had been forced to tend under the threat of execution ... The enraged Zhukov, addressing a group of commanders and local residents, said that history would never forget the Germans' outrages. From a cross, he *carefully* removed a German helmet, which had been penetrated by a bullet, attentively examined it, and satisfied by the edges of the hole that it had been made by an armor-piercing bullet, he *just as carefully returned it to its place.*" (Emphasis the author's)

Let anyone who has a problem with Zhukov's character re-read this story now. We sometimes are missing the best sides of ourselves. Well, perhaps that's how we must be.

39

Stalin and His Generals

D igressions from a theme are always awkward. An amusing story from Zhukov's memoirs has plunked this chapter into a place that had been intended for Leningrad.

There's no need to speak about Zhukov's participation in the defense of the great city. Zhukov demonstrated his usual rigor there. However, there was no room to maneuver around the walls of the city, and nothing with which to maneuver. Leningrad is the heroism of famished despair and frost-bitten frenzy. In the chapter about Leningrad, recounting the measures taken to establish concert of action between the fronts, Zhukov tells a story, which might even move one to laughter, if we weren't speaking, ultimately, about human lives.

Among Stalin's Marshals only one has been scarcely even mentioned in this sad tale – Grigory Kulik, one more tragic figure (who according to some absurd rumors was granted a Marshal's rank due to the uncommon beauty of his wife, Kira Simonych, an aristocrat and the daughter of a count. Kira Simonych was later abducted and killed allegedly by Beria's agents). Kulik commanded Vokhlov Front's 54th Army. Leningrad was already encircled. Zhukov was trying to break the enemy ring around the city, before the Germans managed

In besieged Leningrad.

to dig-in.

Below is his narration with my own parenthetical comments:

If Leningrad was to be relieved in September 1941, the 54th Army would have to operate more energetically and in complete cooperation with the units of the Leningrad Front ... I take the liberty to cite a conversation I had over the wire with Marshal Kulik in the early morning hours of September 15, 1941:

Zhukov: 'Greetings, Grigory Ivanovich ... I would like you and me to get down to clearing the territory more quickly, over which we might be able to shake each other's hands. Please tell me briefly what the situation is in your sector. For my part, I want to inform you of what is going on around Leningrad. ... (Zhukov's first two points, omitted here, proceed to paint a pretty sad picture of the situation ...) Third, we are organizing actions in all sectors of the front. Much hope is being pinned on you. That is all I have to say so far. Please tell me briefly what the situation is in your sector.'

Kulik: 'I wish you health, Georgii Konstantinovich. I am pleased that the two of us have the same proud mission of relieving Leningrad. I, too, look forward to the moment when we'll shake hands. Here's the situation on my sector ... (Kulik goes on to describe the day's events, using the points made by Zhukov as a framework for his response.)

It followed from what Kulik said that his army was not going on the offensive in the immediate future. This was distressing, because the situation in and around Leningrad was becoming critical. Apart from direct action by the 54th Army, I had also been counting on its air arm hitting important targets on the approaches to Leningrad. I needed to make this clear to Kulik.

Zhukov: 'Thanks for the information, Grigory Ivanovich. I have a most insistent request: don't wait for the enemy to attack; organize a preliminary shelling at once, and take the offensive yourself in the general direction of Mga.'

Kulik: 'Certainly, I am thinking of the 16th or 17th [of September].'

Zhukov: 'The 16th or 17th will be too late! We are dealing with a highly mobile enemy, and we must jump on him first. I'm sure that if you mount an offensive, you'll get some good spoils ...'

Kulik: 'I cannot mount the offensive tomorrow because the artillery hasn't yet arrived, and we haven't rehearsed joint action. Besides, not all the units have arrived in their starting positions. I have just been informed that at 2300 hours the enemy mounted an attack in the Schlüsselburg-Lipka-Siniavino-Gontovaia Lipka area. The attack has been repulsed. If the Nazis don't launch a general offensive tomorrow, I'll have my air force do what you have asked ...'

(Oh, how badly noticeable is the absence of one of the repressed commanders on the other end of the line ... Entice Kulik to launch an offensive with captured booty? Ha! However, it is possible to understand him. He wasn't Zhukov. He was still a Marshal. He was no longer a *Stavka* representative, but all the more so – why risk anything? An offensive means risk, and he doesn't have any such skill to attack. Plus the Boss is strict, so strict! You make a mistake – and you will find yourself shot, like Pavlov and Klimovskikh. If the Master forces him to attack, well, that is a different matter ... But even though the circumstances are burning in Zhukov, they weren't in Kulik: Once we bring up the artillery, work out the cooperation in place, and if the enemy doesn't go on the offensive himself, then ...)

... I did not hide my annoyance any longer, and said:
'The enemy did not mount an attack; he was merely reconnoitering in force.'

(Unfortunately, some people mistake reconnaissance and skirmishes for an offensive ... Perhaps, one doesn't need to be a Zhukov, but, at the very least, one doesn't need to be even Kulik either in order to understand that if a German advance in 1941 had been repelled, then it was not so much an advance as it was a reconnaissance probe. I can't refrain from interrupting Zhukov's philippic by noting what Kulik was doubtlessly thinking during this next piece of dialogue...)

'... It is clear to me that you are worried above all about the welfare of the 54th Army, and, evidently, insufficiently worried about the situation in Leningrad. (Kulik's thoughts: 'True, Egorii [a diminutive form of Zhukov's first name Georgii]! Both the first is true and the second! Of course, you know, people look out for their own skins first.') I want you to know that I have to send people from the factories to meet the attacking enemy, and have no time to practice joint action on site. (Kulik's thoughts: 'Well, Egor, those are good reasons, you are really smart ... Are there people in the factories? Well then, send them! The Badaev warehouses[1] have burned; there's nothing to feed people anyway. Send them!') I have understood that I cannot count on any active maneuver by your Army. I will rely on myself only. Let me add that I am astonished at the lack of cooperation between your group and the Front. It seems to me that Suvorov, if he were in your place, would have acted differently. (Kulik's thoughts: 'Is he that Field Marshal, as it were? Well, he was a Field Marshal, yet I'm only a Marshal. Be healthy, Egor!') Pardon me for speaking my mind, but I have no time for diplomacy. Best wishes ...

For the evacuation of Feodosiia, Marshal Kulik was later tried by a military tribunal and demoted to the rank of private, but was soon conferred the rank of major general again and even took over the command of an army. He finished the war as a Lieutenant-General, but at least he did finish it. He hadn't wound up in a penal battalion, and he wasn't sent to command the 2nd Shock Army ...[2] Failing to appreciate the mercy shown to him, he was caught making sharp comments about the Leader after the war and was arrested and shot, else we wouldn't have learned anything about his inactivity from the mouth of Zhukov, just as we wouldn't have learned the commander's opinion of Golikov, the chief of the GRU [the General Staff's Chief Intelligence Agency], who had accompanied the evidence about the concentration of German forces on the Soviet border with such soothing commentary

1   Editor's note: These were closely-spaced, large wooden warehouses that covered several acres in the southwest quarter of Leningrad that were holding the city's food supplies, which the Germans bombed and destroyed on 8 September in their first major air attack on the city.

2   Editor's note: The author is alluding to General A. A. Vlasov's bitter experience with the 2nd Shock Army, which was encircled by the Germans in early 1942. Vlasov became a German prisoner-of-war and later turned to support the Germans by organizing and leading the so-called Russian Liberation Army, comprised largely of former Red Army prisoners-of-war who were released in exchange for service in this army.

for the Leader. (When Golikov, now a Marshal, in his high office at the Soviet Army's Main Political Directorate was later shown old dismissive comments of his, designed to please the Leader, on the warning telegrams from Sorge before the war, Golikov went on his hands and knees on the table and, according to Geller and Rapoport, began to bark, feigning insanity. Perhaps he wasn't acting, but had been truly shaken to the point of loss of reason. After years of living in fear that his dismissive comments would turn up, he was finally confronted with them. Such a reaction would be natural, more natural than resorting to acting like a madman.)

Kulik has been mentioned not because he was worse than the majority. No, he exemplified the majority.

Our combat losses in the war stemmed from our generals' toadying and compliance; from of their faith in the Leader and the artificially-created surprise at the war's start; from of the Leaders's disregard for technology and his reliance upon cannon fodder; from the troops' lack of training. Greenhorns, bespectacled professors and militiamen from the factories ... I, myself, came from a factory, I knew them, the scrupulous norm-setters and mechanics; persevering, yes, responsible, yes, but what did they know about entrenching and advancing in bounds? They'd become accustomed to moving sedately and to arguing over any matter ... They stood to the death; that's all they could do. So they did.

Setting aside Kulik, I will cite a place from the Marshal's memoirs, where Zhukov talks about the adversary:

> The interrogation of prisoners showed that the German Command and troops were operating according to a set pattern, without creative initiative, only blindly following orders. That is why as soon as the situation changed, the Germans became confused, acted very passively waiting for orders from the higher commander, which could not always be obtained timely in the existing combat situation.
>
> Observing the course of engagement and troop actions personally, I saw that where our troops did not merely resist but at the first opportunity counterattacked the enemy by day and by night, they were almost always successful, particularly at night. The Germans acted with extreme uncertainty at night, I would even say, badly.

Is any commentary necessary? I'll let the reader judge. As for me – what sort of night fighting is Zhukov talking about? The Germans became confused at night? Our guys became confused even in daylight! Weren't the Red Army troops confused in 1942? In the winter of 1943, in the Caucasus Mountains and in the Kalmyk steppe? (Look at the memoirs of Marshal Grechko about the corresponding period of the war in the Caucasus.)

☆ ☆ ☆

The title of this chapter promised more than it was possible to encompass. However, one issue must not be neglected: the issue of Stalin's creation of an atmosphere of envy and rivalry among the commanders. For an analysis of the Leader's creativity, so to speak, in these matters, Zhukov's memoirs yields material like no one else's. However, Marshal is not too outspoken, so, it would not be a great sin to draw upon alternative sources.

The men that Stalin promoted to command shared common characteristics: spite, suspiciousness, and long memories of perceived grievances, which are common to people who lack roots and confidence, and who have no firm notions of honor. These, let's call them, qualities can indeed be inherited, but the way these people were promoted, together with their service conditions had sharpened these qualities significantly. Any Johnny-come-lately who didn't know how to spin or sustain a conversation, and indeed was unprepared professionally (and every man was acutely aware of gaps in his knowledge and his dependence upon some frump, say, a chief of staff, or else someone in the rear) was really screwed. Where could they acquire that air of modesty, which is so befitting and so adorning to grandees? The upstart understands the happenstance of his rise and dreads a fall. Especially after such a purge! It is in this fear that one should search for the roots of the quarrels and the fleeting alliances among the Red Army commanders – and their sensitivity to slights. Stalin took full advantage of this.

A similar theme has come up during the dispensation of the first Marshal titles. Here's another story from Zhukov's memoirs:

> In his interesting book *On the Eve* Admiral N. G. Kuznetsov writes in connection with my appointment to the post of Chief of the General Staff: 'At first I thought I was the only one who could not get along with G. K. Zhukov, and that his colleague, I. S. Isakov, Chief of the Main Naval Headquarters, would be able to work with him but nothing came of it.'
>
> "I do not remember now whether it was a case of these two comrades not being able to get along with me or whether I was unable to work with them, but it makes absolutely no difference. However, for the sake of *historical accuracy* (author's emphasis) I should point out that in general, when naval questions were discussed with J. V. Stalin, neither People's Commissar for Defense S. K. Timoshenko, nor the Chief of the General Staff was invited.

The Army and Navy in Russia have traditionally not gotten along. Have even the Fleets? My brother-in-law has been a witness to fatal – and not in a figurative sense – brawls between Black Sea Fleet sailors and Northern Fleet sailors, who had taunted their southern colleagues as "vacationers". Yet for this there's no reason to blame the Leader. However, the Marshal's testimony discloses a major failure in the organization of the country's defense. Ground force commanders were not invited to meetings with the naval commanders, and the naval chiefs were not invited to meetings with the army chiefs ... this is just like some sort of Port Arthur![3] Yet it was not so much that the personalities were complicating relations, as much as it was the separation that Stalin created between the different types of forces. One can even search for a loophole here, as if this occurred not according to a deliberate desire, but was due to the Leader's ignorance, to his inability to understand the importance of contacts between the Army and the Navy. However, is this really an excuse for the Supreme Commander? Cooperation between the Army – especially the Air Force – and the Navy emerged only toward the end of the war.

The lack of coordination yielded a lot of bitter fruit. In the autumn of 1943, in the Red Army's victorious surge after Kursk and during the crossing of the Dnepr, a black day occurred for the Soviet Navy. On 6 October in the course of just several minutes, three

---

3   Editor's note: Port Arthur was a deep-water port and bastion in the Russian Far East and the site of a successful Japanese siege in the Russo-Japanese War (1904-1905). Disputes between the Russian fleet commanders and the ground troops' commanders contributed to the Russian defeat.

combat ships of the Black Sea Fleet were lost as they sailed along an enemy-occupied coastline without air cover[4] – the destroyer leader *Khar'kov* and two destroyers, *Besposhchadnyi* and *Sposobnyi*. During the terrible days of the defense of the Crimea and the Caucasus, their crews had served as marines at the hottest defense sectors of the frontline. These heroes had accomplished incredible feats of valor, most of which were never noted with honors.[5] The toilers of the war died, just as they had lived – not shunning danger, going to the aid of one of their sinking ships, where their combat friends were dying. So, they were all sunk together. The result was not an order to improve the cooperation between the Navy and the Air Force, not a ban against sending ships to sea without air cover, but a ban against assisting a sinking ship to avoid even greater losses.

Intrigues had been an essential part of the Leader's nature from his childhood days, and had been well-honed in elaborate political combinations. It is a mistake to believe that the war sharpened his skill. The war only expanded the opportunity for pitting people against each other; all the more since the military is the ideal field for such activity.

Zhukov again:

In late July, A. N. Poskrebyshev called me on the phone and asked:

'Where is Timoshenko?'

'At the General Staff, we're discussing the situation at the front.' I replied

'Stalin orders you and Timoshenko to come to his villa right away!' Poskrebyshev said.

We had thought that Stalin wanted to consult with us as to possible future action, but we soon found out that his summons pursued a totally different objective. When we entered the room, we saw that almost all the Politburo members were present. Stalin, wearing an old jacket, was standing in the middle of the room holding an unlit pipe in his hands – a sure sign of bad temper.

'Now then,' he said, 'the Politburo has discussed Timoshenko's activities as commander of the Western Front and has decided to relieve him of his post. It proposes that Zhukov take over. (This on the eve of Zhukov's own replacement. First the People's Commissar, then his deputy, the recalcitrant of 3 July ...) What do you think about that?' asked Stalin, turning to Timoshenko and myself.

Timoshenko said nothing.

'Comrade Stalin,' I said, 'frequent replacement of front commanders is having a bad effect on the course of operations. With hardly any time to familiarize themselves with the situation, the commanders are compelled to conduct exceedingly severe

---

4   Editor's note: On their return voyage after bombarding Yalta and Feodosiia, the Soviet ships were attacked in repeated waves by Stukas of III/StG 3.

5   Petty Officer First Class Aleksandr Beliakov before the war had served on a battleship. He was a strapping fellow and officially received double rations. During training gunnery, when shells were being carried on stretchers to the main guns, a mate was stricken with diarrhea. In order not to betray his comrade, Beliakov schlepped both the mate, like a puppet, and the 80kg shells. While serving in the 2nd Separate Marine Battalion in the fighting for the Shockworkers' Homes during the defense of Novorossiisk, he was wounded but remained with his unit. The Germans unleashed their panzers. Beliakov destroyed one with an anti-tank grenade and hit by a burst of machine-gun fire from a second. Coming to his senses, he damaged a second panzer with a close assault from behind and killed the surviving crew as they emerged from the tank, then manage to make his way back to his own. Wounded three times, he refused to leave the frontline. He went down with the *Besposhchadnyi* together with his comrades. Not a single man was rescued from the crews of these ships.

battles. Marshal Timoshenko has been in command of the Front for less than four weeks ... He has done all anyone else could do in his place and for almost a whole month the enemy has been held up in the Smolensk area.'

In essence, the fall and even the death of both Timoshenko and Zhukov would have been unavoidable, had Stalin been able to find a replacement. The military commanders were saved by the complete impossibility to find any replacements for them and their absence of contacts with the political leadership. After all, the main goal of the purge had been the elimination of military commanders with the qualities of politicians and the simultaneous destruction of ties between the commanders and politicians. However, Stalin also simply feared determined people. He feared them even more than analysts. That's why he wanted to keep Zhukov out of Moscow. Was this though the first attempt to keep him at a distance?

In this situation Zhukov's behavior was beyond reproach. (He, incidentally, was also protecting himself. It would not have been pleasant to trade the post of Chief of General Staff for the duty of front commander ...) What about Timoshenko? He was humiliated in front of many witnesses.

Now, let's turn to the case of Stalingrad; Eremenko's role in the Stalingrad epic is well-known. Now we are at the victorious epilogue to the efforts, in which the country had invested everything.

Zhukov writes: "In late December the State Defense Committee [GKO] met to discuss further action. Stalin suggested, 'Only one man should direct operations to destroy the encircled enemy grouping. The fact that there are two front commanders is interfering with this ...'

The members of the GKO supported this opinion, and Stalin asked to whom to entrust the completion of the operation. He always did this, the wise Leader – he asked. Perhaps he'd find a smart fellow, who would guess his wishes, so the choice would seem not to have been Stalin's.

In this case, a smart fellow proposed Rokossovsky – a new favorite, a rising star. As for the elimination of the Stalingrad pocket, this was something for which the entire country was waiting, holding its breath, fearing until the last moment that something might go wrong, alternately rejoicing and disbelieving. The country was living by this. At the time people were talking and thinking about this in every family and in each combat squad: Really? ... When? ... It was clear that the name connected with this victory would forever enter the country's heart. That's how the name of the handsome and cavalier Konstantin Konstantinovich Rokossovsky entered it – the victor over Paulus. Rokossovsky would have taken Berlin as well, had the Supreme Commander permitted it.

There are various opinions about Eremenko and his talents. However, what was it like for him, the one who had held out at Stalingrad from beginning to the end, to be passed over for the honor of the final victory over the German Sixth Army?

Zhukov continues:

'Why don't you say anything?' Stalin turned to me.
    'I think both commanders are worthy,' I said. 'True, A. I. Eremenko will feel hurt if we put the forces of the Stalingrad Front under K. K. Rokossovsky.'
    'It's not the time for feeling hurt,' Stalin retorted curtly. 'Call A. I. Eremenko and

notify him of the State Defense Committee's decision.'

There you are. It is not Stalin's, but the GKO's decision.

Those desiring to do so can pick up the Marshal's memoirs and find out what happened next, and can imagine the degree of Eremenko's life-long, undeserved grievance and his resentful feelings – which also lasted a lifetime – toward the totally innocent Rokossovsky and toward Zhukov, who had transmitted the order to him. Eremenko, of course, decided that this was Zhukov's scheming, in connection with Zhukov's old friendship with Rokossovsky. Stalin, though, at one fell swoop had embittered Eremenko with both Zhukov and Rokossovsky.

The Leader liked this technique, and he made it a custom: to begin an operation with one commander, but finish it with a different one. In the Korsun-Shevchenkovsky operation the Leader pitted Konev against Vatutin. Once again, there was the analogous Order No. 22022 from 12 February 1944. Zhukov writes:

> "N. F. Vatutin was a highly emotional man. Having received this directive he immediately called me and, under the impression that this was all my doing, said with overtones of chagrin:
>
> 'Comrade Marshal, you of all people surely know that I've been going without sleep several days on end and putting my all into the Korsun-Shevchenkovsky operation. Why then have I been brushed aside from the completion of this superb operation? I am proud of my troops too and I want Moscow to salute the soldiers of the 1st Ukrainian Front.'
>
> "The capital of our Motherland had saluted the troops of the 2nd Ukrainian Front on 18 February, but not a single word was said about the troops of the 1st Ukrainian Front. I believe that this was an inexcusable mistake of the Supreme Commander's."

Ah, Georgii Konstantinovich, Georgii Konstantinovich ... We've needed years to understand the motives lying beneath the deeds of our sovereign. Weren't you, though, an old hand in the command intrigues? You knew the point of these command shuffles, so why did you keep covering for your chief to your death? *De mortuis aut bene, aut nihil* (Of the dead be nothing said but what is good)?

Incidentally, in the 1960s in contrast to the dissidents, the regime was full of resolve to support the authority of the state, even Stalin's, and censorship suppressed any comment about the machinations of the Great Leader. Thus even this observation of Zhukov's in those times was a substantial Voltairism.[6]

However, we also need to recognize that the Boss was nobody's fool in these matters, and was not making mistakes. Everything was calculated. The generals had to be set at odds with each other, while glory had to be allocated so as not to create a halo around any new genius commander and potential – on the basis of military honor, the most lustrous of splendors, especially after such a war – new great leader and teacher. Already even with Zhukov you don't know what to do, and now here's this Vatutin. It is more than enough for Vatutin to take Kiev, the capital of Soviet Ukraine, especially on the eve of the October Revolution anniversary, you understand ... If he is recognized for the Korsun-

---

6   Editor's note: This is a reference to the doctrines of Voltaire, which were marked by religious skepticism.

Shevchenkovsky operation, then altogether ...

In a word: NO WAY!

The injustice shook the emotional Vatutin. I think that Zhukov's account of his conversation with Vatutin only faintly reflects its real vocabulary ...

Here's additional speculation. It is my opinion that the 1st Ukrainian Front commander's trip to the 13th and 60th Armies, which cost him his life, he undertook on 28 and 29 February 1944 with the aim to converse personally – not over the telephone, into the ears of SMERSH agents! – with the army commanders, his peers, who like him hadn't slept nights and had been deprived of their share of the deserved glory for successfully conducting a most difficult operation. Privately, *tete-a-tete*, they could lament over the insult and, as they say, down some vodka to commiserate together. This folly is understandable in human terms. The venture of a risky trip within range of the front wasn't necessary, but the front commanders were only human too. Even they were naked under their clothing – less ugly, by the way, than their Supreme Commander. (Let it not be forgotten that Stalin, the Great Healer, just as he was the Great Commander and the High Priest of Linguistics and of All Sciences, refused to allow the amputation of Vatutin's leg against the entreaties of the doctors who had diagnosed gangrene in it. When he finally permitted it, the operation in its timeliness is comparable only to the operation to withdraw the troops of the Kiev Fortified District ...)

In the same fashion Stalin pitted Zhukov against Konev and even Rokossovsky. The 1st Belorussian Front was aimed at Berlin. Before the final assault, Rokossovsky was transferred from command of this Front to the 2nd Belorussian Front. This indeed put an end to the cordial relations between the old comrades. Their friendship couldn't endure this. (It didn't result in bitter feelings between them, but something more like awkwardness.) Meanwhile, the initial boundary line between the Zhukov's 1st Belorussian Front and Konev's 1st Ukrainian Front was drawn in such a way that Konev's forces were excluded from the final assault on Berlin – and likely Zhukov had a hand in this.

Here it should be noted that among his comrades-in-arms Zhukov didn't stand out for his talent. Vasilevsky, Antonov and Rokossovsky were just as strategically gifted as he was. Character is what distinguished Zhukov. However, there is not the slightest doubt that his character in the course of this terrible war was corrupted in proportion to the character of his Leader. They definitely influenced each other. Stalin only at the end of April 1945 testily erased the boundary line between the 1st Ukrainian and Belorussian Fronts in a 60-kilometer sector, and this only at Antonov's insistence, which cost him a Marshal's title.

Likely, Zhukov had requested the honor of taking Berlin – to his misfortune. The cunning Stalin didn't object, and immediately after the victory, already in 1945, Zhukov found himself isolated. He was an excellent commander and a poor diplomat. Stalin relished both his one trait and the other, pitilessly, like the Nazi pilot who had strafed the Red Army recruits rushing around the empty field. Using the prism of intrigue, one can try to read through anew all the misdeeds of Stalin in his post as Supreme Commander and in many others, which his Party comrades had rashly entrusted to him before the time came when he began to appoint himself to posts. Not one of them had taken it upon himself the mission of a final friendly embrace with Stalin while wearing a belt of dynamite around his body. The people residing on one-sixth of the world's landmass would have been spared many problems and, perhaps, other peoples as well.

We were taught properly: personal terror is not a proper instrument of politics.

Ia.B. Gamarnik, V.K. Bliukher and G.A. Ovsepian among the delegates
to the All-Army Conference of Female Command Staff, 1935.

What about mass terror, though, is it a suitable instrument? Indeed, who was directing the teaching? Those, who through this instruction were looking after their own personal security? The bullets that cut down Gamarnik and Goriachev struck the wrong targets. No von Stauffenberg was found in the RKKA before the war, before the terror, before it all. Except that one mustn't leave behind the briefcase. One must remain with the briefcase. It is simple – cancel your future schedule and that's all. Nowadays there is no point to propagandize such a method. Those who desire to die with a belt of plastic explosives around their body for the purpose of taking with themselves as many innocent lives as possible are waiting in queue. Would it be surprising, if this practice became reciprocal?

I conclude this messy and, even to me, somewhat unexpected chapter with the assertion that the Leader didn't succeed in everything. The eliminated commanders had been friends. For this friendship they were indeed killed: Gamarnik, Iakir, Bliukher ... Bliukher had been Iakir's subordinate in the Ukrainian Military District. His acquisition of the title of Marshal didn't ruin his friendship with Iakir, as Stalin had calculated. If they weren't friends, they were good acquaintances: Tukhachevsky, Gamarnik ... Even to the end. If not acquaintances, then they were mutual adherents of modernizing the Red Army. In any case, they believed in the integrity of their colleagues. This belief couldn't be shaken by dossiers or by peeping through the keyhole of their private rooms.

I will cite an extract about Gamarnik from the memoirs of one of his co-workers in the RKKA's Main Political Directorate, I. I. Geller. Ian Gamarnik, "a fellow with a sinister face and kind eyes," was bedridden with diabetes immediately after the 1937 1st of May holiday. Diabetes is an illness that is exacerbated by stress. Gamarnik was under enormous personal stress: friends of his had been arrested, the purest people, and even he, the Chief of the Red Army's Main Political Directorate couldn't see them:

> Often one of us secretaries would go by his house with papers, and sometimes he himself would come to his office and work far into the night. One time Marshal Tukhachevsky dropped by to say good-bye, before he left for his new post in the Volga Military District.
> I remember them as they stood in the doorway, their appearances so different from each other but each handsome in his own way:
> '*Bon voyage*, Mikhail Nikolaevich [Tukhachevsky] ... '
> 'Get better, Ian Borisovich ...'
> This was their last encounter ...

What was lying beneath these parting words? What were these two honorable old hands thinking about? They shouldn't have hesitated! The flower of the army was being destroyed! Arrests were ongoing, and now they no longer had the opportunity even to approach the tyrant. It is unpardonable that they, educated men with knowledge of history, didn't foresee this. Incidentally, knowledge of history is one thing; the creation of history in a country, where the Leader had become the Father of the People while you, his foe, were becoming "an enemy of the people", is another thing entirely. That's what caused the hesitation. Farewell, Mikhail Nikolaevich. I'll not turn myself alive over to the Lubianka's special agents.

On 31 May the legendary man, the prototypical man, the man who it was a blasphemous dream even to imitate, Ian Gamarnik shot himself, when the Lubianka agents were clawing at his door. He understood that they wouldn't allow him to speak, and his hand didn't waver.

Stalin established this system of backstabbing relationships between people. He couldn't achieve the pinnacle, so he imploded the apexes. The liquidation of personalities became his primary work. Mountains were reduced to hills, and he became the tallest hill among them. The level of intellect fell. Posts were offered to mediocrities, and they were running the show.

The war required a screening process. The demands of war had to be met. Even so, did everyone who demonstrated the most outstanding qualities become Marshals? The promotions were implemented with regard for their manageability. If a general could be prodded into launching an unprepared offensive, in which his troops would suffer grievous losses – this was a good, controllable general. If he was stubborn and insisted on his own time schedule, then he was an unmanageable general and a bad one. Konev became a Marshal and was showered with decorations, like Zhukov. Tolbukhin became a Marshal, but never received the title "Hero of the Soviet Union" from Stalin. Antonov, the dispatcher of the Soviet-German front, didn't even become a Marshal, although he served more than once as a *Stavka* representative.

Repressions in the Red Army, which subsided after the first catastrophe of the Western Front (there was no one left to repress, and indeed it was impossible to continue fighting this war with his own men in command!), resumed after the war ended. Those dissatisfied with the Leader were shot. He also executed the witnesses to the shame of 1941 – the generals who became German prisoners and who had sufficient time to reflect upon how all of it had happened. To Stalin these men were particularly dangerous, and it didn't matter that they had remained loyal to their oath and hadn't joined the Vlasov movement. People close to Zhukov were suppressed. Punishment of Zhukov was hindered by the fact that he was popular, while the Red Army, which was obedient to the Sovereign, had become an army of victors and had regained pride in itself. That's why the session of the Higher Military Council in 1946, at which the fate of the Marshal who had saved the Motherland was decided, was different from the 1937 session, which had decided the fate of the army commanders. Although primarily those who envied the Marshal had been assembled for the session, a declaration rang out at the meeting at a critical moment, which nine years earlier might have averted the tragedy of the Great Patriotic War: "The Army will no longer permit the meddling in its own affairs!" Counter to those reckless at war, but not in front of their Leader, that's what the Marshal of Tank Forces Pavel Semenovich Rybalko interjected. Neither the floor nor the ceiling collapsed, the walls kept standing, while the Lubianka gunmen didn't burst in and didn't start wringing their hands. In the meeting hall there were now two, ready to stand back to back.

Did Stalin forget this interjection? He never forgot anything. Rybalko, twice Hero of the Soviet Union, the Commander of Armored Forces in the Soviet Army, died two years later, in August 1948, even before the executions of the generals who were the witnesses of 1941 ... He was, at the time, all of 54 years of age.

It is not likely that Stalin intended to destroy Zhukov physically. In the war the Leader had grown to understand the value of military talent. World rule was still tantalizing Stalin, but the results of the purge were still lingering. Even after such a war, there were still just a few commanders on par with Zhukov. Possibly, the Boss only tried to break the Marshal's character and reduced the public adoration of him to a point commensurate to his own. Having taken control of the Army and recalling the fear that he had much suffered first in 1937, then in 1941 (he wasn't grieving for the population; women would produce a new population), he treasured his domination over the Army and had no intention to release his grip over it. However, Rybalko's statement had been loud and clear, everyone had heard it, and its consequences were both evident and improvable.

During the war, though, this was all still in the distant future, and the generals, isolated and supervised by commissars, who were personally dedicated to Stalin, were vigilant in their communications with each other. Sometimes, however – sometimes! – vigilance was inoperative and a sense of trust remained among the military commanders. Human needs are ineradicable. We need to trust somebody! To consult with someone!

Fortunately for the Leader himself – if there had not been friendship between two of his promotions, much in the war would have turned out differently. We'll get to this in good time.

40

Moscow ... There is Much Meaning in this Word

In table talks, when speaking about Stalin, the Führer made quite a few comments worthy of attention. They never met in person, but both these villains had the measure of each other. The Führer, in particular, observed that the ideological aspect of rule had no value for Stalin, that he more than anything else personified tsarist Russia and ruled so effectively that it would be reasonable to commission him as a Gauleiter in the remaining, unoccupied part of Soviet territory.

In Klaus Reinhardt's fundamental book, *Moscow: A Turning Point?*, there is one remark that indirectly relates to this matter:

"By the end of October at least 13 rifle divisions and 5 tank brigades from the Far East, Central Asia and Siberia had been transported to join troops west of Moscow, a move that contributed significantly to the stabilization of the front. Besides this direct replacement for the front a series of divisions which were to form the backbone of armies that were to be raised were transported at the same time to the Volga region. These troops had to train units, dig defensive positions that were echeloned in depth in the areas where they were raised and plan their manning, so as to be able to continue the battle on the Volga in the event of a German breakthrough near Moscow. *This proves that even if Moscow had fallen, Stalin would not have admitted defeat, as the German leadership was hoping, but was ready to continue fighting in the depth of the country.*" (Emphasis the author's)

In my view, the statement that I have emphasized in italics is dubious. The question about whether or not resistance would have continued after the fall of Moscow remains open. If resistance would have continued, then it would have taken some other form. The evacuation of the People's Commissariats and government bureaus was a fictitious measure. The bureaucrats were whisked away from Moscow, depriving the Germans of informers and accomplices: potential collaborators were put out of German reach. The evacuated Commissariats in the cities in the rear, given the horrible condition of the intercity phone lines, which were not at all like those in the West, and the cramped offices, wherever they'd been hurriedly deposited together with their archives, could not have restored normal operations. A total loss of control was threatening the country. It is commonly known that Stalin communicated *directly* with the directors of major factories.

As a witness, I can testify to the following: the hatred toward the Nazis was beyond limits, but the despair in the autumn of 1941 was even greater. It was growing commensurately with the *Wehrmacht's* progress toward the capital. Its fall would have been a devastating blow, no matter how the Party propagandists might have shrilly tried to spin it. Television was still only a fantasy, and news traveled in its most ordinary form – as facts.

Glancing at a map of the country's railroad system is sufficient to see that the fall, or even the encirclement, of Moscow would have disrupted the communications in the European part of the country, which would have triggered the inevitable collapse of the front because of the inability to shift troops rapidly to threatened sectors. The resistance then would have formed on its own, as happens in catastrophes as the situation unfolds – not without emotions and moreover not without the participation of the opposite side! – but influenced by the following factors:

- The potential of the USSR beyond the Urals was unknown. That means it would not have been safe to leave the industrial regions of the Urals and Siberia to Stalin or to someone else (in a catastrophe, all sorts of changes are possible). However, if all the same the *Wehrmacht* didn't have the strength to continue the campaign and needed a rest, then temporary concessions were possible with an eye toward the idea that he, Hitler, would make a dash to the west, to finish off or come to terms with England and then return to Russia, giving it just as much notice as he had in the summer of 1941. In the meantime, possibly, Hitler needn't demand the removal of Stalin, who would be ready for an armistice on any terms; perhaps it would be even better to guarantee his personal security (and his obedience to Hitler at the same time) and retain his power over whatever remnant of the USSR that Hitler would have considered safe to leave to him. Of course, no remnant of the giant country would have been safe and Hitler understood this, and would not have given Stalin time. However, if the Führer had seized the line Leningrad-Moscow-Odessa, rested and fully refitted the *Wehrmacht*, and started a fresh campaign from that line, there would have been no end to the war by 1945;
- The preservation of the lend-lease routes (the keys to which were Murmansk and the border with Iran, which was occupied by the Allies in September). Hitler would doubtlessly have demanded both one and the other, as well as control over the remaining industry;
- The readiness of the Allies to assist the USSR in its desperate struggle, given its inability to contribute sufficiently to the common cause under such conditions as has been described.

However, over all the logical factors, such as Moscow as the hub of communications, the center of power and industry, and the source of human resources, there hung an emotional factor: Moscow the capital city, which we dwelled upon endlessly in our conversations in the autumn of 1941; Moscow of the May Day parades; "my Moscow" (which most Soviet citizens had never visited personally, but had seen repeatedly in films), with its cult of the Leader, the Kremlin, the Lenin Mausoleum, the entire image of the city and its history, which had been elevated in a unique fashion in a popular song of the times: "I'll never forget a friend, if I became friends with him in Moscow!" A person, who had been to Moscow and had taken in its sights, became the subject of awe. People would ask about the city, and take in every word of fumbling and inarticulate descriptions of this special city, which was, in a way, not as beautiful as Leningrad, but had something about it, something special! The attention of the entire nation was focused on Moscow. Surrender Moscow as a matter of pragmatism? The loss of Moscow wouldn't mean the loss of the Army and the entire country?

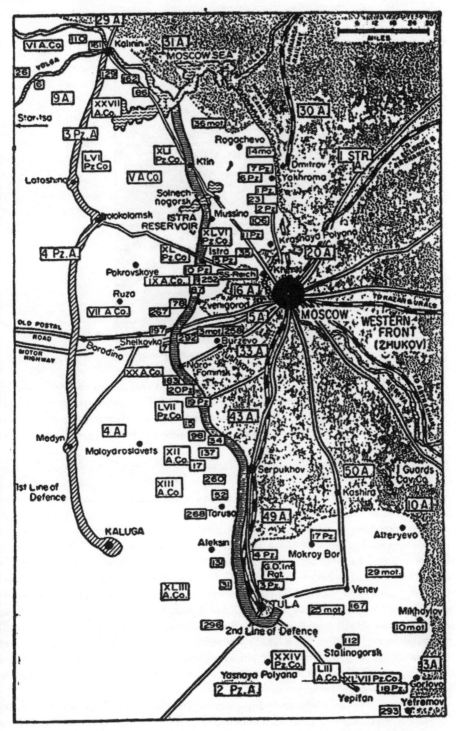

Moscow 1941, emphasising the city's importance as a hub of road and rail links

'You will only pass over my dead body!'

Our resolve, weakened by the evacuation in railcars stuffed beyond capacity, homelessness, the separation from family and friends and our concern for them, the absence of news, illnesses, and the growing list of surrendered cities, was then in 1941 already at its lowest point. In our family, the capitulation of Moscow would have triggered suicides.

☆ ☆ ☆

Now, when debates over Barbarossa have reached a point where there are almost as many opinions about its possible outcomes as there are discussants, one aspect of it generates no dissenting voices: events would have developed in a completely different fashion had the Germans appeared in front of Moscow in August. Just why didn't the Führer make the taking of Moscow the main objective that month, when the city was much more vulnerable to attack? Mobilization had only started, the city wasn't bristling with fortifications yet, and the divisions from the Far East had just begun to prepare for the journey west, while the *Wehrmacht* was fresher, fuel was ample, and the roads were dry and passable. Yet the main thing was that the population had still not adapted to the war. The population, still spellbound by the myth of the RKKA's invincibility, wasn't ready for such a course of events, hadn't yet become embittered by the losses, and easily succumbed to panic. Moscow could have been taken then, not later. So why, instead, was Hitler aspiring for the Ukraine, the Caucasus? There are two reasons.

First, the Führer didn't listen to his generals. The clever Von Bock understood the effectiveness of a blow to the head, after which the entire mass of the Red Army would have been made no more effective than the muscles of an athlete, felled by a stroke. Military

Over open sights

commanders are accustomed to holding the reins. An order is justified (or condemned) by its result. A commander doesn't know how to explain everything that leads him to a particular decision, which is often reached intuitively. Von Bock didn't know how to impress upon the maniacal Commander-in-Chief the importance of taking Moscow, even though he [von Bock] was assessing the situation from a political standpoint. However, in politics Hitler had the reputation of being a master – a nothing in strategy who imagined himself a master of that as well in light of his diplomatic achievements. Hitler was haunted by the fate of Napoleon. If you please, what had the taking of Moscow given to Napoleon? The demoralization and collapse of his *Grande Armée*!

The second reason was oil, the Achilles' heel of the German war machine. The striving for oil upset the priorities. He had to seize the Caspian oilfields before the British managed to reach them! Even now, while the Soviet government survived, the Brits were working out plans in their War Cabinet in case the Soviet government fell, to seize the Baku oilfields, a source that was feeding the engines of war. This seemed more important to the Führer than anything else.

No, in 1941 the Brits, who could barely scrape together enough strength to hold the Suez Canal, were in no condition to undertake an expedition to Baku. Even if the *Wehrmacht* was still stuck at Odessa, given the correlation of forces and the difference in the relative length of the supply lines, such an expedition would have been fatal for the British. In the best case, it could have been taken for a diversion only.

However, while scornful of Russia, the Führer was in awe of England. Commingling with the British ethnos was the dream of his life: to proselytize the British yeomen in his faith and to turn them into Nazi supporters! He disdained Russia and overstated England's power. The fragility of its power in that pastoral era still wasn't apparent, and the Führer compared the monolith of Great Britain on the scale of the Reich's. If we take the durability of the Reich as a basis of comparison, then how did Great Britain's durability stack up? Great Britain had hundreds of years of traditions and had endured great trials. Germany, in contrast, only rose as a power in 1866, and the Reich's only tradition was a hen in an every pot and a breakaway from traditions.

It is time again to recall the main idea of Barbarossa, which was a plan for a *Blitzkrieg* war against the USSR: not being diverted by opportunities that arose (which given the tactical superiority of the *Wehrmacht* on the ground and the Luftwaffe's supremacy in the air would come in multiples), to slaughter the Soviet divisions sent to intercept the *Wehrmacht* and to continue the advance until the encirclement of Moscow and the seizure of Gor'kii's industrial region.

Nevertheless, Hitler was distracted by just such presenting opportunities. The southern flank of Soviet forces was weaker, so it was decided to seek successes precisely there. As a result new opportunities arose, and exhilarating ones at that. On 25 August the *Wehrmacht's* 1st Panzer Army and 17th Army crossed the Dnepr River and seized Nikopol' and Dnepropetrovsk. Now Rostov and Groznyi were just a stone's throw away! Baku too! On the map, everything is flat and looks close together. The British were closer to the oilfields than they were to Moscow. *They* weren't able to defend Moscow, but they might seize the oil. Moscow wouldn't run away; the oil was more important.

The Führer was mistaken. In 1942, the fall of Moscow would no longer mean victory: the embittered, aggrieved people were now in it for the long haul. In the autumn of 1941, though, nothing was more important than Moscow. The seizure or blockade of the Moscow hub would have severed the state transportation network. The bureaucratic apparatus would have crumbled. The defense industry would have been weakened, both in terms of personnel and output. The Army reserves had been gathered together at Moscow, and they unavoidably would have been ground down. However, even all of this taken together doesn't outweigh the loss of morale had Moscow been lost. In August-September 1941, obstinacy toward the Germans hadn't yet encompassed the nation. The fall of the capital would have filled the cup of our fears and sufferings to overflowing.

The start of Operation Typhoon was magnificent. Von Bock and Guderian struck the Briansk, Western and Reserve Fronts (commanded by Eremenko, Konev and Budenny respectively) with enveloping attacks. According to Zhukov, the fronts had approximately 800,000 troops, 782 (?) tanks, 6,808 (?) guns and mortars, and 545 aircraft.

Where did Zhukov find these numbers? Probably, they'd been supplied to the Marshal in response to his request to the Ministry of Defense's Central Archive. However, six years after the first publication of his memoirs, the strength figures had changed radically. The Soviet *Istoriia Vtoroi mirovoi voiny, Tom 4* [*History of the Second World War, Volume 4*], a solid publication that came out only after the commander's death, gives some substantially different (and judiciously rounded) figures: 1,250,000 troops, 7,600 guns and mortars, 990 tanks and 677 (not rounded!) aircraft.[1]

1   Editor's note: Later editions of Zhukov's memoirs, both in the original Russian and the English translation, carry the corrected figures as published by the Soviet *History of the Second World War*.

Based on his lower numbers, the Marshal writes:

After regrouping his troops on the Moscow sector, the enemy had a force superior to the combined strength of our three Fronts. He had 1.25 times as many men, 2.2 times as many tanks, 2.1 times as many guns and mortars, and 1.7 times as many aircraft.

The figures from the Volume 4 of the *History of the Second World War* refute the Marshal's calculations. The Red Army actually outnumbered the *Wehrmacht* on the Moscow sector.

However, the essence of the matter doesn't lie in this, nor in the fact that Soviet troop strength figures were always based on the number of men reporting for duty, while the German estimates of manpower strength were often expressed in terms of ration strength, which includes non-combat personnel, men in hospitals and even prisoners of war. There was no German superiority in manpower and there could not have been. The notorious "overwhelming superiority" of the *Wehrmacht* is a Soviet myth created to excuse the weakness of the Red Army. On the contrary, at the moment of the invasion, the "overwhelming superiority in equipment" was precisely on the Soviet side. In skilled hands, the available T-34s and KV-1s could easily kill all the German "Marks", but time and again the Germans emerged victorious in tactical encounters.

The point is that the Soviet equipment and men were being controlled by unskilled hands. The crews hadn't been trained to handle their vehicles. Vehicle commanders didn't know how to give orders to their subordinate crews and didn't know all the equipment's possibilities. Stalin, relying on his own logic, had placed the initiative in the hands of the foe. The Germans had taken advantage of this. The Luftwaffe began to reign supreme in the air in the very first hours of the invasion. The lack of air cover doomed the Soviet tanks to becoming heaps of jumbled metal. Only then did the Soviet generals recall – Zhukov was among the first – Romanenko's admonition: give the tanks air cover!

References to German superiority in equipment and manpower must be understood in the sense that with possession of the initiative, the *Wehrmacht* repeatedly created local superiority on the axis of an attack when launching it. Then forces would be shifted (do you recall Zhukov's outcry to Kulik, "The enemy is mobile!"?) in order to create an advantage on a different sector – in the face of the numerical superiority of the RKKA, which was like a fat giant confronting a small but nimble foe. The Red Army only began to win victories once it began to maneuver. Thus from 12 July 1943 the strategic initiative passed totally into the hands of the Red Army, and only at times – like at Zhitomir in late 1943 and at Lake Balaton in Hungary in 1945 – did the *Wehrmacht* manage to stagger Soviet forces by means of an extreme exertion by its troops and masterful maneuver.

By the time of the battle for Moscow, the *Wehrmacht's* numbers were not at all growing. The aggregate German losses since the start of the war had reached 534,000 men. A half a million superbly trained soldiers! The only good news for the *Wehrmacht* by the end of September 1941 was the fact that the combat strength of the panzer divisions had reached 70% of the authorized establishment.

Thus, Guderian attacked in the direction of Briansk, Orel and Tula. The weather was dry and clear. Practically without meeting resistance, von Schweppenburg's XXIV Panzer Corps rolled into Orel, which was located 200 kilometers behind the front line and was being defended by a women's battalion. Life was going on in the city as normal. Shops were open, trolley cars were stuffed with people, and factory equipment was standing on the rail platforms waiting to be loaded onto trains to be moved to the East. Von Schweppenburg didn't continue his magnificent raid on to Mtsensk and Tula only because he'd become separated from his supply base and had exhausted his fuel, and couldn't procure more of it in Orel, which characterizes the limited administrative capabilities of this impetuous warrior, and likely explains why he hadn't risen any higher in the *Wehrmacht* command hierarchy. He became stuck in Orel, while the Luftwaffe brought up more fuel for him *by air* in order to continue his dash. The Germans had to take Mtsensk with fighting and once it had been reached the rains began to fall, the Russians came to their senses and .... And Tula they never managed to take. The Russians had a new ditty: "Tula, Tula, you turned things around, and we found ourselves on the attack!"[22]

Zhukov at the moment of disaster (I can't find any better word to describe the enemy's seizure of a critical transportation hub lying 200 kilometers behind the front lines, in the rear of a million-man army!) was located far from the scene of action. Only one thought comes to mind: had he (if not he, then some other Zhukov) been in command of the Briansk Front, von Schweppenburg would not have been able to boast about such an eye-popping (from Konotop to Orel!) and victorious march. Zhukov, however, was in Leningrad at the time, and there was no one else comparable to him in the role of front commander defending Moscow.

In a word, Zhukov gives no explanations for what happened. One must turn to parallel sources. From them it is clear that on 26 September 1941, the command of the Western Front reported to the *Stavka* about the enemy's regrouping and the anticipation of a new German offensive sometime around 1 October. The Front command ordered the troops to get ready to repulse the attack and requested reinforcements and the coordination of defensive measures from the *Stavka*. The *Stavka* reacted with a directive issued on 27 September, which indicated the need to go over to a set defense.

What sort of set defense? The enemy was going to drive panzer wedges into our defenses. We had almost a thousand tanks, and what tanks! Suppose the Germans really did have twice as many. We, though, were on the defense. Let's be mobile! Let's keep tanks ready to intercept the adversary on the lines of advance vulnerable to tanks. Let's set up ambushes on the main roads. Let's maneuver with our tanks, using the superiority of our T-34s or KVs; the Germans hate them with all their hearts!

However, even this *Stavka* directive didn't reach the troops in time (strangely, three days prior to the offensive and it was still late?!), and the German attack once again caught our forces off-guard. The Germans again toyed with the Soviets, launching diversionary attacks here and there, while the front commands once again couldn't determine the axis of the *Wehrmacht's* main attack, once again couldn't use their tanks for defense, and the fronts' reserves were out of position. As a result of this, the enemy exploited gaps in our defenses to penetrate quickly into operational space, which caused Zhukov to chide the command of the Western Front (Konev), considering him responsible for the consequences.

He knew about the errors and blamed Konev, though only in an article he wrote entitled *"Bitva za stolitsu"* ["The Battle for the Capital"]. He didn't repeat the rebuke in

---

2   Tula is a city, famous for its small arms factory. The workers, used to practice shooting, formed strong militia forces with sharpshooter teams. For 45 days Tula was almost completely cut off by German encirclement. The entire city population participated in repulsing Germans. In 1976, the city was honored with the title of Hero City.

his memoirs.

Do you sense, reader, the absence of resolute men like Zhukov in the *Stavka* at this difficult hour for our Motherland, and the absence of similarly capable men in the field? They'd been buried, dumped into the ground, and no one will lay flowers on the graves of the legendary army commanders, who'd been preparing a war "with little blood and on the aggressor's territory."

But what do we call a Supreme Commander, who doesn't learn from mistakes? Who doesn't learn from his own costly blunders? Costly? He didn't pay for them with his own blood and was not stingy with the blood of others. In the summer of 1942, the same situation repeated itself.

Zhukov appeared in the *Stavka* on 7 October. Pride hadn't allowed the Leader to confess earlier that "... we there and then consulted with the Politburo and ..." – and again, excuse me, they shit their pants. Perhaps only at this time the Leader became aware of the dimensions of the catastrophe? According to Zhukov, Stalin had a cold, didn't look well, and greeted him curtly:

'And where do you think they are going to send those tank and motorized forces that
Hitler moved out of the Leningrad area?'
'Obviously in the direction of Moscow. But only after they've been brought up to
full strength again and repairs made to the equipment.'
'Apparently they've already been moving in that direction.'

The honesty of Zhukov's acknowledgment is praiseworthy. Even he hadn't considered that the Germans were so mobile. Here, though, is what one can draw from this dialogue: Zhukov, as a *Stavka* representative in Leningrad, had no idea about what was happening around Moscow. Only now was he being informed that the troops of the Western and Reserve Fronts (Konev and Eremenko) had been encircled, and that there were no communications from the Mozhaisk line (Marshal Budenny). A deep concern had to arise that the confusion that had occurred in Orel might be repeating itself, but this time in Moscow ...

On the night of 8 October, Zhukov departed for Maloiaroslavets. He relates what he found when he arrived there:

I entered the District Executive Committee building, and saw Budenny poring over a map. We shook hands warmly. One could tell that he had gone through a lot in those difficult days.
'Where are you from?' Budenny asked.
'From Konev.'
'How are things with him? We've been out of touch for two days. While I was at the 43rd Army's headquarters yesterday, [Reserve] Front HQ moved. To where, I don't know.'
'I've found it in a forest beyond the railroad bridge across the Protva. They are waiting to hear from you. The bulk of our forces on the Western Front have been encircled ...Go to Front headquarters now, see what's there, and inform General Headquarters of the situation. I'll go to the Iukhnov area. Report our meeting to the Supreme Commander; tell him I went to Kaluga. We've got to find out what's

happening there.'

The delicate description of the encounter raises no doubts that General of the Army Zhukov was thoroughly coming to the rescue of his former commander, Marshal Budenny, who had lost his headquarters and his grasp of the course of events, and was now blankly looking over a map, upon which there was nothing of the current situation depicted, and awaiting Pavlov's fate. Zhukov finds him, gives him a shake, wipes his sniveling nose, and sends Marshal Budenny, his senior by rank, in his stead to report to the Kremlin: "Everything's under control, Comrade Stalin; I'm at my headquarters and reporting the situation, while I've authorized Zhukov to proceed further, to Iukhnov, and then to Kaluga, so he can find out what is happening there ..."

The word to a witness of the meeting's aftermath, Aleksandr Buchin, Zhukov's driver:

Approximately a half-hour later Georgii Konstantinovich [Zhukov] emerged stiffly, with a certain sharp expression in his eyes. A limp Budenny tumbled out after him, his famous whiskers sagging, his countenance puffy and swollen. With an ingratiating appearance, he tried to scurry around in front of Zhukov and was babbling something in a most sycophantic tone. Georgii Konstantinovich, paying him no attention, literally leaped into his car. We set off. Stuck in my memory is the sight of Budenny, stopped short in his tracks, his mouth gaping, and with an outstretched hand, which Zhukov hadn't shaken. A Marshal! Behind him was a crowd of bodyguards, who had bundled out the door ...

Yes, they may have greeted each other warmly, but had parted not very much so ... And there was a reason for it. The meeting speaks volumes. Accompanied by two or three men, Zhukov, at the risk of bumping into Germans at any turn, had driven almost blindly around the Reserve Front's forces and located its headquarters, while Marshal Budenny, with a mob of bodyguards, didn't bother to detach a few in order to search for his own headquarters. Is it so absurd to presume that he didn't want to find it? That he was afraid to find it, since if he did locate it, he would also find a phone there, which would mean he would have had to call Comrade Stalin: "Such and such, and even I don't know much ..."? That is to say that Zhukov's conversation with a different commander, who had lost his headquarters, his neighboring formations, and his troops and was grieving over a map, would have gone differently. They say Zhukov even shot a few ... However, one good turn deserves another. He had fully squared accounts with Budenny. Budenny, likely, had saved Zhukov in 1937; Zhukov, inarguably, saved Budenny in 1941.

In 1942, however, Budenny again was given command of the Southern Direction – Mercy me! – Again with just the same disastrous outcome! You say, "The strangest things happened in the Red Army!" Yet there were no decent commanders available to appoint!

However, the German Army also wasn't forsaken by acts of Providence. At the moment of Guderian's most extreme exertions, when he was lunging ahead on the southern flank of Army Group Center, at a moment when the fate of Moscow was still hanging by a thread, his troops lost support from the south: the Führer ordered von Rundstedt to attack toward Rostov, and further on, toward the Caucasus. Doesn't this surpass even Budenny's appointment for his feats of 1942?

My generals know nothing about economics ...

After the removal of Khrushchev from power, there was a wide-spread joke that among the list of acts, which Nikita didn't have time to finish while he ruled (and he managed to do plenty, even to shoot a lot of people, who might have become the foundation of honorable business after the collapse of the USSR) was the awarding of the title "Hero of the Soviet Union" to Tsar Nicholas II for creating the revolutionary situation in the country. The aforementioned order to von Rundstedt offers up one more candidate for the highest honor of the country of the Soviets – the German Führer. His decision to assault Kiev was *fatal*, but there cannot be two fatal decisions, so the title of *the most stupid decision* will remain the decision to turn von Rundstedt southward at the same time as the advance on Moscow. It not only practically abandoned the single realistic aspect of the plan of Barbarossa: not to get distracted by opportunities as they came up! It ignored a fundamental principle of war: the decisive blow must be inflicted with a fist. Even now, Hitler was striking with an open palm – now, when a matter of days remained until autumn with its rains, until the Russian winter, which eliminated the last chances to take the capital. Instead of covering Guderian, von Kleist's First Panzer Army and its flanking Sixth and Seventeenth Armies diverged from him, exposing Guderian's lengthening right flank and forcing him to detach troops from his attacking wedge to defend it at the most decisive stage of the Moscow offensive.

This decision is so strikingly stupid that it suggests that it is not so much stupidity as it is an act of desperation, a play *va banque*. A possible explanation of this is the entirety of the information about the overall situation, to which the Führer and nobody else had access. (Like, for example, the upcoming war between Japan and the USA, which deprived the Führer of hope for Japan's assistance in tearing apart the USSR – help that back in June he didn't want in the confidence that everything would accrue to him alone, including both Siberia and the Pacific coastal area. Now the Führer would have been thirsting for the assistance of an ally, but it was too late!) On the basis of the entirety of information, he likely understood as well that Barbarossa had failed. There would remain only to prolong the war, to seize resources, and to use time no longer for the construction of the 'Thousand Year Reich', but to achieve his personal and cherished goals. The Wannsee Conference underlined these.[3] There was no longer any return path to reconciliation with civilization ...

However, at the start of Operation Typhoon, the fall of Moscow seemed to be a matter of days. As the result of the destruction of three fronts, two Red Army groupings were encircled west of Viazma, on the north (four armies of the Western and Reserve Fronts) and on the south in the area of Trubchevsk (two armies of the Briansk Front), while in the region of Briansk their battered units with the wounded Eremenko, the might-have-been victor over Guderian were breaking out of encirclement toward Belev. The Western Front suffered the greatest damage – approximately 600,000 men. The loss of Moscow seemed unavoidable, a catastrophe irretrievable. Indeed, it would have been such in any other country.

---

3   Editor's note: This was a conference of leading Nazi officials, which took place on 20 January 1942 in Berlin in the suburb of GrossenWannsee on the subject of the "final solution to the Jewish question". It becomes tempting to suppose that the addressing of such a massive project at such an unsuitable time, when the Eastern Front was cracking apart, while Germany was exerting all its strength, that the conference had as its aim to put the German nation at odds with all mankind, making any peaceful initiatives impossible while at the same time embittering the resistance of the German people to the Allies to the utmost.

It was in this situation when Zhukov, assuming responsibility for the defense of Moscow, was completing his courageous reconnaissance in the forward lines, having no troops, no communications, and risking the possibility of running into the enemy every minute. However, it is impossible to put together the overall picture from Zhukov's memoirs. We'll have to turn to Kurt von Tippelskirch and his book published in Russian under the title *Istoriia Vtoroi mirovoi voiny* [*History of the Second World War*]:

> On 7 October the forward units of both enveloping panzer armies linked up in the enemy rear ... By 13 October, this pocket had been cleared. In the summary of the German command, it was announced that the Russians lost 67 infantry divisions, 6 cavalry divisions and 7 tank divisions – 663,000 prisoners, 1,243 tanks (against the 990 reported in Volume 4 of the Soviet *History of the Second World War* – author's note), and 5,412 guns. This was a new stunning success. But did it justify the announcement on 9 October by the Reich's Propaganda Ministry that 'the outcome of the war had been decided and Russia was finished'?

It is possible to understand the German propaganda apparatus; they were delightedly stunned: two victories in two weeks, and the number of prisoners and captured equipment exceeded half the *Wehrmacht*'s power. Is this not a victory?

The American Albert Seaton writes:

> In the bright clear skies the Luftwaffe reconnaissance and close support were excellent, and yet Hoth was to complain on 4 October of heavy Red Air Force activity. Near Kholm the brigade was counterattacked in strength by a Soviet tank division from the Far East, *on the old style establishment* and completely equipped with *new* American tanks (emphasis added). This tank formation, which had never been under fire before was almost destroyed and lost sixty-five tanks in a few hours.

This is how hours were won for the Soviet side. Even more terrible is his description of a German breakthrough of a Soviet front, isolated but densely packed with troops:

> Enemy dead and dying lay in heaps where they had been caught in the machine-gun fire of the German tanks, which were then many miles ahead. Abandoned equipment was everywhere, including American quarter-ton jeeps, never before seen by German troops. In two days the panzer forces advanced eighty miles, German casualties being very light. The fine weather held.

This scene, incidentally, is inconvenient for those who try to prove that the Red Army offered no resistance in the initial period of the war. They lay dead, but hadn't retreated. The Soviet *Istoriia Vtoroi mirovoi voiny* relates:

> It was necessary to create a new defense front and at whatever the cost halt the foe on the approaches to Moscow...*Stavka* reserves were brought up, a number of formations and units of the Northwestern and Southwestern Fronts, and almost all the strength and resources of the Moscow Military District. Altogether in the course of a week, 14 rifle divisions, 16 tank brigades, more than 40 artillery regiments (the strength

of each was equivalent to a battalion, but they were called regiments – the author) and other units arrived at the Western Front ... On 10 October the troops of the Western and Reserve Fronts were consolidated into one, the Western Front. General G. K. Zhukov was appointed as the Front commander. ... By 10 October, at the height of the work to create the Mozhaisk line of defense, the situation at the front grew even more acute. Hostile troops seized Sychevka, Gzhatsk, reached Kaluga, and were fighting for the cities of Briansk and Mtsensk and on the approaches to Ponyri and L'gov. ... They had succeeded in breaching the Volga River to the northeast and on 14 October burst into Kalinin.

However, that's how it went as long as the effect of the breakthrough was operative. Yet then the transfer of forces from the Southwestern Front in order to plug the gap in the center didn't slip the Führer's attention, and he began to waver. The pace of the advance on Moscow slowed. Was it then that the Führer understood – the first among his entire clique! – that Barbarossa had failed, and that it was time to change plans? Incidentally, a new opportunity had arisen in the direction of the oilfields; how could he not take advantage of that?

However, even now the burning question remains: Was it really the time to change plans? Just a few days later, Zhukov himself recommended the evacuation of government institutions, not excluding by this the possibility that Moscow would fall. Not excluding – given what circumstances? Plainly, if the pressure on his front continued to grow. Zhukov was conceding that the, given satisfactory *Wehrmacht* weather – and the weather, as ill luck would have it, remained dry! – and the assistance to Army Group Center with the northern wing of Army Group South, would still crush the resistance of the weakened Western Front, which still was in the process of consolidating, and force its way into the capital. At a minimum, this would disrupt railroad communications – the decisive factor of the defense. But there was no one who could change the Führer's mind, and so Rundstedt was re-directed to the south.

However, the Soviet command was also presented with certain possibilities. Thus at Mtsensk, after the halt to re-fuel in Orel after that city fell, things really turned badly for the *Wehrmacht*, for the first time since the start of the war. Guderian's panzers were halted. If the Germans had not dispersed their strength, there would have been a second attack on Mtsensk from the south, and the check there would not have reduced the tempo of the offensive toward Moscow. As it was, the halt there became significant. Klaus Reinhardt writes:

The main opposition to Guderian's units came from the 4th Tank Brigade under Colonel M. E. Katukov, equipped with T-34 tanks, which were far superior to German panzers and which gave the attacking 4th Panzer Division a 'hard time'. These rapid counter-measures enabled the Russians to halt the mass of the XXIV Panzer Corps (which had dashingly taken Orel – the author) for a week initially and inflict such heavy casualties upon them as to prompt Guderian to write: 'The severity of the fighting gradually took its toll on our officers and men ... and one was struck by the emotional upset rather than by the physical effects. It is puzzling that our best officers should have been affected to such a degree by the recent fighting.'

What was so puzzling here? The war was continuing for its fourth month, and the wise brigade commander, copying the adversary, was doing only that which the ignorant command of the Western and Reserve Fronts should have done before this. Colonel M. E. Katukov selected an ambush position on the single route useable by tanks, at a bridge across the narrow Lisitsa River, and deployed his combat formation in two echelons – and thus the Germans' numerical advantage was parried. The matter was not in the T-34s, which were clearly better than the German "Marks"; not all of Katukov's tanks were T-34s. The matter was the lack of commanders like Katukov who had been eliminated by the "Father of Nations". Now, after horrific losses, the best remaining commanders of the Red Army were mastering the tactics of a mobile war.

"They had learned," Guderian noted with melancholy laconicism. This he was already acknowledging at the time. He was not acknowledging something else. He was hiding it from himself, in order to fight more stout-heartedly.

Now the time has come for a brief psychological excursion

41

The Spirit of the Army

In our days the majority of historians have come to agree that a preemptive attack by the Red Army, had it been launched in the summer of 1941, would have been ineffective or even catastrophic. There is also general agreement that everything would not have gone like certain Russian authors imagine with lively fantasy, manipulating facts and documents according to their views. I'm not even speaking about the fact that having struck first, the country would have lost the factor of *righteous fury*, essential to a people who are fighting a just war.

Guderian ignores this factor. On the *Wehrmacht's* side, you have the best officers and soldiers, veterans of three stunningly successful campaigns, and a long string of victorious announcements; on the other you have a handful of Russians, 5,500 men, all they could scrape together at Mtsensk, on the road to Tula, not the million-man army that existed before the start of Operation Typhoon, just a brigade of T-34s – and "the 4th Panzer Division had a hard time." Yet the latest announcement from the Reich's Ministry of Propaganda declares that "the outcome of the war had been decided and Russia was finished"? Indeed it looked like that – Orel had been seized without any resistance. Hundreds of thousands of Red Army troops were encircled. Everything was proclaiming that the Russians were finished and the war was over! It was just then, however, that the famous panzer leader should have recalled that this most cruel war of aggression was being conducted on a foreign territory possessing terrible roads and an enormous population that loved their homeland....

Nothing else is as painful as disillusionment. It was extremely imprudent to promise the German Army a rapid victory after Smolensk, Odessa, Kiev and Leningrad. The *Wehrmacht* had indeed been corrupted in this way by the concept of *Blitzkrieg*. Russia, though, was not Poland, and it was not France. The expanses in Russia were not the same, the roads were not the same, and the people were not the same. The Reich's Propaganda Ministry would have been astonished all right: the propaganda organs have their own criteria. The exultations of the Propaganda Ministry were addressed to the German people first and only secondarily to the troops. Could the German command have really taken the Ministry's output seriously? Didn't the command inform the newspaper writers on the condition of the Russians, or did they use the newspapers as the source of information?

Not Guderian, he didn't. He couldn't accept defeat either. How should one fight, once having acknowledged that you are vanquished? Only after the war, recalling "*the lore of ages gone by/in hoar antiquity compounded*"[1] did Guderian address this properly:

> "I decided to visit the 4th Panzer Division at once and find out for myself what the situation was. On the battlefields that had been fought over during the 6th and 7th of October the commander of the battle-group that had been engaged there described the course of the fighting to me. The tanks knocked out on either side were still in

---

1   Editor's note: This is a line from a poem by Aleksandr Pushkin, the celebrated Russian poet.

position. The damage suffered by the Russians was considerably less than that to our own tanks.

"Back in Orel I found Colonel Eberbach, who also told me the story of the recent battles, and then again I talked to General Freiherr Geyr von Schweppenburg and to the commander of the 4th Panzer Division, Freiherr von Langermann und Erlencamp. For the first time during this exacting campaign Colonel Eberbach gave the impression of being exhausted, and the exhaustion that was now noticeable was less physical than spiritual. It was indeed startling to see how deeply our best officers had been affected by the latest battles.

"What a contrast to the high spirits in evidence at the OKH and at Army Group Center! Here was a radical difference of attitude which as time went on grew wider until it could be scarcely bridged; though at this time Second Panzer Army was unaware that its superiors were drunk with the scent of victory."

It is impossible to believe the last paragraph of Guderian's statement. The *Wehrmacht* shared the jubilation in the ether. The panzer crews were listening to the radio; the German tankers had excellent equipment. After such exultant propaganda broadcasts, could one be surprised by the low morale in the units, after encountering such enemy resistance following the announcement that "Russia was finished"? One needs to be sparing with such declarations; they are demoralizing.

The spirit of an army is a delicate matter. To retain confidence in themselves, to find the strength for victory after suffering defeats – it had been intrinsic to Rome's Legions. Nazism had adopted so many Roman rituals and traditions, but it neglected this one. Meanwhile the Russians, beaten so severely, had managed to catch their breath.

Only now it wasn't June with its dazzlingly successful start to the war, and it wasn't Minsk behind the backs of the Russians. Moscow was now behind them! Indeed it was clear that the *Blitzkrieg* was finished. The line Arkhangel'sk-Kuibyshev-Astrakhan' was unobtainable, and a winter campaign was now unavoidable. Now should have been the time to prepare the lightly dressed and bootless German Army for difficulties. That didn't happen, and instead they weakened it further with the announcement of victory. Rundstedt was re-directed to the south, instead of helping von Bock to manage at least with Moscow before the onset of winter. All this was really going off the tracks.

Meanwhile the Russians were marching to their deaths. They had no other choice. There was an enemy in the Kremlin, the worst tyrant ever, but an adversary was at the gates of Moscow – a stranger, who had no grasp of Russian, who treated Russia with contempt and trampled upon its national dignity. There was no choice.

42

The Defense of Moscow

In the 1st edition (1996) of this book I lamented that Hitler's fatal turn toward Kiev had not been assessed by historians, although I pointed to von Tippelskirch's remark:

> The battle ended on 26 September. In the summary of the German High Command it was reported that 650,000 men had been taken prisoner, and 3,718 guns and 884 tanks seized. The size of the success was saying that Hitler had been correct. However, only the outcome of the entire war could show whether the achieved tactical victory justified the loss of time needed for further operations. If the aim of the war should not be realized, then although the Russians lost this battle, they won the war.

My concerns proved to be idle. Not only von Tippelskirch, but indeed all the literature on the war, other than the Soviet literature, has done justice to the Führer's talents – just as it has to the self-sacrificing dedication of the Soviet soldier, who has collectively been referred to as the *Russian* soldier by foreign authors (other than David Glantz with his remarkable book, *Colossus Reborn*).

First Hitler engaged in the Smolensk battle, confident that there he would grind up all the remaining Soviet forces. Japan, the third member of the Axis, understanding that the war was dragging on, made the decision to turn its military forces to the south. This time Stalin didn't ignore Sorge's information. However, the tank divisions from the Far East didn't make it in time to Kiev to intercept the Führer's folly, and only appeared on the fields around Moscow. Insufficiently trained and poorly led, they for the time being continued to share the same fate as had befallen the other scraped-together units, which had been hurled under the wheels of the *Wehrmacht* in order to slow it down. Time, though, was slipping toward winter, no end was seen to the German victories, and the Red Army was learning – at least that which it had already known previously, before the purge ...

The success of the defense of Moscow was determined by the bravery of the defending Red Army fighters and militiamen on the one hand, and the exhaustion of the *Wehrmacht's* soldiers on the other. This was the psychological backdrop to the events.

The real backdrop was the concentration of the efforts of Soviet forces, on one hand, and the dispersal of the *Wehrmacht's* efforts on the other, as well as the *Wehrmacht's* unreadiness for winter both psychologically and in terms of its entire material and technical supply. Back at the Borisov conference, Guderian had asked Hitler for tank engines (alluding to the dustiness of the Russian roads), but received only 300 of them, which prompted his bitter laughter. Yet the panzers before the offensive on Moscow had to complete the thrust to Kiev and then return to their starting point on the Moscow axis. All their motorized transport had to do the same thing. The shipment and delivery of fuel over the railroads given the increasingly long distances to the front turned into a flaming drama. In the biting cold, the synthetic fuel decomposed and wouldn't ignite. The engines refused to start in the extremely cold temperatures and the hydraulic systems worked fitfully. The army was undressed.

The weather backdrop was the autumn rains that turned the dirt roads into seemingly bottomless mud. If the weather indeed could not have been credited to the Soviet command, which was hungrily waiting for winter, then it had to be incriminating to the German command, which was not anticipating winter. One doesn't have to be a soothsayer to foretell the change of seasons. You, sir, had better get ready for the condition of the roads. Call upon the air force, but, as much as you can, create a reserve of fuel and ammunition. Just don't cry if the horses drowned, the tanks bogged, the aircraft were left with no fuel, and the offensive dragged due to the infantry alone, which was worn out and wearied by the prolonged *Drang nach Osten* [Drive to the East]. Don't complain about the never-before-seen and unimaginable road quagmires, or the sudden, cruel freeze that immediately followed them.

A comparison of seasonal weather averages over the decades shows that the autumn of 1941 was typically dry.[1] The early arriving frost reduced the time of muddy roads.

Thus the frost was just what was wanted. What then? If the summer was spent fighting in the Ukraine and the south, and only then with Moscow as the objective, was it really unexpected that the *Wehrmacht* would face cold weather? Or had the Führer supposed that the seizure of the Ukraine would warm up the winter? Trigger the collapse of the USSR? Stupid, stupid ...

☆ ☆ ☆

Just as clearly Zhukov details the operations he personally directed in 1941, he writes just as murkily about the defense of Moscow. The Leader was meddling in everything and giving his marching orders, which made some sense when you consider the main and most worrying aspect to him: Was control in his hands and was there a guarantee that German troops wouldn't enter the Kremlin, as they had entered Orel, and that a stern prisoner escort guard wouldn't show up in his doorway together with his obliging secretary? There should be no doubts that such thoughts were troubling the Leader. Perhaps in the NKVD archives a checklist of measures still may be found. This is indirectly confirmed by the fact that in Zhukov's description of the defense of Moscow, there is nothing more striking than the following episode:

> The Supreme Commander somehow received information that our troops had given up Dedovsk northwest of Nakhabino. This was now ever closer to Moscow.
>
> Naturally, Stalin was extremely worried by that report, especially since on November 28 and 29, the 9th Guards Rifle Division under Maj.-Gen. Beloborodov was successfully beating back the enemy's repeated and fierce attacks in the area of Istra. And now, twenty-four hours later, it was reported that the Germans had taken Dedovsk.
>
> Stalin got me on the phone:

---

1   The amount of precipitation in October 1941 was 51mm [2 inches] against an October average of 59mm [2.3 inches]. In November 1941, the precipitation amounted to 13mm [0.5 inches] against an average of 45mm [1.8 inches]. The average temperature in October was -2.1C [28.2 F.] against a typical average of -3.2C [26.2 F.]. However, in November the average temperature fell to -5.3C [22.5 F.], compared to a typical average of -2.8C [28.4 F.] These data come from Klaus Reinhardt.

'Do you know that Dedovsk has been captured?'

'No, Comrade Stalin, I don't.'

The Supreme Commander was quick to give me a piece of his mind. 'A commanding general should know what's happening on his front. Go to the spot at once, and organize an attack personally to recapture Dedovsk.'

I tried to argue: 'Leaving Front Headquarters in a situation as tense as this would be rather ill-advised.'

'We'll manage, don't worry. Let Sokolovsky stand in for you for the time.'

The continuation is also interesting, but I'm afraid to blur the effect of this "We'll", so I will give the remainder in my own words.

After the conversation, a phone call to Rokossovsky revealed that the Germans had taken not Dedovsk, but Dedovo, a tiny village of no more than several huts. When Zhukov called Stalin and explained the mistake, however, the General Staff's straight-A student flew into a rage and demanded that the hapless settlement be taken back from the Germans immediately. (And you're saying this is logical ...) So now not only Zhukov, but also the commander of the 5th Army Govorov in the role of an artilleryman had to go to Rokossovsky, even though Rokossovsky had his own artilleryman, Kazakov, and not a bad one at that, since he later became a Chief Marshal of Artillery. It wound up with Zhukov ordering Beloborodov "... to send a rifle company with two tanks to dislodge the German platoon holding the houses, which was done."

There are no grounds to distrust the Marshal's words. Together with them, however, let's recall the testimony of an eyewitness and participant of the fighting near Moscow, the author Grigorii Svirsky, who has described a similar quirk of the Supreme Commander's, only without tanks and with a more tenacious platoon of Germans, in his book *Proshchanie s Rossiei (Farewell to Russia)*:

The green Douglas from General Vlasov's army reserve picked us up at Volokolamsk and deposited us all on the fringe of a birch grove – the aircraft machine gunners, drivers and in general all the bit players of our aviation regiment. Engineer-Capitan Koniagin, with burnt and bandaged arms, was a bit unusual and something of a hysteric. He was wearing a strange cap from beneath which his ears were sticking out and was tugging at something under the snow and swearing furiously, something which he'd never done before. It turned out that the entire fringe of the grove, which had been allotted to us as an airfield staging base, was piled with soldiers' corpses. The soldiers were ours, with closely-cropped haircuts, in green quilted jackets and army-issued gray fur caps with earflaps. Some we dragged by their feet away from the landing strip, others we carried off on canvas tent-halves which were crackling with frozen blood.

An infantry major, who out of consolation offered each of us a mug of alcohol and a piece of bacon in his dugout, explained to the Engineer-Captain that two weeks before they had taken a village offhand, next to which was now our airfield. At dawn they reported this to the division. The division reported it to the commander of the 20th Army, General Vlasov. Vlasov reported it to the Front commander Zhukov, and Zhukov had passed the news up to Stalin. Stalin shifted a little flag on a map. In the *Stavka*, they were marking every step on the Moscow axis ... But then the Germans brought up tanks and chased our guys from the hill. They rolled back downward on the built-up ice. Some were fleeing without their felt boots and some had lost their caps. The snow was covered with blood ... Then they went on the attack again, and how! Out of the company only three men returned. One of them had lost his mind.

The wheel began to spin in the opposite direction. Vlasov reported to Zhukov – 'We couldn't hold the hill.' The Front commander didn't even want to hear it: 'Hill Number ... is ours. It has been reported as such to Comrade Stalin ... and you're scuttling backwards, like crabs??'

Zhukov announced that he was sending the 20th Army two more infantry divisions, which were now disembarking from trains in Volokolamsk. 'Load the men onto trucks and right from the march send them straight into battle. At 1700 hours you are to report: "The hill is ours!" Carry it out!'

'That's how it went,' the infantry major finished his story. 'Without artillery, without tanks ...'

As a result, the future airstrip was piled with the corpses of young soldiers in green quilted jackets.... There is little difference between this episode and the overall description of the Red Army's counterattacking phase of the battle for Moscow. The story about Dedovo confirms that Stalin was putting pressure on Zhukov, although Belov, the commander of the 1st Cavalry Corps, remarks upon Zhukov's independence in dealing with Stalin. There are no doubts that Stalin would have crushed any other commander from among those recently promoted under similar circumstances.

However, in the initial period after the Germans launched their attack, the Leader no longer meddled, and those urgent measures which had to be taken were in fact taken. Only staff arguments over where to expect a new German thrust explains why the needed forces weren't committed in time to the Mozhaisk line, and why the Germans were able to penetrate it and capture Mozhaisk without heavy losses.

In general, Zhukov's voice in the Moscow defensive operation was decisive only in its October stage. The word to Klaus Reinhardt in his book, *Moscow: The Turning Point?*:

In mid-October the Soviet leadership also realized that the capital was in very great danger. During this period any available *Stavka* reserves were being employed or sent directly to the front. The raising of new units and the transfer of more divisions from the east had not yet been completed. When, therefore, the German panzer spearheads appeared before the Moscow defense lines the Russians had no troops equal in strength to pit against them. Zhukov advised Stalin to evacuate Moscow. As early as 13 October the secretary of the Central Committee and the Moscow Civic Committee of the Soviet Communist Party, A. S. Shcherbakov, had already stated openly that Moscow was in danger, and new forces would have to be mobilized to defend the city. There was feverish construction of defensive positions in and around the capital and an additional 12,000 men were called up to occupy them.

However, as Stalin was not really convinced that these measures would work, the evacuation of Moscow began on 16 October. Most of the government, military and party organizations as well as the diplomatic corps moved to Kuibyshev on the Volga. The removal of these services had such a demoralizing effect on the people of Moscow that there was widespread panic and people tried to flee to the east. Some of those who remained began to plunder the empty shops and dwellings and steal foodstuffs, which had become scarce. Even Stalin's continuing presence and that of his closest advisers did nothing to reassure the Muscovites, so that on 19 October Moscow and its surroundings were proclaimed to be in a state of siege and martial law was declared.

It wasn't simply panic – it was pillaging. All of Moscow's underworld and filth emerged, in order to profit in the abandoned capital. The government is fleeing, it's the end! Institutions were burning their papers. The weather, as bad luck would have it, was dry, and the ashes wafted above the city. Vehicles were hurriedly being loaded by workers, primarily women. Bundles, boxes, safes, typewriters and office desks were being piled onto the backs of the trucks. Meanwhile certain characters were trashing store windows and hauling away bags of sugar and flour, canned goods, dry goods, pieces of furniture... and vodka, and more vodka! Ashes swirled in the air, and on the ground were broken jars with jam and spilled flour and sugar; here and there scuffles broke out, people were shouting with drunken voices, and in some places shots were fired.

Moscow had no chance to become a Stalingrad at that moment. What if all of this had occurred in August or September?

On 16 October, Radio Moscow transmitted: "On the night of 14 October, the situation on the Western Front deteriorated ... despite heroic resistance, our troops were forced to retreat." There's the Germans' "extreme uncertainty in night fighting" for you ...

How far had they penetrated? Obviously, to a dangerous depth, if there was such a panic in the capital. How far exactly?

For years I have searched for some references about this. I haven't found them in either Soviet or foreign sources. Reliable eyewitnesses are daily departing in front of our eyes. Yet how many of them were there? The odds of remaining alive of those who were mobilized at the beginning of the war and were still reporting for duty by the end of the war ... well, such things only happened in Soviet novels. Katukov, when decorating the heroes of the 1st Tank Army in Berlin in 1945 called for veterans of the Moscow fighting to step forward. The ranks didn't stir. There weren't any. Only the generals remained. The generals, though, weren't eyewitnesses to how far the German forward units penetrated. Their headquarters were far behind the front lines ...

Fate has preserved one eyewitness – a contemporary of those times, who didn't dodge his civil duty and who by some miracle remained alive. Abram L'vovich Portnoi was studying at the Stankin, in Moscow. This was a prestigious institute, the alma mater of a good half of all Soviet machine tool builders. Portnoi, an eminent mechanical engineer, the owner of many patents for die cast machines, a real grease monkey by his own acknowledgment, retains a tenacious memory. Stumbling across such eyewitnesses is a stroke of fortune for the historian.

On 9 July, the students of the Stankin in response to some initiative went *en mass* to the *voenkomat* [military registration office] in Moscow's Oktiabr'skii District. Portnoi was assigned to a firefighting unit in the Oktiabr'skii District, as a member of which he distinguished himself when putting out fires during the first air raid on Moscow on 22 July. (The Germans struck covered marketplaces, apparently taking them for hangars or assembly shops.) From 27 July he served in the 57th Reserve Regiment in Belev, as a member of which on 27 August he took part in intercepting a German airdrop near Tula – ten men dressed in Soviet police uniforms. Recruits fired at the Germans as they dropped to the earth. Only two survived, both of whom spoke fluent Russian. They were carrying Soviet internal passports with a Tula registration. They asked for no mercy, didn't raise their hands, and said: "All the same you're finished!"

On 30 August, after a bombing of Belev, which had damaged the railway station's pump-house, Portnoi was on duty in the kitchen and, while distributing hot water, he scalded his hands and spent the next four days in the hospital. On 3 September, all the students of the senior classes of five Moscow technical higher education institutions (the Stankin, the Moscow Institute of Railroad Engineers, the Moscow Higher Technical School and others) who numbered among the 57th Reserve Regiment, at an order from the Commandant of the Riazan' Infantry School who was passing through the Regiment's position, were assigned to the school for military education. On the night of 3 October they were awakened, changed into civilian dress, and were ordered to return to their higher education institutes to complete their studies.[2]

The day of 16 October – Portnoi's birthday – is memorable for him because of the ashes swirling around the city and the looting. Items were being distributed for free. Abram got hold of a quilted jacket, but saw how others were carrying off valuables, which no one had offered to them. He didn't take part in any defensive measures on that day. He together with two bosom buddies polished off a bottle of wine to mark his 22nd birthday (he even remembers the label – *Kuchuk-uzen'*, a Crimean Madiera that was around at the time, and perhaps still is.)

On the morning of 17 October, the students were bustled into the entrenchments outside the city. West of the Khimki riverboat station they worked to deepen anti-tank ditches. Firewood storage facilities were situated in front of the ditch. It wouldn't have been much for the German tankers to fill the ditch with the corded wood. Students began to haul away the wood. That night the students, quick-witted people, blocked the highway with cables stretched between the trees at a height of one and a half meters.[3] In the darkness, two German motorcyclists were killed by these cables. Portnoi didn't see their bodies; he's relating in this instance what he learned from comrades.

Is it possible that solitary German scouts reached Khimki or any similar Moscow suburb? Who knows … the important thing is not whether they did, but the mood of Moscow's residents. They were ready to believe in the sudden appearance of the Germans. Indeed, the rumor swept the capital: The Germans are in Khimki! The effect of solitary motorcyclists; panic … and what panic!

On 19 October, at Zhukov's recommendation, a state of siege was introduced in the capital, and order was abruptly reestablished. The mobilization of the population continued. Back on 4 July, the State Defense Committee had adopted a decree "On the voluntary mobilization of the workers of Moscow and Moscow Oblast' into divisions of people's militia." Such decrees were adopted only a day later by cities in the front zone. The word "voluntary" shouldn't cause any confusion: the mobilization was forced. Even in those days when Moscow was not under direct threat, of the 168,430 men who arrived with petitions to be enrolled in the militia in the course of four days, "after thorough examination" 160,000 men were selected.

---

2   All these sporadic moves may tell the reader a lot about the overall state of confusion reigning in the Soviet government at the time.

3   This act of stretching cables across roads indicates that people in the zone of the front lines were already aware of the operations of German reconnaissance motorcyclists.

That amounts to 95 percent – *after thorough examination*? It appears that only those with crooked arms and crooked legs were screened out. Scientists were taken in, who were unique experts in their fields. The *voenkomats* enlisted technical managers from the factories and plants, sometimes the only specialists, without considering the needs of production. Later they came back to their senses and brought some of those who survived back from the trenches, like happened with my boss and colleague S. A. Kosonogov. Psychological pressure prodded the relatives of those who'd been repressed in the purges (Sergei Afanas'evich lost his father in the purges) to volunteer first, so they wouldn't be suspected of waiting for the enemy's arrival. They were patriots, but they also emphasized patriotism. Their situation compelled them to do so. That's how the female Komsomol member Zoia Kosmodem'ianskaia[4] also went off to war. From her last name it was already clear that she descended from a line of priests; both her grandfather and father were priests and victims of Bolshevism. Everyone was taken in without a glance, although the shortage of professional cadres was acute (as demonstrated by the story about the student-techies). Several more waves of "voluntary" mobilization followed, when the Germans were approaching the walls of Moscow. In the first half of October, 50,000 people were mobilized. There were no longer the hundreds of thousands that had been available in July. A half million women and adolescents were digging trenches and anti-tank ditches. (Let's recall the 140,000, who were occupied with building fortifications along the entire frontier on the eve of the war. What a trifling number that was ...)

The fate of the Moscow people's militia was horrible, indescribable. People were driven to meet the *Wehrmacht* without training and often without weapons, winning for the regime no longer hours, but literally minutes. Once I happened to witness a meeting of veterans of the Leningrad people's militia divisions around the bed of my literary mentor, Sokrat S. Kara, who'd been paralyzed as a result of a wartime concussion. The Leningraders, recalling their lack of preparation and the pitilessness of their own command, were grieving not about their own losses, but about their friends from the Moscow people's militia: they had perished completely in vain ...

However, troops were hurrying from Siberia, about which the German intelligence had no suspicions. Within Hitler's inner circle it was believed that the Russians were committing their last strength to battle, and that the German soldier, even inadequately clad, would overcome the Russian horde. Only General Field Marshal E. Milch ordered on his own responsibility the preparation of winter uniforms and gear for his million-strong Luftwaffe servicemen, and thus only the personnel of the Luftwaffe were well-dressed by the start of winter.

In contrast, the soldiers of the *Wehrmacht* greeted winter in tattered summer uniforms. Reinhardt's book cites the numbers: 30 percent of the soldiers' footgear was unfit for wearing, and 50 percent required repair. The soldiers had almost no socks. There was a shortage of underwear, and there had been no change of it in weeks. The German propaganda concealed the lack of adequate clothing from the German people. Yet nevertheless the soldiers were

---

4   Editor's note: Zoia Kosmodem'ianskaia was an 18-year-old girl from Moscow, who became a partisan and was purportedly caught by German sentries when trying to set fire to buildings in a German-occupied village. She was tortured and then executed, and the Germans photographed her being led to the gallows. One such photo appears in Rodric Braithwaite's book *Moscow 1941*. She became a celebrated martyr of the Soviet people after an article about her was published by the Soviet newspaper *Pravda* on 27 January 1942, though controversies about her life, capture and death erupted in the 1990s.

full of enthusiasm. At night they could see the explosions of anti-aircraft shells in the skies above Moscow. The Russian capital was close, a stone's throw away, and the soldiers were looking forward to rest under the roofs of warm Moscow apartments.

Meanwhile, the tall, intelligent, stooping von Kluge dragged himself through the muck out of the hut where he was living to the hut that housed his headquarters,[5] always clutching the memoirs of General Armand de Caulaincourt, from which he never parted in these days, and which became a favorite book of many German generals in the gloomy environs of Moscow. They didn't share the Führer's jubilation and didn't believe that the remaining kilometers would be easy ones. They understood that Russia hadn't really changed from the times of Napoleon, and that having lost the mastery of warfare together with the repressed commanders, the Russians were ready to fight on without any skill, at any cost. The dark shadow of Napoleon's fate was hanging over the *Wehrmacht*.

---

5   In these days von Kluge couldn't help but recall how in July during a discussion of the movement of his army he had spoken up against the Moscow axis in favor of the Kiev diversion. When Blumentritt, his chief of staff, expressed surprise at such a strange opinion, von Kluge replied with emphasis that such a turn of events would mean a switch from his subordination to von Bock to being under von Rundstedt's command. Notes Lidell-Hart, "It was not easy to serve with von Bock, and von Kluge was happy to get away from his sphere. This was an interesting example of the influence of the personal factor on strategy." This means that some commanders for whatever the reasons nevertheless supported the Führer's decision to go for Kiev...

On October 28, 1941 ...

.. against the backdrop of a lull in the environs of Moscow and the halting of Army Group South's offensive after capturing Khar'kov, the *Wehrmacht's* Eleventh Army broke into the 'unsinkable aircraft carrier" of the Crimea and was pursuing the adversary in the direction of Sevastopol'.

On this day, 28 October 1941, at the height of the defeats in the course of the Great Patriotic War, leading government figures and military commanders were shot without trial, including Doctor of Technical Sciences and chief of the Armaments Directorate of the Red Army's Air Force I. Sakrier; former commander of the Baltic Military District General Colonel A. Loktionov; General Lieutenant of Aviation F. Arzhenukhin; General Lieutenants of Aviation and Heroes of the Soviet Union P. Rychagov and I. Proskurov; chief of the Anti-Aircraft Defense Directorate of the Red Army's Air Force and Hero of the Soviet Union General Colonel G. Shtern; and deputy chief of the General Staff for Aviation and Twice Hero of the Soviet Union General Lieutenant Ia. Smushkevich (both of the latter were heroes of the Spanish Civil War, and both were heroes at Khalkhin-Gol).

Iakov Smushkevich commanded the aviation at Khalkhin-Gol. Grigorii Shtern commanded the Trans-Baikal Front Grouping, and thus was the superior to both Smushkevich and Zhukov. They'd been arrested one after the other, Shtern on 7 June, Smushkevich on 8 June ...[1]

On 28 October 1941, at a moment of the nation's greatest exertions and tribulations, at a moment of the most bitter doubts in the war's outcome, when the beggarly Voroshilov and Budenny were dragged along by the flow of events and making no effort to control them, these standout military commanders were shot.

Eternal memory to the heroes who fell in the battles for freedom and the independence of our motherland! Death to the fascist aggressors!

But strictly speaking, why only to them?

---

[1]   Göring, the head of the Luftwaffe, danced on a table when he learned the news of Smushkevich's arrest, just as he had a year and a half before on the occasion of the signing of the Non-Aggression Pact with the Soviet Union. He chuckled, "For us, that's the equivalent to the destruction of four full-strength aviation divisions." The unmotivated nature of the arrests and the savagery of the suppression measures at a most unsuitable time for the country prompts the thought that in addition to the disagreement with the Leader over questions, in which the executed commanders were top-notch specialists, they audibly didn't refrain from giving their opinion on what had happened and was continuing to happen in the Red Army and the country.

An Interlude: The Motive behind the Purge ...

... was the fear that seized Stalin when he woke up one fine midday (the carnivore couldn't stand daylight, kept the windows covered, went to bed before morning and rose late) and realized how high he had climbed and how frightening was the fall he faced. This fear reverberated on the life of the country. Likely, Hitler was experiencing the same thing. There could no longer be any talk of retirement, resignation or capitulation.

The villains are comparable in their identical indifference to the lives of their country's citizens. One seized power in an industrialized country, accustomed to militarism. Exhausted by economic collapse, humiliated by defeat, galled by the divestiture of territory and the post-war occupation of the Ruhr, the country was ready for revenge. The other was atop a country with a population that spoke different languages, with a periphery that was half-wild in places, with a culture more ancient than the Germans in other places. Impoverished by a civil war and deliberately devastated by the Leader, this country seemed to be the ideal target for the application of German strength on the path to the cherished East.

People are defenseless, if villains come to power. A civilized nation isn't ready for this. Soon, however, the citizens discover that they've been drawn into conflict with their consciences, even with humanity, but – too late. Slogans are ancient history. The new ruler commands such an apparatus of oppression and employs such methods, that not only the potential Bravehearts but even their families become his hostages. The villains betray themselves by their cruelty already in the stage of the struggle for power, but then the man in the street, for the sake of his peace of mind, prefers to consider cruelty a sign of the contender's strength and his capability to uphold law and order. When a matter affects the man in the street himself and he discovers that the regime needs urgent repairs, he finds that he no longer has the tools. This mistake has caught many off guard and will still catch many more unawares. It's a stroke of luck when a new movement makes its own brutality known on an international scale; this guards against illusions. Brutality within the country, however – this is commonly accepted as a sign of strength, an ability to control the situation .

A group of *old friends* importuned Hitler in his seat of authority. They allowed themselves what Hitler might have stomached as a private person, but he couldn't endure such an attitude as the Führer of a Thousand-Year Reich. He decided to eliminate the associates, decided not without hesitations: they were Party comrades, and in an extreme situation the precedent might provide the justification to make an attempt on him as well Hitler implemented the "Night of Long Knives" and ruled singly until the Reich's demise but in a way so that even his denouncers didn't call him a dictator.

Not so, Stalin. He wasn't a chancellor, only a General Secretary. There was not even yet an article in the constitution that said the Party was the leading and guiding force of the country. The Party prattled unintelligibly about a dictatorship of the proletariat, without explaining what a proletariat was; the definition of which was not given by Marx, much less Stalin. Formally speaking the General Secretary wasn't the head of the country, and his cruelty seemed simply unintelligent.

Yes, it turned out to be unintelligent. However, after all it was pursuing a different goal – not the building of communism in USSR, but the consolidation of a personal dictatorship. The screen of "the dictatorship of the proletariat" served ideally as its cover. The faithful pupil of Lenin had been prepared for terror by the environment in which he grew up – for terror not for ideological, but for personal reasons. The theory and practice of the regime justified terror in the struggle with the class enemy. What, though, obstructs calling a friend a class enemy? *"Amicus Plato, sed magis amica veritas"* [Plato is a friend, but truth is a better friend.] If the enemy doesn't surrender, he is destroyed. If he does surrender, is it not more secure to destroy him anyway? Civilization, laws? "The dictatorship of the proletariat" – that's the law.

The exile of Trotsky made the word "Trotskyist" a slanderous label. They dealt with labeled people without hesitation. Opposition had ceased long before, but it had existed at one time! If there ever was opposition that means it might arise again. Stalin desired its physical extirpation. Neither the removal of former oppositionists nor their imprisonment satisfied the Leader. A mountaineer, who grew up with the notion of blood feuds remote from civilization, he wasn't tranquil as long as an enemy lived. In his view, a man who repented was just laying low. "The only good enemy is a dead enemy." The same held for the friend of an enemy, a relative, or someone who had received a post or a rank from the hands of an enemy. The entire nation became Stalin's enemy.

A NEP-man[1] who has money is independent – do away with NEP. A peasant gives part of his crop to the authorities, but controls the rest of it independently – deprive him of both land and bread, turn him into a field-hand, and starve him to death! The worker must work! The government servants must serve! And all must glorify the Leader! Glorify the wickedest antagonist ...

"Fine", opponents were saying (It was unknown to them, just as it is to the author, what sort of further evidence of the Leader's villainy is lurking in the archives), "but what about the eve of the war, when no longer enough generals were available, still shoot them anyway? Such men?? No, this is incomprehensible; there must be something in this!"

Alas, there was nothing in it. Let any reader imagine himself or herself, let us say, in the place of the Chief of the country's Anti-aircraft Defense, Hero of the Soviet Union General Colonel Grigorii Mikhailovich Shtern. You, reader, are now General Colonel Shtern, the hero of Spain, a co-author of Khalkhin-Gol, and a veteran of the fighting in Finland. You are coming to give a report to the Leader:

> German aircraft are continually violating our airspace. Doubtless, they are taking aerial photographs of our airfields. I request your permission, Comrade Stalin, to shoot down the violators. As Chief of the country's Anti-aircraft Defense, I am obligated ...

---

1   Editor's note: A NEP-man was the Soviet slang for a person who engaged in private enterprise under the relaxed conditions of the so-called New Economic Policy (NEP) of 1921-1928, which allowed such activities after the draconian requisitions and rationing of the period of War Communism. If such people did too well under the NEP, they became the target of envy and scorn, and quickly became class enemies when the NEP ended.

You, as Chief of Anti-aircraft Defense, have allowed a German plane to reach Moscow.[2] Shame! Now, as chief of the Anti-aircraft Defense, you are obligated to carry out the orders of your direct superiors."

Just so, Comrade Stalin. But I am obligated to warn you about the possible consequences of our inactivity. The Germans know the location of our airfields, and we don't have time to build new ones within a reasonable amount of time. We must start to build them, we must shoot down the Germans or chase them away, and the aircraft at the air bases must be dispersed and concealed as quickly as possible. In the event of a surprise attack, the Germans will plaster the runways with bombs, but the aircraft will remain undamaged. I request that you issue an instruction on the dispersing and concealing of aircraft at the border air bases."

If we, Comrade Stern, hide our planes at the border air bases, the Germans will have cause to suspect that we don't trust them and that we're planning something. The Anglo-American imperialists are sleeping and dreaming, as if to prod us into a collision with Germany, against which we have protected ourselves by the Non-Aggression Pact. We mustn't panic. We mustn't yield to provocations. In case of necessity, we'll have time to shelter our aircraft."

Comrade Stalin, in order to conceal our aircraft, we'll need days, if not weeks. It is a lot of work! Meanwhile Hitler, as you know, likes to attack without warning."

He won't attack us. We have a Pact with him."

Comrade Stalin, who do you trust more, your Chief of Anti-aircraft Defense or Hitler?

If you, reader, don't say this to the Leader in a conversation like this one, you aren't a patriot of your country. However, you would say it, just as Shtern doubtlessly did. After such a discussion (or the proceedings of a report, or even an utterance in a conversation with someone else, if not the Leader), Shtern was a marked man. After the destruction of the Soviet Air Force in the very first hours of the war, he no longer had a place in life, because he might say later, "I warned you ..."

Decades later, contemporaries of the Boss, whose lives had been mutilated by the senseless cruelty, started after the disgraceful collapse of the country in the early 1990s to go out into the streets with a portrait of the despot bearing the inscription "Correct in everything!" Stupidity? No, an explainable paradox: *having lived through such lives, having sacrificed comforts, their youth and their health, people could not and weren't in the condition to acknowledge that all of this had been in vain*; all the more so, because indeed truly not everything had been in vain. Several generations of romantics were raised and nurtured on abstract ideals, outside of God. The moral qualities of these people have little equal in the history of mankind. These people and their offspring are still alive today and carry

---

2   In view of the ban on intercepting German aircraft, on 15 May 1941 a German Ju-52 crossed the national frontier of the USSR without authorization and without hindrance made a landing in Moscow, on the Khodynskoe Field, this despite the fact that through the efforts of Shtern and his predecessor Ptukhin, Moscow air defenses were superb. As Klaus Reinhardt observes in *Moscow: The Turning Point?*: "A special effort was made to strengthen the Moscow air defence force, thus thwarting Hitler's desire to use the Luftwaffe to 'raze Moscow to the ground'. In fact the air defences around Moscow were on such a scale and so well organized that German pilots considered air raids on the Russian capital to be more dangerous and would involve more air losses than the air raids on London. They also believed that Russian losses in Moscow sustained in the German air raids would remain insignificant."

memories of the war as a great deed ... Whose? Stalin's?

This was an achievement of the people. A people, being driven by hatred and desperation, not by Stalin!

Cities were in ruins, fields were burning, and thousands of defenders of the Motherland were being sacrificed by incompetent commanders on the battlefields, while in prisons people were being finished off with a shot to the back of the head. The Left Socialist Revolutionaries had taken part in the October coup together with the Bolsheviks, and until 6 July 1918 shared power with them. They were the last bulwark of a two-party system. About their leader, Maria Spiridonova, a person of incomparable noblesse, the Great Soviet Encyclopedia informs that she dropped out of political activity and lived in Ufa. That's a lie! In 1937, she was arrested in Ufa and sent to an isolation cell in the Orel prison; that same Orel, into which von Schweppenburg's panzers unexpectedly burst. With the Germans' sudden breakthrough, Spiridonova, who had always hated the Germans, and all the political prisoners being held in the Orel prison were executed by the NKVD literally under the nose of the German tankers. That's how priorities were determined. They frittered away the city – but not the liquidation of political opponents imprisoned in the city. Interesting, isn't it?

Hitler didn't wrap up his dealings with the "old friends" with a massacre of everyone. He judged that having beheaded the *Sturmabteilung* [SA] movement, he would take the place at the head of its storm troopers, merge them into the *Wehrmacht* or even into the SS, and they would serve faithfully and with loyalty.

He set up the "Night of Long Knives". The entire Stalinist period was a "Night of Long Knives".

Hitler initiated a catastrophe with the liquidation of certain nations. Stalin initiated it with a war against his own nation.

An equal sign must be inserted between their two names, but with a footnote: "In treachery, Stalin surpassed Hitler." Hitler was still expounding on this topic, though cynically so. The mountaineer Stalin didn't even ponder it.

Some people maintain, "Yes, he was a villain, but a great one!" The epithet "great" has been customarily applied to designate higher levels of humanity. A poet, a scientist, even a military commander can be great. A villain can only be terrible. Stalin's "greatness" lay in what; his carefully planned the schedule of purges? This was akin to the "greatness" of palace coups. Of all the "greatness" due to Stalin, there remains only the "great damnation" for the fate of a nation, which has long been and continues to face the consequences of Stalin's rule.

Lenin gave the country a sharp trajectory upward. Stalin made it even sharper at a point when Lenin, judging from everything, was planning to relax the stress on the nation. After Stalin, the Party-crats couldn't change the course, which is not surprising, since the control levers were jammed. The Party-crats upheld a pusillanimous trajectory, which proved to be a plunge into an abyss. That's nothing uncommon; such is the fate of despotism ...

45

Turning Point at Moscow

Klaus Reinhardt recounts the reasons for the successful defense of Moscow. According to him, the Mozhaisk Line had deeply echeloned positions that stretched back for 100 kilometers, with both natural and constructed anti-tank obstacles, which permitted the Russians to conduct a gradual, fighting withdrawal to the east. (The Russians paid a dear price for that learned ability to withdraw slowly.) The dense network of railroads and roads facilitated the operational transfer of forces to threatened points. The German Second Air Fleet was targeting an adversary stretched in front of the *Wehrmacht*, but the weather deteriorated,[1] and the Moscow area rail net, attacks upon which were so desirable in order to disrupt the system of movement and flow of supplies, was hardly affected by the Luftwaffe from the middle of October.

The method of conducting combat operations employed by Zhukov also played its role. The Red Army was now fighting on its final line, and Zhukov was doing everything to use his limited forces more effectively. For this purpose he created deeply echeloned anti-tank and artillery defensive strong points on the most dangerous sectors. In addition, tanks were now being used, not only to support the infantry in penny-packets, but also were being concentrated for the fight against German panzers. These measures forced the Germans to break through position after position.

(The reader needs to imagine a patch of terrain with natural and engineered obstacles, and a road with an intersection still distant from the foe. There men and guns would be deployed on the defense, although the men were sometimes barely trained, and the guns had been taken from Moscow's anti-aircraft defenses. These were the forgotten fundamentals of defensive fighting, which the repressed army commanders had developed and been teaching ... Had these principles not been forgotten, the Germans would not have had such dashing marches at the start of the war, even given their surprise attack. There would not have been encirclements, just as there were none in the environs of Moscow after the time when Zhukov assumed command.)

---

1   The weather, of course, had deteriorated, but not to such an extent that a window couldn't be found in it in order to bomb the arteries and concentrations of troops and equipment. The real blessing for the Moscow area railroad net was the Führer's decision on 27 October to relocate the Second Air Fleet to the Mediterranean Sea, while at the same time designating Luftwaffe Field Marshal Kesselring as Commander-in-Chief South. For some strange reason this fact hasn't received sufficient attention in the literature. This decision, which was so timely for Rommel's Afrika Korps, was just as untimely for the offensive on Moscow. Probably the Führer reached this decision on the basis of two factors: the growing difficulties in supplying the air force with fuel in the Soviet Union and the meteorological conditions of the Russian autumn and winter, which were generally unsuitable for flying. The analysis to determine whether this decision was fatal for the course of the war in Russia or had little influence on it is possible only with consideration for the availability of aviation fuel and the Reich's means to supply it to the Eastern Front, and the weather conditions around Moscow between 27 October 1941 and 6 December 1941. One thing which is absolutely clear is that Germany was not prepared for a war of such enormous scale and its resources were too limited relative to Hitler's ambitions.

Reinhardt also points to the factor of morale, and the harsh measures taken by the Soviet administration to strengthen discipline in the troops. These human factors were no less important than the terrain.

The remark about the "limited forces" in Zhukov's hands is accurate only for the first stage of the defense. As the Germans drew nearer to Moscow, their strength was melting away, while the strength of the Red Army was growing. Day and night, reinforcements from Siberia and the Far East were arriving. The fighters were in felt boots and short fur coats. To the east of Moscow, lightly trained but large armies were gathering. They were only grudgingly thrown into the fighting. Stalin was handling the reserves. Did the General Staff even know about them? Zhukov wasn't aware of them, that's for sure. Secrecy!

The Germans supply lines had grown, while the Soviet supply lines had shortened. The Soviet troops maneuvered on the lateral roads behind the lines with great efficiency. Meanwhile, the *Wehrmacht* confronted the winter and fatigue. After all, it had been conducting nearly uninterrupted fighting for many days in order to chew through the Soviet defenses! Without replacements, without rest, without warm clothing, in conditions not typical for a European, in endless expanses, under a gloomy, foreign sky ...

The Red Army troops weren't getting as exhausted. They were being expended too quickly.

In the summer of 1986, I had the opportunity to travel across Germany by train along the Rhine River. I kept my Nikon camera dozing on my lap, just as I had in Switzerland, I could photograph the attractions of Old Europe through the window of the train. Orderly, toy-like little towns, nestled along the cobbled channels of streams and centered upon ancient churches standing in front of little squares, floated past.

I never removed the lens cover. A feeling of dark anger, which I thought I had lost long ago, was gnawing at me. I looked out the window and was struck: Just *what* had dragged them from such beauty and tranquility into the impoverished Russian depths? I didn't take a single photograph, although I had known long ago about the castles along the train track, even though I, as a person banned from travel abroad in the Soviet years, had never even dreamed about such a trip before emigration.

I was also thinking: How had they managed to penetrate so far? However, the objective had been given to them – to reach such a depth, where even scholars feel themselves lost. The *Wehrmacht* was to plunge into an endless wilderness, in comparison with which the Moscow area was a suburban zone. They had even reached this far.

Heroes ...

And more: what sort of inhuman flung them there, as if they truly were those supermen, after which in their wake, ordinary husbands and brothers would be gathered to be nurtured on the lands conquered by them, just like chicks in an incubator under the warming light of Nazism?

Eternal memory to the honorable *Wehrmacht* soldiers, who fell on Russian battlefields! Eternal memory, as a lesson to those who might conceive such ideas! The Nazi leadership persuaded the soldier that the cause was a good one: the eradication of sub-humans. By eradicating them, the soldiers would be carrying out a duty before mankind. However, the soldiers collided with people, with humans just like them. They saw that these humans were no less brave and no less capable of rendering desperate resistance and ready to die in the very heart of their devastated Motherland. It didn't take the best of the German soldiers long to see that they'd been tricked. However, the soldier has no way back. All that he can do is to refuse to take part in matters, for which volunteers are being called and for which volunteers can always be found, because to kill the unarmed is a safer business. As for the adversary, well, his cause was just, and he indeed expected no mercy.

Meanwhile, the temperatures were plummeting. On 5 December, the temperature dropped to -28° Celsius [-19° F.]. The pendulum had swung to its full extent – and had become frozen. The Soviet command knew how it was to the German soldier, unhabituated to such a winter, dressed in a summer uniform and tattered boots.

46

Interlude: The General Staff ...

.. in the meantime was intensively teaching the Leader to fight, giving him the grade of A for defeats, while it was scratching along between Cs and Fs itself. Such training, naturally, didn't come cheaply, but after all the country was rich in resources: ores of different metals, massive forests, oil here and there ... and certainly not short of people.

The contributions of the Boss to the defense of Moscow are doubtless. He fully demonstrated the know-how to pressure and to squeeze. Troops were hurrying from the Far East and from neighboring fronts. Already in the two weeks immediately following the destruction of the Western and Reserve Fronts, seventeen divisions and all the available artillery were concentrated at the area of the breakthrough. The troops were moving with haste, limited only by the capabilities of the railroad and the endurance of the soldiers' feet. The city was bristling with anti-tank obstacles, ditches, scarps and counterscarps, earthen bunkers and concrete pillboxes.

In the list of factors that played a role in the defense of Moscow, the presence of the Leader has been intentionally placed at the end by me. His main merit was the fact that he didn't flee. He was about to abandon the city, but realized in time: Moscow was his shell; without Moscow, he was as doomed as a mollusk left without its shell. However, by remaining in Moscow, he could contribute to the holding of the habitable bastion with his qualities as an administrator. Thus it was out of these considerations, not at all out of bravery, that Stalin chose not to abandon the capital. He wasn't brave. His years of underground training had made him clever.

For the defense of Moscow, the Leader became so skilled in using the blood of Red Army troops that he began to understand a smattering of the respectful explanations of the General Staff officers: "They say that the idiot Hitler has even now split his forces, directing them both against Moscow and toward the Caucasus. He wants, Comrade Stalin, for us to do the same thing ... However we, pursuant to your genius instructions ... right? ... won't split our forces; we have enough as it is, and we'll give him a hard rap, right? Then we'll seize the initiative in the south, right?"

I will refer those who are interested in the Red Army's counterattack at Rostov to the memoirs of one of its participants, Marshal (at the time Major-General) Bagramian. The Soviet forces, as they had done at Smolensk, were trying to catch the enemy's pincers with tongs of their own, but they were still unable to operate in a coordinated fashion, and didn't venture to act as inexorably as they would a year later, at Stalingrad, and indeed they didn't have enough strength yet. Replacement tanks had all been drawn into the battle for Moscow, and it wasn't simple to attack an enemy equipped with panzers without this shock weapon, or even to plan such an attack by replacing the armor with cavalry. Yet nevertheless the counterattacking Red Army seized the initiative from the hands of the attacking enemy in the south. I bring this to the reader's attention for three reasons.

First, the signal for the Moscow counteroffensive was given by what happened at Rostov. There the Red Army counterattacked the still attacking von Kleist – and succeeded![1] Now God himself was ordering to go on the offensive against the frozen enemy in front of Moscow.

Second, for an illustration of the fact that the Stalingrad pocket wasn't conceived out of thin air by the genius of the generals (and, of course, the Leader together with them); the generals had their own achievements in the Stalingrad operation, but the reader by no means can guess yet what the nature of these achievements were ....

Third, in November 1942 Hitler ordered Paulus to dare not retreat his Sixth Army, recalling a similar situation, from which von Kleist had emerged with honor a year earlier. (Possibly he also recalled Kiev, which saved Moscow, and understood: the Sixth Army was now for him what Kiev had been for Stalin.) It wasn't Hitler who ordered von Kleist to abandon Rostov, but von Rundstedt. With the capture of Rostov, the Führer saw himself as on the doorstep of Baku; von Rundstedt's order threw him into hysterics, and he removed the Field Marshal from command of Army Group South. Von Rundstedt had been correct, but this didn't serve as a lesson to Hitler. After Rostov, by demanding his troops to defend fixed positions to the death, he averted a German catastrophe at Moscow!

He prevented one – and became unapproachable, which prepared the grounds for the disaster at Stalingrad. In the 1942 campaign he gave orders autocratically, and didn't take into account that a year had passed since the Moscow battle, and that he no longer faced Budenny, but a Pleiades of new stars of the Red Army.

Of course, it is easy to slap von Kleist with the accusation that he shouldn't have taken Rostov in the first place. However, as it happens, the military profession, as Bagramian noted, is unavoidably a risky one. If von Kleist doesn't deserve any particular merits for capturing Rostov, then in the retreat from the city he demonstrated top-notch skills. That's just what the Führer had been expecting Paulus to try, that he would try to break out at any moment, unaware of the toughness of the Russian jaws around Stalingrad and assuming that it was never too late to retreat.

The reader might recall how the great von Moltke commendably rejected a comparison between himself and Frederick the Great, by saying that he, Moltke, never had to conduct a retreat – the most complex maneuver in war. Von Rundstedt didn't ignore the movements of the Southern Front and didn't dally with the order to retreat. However, von Kleist was forced to retreat directly from the attack, without a transition. In the withdrawal, he demonstrated superb skill and an iron resolve.

In contrast, the Red Army General Staff wilted under the fixed gaze of its menacing pupil. That is something understandable: there was no Knights Hospitaller of St. John of Jerusalem on the General Staff. Better to tear a rag than to lose one.

However, this wasn't a rag they might have picked up. Kleist was fortunate. (Fortunate .. he died in a Vladimir prison in 1954.) Well, it's an honor to fight against such a commander as Ewald von Kleist.

---

[1]   Theoretically the same thing could have threatened von Bock had he attacked Moscow in August, leaving Kiev uncaptured. The decisive difference is in the much worse shape of the *Wehrmacht* in November relative to August, when the correlation of forces had been much more in its favor; Guderian's, Hoepner's and Kleist's tanks were less worn out; the supply of fuel was made easier by the dry weather and roads; and the men were less exhausted.

Kleist, though, couldn't hide one thing: the *Wehrmacht* was played out. A signal came to the General Staff and its pupil from the south; this helped eliminate their remaining doubts about the enemy's ebbing activity on the frozen fields near Moscow.

47

The Turning Point at Moscow: The Conclusion

It didn't come to this, but it almost happened; almost spontaneously, like a horse compressing a powerful steel coil. It was moving against it, always forward, onward, pressing its chest against the spring, digging its weakening hooves into the slightest molehill and uneven bit of ground – and suddenly the earth freezes, the molehills vanish, the hooves slip without the traction. The spring hurls the exhausted horse backward, backward! Simply with the Red Army's next counterattack – they had never ceased, disregarding the losses – the Germans began to give way. Then the Red Army command increased the pressure, added more strength; the reserves were nearby and available. Ultimately the Soviet command began to improvise: there was no plan.

There was no plan! Let's jump ahead, and there you can judge for yourself, reader. These excerpts are from Zhukov's memoirs.

> April 1943:
> ... the situation on the Kursk Bulge stabilized, both sides getting ready for the decisive battle. It was time to get down to planning the Kursk battle."
> April 1944:
> In outlining my suggestions for the plan of the summer campaign of 1944, I particularly drew Stalin's notice to the enemy group in Belorussia, with whose defeat the enemy defenses on the entire western strategic direction would collapse.
> 'What does the General Staff think about that?' Stalin asked A. I. Antonov.
> 'I agree,' said the latter.
> I did not see Stalin press the button of the buzzer which summoned A. N. Poskrebyshev. The latter entered the office and stopped, awaiting orders.
> 'Put me through to Vasilevsky,' said Stalin.
> A couple of minutes later, A. N. Poskrebyshev reported that A. M. Vasilevsky was on the line.
> 'Good day,' Stalin began. 'Zhukov and Antonov are here with me. Do you think you could fly in for some consultations about the plan for the summer? ... What is the situation at Sevastopol? ... Very well, stay there then, but send your suggestions for the summer period to me personally.'

This is what must be called planning. Now let's go back to where we started, in November 1941:

> On December 1 the German forces unexpectedly made a breakthrough in the central sector at the boundary between the 5th and 33rd Armies and began advancing along the highway towards Kubinka ... Elimination of the breakthrough was completed on

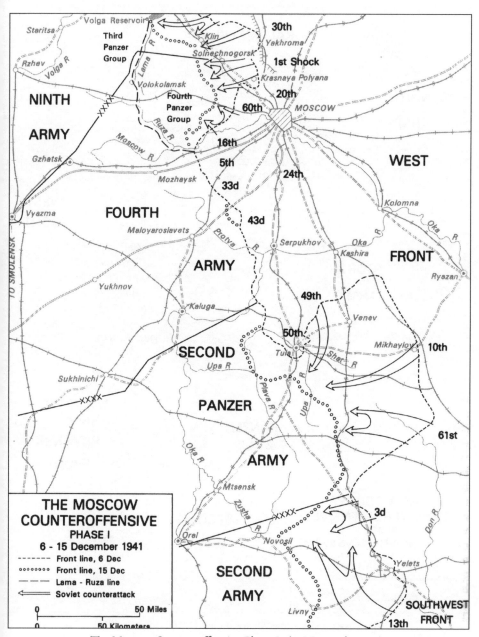

The Moscow Counteroffensive Phase I, 6-15 December 1941

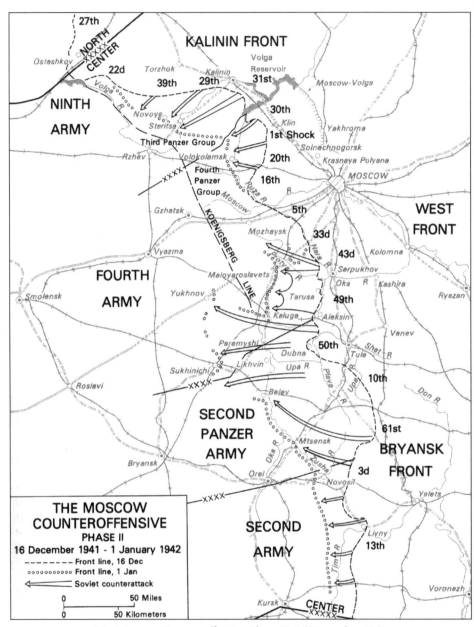

The Moscow Counteroffensive Phase II, 16 December 1941

December 4 ...

From the nature of the operations and the strength of attacks of all the enemy groupings it became obvious that the Germans were losing strength and did not have either the manpower or the weapons to continue the offensive ...

On November 29 I called up the Supreme Commander and, having reported the situation, asked him for orders that would put the 1st Shock Army and 10th Army under the control of the Western Front ... Stalin said he would discuss this with the General Staff.

Late on November 29 we were informed that the 1st Shock and the 10th Armies as well as all the units of the 20th Army passed, by GHQ decision, to the control of the Western Front. At the same time General Headquarters ordered us to send in our plan of operation for these armies.

In the morning of November 30 we reported to GHQ our plan of action ...

Indeed, this is what must be called improvising. Incidentally, it is in the description of the Moscow battles that Zhukov first mentions von Mellenthin (in connection with the assertion that an attack on Moscow instead of Kiev would have been a stab in the heart. Zhukov responds emotionally, but not argumentatively.) It is precisely in this section that there are the fewest insertions in the latest edition of Zhukov's memoirs ...

The British historian Richard Overy gives a description of the events different from Zhukov's on the basis of General Belov's testimony. Early on the morning of 30 November Stalin called Zhukov and ordered the planning of a counterattack, which would end the threat to Moscow. Zhukov replied that he had neither the men nor the equipment for such a counterattack. Stalin ordered him to come for a meeting. The evening of the same day, he received Zhukov and Belov and announced that reserves from Siberia and the Far East had been gathered at Moscow. Zhukov didn't even know about these reserves or their numerical strength.[1] Overy, without naming his sources, believes that *there were no less than twelve armies*. They weren't rich with either artillery or tanks, but the troops were warmly dressed, equipped with skis and sledges, and the horses were accustomed to overcoming deep snow and snowdrifts.

Belov-Overy's version explains Zhukov's lack of psychological readiness for a major offensive operation. What's there to plan, having at hand 240,000 thousand troops, when back in October a million more had been dug-in on the defensive, expecting a winter offensive and finding themselves in a complete debacle? By preparation comes the result. Again the Leader was being overly secretive.

Yes, for Hitler the presence of enormous Russian reserves also came as such a surprise that he didn't believe the aerial reconnaissance. He literally didn't trust his own eyes. After all their losses, the Russians couldn't have such reserves! (To disbelieve facts is a privilege of despots. A half a year later, Stalin refused to believe in Operation Blau, and with the very same results.) However, these reserves came as such a surprise to Zhukov as well that

---

[1]   This isn't the only thing that Stalin kept concealed from Zhukov. Only at the end of his life did Zhukov find out that Hitler's corpse had been found. Yet he didn't learn this from official sources, but from the writer Elena Rzhevskaia, who had been serving as a translator at Front headquarters in 1945 and was brought to identify the body. The Marshal muttered, "Stalin was close to me like with no one else." He was sadly bewildered. He couldn't understand why Stalin had hidden this from him. Who can understand the long range logic of a tyrant?

his plan, worked out in great haste while the *Wehrmacht* still hadn't entrenched, didn't become the plan of the general offensive. There was nothing for such an offensive, other than cannon fodder. No aviation, no ammunition, no intelligence. Moreover, the Red Army was compelled to begin with clipping off the pincers around Moscow. Thus there was no cooperation between the fronts. Alternatives were not exploited. They didn't know what to do once certain lines were reached. They didn't agree to a timetable for reaching phase lines in order to enable joint development of the success. Since there was no plan, the Leader had scope to stick his nose into any ostensibly successful moment with orders – to drive a wedge in both here and there, and somewhere else, dissipating strength in a spasmodic drive to the west.

Drive a wedge without armor wedges? The Germans were fighting desperately, trying not to be outflanked. Oh, how the Leader meddled with his improvisations! Emboldened by the freezing temperatures, the General Staff's star pupil decided that he no longer needed the advice of the military commanders and began snatching armies away suddenly (as he did with the 1st Shock Army) from directions that held out promises of success; he in alliance with the winter would teach his military a thing or two!

The *Wehrmacht*, recoiling, received an opportunity to retreat and got organized. Once they reached a suitable line, they turned and put up a ferocious defense.

However, setting aside all of this, how can I express what the turning point at Moscow became for all of us, the refugees who'd become dejected and depressed with defeats? How can I express our despair in October and our jubilation in December? Except perhaps to use a far-reaching comparison and call it that drop of water, in which one can see the ocean.

48

From the Point of View of a Water Drop

It had turned warm by the beginning of June 1941. On the occasion of an excellent finish of her academic year, my parents allowed my sister to have a party. I was playing on the balcony, while in the dining room, a gramophone was playing such songs as the fox-trot "*Rio-Rita*" and the tango "*Utomlennoe solntse ...*" ["*The Tired Sun*"] and a song with the lines "*Chaika smelo proletela ...nu-ka chaika, otvechai-ka, liubit ili net?*" ["The seagull boldly flew over ...Now then, seagull, answer me, does she love me or not?"]. The evening was warm, the sun was glowing at the end of our avenue and illuminating the balcony, on which my toy soldiers were engaged in a bloodless war. My sister's classmates were chatting and dancing in the dining room, but every now and then she would come out onto the balcony and introduce me to the older boys. Two of her classmates, Arnol'd and Apollon, both good-looking lads, gave me the latest the MOPR and GTO[1] pins to add to my trading collection. The handsome Arnol'd was going out of his way to impress my sister, striking poses and singing arias. Alik, with his buzz cut and dressed in his naval cadet uniform, was behaving modestly. My sister had become acquainted with him at the skating rink in the Dinamo Stadium. The older boys treated me condescendingly; only Alik talked with me as an equal. At his 19 years-of-age, Alik was a well-grounded, mature young man. Arnol'd, sensing that Alik presented serious competition, stretched his hand toward my sister and was swearing that he would leap from the balcony if she rejected his love for her.

The party broke up early, even before it grew dark outside. My sister complimented me; her classmates had liked me, but her mood was somewhat somber. She didn't know which one to choose. Arnol'd was more sophisticated, but such a chatterbox! Alik was solid, but a bit too serious. My sister had never before consulted with me in this way. I spoke up for Alik.

Who could know then what lay in front of these lads? Only Alik returned from the war. As it was back then, of every 100 young men from the same recruitment class, only four came back from the war. Meanwhile my sister, a pampered city girl, already within a month after the party was working alongside adults at a collective farm ...

... We drove out of Kiev on the evening of 4 July. The Germans were 65 kilometers from the city center. There were several families in the back of the one-and-a-half ton GAZ-MM truck. We drove along desolate country roads and on the evening of 5 July we arrived in Konotop. The railway station was jammed with trains and refugees. A freight train was brought up on the afternoon of 6 July on one of the last available routes. The boarding was frenzied, the situation nerve-wracking. We didn't wind up in a *teplushka* [a freight car refitted to carry about forty-odd people and often weakly heated by a small iron stove] but instead on an open flatcar.

The train set off, having boarded all the refugees, and immediately it began to pour with rain. I was sick. My parents took out the things from the single suitcase in our baggage and distributed them among bags, and then having spread a blanket in the suitcase, they

---

1   Editor's note: MOPR – *Mezhdunarodnaia organizatsiia pomoshchi rabochim* [International Organization of Assistance to Workers]; GTO – *Gotov k trudu I oborone* [Ready for labor and defense].

arranged me inside it. They closed the lid and I had shelter from the rain. An hour later the train stopped. The train commandant and his team started running down the length of the train. Soon they ordered us to get off the flatcar and distributed us among the *teplushkas*: they were crowding those, who had already situated themselves comfortably in them. The trains back at the railway stations had crowded the tracks and were a juicy target for the Luftwaffe. It is striking, but already by then, just some two weeks after the start of the war a method of quickly loading and dispatching trains from stations had been worked out. These open flatcars were attached to each train as a temporary accommodation, only for the purpose of getting people away from the station and the danger of air raids. Once away from the station, they would pack the boxcars with people, and this promptly developed methodology was one of the features of that enormous accomplishment of the Soviet railroads, the evacuation of people and loads, which still awaits adequate description.

The train idled and the train crew packed the *teplushkas*, while the sound of heavy, muffled explosions carried to us from the direction of Konotop. A day later, we learned from people on the following train that just after we had departed, Konotop was subjected to a heavy bombing, and movement along the Moscow Southwest artery was halted for more than a day. An indirect confirmation of the success of this raid is the fact that the train, which evacuated my cousin Liubov' Zhivotskaia-Kats with her sister and mother from Kiev on 6 July, didn't head to the northeast out of Kiev (toward Konotop) or to the east (toward Iagotin), but south, toward Belaia Tserkov', and only after reaching that place did it head east. During the stop of their train in Belaia Tserkov', that place also underwent a bombing and strafing attacks that resulted in numerous casualties. The spreading of terror and panic became one of the *Wehrmacht's* tactical novelties, and the Luftwaffe took advantage of this in full measure. During one bombing attack east of Konotop, a young boy, who was my age was killed; we had left Kiev together on the same truck and were riding from Konotop in the same boxcar.

On 12 July we were unloaded at some out-of-the-way station and trucked to different villages in the area. Our family wound up in the village of Chuvakhlei, in Gor'kii Oblast's Vadsky District. The village was near a forested area, where there was logging work.

On 2 or 3 October, rumors about the latest German offensive reached us – it is interesting that rumors traveled so quickly from the Moscow area to a backwater village!! It hadn't been announced over the radio, much less in the newspapers!! We set out on a new stage of evacuation. In a wagon, covered with burlap, under an autumn drizzle we were hauled half the day to some railroad station, and there we waited for a train heading to the east. We spent the night waiting on wooden station benches with hard armrests. I weakly lolled on one of them, trying to fall asleep, and the bench planks kept digging into my ribs.

The train – a real one, a passenger train – pulled into the station that night already overfilled, and the process of boarding it proceeded like a brawl. We elbowed our way into one car only thanks to my uncle, the husband of my mother's deceased sister; he was a sinewy fighting cock of a man, who didn't yield to anyone. We traveled two nights and a day, though possibly just one night. I lost track of the days because of my sleeplessness. I remember that we arrived in Cheboksary in the morning. Most likely, we spent that night in the station armchairs in Cheboksary in the unsuccessful attempt to buy tickets for a train: a gloomy torrent of evacuees was streaming to the south and east and there was no possibility to leave Cheboksary aboard a train.

The adults by that time had heard all the stories. You see, after the boarding of the train had finished, almost all of those who'd been working with their fists and elbows turned out to be the kindest sort of people. Hardly had the train set out when the process of reconciliation began, and even the sharing of boiled water and bread, or else even pieces of hardtack. Sufferings were being shared, our own and others' experiences, and people talked about their misfortunes and losses. Still on the approach to the Volga, my parents learned of the advantage that trains had over steamboats and barges. The edge was only one: at the signal of an air attack, one could leap off the train and hide in a field or forest. The fall of a bomb on a boat meant certain death for everyone. There was no way out, yet the adults probably considered the immediate death of all to a certain extent as a preferable outcome.

I dimly recall the embarkation on the paddlewheel steamboat *Semnadtsatyi god* [Year 1917]. The boat was full of passengers beyond capacity. We headed down the Volga. In October on the Volga, it wasn't very comfortable out on the open deck. Some member of the ship's crew took pity on us (I was 7 years-old, my cousin 9) and let our family onto the staircase leading down to the engine compartment. We settled with our belongings on a flat steel platform that had a surface textured with little diamonds (to prevent slips), trying to take up as little space as possible. The engine compartment down below exuded the smell of heated engine oil and lulled us with the rhythmic clatter of the steam engine. On the second day, the crew squeezed us into the crowd of people on the lower common deck.

The first day of our voyage, a Messerschmitt strafed the steamboat. It was flying just above the river and attacked us from the stern.[2] On the second day we floated past the Zhiguli Heights, which were drenched with the rosy light of the setting sun and struck me with their beauty.

We sailed for three days to Kuibyshev and spent three more days in the city – one day on the streets under light snow flurries, then on suitcases and bundles in dark, cold entryways. The weather was sullen, and flurries alternated with rain. The last evening we warmed ourselves up for several hours in a local family's apartment. The hosts sent the last batch of refugees on their way and invited us inside. There, before our trip to the railroad depot, my sister and I for the first time in three days drank hot tea and listened through our dozing to the cheerless conversations of the adults. The city was overcrowded and filled with gloomy rumors. Nobody believed the newspapers. This was still a week before the Moscow panic. With such chaos unfolding in the rear zone, one can imagine what the effectiveness of the evacuated governmental agencies in Kuibyshev, Kazan' and Ufa would have been, as indeed the effectiveness of all the resistance in general, had the capital fallen.

What about in the zone of the front lines? Here and there, the population, embittered by the retreat of the Red Army, developed a hatred for the occupiers, and in those places the popularity of the collective farms even grew. However, in other places the Germans were greeted as liberators – with icons and prayers, celebrating the opening of churches and the end to Bolshevik atheism, and hoping for the dissolution of the collective farms.

Today Western historians, even the most insightful, allow no thought to the possibility of a Soviet defeat (though in 1941, Western military experts gave the Soviet regime only

---

2   This happened somewhere between 4 and 7 October 1941. For some time I deliberated over whether or not to tell the story of what occurred to me in that area between Arzamas and Gor'kii with the Messerschmitt. Then pilots, veterans of the war, explained to me that with drop tanks, the German fighter could fly as far as Gor'kii (Nizhnii Novgorod). A cousin reminded me of the episode on the steamboat, when out of curiousity I clambered up onto the deck in order to get a better view of the strafing Messerschmidt, and my cousin dragged me by the feet back down into the ship's hold.

three weeks to three months of further survival). Mesmerized by the Soviet expanses, the Soviet efforts, the Soviet losses and, in the final result, the victory, historians can't imagine the situation in October 1941. Yet what if the attack on Moscow had taken place in August?

The men in our group spent two days around the clock, standing in lines to purchase tickets at the train station in Kuibyshev. Self-appointed guardians of order kept track of the number with chalk on the backs of jackets and coats. We boarded the train at night. It was full, but everyone had a seat. That meant that in Kuibyshev, the sale of tickets and the loading of the trains remained under the control of the railroad administration. Ten days dragged along in the passenger car on the way to Tashkent. There was general hunger. Evacuation points supplied the refugees with boiled water and served as places where people could leave behind notes in the hope of finding loved ones. Evacuation points were places for checking in the sick, but only singletons. Families were trying to conceal their sick members, fearing that they'd become separated or kicked-off the train. The evacuation points at train stations and city post offices became places where fates crossed paths. Heartbreaking scenes became common there – the reunion of families and the receipt of news about individuals long gone missing. People were always milling around these places, and the walls were festooned with notes like: "Sofochka, we're going to Alma-Ata. David was killed near Kiev. The Fridmans."

The evacuation points must be mentioned in particular in connection with the emptiness gaping on this great page of the evacuation. Already by the first stage of our journey, they'd been set-up in all the major rail stations. Interestingly, they'd been organized even before the Leader had recollected himself and begun to lead again; even before his henchmen had dragged him in front of the microphone for his celebrated speech. Thus, the decree of the Cheliabinsk City Soviet's Executive Committee on the reception of evacuated people was adopted on 27 June 1941, with the instruction that reception stations for the evacuated must be ready by 7:00 pm. on 29 June. This took place before the State Defense Committee was created on 30 June, while the Leader made his address to the nation only on 3 July.

In a word, the evacuation points were created almost spontaneously even before we set out on our way. The initiative for their creation plainly goes to the railroad workers and medics, veterans of the First World War. Detecting the sharp increase in population migration and recalling the Civil War with all its charms – the overcrowding, which threatened the sudden outbreak of epidemics, the infant mortality, and the constant stream of wounded – they right away, perhaps even in the first hours of the war issued a departmental order about evacuation points. They came under the control of the Main Military-Sanitary Department of the Red Army. Their aim initially was to serve trains carrying the wounded, but seeing the effectiveness of them, their functions were expanded, and they quickly began to offer various forms of assistance not only to trains carrying the wounded, but also trains carrying the evacuated families and people.

How far did the responsibility of the evacuation points extend for supplying boiled water? The chief of the evacuation station was responsible for everything other than traffic and track maintenance, and boiled water was the first among his concerns – and the main objective for refugees at stops. The majority of refugees were evacuated in *teplushkas*, which were not equipped with water boilers. Without this boiled water, without the boiling of water, it would have been impossible to count the human losses of the war. Indeed in general, against the backdrop of the total confusion, these evacuation points were focal points of organization and order, where one could obtain both information and some sort of food, even if it was meager. They not only saved hundreds of thousands of lives, perhaps even millions of them, but they also played an enormous role in keeping up morale.

Those, who will be reading these pages, will likely think that the boiled water on the journey was used in order to dissolve soup concentrates or make oatmeal and will be surprised to find out that nothing like this existed in the USSR. That is to say that there might have been such things for Arctic or Antarctic expeditions. However, in everyday life food concentrates in the form of porridge and soups appeared only after the war, most likely from unused military stores of Lend-Lease items. In the war, the first concentrate, with which we became familiar and elicited our delight, was powdered eggs from American food shipments. But en route to our destinations during the evacuation, the boiled water was used directly: we drank it. It was fine, if you could camouflage, so to speak, the boiled water with dried carrot chips or traces of milk under the guise of "tea with cream", which had not even a whiff of tea in it. If there was sugar, even just a small piece, this was considered a luxury. Most often we drank the boiled water accompanied by a piece of bread, and sometimes even without that.

In Tashkent, the square in front of the train station appeared to be a bivouac of soldiers of General Anders' Army.[3] They were sleeping on the grass of the square, sitting in little circles or alone, or wandering around the square. Greenish greatcoats, perplexed faces and searching glances from under the bills of their caps ... Our parents, scarcely having made arrangements for us for the day, rushed off to the post office. There they found a note waiting for them from my aunt: she and her son were heading to Namangan. This was ominous news. It meant that her husband and mother, my uncle and grandmother, remained in occupied Kiev. Nothing was known about what was happening there.

We stormed the train to Namangan. My parents shoved me into one railcar through a window. The overcrowded trains became the incubators of diseases.

On our way, news became totally inaccessible, but the rumors were becoming more horrifying. There were rumors about everything. According to them, life had already gone to ruin. There wasn't a single popular artist or singer, about which people were not saying that either he or she had died or had gone over to the Germans. Among the deceased they counted such stars of the screen as Leonid Utesov and Mark Bernes; among the turncoats they listed Lyubov' Orlova and Ivan Kozlovsky.[4] In these conditions, being impressionable was deadly, while skepticism and incredulity were saving.

On 25 October, at 6:00 pm, we arrived in Namangan. The Fergana Valley is a dead-end; there was nowhere to proceed. It was the wondrous Central Asian autumn. The wave of evacuation had reached a city, in which the food prices hadn't risen yet, and the flapjacks that I feasted upon at the bazaar the next morning, after being hungry for so long in the

---

3   Editor's note: This is a reference to the Polish Armed Forces in the East, formed almost totally of thousands of Polish prisoners of war released from Soviet prisons after Stalin abrogated all of the existing pacts with Nazi Germany, including the Non-Aggression Pact, following the German 1941 invasion. The Polish ultimately formed four infantry divisions and were commanded by General Wladislaw Anders, who was released from the Lubianka prison on August 4, 1941. Anders Army eventually was allowed to go to Iran, where it came under British command as the Polish Second Corps.

4   Editor's note: Happily, Utesov and Bernes survived the war and lived for many years after it, while Kozlovsky remained a favorite of Stalin's throughout the war, often invited to Stalin's dacha for private performances, and Liubov Orlova continued to act in Soviet films after the war – something quite unlikely if she had betrayed her homeland during the war.

passenger car, were delectable. My joy was short-lived. On 28 October a red rash broke out on me and I was sent to a hospital with a high fever (the same day Shtern, Smushkevich and Loktionov were executed ... what did we know about that?)

Hospitals had the reputation of being a direct route to a morgue, but there was no choice. The doctors' diagnosis was scarlet fever and measles. With this bouquet they placed me in a ward with one other bed. On it, laying on her back, a young girl about my age was quietly dying from pneumonia. She wasn't moaning, and I didn't understand that she was dying, but I'll never forget her pallid little face with its delicate features in a cloud of blonde, disheveled hair. She passed away on the third day. I recall the bustling around the bed on the opposite wall and the ominous silence that descended. Nurses began to scurry, they draped sheets around the bed, while they rolled me into a small room without a window, a tiny utility room. I was doing poorly. From an outside perspective, I was also dying quietly: to add to the combination of scarlet fever and measles, which caused the doctors to furrow their brows, I developed bronchitis.

I woke up and saw my mother and father. The hospital was kept under strict quarantine; no one was allowed to enter it. I understood the meaning of this visit only years later. At the time it cheered me up that, in distinction from the ordinary visits which involved standing mournfully under the window of the ward, my mother hadn't brought me anything to eat. The thought of food was repugnant to me. We were fed something, but I remember only kasha. The doctors were luminaries from major cities in the western part of the country, but as medicines they had only aminopyrine, streptocide (white and red) and sulfonamide – in limited quantity. They had limitless amounts of castor oil. They were going to give me a blood transfusion – if they could find someone to donate blood. They tried to get some from Mama, but her veins had collapsed out of lack of food and weakness, so the nurse couldn't collect any blood from her. My father offered his arm, the nurse immediately found a vein, and the syringe became filled with blood. I remember watching the syringe filling with blood, but I don't understand how this became stuck in my memory. The nurse transfused this blood into one of my buttocks. My parents departed, I fell asleep – and I woke up two days later.

I was transferred back to the common ward, where I came under the charge of a gaunt old man with a shaved head, like everyone else's, Kuz'ma Timofeevich, a soldier of the First World War and Civil War. He had persuaded the doctors to allow him to care for his four-year-old grandson, with whom he situated himself on the same bed. In the dry, spacious ward, he, obviously accustomed to poverty, literally felt as if he was in a palace. He looked after me, like he did his grandson, and distracted me with conversations. I didn't have much to say, but I listened to him gratefully and often fell asleep to his words. Waking up, I would see the slumping Kuz'ma Timofeevich on his grandson's bed, and in the window beyond a wasteland, a long, two-story building, with its windows all lined up in rows. I don't recall a single sunny day; only the building's gray façade and the gray sky. I spent hours gazing at the darkened windows of the façade. They became for me a melancholy symbol of the autumn of 1941.

The sick children were silent; it was never noisy in our ward, although there was a whole kindergarten of us in it. A loudspeaker transmitted the ticking of a metronome, interrupted occasionally by reports; from the mumbling of the announcer there was nothing cheery. The winter for the Fergana Valley was unusually severe; snow was falling already in December. As it happened, even Kuz'ma Timofeevich had run out of words to say.

Then suddenly the radio speaker came to life. A festive, joyous voice announced: "From the Sovinformburo! In the last hour!"[5] I don't remember the words, but the music! Parade music ... Ippolitov-Ivanov's *Triumphal March*. That is how the turning point at Moscow arrived for me, though I didn't understand the significance of the music. There was no longer the ticking of the metronome. Marches!

A wave of fever accompanied the wave of refugees. They were being hauled along in packed trains, without washing, for long weeks. The only hospital in the city was overflowing with patients; recovering patients were placed two to a bed, foot to head. I was laid together with a sharp-nosed little boy, who was agile and really helped me manage with the semolina we were often fed. Close to 20 December, Mama came for me, but the doctors cancelled my discharge: they had detected another rash on me and held me, to make sure that it wasn't endemic typhus. In return, Kuz'ma Timofeevich filled me with his wisdom for another two days. (In 1943, we met in the city and chatted: how to scrounge food, who had recovered, who had died ...)

Then my Mama came for me again, took me by the hand, carried me off, then set me down, in order to catch her breath, and I said that I could walk on my own. So off we went. Our household turned out to be a tall, damp adobe storage building with an earthen floor dotted with puddles, and there were five families living in it. At an offer of something to eat I asked for a two-egg omelette, which was presented to me without a murmur, and I gobbled it down quickly, since fifteen pairs of hungry eyes were contemplating my feast.

In February Mama and my sister took me to a public bath. The water was barely warm. They washed their hair with kerosene, then with water and household soap. Right there, in the women's section, they washed me as well: my father had gone as a volunteer to the labor front. From the bath we went to a cinema, and I watched the documentary film, *Razgrom nemetskikh voisk pod Moskvoi* [The crushing defeat of the German troops at Moscow].

The local Uzbek population didn't go to the movie theaters. There were around twenty of us evacuees in the theater. Mama and my sister sat on either side of me and held my hands in theirs. Mama kept silent and my sister cried quietly. The theater wasn't cheering the victorious scenes in the film, and gasped only twice – when gallows in Volokolamsk appeared on the screen, and then the face of the tortured and hanged Zoia Kosmodem'ianskaia, frozen in unendurable and most noble suffering, her head shorn like a little boy's.

The *Marsh zashchitnikov Moskvy* [*March of the Moscow Defenders*] played throughout the entire film, a composition of words and melodies incomparable in the strength of its emotional impact. It was the second most popular song after *Sviashchennaia voina* [*Sacred war*], which prompts shivers even in the young contemporary listener.

German songs are fine. They are sung in a bouncy major key with a broad smile, like the famous *Deutsch Soldaten und die Offizieren* ...

The Russian singing tradition is in the minor key:

We'll not flinch in the battle,
Moscow warms our hearts,
Precious capital, dear to us all.
With a defense – a wall of steel,

---

5   Later as an adult, I learned that the date of this broadcast was 9 December 1941.

With invincible will
We will smash and extinguish the foe.[6]

From this menacing song in the minor key, which accompanied the footage of war ruins, corpses and the desecration of valuables, blazed up something that was impossible to overcome and which later needed to be suppressed by an active mental effort for an entire lifetime.

Not the evacuation under fire, not the death that passed by me three times, but the gallows at Volokolamsk and the women wailing over the frozen corpses of their loved ones to the accompaniment of that menacing song in the minor key became for me the start of the Great Patriotic War of the Soviet people against the Nazi aggressors. (Later in emigration I found out that this documentary film became the first Russian film to be awarded an Oscar. It was not without reason. The film did a good job ...) The documentary's scenes ignited my feelings of wrath toward the Germans, and they remained fixed on them until I saw a second film: *Geroi ne umiraiut*. The maturation of my feelings runs between these two films. The latter film began the erosion of my hostility toward the Germans, who were following their Führer. My antagonism toward them found a solid footing on the factor of causation and began to swing toward the main guilty party in the tragedy – toward the Genius Leader, "who was correct in everything", and who offered the Germans an opportunity that was hard to resist.[7]

---

6   Translation by Valentina Kucher.
7   On 5 May 1941 the German military attaché reported to Franz Halder, the Chief of Staff of the OKH, that the Soviet military leadership was "decidedly bad".

49

The Genius

The Germans were driven back from Moscow, and the Genius of All Times and Peoples became encouraged. He ordered a general offensive along the entire front, with the goal, not only to liberate the area between Moscow and Smolensk, but also to win back Khar'kov in the south and even to force crossings of the Dnepr to create bridgeheads for taking Dnepropetrovsk and Zaporozh'e. With this order, he began to teach his generals, though not without the benefit of hindsight. Here is an example of his instructions from a Directive of the *Stavka* of the Supreme High Command. I cannot refuse myself the satisfaction of citing this directive, if not in full, then at least to the extent cited by Zhukov, who doubtlessly considered this pearl of military wisdom to be significant. Otherwise, why would he have quoted it? I cannot refrain from adding my own accompanying acidic parenthetical comments:

> To secure successes in 1942, our troops must learn to break through the enemy's defense line, to organize the breaches to their entire depth, and thus open the way for our infantry, our tanks, and our cavalry. (Stalin: 'If I fail to add the word "our", then I'm afraid that my dunderhead generals will think that we must open the way for German infantry, German tanks, and German cavalry.') The Germans have more than one defense line – they are building and will soon have a second and a third. If our troops do not learn to breach swiftly and thoroughly (Stalin: 'Given the following verb, it is possible to get by without these words, but then something will be missing; it won't sound emphatic, and I am loathe to discard the word "breach", which is a good word, a meaningful word.) and to break through the enemy's defense line, our advance will become impossible ...[1]

Penetrating analysis, one may say. Yes, the Germans were building so many defense lines, so extending their defenses in depth, so fortifying hills and so registering the hollows and depressions between them that an advance to the west truly became impossible.

Next, Stalin laid out the conditions for a successful counteroffensive. The General Staff's pupil grasped them not without effort, and expressed them to the extent of his understanding, and moreover in the form of precepts.

The first precept was the use of shock formations (and again, I add my own parenthetical comments):

> Our troops usually advance as separate divisions or brigades deployed along the front in chains. (If it had really been this way, then he wouldn't have had to write any instructions. Military actions would have ceased long before this, the Leader himself would be sitting in a cage, like a monkey, and Hitler would be displaying him

---

1   Here and subsequently I am citing from the 2nd Edition of Zhukov's memoirs, published by APN in Moscow in 1974.

to visitors: 'Take a look at this idiot, who destroyed his own military leadership on the eve of the war!' It is totally unclear where the Leader had heard about such a tactic. After all, this Generalissimo during the years of the war never even once visited the front.) It is understandable that this organization of an offensive cannot be effective, of course, because it gives us no superior strength on any particular sector. Such an offensive is doomed to failure. An offensive can be effective only if we concentrate a considerably superior force vis-à-vis the enemy in one of the sectors of the front. (Stalin: 'Did I repeat the word 'superior'? If I didn't, you know, my bone-head generals wouldn't understand my contribution to military science; oh, they wouldn't grasp it ... Well, that's OK, I'll hammer it into them.') It is essential for this that *each army setting out to breach* the enemy's defense should have a shock formation of three or four divisions massed for a strike at some specific point along the front.

The emphasis is mine, of course... Forgive me, reader; I can't restrain myself. It is *my* impressions that the maniac is pounding *into my head* the ABCs of war interspersed with a thick-headed raving: *each army!* Yet he understood *sectors of the front* to mean the entire Soviet-German front, since the Genius ordered nothing more and nothing less than a general offensive. Indeed, it is in this dispersion of strength that resides the secret of the Red Army's modest success on the snow, turned red with blood, of the winter of 1941-1942. The winter offensive might have become the turning point of the war under proper leadership prior to the terrible summer of 1942 – before the loss of the Crimea and the Taman Peninsula, before the *Wehrmacht*'s penetration to Stalingrad, Tuapse and Novorossiisk. The initiative that winter had passed into the hands of the Red Army. It isn't strange that the Germans began to retreat. It is strange that they didn't run, as the French did in 1812. Yes, it wasn't a simple matter for the Red Army to make good the losses at the start of the war. Even that which they had managed to gather by December 1941 under proper command should have yielded much more success.

There is a technical and scientific concept – an efficiency coefficient, a ratio: useful output energy is always lower than input energy. There is an efficiency coefficient in military affairs as well. It is the most awful of all efficiency coefficients. It is achieved at the cost of lives, primarily young lives. The military efficiency coefficient of actions of the winter of 1941-1942 is a disgrace and a disaster. Reinforcements were thrown into battle from the march; it is embarrassing and awful to write about the losses. Moreover, the reinforcements were thrown into battle not where Zhukov recommended (the General Staff was cowardly silent), but wherever the Leader ordered. The misaligned offensive went on simultaneously everywhere. There were no diversionary or demonstration attacks; they were all real ones. Instead of maneuvering, there was the scattering of force. The amateur Stalin, just like had the amateur Hitler, struck not with a fist, but with an opened palm. However, the *Wehrmacht* was highly trained; its encircled troops didn't go to pieces, the field officers demonstrated resolve, the staff officers showed calm, communications were maintained by radio, supplies were air-dropped, and lines weren't abandoned. The Germans were worn out, hungry, frozen, and had neither superiority in the air (weather and the lack of fuel) nor on the ground (the lack of fuel and the pitiful condition of the equipment). Yet they managed to hold out.

I think it is clear that Zhukov cited the Genius of All Times' directive so abundantly not only because of the pettiness of his style, but also for the pettiness of his thoughts.

What chutzpa must one have to give such instructions to the General Staff, when one doesn't understand anything about military affairs! Yet then, after the war, he shoved his didactic work *Marxism i voprosy iazykoznaniia* [*Marxism and questions of linguistics*] upon linguists – linguists, the most educated people on the planet! Then, moreover, he forced his work *Ekonomicheskie problemy sotsializma* [*Economic problems of socialism*] upon economists. Yet for the sake of his homilies, lakes of blood were spilled, because *our forces had to learn on their own*, rather than being trained before sending them to the front! For the sake of this, the flower of the Army perished and Soviet military thought was buried! So that, having crushed the RKKA, he could plunge the country into a terror, inestimable in its consequences, and to lose an unknown number of tens of millions of people in a war (according to one calculation, 27,000,000, but to others, 46,000,000 ...). An estimate cannot be contested, even if it is absurd. A count was never conducted. Back then, no one dared look the terrible truth in the face. However, he didn't dread expending the lives.

So, the first of Stalin's conditions precepts for success was the operation by shock groups. And the second? It turns out to be an "artillery offensive":

Often we send the infantry into an attack against the enemy's defense line without artillery, without any artillery support whatsoever, and after that we complain that the infantry won't go against an enemy who has dug in and is defending himself. It is clear, however, that such an 'offensive' cannot yield the desired effect. It is not an offensive but a crime – a crime against the Motherland and against the troops which are forced to suffer senseless losses ...

Huh, that was how he called it! A "crime against the Motherland" ... So, the cat knew whose meat it was eating, but kept eating for another three and a half years with an increasing appetite, issuing orders to take Kiev by a certain date, to take Sevastopol by a certain date, etc.... The Soviet press labeled Hitler a cannibal, while Goebbel's Ministry – justifiably! – labeled Stalin the same thing.

"We often send the infantry ..." Who? Not he, God forbid; someone else. May everything be observed and ruled out of the Kremlin!? Well, the infantry, you understand, doesn't rush forward into enemy fire ...

Under the burden of Stalin's accusations, the thought of anyone familiar with the Leader's dealings dips into the past, to 1930 it turns out, the year of the Great Change, and there bumps into the "excesses" of collectivization and Stalin's article on the subject, "Dizziness from Success".

Not all Party members felt comfortable carrying out the duty entitled "the war against the kulaks". This literally was a war, a war against the peasants. The rapidity of the operation by itself gives a picture of its inexorable ferocity. Of course, the peasants resisted the plundering. The result? A disastrous fall in the livestock of horses and cattle, which the peasants slaughtered in the tens of thousands: better to eat them, than to turn them over. The USSR population was still feeling the results of this shortfall in cattle even in the 1950s. So lo and behold, on 2 March 1930, *Pravda* publishes an article of Stalin's: it was senseless to create the collective farms by force, Stalin maintained, and excesses were a result of "dizziness from success". I don't have anything to do with it! These are the results of local arbitrariness.

The ruin of agriculture is a success? In the same way the war with Finland was pronounced a success, the Moscow counteroffensive was a success ... and just who was saying this?

Let's continue with the wise Leader's precepts, however. We'll clench our teeth, and continue to the end of this shameless shifting of blame and slander onto his generals:

> This means, first, that the artillery must not confine itself to separate actions for an hour or two before an offensive, and that it must advance together with the infantry and must sustain the shelling all through the offensive with just short breaks until the enemy's defense line is broken up to its entire depth.
>
> "This means, second, that the infantry must not wait until after the shelling to attack, as occurs after following so-called 'artillery preparation', and that it must attack together with the artillery, *to the thunder of gunfire, to the tune of the artillery.*

This is a trope, a figure of speech, where words are used in a figurative sense. I don't recall whether this is an example of metonymy or of synecdoche. Well, whatever it is, we're dealing with a genius! In his youth, he, they say, relieved himself on a Bible and was expelled from a seminary, while he simultaneously wrote verses about the nightingale and the rose ...

> "This means, third, that the artillery should not fire at random, but massively, and it should be concentrated at not just any point of the front (Stalin: To repeat! My military commanders are dunces. Well, that's OK, I'll teach them ...) but in the zone of the shock group of the army or front, and exclusively in that zone (Huh? Denude the others? But what if the impudent adversary goes against the rules and attacks those places?) because otherwise the artillery offensive is inconceivable."

Here you can catch a glimpse of what prompted the Genius to create a new form of offensive, in which the infantry almost doesn't even take part. No way, they were ending in a bad way with the infantry, with the young men with the closely-cropped haircuts, who were fated never to kiss a girl or to become fathers. From 5 December 1941 to 7 January 1942 in the course of the Moscow counteroffensive operation, the irrevocable losses of the Red Army amounted to 139, 586 men.[2] (Precisely so – 586 ... but did they count all the lads' corpses buried under the snow on the fringe of the birch forest?)

All for one month of victories. There still remained 40 months until the final victory. Something about this figure whispers to me that a simple multiplication of these figures will give us the first approximation of the *official* number of irrevocable losses. However, this turned out to be only the number of *killed in action*, although the tabulation for irrevocable losses includes also everyone who failed to report for duty as well, which means prisoners as well.

The Marshal phlegmatically notes:

> The instructions contained in the *Stavka* (the Leader's! – the author) Directive were adopted for unconditional fulfillment. I take the liberty of saying once more, however, that in the winter of 1942 we didn't have the requisite strength and weaponry to

---

2   This casualty figure is taken from G. F. Krivosheev's *Grif sekretnosti sniat: Poteri vooruzhennykh sil SSSR v voinakh, boevykh deistviiakh i voennykh konfliktakh* [*The seal of secrecy has been lifted: Losses of the armed forces of the USSR in wars, combat operations and military conflicts*] (Moscow: Voenizdat, 1993).

put those ideas of a broad offensive, which were in general correct, into effect. And lacking such strength, the troops could not form the desired shock forces and carry out an artillery offensive effectively enough in 1942 to crush an enemy as powerful and proficient as the Nazi *Wehrmacht*.

The Leader didn't want to see the reality and squandered the troops in penetrations which his troops were obviously not able to keep open. Between 27 January and 1 February 1942, General Belov's 1st Cavalry Corps and Lieutenant-General Efremov's 33rd Army were thrown into a breach in the German defense line in the area of Viazma with the order to take the city. Both formations wound up encircled. Remnants of the 1st Cavalry Corps with great difficulty and enormous losses managed to escape the pocket only on 18 July 1942, while the 33rd Army during the withdrawal perished together with its commander. The fate of Vlasov's 2nd Shock Army is well-known.

Zhukov continues:

In February and March [1942] the General Headquarters (not the Headquarters, the Leader! – the author) demanded a stepping-up of the offensive in the western zone of operations, but the Fronts had neither sufficient manpower nor equipment.

"The country's entire resources were strained to the utmost at the time. Requirements of the armed forces could not be met as the situation and current tasks demanded. It got so that every time we were summoned to the General Headquarters we took the opportunity to coax from the Supreme Commander at least 10-15 anti-tank rifles, or anti-tank guns, or submachine guns, or what was to us a bare minimum of mortar and artillery shells. Whatever we could thus obtain was loaded on trucks at once and sent to the armies that needed it the most.

"Ammunition was especially in short supply. Out of the total amount of ammunition supplies planned for the first ten days of January, the Front actually received 1 percent of the 82-mm mortar rounds and 20-30 percent of the artillery shells. The percentages for the whole of January were: 50-mm mortar shells, 2.7 percent; 82-mm mortar shells, 55 percent; 120-mm mortar shells, 36 percent; artillery rounds, 44 percent. Things were still worse in February: out of 316 [rail] car loads of ammunition scheduled for the first ten days of the month we got none. Because of the ammunition shortage, part of the rocket artillery had to be sent to the rear.

"Believe it or not, the rate of ammunition expenditure we had to set was one or two rounds per artillery piece per day. And that during an offensive campaign!

This is the testimony of Front commander Zhukov, not just anyone. Nobody knew the miserable situation with ammunition production better than Stalin. Yet he had ordered "an artillery offensive" – Nonsense!

Thanks to Stalin, Hitler avoided worse possibilities in the winter of 1941-1942, and perhaps even the worst. However, a turning point at Moscow did happen. The battle of Moscow – despite Stalin! – did end successfully in a strategic sense. Indeed, in the book of his life, Zhukov describes it as his most memorable event. I'll say! In order to achieve the turning point in the war, he had to contend with two supreme commanders – the enemy's and his own. The one didn't want to let victory slip away. The other didn't allow victory to happen.

It's a pity that the Marshal didn't write about all the nonsense that he had the occasion to hear from the lips of Leader. The pages would have been *sui generis*.

It seems that because of Zhukov's opposition to the amateurishness of the Leader (for Khrushchev, scientists later introduced a more resonant term, voluntarism, but during the Leader's time, they didn't hazard using it), Zhukov's standing in the eyes of the Supreme Leader fell for quite some time – as punishment for the Supreme Commander's own mistakes. Zhukov, as a member of the *Stavka*, would be remembered only when things reached so far as the Volga. However, at that time he would be installed in the *Stavka* until the end.

50

On the Question of Losses

This frightening question is what prompted me to write this book.

A casual attitude toward losses is traditional for the Russian Army. In the pre-Napoleonic West, the military was hired, professional and expensive. Pensions had to be paid to those maimed and disabled by war, and support to families of those killed. Capitulation wasn't considered such a dishonorable thing. The enemy outsmarted us, outplayed us; so, why pay for a mistake on our part in soldiers' blood ... (By the way, the word "soldier" comes from the Old French word *sol*, which referred to a coin and also meant "pay".) In the painting by Diego Velazquez entitled "The Surrender of Breda" the vanquished commander is crestfallen, but the victorious commander is amiable and gallant. Revolutionary times later overtook this, and the enthusiasm of the masses "heated war with a red fuel," in Kunikov's trenchant expression. Indeed, what sort of compromises could there be when wars are not "a continuation of policy by other means", but a revolutionary spasm for the eradication of dissenters?

However, in Russia cannon fodder has been cheap from time immemorial. The thought to fight not with numbers, but with skill, was exotic and somewhat foreign to the Russian military mind. "To defeat the enemy with little blood on his territory" – the principle of the commander-idealists, gleaned from the painful experiences of the First World War and the Civil War, corrupted even such an expert of Russian history as Alexei Tolstoy. He truly prophetically, before the war, and influenced by this slogan, let slip the word about the traditional Russian approach to war in the pages of his *Peter the First*: "It's nothing, we have lots of folks!" Even the most gifted Russian commanders were not stingy with their men – not Potemkin, not Rumiantsev, not even Kutuzov, the strategist and diplomat. It is true, as with Zhukov that they didn't hide behind the backs of their soldiers. What about that insanely brave Skobelev? Just take a look at Vereshchagin's Shipkinsky cycle.[1] What about Kuropatkin with his bloody campaign against Japan in 1904-1905? Thus there is no reason to expect something that in general has never existed in Russian tradition. Even less so from Zhukov, who was being directed by Stalin.

Incidentally, even Stalin has an excuse. It is a venomous one, like everything else connected with this poisoner, intriguer and killer, but it is objective nonetheless. A multitude of repetitions doesn't beautify a style, but in our case the multitude is justified by the enormity of losses dumped upon Stalin's commanders, Zhukov first of all. As it was, in the war that the USSR had to fight in 1941, there was no other choice. In that war, which Stalin incurred upon the country, in the circumstances in which he placed it under attack, there was no other tactic than to stand to the death in either fronts or thin blocking detachments, and at the slightest opportunity to counterattack the enemy, so that at any cost to disrupt if not the plan of Barbarossa, then at least the timetable of carrying it out,

---

1   Editor's note: Vasily Vereshchagin (1842-1904) was a famous Russian painter, who accompanied Russian troops on their campaigns in Central Asia and in the Russo-Turkish War. His colorful and highly realistic paintings showing the horror and depravities of war prompted considerable controversy.

otherwise despite all its adventurism the plan would have become a success.

However, this excuse is justifiable only for the period prior to the completion of the Battle of Stalingrad. The waste of lives after achieving this – for the second time! – turning point in the war has nothing in common with the country's survival, and is only connected with the Leader's reveries about controlling Europe and the world.

Of course, given any other high command matters would never have reached this far, nor would they have even reached as far as war. And if the war had happened anyway, even unexpectedly, the losses under any other high command would not have been so high. Indeed, no surprise would have been so total, as that which the Great Leader brought down upon the country. However, this is what the entire book is about ...

There was not a single successful operation of the Red Army in the Great Patriotic War, in which an overwhelming superiority in men and equipment had not first been created. That's how it was at Moscow and Stalingrad, that's how it was at Kursk, where only a deeply echeloned defense and an abundance of reserves were able to withstand the *Wehrmacht's* battering-ram attack. German sources give more reliable statistics on Soviet losses, and therefore it is possible to speak with greater confidence on the losses of the defensive period of the war, than on the losses in the years of victories.[2] In the former case, Germans were conducting the counting, while in the latter case, the Soviet side was. For an example, we'll compare if only the losses generated in the tank engagement at Prokhorovka on 12 July 1943, which was incomparable in the valor demonstrated by both sides. In the dust kicked up by the tank armada and the near-zero visibility, command and control became impossible, artillery fell silent, and the engagement dissolved into individual tank duels. The fury of the fighting reached the point of frenzy, the Tigers were invulnerable, Soviet tanks maneuvered to ram German panzers, and the German advance was halted in light of other problems they were facing. Soviet statistics acknowledge the Red Army's numerical superiority at Prokhorovka, but misrepresent the data on losses.[3]

This clash is a fine model of Stalin's piling-on tactics. Other tactics were repressed.

I've already named one of the Soviet wartime commanders – Marshal Fedor Ivanovich Tolbukhin. Sick with diabetes, he would spend days and nights sitting over plans of operations and conducted them without regard for his health. All the front commanders objected to having limited time to prepare an operation. Tolbukhin, such a gentle man, was relentless. He foresaw what was possible. He strove to see even the impossible. He was the first to use a deceptive double and even triple artillery preparation with feint attacks after each of them, in order to disclose and immediately suppress enemy firing positions. He lost fewer men than other commanders and as a result was the last front commander to become

---

2   According to German data, which doesn't include those who died in Soviet hospitals and therefore are incomplete, the Red Army's losses from 22 June 1941 to 31 December 1941 amounted to 2,663,000 killed and 3,500,000 prisoners.

3   The Soviet side hurled 130,000 troops and 597 tanks into the battle against 70,000 German troops and 311 panzers. Soviet losses were 343 tanks and more than 10,000 killed, wounded and missed in action, whereas German losses were 70 tanks and 842 killed, wounded and missing. The bloody "victory", if it can be called that, was the result that along with other factors it neutralized the II SS Panzer Corps' initiative and arguably thwarted its drive to reach operational space. (Source: http://dic.academic.ru/dic.nsf/ruwiki/287058)

a Marshal. But his Gold Star as a Hero of the Soviet Union came only posthumously, on the 20th Anniversary of the Victory Day.

The most successful commanders of the Red Army were ruthless commanders, and not only at the level of front commanders. Exceptions were rare. War time commanders who spared their men primarily came out of the Army reserve. Education of whatever sort is not superfluous to the principles of humanism, which are distinct from the principles of Leninism. Tsezar' Kunikov is the brightest example. He refused the post as Deputy People's Commissar for Ammunition and became the commander of a water barrier detachment, which was a blocking detachment.[4] It wasn't intended for combat operations. It had a disciplinary role. Kunikov was shown the greatest trust, which he did not care to relinquish. He was purely in a formal sense carrying out an order to occupy a rear line on the eastern bank of the Dnepr River in the area of Zaporozh'e, as the Germans were already forcing a crossing of the river, and came under fire. At that moment, the punitive unit became a combat unit. After head-spinning adventures, the unit completed a 60-kilometer march aboard vehicles with extinguished headlights on a moonless night, without losing a single man, in the process extracting another unit that had gone astray, this one, by the way, a real combat unit. A civilian official, a political worker, not even a combat commander, who had never sniffed gunpowder, Kunikov had passed Zhukov's harsh exam at Khalkhin-Gol, thereby proving the full legitimacy of Zhukov's method. It is a simple truth: *A commander must know his business and be able to think.*

---

4   Blocking detachments were detachments positioned behind the main body of troops. Their task was to prevent the fleeing of military servicemen from the battlefield, catch spies, enemy infiltrators and deserters, and for returning those who were fleeing the battlefield or lagging behind back to their units. They were created in critical situations. The blocking detachments of Kornilov in the First World War, of Trotsky in the RKKA, and the NKVD troops in the Red Army are well-known. Already on 27 June 1941, the Third Department of the People's Commissariat of Defense (NKO) of the USSR published a comprehensive Directive No. 35523 on the work of its organs in wartime. In particular, it directed the creation of blocking detachments on roads and at railroad junctions, for sweeping through forests, and so forth, detached with a command that included operatives of organs of the Third Department with the assignments: apprehending deserters; apprehending a suspicious element operating on the front line; and conducting preliminary investigations (1-2 days), with the subsequent handing over of the materials of the investigation and the suspects for trial.

Apparently, soon after their creation, control over the activity of the blocking detachments passed from the NKO to the NKVD, about which a completely secret report from the deputy chief of the NKVD's Special Department, Commissar of State Security, 3rd Rank S. P. Mil'shtein to People's Commissar of Internal Affairs of the USSR L. I. Beria testifies:

"From the start of the war to 10 October of this year (1941), Special Departments of the NKVD and blocking detachments of NKVD troops for securing the rear have detained 656, 364 military servicemen, who had lagged behind their units or fled from the front. Of those detained, 25, 878 were placed under arrest, while the remaining 632, 486 men were formed into units and again sent to the front. Among those arrested include: spies – 1,505; diversionists – 308; traitors – 2,621; cowards and panic-mongers – 2,643; spreaders of provocative rumors – 3,987; others – 4,371; altogether – 25,878. According to the instructions of the Special Departments and the sentences of the military tribunals, 10,201 men were shot. Of them, 3,321 men were shot in front of the formation. RGANI, F. 89, Op. 18, D. 8, L. 1-3. Authentic text. Typed. This document can be found at http://www.alexanderyakovlev.org/

How did semi-literate lieutenants, who acted as judge and jury both, distinguish spies from diversionists, traitors from cowards and panic-mongers, the latter from the spreaders of rumors and all of these from mysterious *others*? How did the categories ascribed to them or to others affect their fates – who would live, who would be shot in secret or go back to the front? The readers will have to judge this for themselves. Looking at these cruel numbers, he, like I, will definitely come to the conclusion that in the majority of cases, justice was not served.

It is precisely because of this, if they weren't killed in the first battle, that sailors operated more successfully in land battle than others. Better educated and prepared, not knowing the routines on land and not considering themselves competent, they approached their tasks more thoughtfully. The naval infantry, which consisted of crews who had been knitted together by years of common service aboard ships, was a formidable force. The value of each life in such formations is higher, and the mutual support is more cohesive. This is apart from the fact that even today the very best men are selected for the Navy.

However, even men like these were sent to their deaths. It was war! Were King Leonid's 300 Spartans in the pass at Thermopylae not a justified sacrifice? However, there is no need for crocodile tears.

In the critical days for Leningrad, a naval landing was made at Peterhof in the rear of the enemy forces with the aim of cooperating with a coastal group. That is, they were sent as a diversion, without any hope of extracting the force once it had landed, where it was discovered even while disembarking. So it is obnoxious to read the Marshal's following statement:

> ... Carried away by their initial successes, the sailors pursued the fleeing enemy, but by morning they themselves were cut off from the sea and most of them fell in battle as did their commander Andrei Trofimovich Vorozhilov.

"Carried away by their initial successes ... they themselves were cut off from the sea ..." The Marshal is implying that they themselves were responsible, as if the numerical strength of the landing force was such, that it was able both to drive the enemy and to hold open a corridor back to the sea. The sailors wouldn't have been pursuing the enemy, if the combat assignment had been otherwise. The orders, though, had been to drive them! So that is what they did, isolating themselves from the sea, fully knowing where they were going. It was war! The Marshal also knew this. It was not for nothing that having arrived in Leningrad he promised to restore order there, not stopping at anything. So he did. It was war! Only he ought not to have made a statement like that here.

Incidentally, it is possible to understand him. The losses were so painful! Thus Zhukov and Vasilevsky didn't even try to explain the tactics of stealing the initiative in the first and second years of the war. They wouldn't have been understood. They wouldn't even have been heard.

However, let's return (not for the last time) to the accusations that Zhukov was cruel. It has already been said that Zhukov was not a military commander of the Western profile. However, there is an amusing incident. At a conference that took place in the Russian Embassy in Washington D.C. in November 1996 which was dedicated to the Marshal on what would have been his 100th birthday, a certain American historian venomously mentioned the Soviet methods of attacking across minefields. After the ironic reply of the head of the Russian delegation General of the Army M. N. Lobov about how American convicts were given more comforts and conveniences than the conscientious soldiers at the front line, Ambassador David Eisenhower, the son of President Eisenhower, took the side of the Russians: "We don't fully understand what sort of war the Soviet Union was leading. We treated our own cowards and deserters with kid gloves." Then the burning question arose: Which of the Allied commanders could be named among the Great Captains, which is how Ambassador Eisenhower put it. The conference couldn't find any, and the venomous historian began to protest the proposition that with consideration for the enormous span of East front operations, only Zhukov had a claim to the title. Russian veterans who couldn't speak English leaped to their feet: *"Da znaete, chego bol'she vsego zhdal soldat? Kukhni? Bani? Shish, nastupleniya! Zhukova! Gde Zhukov, tam nastuplenie!"* ["And do you know what the soldier was waiting for most of all? Kitchens? Baths? Nuts, for offensives! For Zhukov! Wherever was Zhukov, there was an offensive!"] The historian withdrew.

That's how the ones who survived spoke up. What would those who didn't return have said?

Only those who have experienced war and who have fought in one (wherever it might have been, they know the stench of death) understand that the past can't be judged by contemporary criteria. How is it possible in the security of an average life to understand that an order was once given to take panzers with the blades of a cavalry division? In that instance, would even just one enemy tanker be killed? What would happen to the division? Yet here is the field, covered with the bodies of people and horses, but not a single casualty among the enemy tankers – and the cavalry division commander is acquitted by a court! Huh?! His own cavalrymen didn't cut him down for the absurd order?

Absurd?! A nightmare! War.

The head-on attack by Polish cavalry on German tanks is well-known. I hope that Zhukov didn't issue any such orders. However, there were situations in 1941 when not hours, but minutes decided – a pocket would form or it wouldn't. Was the advance of Soviet tank columns without air cover to intercept the Germans really so different from the above-described cavalry attack on tanks?

Now, however, the war was turning after Stalingrad, and especially after Kursk – but what happened? The losses in prisoners were replaced with losses in killed and wounded. Of course, even these losses could be justified by referring to orders of the Supreme Commander. To Zhukov's honor, he never invoked this justification. Nevertheless, it seems, judging from his interviews and talks in retirement, there was a lot which he later bitterly regretted.

Again on the question of casualties, but now applying to all the commanders of *fronts* ...

(As it were, I would like for this entire book to be printed on paper, so that each page has enormous pale-blue or pale-gray letters as a backdrop to the text, stating: **RUSSIAN TRADITION HAS NO REGARD FOR LOSSES WHEN STRIVING FOR VICTORY.** In letters a bit more compact and smaller: THE WISE AND GREAT LEADER OF THE WORKERS OF THE ENTIRE WORLD COMRADE STALIN. In the third layer, still a bit smaller: THIS BOOK IS NOT A JUSTIFICATION OF THE GENERALS. IT IS AN ACCUSATION OF THE LEADER. IT IS ABOUT THE ARMY WITH WHICH HE ENTERED THE WAR, WHICH WAS UNPREPARED FROM TOP TO BOTTOM, INSTEAD OF WITH THE ARMY THAT WAS PREPARED, BUT WHICH WAS DESTROYED BY HIM ON THE EVE OF THE WAR. The text would be printed over all this. Even then, when the topic is people's lives and such losses, what text could satisfy even the author himself?)

Now then, the front commanders ... All of them in the victorious stage of the war became experienced military tacticians. They prepared an offensive before giving the order, "Attack!" Once that order is issued, just as God is not able to look after the fates of all his saints, the commander is unable to follow the fate of his privates, nor even the actions of his subordinate commanders. He has a lot of subordinates; they've been preparing for years, training to understand an order or an elliptical suggestion. Yet even these bits of advice or recommendations aren't given to each commander in the decisive hours of an offensive, since the front commander can't see the situation in each and every sector. Even if he could see it and offer some guidance, then the time spent on this, when multiplied by the number of those subordinate commanders waiting for prompts, would turn into hours that are catastrophically lost for an operation.

Combat is not a time for classroom lectures. It is a time for swearing. The commander plans an operation and then executes it according to the situation. A combat order consists of two components: the first designates an objective, and the second, the time it should be reached. Commanders keep a picture in their mind – good commanders at least: by a certain hour, a necessary line should be attained. This is an imperative, lest gaps and salients form in the line, which the enemy will exploit through counterattacks. Then losses will become even more terrible and wasteful. The overall commander also oversees the reserves, holding them back until the needed moment and committing them wherever the advance is lagging. This may be where his troops face an enemy fortified area, or a sector, where the troops are being led by incompetent officers. Those are the places where the heaviest casualties occur.

It isn't worth even criticizing the hasty training of soldiers and officers during the war years. The weakness of the middle-level command in the Red Army contributed to greater losses, although to a lesser degree than the incompetence of the generals. The Red Army command didn't glitter with originality, experience or erudition. There were cases where troops, taking the wrong direction in a battle, became entangled, even resulting in friendly fire. Terrain and available means were used haphazardly, and troops were committed straight into the teeth of German defenses. German authors observe that the straightforwardness of the Red Army's attacks, in serried ranks, was an indication not of confidence in success, but of commanders' fear of being accused of passivity. The radio waves seethed with threats from higher commanders, the seriousness of which could not be doubted. Military tribunals continued to work until the end of the war. Could Zhukov or any other *front* commander replace incompetent officers? With whom? However, on a front of such length, to advise everyone, who hadn't received adequate training and with whom the repressed commanders had been replaced – this was beyond utopia.

In order to finish with the losses and no longer have to return to this painful question, I will note that Major Kunikov, who'd been appointed (after disembarking colonels with wide ribbon bars into a bridgehead captured by his remarkable operation) to the fatal post of senior naval commander, perished on the tenth day of an extremely unsuccessful combination of circumstances, including a wound and his strangely delayed evacuation from the bridgehead later called Malaia Zemlia. He earned posthumous glory, and was mourned and buried with the rarest honors for military time.[5] With him was buried the

---

5   Kunikov, an idol of his men from the very beginning of forming of his detachment, was a master of diversion, and during the fall and winter of 1941-1942 caused a lot of trouble to German communications in the Azov Sea area. The night raids, which he carefully planned with help of local partisans, inflicted heavy casualties on the Germans; in return he would rarely lose even a single man. His ingenuity seemed to be boundless. When the Sea of Azov had frozen over, his men donned skates, and these shadowy patrols terrorized the Nazis. In the summer retreats, always in the rearguard, his battalion had shown a real mastery of maneuvering defense, combining bravery with shrewdness. Kunikov, facing a lack of artillery, mounted 45mm antitank guns on the reinforced platforms of regular GAZ-MM trucks. These impromptu self-propelled guns quickly moved from one defense sector to another and kept successfully repulsing German and Rumanian tanks. Today sources shows Kunikov decorated by the Order of the

secret of how this Major and former civil servant had been vainly trying to persuade the meritorious colonels to stop launching daytime attacks and wastefully expending the golden men of Odessa and Sevastopol, who had passed through the hell of Kerch, Taman and Novorossiisk, but instead to expand the bridgehead, not allowing the enemy to dig-in, with nighttime probes, familiar to the naval infantry and terrifying to the foe. This example of the attitude toward losses is both striking and unique.

Red Banner and the Order of Aleksander Nevsky. One falsified image depicts him wearing a naval high-collared tunic, which he never wore during the war, with the two Orders on his chest, but without the medal that he truly valued. This medal was the only decoration that this beloved commander was actually wearing on his simple tunic, the medal *Za trudovoe otlichie* [For labor distinction], which he received back in 1938 (instead of the Order of Lenin) for his hard work in the machine-building industry. Men of his detachment were taken from Malaia Zemlia in order to attend Kunikov's burial in Gelendzhik (he was later re-buried in Novorossiisk). Unbelievable, but this is a fact. They were considered irreplaceable, but they were pulled out of a front of ceaseless, savage fighting and given a torpedo boat for crossing the Tsemess Bay, which was under constant fire from all types of guns.

51

The Victories in the Spring of 1942

Unfortunately, we now have to speak about victories of the German arms....
By the spring of 1942, on the Soviet-German front, a balance of force had been established. This was a shaky balance. After the futile efforts of the Red Army to sweep clean all of the territory occupied by the *Wehrmacht* in one grand offensive along the entire length of the front, the initiative again passed into the hands of the Germans. By now, the seasoned Red Army soldiers were a good match for the *Wehrmacht's* soldiers. However, commanders aren't grown so quickly. A soldier, if he survives his combat baptism, especially if he is surrounded by combat-seasoned "old men", becomes much less vulnerable. Even a lieutenant after his first battle still doesn't become a commander, but at least a soldier. For a soldier, combat is always combat.

For a general, battle is a chess game. So many games must be played, both openings and endgames, in order to gain experience – but on the battlefield it is all in blood. That's precisely why it was not in the panic of 1941, but in the daily grind of war, when the difference between the miraculously surviving flower of the RKKA and Stalin's promotions with an NKVD background began distinctly to emerge.

Zhukov should have again mentioned the consequences of the repressions in connection with what was happening at the front in the spring of 1942. It might have sounded like this:

Since in the spring of 1942 I was the only capable man in charge in the higher echelon of the RKKA at the level of front commander, and since I was sitting around Moscow because of the Leader's fear of leaving this direction without close attention and of overlooking the *Wehrmacht's* preparations on it, the remaining directions were entrusted to simple-minded Marshals, as a consequence of which the Red Army could not successfully conduct large scale operations ...

Of course, Zhukov couldn't write anything like this. He didn't dare; but he could think it, because it was the truth. That's why he valued Vasilevsky: not a commander yet, a staff strategist, no combat experience, no cruelty – but he understood an idea lurking within an elliptic suggestion! He had a nose for the situation! He knew the value of Zhukov himself! At least one more like-minded individual existed!

I don't exclude the possibility that Stalin was holding Zhukov on the Moscow axis intentionally, so as to squelch even a feeble impulse in Hitler toward the capital. Knowingly, *Krasnaya zvezda*, the Soviet Army's central newspapers from the very origins of the RKKA, published a large portrait of Zhukov on the front page in October 1941. Not only in order to find a handy culprit in case of a defeat, but also to let the Germans know that the hero of Khalkhin-Gol was there. The Germans already respected Zhukov's grip on things. Meanwhile, in this particular case Stalin rejected the principle of "No one is indispensable". Had Zhukov surrendered the capital in 1941, possibly Stalin would have shot him, if only to demonstrate, as he did with Litvinov's replacement, his obedience to Hitler and his readiness for peace under any circumstances. As if to say, "Here, in order to please you I've even shot my last commander; I have no intention to continue the war against you, everything is now at your service – the population, the territory, the resources." In his ability for making any compromise, Lenin's faithful pupil was the equal of his mentor.

At the General Headquarters there were Shaposhnikov and Vasilevsky. They understood the situation. To understand, however, is one thing; to stand up for that understanding is something else. (Zhukov defended his views, although, of course, not as heatedly as he had on 29 July 1941. However, Stalin didn't allow himself anything like the July episode with Zhukov – until the final outrage over the Marshal in 1946 ...) The lesson that the Leader had drawn from 1941 was that he must not give Hitler the initiative. So in the summer of 1942, he decided to keep it for himself. Iakir's strategy to wear down the enemy with an active defense, which should have been used from the very beginning of the 1942 summer campaign, and which turned out to be applied – unwillingly! – at Stalingrad and later, in 1943, at Kursk (after the new bloody experiences at Zaporozh'e and Khar'kov in the winter of 1943), remained in the meantime unused. As a result, instead of an active defense Stalin ordered not the preparation of harassing attacks, but a broad-scale offensive in both the Crimea and in the area of Khar'kov, on the L'gov-Kursk and Smolensk directions, and on top of that in the regions of Leningrad and Demiansk. Let's grab the initiative!

This topic was discussed in the *Stavka* on 5 January 1942. Zhukov raised objections, and requested that he be given the forces to crack the German lines in only one decisive, central sector. According to Zhukov, after the meeting, Shaposhnikov tiredly told him "You shouldn't have argued, the Supreme Commander had settled that question." When Zhukov asked then why his opinion was asked, Shaposhnikov replied with a heavy sigh "That, my dear fellow, I do not know."

This meeting didn't go easily for Shaposhnikov. Its outcome was even more difficult for the Soviet people and the Red Army.

The Red Army had neither the sufficient power for operations along the entire front, nor the skill to retain the initiative. It didn't have the operators for the planned operations. Yet there was Leningrad, a fortress, and Moscow too, and Zhukov was in the role of a commandant of besieged fortresses – both of them. He wasn't handling things in the south, nor was the General Headquarters. The ill Shaposhnikov and the still timid Vasilevsky didn't intercede in the matter with the Leader.

The Germans were marking time. Moscow wasn't the goal for the 1942 campaign. Now, when the war had become "deep" (the poet Evgenii Evtushenko's expression), a campaign for Moscow meant grinding through a prepared defense, and then a siege as well, similar to the one at Leningrad. Moreover, it was precisely on the Moscow axis where the *Wehrmacht* couldn't boast of possessing the initiative. Indeed, the fall of Moscow, which would have been fatal in 1941, in 1942, when the civil servants had straightened out their work in the rear, when reserve command posts had been established and the flow of Allied assistance had increased, now would have meant only one more Russian defeat in a long war. Oil! That remained the Führer's goal, and he accordingly selected the direction of his 1942 campaign – in the south. Operation Blau had the twin target of cutting the Volga and seizing the Caucasus.

The *Wehrmacht* wasn't in a hurry. As in the previous year, the factor of surprise was at the forefront of their plans. In essence, to the *Wehrmacht* it made no difference where to launch its attack. Any place was suitable for a breakthrough with a subsequent exploitation in the direction of success – not excluding even Moscow, should the opportunity present itself. Indeed plans were ready for all contingencies, if only to assure themselves that the Red Army's movements weren't feints. For a decisive opportunity, the Germans needed a conclusive dislocation of the Soviet forces. In the meantime, they were securing their flanks, particularly the Black Sea. Crimea, the unsinkable aircraft carrier, concerned the Führer.

The Crimea became the prologue for the 1942 campaign. The Crimean Front command displayed ignorance unprecedented even for the Stalinist school. Possessing a significant numerical superiority, the Kerch grouping attempted to relieve Sevastopol. It attacked and immediately became bogged down. At just the moment when the Soviet front congealed, that's when the *Wehrmacht* went on the offensive to destroy the Kerch grouping, occupy the Crimea, and neutralize the Black Sea Fleet.

On 8 May 1942, the *Wehrmacht* launched an attack on the Kerch Peninsula along the Black Sea coast, broke through the front and penetrated 8 kilometers into the Soviet defenses. This still would not have been a disaster, had appropriate measures been taken immediately. Here's how a most authoritative witness, the acting Chief of the General Staff (and at the time still only Lieutenant General) A. M. Vasilevsky described these, if you'll permit me to call them, measures; (the few parenthetical comments are mine):

> Towards evening on the first day of the enemy offensive, Stalin received a telegram from L. Z. Mekhlis ...

(Ahh, an old acquaintance! Do you remember him, reader? A witness to Zhukov's finest hour, as yet still the Chief of the Red Army's Main Political Directorate, but in the purges he was Stalin's *oprichnik* [one of Ivan the Terrible's "guards", who were entrusted with the torture and murder of the Tsar's internal enemies], a permanent member of the so-called "Extraordinary Troika", which replaced the system of justice under Stalin.)

> ... who was then the GHQ representative on the Crimean Front. The telegram went as follows:
> 'This is not the time to complain, but *I have to let the GHQ know about the Front commander.* (This is a style typical of a NKVD informant!) On 7 May, that is, on the eve of the enemy offensive, Kozlov summoned the Military Council to discuss the plan of an operation to take Koi-Asan. I recommended that this project be abandoned and instructions immediately given to the armies with regard to the expected enemy offensive. In the Front Commander's signed order he had indicated in several places that the offensive was expected between 10 and 15 May and instructed all commanding staff, commanders of formations and staffs to work out and examine, before 10 May, the defense plan of the armies. This was being done when the entire situation of the previous day showed that the enemy was going to attack that morning. On my insistence, the erroneous dates were altered. Kozlov also resisted moving additional forces to the 44th Army sector.'

Good God, how low must things have fallen, for a Mekhlis to become a *Stavka* representative ... Mekhlis, the ignoramus and executioner!? The plot unfolds – a comical one from the point of view of a far-removed historian, but a macabre one for the soldiers of the Red Army.

Or else the *Stavka* didn't know that Kozlov was not an Uborevich or an Iakir – and just where could you find them now? Thus you are there now, Mekhlis, you bloody guy, so you can make a sugar candy out of all this filth. Ah, you yourself, it turns out, are part of this same filth. That's just the way the Supreme Commander reacted to Mekhlis's telegram – in a restrained manner, of course, as far as the telegraph would allow:

> You are taking a strange position like an outside observer who has no responsibility for the Crimean Front affairs. This position may be convenient but it is utterly disgraceful. You are not some outside observer at all, but the responsible representative of the GHQ, responsible for all of the Front's successes and failures and obliged to correct command's mistakes on the spot. You together with the command are responsible for the Front's left flank being weak. ... You demand that we replace Kozlov by someone like Hindenburg. *Yet you are bound to know that we do not have any Hindenburgs up our sleeve ...*

The emphasis is mine, but the outcry is whose? Perhaps it is even a veiled reference to the zeal shown in the purge. This "You are bound to know ..." Stalin remembered!

During this verbal tussle the Luftwaffe was accurately pulverizing headquarters and cutting communications lines, while the panzer wedges, just as in 1941, were dismembering masses of troops – and tanks! Twenty-one divisions! Yet they were doing this with ten and a half German divisions, against a canon of war, which requires the attacker to have a 3:1 advantage in strength. A *Wehrmacht* infantry division had double the numerical strength of a Soviet rifle division, but this doesn't explain the German success. The *Wehrmacht* had no superiority in tanks or artillery here. They did not even have the advantage of surprise: the attack was expected! Yes, the Luftwaffe reigned supreme in the air, but the main difference was the German superiority in the quality of command.

The Germans were rampaging in the rear and overran the Kerch Peninsula. The Soviet forces had disintegrated. The defeat was total and terrible. Germans in captured tanks fired upon the fleeing Red Army troops, trying to avoid taking prisoners (but they still managed to capture 170,000 of them). People were flinging themselves into the Kerch Strait on barrels, pieces of wreckage and simply by swimming, while Luftwaffe aces were diving not only on boats, but even on solitary swimmers...

Even thirty years later, Crimean residents who had witnessed this debacle, were crying as they shared details with archeologist Mikhail Kublanov, who was conducting the excavation of ancient ruins at Kerch. Those Red Army men who took shelter in rock quarries doomed themselves to agony. The Germans unerringly seized anyone who left them in search of food: they recognized them by their inflamed and swollen lips. There was no water, and prisoners of the quarries were sucking on rocks from aquiferous layers of limestone. Kerch, the Hero City ...

A *Stavka* directive dated 4 June 1942 observed:

> The major cause of the failure of the Kerch operation is that the Front command – Kozlov, Shamanin, Vechny and *Stavka* representative Mekhlis, the army commanders, and particularly the 44th Army commander Lieutenant-General Cherniak and the 47th Army commander Major-General Kolganov displayed a complete misunderstanding of the nature of modern warfare.

This acknowledgement is unprecedented. Who is responsible for the fact that generals with no understanding of "the nature of modern warfare" were in command? This is a rhetorical question, of course.

☆ ☆ ☆

It would seem after the bloodbath in the Crimea, it was time to ponder the *Wehrmacht's* next move. The fall of the Crimea had changed the situation dramatically. With only a glance at a map, the following question arose on its own: Was this swift and pitiless operation, in which the *Wehrmacht* once again dazzled with the same energy of 1941, a stage in some sort of plan? It is unbelievable, but a fact: *a question like this one was never raised*. Orders directed that the *Wehrmacht's* next step would be toward Moscow.

Storm the Crimea in the summer, thereby postponing an attack on Moscow? A similar loss of time the year before had already been punished by the Russian winter. These two objectives were located far apart. The Germans would have to shift a lot of forces a very long way in order to return to the Moscow axis. So, just perhaps, Moscow was not the *Wehrmacht's* goal in the 1942 campaign? The narrow Kerch Strait beckons a landing on the Taman Peninsula, and that's already the Caucasus. Or was there no longer any concern for the Baku oilfields, so desired by Hitler? *The Wehrmacht's next step will be toward Moscow!*

Fine, let's assume that was the case. Yet shouldn't we in the meantime refrain from offensive operations? The generals are unskilled, and they'll use up their armies in vain ...

The Wehrmacht's next step will be toward Moscow. Preempt it!

On 12 May 1942, at the height of the Crimean drama and without the slightest connection to it, without any hope to ease the situation there, the Southwestern Front launched an attack in the direction of Khar'kov designed to forestall a German attack toward Moscow. It did so with the full knowledge of the enemy grouping in front of it and over timid *Stavka* protests, but in accordance with the Leader's decree that a diversion away from the Moscow direction was necessary. The operation was removed from *Stavka* oversight; it was ordered to be handled as a matter for the Southwestern Front only. This was Stalin's personal contribution to the 1942 campaign ...

The Leader urgently needed a success in a major operation. In addition to military aims, he was also pursuing political goals.

The offensive, which caught the Germans off-guard, began spiritedly. The Red Army, which outnumbered the *Wehrmacht* here, especially in tanks, spryly advanced on Khar'kov. The tempo of the advance, however, ominously slowed. In a classic, five-day defensive struggle, the *Wehrmacht* battered the attackers, and on 17 May, eleven divisions under von Kleist launched a counteroffensive from the area of Slaviansk and Kramatorsk at the base of the Russian salient, and punching through the defense of the 9th Army, they began to close the breach.

The *Stavka* didn't overlook what was happening. Vasilevsky, who had not been permitted to direct the operation but was nevertheless closely monitoring it, immediately recommended a switch to a tough defense. (Stalin ignored his advice, but ten days later, at the culmination of the German victory, the Leader promoted him to Colonel-General...) In Soviet books on this operation it is written that the Southwestern Front headquarters under Timoshenko's command, with the *Stavka's* (with Stalin's!) agreement clung to a differing opinion: the situation was under control, but reinforcements were needed. I don't believe this. It is more likely that this was not truly the opinion of the Southwestern Front headquarters, but only a timorous recitation of the Leader's wishes, just as had happened a year before at Kiev. Stalin authorized the commitment of the reserves and ordered the continuation of the advance into the German rear. He added that the reinforcements wouldn't arrive for three more days. Three days ... not a big deal ...

Already on the next day, though, from the morning of 18 May, the situation in the Barvenkovo salient became disastrous. Von Kleist expanded the 100-kilometer breakthrough and formed a defense against any possible liberation of the encircled Soviet troops from both within and without. The Southwestern Front command was no longer handling the course of events. Vasilevsky beseeched Stalin to halt the offensive. The Leader replied with a blunt refusal. The armies continued their fatal swing dance in the *Wehrmacht*'s rear.

By the evening, the Front headquarters was no longer playing up to the Leader. The frightened Khrushchev, a member of the Front's Military Council, called Vasilevsky. The latter attempted to change the Leader's mind. Stalin again answered with a refusal, and the General Staff again didn't insist on its opinion. (Later that autumn Vasilevsky, balking at openly challenging the Leader's opinion, under the pressure of circumstance would make his own decision.) Again and again, one regrets the absence of the more willful army commanders.

Was it frightening to oppose the tyrant? Was it not frightening to lose hundreds of thousands of soldiers in encirclements in the heart of the country?

What was behind the Leader's insolent refusal to listen to the opinion of his generals? It was no longer his buddies from the 1st Cavalry Army that were making the requests; he had long ago lost faith in them. Now he was being begged by his own protégées, the leading talents of Uborevich's school (mentioned here, since the Leader once demanded in a fit of temper: "... teach the troops like they were under Uborevich"). He knew the opinion of Shaposhnikov, a man who'd been coerced into silence, but who remained for Stalin the highest military authority (excluding himself, of course). In my view, Stalin's refusal to listen is transparent: after the muddle in the Crimea and in view of Molotov's pending trip to London to conclude an agreement between the USSR and Great Britain, the Leader urgently needed a military success. There was going to be a need to defend the territorial acquisitions at the expense of war-torn Poland, which would be simpler with an offensive underway back home, thereby reminding an ally that the fate of the war – and the fate of the ally as well – was being decided on the Eastern Front, where the Red Army was attacking without regard for losses. With an enemy in the heart of the country, a hundred thousand lives were being expended, in order to gain a bargaining position in the haggling over future borders ...

Molotov flew off on the evening of 19 May. Only then, having let 24 hours pass since the General Staff's entreaty, did the Leader permit the withdrawal of forces. It was too late! Paulus, going over to the offensive from his defensive posture, attacked toward Balakleia, closing the ring. The pullback of the Soviet armies and the violent attacks on the enveloping German prongs didn't alter the situation. Infantry in closed ranks with the support of tanks attacked into deadly fire, trying to hold open the road to Izium, but on 23 May the jaws clamped shut, while the Soviet tanks had used all their fuel. A mass of troops remained trapped inside the pocket, which were destroyed "with improbable rapidity".[1]

Why this "with improbable"? It was inevitable! The Army had gone on the offensive without having defensive lines behind it!

On 28 May one of the Southwestern Front's armies at the cost of horrendous casualties managed to break into the pocket and to create a hole 800 meters wide in the German defenses. A group of 22,000 men slipped out of the pocket. The slaughter of those still entrapped continued for a week. The higher command staff perished. Generals Podlas, Kostenko and Bobkin with his 14-year-old son all fell in hopeless combat. The brightest figure of the Smolensk battle, General Gorodniansky, whom the soldiers liked to say that no bullet would ever strike, shot himself. Three armies ceased to exist. According to German data, 241,000 Red Army soldiers and officers were taken prisoner. The number of killed was estimated in the range of 150,000 – 200,000.

Grif sekretnosti sniat [The seal of secrecy has been lifted], upon which we have to rely, since it is the only source which uses available (or authorized) archival documents, gives a figure for the irrevocable losses in this operation (which is naturally called the Khar'kov *battle*, and not the Khar'kov *massacre*) of 170,958 soldiers and officers. What about the prisoners, though?

The agony of Sevastopol inevitably followed the fall of Kerch. The released forces of the *Wehrmacht* headed to the south. Khar'kov had created an excellent situation for the start of the summer campaign. The Führer now was convinced that Operation Blau was the right plan, and that the southern flank was the Achilles heel of the Soviet defense.

The offensive began with feints. The German masters of the military game maneuvered their forces to create the impression that the goal was Moscow. The frightened Stalin now without Zhukov's reminders ordered the strengthening of the Moscow defensive zone at the expense of other sectors. This is revealed in Vasilevsky's memoirs. However, even he didn't say how they had let slip Operation Blau ...

In the middle of June, Briansk Front's aerial reconnaissance reported on the concentration of German forces in the Shchigry-Kursk area. The General Staff's Intelligence Department responded: "You're looking in the wrong direction. The German offensive is being prepared not on your southern, but your northern flank, where they've assembled four panzer and ten infantry divisions for an attack on the boundary of the Briansk and Western Fronts." (In the same way Hitler didn't believe his aerial reconnaissance on the eve of the Soviet counteroffensive at Moscow ...) The reaction of the General Staff[2] was the result of the *Wehrmacht's* demonstrations. The Germans deceived not only Stalin, who was predisposed to take the feint, but also Vasilevsky, who was goaded by him, and even Zhukov, who can be exonerated, incidentally, by the fact that he only had a superficial knowledge of the general situation, and as a front commander, was more concerned with his own more narrow responsibilities.

---

1   V. Rapoport, *Khar'kov-Stalingrad-Khar'kov*, NRS, 7 August 1987.

2   Two years later, Soviet planners, who had learned from the Germans, deceived the *Wehrmacht* in the same manner, but even more bitterly, prior to the offensive against the "Belorussian Balcony" (Operation Bagration), by secretly assembling tank formations further south, on the axis of the planned attack, while at the same time filling the southern direction with dummy tanks and leaving that area accessible to German aerial reconnaissance flights, in distinction from the Belorussian direction, which was sealed from the air and closed to ground reconnaissance. The Soviet offensive was launched in part through those same swamps, which had been an obstacle for the narrow-tracked German tanks in 1941. The result for the *Wehrmacht* was truly devastating.

However, the Briansk Front was rudely awakened by the crash of a German signals airplane, carrying a staff officer of the 23rd Panzer Division, Major Reichel, on board. The pilot was killed in the crash, while Reichel attempted to flee with a portfolio and was shot. Inside the portfolio were instructions to General of Panzer Troops Stumme, the commander of the XXXX Panzer Corps, about the first phase of Operation Blau. That same day, the contents of the portfolio were handed over to the General Staff. The goal of the offensive was revealed: the seizure of Voronezh with a subsequent pivot to the south, toward the Don River. The offensive was aimed not at the boundary between the Briansk and Western Fronts, but at the boundary between the Briansk and Southwestern Fronts. Stalin, just as he had before, believed this was a provocation. Reichel? A major? Yes, he would have sacrificed a hundred majors in order to deceive the enemy. He believed the Germans would do the same thing. Literally as if by an accord with the Führer, he was anticipating a direct assault on Moscow.

Again and again, Lieutenant General Golikov, commander of the Briansk Front, reported on the *Wehrmacht's* concentration at Kursk and the increasing activity in the area, and on the doubtless transfer of German troops from Orel. In vain! On 20 June the front commander was summoned to appear at the *Stavka*, where the enraged Leader swept the papers of the ill-fated Reichel off the table and said that he didn't believe a word about Operation Blau. He lambasted the military intelligence for its gullibility, forgetting – no, remembering (but taking revenge against Golikov, who had been directing the GRU on the eve of the war!) – that before the war he had received intelligence about the possible invasion dates, although it was his, the Leader's, responsibility to interpret that intelligence.... With a heap of abusive language and an order to prepare the taking of Orel no later than 5 July in a concerted operation with the Western Front, Golikov returned to Voronezh.

At 0300 on 28 June, a draft of the plan for the offensive on Orel was ready. Three hours later, the general German offensive to the south (Operation Blau) began. This time the wise Leader Comrade Stalin, "who was correct in everything", had no less than eight days available to him from his stormy session with Golikov until the start of Operation Blau to reach an accurate decision...

The strengthening of the Moscow zone doesn't at all mean that the *Wehrmacht* had superiority in the south. In personnel and the number of tanks, the Briansk Front was twice the size of the attacking *Wehrmacht* in its sector. However, as before the Germans dominated in the air – and in operational-tactical thinking. The Front's prepared defenses were breached. Over two days, the *Wehrmacht* advanced 40 kilometers. (The scale of this disaster becomes clear, when one recalls that on the first day of the Stalingrad counteroffensive, Soviet troops advanced 30 kilometers.) The *Wehrmacht* broke into operational space: a defense extending even 10 kilometers in depth along the entire Soviet-German front would have been beyond even China's strength to crack, with all its human resources. Marshal Zhukov comments, "By the middle of July, hurling our troops back across the Don from Voronezh to Kletskaia, and from Surovikino to Rostov, the enemy forces engaged ours in the bend of the Don, seeking to break through towards Stalingrad ..."

☆ ☆ ☆

Who knows what the Leader was thinking on these short summer nights, as he was heading to bed to sleep at daybreak. Was he pondering his repressed cadres? He remembered everything, all the "wheres" and "whens". He didn't forgive. He didn't repent. He was simply thinking:

"This one I might well have left alone ... and this one ... and that one. Not Iakir with Uborevich, not Primakov together with Eideman and Putna, not Tukhachevsky with Fel'dman. With Bliukher, though those Chekists got into a rage... what do you do with him, having poked out his own eye? ... and just shot him. Ay-ay, such stubbornness ... just not to give any evidence at the trial, you understand. ... and without Bliukher, what kind of trial would it be... Ezhov, that nasty, bloody egg ... He should have been a bit gentler, given things a bit more time; he should have thought a bit more and lightened up. The pilots too ... Well, with them it was fully up to me ... But my protégés, they didn't hide the aircraft away under cover; they waited for directions, damn it! Couldn't they have put two and two together and seen that they had to do it without instructions!? ... Even against instructions! So that the Boss didn't have to know what he didn't want to know? So that when facing an enemy, if any questions suddenly arose, he could more sincerely feign surprise: 'Just what are you saying, dear sirs, why, we know nothing about anything, and don't have anything in mind like something we'd have to hide from you.'

"They were afraid for their own skin, you understand. They weren't supposed to think first about the Motherland, about the great Stalin! Yet what was one to do when Rychagov, a whippersnapper, you understand, this brat, in front of everyone said: 'We're flying in coffins!'[3] He was speaking for all of them, so they all had to be eliminated. Smushkevich, the bloody scoundrel, had given the same sort of alarm: we had to teach the young pilots how to fly! Bah! Just where's the time to train them so intensively? He also was disgusted with the arrests; you understand, he had once vouched for the arrested, for their dedication to the Motherland!! This ace on crutches they had arrested, in plaster after a crash ... Never mind, we'll grow a replacement batch. This Vasilevsky and Antonov, for example ... I have to check, by the way, whether he's related to the other Antonov, who arranged that Tambov Rebellion mess.[4] Others will show up as well. As for the losses, well, this is war."

That's how Stalin both thought and acted. The lack of success with the selection of Vlasov as the commander of the 2nd Shock Army ("He didn't shoot himself in encirclement, the whore!") didn't halt the promotion of new commanders. The main concern was the General Staff. Shaposhnikov wasn't a worker, while Zhukov was needed at the front. He may return to Moscow only for consultations. Except that he may be called back more frequently ...

The Leader had been trying out Vasilevsky in the role of *Stavka* representative before

3   The accident rate after the purge had risen dramatically.
4   Editor's note: The Tambov Rebellion was a large peasant uprising against the Bolshevik conscription of grain and Bolshevik rule in 1920-1921. It took place in an area covered by the modern-day Tambov Oblast and part of Voronezh Oblast. In Soviet historiography, it was referred to as Antonov's mutiny, though Aleksandr Antonov was only chief of staff of one of the rebel armies. However, since he had been an official in the Left Socialist Revolutionary Party who'd grown disenchanted with the Bolshevik's policy of grain conscription, he offered a convenient way to smear the rebellion as a crisis manufactured by "counter-revolutionary plotters". The Red Army under Tukhachevsky brutally suppressed the rebellion, not stopping short of executing civilian hostages without trials and the use of poison gas.

urging him to take over the General Staff, which Vasilevsky accepted after long persuasion. While he was working on probation on the Northwestern Front, still clumsily resolving the task of liquidating the encircled German grouping at Dem'iansk, and Zhukov, the Red Army's sole Hindenburg, was commanding the defense of the Moscow sector, the Germans were easily demolishing the entire southern Soviet front.

There were no Hindenburgs ... but there had been.

After the new fright, the Leader took heart: the Germans weren't aiming toward Moscow! Measures were taken. At first, of course, there ensued the usual game of leapfrog with command posts. Army commanders and front commanders were shuffled. Part of the Briansk Front was transformed into the Voronezh Front. Because of the lack of field generals, Vatutin of the General Staff was appointed to command this new Front. The Southwestern Front was renamed the Stalingrad Front. The Southern Front was liquidated and its forces were handed over to the North Caucasus Front. The swashbuckling Budenny became its commander. A comment? No, no comments are necessary here, with the exception of one: Zhukov had learned to hold his tongue! The man was strong. This one, God forbid, in order to avoid being a witness at the next trial might repeat Bliukher's trick of poking out his own eye... Obviously, the Leader hadn't yet learned about the Maloiaroslavl' achievements of his swashbuckling buddy Budenny, which increases the value of Zhukov's beneficence: it was long-lasting. At the head of the RKKA's Main Political Directorate, the more flexible Shcherbakov, the former head of the Writer's Union, replaced Mekhlis.

However, the main thing isn't these reorganizations; the main thing is the following: portraying the abandonment of Rostov as a voluntary act against orders, Stalin made a radical amendment to *Stavka* Order No. 002, written by Vasilevsky and dated 28 July 1942, and it became ominously known worldwide as Order No. 227: **"Not a step back!"** This order has been recognized by several contemporary writers as a highest product of thought, and even as a model of style.

52

Interlude: The Tools of Power

Yesterday, 11 June, the Supreme Court of the USSR consisting of Comrade **Ulrikh**, the Chairman and Chief Justice of the Military Collegium, as well as members of the Court A. M. Alksnis, Deputy People's Commissar of Defense **S. M. Budenny**, V. K. Bliukher, **B. M. Shaposhnikov**, P. E. Dybenko, N. D. Kashirin, E. M. Goriachev, and I. P. Belov according to the law of 1 December 1934 examined the matter of M. N. Tukhachevsky, I. E. Iakir, I. P. Uborevich, A. I. Kork, P. M. Eideman, B. M. Fel'dman, V. M. Primakov and V. K. Putna. The above listed men have been accused of betraying their military duty and military oath, of betraying the Motherland, of plotting against the peoples of the USSR and the Workers and Peasants Red Army.

All the accused have been sentenced to be shot.

The sentence has been carried out."

Izvestiia, 12 June 1937

Only those names that I have boldfaced in the text are men who survived the purges. All the others were shot soon after this trial. (Goriachev shot himself.)

They were sentenced one day – and the sentence was already carried out on the following day!? No, the same night! Someone is gasping: "Wait, wait, just what are you saying? Uborevich is a traitor? Iakir, Tukhachevsky???" They were now gone, they'd been shot. They couldn't be brought back to life, even if you advanced all the troops on Moscow. It wasn't a mix-up – terror was sown by this liquidation of the first heroes of the nation, the most necessary people, who personified the "tranquility of our borders"[1] – and who just the day before had been the purest, the most beloved, the most-most!

The tools of power: multiply the vacancies, eliminate personalities, chum the nonentities (it's a blessing they're the majority), and do all this with such rapidity, so that honorable people, appointed to the courts, don't have time to examine the indictments. While they are figuring out that an accused man's confession is not a proof of his guilt, that a confession can be forcibly extracted, the accused is executed and then there is no longer any point to checking into it. So now the members of the tribunal become criminal collaborators. People with such a troubled conscience are now mentally ready for their own executions, but it is preferable to liquidate them before they've come to their senses and plot something together.

From there it is simple. You were a friend of the executed? You must be guilty too! A relative? You too! A co-worker? We'll check you out!

The accused people, standing in front of their judges, with some of whom they had been friends, companions in arms, behaved pathetically. They acknowledged their guilt,

---

1   This is a line from the Aviamarch, a Soviet song in the form of a march, written in 1921. The music was attributed to Iu. Khait (though he may not be the original composer), the lyrics were written by P. Herman. The song was often played at parades and was the official hymn of the Soviet Air Force. The same song with different lyrics became very famous in Germany, and it was... the Horst Wessel Lied.

plainly in the effort to save their families. (Perhaps also their friends, the members of the tribunal ...) Meanwhile the judges became convinced that they'd been deceived, only by the hastiness in carrying out the sentences. Then it hit home – just whom they'd sentenced. Then they understood the despairing words of Tukhachevsky, who had cried out as his sentence was being pronounced: "You are not shooting us; you're shooting the Red Army!"

"We are beheaded!" – that was most likely what judges had thought.

A purge of the Party apparatus preceded the massacre of the military commanders. During the trial stage a link between the military and the Party became impossible even down at the oblast committee level, not even speaking about the republic or the state level. The war against "enemies of the people" had reached a zenith, and even the deaths of Kuibyshev and Ordzhonikidze passed almost unnoticed.

The leading military commanders had been liquidated – but in the country there was widespread jubilation. The Stalininst Constitution, a false guarantor of the rights of workers and peasants, was being glorified. Heroes of the Russian Civil War had been the Order bearers, but now Stalin was hastily devaluating the title by creating a new class of Order recipients: writers, scientists, artists, even clowns[2] .... New Orders were introduced, of higher merit than those that decorated the heroes of the Civil War. The Leader was in process of creating celebrities in the country. Their names now and then flashed in the newspapers and in the titles of films, and rang out over the radio with the mandatory reference – the Order bearer such and such! The entire propaganda apparatus was heavily involved in the process of forcefully promoting this new category of Order bearers as the most popular people in the country. On the days of the session of the Main Military Council (about which the newspapers didn't report), the newspapers printed lists of those who had been awarded with Orders – the longest yet since they had begun to award people of the arts with them. On 2 June, 86 names; on 3 June, another 21 names. Among them were the opera singers Reizen, Lemeshev, Kozlovsky; the musicians Oistrakh, Gilels, Oborin ... Soon they were summoned to sign letters: they had to earn their awards! So the signatures appeared. May the Father and Leader of the working class Comrade Stalin live and be healthy! We no longer need anyone else on the earth, as long as he exists.

And he? "Believe, don't believe, but be afraid! Are you aware? Do you grasp what is going on? Oh! Then don't say a peep! All of you, don't say a word!! I'll deal with you one by one."

Here is how the national press in the Soviet Union fell all over itself when reporting on the show trial of the Trotskyist bloc:

> These people raised their filthy paws against Comrade Stalin. Having raised their paws against Comrade Stalin, they had raised them against us, against the working class, against the workers of the world. Having raised their paws against Comrade Stalin, they had raised them against the teachings of Marx-Engels-Lenin. Having raised their paws against Comrade Stalin, they had raised them against the humanism's greatest accomplishments. Stalin is our hope. Stalin is our future. Stalin is the helmsman of all progressive mankind. Stalin is our banner. Stalin is our will. Stalin is our victory.

That was the tone of the diligent media a year before, in 1936. What sort of plot or even

---

2   Among the Order recipients was Iurii Durov, a circus animal-trainer and clown from a famous family of Russian clowns.

intent could there have been against the Leader, given such an indicative outpouring of propaganda glorifying him and such a broadcast to the broad masses of the workers, raving with love for him?..

There is little reason to doubt in the authorship of this shamanistic ritual. Such zeal isn't inspired by honorariums, nor by fervent love, for which there was, incidentally, not any justification. These lines were inspired by a concern for oneself, for someone of genius and ardent narcissism. The Leader didn't dictate them; there was no need for this. Simply, while reading the latest version of the script a beautiful hand stroked a mustache and a kindly smile touched a pair of lips.

That's how the first recording of the choir of the humanists of the new epoch, of scientists, writers and artists, whose mission has always been, at all times, compassion even for notorious criminals, began to play a nasally song. The destruction of heroes, whose autographed photographs decorated their writing tables, stunned the humanists. If these are killed, on whom the country's defense relied, what were the artists and writers in comparison with them!? Terror gripped their throats. Having come to realize their own defenselessness, they began to sing a song of mercilessness, which was dictated to them, in their frantically high voices, even surpassing the stridency of the tyrant's own curses:

Death to the bloody killers!
Death to the traitors of the Motherland!
No mercy to the nefarious bastards!

Who, however, were the real bastards?

53

The Stalingrad Axis

The Leader's minions and the Deputy People's Commissar of Defense and Chief of the General Staff Colonel-General A. M. Vasilevsky are sent to Stalingrad. Meanwhile, the enemy is rolling through the Kuban and drawing quite near to Stalingrad. At this alarming hour for the Motherland, when the Red Army is retreating, while tribunals on the basis of Stalin's "genius" Order No. 227 are, as always, without hesitation, training the Red Army with bullets to the head – where is Zhukov?

As before, he is near Moscow, with the Western Front. So what is he doing there? Indeed nothing special; he is attacking.

Attacking – how? Attacking while the Red Army is retreating!?

Well, yes and no; the Red Army had learned a smattering about war, and it was attacking in those places where a commander had seized the initiative. It was not a simple thing to grab it back from a skilled adversary. Why? The Red Army had plenty of unskilled operational commanders.

The German command's planning of the 1942 summer campaign differs from Barbarossa by its clear-cut sense of realism. Obtainable goals were set. Moscow had ceased to be the primary object; its fall wouldn't open the same prospects, which would arise with the seizure of the Caucasus and by drawing Turkey into the war (as long as Japan refused to be drawn into it). However, it shouldn't be excluded from the OKW's calculations that the Germans knew that the single operational commander of the Red Army comparable to them in skill was holding Moscow. There, on his sector, he possessed the initiative and was using it to attack, while the Germans were defending and bringing up reserves that had been designated for use elsewhere. In the Sychevka – Pogoreloe-Gorodishche area in the middle of July, as the Germans went all out in their efforts to clear the Don River bend, savage fighting had flared up. The reinforced 20th Army (which had previously been Vlasov's) was attempting to break through the German front – and did so. There, where they had broken through, in the Kalinin swamps, the greatest tank battle to that point in history erupted, with more than 3,000 armored vehicles from both sides participating. The next clash of armor on that scale occurred a year later at Prokhorovka.

I'm skipping ahead, because I'm finishing this book with Stalingrad. Zhukov didn't have time to reach Prokhorovka before that battle started. The victory came at a heavy cost. The Red Army generals there still hadn't learned their craft, and were still undergoing training. The commander of the 5th Guards Tank Army Rotmistrov went straight into battle from a long march, and in his haste didn't manage to issue accurate assembly areas and clear lines of attack to his tank columns. In contrast, Zhukov in 1942 was still personally crawling around the front line under fire, when, as it happened, one couldn't even raise his head or, as Mikhail Svetlov joked, "One could raise his head, but only one separated from the body." He had to show the tank commanders what they were obliged to know how to do. In contrast, by the time of the Berlin operation, the commanders had been trained up to their ears, and Zhukov didn't have to crawl around the front line, pointing out jumping-

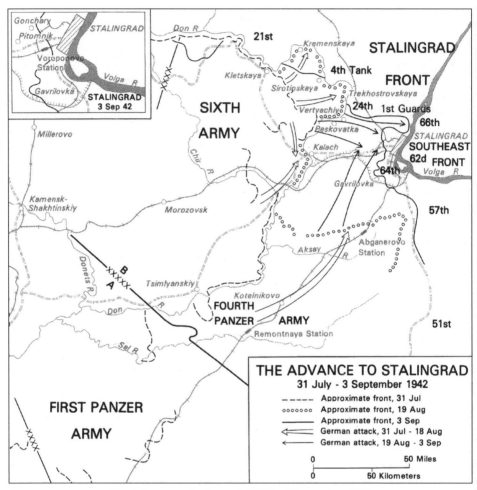

The Advance to Stalingrad, 31 July-3 September 1942

off positions. Indeed, there the Red Army's best troop leaders had been assembled under his command. The genuinely strongest army of all time and nations moved out for the final assault on Berlin. However, two years of war remained until that time, two years of bloody training for the generals. The losses were pinned upon Zhukov. Of course, he wasn't sinless, although the losses were achieved by combined efforts. In addition to that, by the end of 1942 Zhukov had become insensitive to losses, it seems that this cast a shadow over his old age. Incidentally, an analysis of Zhukov's spiritual changes is truly far off-topic. After all, this book isn't about Zhukov ...

The Marshal speaks about the events of 1942 with restrained pride:

> The enemy sustained heavy losses in the Pogoreloye-Gorodishche – Sychevka sector. In order to halt the thrust of the Western Front troops, the German command was forced to rush to there a considerable number of divisions, previously intended for the development of the offensive on Stalingrad and the Caucasus. K. von Tippelskirch, a German General, wrote on this matter: 'We managed to prevent a breakthrough due to the fact that three Panzer divisions and several infantry divisions which were ready to be transferred to the Southern Front, were held behind and committed first to localize the breakthrough and then to counterattack.'
>
> If we had one or two armies at our disposal, we could have, in conjunction with the Kalinin Front under General I. S. Konev, defeated not only the Rzhev group but the entire Rzhev-Vyazma German force and thus considerably improved the strategic situation in the Western strategic direction as a whole. Unfortunately, this opportunity was missed by the Supreme Command.
>
> True, I must say Stalin realized that the unfavorable situation in the summer of 1942 had resulted, among other things, from his own personal error made when approving the plan of operations of our forces in the 1942 summer campaign. And he did not seek any other guilty party among the leaders in General Headquarters or the General Staff.

The Leader understood: he wasn't Zhukov, and this wasn't the time for a new 1937. You finish off the remainder – and what, fight by yourself? Thus even the former commander of the Crimean Front, Kozlov, resurfaces in the area of Stalingrad – and fights. One beaten general costs as much as two unbeaten ones. Kozlov is not Zhukov, of course, but ...

54

Interlude: Zhukov ...

... was imposing his will on those same German generals, in front of whom the Soviet troops of the southern wing of the Soviet-German front were retreating. The training in the ranks of the RKKA of at least one such commander characterizes in the best possible way the high professional capabilities of the executed army commanders. There had been a many such pupils. The greater portion of them perished in the purge together with their mentors. Whose fault was it that at the moment of the start of the war, there were no other men like Zhukov in the higher command posts of the Red Army? Only because of the suspicion in the guilt of Tukhachevsky, Iakir and their comrades, the Army's best officers were arrested and eliminated. According to the evidence of one of the surviving veterans of the Red Army, Lieutenant General Todorsky, who squandered 18 years of his life in jail cells and prison camps, but after the death of Stalin headed the commission that oversaw the rehabilitation of military men, the number of commanders who perished in the purges were as follows: three of the five Marshals; three of the five Army Commanders, 1st Rank; both Army Commissars, 1st Rank; both Flagman of the Fleet, 1st Rank; all ten Army Commanders, 2nd Rank; all fifteen Army Commissars, 2nd Rank; and both Flagman of the Fleet, 2nd Rank. In addition, 60 of the 67 corps commanders were repressed (57 of whom were executed); all six Flagman, 1st Rank and nine of fifteen Flagman, 2nd Rank were destroyed; 25 of 28 corps commissars were repressed (23 of whom were shot) and 136 of 199 division commanders (of which only eleven returned from imprisonment). Finally, out of the 397 brigade commanders, 221 were repressed (200 of whom perished).[1]

Almost all the arrested were shot after brief investigations, accompanied by beatings and humiliations.[2] The execution by a bullet to the back of the head immediately followed a 15- to 20-minute reading of the absurd and false charges, fabricated by the Chekists. A commission of three men, the notorious "Extraordinary Troika", which replaced the judiciary in Stalin's USSR, read out the sentences. Others of the arrested were beaten to death by the interrogators in the torture chambers, or killed themselves, being unable to endure the torture, or died in prison camps. The obvious fault of all these people was one and the same – they were people of character who had their own opinion about what was happening in the Red Army.

When brigade commander G. K. Zhukov was still little known to anyone and not more than an a commander of a cavalry division with an average education, brigade commander S. P. Obysov was serving as the Chief of the RKKA General Staff's Operations Department (a position later occupied by A. M. Vasilevsky), and judging from the recollections of the military commanders who knew him, he was a quite extraordinary military chief. Zhukov survived, triumphed at Khalkhin-Gol, and became famous in the Great Patriotic War.

---

1   *Ogonek*, No. 13, 1989, p. 29.
2   According to K. A. Meretskov, Zhukov's predecessor in the General Staff and who later became a Marshal and Hero of the Soviet Union, the interrogating officer urinated on him in order to bring Meretskov back to consciousness after he had knocked out all of the General of the Army's teeth.

Obysov, however, after escaping an execution by White Guards in the Civil War (he was captured, shot together with a group of others, then covered with blood, but still alive, he dug his way out of the fraternal grave, crawled back to his own lines, fought, completed both the Soviet and German military academies, and served)[3] received a bullet to the back of the head. What memoirs might brigade commander Obysov have written, had he passed through the Great Patriotic War! But of course there wouldn't have been such a war, and Mister Hitler would have behaved much more circumspectly, had Stalin not destroyed his magnificent Army.

Wherever Zhukov was, there was an offensive ... yet it might have been everywhere, where the fronts would have been commanded by men who understood each other's half-words, like Iakir, Uborevich and Bliukher, together with their noted, promoted and fully-trained Zhukovs and Rokossovskys, while Tukhachevsky and Egorov were in the General Staff with their protégés ... and then not only would there have been nothing like Zhukov's clash with Kulik at Leningrad or the Crimean and Khar'kov calamities, but also nothing like the entire nightmare of the summer of 1941, not to mention the disaster and dishonor of the summer of 1942.

In the summer of 1942, the RKKA was deprived of even a single commander like Zhukov. Zhukov was available, but he was commanding the Western Front. In this role, excluded from discussions of the general situation on the fronts, he was prevented from participating in the defense of those ideas, which Shaposhnikov and Vasilevsky were unable to defend. In their case, the matter was not a lack of understanding, but of character.

Perhaps even the entire situation in the country would have been different? And the entire system would have been turned around by a different face? After all, the civilian government bureaucrats had also been "cleansed", just like the military commanders ...

---

3   O. F. Suvenirov, *Tragediia RKKA* [*Tragedy of the RKKA*] (Moscow: Terra, 1998).

55

Summer 1942

As a result of the bungling at Voronezh, fighting the likes of which mankind had never seen before developed in the expanses of the USSR. The country was exerting all its strength. The dead were piling up a thousand kilometers behind the front – dead from exhaustion, dead from illnesses, from diseases, from despair. Enormous smoke columns from conflagrations were rising into the cosmos. The planet was shaking, seized with the flames of war, and millions of souls reverently rose to heaven. The *Wehrmacht's* finest forces were bearing down on Stalingrad. The city was burning, shattered by a beastly bombing raid. Its fate was hanging by a thread. On 27 August Stalin requested for Zhukov to appear at the *Stavka*. By the way, the evening before Poskrebyshev had called Zhukov to inform him that the GKO (the GKO ... not Stalin ...) had decided to appoint Zhukov (a General of the Army, bypassing Marshals!) as First Deputy of the Supreme Commander.

Hmm, the scapegoats were not being prepared on the eve of victory, but on the precipice of disaster. In addition, the appointment also worked to encourage Zhukov, officially erasing his fall from grace, which is what his appointment to command the Western Front had actually been. It was also time to save Stalingrad. Stalin now understood that Moscow wasn't Hitler's goal, so it turned out that Zhukov had nothing to do in front of Moscow.

The plan of Operation Blau foresaw the destruction of Soviet armies in the course of seizing Stalingrad in passing, with a subsequent, now unobstructed advance toward Astrakhan and into the Caucasus. It is interesting, and in a strange fashion it has not been noted: now the Führer had no concerns about the Moscow flank hanging over Kleist's advancing group, like a year before the much weaker Kiev flank had so troubled him. The configuration of the front lines, as in 1941, had become a result of operational circumstances, but now there was confidence that the Soviet "fist" in the north couldn't hinder Army Group South from reaching the oil fields.

This had not happened only because of the Führer's nervous opportunism. The resistance of the Soviet troops in the great bend of the Don River had disrupted the *Wehrmacht's* timetable, but the oil was beckoning, so the Führer ordered a drive into the Caucasus without waiting for the fall of Stalingrad, but for the city to be taken without delay – yet this was a twin departure from the plan for the campaign. While Hoth's 4th Panzer Army, raising clouds of dust, exhilaratingly rolled across the Kuban, which is as flat as an armor training ground, Vasilevsky in the bend of the Don River, given a certain freedom of maneuver after Hoth's departure, was directing desperate maneuvers with semi-encircled armies just like in 1941: pinning down the *Wehrmacht's* forces, delaying their advance, and hurling troops into counterattacks without waiting for them to assemble, which given the Luftwaffe's supremacy in the air was still impossible, and as a result, although at the cost of great losses, he managed to hold the Germans on the Don for almost a month.

A new chapter of the war ... from where did it stem? Seemingly from an alarmed comment of one of the German generals: "The Russians have resurrected their old skill of rear-guard fighting." What had prompted this statement? Although Operation Blau had been a surprise at the courtesy of the Leader of All Nations, it didn't result in the encirclements of 1941. The Red Army fell back, snarling. It didn't allow itself to be encircled, and its rearguards clung to critical lines to the last man.

The Southwestern Front (commanded by Marshal Timoshenko) hadn't prepared reserve lines of defense. The Voronezh Front was commanded by Lieutenant General F. I. Golikov, the same Chief of the GRU, who before the war had accompanied intelligence data pointing to German preparations for an invasion of the USSR with comments pleasing to Stalin.[1] There are different opinions about his performance as the Voronezh Front commander. However, for the sake of justice it should be noted that the counterattacks by his *front* – though it is true, under pressure from the *Stavka* – allowed Timoshenko to withdraw the armies of his Southwestern Front behind the Oskol and Donets Rivers. Since there were no prepared fallback positions (just as prior to the Khar'kov catastrophe, the *Stavka* was still ready only to march unceasingly forward, to the West!), the withdrawing troops clung to any natural obstacle. Order № 227 proved to be effective ... It was precisely on the subject of Southwestern Front's withdrawal that the aforementioned comment by the German general was uttered about the Russian skill in rearguard fighting. This remark doubtlessly testified to the fact that the toughness of the Red Army in the fighting in the summer of 1942 once again directed the German generals' thoughts toward the fate of Napoleon.

During the month of tussling in the Don River bend with the Southwestern Front,[2] which was being strategically directed from Moscow by Vasilevsky, but tactically, in the field, by Marshal Timoshenko, the *Wehrmacht's* Caucasus spearhead drove ever further to the south, and the insecurity of the spearhead's elongating northern flank made both the Führer and his Headquarters nervous. It can be assumed that in order to distract (with the silent consent of his patron?) Hitler from the Caucasus, Vasilevsky provoked him with Stalingrad, with these uninterrupted attacks on the periphery of the city's defenses, and with this activity he fully succeeded. From an intermediate point, which it had been according to the OKW's plan, Stalingrad became a threat to the distantly separated Army Group South, while for Hitler it had grown into a matter of principle: this was Stalin's city! The Führer pulled the Fourth Panzer Army back from the Caucasus to the Stalingrad axis, while there in the course of one single day, 23 August, a German panzer wedge outflanked the Red Army troops fighting along the Don and crossed the interval between the Don and Volga Rivers, and emerged on the Volga on the northern outskirts of Stalingrad. The sudden advance prompted jubilation in the OKW and seemed to be a decisive step toward seizing Stalingrad. However, I assume that its main significance turned out to be the instructive role that it played: the Soviet General Staff received a priceless lesson that later proved costly to the *Wehrmacht*. It was just at this point that Zhukov was plucked out of his "exile" with the Western Front.

When the Führer's obsession with Stalingrad had become clear, the propaganda machines on both sides kicked into full gear. One revived the legend of Tsaritsyn' – here, one side said, was where the fate of the Civil War had been decided. The other asserted that here was the heart of Russia, and on the Volga its fate would be settled. Hitler knew that it wasn't so simple for Stalin to give up the city bearing his name. That meant that the fight

---

1   Golikov subsequently became a Marshal and Chief of the Main Political Directorate of the Soviet Army.

2   American newspapers in July and August 1942 came out with large headlines: "The Russians have Stopped the Germans on the Don!" and "Defensive Fighting of the Red Army on the Don!"

for this city was an opportunity to crush the remaining Soviet armies. Crush! The Führer couldn't give up this illusion ...

The Southwestern Front's 62nd Army retreated back to the city. General Lopatin had preserved it, but after all the perturbations, General Chuikov, who was not timid when on his own and also fearless of the Germans, was appointed to command the Army. Prior to this he had served as an advisor to Chiang Kai-shek. On the Don River and in Stalingrad, he acted with the zeal of a neophyte, who had resolved not to recognize the possibility of defeat. About him it can be said without any stretch that "victory or death" was his slogan. He had fallen back to Stalingrad after doing his part in the vitally important Don battles, which had taught him every aspect of the adversary.

Somehow managing to stabilize the situation in Stalingrad with the reserves he requested, Zhukov became imbued with confidence that Stalingrad was now Hitler's objective. With that, he returned to the *Stavka*.

With Stalingrad as its goal, the German command bound hand and foot of its own initiative and deprived itself of freedom of maneuver. Meanwhile at the start of August, it was in the Caucasus where the *Wehrmacht* was plainly finding success. Easily forcing a crossing of the Kerch Strait, as could have been expected, the Germans seized Temriuk and Eisk (eliminating the Soviet Azov Flotilla at the same time), and with a strike from the north, took both Armavir and Stavropol. However, Hitler refused to go on defense in the Don River bend, and an offensive required a lot of reserves. Between 1 and 15 August, the Führer threw 15 infantry divisions and three panzer corps into the fighting there. Most of these troops might have been committed to the Caucasus, decisively changing the strategic situation. Stalin, in his turn, still withheld most of his reserves closer to Moscow. The Caucasus remained exposed.

Neither I, as I write these lines, nor anyone else, will ever find out how close the USSR had been to collapse in 1941. What opportunities did the *Wehrmacht* miss by failing to send just one reconnaissance battalion in a certain direction? What sudden downpour delayed the advance of Barbarossa before the arrival of reinforcements from the Far East, and where did it take place, thereby sparing a weak Soviet blocking force, and with it the USSR? The opportunities that the Führer missed in the Caucasus in the summer of 1942, by failing to concentrate on one goal, will remain just as unknown. We will not talk about miracles; this isn't seemly to the valor of both the German and Soviet fighting men. Fortunately, fate itself wound up on the Soviet side in both 1941 and 1942.

Human resources in the Caucasus and Transcaucasus were limited, and the road network was poor. The Supreme Commanders had believed that they could always reinforce a critical axis, as long as they possessed reserves. Indeed, reserves were available. However, in September 1942, the military situation blocked both the overland and sea routes for shifting Soviet reserves to the Caucasus. The emergence of the *Wehrmacht* on the Black Sea coast created a strategic *cul de sac*. Soviet troops could not be delivered to the Caucasus or evacuated from there. The Caucasus region became isolated, and with its volatile ethnographic mix, an explosive situation had been created. The Muslim mountain nationalities and Turkey were all waiting to see what would happen. Only in 1991, when the USSR broke up and the Caucasus began to boil did it become clear what opportunities Hitler had missed in the summer of 1942. To trigger Turkey's intervention into the war, the appearance of the *Wehrmacht* on its border would have been a much more compelling achievement than the taking of Stalingrad. Even if the combat capabilities of the Turkish army could not be compared with *Wehrmacht*, or even with the Red Army, it had one thing that could not be taken away from it: It carried out police functions impeccably well, and Hitler wouldn't need any more than that. The *Wehrmacht* could then commit all its strength for a lunge at Baku, leaving behind the Caucasus, torn by national ambitions, to the merciless Turkish rule. Stalingrad – this was a transient name. Illusory propagandistic aims obstructed the Führer's vision of realistic political goals. The disastrous 1941 winter campaign hadn't taught him anything. Failing to take Moscow, he decided, as if in revenge, to take Stalingrad.

Would the seizure of Stalingrad yield so much? Hitler could hardly have been seriously contemplating such a utopian idea as the establishment of a bridgehead beyond the wide Volga River in the vicinity of the city. By taking Stalingrad, the river traffic from Astrakhan to Nizhnyi Novgorod would have ceased functioning, but it had already been paralyzed anyway. However, the roads in the rear would have been still operational, and they could feed the front with Baku oil.

On the other hand, a blockade of the Caucasus – in the extreme case, even without seizing it – by means of driving to the Caspian Sea across the Kalmyk Steppes would have been even more effective than the capture of Stalingrad. Several Luftwaffe squadrons based near the Caspian Sea would have been capable of interrupting both the supply of oil to the Red Army, and the transfer of forces, even by sea. With the severing of connections with the central authority in Moscow, a blockade would have led to unavoidable internecine wars and a collapse of local Soviet authority. That's why the 1942 campaign should have been directed at the very least toward a blockade of the Caucasus by reaching the Caspian Sea and the border with Turkey. This advance could have been successfully conducted with Field Marshal List's Army Group A and Hoth's Fourth Panzer Army. With the Führer's decision, the Fourth Panzer Army left the Caucasus but was too late for the maneuvering stage of the offensive on Stalingrad.

The bitterness of the fighting in the Caucasus was no less than that of the fighting in Stalingrad. At the Novorossiisk cement factories and on the approaches to Tuapse, there was the same hell. In just the same way, brick buildings and tool sheds changed hands many times as the two sides fought over them, dying men behind their machine guns continued to fire while their life blood drained away, and men with bundles of grenades threw themselves under tanks. The difference was in the complete lack of Red Army reserves in the Caucasus. Now not only ships' crews were thrown into the fighting, but also intelligence units, military cadets, and the staff of army rear departments and even headquarters: there were no reserves![3] In the list of the defenders of Novorossiisk, there are not divisions and regiments, but battalions of naval infantry, artillerymen of the coastal defenses, even blocking detachments – "Captain Matveichuk's battalion". Some units remain forgotten even up to the present time.[4] Shuffling commanders and as a result losing the picture of

---

3   The commander of the Novorossiisk naval base, G. N. Kholostiakov, was ordered to gather together all the headquarters' staff and lead them personally into battle, which was in fact done – with no result, of course.

4   I can't forget the subterfuges I used through my friend, the writer and war veteran Grigorii Glazov and his acquaintance, a special correspondent with the *Krasnaia zvezda* newspaper in the Prikarpatskii District, Colonel Arkadii Pinchuk, to try to publish materials in *Krasnaia zvezda* about a forgotten military unit, the 2nd Separate Naval Infantry Battalion, which played a decisive role in the defense of Novorossiisk – event to the point of appealing to the USSR Commander-in-Chief of the Navy Admiral S. G. Gorshkov. Even Gorshkov's note on the margin of my article, "That's correct!" for a long time had no effect. The authority of the Commander-in-Chief of the Navy, a veteran of the fighting and the chief of the

the situation in this region, the General Headquarters informed the Sovinformburo that Novorosiisk had fallen, and in its summary of latest events the Sovinformburo made this announcement on 10 September. They might as well have reported the same thing about the surrender of Stalingrad. In comparative terms, by the end of the defensive stage of the fighting, the Red Army held less of Stalingrad than it did of Novorossiisk, where between 7 and 10 September sailors and coastal artillerymen stood fast on the line Red October Cement Factory – Adamovicheva balka and from this line never retreated. However, Novorossiisk didn't carry the name of the Leader, so they weren't ceremonious with it.

If Hitler hadn't been diverted by Stalingrad, he would have understood where the outcome of the campaign would be decided. Oil, in the autumn of the previous year, had diverted him from Moscow. Now it was within reach, but the Führer became mesmerized with Stalingrad. The return of the Hoth's Fourth Panzer Army from the Caucasus to the Stalingrad axis was similar to the diversion in 1941 of von Rundstedt toward Rostov, rather than assisting the right flank of von Bock as his Army Group Center thrust toward Moscow. This order causes one to ponder a rather trivial topic – the role of personality. In truth, one of Stalin's actions must be given its due – the renaming of Tsaritsyn into Stalingrad. If the city had carried a different name, it is unlikely that a major struggle would have developed in this area.

Regarding Soviet historiography's conceptualizing of the war, the English historian John Erickson, who has been previously mentioned in this book, with the tact of an ally divulged (in passing, in the notes to the text of his book *The Road to Stalingrad*) that the goal of Soviet historians was not an accurate description of the war, but the creation of an heroic myth. I would rather say that it wasn't the aim of the historians, but the aim of the CPSU apparatus. The historians' hands were tied, and they weren't allowed to work. Instead, heroic mythmaking was favored! Having fallen into disfavor, even top-notch authors, after writing something that was declared seditious, and given no possibility of publishing original works, took up the writing of history. They could earn some money for this. As a result, Soviet books about the war consist primarily of pulp fiction, which grandiosely glorify the role of the Party. War veterans' memoirs were fiercely edited and didn't always contain the very essence of that which the veterans knew and wanted to tell. There were no consistent, day by day descriptions of the basic course of combat operations on the Soviet-German front published, nor any writing about the administrative and social history of the war. Yet after all, considering the enormous wave of evacuation, this would have been an important page on the war. Its absence gives some historians the justification doubt the very fact of that unique rallying of efforts nation-wide, which by right attained the name "Great Patriotic War".

An interesting aspect of this for us is the fact that as a result of the tendentiousness of the Soviet historical science, even academic Soviet history books absolve the Führer of charges of incompetence. The Führer, in the Soviet interpretation, made no mistakes. His

---

Novorossiisk garrison, could not contend with the stubbornness of the ideological apparatus. The chief editor, a Lieutenant General, kept growling that we didn't have any unknown heroes. Only the sympathy and assistance of employees on the newspaper staff (who were primarily Fleet officers) and especially its conscientious secretary Captain, 1st Rank Oleg Borisovich Baronov, made this and subsequent publications possible. Even in the military literature of today, there is no mention of the 2nd Separate Naval Infantry Battalion, with the exception of Gorshkov's own book, *Na iuzhnom primorskom flange* [*On the southern maritime flank*] (Moscow, 1989).

only mistake was the invasion of the USSR. The war was won not as a result of the sum of circumstances, including the Führer's miscalculations, but as a result of the managing role of the Party and the wise decisions of Comrade Stalin. The heroic efforts of the people – this was secondary.

Yet the staggering dimensions of its losses speak to the heroism of the people. In contrast, Stalin did his work in the role of a fiendish administrator, working to save his own life.

As for the role of the Party, it is only possible to deny it in a polemic fervor. After all, the Party, at the time of the Great Patriotic War, wasn't that flabby and greasy body, which later infected the empire with gangrene. It was the living nerve of the steel muscle, which controlled the fist that Stalin manipulated and died together with him. Oh, how Soviet power grew irritated at the mention of such components of the victory as lend-lease, the factors of non-existent roads and the climate, or the Führer's mistakes! Indeed, everything was done to strengthen the heroic myth.

This is how the opinion took root that the transfer of the Fourth Panzer Army from the Caucasus to Stalingrad "did not represent a free play of mind of the German General Staff officers" (D. Proektor, *Aggressiia i katastrofa* [*Aggression and catastrophe*]; we'll return to this work...). So the transfer was not a mistake, but a compulsory response to the Supreme Commander's deployment of reserves to the Volga, which caused Hitler to fear an attack into Army Group South's rear.

Hitler didn't know about the shift of Soviet reserves to the Volga (the shock of the Soviet counteroffensive for him testifies to that). At that time, the *Stavka* still had no intention of a counteroffensive at Stalingrad. The Moscow axis was regarded as the critical one until the German forces became fully bogged down in Stalingrad. Indeed, the Fourth Panzer Army's shift from the Caucasus to the Stalingrad "did not represent a free play of mind" of the German generals. This venomous comment is accurate, though it was the Führer's own personal decision. After the diversion toward Kiev – and even more so after splitting his forces near Moscow! – it is hardly worth speaking seriously about a triumph of the Führer. The United States was already fighting and putting itself on a war footing. The British Empire had also won a year. However, had Hitler set the goal for the 1942 summer campaign as the isolation of the Caucasus, the course of the war might have gone differently. The point is, however, that the successes of Operation Blau rekindled a hope for victory in the Führer. So as in 1941, he coveted the crushing of the *entire* Red Army. He couldn't imagine that an *entire* nation could be placed under arms. At the time he couldn't. Later he would do the same thing even more mercilessly – he would call young boys and old men to duty.

Stalin is defending Stalingrad? Then that's where we'll head! We'll put an end to the Red Army – and that will be the end of the war.

The losses of the Red Army were horrendous. However, the losses of the *Wehrmacht* had also become commensurate, and this was much greater than Germany could afford, especially in a war which for it had not yet become total. By selecting Stalingrad as the goal, Hitler chose a hopeless option. This move was predictable. At Stalingrad he was awaited.

The stubbornness of the Führer in committing blunders is striking: the dispersal of forces in 1941 and 1942; and the head-on collision (which was totally against von Schlieffen and German military doctrine) with the defending Red Army both at Stalingrad and Kursk. Just as did Stalin, Hitler considered himself to be his army's top strategist, but in contrast with Stalin, he never woke up from this misconception.

The *Stavka* reserves remained in the center of the country, so Hitler headed for Stalingrad. However, at both Novorossiisk and Tuapse there were no reserves and the Germans by redirecting the Fourth Panzer to Stalingrad lacked that straw to break the camel's back. With respect to these circumstances it is possible that the shift of Hoth's Fourth Panzer Army from the Caucasus to Stalingrad became the turning point of the 1942 summer campaign on the Eastern Front of the Second World War.[5]

---

5   Von Mellenthin concluded simply and flatly: "There followed one of the greatest misfortunes in German military history – the splitting of our effort between Stalingrad and the Caucasus. ... In the autumn of 1942 Hitler committed the oldest and the simplest mistake in warfare – neglect of the principle of concentration. The diversion of effort between the Caucasus and Stalingrad ruined our whole campaign."

56

The Stalingrad Defense

In justification of the fact that only the wartime name of the city is mentioned in this book, I will cite the words of Aleksandr Bovin.[1] To a question as to whether it was true that Volgograd would be renamed as Stalingrad again, Bovin replied that he didn't know, but stated "... it is necessary to rename it. The majority of Soviet people have been born since the war. They should know the name of the person, who allowed the Germans to reach Stalingrad." In its tone, this is one of the best sarcastic comments I've ever heard. In essence, Bovin meant, of course, not the refurbishing of the county's memory of the despot, but the immortalization of the people's achievement.

From the start of the defense of Stalingrad, Soviet propaganda resurrected the myth of Tsaritsyn and adorned it with fabricated details. Was this the first instance? The Panfilov heroes[2] are an exemplary example. What's the importance that there weren't 28 of them, that they weren't Guardsmen yet, and that it was only the 4th Rifle Company? Really, did not thousands of unknown men prior to this lay down their lives not in companies, but in platoons, in squads, or else even in just twos and threes, refusing to retreat? Propaganda isn't history, it is a work horse. Who ventures to judge the desperate propaganda of war times ...?

Again we'll repeat: the place was already sacred before the epopee. For a defense it was suitable not only ideologically. A sprawling city in a bend of the broad Volga River, it was ideally unsuited for assaulting and reliably connected to the rear. The river secured both flanks and prevented soldiers from fleeing. The invulnerable water surface served as a route for ferrying supplies and let down the defenders only on one occasion – when it began to freeze-up and slush ice formed. By then, however, the counteroffensive was ready and the Germans were worn out. The city, which stretched along the river for almost 50 miles, stretched the assault forces. Its layout lent itself to the defense: several streets parallel to the river were like lines of redoubts. Everything was favorable for carrying out of Order No. 227. In this battle, which reached animal ferocity, the brave men and cowards became warriors of the same intensity of fury and despair. The streets of Stalingrad turned into fortified lines. Ravines turned into shelters. The reinforced concrete hulks of factories with underground basement levels became fortresses, sheltering the forces for counterattacks and even for local counterstrokes. The majority of the population of the city consisted of workers. They played their role in the first stage of the defense.

---

1   Aleksandr Evgen'evich Bovin (1930-2004) was a Soviet and Russian journalist, publicist, political analyst and diplomat.

2   Editor's note: Supposedly, twenty-eight men of the Major-General I. S. Panfilov's 316th Rifle Division opposed a German offensive column, destroyed several German tanks and delayed the German advance on Moscow in November 1941, fighting in a self-sacrificial manner to the last man with no survivors or witnesses. They were quickly immortalized by Soviet propaganda and labeled "Pantsilovtsy" in honor of the General, who was later killed in action in the Moscow counteroffensive. However, with the breakup of the Soviet Union, this legend has received enormous scrutiny and been largely deconstructed.

These are the factors that determined the course of events. It is unknown if they were considered in the initial decision to hold the city. Probably, Stalin had at least some of them in mind when back on 20 July in a discussion with the Secretary of the Stalingrad Oblast committee Chuianov he forbade the evacuation of the civilians.[3] Doubtlessly, these combined circumstances weren't considered by Hitler. The Führer in his imagination could overcome anything. He remembered that the mere threat of bombing Rotterdam had prompted that city's capitulation. In Stalingrad, though, the brutal bombing (described by Vasilii Grossman with startling effect, just like he did the entire battle) produced a reverse effect. The destruction of the city enraged the living. Wrath is stronger than fear. It was the rare family in which a mother, child, wife or all of them together weren't killed. Yet cities, which do not fall immediately, become fortresses, and that should never be forgotten.

However, if Stalin is to be credited, it is better to forget. Those who cannot separate citizens' self-sacrifice from the cynical use of their lives by their leader should refrain from discussing this altogether. Because the leader's greatest accomplishment lies in the fact that in the summer of 1942 the Nazi hordes ended up in the middle of the country's heartland, from where the people of all nationalities, both Communists and non-Communists, at the cost of their blood and their lives flushed them out over the course of nearly three years.

---

3   Stalingrad was full of children, who had been evacuated to it in the spring from blockaded Leningrad. The Leningrad resident Aleksandra Vasil'evna N., the landlady of the apartment where I stayed on my visits to Leningrad, spent the entire siege with two children aged 3 and 5 in the tunnels and basements of Stalingrad, fed now by Soviet soldiers, now by German soldiers. For a description of what she experienced, more than a book would be required.

57

Interlude: The Author ...

... is approaching the end of this narrative. Now it is no longer necessary to follow the outline of the memoirs of the one to whom history handed the role as the greatest commander of the Second World War. The narrative was linked with him only to expose the circumstances that propelled him to a place about which he had never even dreamed.

Not everyone will accept the attribution to him of such a decisive role. However, it may be argued relatively simply.

It is impossible to deny that the damage inflicted upon the enemy is the main criterium for evaluating a commander. As such, even without resorting to statistics, one can safely assert that neither the scale of the operations nor the *Wehrmacht's* losses on the Western Front were comparable to what they were on the Eastern Front. So given Zhukov's known and acknowledged decision-making role on the Eastern Front, it automatically places him on the top pedestal in the history of the Second World War.

There are other opinions, however. Veteran I. Saksonov, a Colonel in the Reserve who was the deputy technical officer to a corps commander in Rybalko's 3rd Tank Army in the war, bitterly rebukes Zhukov for the enormous casualties and characterizes him as a commander, who " ... cannot be placed significantly above Konev, Rokossovsky, Vasilevsky, Shaposhnikov, Malinovsky, Antonov, Petrov ..."

The individuals in this list are quite unequal in merit, but that is not the point. There is another question: "cannot be placed significantly above" – when? In 1944-45? Yes, it is true, at that time Zhukov had some equals. (After all, though, in years of victory even generals' courage is different ...) Or are we speaking about 1941, in June, when Shaposhnikov was trembling, like everyone else, while Zhukov was squandering his tankers without air cover in counterstrokes against the *Wehrmacht's* panzer aces? Konev even in October 1941 still didn't understand how to employ his tanks, and was learning at the expense of his soldiers' blood. When did Konev become a tank general? In the summer of 1944, when he also had Rybalko under his command? When did an alternative to Zhukov as a frontline operational commander first appear? In the summer of 1942? Yet prior to this, whom could you mandate to fight, especially under Stalin?

Yes, Zhukov inflicted terrible losses upon the *Wehrmacht* at the cost of even more terrible losses to the Red Army. However, can he really be blamed for the fact that in the six months at his position as the Chief of the General Staff, he was unable to grow a generation of generals and officers to replace those murdered by Stalin? That he couldn't produce enough radio sets for headquarters? That he couldn't train soldiers, as they had been trained before the purge? That he didn't show peasant-infantrymen how to operate in a loose formation according to the situation? That he didn't instruct pilots to fly, and teach tankers how to find suitable positions? The knowledge of the *Reichswehr-Wehrmacht* panzer drivers had been honed and polished over the years. The *Wehrmacht* had been tempered in battles against weak armies in Poland, France, Yugoslavia and Greece. In contrast we sent young lads with only five hours of driving experience into battle, and pilots who only knew how to take off and land. In Joseph Brodsky's ingeniously brief summation, Zhukov was "... As a commander, making walls crumble, he held a sword less sharp than his foe's." Shall we forget about this? Disregard it?

Zhukov's achievements on behalf of the country are first of all (and even exceptionally) his achievements of 1941-42. The Soviet casualties, especially in the first period of the war, are direct consequences of the purge of the RKKA. This cruel war could have been ended by others, who'd been whipped into shape by Zhukov – and the *Wehrmacht*. Could they have brought it to an end with less bloody fighting than Zhukov? Under Stalin? Hardly. Yet first someone had to stabilize the situation, to save the country, even at the cost of blood and with the assistance of the elements. An entire year passed before a person fully equal to Zhukov[1] developed in the fighting; then such generals appeared in a full bouquet – but now in a different stage of the war!

One more thing: an abyss separates these two capabilities – the ability to see a correct decision, and the ability to adopt a decision; or to give advice and to take advice, and along with it the responsibility for its implementation. Both Shaposhnikov and Vasilevsky could see correct decisions. However, to defend such decisions, to insist upon them, to implement them, despite all obstacles and setbacks, for this one needs character in addition to decision-making ability. Not one other general in sight at the start of the war possessed such character. Dispute? With whom, the Leader? To stand firm on one's own opinion after such a devastating purge? There's no better indicator of the purge's success: not only a second Tukhachevsky couldn't be found in the country, but a second Zhukov either. He had not experienced the torture chambers, but he was so hardened that he would have even accepted time in one – and he wouldn't have signed any confessions of guilt.

---

1   The author means first of all A.M.Vasilevsky, who at the beginning of war was a Major-General and Chief of the Operations Department of the General Staff.

58

The Concept

For some reason I always thought that when bringing the Leader around to thoughts of conceiving an offensive operation at Stalingrad, Zhukov and Vasilevsky had calculated that the city's name would tickle the Leader's narcissism with the possibility of entering history with a major military operation at a city bearing his name. The Battle at Stalingrad! As it has become clear, this wasn't so. The name of the city first of all entranced the Führer, and in the attempt to seize the city, he had, as chess players call it, left the Sixth Army *en prise* [French, meaning "exposed to capture"] in Stalingrad. The Red Army had only to take advantage of this blunder.

Now, the question was how the Red Army could take advantage of this. The terrain between the Don and Volga Rivers is ideal tank country, which the Germans themselves unwittingly made known to Soviets back on 23 August 1942 with their own breakthrough toward Stalingrad. At that time, as if putting an end to the Red Army's tenacious resistance in the bend of the Don River, a German panzer corps in the span of one day crossed the entire interval between the Don and Volga Rivers and emerged on the Volga on the northern outskirts of Stalingrad.

Now, when the Germans had become bogged down in the bitter street fighting in Stalingrad of a sort unknown in history, the situation called for a scheme of concentric attacks, which would create a double ring and form inward-facing and outward-facing fronts in order to prevent attempts to liberate the encircled German forces from any direction. The ring was planned to slam closed in the 6th Army's deep rear, beyond the Don River, so as to hamper German efforts to bring up reserves and to parry the Soviet attacks. Elementary!

Here's how Vasilevsky described the planning process:

> ... Zhukov and I summed up the work done among the troops. On 13 November,[1] we presented the amended plan at a session of the Party Central Committee's Politburo and the GHQ. In brief our conclusions consisted in the following. The German troop

---

1   My suspicion of some secret, hidden in the Stalingrad operation, arose precisely from this date of 13 November given by Vasilevsky, when I was doing a second reading of Marshal Vasilevsky's memoirs. The date 13 November 1942 is almost on the very eve of the operation! Yet what had happened previously? How was such a glittering plan for the operation conceived? From Zhukov's memoirs it becomes clear that the general plan of the campaign was formulated at a meeting involving Stalin, Vasilevsky and Zhukov himself on 12 September 1942. Two months prior, yet Vasilevsky doesn't have a word to say about the plan?! The period from the beginning of September until the middle of November has simply been dropped. The same gap yawns in Zhukov's memoirs as well. Why? The well-versed Soviet reader knows: if a Soviet military commander in his memoirs suddenly switches to a discussion of the increase in military production, to praising the efforts of the Soviet people, or to describing the heroism of the defenders of the Motherland and the significance of the Party in organizing the resistance at the front and in the rear, that means he wishes to hide something important that took place in the period that he is neglecting. Both Marshals do the exact same thing in their memoirs. The same sort of gap in the memoirs of both commanders is discernible as well in their account of the year leading up to the German invasion in 1941.

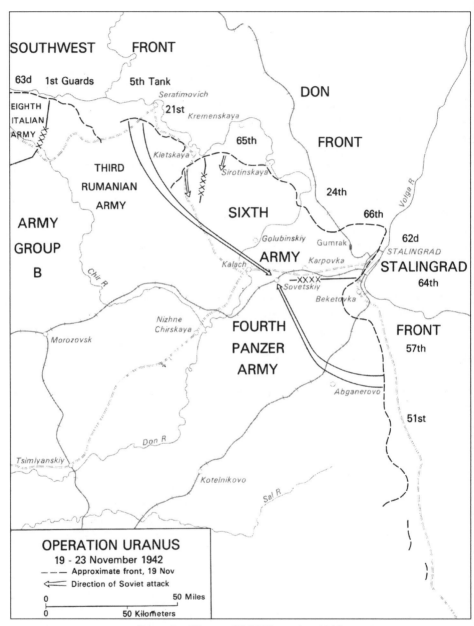

Operation Uranus, 19-23 November 1942

grouping would basically remain as before: the main forces of the Sixth and Fourth Panzer Armies would continue to be involved in protracted fighting in the area of the city. The Romanian units would remain on the flanks of these forces (that is, in the areas of our major attacks). We had not observed any more or less substantial reserves being brought up to the Stalingrad area from the interior. And we had not noted any essential regroupings taking place in the enemy troops operating there. *On the whole the strength of both sides at Stalingrad, as far as we could judge, was roughly equal at the beginning of the offensive.* (Emphasis the author's)

The *Wehrmacht's* ability not to be at a loss when encircled was taken into account, and determining the numerical strength of the German groupings doubtlessly received particular attention. Participants in the operation recall the *Stavka's* strictness in assembling intelligence and identifying enemy formations and even units in the theater of the forthcoming operation. Scout teams, servicemen who had emerged from the German encirclement at Stalingrad, aerial reconnaissance and information from prisoners – evidence from every possible source were compiled. Ordinarily, it had been the practice to add a certain margin of error to intelligence estimates of enemy strength, depending on the reliability of the information.

More than two months was spent preparing for the Stalingrad offensive operation, which was sufficient time for the collection of intelligence. The Supreme Command developed a list of the opposing field formations. It also knew about the presence of auxiliary units. The exhaustion and level of morale of the opposing troops were also known from prisoners, but this factor was treated conservatively. Calculations of enemy troop strength had been performed in such a way to ensure it wasn't underestimated. In making the calculation, an error estimate could not exceed 25 percent – always on the side of exaggeration, naturally. However, not 50 percent, not 100 percent, not 150 percent, not 300 percent – and certainly not on the side of underestimating!

Zhukov writes about the German group in the area of the Middle Don, Stalingrad, and to the south along the Sarapinsky Lakes: "The effective strength of this group totaled more than one million men, plus 675 tanks and assault guns and upwards of 10,000 guns and mortars. *Numerically the confronting forces were almost equal* – with the exception of a slight superiority in tanks on the Soviet side." (Emphasis the author's)

We have reached the main achievement in the lives of two commanders, which they never even confessed after the completion of it. Fearing – and not without grounds – that the Genius of All Times and Peoples, frightened by the *Wehrmacht*, would again stick his omnipresent nose into the operation and hinder them in one terrible stroke (which they were confident would succeed) and change the outcome of the war, Vasilevsky and Zhukov in their report to the Leader deliberately undercounted the number of German troops that would be encircled in the Stalingrad pocket. Otherwise Stalin, having learned of the scale of the proposed operation, might have refused to authorize its implementation, so that all the enormous preparatory work of the Army and the people would be wasted. Their dedication to the venture was stronger than their fear of the Leader and his punitive organs. Just imagine how strong their mutual trust was, since they agreed to collude with each other – even if it was in the interests of the Leader. However, this didn't matter, because heads had rolled over less important reasons. (There is the temptation to believe that this was Vasilevsky's act alone, since he was directly overseeing the Stalingrad operation. However, even if this was so, he would not have decided upon this without Zhukov's consent ...) It is for this that we are obliged for the magnitude of the Stalingrad victory.

Such a startling proposition must be supported. The sources are not from the bowels of the Secret Intelligence Service (SIS); they are accessible to everyone. I'm speaking of Zhukov's *Vospominaniia and razmyshleniia* and Vasilevsky's *Delo vsei zhizni*.

"Aleksandr Mikhailovich [Vasilevsky] and I preliminarily reconciled our proposals in this respect ..."; "Having discussed this with Vasilevsky, we designated the offensive ..."; "I was kept well-informed by Vasilevsky ..."; "Vasilevsky and I ..." – Zhukov's memoirs are strewn with similar expressions. The relations between these two pillars of the *Stavka* left nothing to be desired until the end of their lives. Besides the fact that Stalingrad bound them together with their illicit act (if you consider the case formally), Vasilevsky's analytical gift was supplemented by the operational thinking of Zhukov, an executor both decisive and merciless.

Their deception almost became revealed. Vasilevsky relates:

> ... a leadership post had been prepared for me by the General Headquarters over the Southwestern, Don and Stalingrad Fronts, which had been designated to take part in the offensive operation; I planned to travel to it on 17 November. However, Stalin over the telephone proposed that I come to Moscow on 18 November in order to discuss one of the questions touching upon the pending operation. He told me nothing more specifically.
>
> At 1800 hours, a meeting of the GKO convened in Stalin's Kremlin office. Stalin immediately received me and proposed that while a discussion of a number of important administrative questions proceeded, I familiarize myself with a letter he had received from the commander of the 4th Mechanized Corps, V. T. Vol'sky, who had been given a decisive role to play in the forthcoming operation on Stalingrad Front's sector. The corps commander was writing to the GKO, that the planned offensive at Stalingrad *given the correlation of forces and means as it existed at the start of the offensive* not only excluded any possibility to count upon success, but also in his opinion, was unquestionably doomed to failure with all the consequences flowing from that, and that he, an honest Party member, *knowing the opinion of other responsible participants* in the offensive as well, was asking the GKO immediately and thoroughly to assess the feasibility of the decisions that had been taken for the offensive, to delay it, or even perhaps to reject it entirely. ... I expressed surprise at the letter's subject: in the course of recent weeks its author had actively participated in preparing the offensive and hadn't once expressed the slightest doubts about the operation as a whole, or about the tasks given to the troops of the corps that had been entrusted to him. Moreover, at a final conference on 10 November he had assured the *Stavka* representatives and the Front's Military Council that the corps was ready to carry out its assignments, and then reported on the formation's full combat readiness and the excellent, pugnacious spirit of its personnel. In conclusion, I declared that there were no justifications not only for a cancellation of the readied offensive, but also for any re-examination of its schedule start.
>
> Stalin immediately ordered that he be put in communication with Vol'sky over the telephone, and after a short but not at all sharp conversation with him, recommended that I disregard this letter and leave its author in command of the corps,

since he had just given him his word that he would carry out the task given to his corps at whatever the cost.[2] (Emphasis the author's)

In my view, there's no need for additional commentary here.

The Stalingrad commanders were not those novices of 1941. They understood that they would be encircling an entire army of the *Wehrmacht*. The German assault on Stalingrad was continuing. The Volga River was icing up, and the supply line across the river had been cut by forming ice. Paulus wasn't anticipating a Soviet counteroffensive; he had reason to assume that precisely now the time had arrived to take full possession of the city, and now his assault groups had been reinforced for the final push.

Why did Vol'sky speak up, while everyone else remained silent? After all, he had referred to "other responsible participants in the offensive."   His corps was on the axis of the main attack. He understood the size of the operation. Was he being more responsible than the others ... and more courageous?

We'll never know. It is possible that during the telephone conversation, he learned that which the reader would soon come to know and which, undoubtedly, could convert anyone ...

I don't believe that Vasilevsky and Zhukov truly deceived Stalin. The Leader allowed himself to be deceived: if you will, a victory will be my accomplishment; a defeat will be their fault. The punishment would also be theirs, naturally. Then, just in case, he could conclude a truce with the weakened Führer, reinforce and re-equip the Army, appoint new generals ... and then crush the foe.

The underestimate was revealed almost as soon as the ring was closed and the troops had to begin the process of reducing the pocket and eliminating the defending German grouping piece by piece. Vasilevsky testifies:

> The troops commenced to fulfill their missions on the morning of 24 November. Unfortunately, the offensive did not bring the expected results. In our initial calculations on which we had based the decision to destroy the surrounded enemy by a single drive, we had made a serious mistake. According to intelligence information from the fronts participating in the counter-offensive and from General Staff intelligence agencies, the total number of men in the surrounded grouping commanded by Colonel-General Paulus was put at 85,000-90,000. In fact, as we learned later, it had over 300,000 men. Our notions of enemy equipment, especially artillery and tanks, and the arms available to the surrounded Germans also fell far short of actuality. We had not taken into consideration ...

I'll say! That means in the course of two months, three fronts had been preparing in complete secrecy for the excision of an enemy group numbering 90,000 men. The generals, who had experienced defeats in the Kiev, Briansk, Khar'kov and many other pockets were venturing to take on only 90,000 men of the entire Sixth Army with all of its attached units

---

2   When checking for the translation of this passage with the original Russian text, I noticed with surprise that the entire episode had simply been dropped from the English translation of Marshal Vasilevsky's memoirs, which had been obligingly prepared for Western readers in Moscow by the Progress Publishing House in 1981. This is a technique characteristic for Soviet historiography, as if to say, "Let's forget the undesirable".

... and after the weighing of all the factors and the numerously repeated assessment of the intelligence information, we get this "in our initial calculations ... we had made a serious mistake." All right, sirs, we regard you too highly, but don't give us all that baloney.

However, we'll give an ear to the justified prattling of the heroes, whose modesty and silence is truly becoming. We don't hold these escapades against them. Their triumph will shine brightly, as long as the triumph of Stalingrad doesn't fade. It substantially depreciates the achievements of their patron Stalin; however, because what kind of Supreme Commander was he, if for the sake of victory it was not only necessary to outwit the foe, but also him?

Accordingly, here is Vasilevsky, with my parenthetical comments:

> We had not taken into consideration the reinforcements which joined the formations of the German Sixth and Fourth Panzer Armies in the process of their offensive and the defense, and ... (Do you recall, reader, what he had stated above? "We had not observed any more or less substantial reserves being brought up to the Stalingrad area from the interior.)

... And?

> ... and the huge number of units and subunits of all types of special and auxiliary troops that had become involved in what was known as the 'cauldron', or pocket. What is more, the personnel of these troops were mostly used subsequently for reinforcing the combat units. Thus we had completely left out of consideration the Anti-Aircraft Defense Division (Let's give it 30,000. A little bloated, perhaps, but we won't be stingy), more than ten detached sapper battalions (Assume 1,500-2,000 in each), medical organizations and units, numerous construction battalions and engineering detachments ('numerous' ... 'construction' ...) from the former Todt Organization (headed after Todt's death by Speier), units of the field gendarmerie, the secret military police, and so on.

Sapper battalions, construction battalions, engineering detachments...; that's just it, "and so on". Just as they made excuses to the Leader, that's how they spelled it out in their memoirs.

Any book that mentions Zhukov doesn't dare pass over the name of Aleksandr Mikhailovich Vasilevsky. Zhukov began the war as a General of the Army, Vasilevsky as a Major-General, but the associates became Marshals almost simultaneously, in the winter of 1943.

Marshal Vasilevsky talked about himself with his book *Delo vsei zhizni*. He didn't say much about a lot of important things. He couldn't, because of censorship and his characteristic modesty. He was the co-author of ALL the strategic decisions of the Great Patriotic War, even when he was spending time in the modest rank of major general, since his post at the time was Chief of the Operations Department and Deputy Chief of the General Staff. Vasilevsky was a gifted military thinker. Without him there would have been no Stalingrad, nor any of the later planned operations of the summer of 1944 (where – not for the first time – shined the talent of K. K. Rokossovsky, who had survived the purge by a miracle), and indeed Stalingrad would have cost a far higher price. Vasilevsky was later the conqueror of the Japanese Army in Manchuria, and this superb operation is a model of a nearly bloodless battle.

Vasilevsky was a congenial conversation partner, who in a soft, confiding voice would gently, not annoyingly, put forward alternative approaches. His nature was to suggest, not to insist. It wasn't easy for him, the son of a priest, in the disciplined army environment. A lot of time passed, before he had learned to defend his opinion and even to insist upon it. The main honors in the Stalingrad offensive operation belongs first of all to him. He directed the Don epopee, poring endlessly over maps together with his operational assistants and listening to their opinions. It was he who in these critical days for the city, exchanging a few words with Zhukov in Stalin's office while the Leader was engaged in studying maps, and aware of the Leader's fox-like sense of hearing and constantly apportioned attention, would deliberately let slip a phrase just loud enough for Stalin to overhear, which would prompt a fresh round of deliberations over the Stalingrad offensive: "We must search for a different solution ..."

The preparation and execution of the Stalingrad operation was wonderful, but there was nothing particularly special about its conception. This intelligent decision was in the mainstream of the RKKA's school, of which Vasilevsky was a protégé, and later even an instructor: an amputating strike at an enemy worn down after battling a sturdy defense. The Kiev maneuvers of 1935, which shocked the military community of the planet, was its model, with the exception that there was no airborne landing at the point where the attacking spearheads linked up. The timing of the operations (plural; is this a mistake? This will become clear ...) was extraordinary, the extent to which has only now become known. To plan such an operation, when the fate of the city was hanging by a thread, and the Germans were storming Novorossiisk and Tuapse!

Incidentally, who else other than Vasilevsky was in a position "to search for a different solution"? He, the Chief of the General Staff, was precisely the person who formed the reserves and knew better than anyone else in the country the main thing that a commander goes by when deciding upon battle – the strength of his own forces. The second point in making the decision to offer battle is the evaluation of the enemy's strength. A born staff officer, Vasilevsky could not help but know everything necessary about the adversary.

Before the appearance of the second volume of David Glantz's majestic work on Stalingrad, *Armageddon in Stalingrad*, I was puzzled: On what did Vasilevsky and Zhukov base their deliberately low enemy troop strength estimate that they presented to the Leader? The second volume of Glantz's study on the battle of Stalingrad provided the answer: 85,000 to 90,000 was the number of German troops directly involved in the fighting for the city. This number repeatedly appeared in summaries and was familiar to the Leader, so the creators of the Stalingrad offensive operation drew upon it in their report to him.

With a glance at the operational map, however, it was clear that the ring of encirclement would enclose not only the city, but also the *Wehrmacht*'s deep rear, which was dense with troops. What was their strength? Why didn't the shrewd Leader ask this question? This will always remain a riddle. Had he asked, how would Vasilevsky have answered? The risk Vasilevsky was taking was great!

Only with deliberate blindness, which is so characteristic to Soviet/Russian historiography, is it possible to explain how despite the incident with Vol'sky, the Vasilevsky-Zhukov version of events had a long life. With an analytic approach to history, it wouldn't have survived its infancy.

Returning to the justifications and refusing to accept them, I am seemingly accusing the Marshals of a most serious military crime, which they, as military men, would simply not want to recall, even if to take credit for themselves in the triumph. This deed was nothing less than the misinforming of a superior commander in order to obtain his authorization for a planned operation, to which the commander would not consent, had he been presented with objective information. These smart people recalled how their superior had used accurate information presented to him by the intelligence on the eve of the war. They knew about his dilettantism. They considered his mistrust in the rising level of generalship and of the troops. He read a map like a plan and trusted only the numbers of numerical superiority. Could they have been assured that the presentation of objective information would lead to a sensible decision?

In a word, think what you wish, but I won't condemn the Marshals. Moreover, I bow before them for this deed. On Vasilevsky's and Zhukov's own hook, the Stalingrad operation took place according to their plan variant. Although, they were assuming that the Germans in the pocket would be more acquiescing, and that their attack would push on to the south. Then they might have succeeded in pressing von Kleist to the sea, where the Soviet Black Sea Fleet dominated. A mass of troops would be freed up, including Malinovsky's reserve 2nd Guards Army, the same one that eventually halted von Manstein's drive to free Paulus in Stalingrad. Oh, what it might have done in the rear of von Kleist's group, which had been weakened in the fighting for the Caucasus!

However, the 6th Army pinned down the forces of two fronts, while the 2nd Guards Army had to be sent to intercept von Manstein. Vasilevsky made this decision on his own authority, and then spent all night pacing from corner to corner in the hut that held his headquarters waiting for a call from the Leader, which would approve that which was already underway. (Here indeed is an instance of disobedience, foretold by the supposed disobedience of the repressed army commanders!) At 5:00 in the morning, the phone rang. Vasilevsky picked it up. "To hell with you, take it!" Stalin spitefully spat out before slamming down the phone. Yet what if he had said, "No!"? Was this why Vasilevsky received his first Gold Star of Hero of the Soviet Union – for courage in the face of the Leader? This was an act of bravery.

The main figure in the Stalingrad operation was Vasilevsky, so he is explaining things. Zhukov in his memoirs avoids a discussion of the matter, but one phrase in *Vospominaniia* causes one to think that he was involved:

> In late September I was again summoned by Stalin to Moscow to discuss the plan for a counter-offensive. (Likely, it was then that the Leader determined the size of the anticipated pocket – the author.) By that time, Vasilevsky had also returned to Moscow after a tour during which he had studied the conditions for the counter-offensive on the left-wing of the Southeastern Front. *Before arriving at General Headquarters* (! – the author) we met to discuss the results of our studies of the conditions for effecting the counter-offensive.

It would be nice for posterity to know what the two men said in this discussion. It was a genuinely historical exchange. It was such in a human sense as well. It demonstrated that even in a time when any conversation might be dangerous, human feelings and relationships don't disappear – even if they conflict with a sense of prudence. Because, thinking prudently, highly-placed officials under the vigilant gaze of the Tyrant and his entire apparatus didn't enter into secret deals, they didn't dare. For the sake of what? To hell with him, by agreeing with his instructions you'll achieve less success, though without risk.

Vasilevsky and Zhukov didn't have time to parse motivations. It boiled down to a choice between "I don't trust you, I'm afraid" and "I trust you". That's all that was left to them. Genuine patriots of their country and military professionals, they chose the latter.

If someone in our time has lost hope in humanity, if it is assumed that the reserves of the human spirit have been exhausted and we are doomed to only miserly empiricism, let them recall this historical episode, and how two men trusted each other in a land of tyranny in a dark hour for it.

Possibly, this secret deal became the beginning of that relative freedom of action that the Soviet generals acquired, about which, according to Iurii Nagibin, Rokossovsky subsequently spoke so sharply: "This untutored priest [Stalin] only interfered with everyone. We deceived him. Whatever sort of foolish instruction he might give, we'd play along, but do whatever we thought best."

59

Were they really Allies?

With respect to the laying out of *permitted* facts, the books of Soviet publishers have attained a solid reputation among their circle of readers. However, Soviet historians were forced to engage in myth-creation. One of the myths that they were ordered to create is the myth about the stinginess of Allied operations that took place during the battle of Stalingrad.

In contrast, Western historians, even during the years of the Cold War, paid due to the contribution of the USSR in the ultimate victory. Sometimes they even did this with impressive forcefulness:

> The German invasion of Russia opened a new phase in the war; though its full importance was not obvious at first, it was a real turning-point. From 22 June 1941 Germany was inextricably involved in an eastern war from which she knew no respite until the Russian hordes overran the ruins of the Wilhelm-strasse ... For twelve months the British Commonwealth had resisted the triumphant Axis without a major ally, though sustained by increasing material help from across the Atlantic. For twelve months London had been the acknowledged capital of all who fought for freedom, her scars a visible proof of what the enemy could, and of what he could not do. For twelve months, and this touches the plan of the present history, the strategic decisions had been taken by Britain alone ...

That's what the British historian J. Butler, wrote in his fundamental book *Grand Strategy* in the 1950s at the very height of the Cold War.[1]

My kind friend, a Londoner, Mike Bradshaw told me that Tchaikovsky's First Piano Concerto once became a beloved melody of the English people not only because of its beauty, but also because the central broadcast of the day in the war years began with this melody – the transmission of news from the Eastern Front.

Soviet historiography passionately dislikes speaking about the Allied assistance in the war, but Zhukov, in his memoirs, defended the talking point about the importance of Allied help even in those years of censorship. Of course, the Allies provided help out of the complete recognition that if the USSR crumbled they would have to expend much more of their own blood. However, there is no point in closing our eyes to the fact that without this assistance – without the food, explosives and vehicles, not to mention the weapons (Pokryshkin[2] after all flew in a Bell Airacobra ...), the war would have been lost.

---

1   "Russian hordes" in the Soviet edition of Butler's book is translated as "the Soviet troops". This is an offensive generalization for a liberating and at the same time multi-national Army, but after all Soviet soldiers in Germany now and then didn't behave in the best manner, especially with women ...

2   Editor's note: One of the top Soviet aces and a three-time Hero of the Soviet Union, Aleksandr Ivanovich Pokryshkin in January 1943 began flying the Bell P-39 Airocobra received through Lend-Lease. He liked its firepower, and at the low altitudes that characterized aerial combat on the Eastern Front, found it was

There's also no point in casting thunderbolts at the Western leaders – at Churchill as if he was wearing a bulls-eye – for dragging their feet with opening a second front and their insufficient compassion for the miseries of the Soviet people in their terrible struggle. It is like saying that the leaders of the United Kingdom and America were obliged to sacrifice their own compatriots for the safety of Soviet citizens. It is like saying that the Soviet people didn't have a leader to look after them. Instead, they had a Leader who cared about himself and who wasn't troubled by losses, which the Western leaders in fact considered and exploited by supplying the USSR with war material while preserving the lives of their own people. Let me ask, why not? Didn't Stalin, with his bloody politics, invite the Western partners to see in the USSR's large population one of the pillars of Mother Russia's power? Didn't Stalin with his pitiless process of collectivization and executions of the country's best people disclose his indifference to casualties? Of course, pity the people that has such a leader, but as long as the people tolerate him and call him "Father", who legally determines their fate, there is nothing left to do but to take advantage of this.

Such is the logic of national boundaries. It is amusing to hurl accusations at Churchill. A leader is called upon to preserve and protect *his own* population, to conduct a foreign policy so as to provide the maximum protection of *his own* citizens, even in a war for national survival. Concern for other peoples rests upon the shoulders of *their* leaders. Is it shocking to fight with the blood of allies, whereas with the blood of your own citizens, no, it's not shocking? The United Kingdom's combat losses in the Second World War have been calculated *down to the individual* soldier. They comprise 144,079 killed, 239,575 wounded and 152,076 taken prisoner. The British would hardly have considered Churchill a great leader, had he lost 14,500,000 soldiers in killed alone (and that's only highly approximate!), while exterminating and killing those who had wound up as German prisoners in concentration camps after the war – 339,000 of them, in fact, more than twice as many as the United Kingdom's losses in killed in the entire war! Well, it is clear that the *Wehrmacht's* losses on the Eastern Front of the war were proportional to the Soviet losses ...

Yes, the outcome of the war was decided in the East. Yes, Stalingrad broke the back of the *Wehrmacht*, which one can hardly say about El-Alamein before it. However, the myth of Soviet historians has gone just as far as Churchill's own: it is as if operations on the Western Front played no role whatsoever in the war!

I'll now carry out my earlier promise and return to D. M. Proektor's book *Agressiia i katastrofa* [*Aggression and catastrophe*] (Moscow: Nauka, 1968). Proektor is a typical Soviet historian, but he was not involved in the process of denying the Allies' their role. In his book he creates a colorful scene with the following description of the atmosphere in the Führer Headquarters in November 1942, which I have taken the liberty to condense somewhat:

> Montgomery has broken through the Italian-German defenses in the area of El-Alamein and has emerged in Rommel's rear. The latter is requesting reinforcements, and he has warned ... 'Tell him,' Hitler gloomily says, 'that it is happening not for the first time in history that a strong will is overcoming larger battalions.' His order – no retreat! That night news arrives that the Italians are retreating; therefore the German army had been compelled to withdraw as well. The report doesn't reach the Führer's attention at once, but only together with other telegrams in the morning. An

---

equal to the Me-109 and superior to the Fw-190 in maneuverability.

explosion follows. If he had been handed this at once, Hitler howls, with his own will he would have averted the collapse. He bawled out his favorite Keitel and removed General Warlimont from his post. (Two days later he returned him to it again.) The atmosphere was becoming heavy. In the bunkers of the *Wolfsschanze* [the Wolf's Lair, Hitler's military headquarters in East Prussia], whispers have begun about a "sharpening crisis of the will".

"Field Marshals Küchler and Busch arrived with a request for reserves for Army Group North.

A messenger from Rommel flew in from Africa. Rommel: The Field Marshal has halted the troops at a reserve position, but the British are attacking with massive forces. He has managed to allocate a paratrooper detachment, an infantry battalion and in the form of special dispensation 12 of the recently arrived Tigers to man the line.

The Headquarters is in feverish expectation of a Russian offensive by 7 November, the anniversary day of the Russian Revolution. Zeitzler back on 27 October had reported on a wave of Russian propaganda and on a possible major operation on the Russian front. The Red Army is attempting to mark the anniversary of the Revolution with a military success. The Führer agreed with Zeitzler's conclusion.

It is 7 November. Even before sunrise, everyone is on their feet. They waited for the dispatches. They began to arrive – and nothing. It was quiet on the Eastern Front!

The release of tensions brought with it a void. The Führer can no longer be found in this out of the way place. He needed a change of scenery. Where? Of course, in the Munich Löwenbräukeller beer hall, where his fellow comrades-in-arms of the 1923 Beer Hall Putsch annually gather. He had to regain the equilibrium necessary for new actions, and from Munich he wouldn't return to this place, but would instead spend a few days at his villa in the mountains. He would take with him some staff officers. It was nothing – for a certain time he would not issue his orders from East Prussia, but from Bavaria.

Zeitzler brings a telegram: 'On the Eastern Front, it is becoming ever clearer that the sector of Army Group Center is the focus for the forthcoming Russian operations.' The document has been signed by Gehlen, an experienced intelligence officer.

Yes, of course, the Soviets are preparing an attack in the area of Moscow. But measures have been taken: Manstein's army is being shifted from near Leningrad to the center, and positions are being strengthened ... Let's go! At 1340 hours on 7 November, a special train carrying Hitler, Keitel, Jodl and their staff set off for Munich.

It hadn't even passed the halfway point to Berlin, when Jodl received a report from the *Wolfsschanze* so important that he had to report it immediately to the Führer: 'British armed forces at Gibraltar have linked up with a large convoy of American ships that has arrived from the Atlantic and are moving to the east.'

A meeting gathers in a compartment. What are the Allies' goals? Opinions differed: Africa? Sicily? Southern France? As a result they concluded: 'The enemy's intentions to make a landing in Africa must be acknowledged as established, or at least likely.'

The next day, during a stopover in Thüringen, news arrived about an Allied landing in northern Africa. Immediately, an order goes out from the train to the commander of Army Group West about preparing a march into the unoccupied 'free zone' of France (Operation Antoine) and about strengthening the defenses on Crete.

The train's arrival at the Munich station creates no sense of euphoria among its occupants. Hitler was expecting to meet Italian and French delegates in the city. Keitel and Jodl remained aboard the train, which had been closed off by S.S. troops. They were unable to make any decisions, not even to send orders to the fronts: the Headquarters' field train was sitting in East Prussia. Warlimont, who had been dismissed and called back, was heading with a mission to the residence of the French government. He hadn't even managed to take a seat on the train when he was summoned back to Munich.

A stream of unpleasant news from Africa: the Allies had landed; Petain's troops were putting up only token resistance ... At the same time, Laval [Vice-Prime Minster of Vichy France] and Ciano [the Italian Minister of Foreign Affairs] arrived in Munich. A brief discussion, and at 0700 hours on the morning of 11 November, troops of Army Group West crossed the demarcation line of the so-called Free France.

Measures had been taken. The generals implored the Führer to go to the Berghoff. He would generate forces and find a way out of the new complications. Direct the war? Oh, the field headquarters could be called back from Rastenburg to here! A telegram to the *Wolfsschanze* follows, and late on the evening of 12 November the special train *Atlas*, in the cars of which officers of the OKW's field headquarters were situated, departed the Görlitz Station near Rastenburg, sped across Germany, and at 0200 hours on the night of 14 November arrived in Saltzburg. Here, an hour's journey from the Führer's residence, the field headquarters stopped on a secondary track.

That's where they greeted the news from Stalingrad – on a secondary track at Salzburg Station of the Alpine Railroad in Austria ...

Their attention had been fixed on the Western theater of operations. The Eastern Front, with the Red Army on defense, had slipped into the background to such an extent that a dispatch from the Department of Foreign Armies of the East dated 12 November about a concentration of Soviet forces opposite the 3rd Romanian Army and their preparation for an offensive was never transmitted, neither to the Berghoff, to Keitel's residence, nor even to the train standing on the secondary track at Salzburg Station.

The OKW and Hitler were busy with other matters: French sailors in response to the occupation of the 'free zone' of France had sunk their Mediterranean Fleet. In the best case, little could have been expected from the heavy ships, which were nothing more than large targets with floating gun batteries, but the deed and the Frenchmen's attitude were shocking!

On 18 November, dispatches, as usual, began to arrive in the OKW: the Italian tanker *Giordano* had been sunk, a British convoy was approaching Derna, and a Luftwaffe Field Division had been transferred to Crete ...

Not a single dispatch worthy of attention arrived from Stalingrad. One more frosty night fell over its ruins, split by rare bursts of machine-gun fire and the shaking trails of rockets ...

However even this impressive compendium didn't prevent the appearance of quasi-historical studies in the USSR that ignored facts. Yet the bold list of these concerns that existed at the hour of the Stalingrad counteroffensive is clear evidence of what in reality contributed to the German command's overlooking the grandiose blow that changed the course of the war.

The Stalingrad Triumph

The triumph came about not only so that the Kremlin mountaineer could express his comment: "Stalingrad was the demise of the German fascist hordes. After Stalingrad they were never again able to recover."[1]

Now, however, the Soviet Army had to get down to the work of eliminating the encircled Paulus grouping. Its prolonged resistance averted a German catastrophe on the Eastern Front. There was a reason why Paulus received his Field Marshal's baton: the Sixth Army with a virtuoso defense bailed Kleist out of a most precarious situation. The *Wehrmacht* at Stalingrad demonstrated a heroism which might have been called incomparable, if the Russians hadn't demonstrated the same courage prior to this, and the Poles before them, and the Japanese later. The Germans also displayed a dedication to their oath and a not unfounded fear: of the 91,000 German prisoners taken at Stalingrad, only 5,000 eventually returned to Germany.

There were days in December when von Manstein was trying to break though the Soviet defenses along the Myshkova River to liberate the 6th Army, and the world was holding its breath: which side would win? Then the Red Army unleashed its offensive on the Middle Don, on the northern flank of von Manstein's group, a blow that shattered the 8th Italian Army and was so timely that von Mellenthin referred to it as decisive. The offensive developed to the south, toward Rostov. Had only this attack been as successful, as had been planned!

Von Mellenthin later wrote in his book *Panzer Battles*:

> Manstein was a commander of iron nerve, and if it had been possible to leave the Fourth Panzer Army intact he would have done so. But it was not possible; the loss of Rostov would have been fatal to the 48th Panzer Corps, to Hoth's Army, and to Field Marshal von Kleist's Army Group in the Caucasus. Indeed, it may be that Zhukov, with fine strategic insight, deliberately withheld his attack on the Italians until he was sure that Hoth was fully committed toward Stalingrad; by adopting this course he may well have hoped to trap all our southern armies.

Zhukov didn't accept this version that was so flattering to him. In general, he had nothing to do with what happened here. At Stalingrad, Vasilevsky controlled everything. The offensive on the Middle Don had been delayed due to Voronezh Front's and Southwestern Front's lack of readiness. Meanwhile, Zhukov himself at this time ... but about this in the final chapter.

By the end of December, movement around the outer-ring of encirclement at Stalingrad had stopped, and Paulus's 6th Army was left to its icy fate. However, another month would pass before its grim fate became a reality.

---

1   Churchill evaluated Stalingrad differently. "This isn't the end," he said; "and it isn't even the beginning of the end. But at least it is the end of the beginning." In essence, with this comment on the event Churchill contradicted his own conception of the primary contribution of the West to the victory.

The Frightening Tale of Stalingrad

The name of the place where the war turned is itself symbolic. In the same way, it could have been called Bulletgrad or Deathgrad. With the jesting inherent to history, the place received the name of Stalingrad. The ring of the name, however it came about, is only though the ceremonial aspect of the matter, the end of the *Wehrmacht's* parade through the expanses of Europe and Asia. The mundane aspect is the death of hundreds of thousands of Germans, Russians (collectively speaking), Italians, Romanians, Hungarians and other peoples, who were fighting at the will of Hitler and Stalin. However, the event was the handiwork of the Great Leader, entirely against reason, entirely on his conscience: at an unprecedented cost the Golem [Hitler] was conquered, which Stalin's regime itself had brought forth ideologically (by breaking from German social-democracy, and in this way sweeping the path to power for him) and physically (by conniving and building tanks and aircraft for him at their factories for the sake of acquiring the technology).

There remains to elucidate three points. The first – in what does the true gift of the one whom in his lifetime was glorified as the Genius and Luminary of Science, and whose name was attached to the victory at Stalingrad, consist? The second – at what price was this victory obtained? The third: who were the co-authors of the plan of a grandiose war game on an expanse many times larger than the area between the Don River and Volga River?

A multitude of books has been written in response to the first question. Western historians have analyzed the phenomenon of Stalin in a rational, scientific manner. Two of their names stand out in particular: Leonard Schapiro and John Erickson. I need only briefly scroll through the succession of the Leader's criminal activities.

Again we'll note: everything is within reach of someone, who having donned a fine-looking guise, rejects morality. If two men step into the ring, one wearing boxing gloves, the other concealing a sharp blade in a glove, one needn't be a prophet to predict the winner. Stalin was just such a boxer; the blade in his glove reeked with ruthlessness, and the Leader had only one concern: to strike without exposing the blade. His criminal experience was broad, forged in his years of underground activities, and this turned out well for him. He ruled through underground methods, having become General Secretary, and in the RKKA, which unlike the NKVD he was not authorized to control, his most dangerous rivals in the army were eliminated. That's how Skliansky, Kotovsky, Frunze and others were eliminated – supposedly having drowned, supposedly having been murdered out of jealousy, supposedly dying from a botched operation, or having been killed in supposed aircraft crashes.[1]

---

1   The repressions in the Red Army never ceased, but of course, in the war the Leader, who was busy overseeing the war, didn't have time for them, so only the NKVD apparatus was operating, and concentrating on the routine spies, saboteurs and anti-Soviet propaganda. Immediately at the war's conclusion, at the Leader's order the apparatus revved up, and initially its target were former military prisoners and displaced people. Soon the Boss returned to past methods. On 13 January 1948 Solomon Mikhoels, the chairman of the Jewish Anti-Fascist Committee and the director of the Jewish Theater in Moscow, was assassinated. He was killed in Minsk, to where he had been sent on an assignment (just like the former Skliansky; the handwriting hadn't changed); he was shot, as was his traveling companion, after which they staged a hit-

However, after eliminating the men most dangerous to him, there still remained too much work to be done, which the Leader couldn't carry out by the use of individual terror. At the same time, the Red Army was continuing to develop independently of him. The Army was learning, growing stronger, and gradually shedding the dual command structure, the iron heel of the system of political commissars, which was foreign to it and despised by it. The RKKA was converting the political commissars, which were equal in authority to the commanders, into *politruks*, deputy commanders for political matters. This was an important victory of the military commanders, who were represented by Frunze. The introduction of unity of command, the supporters of which were often hidden and consisted of all the commanders of the RKKA without exception (including Gamarnik as well, though he was head of the GPU), was stripping the Boss of everyday control over the Army's activities. He still hadn't fully consolidated his rule and was conducting his primary struggle in the political arena. Extremely anxious over his own personal security, for which he was feverishly strengthening the NKVD's apparatus, he temporarily retreated. In this period between 1926 and 1934, not refusing on occasion to use the blade in his glove (the apogee was the "villainous" murder of Kirov), the Leader opted to created schisms within the Army as the main method of his struggle with it.

Oh, in this he demonstrated a refined skill, playing on human ambitions. He knew for himself how strong this passion was, and back in 1924-1925 he had insisted on a number of measures for clearing the Army's command staff of "foreign" elements. That's how the first purge was implemented. The military commanders accepted it with little protest: they were forced to yield on what they considered a minor matter compared to the issue of unity of command, and besides, this new policy was opening up vacancies. (A parallel process was occurring in the Party as well ...)

Now the Leader had found the key to the lock, and now turned to resolving Army matters through personnel and staffing measures. If someone in the Army was interfering with him, Stalin would have him transferred to a responsible civilian post, even with a significant promotion. That's how one irreconcilable opponent of the Leader, the Commander-in-Chief of Soviet Navy Muklevich was removed from the military, as well as many, many others.[2] Unsuitable commanders were sent on distant exotic missions abroad.

---

and-run traffic accident to make it look like his death was a result of that. They transported his body back to Moscow and buried him with full honors. This can be considered the beginning of a new wave of terror. In August 1948, a Secretary of the Central Committee and the First Secretary of the Leningrad District Committee A. Zhdanov suddenly died. He had been Stalin's chief ideologist. Rumors circulated that he'd been poisoned. (In a similar fashion, a year later the Bulgarian leader Georgi Dimitrov died, whose celebrated name didn't allow an arrest to be made, and whose unruly nature could not be tolerated by the Leader. Later their deaths would be attributed to the "Doctor Poisoners", but at the time the Leader hadn't yet conceived the Doctor's Plot that supposedly involved them.) After Zhdanov's death the so-called "Leningrad Affair" arose (involving the chairman of the USSR State Planning Agency N. Voznesensky, the chairman of the RSFSR Council of Ministers M. Rodionov, a Secretary of the Central Committee A. Kuznetsov, First Secretary of the Leningrad District Committee and City Committee P. Popkov and others). All of the accused were sentenced to execution on 30 September 1950, and the sentence was carried out on that same day. By now the matter of the Jewish Anti-Fascist Committee was in full swing everywhere, and former Red Army generals who had fallen prisoner but remained loyal to their oath had already been shot. The final act of the drama was being prepared – The Doctor's Plot.

2   Muklevich was arrested on 28 May 1937 (the same day as Uborevich and Iakir). He confessed to the "organization of a Polish fascist plot in the RKKA". On 8 February 1938 he received a death sentence, which was carried out the next day in Kommunarka [a village on the outskirts of Moscow]. In 1957

Much attention was given to improving the military commanders' living conditions. The commanders were literally debauched by the government's largesse. An additional stimulus appeared for climbing the service ladder, and competition in the Army sharpened. It was heated up by the practice of denunciations, and the ceaseless political trials threatened anyone with being labeled as a Trotskyist, an oppositionist, or an agent of a capitalist power. The escalation of suspicions, the fear of being discharged from the Army or to be transferred to civilian work led to a weakening of ties within the upper echelon of the military commanders. In order not to draw suspicion upon themselves and their friends as being part of some conspiracy, the military commanders stopped communicating with each other, which of course is what the Leader sought and which, of course, contributed to the strengthening of his position.

Vacancies continued to multiply with each additional purge, inspired by the Boss through the Party apparatus. "Divide and conquer!" First, commanders of noble lineage were removed from the Army, then commanders of non-proletarian origin. Through transfers to civilian posts, everyone was expelled who could be expelled. At last, there remained only the irreplaceable, whom it was impossible to transfer to civilian work, and upon whom rested the power of the country and its insurmountable defense. And then ...

John Erickson concludes with sagacious insight that the essence of the "Commanders' Plot":

> ... was the sign of minute care and skilled preparation with which it had been mounted by Stalin and his NKVD, rather than the 'lightning blow' against conspiratorial army commanders. Stalin must, therefore, have had weighty reasons for deciding that the Red Army's best brains and leading personalities were expendable. In liquidating the most independent section of the high command, Stalin rid himself of the last potential source of a leadership which could rival his own, having sent or being in the process of sending his political opponents to the wall. The action was not so much to prevent a conspiracy but to block an eventuality.

Thus the last independently-thinking statesmen of the country were killed, who had naively assumed that the army was invincible, that it was impossible to displace it, and who being so convinced, realized their error too late, at the XVII Party Congress, where it turned out that it was impossible to remove only Stalin.

How did the liquidation of the army commanders become prepared so skillfully and carefully? The Leader didn't begin the massacres until Ezhov replaced Iagoda in what was for him a new line of business as the People's Commissar of Internal Affairs. The engine of destruction started to work – and instantly at maximum revolutions! – only when Stalin confided in Ezhov regarding the scripts of the Central Committee's and NKVD's coordinated actions. Until that moment the Army had protected Stalin from the extreme power of the NKVD, and it in turn had kept the Army in check. At this stage, Stalin decided to finish with the military commanders.

First, on 11 May 1937, a Central Committee decree re-established the system of dual command. *Politruks* became commissars, full co-equals of the commanders. In this connection, taking advantage of the commanders' shock after their instant loss of power,

---

Musklevich was rehabilitated and restored to the Communist Party of the Soviet Union. A typical fate for a RKKA military commander-in-chief ...

there was a lightning and wholesale replacement of the former commissars with reliable Stalinists (few of whom would subsequently survive themselves), and the doomed military commanders of the higher echelon were moved around: Tukhachevsky was reassigned from his post as First Deputy of the People's Commissariat to be the commander of the Volga Military District (where he would command all of three territorial divisions and a tank battalion); Egorov was appointed to take Tukhachevsky's place from his previous post as Chief of the General Staff; Shaposhnikov replaced Egorov; Iakir was removed from the Kiev District and reassigned to the Leningrad District, but first, as was Uborevich, he was ordered to come to Moscow, supposedly for a meeting. On these same days, many Party and civilian personalities were arrested (including Muklevich). Gamarnik's suicide was a result of the Leader's success. Next there occurred the previously described session of the Higher Military Council, three-quarters of the members of which would not even survive another year.

The reconstruction of what happened further in light of Stalin's behavior and the few phrases that he was forced to let drop allows us to assume that the repressions took on a scale in which events to a certain extent spun out of control. I assume that the Leader began to fear that Ezhov might want to seize power. Even if this seemed senseless and was doomed to failure, the very notion of an NKVD insurrection against the Leader would be knocking the ground out from under his feet. Given his nature it was natural for him to be suspicious of Ezhov: a Russian with an impeccable background, who had concentrated enormous executive power, while the Army, the NKVD's rival, had been crippled and left without a voice ... Theoretically it wouldn't have been much for Ezhov to take power: the repressive apparatus was in his hands, and he could have filled the vacancies, created once he simply shot Stalin's associates together with the Leader. Naturally, the hour struck for the People's Commissar. He was liquidated and replaced by Beria, who had been timely appointed as Ezhov's deputy and was loyal to Stalin. However, when the clock tolled for Beria, the aged Leader goofed ...

Let's return to Stalingrad.

I'll mention the Soviet myth about the war's turning point:　　　　The wise Soviet Supreme Commander, understanding that a breakthrough of a prepared German defense was still an unfeasible undertaking, detected weak links in the German front lines flanking Stalingrad, which were defended by Hitler's allies. So the offensive targeted those places. Impeccably planned to take place in the area between the Don and Volga Rivers and conducted according to scheme, the offensive became the turning point in the Soviet people's Great Patriotic War against the fascist aggressors. However, there was still an unanswered question for us, the war's contemporaries, who remember Levitan's jubilant voice in his victorious broadcast ("In the last hour!"): Why didn't Hitler extract Paulus's army?

In the retelling of the chapter from D. Proektor's book, the reader undoubtedly noted the statement, "On the Eastern Front, it is becoming ever clearer that the sector of Army Group Center is the focus for the forthcoming Russian operations." Noted and given to wonder: the report had been signed by Richard Gehlen – an intelligence officer with an unblemished reputation, who after the war would go on to direct the Federal Republic of

Germany's intelligence service. To be assigned such a post after such a fatal mistake?

He wasn't mistaken, about which Proektor, of course, doesn't have a single word to say, but about which five years later General of the Army K.N. Galitsky managed to make us aware. In the autumn of 1942, Lieutenant General K.N. Galitsky was commanding Kalinin Front's 3rd Shock Army. In his book *Gody surovykh ispytanii* [*Years of Severe Trials*], which was issued by the same publisher *Nauka* as part of the same series as Proektor's book *Vtoraia mirovaia voina v issledovaniiakh, vospominaniiakh, dokumentakh* [*The Second World War in studies, memoirs and documents*], Galitsky informs readers about Operation Mars, which was conducted by the forces of the central fronts in order to divert Hitler's attention from Stalingrad.

A puzzling fact: Galitsky's book *V boiakh za Vostochnuiu Prussiiu* [*In the Battles for East Prussia*] came out in the same series by the same publisher *Nauka*, but three years earlier. The book's title itself speaks to the fact that this book is about the general's final wartime actions – but it was published prior to the book about the start of his service. Why? Generals are not professional writers. Busy people that they are, they describe their lives and careers in chronological order: where they were born, where they studied, how they entered the service, etc. But if his book *V boiakh za Vostochnuiu Prussiiu* is the second part of Galitsky's memoirs, where was the first part *Gody surovykh ispytanii* knocking about for several years? Do we have justification to assume that it spent those years in the hands of the publisher *Voenizdat*? That there they tried to persuade the author to cooperate and demanded that he write "like everyone else"? Oh, yes, and how – there's justification!

However, the author refused, and recalcitrant are rejected summarily. So they have to take their business elsewhere and seek a different publisher for their manuscripts. Vasilevsky turned to *Politizdat*, where they knew him and where their print runs were larger. *Nauka* took care of Galitsky.

Just who was this recalcitrant? Let's check his biography. Hmmm, he graduated from the Frunze Academy of the General Staff back in 1927, which meant Galitsky studied under the guidance of Tsarist Army generals Svechin and Snesarev. Moreover, he was the academy's adjutant. He served in staff positions; plainly, he could capably handle the pen. But in July 1938, at the height of the purges, he was arrested, and remained imprisoned until May 1939. He never confessed to any guilt – even despite those investigative methods of the NKVD! Galitsky was freed after Ezhov was removed from his post as People's Commissar of Internal Affairs, during a re-examination of the cases of the arrested.

His refusal to confess says a lot about his character. The memoirs of such a man are worthy of attention. In 1942 he was commanding Kalinin Front's 3rd Shock Army, right at the center of our interests. Let's take a look at his book.

Its fate is surprising. Plainly, the manuscript roamed among publishers for quite some time, and the author didn't live to see it come out in print. Perhaps the book was in fact the cause of the general's death, though he was not a young man. The book went to press on 9 March 1973, and Galitsky died on 14 March.

Even its further fate is striking. For almost 40 years, no Western or even Russian author paid it any attention. It gave rise to a multitude of misconceptions. One of them was the fact that it forced a fresh look at Operation Mars, which Soviet history had decided to keep hushed up. At the cost of unbelievable efforts, this was done by David Glantz. His book, which was published in 1999, explains why Hitler tarried in freeing Paulus's 6th Army: even after 7 November 1942, he was anticipating the main attack, and expecting it to land on the central sector of the front. It was closer to Moscow than Stalingrad. The attack did come, and for some time it convinced the Führer that the offensive at Stalingrad was nothing more than a serious diversion. Historians also believed this, as Glantz was digging up the operation that had been deliberately buried by Soviet historiography. Glantz himself also supposed this, when he entitled his book *Zhukov's Greatest Defeat*. Just who could expect that the defeat had been planned? Such a thought was inconceivable. The operation at Stalingrad was started first – that clearly meant that it was a diversion!

If you will, I'll start with an extract from Glantz's work, where he is describing the plan's origins:

> On the evening of 26 September, Stalin announced to his commanders, 'You may continue to plan your offensive. Conduct two efforts. Zhukov will control the Rzhev operation and Vasilevsky the operation at Stalingrad.' During the following days, the General Staff developed outline plans for two two-stage operations; each assigned the code name of a planet. The first operation, Zhukov's **Operation Mars, would commence in mid-October with the immediate objective of encircling German 9th Army forces in the Rzhev and Sychevka salient**. Two to three weeks later, it would be followed by an attack along the Viaz'ma axis by the Western Front's central sector armies designed to link up with the victorious forces of Operation Mars **and envelop all forces of German Army Group Center**. The second phase of Zhukov's operation was possibly code-named Jupiter. **Vasilevsky's initial operation, code-named Uranus and tentatively set for mid-November**, was designed to envelop German Sixth Army in the Stalingrad region." (Emphasis the author's)

Stop, wait a moment ... what about the weak flanks? Where is the genius of the plan, if it first intended to break through the notoriously impenetrable defenses of Army Group Center? Does this mean that a lie has been hammered into us for so many decades? Is this what happened? So they presented the result as an ingeniously planned operation?

Documents testify that Operation Mars, which had been designated to begin on 12 October 1942, was postponed to 28 October due to bad weather. A delay in bringing up forces for it caused the operation to be postponed to an even later date. So during his next trip to Moscow on 29 October, basing his proposal on the fact that Operation Uranus was to begin on 19 November, "... Zhukov now recommended that the offensive commence on 24 or 25 November to derive as much benefit as possible from the possible success of Uranus." (D. Glantz)

I say! Does this mean that Army Group Center remained the primary target?

What does Zhukov have to say? There is a half-hearted explanation in his memoirs: in order to prevent the transfer of forces from the powerful Army Group Center to Paulus's assistance, the *Stavka* decided simultaneously with the offensive at Stalingrad to pin down Army Group Center with the forces of the Western and Kalinin Fronts.

"Simultaneously"? When? Writes the marshal, "In the period between 20 November and 8 December, the planning and preparation of this offensive was completed", and he goes on to say that the directive from 8 December 1942 laid out the cooperation of the fronts and their objectives from 10 December 1942 and beyond. The reader might say that this means Hitler was given 20 days to send help to Paulus – yet he didn't take advantage of this?! A patzer!

Hitler was a patzer, of course, but he wasn't given 20 days as Zhukov intimates. He was given five days. On the morning of 24 November, the formations of the 3rd Shock Army moved out. A day later, the artillery began to roar, and infantry and tanks of the Kalinin and Western Fronts went on the attack. However, the attack was repelled; Operation Mars collapsed and was added to the list of "forgotten battles", in D. Glantz's apt phrase.

Yet just what was thrown into the battle on the Soviet side? The second edition of Zhukov's memoirs says the following about the operation launched by the Kalinin and Western Fronts: "... the operation, which was conducted with the strength of two fronts, had great significance." In the tenth edition, two words were inserted: "... the operation, which was conducted with part of the strength of two fronts, had great significance."

Who touched the text? Zhukov was no longer alive. History is written, history is rewritten ... Still, was it with part of the strength of two fronts, or with the strength of two fronts?

According to A.V. Isaev, who in 2007 wrote the foreword to the Russian-language edition of Glantz's book, and who shares the opinion that Mars was the main operation, while Uranus was a secondary operation, 667,478 soldiers and 1,318 tanks went on the offensive on 25 November 1942 in the Velikiye Liuki-Rzhev-Sychevka area and at Viaz'ma. *Stavka* representative General of the Army Zhukov now and then showed up at field headquarters, while General Katukov commanded one of the tank armadas. Yes, the same man whose name by now was even too well-known to the *Wehrmacht*, the victor over Guderian. In an odd manner there was no real effort to hide their presence, and now and then their pseudonyms, which were well-known to the Germans, were spoken in radio transmissions.

The human losses of the Red Army in Operation Mars were 100,000 killed and 235,000 wounded or taken prisoner. Almost all of the tanks were lost.

The result? We'll only note that in the meantime, Hitler didn't weaken Army Group Center. Probably he already understood that with Stalingrad he had led the *Wehrmacht* into a trap and hadn't left any way out for himself other than to leave Paulus's army to its fate. That was the price of saving the Eastern Front. The Russians in the late autumn of 1942 had repeated what the *Wehrmacht* had showed in the summer: There are two fists; do you know which one will strike? Both of them had. Only having first halted the Russians in the center might it be possible to hurry to Paulus's assistance. It was too late! The entire Soviet front was now in motion. The loss of the initiative normally means that commanders are no longer able to anticipate the enemy's next moves. The Germans now no longer called the dance tune and had to wait for where the Red Army would strike next and try to repel the blow.

However, what in the final analysis was the aim of the Red Army's winter campaign? Where is the truth? Which operation, Mars or Uranus, was the primary operation, and which one was secondary?

It is easy to explain why K.N. Galitsky's book fell out of the field of vision of the Western historians. Given the low reputation of the Soviet memoir literature, one more book by one more general, moreover one who spoke fawningly about Zhukov, could be disregarded. That the memoirs of other generals were eagerly sought out and read makes this explanation somewhat flimsy, but there is no better one. Something else, however, is totally incomprehensible: how could this book have been ignored by Russian historians? The only answer that suggests itself is – intentionally!

Well, with the recreation of ancient events, which have drawn the interest of incomparably fewer people and factors, we collate and merge the sources. That goes without saying about the most recent history. Claims to possess the full truth, where one must put together a broad mosaic out of events that seemingly have no connection with one another, are absurd, and we are left with trying to explain those empty spaces, where the pieces of the historical smalt have been lost. In Soviet history, though, the pieces haven't been lost; they've been concealed (or ignored as in Galitsky's case), and sometimes so artfully that even united efforts do not guarantee that they'll be found.

However, in our case, fortunately, we have a reliable eyewitness. Let's turn to what K.N. Galitsky has to say. This story is so important that I will cite it in full, with only insignificant abridgements:

Intense work began for preparing the operation. As was designated, the army's headquarters shifted to the Velikiye Luki axis and was temporarily located in the village of Kartashevo (20 kilometers west of Toropets). From here it was convenient to direct the troops while they were assembling for the offensive. On the morning of 19 November, however, General M.A. Purkaev and a member of the Front's military council Corps Commissar D.S. Leonov unexpectedly arrived at our headquarters.

Stavka representative General of the Army G.K. Zhukov is on his way from the airfield," the Front commander told me. "Be ready to report the situational assessment, decision, and plan of the operation to him."

I was prepared. But just in case I concisely jotted down a short summary of the report's contents on the pages of a notepad. Even today, as I am writing these lines, the pages of the notepad are laying in front of me, resurrecting the events of those threatening days in my mind.

Soon two Willys jeeps drove up. G.K. Zhukov stepped out of the first one. He was wearing a knee-length, gray lambskin coat with the insignia of a General of the Army, and on his head was a gray, general's astrakhan hat. G.K. Zhukov's face bore the expression of an obdurate man, demanding and imperious.

Having shaken all our hands, Georgii Konstantinovich, nodding at the new collar tabs sewn onto General M.A Purkaev's overcoat, congratulated him on his recent promotion to colonel-general. Then, pointing at his knee-length coat and smiling, he added, "I, as you can see, am in the uniform of a commander of the 4th Don Cavalry Division, which I commanded back in the mid-1930s, and I even have the pre-war general's insignia."

Everyone burst out laughing. This little joke somehow immediately dissolved the tension. But the thought flashed through my mind that this joking comment that G.K. Zhukov had unexpectedly made, without changing the serious expression of his face, revealed in him a man who was not as haughty as it seemed from first appearance.

At the meeting of the Front's military council that took place, I reported on the operational-tactical situation on the army's front, paying particular attention to the grouping that the enemy had created in the Nasva-Velikiye Luki-Nevel'-Novosokol'niki area. I said, "The plan of assembly answers two aims: the continuous combat readiness of the forces to repel a possible enemy attack toward Toropets, and at the same time it provides for an immediate shift to offensive combat operations."

Here I'll interrupt Galitsky's narrative and for the sake of brevity explain the situation. The 3rd Shock Army was positioned between two German salients, protruding in the direction of Moscow. Select *Wehrmacht* formations were holding the front here. The operational plan, as reported by Galitsky, foresaw the rapid seizure of Velikiye Luki and Novosokol'niki, which would sever the only railroad that linked Army Groups North, Center and South. Deprived of this lateral communication line, the Germans would lose the capability of quickly shifting troops and would be forced to evacuate the two salients urgently, thereby freeing not less than 22 divisions that had been tied up in fighting, which could then be sent to any other sector of the front. Now let's continue with Galitsky's testimony:

Although the report took more than an hour – I wanted to lay out everything in detail – G.K. Zhukov didn't interrupt me. I sensed that he knew how to listen attentively, considering carefully all the details. Having then heard the opinion of the Front commander, who supported my evaluation of the situation in front of the army and the decision to conduct an operation, Zhukov said: "The army's combat operations are organically connected with the operations of the Front's forces and all of our Armed Forces. One plan, even if deeply thought out, is not able fundamentally to change the situation. Thus the main thing in the army's operation is its role and significance on the operational and strategic scales."

"Take a look here", he said as he invited us to examine a strategic map hanging on the wall. Pointing at the red arrows that indicated the attacks by the Red Army's forces at Leningrad and Demiansk and at Rzhev and Viaz'ma, the *Stavka* representative continued, "All of these concerted attacks support the counteroffensive of Soviet troops at Stalingrad, which started today, by pinning down the adversary's reserves. Such is the main role of the 3rd Shock Army as well in the forthcoming combat operations on the Velikiye Luki axis."

Here it is necessary to mention that it was just on this day, 19 November 1942, when the described meeting at the 3rd Shock Army's headquarters took place; the Red Army forces launched one of the decisive operations of the Great Patriotic War on the southern sector of the Soviet-German front. We, of course, didn't have back then a sufficiently clear picture of the size of this operation. As concerns its results, even the *Stavka* likely still couldn't fully foresee them. But it was doing everything possible to make it a decisive turning point. The Supreme High Command saw as one of the conditions of this turning point the diversion of the enemy's strategic reserves away from the Stalingrad axis by active operations on other sectors of the front.

"Draw the enemy's forces onto yourself – that's the main task of the 3rd Shock Army", Zhukov said. "Take Novosokol'niki or not – all the same your assignment will be considered fulfilled, if you draw the enemy's forces onto yourself and he will not be able to remove them from your sector for sending to the south. Thus, by your actions for a lengthy time – I repeat, a lengthy time – tie down the forces opposite you and attract the reserves of the nearest German armies and army groups. This is equivalent to disrupting their transfer to the south. This, in fact, is the main task of the 3rd Shock Army."

The objective as formulated by G.K. Zhukov sharply altered the entire character and timeframe for conducting the Velikiye Luki offensive operation. It was clear that it didn't need to be a lightning operation. **The operation was to be deliberately lengthy, in order possibly to grind down the enemy strength in the course of several weeks**. In these circumstances, not only offensive operations acquired important significance, but also defensive actions, which in fact is what G.K. Zhukov stressed, "Don't be afraid of defending; the main thing is to grind down as much of the enemy's strength as possible." [Emphasis the author's]

Understandably, this made it necessary to make substantial changes in the decision ...

In order to prevent the impression that the decision reflected Zhukov's plan only at the beginning of the Stalingrad operation, when its fate was still unclear, I'll note that a similar conversation took place between Galitsky and Zhukov on 4 January 1943, when the fate of Paulus's army had already been decided. The situation on that day required a pressing decision from Galitsky – to go on the offensive with the army, or to defend in place, grinding down the German forces that were striving to reach their encircled comrades in Velikiye Luki. Even the Front commander Purkaev, who arrived at the 3rd Shock Army's headquarters late at night, wanted to attack the enemy forces that were wedged into his lines. But Zhukov, who arrived early in the morning, rejected the proposal:

"The fighting is bitter; a lot of Hitlerites have been killed. This corresponds to the army's assignment. But even in our units the losses have not been small, and indeed the divisions have been in combat for a long time. That means the 3rd Shock Army must be reinforced at the expense of the Front's reserves."

As concerns the launching of a flank attack against the enemy, having acknowledged that this decision was generally correct, and the *Stavka* representative directed that it wasn't appropriate for the given concrete situation. Thus we would only waste the reserves, he said, while the enemy in response to the attack would set up a strong screen and would break through in a different place. Therefore both reserves and units removed from other sectors were necessary, and they should be deployed in echelons in front of the attacking German divisions. Let them smash themselves against our defenses. In this case their losses will be incomparably greater; moreover they will not break through to the city in this way. But, he added, the garrison's remnants must be finished off.

Zhukov didn't spend a long time with us. As is known, he wrote later: "At the beginning of January 1943 the *Stavka* instructed K.E. Voroshilov and me to coordinate the operations of the Leningrad and Volkhov Fronts to break through the German's blockade of Leningrad in the area of Lake Ladoga." He was in fact hurrying off to there, having dropped by the 3rd Shock Army on his way from Moscow.

For those who doubt the auxiliary role of Operation Mars and who offer the objection that it is possible that only the Kalinin Front's 3rd and 4th Shock Armies on the extreme northern flank were making a diversionary attack in order to ease a breakthrough in the center, I will offer an excerpt from a recently published book by Geoffery Jukes, which incidentally brought K.N. Galitsky's undeservedly forgotten book into academic circulation. Dr. Juke's latest work *Stalingrad to Kursk* refers to a statement by General of the Army A.I. Gribkov, who was a participant in Operation Mars as a captain of the General Staff:

> The corps to which he [Gribkov] was attached fought for several days in encirclement, and after the remnants of it had managed to break through to the Soviet lines on 15 December, he and the corps commander [Solomatin] were immediately taken to Zhukov, who conceded that the corps had suffered heavy losses, but said it had "… fulfilled its task. The Germans did not venture to remove the tank divisions from your front and send them to Stalingrad." Here Zhukov may have been making the best of a bad job, but the view he expressed then is consistent both with what he had told Galitsky before "Mars" began, and, of course, with what actually happened.

Thus, Geoffery Jukes's work places a definitive stamp – "Secondary" – on Operation Mars, which David Glantz brought back from obscurity.

However, having clarified one matter, Dr. Jukes confuses another. In the light of his definition of Operation Mars as an auxiliary operation, Jukes misses the essence of the question of the disinformation that he otherwise scrutinizes. The disinformation was supplied to the *Wehrmacht* leadership on 4 November 1942 by the double agent "Max" (the code name for Aleksandr Dem'ianov, a General Staff signals officer and a person with aristocratic roots and links with the arts world, which gave him access to the diplomatic circles back in the years before the war). This carefully screened dispatch didn't reveal the details of the plan of the Red Army's counteroffensive, which was supposed to go into motion no later than 15 November. Its most important aspect was the listing of the areas where the anticipated attacks were to come: Lake Il'men (the Dem'iansk salient), Rzhev, Groznyi and Voronezh. The mentions of the Dem'iansk and Rzhev salient were unassuming, but inevitably alerted the Germans to look at the central sector of the front – and diverted their attention away from the south. It was also not overlooked that Zhukov would head the operation in the center. There was not a single word about Stalingrad! This alone confirms that Operation Mars was a secondary operation.

According to Jukes, Zhukov was unaware that the Germans had received this information about the forthcoming operation, which in fact explains its heavy losses. This statement categorically contradicts the meaning of the conversation that took place between Zhukov and the 3rd Shock Army commander K.N. Galitsky. This also contradicts Zhukov's words of praise for the actions of Major-General Solomatin's 1st Mechanized Corps, which was destroyed in the operation. A contrary conclusion should be drawn from Zhukov's direction to Galitsky about drawing out the operation: Zhukov consciously went for the heavy losses. Thus, he was more interested than anyone else in the transmission of the disinformation.

The secrecy of Operation Mars was not in its fact, but in its hidden objective. It had no intention to drive the enemy from the positions that they occupied. On the contrary, his withdrawal was undesirable. All the same, such a withdrawal wouldn't open any opportunities for a breakthrough in the center. Zhukov, who had recently commanded the western fronts, knew the strength of the German defensive system. An evacuation of the Dem'iansk and Rzhev salients wouldn't weaken the German defenses, but on the contrary would strengthen them. It would only signify that the *Wehrmacht* was losing a favorable position for an offensive, for which all the same it wouldn't have gathered enough strength to launch prior to spring. However, a shortening of the front lines would free 22 divisions, which could immediately be activated elsewhere in the center or in the south. That is why Zeitzler, the chief of the German OKH, had in September 1942 tried to get

Hitler's approval for an evacuation of the salients. It means that the task of the Soviet forces was to divert enemy strength onto themselves, tie it down and to keep pressure on it – but to pressure it in a way so that the enemy didn't withdraw from the salients.

Zhukov's obvious interest in the delivery of the disinformation to the Germans also makes pointless any arguments over who conceived the idea and who gave the order for it to be supplied to the Germans. Any citizen of the USSR of the Stalinist years had no doubts: only one person could give the order to deliver disinformation of such magnitude – Stalin. It is also obvious that its contents were concocted by Zhukov and Vasilevsky, two commanders that were deputies of the Supreme Commander, who conceived and implemented the long-awaited turning point in the war. Dr. Jukes' mistake in interpreting the events arises from a misconception of those relationships, which developed both between Stalin and his generals and among the generals themselves. It seems that except for Glantz, this misunderstanding is part and parcel of every Western historian.

In Dr. Jukes' depiction, Stalin is inseparable from Zhukov and Vasilevsky. In his description, the plans of the operations spring forth, as the Russians say, out of counsel and love. There is unity in their views. There was not the slightest difference of opinion, either in the meeting of 12-13 September 1942, or the meeting on 26 September 1942. In contrast, Hitler always contradicts his generals, insisting on his own notions right up until the very end. The conclusion suggests itself that Stalin had no need to contradict his generals. The Leader was the great commander; the generals agreed with him in everything.

Was this the way it was? No!

The shattering defeats of 1941 and 1942 speak to what sort of commander the Boss was. Agreement and mutual understanding arose in 1943 and 1944, when the Leader began vigorously to promote his more pugnacious generals and to festoon them with honors and medals. Prior to this the two sides had regarded each other with mistrust and even hatred. Initially the attitude of the commanders toward the Leader had been determined by the extermination of their teachers, in whose fealty to Soviet power the commanders had no doubt. Naturally, they were haunted by the fear of being shot for the Leader's own blunders, just as the unfortunate leaders of the Western Front had been shot in 1941. On his part, Stalin had the fear of shooting his last competent commanders.

Hitler's and Stalin's maniacal stubbornness nevertheless doesn't give justification for drawing any parallels between the leaders in their relationships with their commanders. Prior to the assassination attempt on 20 July 1944, Hitler never touched the generals – a profound difference! The generals who were incapable of changing the Führer's mind were forced to submit or to go into retirement. Stalin's generals didn't have such a choice.

In addition, the war was taking place on their territory, not German lands. The situation was desperate. So back then the Soviet generals mastered a new way of behaving – without protests ...

How do I picture the course of events from September 1942? After the 13 September meeting with Stalin, Zhukov and Vasilevsky had been sent by him to Stalingrad to assess the situation there and to conceptualize draft plans for the forthcoming operation; they, friends from before the war who had survived the purge and who fully trusted one another, agreed to act jointly. The Germans were in the Caucasus and on the Volga River. One couldn't take risks. It was impossible to rely only on the order "Not a step back!" Nor in any way could the Leader's military talents be trusted: look at what his high-handedness had produced in the Crimea and at Khar'kov in 1942. They had to act in concert in the interests of conducting an operation at the only place where one could be conducted – on the flanks of Stalingrad, where the enemy had only recently adopted a defense, where it wasn't yet fully elaborated, and where it was being held by less capable German allies, who had no desire to die for Germany. So that the Leader take something else in his head and didn't get consumed with any sort of new ideas, the main attack had to be set up at Stalingrad. Yes, it was difficult to assemble the forces there; the area was desolate, remote from where the reserves were positioned, and lacked good roads. However, the advantages were also doubtless. Moreover, the terrain for an offensive here was much more advantageous than on the Moscow axis.

Having heard the Leader's decision at the 26 September meeting to conduct two equivalent operations at Rzhev and at Stalingrad simultaneously, one under Zhukov's direction, the other under Vasilevsky's, and moreover that Mars, the operation at Rzhev, was designated to take place in the middle of October, the deputies of the Supreme Commander were horrified, but possibly didn't dare even to exchange glances. Their unanimous decision was not to repeat the *Wehrmacht*'s mistakes and not to allow a similar dispersal of forces to happen! It was just this dispersion of forces that had broken the back of the *Wehrmacht*'s summer campaign.

It was dangerous to try to dissuade Stalin. The central, Moscow sector was his main concern. He had not forgotten his fright in October 1941. However, Zhukov knew what an undertaking a breakthrough in the center meant. He himself had crawled there, where one couldn't even raise his head. The *Wehrmacht*'s defenses were so deep, the elevations so fortified, the depressions between them so thoroughly registered by fire, that an advance had become impossible. Zhukov was aware of the *Wehrmacht*'s firepower and its mobility. He was also aware of the Red Army's clumsiness. What else could be done, but to fight with that army, such as it was, and to pay for successes with blood? Taking into account the characteristics of this army, a plan took shape: converging attacks at Stalingrad on sectors being defended by Germany's allies. In addition, a demonstration attack at Rzhev, there, where Stalin conceived of a breakthrough, without letting the Leader know that this would only be a demonstration. Start the offensive at Stalingrad earlier, so that even the adversary would take it as a diversion. At the same time, it would soothe the Leader: if you start at Stalingrad earlier, that must mean it is a secondary operation. Affirm the resolve to break through in the center with stubborn attacks, but don't force the enemy out of the salients that are lengthening his front lines!

There remained a problem: to persuade the Leader regarding the disinformation intended for the *Wehrmacht* command, just as it was conceived by Zhukov and Vasilevsky. The *Wehrmacht*'s obvious vigilance in the center and the lack of movements on Stalingrad's flanks helped this. Stalin personally concerned himself with keeping Stalingrad secret, whereas on the central sector it was impossible to conceal anything substantial. The disinformation appeared legitimate, and judging from the result, they succeeded in persuading the Supreme Commander to approve it.

They were indulging the Leader, who was pressing for an attack in the center. They were humoring him, but also keeping such an attack on the back burner, and Zhukov was focusing all his attention on the south, not the center, where his own fist was gathering. Incidentally, Dr. Jukes also notes this, when he calculated the number of days spent by Zhukov on the different fronts. Zhukov was prepared to be the scapegoat – and subsequently almost became one.[3] He and Vasilevsky moved the launch dates for their offensives closer together, justifying the postponements of Mars either due to a lack of railroad transport for moving the troops or to the weather, until it became logical to propose an amendment: to attack first in the south, where it would be a surprise for the enemy, to divert attention from the center where it was expecting an attack, and then as the enemy transferred forces from the central sector to the south, to break through the weakened center; and then, Comrade Stalin, as you please, straight on to Berlin! But if the enemy doesn't transfer forces southward – well, so what, we'll furrow the ground at Stalingrad. Either way, the initiative is now in our hands!

Meanwhile, behave formally in front of Stalin. Nothing irritated the Supreme Leader more than good relationships among his subordinates. It was proper only to tolerate colleagues, nothing more. However, Zhukov and Vasilevsky understood each other without words. They knew that the enemy would not weaken the center! A breakthrough in the center would mean a collapse of the Eastern Front and a rapid defeat in the war. They were counting upon the enemy's vigilance in the center and less attention on the south.

As mentioned above, the fact that for a rather long time the Führer considered the Stalingrad operation a demonstration contributed to its success: after all, it had started first! This was Zhukov's and Vasilevsky's latest word on tactics: the primary operation begins first and the secondary operation second!

When did the Leader agree to consider Uranus as the main operation? Most likely, on 29 October, when he accepted Zhukov's recommendation to begin at Stalingrad first. To be sure, Zhukov's words about extracting as much advantage as possible from the success of Operation Uranus prompts certain doubts. However, on the other hand, on 19 November Zhukov was not at Stalingrad, but was on the central sector, which could not have been without Stalin's approval. The Leader could not exclude the possibility that the Germans would take the disinformation just for what it was, and in this case Army Group Center would evacuate the salient and rush the freed divisions to Paulus's assistance. Now, though, there was a powerful grouping of two aligned central *fronts* which was hammering the German lines in the center!

After the ring around the German Sixth Army closed at Kalach and the failure of Operation Mars, Stalin faced a settled fact. But a turning point in the war had been achieved. The victorious battle would bear his name! So he didn't punish the marshals for the deception. One more word about the grim tale of Stalingrad: At the end of 1942, the weakness of the Red Army required two equivalent military operations, in order to win at least one of them at a colossal risk.

Dr. Jukes comments on the subject of the inarticulate nature of Zhukov's memoirs regarding the Rzhev offensive. But what could the Marshal write? Yes, in both a tactical and strategic sense, Mars was a delicate operation. Zhukov, against his custom, struck with spread fingers and, in Jukes' expression, "... may have been making the best of a bad job." To

---

3   From David Glantz I learned that in distinction from other folders in the archives of the Ministry of Defense, which contained jumbles of all sorts of files, the folder for Operation Mars was in exemplary order: the documents were bound, maps and diagrams were in separate envelopes, pages had been numbered ... Glantz was puzzled by this difference in managing the folders. Even I couldn't understand it, until my friend A. Kucher suggested: 'They were probably preparing for a trial. Victories – what? But defeats – incriminating evidence!" Apparently the materials were prepared for Zhukov's fall from grace in 1946.

try to defeat the adversary slowly in the interests of the strategic situation on other fronts – a thorough understanding of both the situations at the front and of the way of thinking in the enemy supreme command were necessary for this. But should the commander of the Stalinist school Zhukov and Vasilevsky be praised for the fact that they had mastered the concept of initiative, and with a weak army crushed the foe in one place at the cost of enormous losses at both that place and another? Or should the fact that he and Vasilevsky, risking their lives, led the Leader around by the nose, refusing to accept new fatal decisions from him? Obviously, Dr. Jukes didn't know about the confession made by Marshal Rokossovsky shortly before the end of his life about "this untutored pope."

Ignoring in a strange way the differences of opinion between Stalin and his generals, Dr. Jukes emphasizes the rivalry among the military commanders. Stalin actually encouraged competition between them, but in 1941-1942 he still hadn't reached that point. Indeed, in those years the generals couldn't even compete with the German generals. Dr. Jukes doubts: "It is unlikely that Zhukov would readily play second-fiddle to Vasilevsky, whatever the official status of 'Mars' relative to 'Uranus'". It would seem that when hurling troops into bloody attacks on the Central Front and against the northern flank of the German penetration to the Volga River over the entire summer of 1942, Zhukov wasn't playing second-fiddle!

In the essay *"Chitaia marshala Vasilevskogo"* ["Reading Marshal Vasilevsky"], which was published in 2010[4], I wrote about how Zhukov and Vasilevsky deceived the Leader regarding their estimate of the size of the enemy grouping encircled at Stalingrad. I wanted back then to prove the primacy of the Stalingrad operation over the Rzhev offensive. I didn't have enough evidence. Geoffrey Jukes' latest book supplied it.

There was one more decisive reason for the commanders' triumph: there was no third party in their scheme. They together made up one party. The Supreme Commander was the second party. After the reduction in the number of deputy People's Commissars of Defense from ten to two (according to Vasilevsky's narrative), there was no one left to denounce the two schemers. The secret of Stalingrad remained between them. They couldn't reveal it in the Soviet era. This would have cast a pall over not only their own lives, but also the lives of their children and grandchildren. One cannot censure the marshals for their silence. It is majestic.[5]

---

4   See http://www.berkovich-zametki.com/2010/Zametki/Nomer5/Mezhiricky1.php)

5   Even in such a serious book, Dr. Jukes considered it proper to cite the opinions of former Private V.P. Astaf'ev and General Batov about Zhukov, which were similar to scuttlebutt. Given all of Zhukov's gruffness and even cruelty, along with his other negative qualities we must give him his due for participating together with S.K. Timoshenko in saving the country in 1941, alongside Russia's lack of roads, spells of stormy weather and the Führer's fatal decisions, while in 1942 he made a decisive contribution to altering the course of the war. He was the war's main worker, a tireless officer who slept less than any other front commander, and one of the reasons for his temper was his constant fatigue. Indeed, in places he found affairs not at all in that condition as had been reported to him. He talked with servants like a master. With those who answered invective with foul language of their own, he spoke as an equal. To those who would rebuke me for my personal admiration of Zhukov, I will respond that I am only giving him his due. Of course he isn't my ideal of a commander, and even more so, of a man. My ideal is some sort of impossible hybrid between Iakir and von Stauffenberg.

I flew into Stalingrad in April 1958. My business trip was to the Red October Factory, but unfortunately I wasn't allowed onto the grounds of it; the factory had again become top-secret, and I had to resolve all my questions over the telephone with the guardhouse. I spent the remaining days of my trip strolling around the city. Fifteen years after the battle, the concrete ruins of the Tractor Factory unsuitable for demolition were still thrusting skyward, but the city's industrial areas had been rebuilt and repopulated. The city center remained empty of people. Ruins had been cleared away, and entire city blocks of new apartments were being erected and finished, but hadn't yet been occupied. The empty city was serene and solemn. I climbed the Mamaev Kurgan, which was bare and laced with communication trenches. I visited Pavlov's House (people had moved back into it). I stood for a long time at the ruins of the Grain Elevators, and froze at the low, uniform concrete monuments that stretched along the broad Volga. Each one supported the turret of a T-34, and at the eye-level of the passers-by there was a bronze plate that bore an inscription: "Here stood the last-ditch defense of General Rodimtsev's division"; "Here stood the last-ditch defense of General Gurt'ev's division". A chill ran up the spine, as if the dead were rising up from beneath the monument: "Look where we were standing!" I looked back. From their line of defenses, there remained only 50-100 meters to the edge of the water.

Repeating the question of the Foreword, but now from the perspective of the end of the book, it is time to explain why Zhukov and Vasilevsky were so tight-lipped when discussing that bloody tactic, to which they were compelled to adhere in the war in order to wrench the initiative away from the foe at such a horrifying cost. Both of them – especially Zhukov, who is particularly vilified – have drawn so many accusations of inhumanity, as if reproaching them with the charge that without such losses it was possible to stop the inexorable machine of the *Wehrmacht*, which had lunged across the entire national border into a country that had been lulled to sleep by its Leader in the conditions of an artificially created surprise.

In 2005, David Glantz's book *Colossus Reborn: The Red Army at War, 1941-1943* (University Press of Kansas, 2005) (known in the later Russian translation as *Sovetskoe voennoe chudo* [*The Soviet military marvel*]) came out. It focuses on the Red Army's bloody training in the first two years of the war and its conversion in 1943 into the strongest army in the world. This work changed a lot of minds about the course of Hitler's Eastern campaign, not only in the West, but also in Russia. The book's key aspect and a genuine discovery for us was Glantz's introduction of the concept of "forgotten battles" into the history of the Great Patriotic War. They are changing our attitude toward what in the USSR had been considered the spastic movements of 1941. Glantz's book lists the unsuccessful operations, which disrupted the timetable for Barbarossa and in doing so brought it to its inglorious conclusion in Rostov and on the fields around Moscow. Forgotten battles! Bloody counterattacks in the vicinities of Dubno, Kholm, Rezekne and Grodno (in June!), in the areas of Sol'tsy, Lepel', Bobruisk and Kiev (July), at Staraia Russa, Smolensk and Kiev (August), at Smolensk, El'nia and Roslavl' (September) and Kalinin (October) ... That, which I had understood intuitively while writing the first edition of this book, ten years later received documentary confirmation with only the difference, that my description of Zhukov's tactics in Chapter 35 should have not have been ascribed solely to him (though primarily to him personally, nevertheless), but to the entire General Staff – from the most competent Shaposhnikov and his operators, who at the time were Major-Generals Vasilevsky and Vatutin, to Marshal Timoshenko with his haphazard and helpless, as it still seems to many today, attacks in the area of Smolensk.

Why the attacks were helpless, why the counterstrokes didn't lead to the *Wehrmacht*'s quick demise, but only managed to wear it down and drag the war on into the muddy season of autumn and the winter – a lot has been said about this by me and as I remind you, in a lapidary fashion by Iosif Brodsky in his ingenious ode *"Na smert' Zhukov"* [*"On the death of Zhukov"*]: "As a commander, making walls crumble, he held a sword less sharp than his foe's." The Red Army was immeasurably inferior to the *Wehrmacht* in organization and the quality of command, in armament, in signal communications, and in the organization of the rear services. Justifying themselves by the dullness of the blade at the conclusion of the victorious, albeit one so bloody, war would truly have been inappropriate. That's why the Marshals have been restrained in offering excuses.

However, should they even be the ones to make excuses? Stalin appointed himself as the Supreme Commander. Orders aren't up for debate. There is no such high position that allows a military commander to disobey an order, if there had been no success in changing the plan before the order was issued. (The same goes for Hitler's generals ...) To offer excuses means to accept one's own guilt. However, the Soviet military commanders did carry guilt – Zhukov in particular! – for the victorious period of the war, when they continued to carry out the Supreme Commander's orders *at any cost*. In the period of defeats, they were doing everything possible to avoid a total defeat and the collapse of the state. Why didn't they dump responsibility for the losses on Stalin? While the Leader was living, it was impossible to exonerate oneself even at the cost of one's life. Yet after his death it seemed to them ignoble to pour all the blame onto a dead man. Anyway, they were the victors. The Supreme Commander ... he was also a victor.

They didn't dare audibly acknowledge that he was only the main purchasing agent of the war, the distributor of resources, and an administrator. He wasn't the Supreme Commander. Not him, and not with these losses. He alone was responsible for them.

☆ ☆ ☆

Now I will turn to the last secret of Stalingrad (even if it is now no longer such a secret).

Of course, by Stalingrad the Red Army had learned from the *Wehrmacht*. It was a tradition in Russia to pay tribute to the foe, and Peter the Great's toast to his Swedish instructors after his victory on the battlefield of Poltava is remembered by all Russian school kids. However, we will not hurry to bow before our German instructors. Soviet generals had their own teachers. Corps commanders Rokossovsky and Zhukov themselves were tutors, who had learned the methods of their more educated teacher-contemporaries. Even Colonel Vasilevsky, a second-year student, who rose to a position on the faculty of the General Staff Academy, which had been emptied by arrests and was short of professors, didn't pick his talking points from the ceiling, but from his lecture notes, and through them he taught his own students to pin down an adversary before delivering the decisive blow. However, a second-year is a second-year, and he had to complete his studies in battles. That is why his resolve was slow to mature.

The authors of the winter 1942-43 campaign had many co-authors. Do you recall

Zhukov's comment in his report to Stalin about the presence of tank and armored brigades at Khalkhin-Gol, without which he could not have defeated the Japanese? G. M. Shtern's similar plan frightened the Japanese at Lake Khasan in 1938. There weren't many tanks, it was difficult to employ them in the lake region, and the Japanese escaped from the trap. However, it established a concept, which was doubtlessly kept in mind while working out the Khalkhin-Gol operation, and which by the winter of 1943 had become entirely elementary ... Let us never forget Hero of the Soviet Union Colonel-General Grigorii Mikhailovich Shtern (born 24 July 1900 – shot 28 October 1941).

Together with him, the co-authors of the victors over the *Wehrmacht* were:

- Marshal of the Soviet Union Vasilii Konstantinovich Bliukher (19 November 1890 – 9 November 1938)
- Marshal of the Soviet Union Aleksandr Il'ich Egorov (13 October 1883 – 23 February 1939)
- Marshal of the Soviet Union Mikhail Nikolaevich Tukhachevsky (4 February 1893 – 11 June 1937)
- Army Commander, 1st Rank Iona Emmanuilovich Iakir (3 August 1896 – 11 June 1937)
- Army Commander, 1st Rank Ieronim Petrovich Uborevich (2 January 1896 – 11 June 1937)
- Army Commander, 1st Rank Ivan Panfilovich Belov (15 June 1893 – 29 July 1938)
- Flagman of the Fleet, 1st Rank Mikhail Vladimirovich Viktorov (24 December 1893 – 1 August 1938) For a long time it was not even known when they shot or abused to death this remarkable man, a nobleman, an officer of the fleet, who believed in the possibility of the people's freedom.
- Flagman of the Fleet, 1st Rank Vladimir Mitrofanovich Orlov (3 July 1895 – 28 July 1938)
- Army Commissar, 1st Rank Ian Borisovich Gamarnik (2 June 1894 – 31 May 1937)
- Army Commissar, 1st Rank P. A. Smirnov ...

... and all the rest of the approximately 10,000 officers of the RKKA's command staff who perished in the purges.

Just a few statistics about the scale of the purge: in the Great Patriotic War, the Red Army lost 199 generals either killed or taken prisoner. In the purge, 598 of them perished – an amount of losses equivalent to three wars of such never before seen savagery and fury. This is how we arrived at the war, having only *one* exemplary student, G. K. Zhukov.

When speaking before auditoriums of veterans, it was impossible to leave without giving your personal opinion of Zhukov, so I referred to Iosif Brodsky, who in his *"Na smert' Zhukova"* had made a brilliant paraphrasing of Derzhavin's *"Snegir"* [*"Bullfinch"*] (an elegy on the death of his friend Field Marshal Suvorov). Poets know without even trying to understand. They see everything with a special vision. Given a scrupulous study of the subject, even now with free prose, I cannot say anything about Zhukov better than what

Brodsky said back in 1974. In the extract from it that I offer below, one must try to grasp the meaning of every word. Known for his sniper's accuracy with his choice of words, Brodsky here particularly distinguishes himself. Each word of the ode is significant and each one acquits the Marshal in that terrible mission that fell to his lot – to save the Motherland through the blood of its sons:

> How much dark blood, soldier's blood, did he spill then
> on alien fields? Did he weep for his men?
> As he lay dying, did he recall them –
> swathed in civilian white sheets at the end?
> He gives no answer. What will he tell them,
> meeting in hell? "We were fighting to win."
> Zhukov's right arm, which once was enlisted
> in a just cause, will battle no more.
> Sleep! Russian history holds, as is fitting
> space for the exploits of those who, though bold,
> marching triumphant through foreign cities,
> trembled in terror when they came home.
> Marshal! These words will be swallowed by Lethe,
> utterly lost, like your soldier's rough boots.
> Still, take this tribute, though it is little,
> to one who somehow – here I speak the truth
> plain and loud – has saved our embattled
> homeland. Drum, beat! And shriek out, bullfinch fife![6]

Instead of an Epilogue

Among the songs performed by Sergei and Tatiana Nikitin, there is a special one – lighthearted, in the playful and carefree major key of Peter Tordovsky's "Rio Rita" to the words of the poet and director Gennadii Shpalikov, a man orphaned by the war. The song recreates the visual illusion of a dance floor in a hollow square of freshly leafed-out trees of some park in any oblast or district center, illuminated by dim lamps; of musicians, or else a gramophone, and fellows dressed in pressed trousers and polo shirts or – in those times a polo shirt was a luxury – in shirts with rolled up sleeves, circling around their girls, fresh, like peas from a pod; of the whirling skirts of young maidens' light frocks and the exultation of a young life with all its hopes for love and a bright tomorrow, joyfully panting to the rhythm of a foxtrot.

> Well, the Germans are in Poland,
> but the Country's strong,
> and this war will soon be over,
> in a month, no more …

You still don't see the dreaded closing stanza clearly, but tears are already starting to well up. It is clear that these teens, who devotedly sang at parades, "But from the taiga to the British seas cold, the Red Army's the strongest of all", didn't know the situation and warbled what had been driven into their brains, and their naïve faith in the Red Army and in the fact that they would strengthen it, filling its ranks, tugs at the heart. Meanwhile the song rejoices:

> Rio Rita, Rio Rita –
> Dance revolved round, round …
> On the dance floor in our town
> Nineteen forty-one.[1]

To a broken-off note and a suddenly silent guitar, the song ends – and then silence. A profound silence. It is quiet in the hall. The hall isn't erupting in applause; the hall is in stunned silence: the youth of 1941 are dead, dead. The young female saboteurs, who didn't know how to say words in the rural vernacular; the young infantrymen, who'd only fired a gun once in training; the pilots who had only learned how to take off and to land; the tankers who were barely familiar with the gas pedal and levers; the inexperienced signalers and sappers; the sailors who were unfamiliar with fighting on land; the student-lieutenants, who out of all the tactics had mastered only the words, "Forward! For the Motherland!" the untrained platoons, who had risen to the attack and been cut down, covering the defenseless country with their bodies. There is no more bitter expression of our pain than this silence; it is a voiceless wail, for there are no words or sounds for it. The stillness of death, there where the young people were twirling, who entrusted their only thing of value – life – to a

---

1   Translation by Valentina Kucher

ruler, wise and incomparable, and of course, who knew better than anyone what he did to his Army and country ...

☆ ☆ ☆

In the 1920s and 1930s, there was no Iron Curtain, nor a status of being restricted from travel abroad. Specialists, people accustomed to be observant, traveled abroad and returned, and shared their impressions. Even the army commanders made foreign trips more than once or twice, and they formed their own impressions about countries and politicians, with which they had to co-exist. Intelligence reported the truth, but not that which the Despot wanted to hear.

To such military thinkers as Iakir, Uborevich and Tukhachevsky, Hitler's assumption of power clearly shed light on how the future would unfold. By 1937 the correlation of power in Europe had changed. Poland on the USSR's western border could no longer be perceived as a military threat. Its conversion into a German satellite was considered highly unlikely, but the military commanders who knew German had read *Mein Kampf* with much greater thoroughness than the Leader. (The book had been especially translated into Russian for him.) The hunch of the military commanders was not mistaken. It is not ruled out that they told Comrade Stalin in a gentle (but perhaps in the heat of a debate no so gentle) presentation something like the following:

> Of course, Comrade Stalin, you may let Hitler conquer Europe. He will not do this for you, however, but for himself, and any war with him after he subjugates Europe will be extremely difficult. Germany is a formidable adversary, and we have Japan on our tail ... Hitler, having conquered Europe, doesn't have to tear England to pieces, which would give you, Comrade Stalin, as you suppose, Turkey, Iran and India. More likely, knowing our strength, Hitler will conclude a pact with England and besiege the USSR. It will be fine if he doesn't attack, respecting the equipping of the RKKA and the competence of its soldiers and commanders. However, it is probable that he will put pressure on England and draw it together with America into an alliance against us, whom the entire capitalist world despises and curses. So wouldn't it be more prudent for us not to have a falling out with Hitler, but all the same not to count upon him as an ally?

Something worse occurred. Hitler attacked when the Red Army had neither the army commanders nor the soldiers capable of repelling the offensive, in a situation, when the Rokossovskys, Zhukovs and Eremenkos were commanding not corps and armies, but fronts and the General Staff. There was also no longer the buffer of Poland between Germany and the USSR.

When discussing Stalin's confrontation with the military commanders and the conflicts which now and then arose between them and rose to the level of the Politburo, historians even today disagree. Some believe that the Leader was interfering in matters in which he had no knowledge. Others, that the military commanders were prying into business not their own and preventing the Leader from giving his genius foreign policy combinations a spin. The arguments endure, but meanwhile the most important scholar of the Red Army, John Erickson, long ago grasped the essence of the matter and laid it out succinctly and clearly in his book *The Soviet High Command*:

> The elimination of the Tukhachevsky group from the Soviet command had been primarily a political operation. The state, personified by Stalin and his apparatus of repression, had reversed the normal order by itself turning Bonaparte and marching on the soldiers. In destroying potential opposition and crashing this final barrier to untrammeled power Stalin had done himself a monumental service. Breaching the magic circle of the military, he had hurried the fractious, ambitious, independent minded or critical commanders into the oblivion of death or the NKVD labor camps. He set out to destroy not only their persons but also their policies and prestige. ... The alterations brought about by Stalin were themselves an indication of the enormous pressures of divergence and conflict over strategic doctrine and priorities which had been building up for some time before the onset of the purge ...

This judgment of history was pronounced back in 1962. Not Stalin, but the military commanders accurately assessed the foreign policy realities and the optimal combination of alliances in the case of a major war.

I had already completed this book and had read through the English translation, when a new supposition entered my mind. For years I had wondered why the Army commanders didn't take decisive measures against Stalin. After all, they had witnessed as he had undauntedly destroyed his political opponents. Then suddenly I understood why: after Hitler's assumption of power, the situation in Europe had sharply changed. It was clear to everyone that Hitler would turn his vision toward the East. Who would stop him? Without them, the pillars of the Red Army, Hitler couldn't be stopped. Whatever Stalin was up to with his political opponents, the Army wasn't part of it. This the Army commanders demonstrated to him with their obedience, and they were confident, or at least strongly hoped that the Boss wouldn't dare touch the Army while facing Hitler and his desire for *Lebensraum* in the East.

They were mistaken. The formal obedience of the military commanders didn't beguile the Leader. He hated and feared these lofty, strong men with their military bearing. He also knew from the dispatches of his agents in the military sphere that the higher military commanders also feared and despised him. A national boundary and hundreds of kilometers separated him from Hitler, but the military commanders were right next to him. His maniacal suspiciousness engendered frightening scenes in his mind. There were a lot of them, and he was alone. He had to get rid of these obedient, good-looking men with their independent minds. They had already taught him the direction in which he needed to modernize the Army. They had already put the rapid production of tanks and aircraft into motion. Now they were hindering his aggressive plans.

The Boss contrived his crimes with great foresight. Hitler, Germany? Oh, that's simple: kill the Army commanders, after which it would be possible freely to destroy all the potential opponents – and then make a deal with Hitler. At any cost. In the time he would win through the pact, he could then reorganize the Army, develop a new cadre of commanders to replace the deceased, and wait for a suitable moment to finish off Hitler, Germany, and all of continental Europe.

He ran out of time. Hitler beat him to the punch. Only part of Europe accrued to Stalin.

The dead cannot be resurrected, and victors are not judged. Stalin hasn't been judged. Really, however, will that terrible price be forgotten, that the country and indeed the entire world had to pay for his time in power?

Already in response to earlier Russian editions of this book, there appeared feedback of the following type: "Well, of course, the army commanders are holy, and Stalin is guilty for everything!" (I'm grateful to those who agreed at least with the book's main propositions.) Well, come on; let's return to the beginning of this book. Let the army commanders be unholy. Let's even assume that they were giving some thought to a coup. Why, though, was *everything* so bad? Was it the army commanders who arranged famine in the country? Were the army commanders determining foreign policy? Did the army commanders hound millions of innocent souls into the Gulag? Did they shoot the Polish officers in the Katyn Forest? Did they let slip the start of the war? Did they destroy so many of their own soldiers who had fallen prisoner to the enemy, that their number exceeds all the English losses in the war?

The author Iurii Nagibin wrote in his diary:

Molotov said, 'One can embrace or reject Nazi ideology, like any other ideological system; this is a matter of political opinions. However, it is impossible to destroy an ideology by force. Therefore, it is not only senseless but also criminal to fight a war to destroy Nazism.'

In the Pact there was an article – a mutual obligation – 'not to engage in ideological propaganda against each other'. Stalin assured Ribbentrop that 'the Soviet government could assure upon its word of honor that the Soviet Union would not betray its partner.'

When Hitler approved the Barbarossa plan, Stalin banned any preparation to repulse the imminent aggression. Learning of this, Hitler exclaimed, 'A devilish fellow! Stalin is indispensable.'

Mussolini said of Stalin, 'Indeed he's already become a covert fascist. He's helping us like no one else, undermining the anti-fascist forces.'

Hitler said of Stalin, 'He is savage like a wild beast, but his villainy is human. When I conquer Russia, I'll make Stalin the ruler, of course under German control, because no one knows how to handle the Russian people better.'

Eighteen million people were killed in the Civil War; 22,000,000 during collectivization, the struggle against the kulaks and famine; 19,000,000 people in the repressions between 1935 and 1941[2]; 32,000,000 in the Great Patriotic War; and another 9,000,000 were repressed between 1941 and 1953.[3]

The future clambers over the past and supersedes it, so as to give justification to certain

---

2   According to Olga Shatunovskaya's 64 volumes that document Stalin's crimes in this period, 19,840,000 people were repressed, and more than 7,000,000 of them were shot. Olga Grigoryevna Shatunovskaya (1901-1991) was a member of Khrushchev's Shvernik Commission created to investigate Stalin's crimes. A Party member since the age of 16, she was well-acquainted with both Stalin and Mikoian, but she spent many years in the Gulag from the 1930s to the 1950s. Once the Shvernik Commission's work was completed, Khrushchev, frightened by the range of crimes committed by Stalin and his regime, of which he himself was part, he ordered all the Commission's materials and findings to be archived. Later, she became a member of the Soviet Commission of Party Control and head of a special commission on rehabilitation. After Shatunovskaya death, most of the Shvernik Commission's materials were lost.

3   Nagibin, *Dnevnik*, pp. 562-563.

Russian historians to blot out a millennium from the history of civilization. There was no Methuselah, but had there been – who would have believed the old man? He's as mad as a March hare, they might have said, and spouts nonsense. Soon we too, the final eyewitnesses to the war, will depart beyond the horizon. We however, thanks to our fathers and brothers who gave their lives for us, we have lived our lifetime. It is painful to think about those who didn't get that chance. It is also offensive that Michael Caine, the superb actor, portrayed the Majestic Leader of Peoples so convincingly, that in the mini-series *World War 2: When Lions Roared*, the Bandit of History dominates Roosevelt and Churchill. Yet it was not shown very clearly that he quashes them with the blood of his own citizens, or the ease with which he spilled it on the Eastern Front, and how he intimidates the Allies with this blood, knowing their apprehension of human losses and their revulsion toward them. There was also not even a word about the fact that it was Stalin who was most responsible for the Second World War.

We will depart, but the film will remain, and people will watch it and think, "What a lion! Such character!"

Sadly, there will be nobody to tell them, "Remember! This is just a film. In real life it was a betrayer of the Motherland, a criminal, a scheming bandit, a treacherous poisoner and a cold-blooded planner and dispatcher of Evil."

Do you not agree? Well, then mankind is truly worthy of its own fate.

Appendix: The German Declaration of War on the Soviet Union

The Reich Foreign Minister to the German Ambassador in the Soviet Union (Schulenburg)
Telegram
VERY URGENT
BERLIN, June 21, 1941.

STATE SECRET

BY radio
For the Ambassador personally.

1) Upon receipt of this telegram, all of the cipher material still there is to be destroyed. The radio set is to be put out of commission.

2) Please inform Herr Molotov at once that you have an urgent communication to make to him and would therefore like to call on him immediately. Then please make the following declaration to him.

The Soviet Ambassador in Berlin is receiving at this hour from the Reich Minister for Foreign Affairs a memorandum giving in detail the facts which are briefly summarized as follows:

I. In 1939 the Government of the Reich, putting aside grave objections arising out of the contradiction between National Socialism and Bolshevism, undertook to arrive at an understanding with Soviet Russia. Under the treaties of August 23 and September 28, 1939, the Government of the Reich effected a general reorientation of its policy toward the USSR and thenceforth adopted a cordial attitude toward the Soviet Union. This policy of goodwill brought the Soviet Union great advantages in the field of foreign policy.

The Government of the Reich therefore felt entitled to assume that thenceforth both nations, while respecting each other's regime and not interfering in the internal affairs of the other partner, would arrive at good, lasting, neighborly relations. Unfortunately it soon became evident that the Government of the Reich had been entirely mistaken in this assumption.

II. Soon after the conclusion of the German-Russian treaties, the Comintern resumed its subversive activity against Germany, with the official Soviet-Russian representatives giving assistance. Sabotage, terrorism, and espionage in preparation for war were demonstrably carried out on a large scale. In all the countries bordering on Germany and in the territories occupied by German troops, anti-German feeling was aroused and the German attempt to set up a stable order in Europe was combated. Yugoslavia was gladly offered arms against Germany by the Soviet Russian Chief of Staff, as proved by documents found in Belgrade. The declarations made by the USSR on conclusion of the treaties with Germany, regarding her intention to collaborate with Germany, thus stood revealed as deliberate misrepresentation and deceit and the conclusion of the treaties themselves as a tactical maneuver for obtaining arrangements favorable to Russia. The guiding principle remained the weakening of the non-Bolshevist countries in order the more easily to demoralize them and, at a given time, to crush them.

III. In the diplomatic and military fields it became obvious that the USSR – contrary to the declaration made at the conclusion of the treaties that she did not wish to Bolshevize and annex the countries falling within her sphere of influence-was intent on pushing her military might westward wherever it seemed possible and on carrying Bolshevism further into Europe. The action of the USSR against the Baltic States, Finland, and Rumania, where Soviet claims even extended to Bucovina, showed this clearly. The occupation and Bolshevization by the Soviet Union of the sphere of influence granted to her clearly violated the Moscow agreements, even though the Government of the Reich for the time being accepted the facts.

IV. When Germany, by the Vienna Award of August 30, 1940, settled the crisis in Southeastern Europe resulting from the action of the USSR against Rumania, the Soviet Union protested and turned to making intensive military preparations in every field. Germany's renewed effort to achieve an understanding, as reflected in the exchange of letters between the Reich Foreign Minister and Herr Stalin and in the invitation to Herr Molotov to come to Berlin, brought demands from the Soviet Union which Germany could not accept, such as the guarantee of Bulgaria by the USSR, the establishment of a base for Soviet Russian land and naval forces at the Straits, and the complete abandonment of Finland. Subsequently, the policy of the USSR directed against Germany became more and more obvious. The warning addressed to Germany regarding occupation of Bulgaria and the declaration made to Bulgaria after the entry of German troops, which was of a definitely hostile nature, were as significant in this connection as was the promise to protect the rear of Turkey in the event of a Turkish entry into the war in the Balkans, given in March 1941.

V. With the conclusion of the Soviet-Yugoslav Treaty of Friendship of April 5 last, which was intended to stiffen the spines of the Yugoslav plotters, the USSR joined the common Anglo-Yugoslav-Greek front against Germany. At the same time she tried rapprochement with Rumania, in order to induce that country to detach itself from Germany. It was only the rapid German victories that caused the failure of the Anglo- Russian plan for an attack against the German troops in Rumania and Bulgaria.

VI. This policy was accompanied by a steadily growing concentration of all available Russian forces on a long front from the Baltic Sea to the Black Sea, against which countermeasures were taken by Germany only later. Since the beginning of the year this has been a steadily growing menace to the territory of the Reich. Reports received in the last few days eliminated the last remaining doubts as to the aggressive character of this Russian concentration and completed the picture of an extremely tense military situation. In addition to this, there are the reports from England regarding the negotiations of Ambassador Cripps for still closer political and military collaboration between England and the Soviet Union.

To sum up, the Government of the Reich declares, therefore, that the Soviet Government, contrary to the obligations it assumed,

1) has not only continued, but even intensified its attempts to undermine Germany and Europe;
2) has adopted a more and more anti-German foreign policy;
3) has concentrated all its forces in readiness at the German border. Thereby the Soviet Government has broken its treaties with Germany and is about to attack Germany from the rear, in its struggle for life. The Führer has therefore ordered the German Armed Forces to oppose this threat with all the means at their disposal.

End of declaration.

Please do not enter into any discussion of this communication. It is incumbent upon the Government of Soviet Russia to safeguard the security of the Embassy personnel.

RIBBENTROP

Source for the translation:
http://www.pbs.org/behindclosedoors/pdfs/NaziInvasionDeclaration.pdf

Selected Bibliography

English language sources

Clark, Allan, *Barbarossa* (New York: Quill, 1985).

Deutscher, I., *Stalin: A Political Biography* (New York and London: Oxford University Press, 1949).

Erickson, John, *The Road to Stalingrad: Stalin's War with Germany Volume 1* (New Haven, CT: Yale University Press, 1999).

Erickson, John, *The Soviet High Command*. 3rd ed. (Portland, OR: Frank Cass Publishers, 2001).

Glantz, David, M., *Zhukov's Greatest Defeat: The Red Army's epic disaster in Operation Mars 1942* (Lawrence, KS: University Press of Kansas, 1999).

Glantz, David, M., *Colossus Reborn: The Red Army at war 1941-43* (Lawrence, KS: University Press of Kansas, 2005).

Hoffmann, Peter, *History of the German Resistance*. 3rd ed. (Montreal: McGill-Queen's University Press, 1996).

Hohne, Heinz, *The Order of the Death's Head: The Story of Hitler's S.S.* (New York: Ballantine Books, 1971).

Jukes, Geoffrey, *Stalingrad to Kursk: Triumph of the Red Army* (Barnsley, UK: Pen & Sword, 2011).

Liddell Hart, B.H., *The German Generals Talk* (New York: Quill, 1979).

von Manstein, Erich, *Lost victories* (Chicago, IL: H. Regency Co., 1958).

von Mellenthin, F., *Panzer Battles*, 12th ed. (New York: Ballantine Books, 1990).

Overy, Richard, *Russia's War* (New York: Penguin Books, Ltd, 1997).

Seaton, Albert, *The Battle for Moscow* (New York: Jove Books, 1986).

Stolfi, R.H.S., *Hitler's Panzers East* (Norman, OK: University of Oklahoma Press, 1993).

Warlimont, Walter, *Inside Hitler's Headquarters* (New York: Frederick A. Praeger, Publishers, 1965).

Wette, Wolfram, *Wehrmacht. History, myth, realty.* Translated from German. (Cambridge, MA: Harvard University Press, 2006).

Russian language sources

Военно-исторический журнал [Military-History Journal], No. 8 (August 1966).

Военные архивы России [Military archives of Russia], 1st ed., (Moscow: TOO "Peresvet", "Tserera", 1993).

Вопросы истории [Questions of history], № 6, 1993.

Bagramian, I.Kh., *Так начиналась война* [*How the war began*] (Kiev: Dnipro, 1975).

Bergier, Jacques and Pauwels, Louis, *Утро магов* [*The Morning of the Magicians*] Translated from French. (Moscow: Mif, 1993).

Bezymensky, L., *Гитлер и Сталин накануне схватки* [*Hitler and Stalin on the eve of the war*] (Moscow: Veche, 2000).

Bovin, A.E., *Записки ненастоящего посла* [*Notes of an imaginary ambassador*] (Moscow: Zakharov, 2001).

Buchin, A.M., *170 000 километров с Г.К.Жуковым* [*170,000 kilometers with G.K. Zhukov*] (Moscow: Molodaja gvardija, 1994).

Butler, J.R.M., et. al., *Большая стратегия* [*Grand Strategy*] Translated from English. (Moscow: IL., 1959).

Dubinsky, Il'ia, *Портреты и силуэты.* [*Portraits and silhouettes*] (Moscow: SP, 1987).

Finkel'shtein, Iu., *Свидетели обвинения: Тухачевский, Власов и другие* [*Witnesses for the prosecution: Tukhachevsky, Vlasov and others* (Saint Petersburg: Neva, 2000).

Galitsky, K.N., *Годы суровых испытаний* [*Years of severe trials*] (Moscow: Nauka, 1973).

Grechko, A.A., *Годы войны* [*The war years*] (Moscow: Voennoe izdatel'stvo MO SSSR, 1976).

Guderian, H., *Воспоминания солдата* [*A soldier's memoirs*] Translated from the German. (Moscow: Voenizdat, 1954). Guderian's memoir was translated into English under the title *Panzer Leader*.

История второй мировой войны [*History of the Second World War*], Vol. 4. (Moscow: Voennoe izdatel'stvo MO SSSR, 1975).

История дипломатии [*History of diplomacy*], Vol. 3 (Moscow: OGIZ, 1945).

Итоги Второй мировой войны. Сб. статей. [*Results of the Second World* War: *A collection of articles*] Translated from German. (Moscow: IL, 1957).

Hoth, H., *Танковые операции* [*Panzer operations*] Translated from German. (Moscow: Voenizdat, 1961).

Ian Gamarnik: Воспоминания друзей и соратников [*Ian Gamarnik: Recollections of friends and* co-workers] (Moscow: Voennoe izdatel'stvo, 1978).

Канун и начало войны. Документы и материалы [*The eve and the beginning of the war*: *Documents and materials*] (Leningrad: Lenizdat, 1991).

Karpov, V., *Маршал Жуков* [*Marshal Zhukov*] (Moscow: Veche, 1994).

Krivosheev, G., et. al., *Гриф секретности снят.* [*The seal of secrecy has been removed.* (Moscow: Voennoe izdatel'stvo, 1993).

Людские потери СССР в Великой Отечественной войне. Сб. статей. [*Human losses of the USSR in the Great Patriotic War]* (Moscow: Spb., 1995).

Manfred, A., *Наполеон* [*Napoleon*] (Moscow: Mysl', 1986).

Mezhiritsky, P., "*Сталинградское пари*" ["The Stalingrad Bet"] NRS, 1 March 1991.

Mezhiritsky, P., *Товарищ майор* [*Comrade major*] (Moscow: Politizdat, 1975).

Middel'dorf, E. *Русская кампания: тактика и вооружение [The Russian campaign: tactics and weaponry]* Translated from German. (Moscow: AST, 2002).

Pankin, B., *Четыре Я Константина Симонова* [*The four "I" of Konstantin Simonov*]. (Moscow: Voskresen'e, 1999)

Proektor, D.M., *Агрессия и катастрофа* [*Aggression and catastrophe*] (Moscow: Nauka, 1968).

Провал гитлеровского наступления на Москву. Сб. статей [*Failure of the Hitlerite Moscow* offensive: A collection of articles] (Moscow: Nauka, 1966).

Rapoport, V. and Geller, Iu., *Измена Родине* [*Betrayal of the Motherland*] (Moscow: RIK Strelets, 1995).

Rapoport, V., "Khar'kov – Stalingrad – Khar'kov," HPC, 7 August 1987.

Rauschning, Hermann, *Говорит Гитлер.* [*Hitler Speaks*] Translated from German (Moscow: Mif, 1993).

Reinhardt, Klaus, *Поворот под Москвой* [*Turning point at Moscow*] Translated from German (Moscow: VIMO SSSR, 1980).

Shapiro, Leonard, *Коммунистическая партия Советского Союза*. Russian translation of *Communist Party of the Soviet Union* (London: Overseas Publications, 1990).

Sokolov, B., *Неизвестный Жуков: портрет без ретуши* [*The Unknown Zhukov: A portrait without retouching* (Minsk: Radiola-Plius, 2000).

СССР в борьбе за мир накануне второй мировой войны [*USSR in the struggle for peace on the eve of the Second World War* (Moscow: Politizdat, 1971).

Suvenirov, O., *Трагедия РККА. 1937-1938* [*Tragedy of the RKKA: 1937-1938*] (Moscow: Терра, 1998).

Suvorov, V., *Ледокол* [*Icebreaker*] (Moscow: Izdat. Dom Novoe Vremja, 1993).

Svirsky, G., *Прощание с Россией* [*Parting from Russia*] (Tenafly, NJ: Ermitazh, 1986).

Tarle, E., *Наполеон* [*Napoleon*] Translated from French (Moscow: OGIZ, 1942).

Vasilevsky, A.M., *Дело всей жизни* [*A matter of an entire life*] (Moscow: Politizdat, 1973).

Index

Index of People

Index of Military Units
German Military Units

Soviet Military Units

Related titles published by Helion & Company

Demolishing the Myth. The Tank Battle at Prokhorovka, Kursk, July 1943: An Operational Narrative
Valeriy Zamulin (edited & translated by Stuart Britton)
672 pages   Hardback
ISBN 978-1-906033-89-7

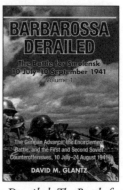

Barbarossa Derailed: The Battle for Smolensk 10 July-10 September 1941 Volume 1: The German Advance, The Encirclement Battle, and the First and Second Soviet Counteroffensives, 10 July-24 August 1941
David M. Glantz
624 pages   Hardback
ISBN 978-1-906033-72-9

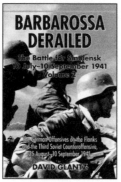

Barbarossa Derailed: The Battle for Smolensk 10 July-10 September 1941 Volume 2: The German Offensives on the Flanks and the Third Soviet Counteroffensive, 25 August-10 September 1941
David M. Glantz
624 pages   Hardback
ISBN 978-1-906033-90-3

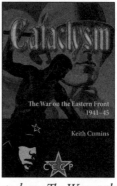

Cataclysm. The War on the Eastern Front 1941-45
Keith Cumins
360 pages   Hardback
ISBN 978-1-907677-23-6

HELION & COMPANY
26 Willow Road, Solihull, West Midlands B91 1UE, England
Telephone 0121 705 3393   Fax 0121 711 4075
Website: http://www.helion.co.uk